"The Bible I Know"
A Handbook for Life

Nina Jean Cameron

How God's Word became my handbook of life.
Teaching me where I came from, who I am and where I am going.

Copyright 2017
By
Nina Jean Cameron

ISBN   978-1-940609-00-3 Soft cover

This book was printed in the United States of America.

Copies of this book are available for purchase from:

Biblestudies@globalministries.org
or
www.Amazon.Com

**For Worthwhile Books
Columbus, Ohio**

Table Of Contents

Introduction

I grew up in a family who went in church every time the doors were opened. The church was the core of our lives. As a minister's daughter, our social life, family life and how we represented ourselves to the world all revolved around the church and its doctrines. My father was a war hero and a man of God who was full of adventure and fun. In my eyes, he could do no wrong, and his word was gospel. Naturally I accepted the doctrines that he and the church denomination we belonged to put forth

I want to tell you a little about how these lessons came to be and how I learned to fall in love with, and develop, an understanding of the Bible in my adult life.

My life as a child felt safe and secure. I always knew my parents loved each other and me and would do whatever was necessary to protect our family. I grew up eager to find a man just like my dad who seemed to be able to walk on water and to be sure we all enjoyed ourselves while following him out into the deep waters of life with his adventures. He always loved my mom well and provided well for our family. He repaired anything and everything, and took the lead in our family's spiritual life. I know he sounds like superman and from my viewpoint as a child, and even until the day he died at age 86 that remained true.

This was a set-up for my mate to try to live up to those qualifications. I married my childhood sweetheart, and it wasn't long before I realized he had not grown up with the same life and belief patterns. His father had died when he was young, and he grew up in a home where the woman carried many of the responsibilities that I had taken for granted were the roles of a husband. This caused me to start a process of trying to adapt to the expectations of another, and reassessing who I was as to be as a wife, and later as a mother in our home.

 Ten years later we divorced, and I was now a single mom with a young son. A new identity once again, and not what I had thought my life would look like although I kept my father's fun spirit and made many wonderful memories with my son during that time.

I later married my current husband of forty-two years. He brought a different set of role models into our marriage and once again I found myself trying to fit into someone else's mold. It was a different mold than the previous one, but I was still not being true to myself or the person God had created me to be.

As we began blending our lives, the question of faith was at the center of both our lives and we now had to figure out where we would worship as a family. We soon realized we had each grown up with a different set of beliefs and doctrines.

 We decided to visit each other's church of origin. I was a Baptist minister's daughter, and he was steeped in Episcopal theology. He was used to a very formal quiet service where the prayers were read from a book and creeds were recited as printed. I grew up in a church where we sang hymns loudly and had people share their testimony or even stand up and request prayer for a problem in their life. A church where at the end of each service the preacher gave an altar call for anyone who felt the Holy Spirit leading them to give their life to Christ when they had reached the age of understanding, or what we called the age of accountability. His church had a different approach and had a pre-ordained service that was full of liturgy and formal instruction for children when they reached that same age.

I soon realized neither approach was right or wrong, but it did present a dilemma that caused me to take a closer look at who I was, and eventually led me on a journey that allowed me to discover the truths in the lessons in this book.

As I reflected on my life up to this point, I realized that I had spent much of my life basing my identity on the perceptions of another. I had grown up as Daddy's princess where I seemingly could do no wrong only to find that as I tried to blend into the lives of others, they did not realize I was a princess and had expectations different from those I had grown up with. I had tried to find my peace in being what others thought I should be, but there was an emptiness that nothing seemed to fill.

Although I thought I knew our denomination had the right doctrine, when I talked to my husband, I found he felt as strongly that the doctrine of his upbringing was right. This brought many questions to mind, and I was getting really confused.

I found I could compromise on most points pretty well. But when it came to turning my back on the doctrinal belief I had grown up with (that my dad had taught me and that all my ancestors as far back as I can find had followed) I had a day of reckoning that I have lovingly called, My Day On The Deck.

I had reached my limit on many fronts and went out on my deck and got on my knees and announced to God that I was tired of trying to be anything and everything. I came to him, and in a not so humble way, announced to him that I had come to a decision that from this day forward I was going to open the Bible and read it for myself. I no longer would identify as a Baptist like my daddy or try to embrace my husband's faith. I would put away any preconceived ideas of who he was, and also that from this day forward no one would ever identify me but him. I reminded him that he had created me and that he was the only one who knew what he had in mind for my life and destiny.

I had now begun the most exciting journey of my life. I was God's child, and he had left me a manual with everything I needed to know about my past, present, and future, and I could not wait to dig in and start this journey.

I got a notebook and started to journal my progress, and I started at the most basic place of asking myself, "Why am I, who am I, and why do we have so many different doctrines if we are all God's children?" I majored in psychology in college and this was going to be fun, as well as a challenging journey of discovering the Bible through my new unfiltered eyes.

The surprising thing that happened was that when I found my identity in God, many of the things that had seemed so big before didn't seem to matter. I knew who I was, and as I discovered who my heavenly Father was, and how he loved and cared for me, everything else seemed to pale in comparison.

I no longer focused on the opinions of others, but in the one who created me. My goal became to be the best that God created me to be, and he went before me every step of the way. I learned that his Word was the place where I could go to find answers when life seemed unfair. It was the place of wisdom filled with promises from a Father who had me in mind when he created the world and who loved me so much that he would willingly die in my place to save me. I was blown away at the thought of being able to talk to and hear from him like a close friend, and yet he was the creator and source of everything that existed. I was, and continue to be, amazed that he cared about my marriage, my children, my concerns, and me

Although we have many differences, my husband has been a huge blessing in my life, and we both became more focused on who God wanted us to be, rather than identifying with a doctrine. God has blessed us in more ways than I can begin to count. We now have four children and nine grandchildren. We have learned to appreciate each other's differences and have even spoken about it on more than one occasion at marriage conferences. One day he came home from work and said he had heard James Dobson on the radio say that God created opposites to attract because if they were alike, one of them would be unnecessary. We have come to know that we are both necessary in each other's lives.

As we were preparing to speak on differences in marriage several years ago, I wrote a poem that sums up what I have learned.

> I don't want to walk before you, for fear I'll block your view.
> I don't want to walk behind you, for all I will see, is you.
> So let me walk beside you, so both of us can see
> Exactly what God had in mind when He created you for me!

This goes for any relationship God brings into our lives. I have learned anytime I base my identity on anything or anyone but God I will surely be disappointed. My hope and prayer for you and each of my children and grandchildren is that they, too, reach a time when they have their "day on the deck" and learn the incredible truths in God's Word for themselves.

As you approach this study of the Bible, I hope you will approach it with an open mind and let God teach you who he created you to be. The Bible was written for each and every one of us to be able to read and understand.

Preface

As I approached my study of the Bible, it seemed incredibly intimidating. Then I remembered what my English teacher taught me in junior high school about diagramming.

If I can just break it down, get the overall theme, and identify the characters, it will be much easier to understand. So the first thing I did was create an outline to work from.

Next, I remembered in school, when I was given a book to read that seemed difficult and knew I was going to be asked to give a report, I would often buy Cliff's Notes. This was the little blue cheat book that summarized the contents of the book. Reading that alone left out many of the important facts and drama of the book, but it did give me a framework to work from. I could then read the book, fill in the gaps, and somehow it made it easier to comprehend.

So first I worked on the diagram. As I reflected on verses I had learned years ago, I remembered the verse where God said, "I am the Alpha and Omega, the beginning and the end." So, I immediately knew that God would be the first line and last line on my diagram.

Next, as I looked back in history I found that before man there were angels. On and on I went following the timeline of the Bible. Once I got to the end of the Old Testament, I took a pause and looked at the 400-year gap between the Old and New Testaments. Then I continued with the same thing beginning with the life of Jesus and the formation of the church in the New Testament. My outline ended in the book of Revelation and the end of time, of course with God, the Omega, (God) living with His children in Heaven for eternity.

So now I had the framework, and next, I wanted to get a quick overview before I dug deeply into the specifics of each time frame.

The Bible is a love story of a Father whose main characteristic is pure love. He is the life force of all creation. Looking at Genesis we see, "In the beginning God created the heavens and the earth. Now the earth was formless and empty, darkness was over the surface of the deep, and the Spirit of God was hovering over the waters." And God said, "Let there be light," and there was light. This started the beginning of all created things on this earth. The next question I asked was, why did he create this beautiful earth and fill it with vegetation, animals and the ability to procreate each species forever? The answer came with his final act of creation, his crowning glory, and that was man. A species created in his own image. Genesis 1:26, "Then God said, "Let's make man in our image, in our likeness and let him rule over all other created things."

That would seem like the second line of our outline, but as we look at the content and timeline, we see there were angels who existed with God before man was created. Psalm 148:2, 5, 6 tell us, "Praise the Lord, all his angels, praise him, all his heavenly host.... Let them praise the name of the Lord, for he commanded and they were created. He set them in place forever and ever; he gave a decree that will never pass away." We will devote an entire lesson on exactly who these created beings were and the purpose of their creation. Because they were the next created things, they are the second line of our outline. It is important to mention them here because it was a rebellion against God among them that the possibility for an evil mindset even exists. God purged the ones who turned against him from heaven, but they were still a force to be reckoned with as they existed as rogue spirits on earth and had access to man.

God gave man authority over them and actually over everything created, but since God wanted man to be free to choose to love and obey Him, he put a tree in the garden and told them not to partake of it. God is love and love needs a recipient to be complete, love that is not forced but given willingly. God wanted man to be family and not be mere robots. After all, when God created man he breathed his very DNA into him. Genesis 2:7, "The Lord God formed the man from the dust of the ground and breathed into his nostrils the breath of life, and the man became a living being."

The rest of the story is that this rogue spirit entered into a serpent and appeared to Eve telling her that if she ate of the tree, she and Adam would be as smart as God. She convinced Adam to listen as well, and they were both deceived into disobeying the very one who had created them. Immediately they felt the absence of God's presence, and for the first time, they felt fear and shame. God had warned them in the beginning that if they ate of that one tree they would surely die. The death he was talking about was spiritual death. You might ask why God did not at this point just destroy them and create another pair. The answer is the love story of the Bible. John 3:16 says it all, "For God so loved the world (man) that He gave His only begotten son (a part of himself), that whosoever believeth in Him shall not perish but have everlasting life." We will look more deeply into the whys as we study the attributes of God in the following lessons.

This sets the framework of the Bible. God is now on the outside looking in at his creation. The ones that he had given over the authority of all he had created, and now they had by their disobedience given that authority over to a rogue spirit and they now had partaken of the nature of the one they obeyed. They were now left with a sense of longing, or heart hunger, because of the absence of the life-giving spirit that had been breathed into them when they were created. Because of God's nature, he could not reside with sin, so he had to withdraw himself from the very ones he had created, at least until he could bring about a plan of restoration. We will get more deeply into the whys of that in our future lessons.

God now found Himself living estranged from his children. He no longer had the sweet fellowship that the spiritual connection had brought. He had to approach them from the outside world working through angels, prophets, and chosen men to bring about a plan to restore spiritual fellowship. But the ultimate way to restore us to himself was to come to earth in the form of a man to once again join humanity and divinity in one body. Man alone could not redeem himself because he had partaken of the very nature of another spirit.

Restoration required a new and pure bloodline to be formed, a bloodline that had not been tainted with the nature of sin running through its veins. This process of restoration is the greatest love story ever told. God once again entered into man by the breath of the Holy Spirit impregnating a young virgin girl named Mary. The result was the birth of Jesus. He had been conceived by the life of God that had no sin nature, and when joined with the seed of the Virgin Mary, once again there was a man who did not have the DNA of sin running in his veins. The very Son of God had entered earth on a mission of redemption.

He alone could come as a representative of the man God had created with a perfect bloodline. He would have to face the same temptations the first man did and not be led astray from the purpose of his Father. He too was given a choice about partaking of a tree, but the tree he had to choose to partake of was the cross that represented the sin of man.

He was created fully human. The Bible tells us he was tempted as man in every way. Then he had to stand before the judgment seat of God as man and be put on trial for man's sin. It was not automatic, it was his choice, and a painful one as we see when he spent an evening in the Garden of Gethsemane so anguished that he sweat drops of blood while asking his Father if there was any other way. We know the answer he submitted when he said, "Not my will but thine be done."

The will of the Father was that we be restored back to the state of spiritual oneness with him. This was the only way. A heavenly intervention had to take place and we know that Jesus suffered unbelievable humiliation and shame as he was beaten, stripped naked, and nailed to the tree. I have often wondered if the cross might have been cut from the same root of the tree God told Adam and Eve not to eat of in the garden. The tree that represented man's disobedience was now the tree that Jesus was hanging on representing all mankind. Now Jesus, in his obedience to be a substitute for the sin of man, offered his righteous nature to destroy the sin nature man had been living with.

Now man had been vindicated and was given once again the ability to choose God's best by accepting what his son had come to earth to restore. Once again, God was saying to all mankind you can freely eat of the tree of life by identifying with Jesus and making the right choice this time. We are told that when we make that choice we are made righteous once again in the sight of God.

So as we look at the Bible we can see the beginning of mankind and the fall of man in the first few chapters. Then the rest of the part that is called the Old Testament is the plan God devised to work through men to bring about a righteous seed once again. Men now had a rebellious nature, so for God go accomplish this, he had to isolate a genealogy to work through to bring about this coup. This is the big picture of the Old Testament. God worked through prophets, angels, and finally isolated a man and his family, Abraham, to be set apart for his purpose.

The New Testament starts with the arrival of God's son Jesus, the one who was sent to take our place and restore us back to the Father. There are four live accounts of his life in Matthew, Mark, Luke, and John. Matthew, the first book in the New Testament, opens with a history of the genealogy that God worked through. That genealogy starts with a man named Abraham and continues through to the time of the birth of Jesus. It is quite an interesting group of people, as you find kings, prostitutes, farmers, businessmen, etc. All had a place in the lineage of Jesus, and in the end, our lineage as we become identified with him. God wants us to know that he loves us all regardless of our background or heritage.

Our lessons follow Jesus to the cross, resurrection, and the start of the church. In the end, we study the fulfillment of prophecies and how they point us to the end time when we will live eternally with him.

On the next page is my outline of the Old Testament. I hope as you get the big picture after you go through these lessons that you will be able to come back later and fill in the many other stories and characters in the Bible.

Old Testament Outline

God
^

Angels
^

Adam and Eve
^

Cain-Seth-Abel
^

8 Generations
^

Noah
^

Ham-Shem-Japheth
^

8 Generations
^

Abraham
^

Isaac
^

Jacob (Israel)
^

Simeon-Asher-Levi-Dan-Gad- Judah-Issachar-Rueben-Naphtali-Joseph- Benjamin-Zebulon
(Children of Israel)
^

Moses
^

Joshua
^

Saul
^

David
^

Solomon
^

Rehoboam-Jeroboam
2 Tribes-Northern Kingdom   10 Tribes-Southern Kingdom
^

Babylon Captivity
^

Daniel (Decree of Cyrus)
^

Jeremiah   Ezra   Nehemiah
(Restore Temple)   (Restored Scrolls)   (Rebuilt Wall)
Jews were back in Jerusalem with the temple rebuilt and this ends the Old Testament

Lesson 1
The Bible & My Belief

When you study any book, the questions you want to know are: What is the subject of the book? Is it fact or fiction? Who wrote it and why? What does it have to offer me as a reader? The Bible is no exception, and before we begin to study it, we have to ask two important questions: What are my beliefs about the Bible as a book, and what role, if any, does it play in my life? These questions are important because the belief we have about anything in our lives is how we will respect and respond to the Bible.

I think if we are brought up in a Christian nation, most of us have an element of respect for the Bible, regardless of how we respond to it. We see it in every home, hotel and government office across our nation. Every court preceding places it as the authority to swear by in giving a testimony. Our nation was founded on its principles, and every President who is inaugurated places his hand on the Bible in taking his oath, as if to say this is the foundation I swear to uphold and abide by during my term of office. The Bible is read at christenings of newborn babies as they begin their life, and at funerals witnessing the end of life.

How you respond to the Bible often depends on the respect and importance it was given in our home as we were growing up. If you were taught to read it and obey the teachings in it as a child, then you no doubt at some level of your being, have a foundation that will always lead you back to it in times of trouble, even if it is not a part of your everyday lifestyle. If it collected dust on the shelf and was never opened, it may be like Webster's Exhausted Dictionary. Every home needs one, but it is referred to only a few times in a lifetime. It may be little more than a convenient place to store information about births, deaths and other family genealogy. It was never read even as a good book, much less for life wisdom and understanding.

This brings me to the next question I want to address. Why study the Bible? To find the answer to this, we have to look at more than just the printed material itself. We also have to spend some time reflecting on our personal development as created beings.

This is true because the Bible is the history of our heritage, an account of our destiny, and a guide for daily living. Why then do so few people ever bother to read it once in a lifetime, much less study it for understanding, as you would any other text containing pertinent information about your life?

We take classes in psychology and read every self-help book we can get our hands on to try to find out what life is all about and help us understand the meaning of our existence. Most of the time this becomes a study of human behavior rather than a search for the internal purpose of our being. Psychology can go a long way in telling us why we behave the way we do, because psychologists have studied the patterns of people's behavior and documented data that has a great deal of consistency. They have also done a great deal of research on the power of parenting techniques and the effects of early childhood memories. This can go a long way in helping us determine the origin of our own behavior patterns and the beliefs we have developed over our lifetimes.

This was brought to my attention several years ago when I attended a meeting where we were handed a sheet of paper with the questions on it: Who am I? What is my purpose in living? As I reflected on my answer to the first question, I realized it read like a job description: wife, mother, Free Will Baptist, Republican, member of different boards, etc. I also began to look at the places in my life where I had a natural drawing, such as being an advocate for the elderly, aiding children with physical disabilities, and working with teenagers.

I began to realize that so much of my life was a process of repeating patterns that had been taught to me by my parents and those around me. The question came to my mind, if I had been born to the people next door, how much of me would I still be? I would be a Catholic instead of a Baptist, I would be allowed to dance, but not eat meat on Friday. I would be a Democrat instead of a Republican. I would not have had the passion for the elderly in nursing homes because my father wouldn't have been there to take me to the nursing homes as a small child to develop that sensitivity. However, I would have had a desire to fight for the life of the unborn since their daughter had an abortion against their wishes and they felt a sense of responsibility to protect other unborn children.

Even the way I care for myself is a reflection of my upbringing. I never will forget working with a girl many years ago who was brought up in the Pentecostal denomination. We talked about our faith a lot, and how God was working in each of our lives. One day she came to me troubled and said, "You are as good a Christian as I have ever met, but I don't understand how you can have such a close walk with the Lord and wear all that make-up. I have come to the conclusion that it must not be wrong." She determined to start adding a little color to her own face. The next day she wore lipstick and a little blush. She sat at her desk all morning looking like she had just stolen the company secrets. By noon she came to me and said, "I can't do this. My conscience is killing me." She went to the bathroom and immediately washed her face. That got my curiosity roused as to the power of parenting patterns. Her dad had taught her that the Bible taught against wearing make-up and if she wore it, she could not be a Christian witness. My dad told me, "If the old barn needs painting, then paint it." (He was a Baptist minister). What was right? Was my dad wrong and was I being an embarrassment to Christ by wearing make-up and calling myself one of his children? Was it really wrong to dance? Was my Catholic friend right and should I be going to mass, not eating meat on Friday, and going to a priest for confessions of my sins?

Why did I go to bed at night as a child wondering if I had unknowingly committed a sin that might send me to hell if I died in my sleep because I did not ask forgiveness of it? Meanwhile my neighbors said, "Once saved, always saved," and they never had to worry about going to hell.

Why did one of my mother's best friends pray in a language we could not understand and feel so much joy saying it was a gift sent from God, while I was taught talking in tongues was just a sham, a type of hypnosis with no biblical basis? They cannot all be truth. They are so diabolically opposed to each other, and yet we all call ourselves Christians (Christ-followers).

We will defend our beliefs almost to the point of death when, in fact, they are often not ours at all. When we are born, we start imitating the behavior of our parents. We watch them walk and start trying to take steps so we can move about like them. We hear them talk and start imitating the sounds until we have developed our vocabulary like theirs. If we are born in France, we pattern that language and grow up speaking French. If we grew up in America, we speak English. Even in our country you can tell whether a child grew up in Georgia or Boston, just by the way he pronounces his words.

Our parents are the two primary people God gave us to pattern our identity after. They gave us the first reflection we have of ourselves. Unfortunately, they too have imperfections and struggle with the truth behind all the patterns handed down to them from generations past.

I think the story about the woman who always cut off the end of the ham at Thanksgiving points this out as clearly as any. One year as she was teaching her daughter how to prepare the traditional Thanksgiving meal, her daughter asked her why she always cut off the end of the ham. She replied, "I don't know that's just the way my mother taught me to do it." Her curiosity caused her to ask her grandmother and she said she too had never questioned why, it was just the way she had been taught. Finally, she went to her 90-year-old great-grandmother and asked her why she cut the end off of the Thanksgiving ham, to which the old grandmother replied, "I did because I did not have a big enough pan to put it in."

I decided to test this theory a few years back and tackle a fear I had by finding its origin. It started when I was giving my daughter swimming lessons. She was terrified of putting her head under water. She was afraid she would not be able to breathe. I panicked when they told me they would have to just throw her in and show her that she would be able to hold her breath long enough to get to the top. This would help her not be afraid, they said.

My mother happened to be visiting that day, and we waited together outside the pool area. We heard water splashing and could hear my daughter starting to cry, and I saw my mother in an even greater panic than I was in. She had to leave and sit in the car. As I looked at all the other little four year-olds jumping in the water and having such fun, I asked myself, why was my daughter so afraid of water? I knew I had always panicked when my head went under and had struggled with that my entire life. I thought about my mother and realized I had never seen her swim. I asked her why she never swam and she replied, "I just can't get my head under water, I start to smother and can't breathe." I began to see a pattern that had been set in motion somewhere in my background and determined to find out where.

I visited my 80-year-old grandmother and asked her to tell me about her earliest memories. After thinking back through her childhood, she first said nothing came to mind that stood out. Then she got this panicked look on her face and said, "When I was just a little girl, we had to cross a stream to get to school. It had been raining and the water was high. They had put a log from one side to the other so we could get across. My foot slipped as I was crossing and I fell in. When I did, the current caught me and carried me downstream. I still remember being pulled under and not being able to breathe. Someone saw me and pulled me out. I was always terrified of water after that. I never wanted my kids to go swimming, I was so afraid one of them would drown."

I could see immediately how the abnormal fear of being under water had been handed down to my daughter. My mother was the oldest, and of course got the full effect of her mother's caution concerning the water. She was so afraid of water, my dad used to tease her about being afraid of taking a bath. She in turn always panicked when she saw me getting in water over my ankles. It was easy to see how, without anyone realizing it; my daughter was terrified of water because her great grandmother fell off a log into the water 75 years earlier. Once I recognized the origin, the fear lost its power. My mother, at the age of 60, took swimming lessons and overcame her fear of water, as did I. My daughter is now as comfortable under the water as she is on dry land.

I share this with you to show you just one small way the power of repeating patterns can affect our beliefs and the way we live our lives. The same is often true in our spiritual lives. Had I never questioned the truth about the origin of the fear handed down in my family concerning water, no doubt it would have continued to be passed on long after grandmother had died, and no one would have known why. Not unless she left a diary with a history of her life experiences. Even then someone would have to take the time to read the diary, looking for the answers to these questions related to their life. When a family passes down a genealogy of past events in a family history, they do so to enable future generations to know more about the people and circumstances that helped shape their family heritage. Each unique event that happened in our family's past has played an important part in shaping who we are today.

The same is true of our study of the Bible. It is a diary left for us by God to help us better understand where we came from and the purpose of our existence. Although the evolution of our belief system is rooted in our particular family heritage, it is important to not dump blame on our parents for hurtful or erroneous beliefs they passed on to us. Remember, they too were handed down a set of beliefs that stemmed from their ancestors. This started when the first set of parents (Adam and Eve) were not attentive to God's Word and disobeyed in the garden all those years ago. There has been a continual heritage of imperfections ever since. They too missed the perfect plan God originally had for them.

It is important for us to understand that our self-esteem and view of God is usually a mirror of our parents' attitudes toward us. If we were loved and affirmed by our parents, we tend to have a fairly healthy self-concept, and usually find it easy to believe that God is loving, merciful and forgiving.

Those whose parents have been neglectful, manipulative, or condemning, usually seem to feel that they have to earn a sense of worth, and they find it harder to receive God's unconditional love. Just as God's love is unconditional for us, it is unconditional for our parents. Just as we would not blame a parent in a wheelchair with a physical handicap for not being able to run and play ball with us, we can't blame those with emotional handicaps for not being able to love us the way we needed to be loved as children. Jesus taught forgiveness, and if we can let him open our eyes to these truths, we can even be a part of the process of our parent's emotional and spiritual growth, as well as our own.

Regardless of our upbringing, it is essential to our adult sense of wellbeing, to take a look at where we came from, whether we feel it was a positive or negative environment. Find out what messages have been given to you to process life with.

In front of every person in the world is a large window through which he or she views everything that goes on. Although it is invisible to the naked eye, it is very real. Not only do we see the world through it looking out, we also use it as a filter through which all of the world's data is passed coming in. This is called your belief window. It is important to see what is written on your particular window, because through it you will view the world. Be sure that the view you have is accurate, whether good or bad. Examine whether your perceptions are based on an accurate view or filtered through the memories and experiences of others.

This reminds me of the story of two men who were sharing a hospital room. Both had to remain flat of their backs for weeks upon end. The one man who came in first got the bed next to the window, and the other man was very jealous. As time went on and the days began to drag out, the one by the window sensed the weariness of his roommate and started sharing what he could see out the window. He told about the children playing in the park, and described them so vividly that you could almost feel you could join in their games. He described flowers as they began to bloom and how two lovers walked through the park and how he stopped to pick a bouquet and hid it behind his back, not thinking anyone was looking, until they were alone, and how he knelt on one knee as he proposed to her. Then how the birds built a nest just outside the window and how he could see the mother bird gather straw and carefully knit it together to form a secure place for her babies to hatch. Then the excitement of the day they arrived and how she carefully brought back worms and dropped them in the mouth of each baby. Then watching them grow and gain their confidence as they began to discover the power of the wind beneath their wings, and watching them fly off, never to return.

There was a parade that lasted for two solid hours and he did not leave out one detail of the vivid colors of the sixty-three floats as they passed the hospital on the street below. As the man listened to all the beautiful sights he was missing out on, the angrier he became, until he began to curse and swear at his roommate. Then the day came the roommate got ill and died. He could hardly wait until the nurse returned to the room to, at last, get to move to the bed close to the window. The nurse obliged him and propped him up so he could see the long-awaited view, only to find the window faced a blank, dirty, brick wall. Then he realized that the things his friend had seen were only memories in his mind that gave him a view of life to pass on and share with those around him.

This is the way we begin our lives. Looking at it through the window of the experiences and memories handed down to us by those God entrusted us to. Many of these are ways of living we would choose if given no outside influence, but we never really know that for sure if we never take a realistic look at what was written on our belief window in each area of our lives.

This was highlighted for me when my husband and I got involved in politics, and I started really looking at the voting record of the elected officials I help put in office. I was somewhat astonished to find out that the candidate that I had voted for year after year did not represent the moral values or the political views that in my opinion would best shape the nation my grandchildren would someday inherit. Up until then I had not given much attention to the person to vote for. I inherited a political party, and therefore whoever that candidate was, was my man.

I was appalled at the power of tradition. As I focused on one particular election, there were some issues that were diabolically opposed to everything my family had believed in that (our) candidate supported.

I will never forget visiting with my grandfather and discussing these issues. I informed him as to the stand that our democratic candidate had taken and pointed out his voting record in the past term of office. My grandfather was also surprised and agreed with me that this was not right and something needed to be done. I was feeling pretty good until I got ready to leave and I asked him about which of the other candidates he was going to vote for that represented a belief more like ours, and he replied: "Oh, I'm still going to vote for the Democratic candidate. You see we have always been Democrats." It was then that I began to examine how the power of tradition had affected other areas of my life. It was not the fact that the Democratic candidate was not necessarily the best guy to vote for, but the fact that tradition overrode logical examination of the important issues that could directly impact our lives and those around us.

This caused me to examine what my belief system was and how it had been formed. First, I was surprised to realize that I really did not want to take the time to look at a political candidate and listen to what he stood for. If he could give a good (general) political speech and look good on the surface, (and they all do, or they would not be running), I was proud to be a Democrat. It amazed me at the defensive attitude I had for my candidate because I was on his team. I wanted him to win, no matter what. It was then that I realized how important it was that we are on a team.

How many people go to a ball game and just watch the game, not caring who wins? We won't watch long before we take sides. Usually one that either represents our heritage (hometown, state, etc.) or someone we might know on one of the teams that we somehow connect with. By our very make-up we want to take a stand and support a team. Unfortunately, we come into this world with our teams already chosen, and if we don't make a conscious effort to examine our own personal make-up and beliefs, we can go a lifetime being on a team and never know why or what it stands for.

As I looked at my Christian life, I realized that it was also very much a reflection of a team that had been chosen for me at birth. Because I was brought up in a minister's family and went to church every time the church doors were opened, I was programmed with the belief system that had been passed down by my parents, their parents, and on and on. I learned the Bible stories and loved identifying with the characters in a fantasy-like way. I was often first in the sword drill (where children were lined up and given a verse to see who could find it first.) I understood the plan of salvation; I believed that Jesus was God's son and that He died for my sins. Going to the altar and making a public confession of that was the beginning of my life as a Christian. From this point on if I died I would not go to hell. It allowed me to sleep better at night knowing my eternal fate had been established.

From this point on, I did like so many others do, and unquestioningly accepted the doctrines, or belief system, of my family. I was assigned a team. Other denominations were close but not quite right. I always knew if Jesus came to live in our town, he would attend our church. This closed attitude toward God's plan hindered me from taking a personal look at what God had to teach me. Don't get me wrong, I treasure my Christian heritage as one of the greatest blessings God has given me. My family's love and acceptance undergirded the foundation my faith was built on.

I remember hearing that at about the age of 12, boys and girls reach the age of accountability (time to take responsibility for their spiritual lives.) That meant, in my church going to an altar and asking God to forgive you of your sins. It was at that point that you became a Christian. Some churches have confirmation ceremonies. Whatever denomination you were raised in determined the process you went through. Then so often we proceed with the manner of worship and continue that throughout our lives, without ever growing and developing our personal relationships with Christ or studying the Bible for ourselves. We just naturally adopt the belief and doctrine of those around us.

I remember asking a young man visiting in my home if he was a Christian, and he replied; "Oh yes, my family are all big church people." It was then that I realized how much of my life I too had planned to get to heaven on my father's coattail. I think somewhere in the back of my mind I felt that Christianity had a legacy system.

It was not until I was out on my own that I started taking personal responsibility for my relationship with God. Even then, I stayed within the confines of the family tradition, never questioning the whys of the doctrinal pattern I had grown up with. As I looked at the difference in theological knowledge and personally inspired knowledge of the Bible, I realized one of the biggest hindrances I had to putting aside the teaching of others and digging into the Bible for myself, was that I felt so inadequate. I felt that the only ones who really were capable of understanding the Bible were the Bible scholars and those who attended seminary.

Then one day I read in Psalms where it says, "God gives understanding to the simple," and I figured that must include me. I began to hunger for more knowledge of the Bible. I read in Hosea 4:6, "My people perish for lack of knowledge." I knew that in a lot of areas of my life I was perishing. I learned that this was not just head knowledge of the Bible, but also heart knowledge. I first had to learn it with my head by reading the information, but the real power of God was released when I asked the Holy Spirit to give me the understanding of those truths in my heart so I could apply them to my life.

It was much the same as learning math. I can memorize a formula to solve a math problem to pass a test, but if I don't understand the process, when I am in a real-life situation, it will be hard for me to adapt that formula to my problem. The same is true of God's Word.

This lesson was designed to help you clear out any clutter that may hinder God's Word from being fully realized in your mind. I'm not asking you to depart from your beliefs, just put them aside while you study the Bible for yourself with an open mind.

As a means of reflection, I will include questions at the end of each lesson for you to consider and share with others for further discussion.

Discussion Questions:

1. Describe your view of God. (What he is like? How do you relate to him, etc?)

2. Write down your three earliest memories. (Think back to the first time you remember an event, regardless of how insignificant it may seem, and remember how you felt. You may have to go back to your first birthday or special holidays to get started remembering.)

3. Briefly describe your father and mother, particularly as you viewed them as a child.

4. What messages are written on your belief window? (Attitudes towards political, social issues, family life, ways you show emotions, spiritual life, particularly your religious doctrinal belief. List as many as you can. For example: My belief window taught me as a result of growing up in a Baptist Church that dancing was wrong. As I examined that as an adult, using God's Word, I found that was a doctrinal belief that I did not share.)

5. What are some of the barriers that prevent you from departing from the belief system that have been handed down you? (For example: Loss of parental approval.)

6. Describe ways your father and mother either affirmed you or rejected you.

7. What beliefs did you have growing up about the Bible? (Whether it was literal, etc. Even if you did not have one in your home that shows it had little importance).

8. Are you willing to set aside past patterns and beliefs and study the Bible with an open mind asking the Holy Spirit to guide you into truth?

Lesson 2
The Bible: Fact or Fiction?

The last lesson we talked about the role the Bible played in our lives and our need to study it for ourselves and take personal responsibility for our own understanding of it. Once we have made the decision to set aside our doctrinal teachings from the past and truly study the Bible for ourselves, it is important that we know in our hearts that the Bible is more than a fine piece of literature.

We are going to find we are being asked to make decisions on how we conduct our lives based on the instructions in this book. That will be impossible to do if we do not first answer the question: is the Bible fact or fiction?

When I was a child, I enjoyed going to church each Sunday and listening to my Sunday school teachers read Bible stories. I enjoyed the heroic story of how the little shepherd boy, David, killed the giant, Goliath with a slingshot and a few small stones. And the story of Joseph being thrown in the pit and sold by his brothers who were jealous of him and how he eventually was made ruler over the country they were dependent on for food to survive. And the Hebrew mother who put her baby boy in a basket and hid him in the bushes of a river to avoid him being killed by the king, and how the princess found him and he grew up in the palace. How he eventually was the hero who saved his people. And the adventure of following the children of Israel as they fled from Egyptian bondage, and how God parted the sea as they were trapped by the army on one side, and the Red Sea on the other.

As a girl I particularly enjoyed the romantic stories of Boaz and Ruth, Jacob and Rachel, and the intriguing story of how Samson loved Delilah so much that he told her his most trusted secret and how she deceived him, and used it to destroy him for her own selfish motives.

These stories were interesting to read about, but were little more than other classic stories we learned as children, and for many years that is how I approached the Bible. I knew it was supposed to be holy (set apart) and sacred and more than mere entertainment by the storytellers of old. However, when I tried to read it, it seemed to be a book of Kohath begat Korah, begat Assir, begat Tahath, begat Uriel, begat Uzziah, begat Elkanah.

I was told that this was the book that I was to base my life on – the inspired Word of God sent to show me the do's and don'ts of living a Christian life. I knew I was a Christian because I had gone to the altar at the age of 11, asked forgiveness of my sins, and asked Jesus to come into my heart. I felt a newness of life come into me at that time and I never questioned my salvation.

I was told everything I would need to know about being a Christian was found in the Bible, and I was to study it and obey the rules, both of the Bible and the doctrinal beliefs of the particular denomination I belonged to. I tried to read it and understand it with my intellect and memorize key verses. I listened to the minister each Sunday interpret the rules of being a Christian and tried to follow them as best I could out of fear of not getting into heaven if I didn't. I was taught that I was to fear God and be surrendered to him, and to be sure there was no unconfessed sin in my life. I was always fearful that I might sin and die in a car crash before I had a chance to ask forgiveness and end up in the deep pit of hell for eternity.

It was like coming to the age of being able to drive a car and being given a driver's manual, but not understanding the concepts or mechanics of handling a vehicle. I studied the rules and knew the appropriate speed limits and how to parallel park but until I got behind the wheel of a car myself, it was only a set of rules someone put down to prepare me for safe driving that, at the time, seemed unimportant except to help me get a certificate saying I could drive.

It wasn't until I climbed behind the wheel of a car and felt the power as it accelerated, the ability the brakes gave me to stop the vehicle, and the control of changing directions at the turn of a wheel, that I fully understood what the laws governing driving were all about. Then I had a healthy respect for the protection and safety that they imposed on me, as well as the other million drivers I was going to encounter on the highways. It is only then that I could call myself a driver.

That is much the way I was concerning the information in the Bible. I learned the basics of the stories and was doing a good job of obeying the rules, but I felt something was missing. I began to search to see if I could find out why Christians all through the ages had lived by and died for the preservation of this book. If I was going to be asked to base my life on the authority of this book, I wanted to know for myself that it was true and accurate.

As I looked at the different denominations, I found that some thought the Bible was a collection of parables and could not possibly be true because of the supernatural things that it told happened, such as Jonah being swallowed by a whale, Peter walking on water, or the parting of the Red Sea. These were not acceptable to the natural reasoning of man's finite mind. So, some decided that the parts that were not possible in the physical realm of reasoning must have just been inserted to make a point. However, these same people believe in the virgin birth of Jesus, the resurrection, and His supernatural ascension into Heaven.

Somehow it did not seem right to me that God would leave it up to man to use his interpretation to know what parts were actually true and which were object lessons. That is like us hearing a presidential speech and then having five different newscasters try to draw a conclusion as to what they thought the president was telling us (using their own biased opinions of course) about the impact it was going to have on our economy and us.

That is how we ended up with so many denominations. People took the Bible and tried to interpret it as something other than the way it was written, often to suit a particular need in their own lives. Each of those views formed a denomination and has been handed down for generations to come. Too often we accept things as truth without ever taking responsibility for studying for ourselves and questioning the basis the truth is established on.

Either the Bible is true and factual, or it is not. So, I think the first step in studying the Bible is to decide if, in fact, it is true.

Men through the ages have been trying to destroy and disprove the Bible, but until this day, every attempt known has resulted in atheists becoming convinced of the authenticity of the Bible and the belief that it was truly inspired by God. When you read it and study it to discover truth, the Spirit of

God bears witness with your spirit and the awareness of truth comes more from somewhere within than on the written pages.

As I researched through many books, papers and writings of Biblical historians I found that by any standard, the Bible is a great masterpiece. How could a book that begins in the Stone Age, and ends in the world of the Roman Empire, still be relevant today?

I was amazed to find its most recent sections are almost 2,000 years old and took approximately 1,600 years in preparation. So why does such an ancient book still captivate us today? Why during this time of space-age technology do people take the trouble to read a book whose authors had not yet witnessed the invention of the light bulb, telephone or automobile, much less the new age of computer technology?

To answer these questions, let's look at the book as a whole. Actually, it isn't a single book, but a collection of books. Some of them are long, some short, some very ancient, some not as old. They contain history, poetry, philosophy, hymns and even personal letters and sermons. Some are really not books at all in the typical meaning of the word. Some are merely letters, while others are messages so short that they could be copied on two or three typewritten pages.

So how did these various books come to be written? Who wrote them? When? How did they come together to make the book we now know as the Bible? It is made up of sixty-six books, which was the work of thirty-five authors. One of the most important was Moses, who was credited with writing the first five books: Genesis, Exodus, Leviticus, Numbers, and Deuteronomy. Paul was credited with writing thirteen epistles (letters): Romans to Philemon and possibly Hebrews. Other prominent writers were David, who wrote many of the Psalms; Solomon, to whom we credit Proverbs, Ecclesiastes, and the Song of Solomon; Luke, who wrote both the books of Luke and Acts; and John, who wrote the Gospel that bears his name, three epistles, and the book of Revelation.

The authors represent a wide variety of experience and background. There was Moses, who grew up in the Pharaoh's palace and had all the training and wisdom of the Egyptian royalty, but who God choose to lead the first freedom movement of all time, leading the children of Israel out from the bondage they had been put under in Egypt. There was Joshua, the valiant army captain who established Israel in the land of Palestine. There was David, who rose from a shepherd boy watching over sheep to a ruler in the palace. He shares his hardships and sorrow in that process and the disappointments that came from Saul and later from his own son, Absalom. There was Solomon, who brought Israel to its highest place of fame and wealth; Daniel, for many years prime minister of Babylon; Amos, the herdsman; Matthew, the tax collector; Luke, the doctor; Peter, the fisherman; Paul, the Pharisee; and many others with varied occupations and experiences.

What an unlikely group to write a book! And the great marvel is that the words they wrote blended together so perfectly that they have stayed together for more than two thousand years.

Why do you think God did not use the scholars, historians, and other educated men of the time to write the Bible? The answer is, because the Bible was intended to be understood by people who were fishermen, tax collectors, doctors, farmers, and every other profession known to man. The experiences they had and recorded not only help us understand the message intended, but because they were like most of us, we can identify with our own circumstances of life.

The atmosphere that it was written in was also as varied. Parts were written in the wilderness of Sinai, others in Jerusalem, and some in Babylon while the Jews were in captivity. Some were written from a prison cell in Rome and one was written on the Island of Patmos in the Mediterranean. Most of it was written under very difficult conditions. The authors had no typewriters, no fountain pens, no smooth paper, and no computers with spell-check. They wrote with pens of quill or bone on parchment, often with no light but that of a candle.

How amazing that the work of so many diverse individuals, living in such widely scattered places, under such different conditions, and separated by thousands of years of time, should, when gathered together, become the greatest, the best-known, and the best-loved book in the world. That could only have been the work of God.

Unfortunately, none of the original writings exist today. All of them have since decayed and turned into dust. However, because of the sacred treasure of these documents, while the original manuscripts were still in existence, men (called scribes) copied them. They were copied so often that many of these copies can be found in the great museums and libraries of the world today. The copying was done with such precise care that when the work is examined today the differences due to faulty workmanship are found to be so slight as to have no essential effect upon the overall meaning.

One of the strongest evidences that the Bible was prepared by God's divine direction is its unity. Though all the extraordinary circumstances, locations, authors and time frame, all sixty-six books have one predominant purpose. Some poetry, some historical records, others truths revealed by the prophets of things to come. Some are missionary reports; others are church letters or personal correspondence. Yet they all speak of the same God, all uplift the same standards of righteousness, all tell of the same plan of salvation, and all look forward to the same Day of Judgment and eternal reward. The same thread of truth is woven in each book, each complimenting the others.

Over the years, men have taken parts of it out of the context it was written in and tried to disprove it this way. But again, if examined as it was intended, it always brings truth. Another proof is the way it has been preserved from its many enemies. If God had not watched over it with special care, it would have been destroyed many times over the years. Because it advocates good, evil men have always hated it. Because it lifts up the poor and needy, wealthy men who wish to exploit them for selfish gain have despised it. Because it advocates the rights of individuals, saying the most humble human being is of utmost value in the sight of God, it has always been an enemy to tyrants and dictators.

Time and again down through the centuries, deliberate efforts have been made to get rid of this book, but always in vain. Angered by its obvious power to turn men from the worship of heathen gods to Christ, Roman emperors decreed its extinction, with that of the early church. All copies were taken and burned. But always a few were overlooked, carefully hidden by courageous Christians.

During the Middle Ages, thousands of godly people were put to death because of their love for and devotion to the Bible. Even possession of a copy of the book was evidence enough to condemn a person to torture and the stake. Yet despite all the senseless killing and suffering, all the burning of all the known books, the Bible lives on, protected by God for His people.

After more copies had been printed and circulated than anyone could ever hope to recover, a new tactic to destroy the Bible arose. An attempt was made to discredit it, and for a time the critics enjoyed a field day. Moses, they said, couldn't possibly have written the first five books, because the art of writing wasn't known in those days. People living in 1500 B.C. couldn't have been more than ignorant nomads and cave dwellers. A global flood, they claimed, was ridiculous. As for the Genesis record of creation, nothing as vast as the earth could possibly have been created in so short a time.

Even firm believers in the Bible were concerned. Could the critics be right they wondered? Could it be possible that the Bible wasn't God's Word after all? Was it indeed inaccurate, unreliable, and untrustworthy?

The answers began to come when archaeologists began to dig into the tombs of ancient Egypt and the long-buried areas of Palestine and Babylon. Soon they were bringing forth amazing evidence in confirmation of even the smallest details of the Bible stories. Biologists, after innumerable experiments, confirmed the simple Genesis declaration concerning the reproduction of species. Geologists and paleontologists gleaned facts from the rocks in widely scattered areas of the earth, which demonstrated beyond doubt that Noah's flood was no fiction.   Nuclear scientists, investigating the power of the atom, came to the conclusion that sudden creation and dissolution even of stars and planets is not by any means unreasonable. Astronomers, with their mighty modern telescopes and technology, revealed a universe in perfect harmony with the concept of the Hebrew astronomers of long ago.

Archeologists repeatedly, are still today, finding proof of accuracy of historical facts of the Bible. One of interest was the discovery of a very ancient city which parallels with Babel in Genesis 10:10. After going down through fifty feet of debris of reed huts and mud-brick houses, they came across the foundations of a great temple and the findings that prove the existence of an educated, highly organized community, with considerable knowledge of arts, crafts, and religion, as far as 2000 B.C. Even today explorers have found evidence that they have possibly found the location and possible remains of Noah's Ark and the Shroud of Jesus.

Ever since the beginning, people have tried to destroy and disprove this book. But God has through all generations brought enough evidence to light to keep it alive in the hearts of those who search for it. Another proof is the fulfillment of prophecy uttered hundreds of years before by prophets who could not possibly have had any way of foreknowing the future, except by the inspiration and prompting of God to record them for us as to have as a sign of encouragement and accuracy of his Word.

There were prophecies given from the beginning of time. They began in Genesis and follow through Revelation. Look up and read a few:
  Gen. 2:17: God warns Adam not to eat of the tree or he will die - Fulfilled in Gen. 3:7, 8 and 5:5
  Gen. 6:3: The flood will occur in 120 years - Fulfilled Gen. 7:10
  Gen. 9:25: Canaan to be a servant to his brothers - Fulfilled Judges 1:28
  Red Sea to part - Ex. 14:13-18: Fulfilled Ex.14:26-31
  Joshua 6:1-5: Wall of Jericho to fall on the seventh day - Fulfilled Joshua 6:20

There are 45 different prophecies made and fulfilled about Christ:
  Gen. 3:15: He would be born of a woman - Fulfilled Gal. 4:4
  Gen. 12:3, 7 - 17:7: He would be from the line of Abraham - Fulfilled Gal. 3:16, Rom. 9:5
  Isaiah 7:14: He would be born of a virgin - Fulfilled Matthew 1:22, 23
  Micah 5:2: That He would be born in Bethlehem - Fulfilled Matthew 2:5, 6, Luke 2:4-6
  Isa.53: 3: He would be rejected by His own - Fulfilled Jn. 1:11-7:5
  Isaiah 53:12: He would be crucified between two thieves – Fulfilled Luke 22:37

On and on it goes as you search the scriptures and find how God spoke through prophets to tell of future events so man would know they were inspired by God. This also gives us a glimpse into our future as we look at prophecies that are yet to be fulfilled by our generation or generations to come. Each fulfillment is more evidence of the Bible being God's inspired Word.

Today the world is beginning to take notice of the prophecies foretold about the events leading to the end times, as they are showing alarming similarities to world events today. Questions about the Bible are making headline news in articles, documentaries, and even scientific journals. They are asking questions about the evidence coming to light about Noah's ark, Jesus, the Messiah, creation, and the validity of the Bible as God's inspired Word.

Books, articles, and television specials have attempted to give light on the subject of Biblical accuracy and authenticity, but the greatest evidence of all is the fact that wherever it goes it has a reforming influence, changing people's lives, filling them with courage and hope. It has universal appeal and its message is for all people. It speaks to the Indian, the Chinese, and the African, with the same compelling power that it speaks to the Englishman or the Australian. It appeals to children and youth, the middle-aged, and the elderly everywhere.

The value of anything is the price someone is willing to pay for it. Not only did God give His Son for us but also Christians throughout the ages have given their lives to protect and preserve this book. Jesus said it all in Matthew 24:35: "Heaven and earth shall pass away but my words shall not pass away."

Discussion Questions:

1. Do you believe the Bible is the inspired Word of God or just a good book given to us to set a standard of living?

2. Do you have problems interpreting the Bible as a literal piece of work? (Ex. Do you believe Jonah was swallowed by a whale?) Why or why not?

3. What doctrinal beliefs about the Bible did you learn as a child that you either did not understand, or you feel you want to learn more about?

4. Why do you think God used such a wide variety of men from so many walks of life instead of the scholars of the time to record the Bible?

5. Have you found a person in the Bible who has been in a circumstance similar to your life? Share a brief example.

6. Name two biblical proofs of the Bible that help you accept it as accurate.

7. How many books are in the Bible?

8. How many authors?

9. Who wrote the first five books of the Bible?

10. Look up and read at least three prophecies that are listed and where they were fulfilled. How does this help validate the authenticity of the Bible for you?

11. List any questions you might still have about the Bible as the inspired Word of God.

Lesson 3
Structure of the Bible

As we mentioned in the last lesson, the Bible is not just one book, but a collection of books that have been inspired by God, and when compiled and put together they each complement each other and complete the story of mankind. It is like a jigsaw puzzle. Without each piece, the puzzle is incomplete. Each piece is different in size and shape but each one is equally important in filling in a space to complete the overall picture.

The Bible is divided into two major sections - The Old Testament and The New Testament. The Old Testament is the new concealed and the New Testament is the old revealed.

The word testament, as defined by Webster, means covenant (settled declaration, contract). That is exactly what the Bible is all about. It is a history of how God created man in his image, to commune, love and obey Him. After man's disobedience in the garden, he lost that unity with God. However, immediately God started the process of restoring man to himself again.

First God found a family (Abraham) of honor and character to work through. Then He gave them a visual understanding of what was to come. He made agreements with them about what needed to happen for the fulfillment of the plan. He had to restore man to the state he was in before Adam sinned and brought spiritual death into the life of every person born after him. These agreements were called covenants and they were more binding than life itself.

The plan, of course, was for God to come to earth in human form (Jesus) and pay the price that justice required for man's redemption. The Old Testament records the covenant relationships God used to bring about the entrance of Jesus onto the earth. The New Testament tells about the unfolding of the plot, starting with His birth and leading up to His death and resurrection.

About 400 years lapsed between the time of the writing of the last book in the Old Testament and the time of the writing of the first book in the New Testament. We are going to look at the structure of each one.

Old Testament

The Old Testament is made up of the first thirty-nine books of the Bible. It begins with creation and tells the story of the Jewish people up to the time of Christ. It was written by approximately twenty-eight different authors, and spans a period of over two thousand years. These books were first written in Hebrew and Aramaic, the ancient language of the Jews. These documents were recorded by Jewish scribes who from time to time would make new copies as the documents became old and deteriorated due to poor quality of paper and the climatic conditions of that day. Therefore, we rarely find old copies of the earlier writings.

Until 1947, the oldest Hebrew manuscript of the Old Testament from the ninth and tenth centuries A.D. was a copy of the first five books of the Bible - the Pentateuch. Then in 1947 came the remarkable discovery of the Dead Sea Scrolls. These were early manuscripts from the library of a Jewish religious group who lived in an area called Qumran, near the Dead Sea about the time of Jesus. They were about a thousand years earlier than the oldest copies we had found until that time. The scrolls, which are what they used for paper, contained copies of all the Old Testament books except one.

What difference does this make to the authenticity of the Bible for me? It is important because these early manuscripts discovered in my lifetime are essentially the same text as the ninth-century manuscripts. They show that the text of the Old Testament has changed very little over a thousand years of being transcribed. It shows that as we read our Bible, we can be confident that the Old Testament, as we have it, is essentially the same as its authors wrote many centuries ago. That could only have happened by the preserving hand of God.

I can hear a story repeated from one friend to another in the period of a few hours and find more distortion in the real truth of the event as it really happened, than that of the Bible passed down through a thousand years. Tradition credits the scribe Ezra with collecting and arranging the books of the Old Testament. However, collections of the first five books (the books of Moses) and some of the sermons of the prophets were in existence much earlier, as were the Psalms and Proverbs.

The Old Testament is divided into three types of writings:

Historical – These books tell about creation and the formation of laws that helped shape the lives of the people of the Hebrew nation, which was Abraham's family. Genesis through Esther can be compared to a book we might read today to study the history of the United States. We would read how Columbus discovered America, how we broke away from England and established new laws and ultimately our freedom. Just as you would study past presidents and how the leadership of each helped shape us into who we are today, the Old Testament traces the lives of men and events God used to establish our heritage and freedom in the spiritual world.

Poetical – These books give us a glimpse inside the people of the time. They tell us about the emotional struggles they endured. David in the Psalms shares his emotional pain while running from Saul; Job shares his grief and pain while being tested by Satan to see if he would remain faithful to God. We also see the wisdom of great thinkers of that day as we read Proverbs, Ecclesiastes and the Song of Solomon. All of these were inspired by God to leave this wisdom for us to base our lives on thousands of years later.

Prophetical – The last seventeen books of the Old Testament are prophesies about Israel. Prophets were men of God with his message that they often spoke using terms such as "I say to you...." They were conscious of being called by God and were inspired by his Spirit and his Word. Their messages were often vividly expressed using pictures, parables and even visions. The word "prophecy" today implies foretelling the future, and the Old Testament certainly did make accurate predictions, particularly about the coming Messiah. But the heart of the Prophets' message was about the present, not the future. Their message was to call the people back to God's ways and to have faith in Him and Him alone.

They all three play an intricate part in the completion of the book. It is important for us to understand the times historically, to clearly follow the process leading up to the application to our lives today. The poetical gives us an understanding that the people of long ago had the same struggles we do today. The prophetical not only gives validity to the Bible but also acts as a guide toward events we are experiencing even today.

Combining these three aspects of the Old Testament gives us an understanding of the context that allows it to speak to us today as it did then.

New Testament

We have looked at the Old Testament and how it was structured. Now let's look at the New Testament. It contains twenty-seven books. Unlike the Old Testament, which was first written in Hebrew, the New Testament was first recorded in Greek. It is clear that by the time of Jesus, most, if not all, of the Old Testament was being read by the Jewish people. Most of the books of the Old Testament are quoted somewhere in the New Testament. This makes it likely that Jesus and his followers were familiar with the Old Testament, as we know it today. In fact at one point, Jesus reads the Old Testament scroll in the temple and tells them that the prophecy he is reading about is coming true by his very presence.

The first printed edition of the Greek text came in 1516, assembled by the Dutch scholar, Erasmus. The King James translation came along in 1611. Before the invention of printing in the West, in the fifteenth century, all writing had to be hand-copied for circulation. This was usually done by a group of scribes. Each wrote out his copy of the manuscript as the head scribe dictated. Very few private individuals could afford to own a handwritten manuscript. They were expensive to make, and Christian churches would usually own manuscripts, which all their members could share. The first copies were made on parchment or scrolls but around the second century the book form, which we use today, was introduced.

Let's take a look at how it took its present shape. The first gatherings of Christians probably followed the practice of the Jewish synagogues and had regular readings from the Old Testament during their meetings. Not only could they read the prophesies of the coming Messiah, they actually witnessed its fulfillment in their generation.

Since they were worshipping Jesus Christ, it was natural for them to add an account of some part of his life and teaching. At first, this may have been in the form of a first-hand account from someone who had known Jesus during his lifetime. But then, as the churches grew in numbers, and as the eyewitnesses began to die, it became necessary to write these stories down. This was the way the four Gospels (Matthew, Mark, Luke and John) came into being, and they obviously had an important place in the worship and life of the early churches.

The gospels are more than simply biographies of Jesus. They contain very little about his early years and a great deal on the last week of his life, and what happened in the days after His death. The word gospel means "good news."

The gospels concentrate on the good news of what Jesus brought to the world by His teaching and healing, but most importantly, the fulfillment of the purpose he came to fulfill on earth: to become one of us and by his crucifixion and resurrection redeem us from the sin state we inherited from Adam, the first created man.

For thirty years after Jesus died and rose from the dead, the apostles declared the accounts of good news about him by word of mouth. Meanwhile, written records of his sayings and actions were being collected. Eventually these records and the word-of-mouth about Jesus in different centers of Christianity were brought together to make the four gospels. These became the essential backup to the apostles' preaching. They steadily increased in importance as time passed and eyewitnesses of Jesus' life became fewer.

Why four gospels recounting the same events? As you tell of memories of a person's life, it will always be selective according to the circumstances of the person telling them. As I listen to my children recalling a particular vacation in our family's past, it always amazes me as one will tell of one thing that happened and then another will chime in with another story. If you ask each of them to write in a letter about the trip, each will remember something different than the other, and it is the combination of these that give a more accurate account of the vacation. The same is true of the apostles recalling the events around Jesus' life.

The accounts of Matthew, Mark, and Luke, have a considerable amount of material in common, but John's gospel takes a different approach. We can be thankful that there are four gospels, giving us a much more comprehensive picture of Jesus, than if there had been only one. Each one has something special and important to bring to the whole.

The book of Acts was added to the gospels in the New Testament because it continued the story of Luke and preserves the only full account of the beginnings of Christianity. Then the apostles and other leaders wrote a number of letters to various churches and individuals. Since these often gave general guidance on Christian life and beliefs, their usefulness for the whole church was recognized.

By the year 200 A.D. the gospels, as well as the letters of Paul were accepted as an important part of church history. It was not until the third century that Revelation was widely circulated. Although Hebrews was read in the first century, it was not until the fourth century that it was more readily accepted. It took longer for 2 Peter, 2 & 3 John, James and Jude to be accepted by the church as basic scripture. One reason for this was that the New Testament books were mainly used at first for public reading. If they weren't suitable for this purpose, their usefulness seemed limited.

It is obvious God inspired men as to which books would ultimately compose the New Testament. Over a period of time the church discovered that certain writings had a clear and general authority and were helpful and necessary for their growth. When put together they harmonized and completed the puzzle of the overall book. Above all, the churches were concerned that the documents they included in the New Testament truly represented the witness and experience of the men who lived closest to Jesus, and those that God had appointed to preserve His teachings.

Whether you are reading the Old Testament to study the creation of man, the historical background to the coming of Jesus, the prophecy of ancient prophets, or the New Testament, to study the life of Christ and formation of the church as we know it today, your Bible is your greatest treasure. This is true because it is the written will of God to tell His children why they are here and what their inheritance is presently and after death.

From ancient Greece comes a story of a rich farmer who on his deathbed said to his sons, "My treasure is buried in my fields. If you would be rich, dig for it." Upon the old man's death, the two sons, presuming that their father had hidden his money in an ironbound chest somewhere on his farm, set out eagerly to find it. Equipped with spades and shovels, they dug with great enthusiasm and perseverance, but seemingly without success. Carefully they turned over the soil in every field, digging to a depth no plow had ever reached. But no sign of a treasure chest did they discover. When spring came, the search was abandoned in order that the land might be sown with corn. Then came summer and harvest. And what a harvest! One like they had never seen before. In digging the land so thoroughly, the boys had won the riches they had sought. Their wise old father's plan had succeeded. God reveals the same truth in His Word. Read Proverbs 2:1-5

We, too, have a wonderful inheritance that has come down to us through many generations. It. too, is buried. Not in a field, but in a book. He who left it to you said in Joshua 1:8: "Do not let this Book of the Law depart from your mouth; meditate on it day and night, so that you may be careful to do everything written in it. Then you will be prosperous and successful."

There are a lot of times in life when we are not sure which way to turn, or even where we are in relationship to things going on around us. I compare the Bible with the directory in a shopping mall that has a red dot on it that says _**you are here.**_ It not only helps you establish where you are but allows you to map out a plan to get where you are going.

The Bible is the standard God left for us to anchor our lives on. It is the nature of man to live his life based on a standard established for him in every aspect of everyday life. Our cash flow is based on a standard that is set for our currency system (amount of gold stored somewhere.) Our conduct in society is based on a standard of laws and regulations set by our judicial system. Our standard of intelligence is based on a standard set by our educational system. Even the way we dress and wear our hair is based on standards set by designers and the fashion industry. We often base our self-worth and happiness on how well we measure up to these standards that have been set by the world and are constantly changing. The Bible is the only standard that has truly passed the test of time.

God said in Matthew 24:35: "Heaven and Earth will pass away, but my words will never pass away." It is important that we study the Word for ourselves, asking the Holy Spirit to guide us in understanding and truth. Next, we have to know in our hearts that the Bible is a written legacy left for us by the one who created us. Then we have to make the decision to let it be the red dot in our lives showing us not only where we are, but allowing it to map out a path to end up where we want to be.

Psalm 119:105 promises to do just that. It says: "Thy Word is a lamp unto my feet, and a light unto my path." Also Proverbs 3:6: "In all thy ways acknowledge him, and he shall direct thy paths." Next, focus your eyes steadfastly on its teaching. Let it be the anchor for your soul. If not, we will be led astray by the world we live in. Much like when we are stopped at a stop light and not looking at the light but on the car next to us. Suddenly he starts to move and we will find ourselves disoriented for a moment thinking we are the one who is moving, because our eyes were not focused on a stationary object. The same thing can happen when you take your eyes off God's Word and put them on someone or something else.

Another danger is often if you are looking ahead but not paying much attention, when the other car gets a green light next to us and starts moving we might instinctively accelerate as well. We can find ourselves in the middle of a busy intersection in danger of a collision. That is what happens when we try to keep up with someone else in his or her Christian walk.   Only the Holy Spirit can direct and mature us as we are submissive and obedient each step of the way.

Don't take anyone else's Christian doctrine as a basis for your life. Psalm 119:130 tells us "the unfolding of God's words gives light: it gives understanding to the simple." Don't think that you have to have a degree from a seminary to be able to understand God's message to you.

Jesus spoke in everyday language and sometimes with parables (illustrations to make a point or give understanding) of everyday things in which we can relate. He compared faith to a mustard seed and our relationship with Him to that of a bride and groom. He used stories of a boy who ran away from home (prodigal son), a beggar on the side of the road who needed help (Good Samaritan), a widow woman and her son who were out of food, fishermen caught in a storm, and a prostitute who had been rejected. It was not intended to be complicated.

Men have tried to make it a theological, philosophical, hard-to-understand book, but that was not God's plan and often the more we try to tear it apart and formulate a doctrine out of it, the less we understand it. To try to make it through life without an understanding of the Bible is like trying to put a puzzle together without the top of the box to look at. You might manage to get some of the pieces in place over time, but it is almost impossible to do so completely and with any degree of enjoyment.

Discussion Questions:

1. How are the books in the Bible like a puzzle?

2. What does the word "testament" mean?

3. Describe the difference between the Old and the New Testament.

4. How many books are in the Old Testament?

5. What languages were they first written in?

6. What three types of writing is it divided into? Briefly describe what each one adds.
   1)
   2)
   3)

7. How many books are in the New Testament?

8. What languages were they originally written in?

9. What does the word gospel mean?

10. Who wrote the four New Testaments gospels?

11. What is the overall theme of the New Testament?

12. How can the story of the farmer's inheritance be related to your study of the Bible?

13. Do you have any hesitation about being obedient to the teachings of the Bible as the standard for your life? If so, what are they?

Lesson 4
Who is God?

One of the most important things you do when you study a book is find the main character. The Bible is no exception, and the first verse in the Bible names the central figure that everything is based. I suggest that you get a color highlighter and start to personalize your Bible with your own markings. We are going to start looking up and marking verses to help you get used to studying on your own.

Look up and read Genesis 1:1. "In the beginning was God." We have to establish first, that before God, there was nothing. Colossians 1:17 tells us that "He is before all things and by Him all things exist." That is hard for our finite minds to even conceive, but is one of the first and most important facts you need to establish for your study of the Bible. He says in Rev. 1:8, "I am the Alpha and Omega (meaning the beginning and the end), who is, who was, and who is to come, the Almighty."

So one of the characteristics of God is the fact that he is _Infinite_ (limitless, non-ending). Psalm 147:5 says: "Great is our Lord, and of great power; his understanding is infinite." This means that he has no limitations as we do. Isaiah 55:9 tells us, "For as the heavens are higher than the earth, so are my ways higher than your ways, and my thoughts higher than your thoughts." God has no boundaries. He is bound only by his own nature and will. What does that mean to me as I accept him as the Lord of my Life? It means that when I come to the end of my ability to handle life's problems because of my finite knowledge, I can go to God and know that there is no limit to His ability to handle even the most difficult circumstance. Read Psalm 46:1.

God is _Omnipresent_ (ever present.) Proverbs 15:3 says, "The eyes of the Lord are in every place, beholding the evil and the good." Proverbs 5:21 also tells us, "A man's ways are in full view of the Lord, and he examines all his paths." This means that He is present everywhere with his whole being at the same time. This gives me the confidence that when I need to talk to Him about something or just want to enter into a time of thankfulness and praise to Him, that I do not have to wait in line for my turn. Look up and highlight Jeremiah 23:24.

God is _Omnipotent_ (all-powerful.) This means that God can do anything that does not contradict his nature. For instance, God cannot lie or steal because these things would contradict His word or character. Hebrews 6:18 tell us that it is impossible for God to lie. Hebrew 30:5 tell us that "Every word of God is flawless; He is a shield to those who take refuge in him." That gives me the security that I can trust God's Word to always be accurate and steadfast. Hebrews 13:8 tel me he is the same yesterday, today and tomorrow. He can't change his mind one day. It instills confidence and trust that is beyond anything we can experience from another person here on earth. Jesus sums it up in Matt: 19:26: "with man this is impossible, but with God all things are possible." Read and highlight Titus 1:2.

God is _Omniscient_ (all knowing.) He possesses complete and universal knowledge of all things past, present, and future. This includes not only the actual things that already exist, but also the things that we only dare to dream about. Hebrews 4:13 tells us "Neither is there any creature that is not manifest in his sight: but all things are naked and opened unto the eyes of him with whom we have to do." Luke 12:7 tells me that he knows exactly how many hairs are on my head.

As I reflect on these characteristics of God, I realize that there are many people in my life who know many things about me. But only God knows the good, the bad, and the innermost secrets of my thought life, as it tells us in Psalm 44:21, "He knows the secrets of the heart". Psalm 139:2 also tells us that "He understandeth my thoughts afar off." That is a great comfort to me knowing I can talk to Him about anything going on in my life because he already knows every thought, every need, and every sadness I have. He has known me at my best and known me at my worst and still loves me unconditionally. Look up and highlight these verses that give more insight into His omniscience. Proverbs 15:3, Matt: 6:32, Psalm 69:5.

God is _Sovereign_ (complete power over all.) This means that he is the absolute and sole ruler in the universe. It means that he has total freedom, power, knowledge, wisdom and determination to carry out any course of action. For me this means that I can know that no other force I come up against will ever usurp God. Isaiah 54:17 tells me, "No weapon formed against me can prosper." That instills great confidence in me as I put my trust in Him with the circumstances in my life, knowing that no problem I come against is too great for Him to handle. 2 Cor. 12:10 tells me that when I am weak (flesh), I am strong (The Spirit of Christ in me).

David understood this when he came against the giant, Goliath. The other well-trained soldiers looked at the size of the giant in comparison to themselves. David looked at the giant in comparison to the allies he had backing him (God and all the forces of heaven). If he had looked at the size of the giant in comparison to himself or his abilities, he too would have tucked his tail and ran like the others. But notice how he views the giant in 1 Samuel 17:36. "I have slew both a lion and a bear, and this uncircumcised Philistine will be as one of them, seeing he hath defiled the armies of the living God." Calling him an uncircumcised Philistine was saying he not only was not under the covenant protection of God (because circumcision was a sign of covenant relationship), but that he was coming against the armies of the living God. David knew that he was not facing the giant, but the sovereign God of the universe was actually working through him. That same covenant relationship exists between God and me. I can say with David in Psalm 56:4, "In God I trust; I will not be afraid. What can mortal man do to me?"

God is not only sovereign over our life, but also over death. Psalm 68:20 expresses it well, "Our God is a God who saves; from the Sovereign Lord comes escape from death." When we walk in the light of his law and love, we will never experience spiritual death. We are essentially spirit beings with a body that gives us access to the environment we are born into. However the day comes when each of us drop off our bodies, and our spirits will be returned to God from where they came, and will reside eternally in heaven with him. Psalm 49:15 tells us that, "But God will redeem my life from the grave, he will surely take me to himself." Jesus tells us this in John 5:24 "I tell you the truth, whoever hears my Word and believes him who sent me has eternal life, and will not be condemned; he has crossed over from death to life." Look up and highlight Psalm 27:1-3 and Psalm 30:1.

God is _Holy_ (set apart). He is like none other. The English word "holy" is derived from the Anglo-Saxon _halig, hal_, meaning, "well, whole." To be holy means all-inclusive, set apart. He does not conform to a standard, but He is the standard. His desire for man was to be holy and set apart from all creation. We are to be holy in body, soul and spirit. Set apart from sin, which separates us from the state we were created to live in. This can only be done if we allow his law and love to sanctify US (cleanse, purify, make holy) in every area of our lives.

1 Thessalonians 5:23-24, say, "May God himself, the God of peace sanctify you through and through. May your whole spirit, soul and body be kept blameless at the coming of our Lord Jesus Christ. The one who calls us is faithful and he will do it." This is referred to as our standard both in the Old and New Testament. Leviticus 19:2 tells us, "Ye shall be holy; for I the Lord your God am holy." 1 Peter 1:15 "But as he which hath called you is holy, so be ye holy in all manner of conversation." Look up and highlight Psalm 99:9.

He is _righteous_ (standard of right-ness). The word "righteousness' means right standing. In the physical sense, we say we are righteous with the law if we have no criminal record. That enables us to have certain privileges and freedoms. The standard by which we measure right or wrong is the law that represents the right way. If the speed limit on the highway is 55, then that is the law by which you are driving will be judged. Anything over that will be subject to punishment.

God represents, in the spiritual realm, the law, or our standard for righteousness. He represents all that is good and right. When we obey him, and live within the laws he has set down for us, we are in right standing with him and we have access to all the privileges and freedoms in the spiritual realm. Look up Isaiah 5:16,. 1 Samuel 26;23, Psalms 145:17

This brings us to the next characteristic of him being a _just_ God. This shows the justice system established by God brought about a sense of order to our universe. This was one of the first things he did when he made man. He laid out the rules to Adam and Eve. He told them their privileges if they obeyed the rules. The list was endless. They had access to every good thing and dominion over all things in the earth. He told them to freely eat of every tree but one.

Then came the rule concerning the justice system. He said, "If you eat of this one tree, you will surely die." As we look back at it now, we can see that God set up that rule both to test their obedience and for their protection. If they had obeyed him, sin would not have entered the world and we would not have had the suffering it has brought to all mankind. However, since man was given a free will with the potential of disobedience (sin) entering his life, and since because of God's nature he cannot reside with sin, he set up a plan B to establish a penalty to be paid so man could be restored to oneness with him if he chose that wrong path.

Just as we pay a fine or have our license revoked when we choose to go over the speed limit. After we receive a punishment, (whether it be payment, jail, etc.), we then are given our license and restored to good standing with the law. Likewise, God set a plan of redemption in motion for man. So, you can see how it was an act of love that God set forth the system of sacrifice and redemption. It always gives us a way back. That's justice. Psalm 36:6 says it all. "Your righteousness, O Lord, is like the mighty mountains, your justice like the great deep." Look up and highlight Deut. 32:4, Psalm 145:17 and Proverbs 8:20.

One attribute we have not discussed is the very essence of who God is. His main characteristic is _love._ 1 John 4:16 tells us, "God is love; and he that dwelled in love dwelleth in God and God in him." It is from this one characteristic that all the others are derived.

He is _sovereign_ and _just_, all because he is _love_ first of all. He created man because he is love and love desires a recipient to be complete. It was that same love that restored man after the fall. John 3:16: "For God so loved the world that he gave His only begotten son, that whosoever believes in Him should not perish but have everlasting life." Romans 5:8: "God commanded his love toward us in that, while we were yet sinners, Christ died for us." It is from this attribute the Bible unfolds. It is expressed starting in Genesis with man's creation and ends in Revelation with his restoration.

We could spend pages just looking at the many attributes of God and still only have a glimpse of the complexity of his nature. We were not intended to fully understand God, just to walk in His ways. He tells us that in Isaiah 55:9, "For as the heavens are higher than the earth, so are my ways higher than your ways, and my thoughts higher than your thoughts."

The last thing we want to talk about is the three ways God presents himself to man. This is called the Trinity _(three in one)_. God is referred to as the Father, Son, and Holy Spirit. They are one; yet operate in three different capacities.

This is a hard concept to understand until we take a look at our own make-up. The scriptures tell us that in the beginning was God, and out of the heart of God's love, he created man in his image. Genesis 1:27 tells us "So God created man in his own image, in the image of God he created him; male and female he created them." Like God, we, too, operate with a threefold nature. We have a body, soul, and spirit. Paul refers to our three-fold nature in 1 Thess. 5:23, "May your whole spirit, soul and body be kept blameless at the coming of our Lord Jesus Christ."

In the beginning God created a physical planet out of dirt, water and air. Then he took some of the physical material and created man in a physical form. We call that our physical body. This enabled him to move around and enjoy the beautiful environment that had been created for him. This body was just an empty shell until God breathed his breath into him. Genesis 2:7 states, "The Lord God formed the man from the dust of the ground and breathed into his nostrils the breath of life, and the man became a living soul."

That breath of God that gave him life is the part of our being that we call our spirit. The compartment that connects our body and spirit is our soul. We could compare it to a new car rolling off the assembly line, fully equipped with every piece of equipment and gadget for peak performance, but until a charge is put into the battery it is just a useless vehicle. That spark in the charge represents the spirit of God that makes our body more than a useless form. The battery transfers the spark to the body, as does our soul. When we do not use our will to choose to obey God by renewing our mind according to his Word, we like a car battery, can lose the charge of God's life working through us. It is by continual use that a car battery stays ready for service.

Likewise, our soul must keep our spirits linked to God. Jesus tells us in John 15:5: I am the Vine; you are the branches. If a man remains in me and I in him, he will bear much fruit; apart from me you can do nothing." The spark of God that dwells within us by his holy spirit is the way God communes with us. John 4:24 tells us "God is a spirit and those who worship Him must worship him in spirit and in truth." Proverbs 20:27 tells us "The spirit of man is the candle of the Lord." It is the way he enlightens us, relates to us, and shows his love to us. 1 Corinthians 2:14 tells us, "The man without the Spirit does not accept the things that are from God, for they are foolishness to him, and he cannot understand them, because they are spiritually discerned."

It is hard for us to understand the fact that our body, the actual physical part we see, is only temporary housing for our spirits. Ephesians 2:22 states it clearly, "And in him you too are being built together to become a dwelling in which God lives by his Spirit." In Genesis 3:19, God tells Adam, "By the sweat of your brow you will eat your food until you return to the ground, since from it you were taken; from dust you are and to dust you will return." Yet we live so much of our lives according to the dictates of our physical bodies, instead of being spirit-led in the driving force leading us in the lives we were created to live.

To sum it all up, I am a spirit, I live in a body, and I have a soul. Likewise, God is a spirit, he came to earth in a body, and his Holy Spirit guides and directs our souls. I heard it described to me like this one time. If you saw me driving down the street in my car, you would wave and tell a friend there goes Nina. That would be accurate. However, if you passed the shopping mall later and saw my car parked in the lot, you wouldn't point to the car and say there's Nina. That would have only been the vehicle that had moved the real me around. The real me would be inside. That is what our bodies are like. They are only vehicles to give us access to the beautiful earth God created for us to enjoy. He wanted us to be able to enjoy the physical pleasure he had created for us while at the same time be in fellowship with him in spirit. We were intended to have God's spirit communing with our spirit, which would inspire our soul, and the soul would direct the body. When we live in harmony of that order, we fulfill the purpose for which we were created and experience the complete joy and peace God intended for us to have.

I hope this helps you understand not only more about God but perhaps more about yourself, as well. It is essential to understand the aspects of our make-up to truly understand how God deals with us, and what the Bible is all about.

The Trinity is woven so tightly together throughout the Bible that it is impossible for man to fully understand the nature and purpose of one Godhead, yet they are eternal and co-equal persons within that Godhead. They are spoken of collectively starting in Genesis 1:26, "And God said let _us_ make man in _our_ image, after _our_ likeness..." And in Genesis 3:22, "And the Lord God said, Behold, the man is become as one of _us_, knowing good from evil..." In Genesis 11:7, God says "... let _us_ go down, and there confound their language."

They are referred to individually: Matt: 28:19, "Go ye therefore, and teach all nations, baptizing them in the name of the Father, and of the Son, and of the Holy Spirit..." John 14:26 - "But the comforter, which is the Holy Spirit, whom the Father will send in my name, he shall teach you all things, and bring all things to your remembrance, whatsoever I have said unto you." Matt. 3:16-17, "And Jesus, when he was baptized, went up straightway out of the water: and, lo, the heavens were opened unto him, and he saw the Spirit of God descending like a dove, and lighting upon him: And lo a voice from heaven, saying, This is my beloved son, in whom I am well pleased."

Some other scriptural summaries of the Trinity you may want to look up are:
    A. The Father is God (John 6:44-46; Romans 1:7; 1 Peter 1:2)
    B. The Son is God (Isa. 9:6; John 1:1; Heb. 1:8;
    C. The Holy Spirit is God (Acts 5:3-4; Heb. 9:14)

Below is a comparison of the Trinity of God and man.

God is Spirit
John 4:24 "God is spirit and those who worship him must worship him in spirit and in truth."

Man is Spirit
Zechariah. 12:1 "The Lord formed the spirit of man within him." Heb.12:9 refers to God being the "father of our spirits."

God is Flesh (Jesus)
John 1:14 "The Word (God) became flesh and dwelled among us." (Jesus)

Man is Flesh
Genesis 2:23 records Adam's words about the new woman God had created for him. "This is now bone of my bone and flesh of my flesh."

Now we have seen God create a spirit being in the likeness of his spirit. We have seen him create a physical housing for that spirit to give it access to the world he had created for him. Genesis. 2:7 tells us, "then God breathed into man the breath of life, and he became a living soul." The Greek word for soul is "psyche." That's where we get our term psychology. It means the science of that which concerns the psyche, or soul. The soul makes up the mind, will, and emotions. Within the soul resides our ability to think, make choices, and feel emotions. This freedom of choice keeps us from being mere robots. We have a choice to love and obey God or not to obey Him

The soul is the bridge between the spiritual world and the physical earth, for within it lies the power of choice where the dictates of our life are established. Satan understood this when he came to Eve. He could not physically make her do anything to disobey God, nor did he have spiritual access (he lost his spiritual access and became a dead spirit when he rebelled against God and was cast out of heaven), so the only thing he could do was to appeal to her soul. He appealed to her pride "If you eat of this tree you will be as smart as God." He appealed to her emotions telling her God had lied to her, and through that deceit, he caused her to purposefully choose to disobey God.

We, too, have the same choice as Eve to make in our lives. Paul talks about it in 2 Corinthians 11:3, "I am afraid that just as Eve was deceived by the serpent's cunning, your minds may somehow be led astray from your sincere and pure devotion to Christ." He also warns in 2 Cor. 10:5, "Take every thought captive to make it obedient to Christ." Matthews 12:34"...Out of the overflow of the heart the mouth speaks. Proverbs 23:7, "As a man thinketh in his heart, so is he."

God has a Soul (Holy Spirit)
He has a mind: Romans 8:27 "He that searcheth the heart knoweth what is the *mind* of the spirit."

Man has a Soul
Man has a mind: Romans 12:2 tells us "be transformed by the renewing of our *minds.*"

He has a will: 1 Cor. 12:11 "But all these worketh that one and the self-same spirit, dividing to every man as He *wills.*"

John 7:17 shows us man has a will. "If anyone chooses to do God's will..."

He has emotions: Romans 15:30 "...for the *love* of the spirit, that ye strive together..." Eph. 4:30 "*grieve* not the Holy Spirit of God,.."

Psalm 39:2 is only one of the many emotions we can read about in psalms. "When I was silent...my *anguish* increased."

When you examine our makeup, you can see how sin has distorted the order of man's life. We were created to walk in spirit-to-spirit harmony with God. Our spirits, (being united with God) influence our minds, (take every thought captive to the obedience of God) and our souls, direct the actions of our body.

This was God's original plan for man, and is the only way man can live in harmony with Him. He told Adam (Spirit-to-spirit) not to eat of the one particular tree. Ideally Adam would have processed this with his mind and used his willpower to refuse to disobey God, no matter how tempted the body was with the sight of an appealing fruit and the temptation to let peer pressure (Eve) take over. Had he obeyed God, he would not have been separated from God and would have lived out his life fulfilling the purpose God intended for him when he was put on this earth.

God's original plan   Communion after the fall

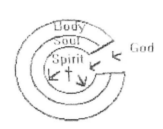 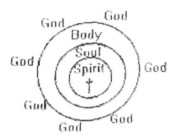

After man let sin enter his life, God had to immediately shut off His spiritual connection. Remember, one of God's attributes is the fact that he is *Holy*. That means he cannot reside with sin. From that day on, God had to approach man from the outside environment, the same way Satan did. God had to appear to men's physical senses (letting them see angels who delivered messages, hearing prophecies, using talking donkeys, burning bushes, etc. to get man's attention).

Then God had to appeal to man to trust him and yield his soul to be used by God to help bring together a plan that would eventually include coming to the earth himself to make available a plan for us to once again open the door to spiritual oneness with God. In Matt. 7:7 Jesus states clearly "Ask and it will be given to you; seek and you will find; knock and the door will be opened to you." The door is the door that was closed when Adam sinned, and now we once again can communicate with God, spirit-to-spirit the way he intended us to when he created us. We call that communication prayer.

People are always trying to put God in a finite box to understand Him. I think Isaiah 55:8 tells it all; "For my thoughts are not your thoughts, neither are your ways my ways, declares the Lord. As the heavens are higher than the earth, so are my ways higher than your ways, and my thoughts higher than your thoughts."

The Bible starts talking about God in the opening of the first book of Genesis, "In the beginning was God." It continues throughout, and ends with the last book of the Bible stating in Revelation 1:8 "I am the Alpha and Omega, who is, who was, and who is to come, the almighty."

There are many who imitate God and try to set themselves up as gods in our life. Isaiah 45:5- 6, says it all. "I am the Lord, and there is none else, there is no God beside me: I girded thee, though thou hast not known me: That they may know from the rising of the sun, and from the west, that there is none beside me. I am the Lord, and there is none else."

We are given the same choice as Adam. We are put here on this earth for a purpose. Each one of our missions is different, but to love and obey God is always the plan. There is no peace outside of fulfilling that plan. There will always be an emptiness left at the end of the search for our identity anywhere outside of God.

Discussion Questions:

1. List the nine attributes of God in this lesson and write the brief description of each.

2. Can you give an example when you have had to place your faith on the truth of one of these attributes?

3. Which of the attributes of God are the most reassuring as you look to Him for answers in your life?

4. Can you see the comparison of the Trinity of God and the trinity of your own life? Explain

5. As you look at the body, soul, and spirit, which area do you focus most of your attention and time on?

6. Understanding that we are spirit beings and that is the part of us that will live throughout eternity, what changes would you like to make in your life to have more of an eternal focus?

7. Understanding that God, the creator of heaven and earth, is our heavenly Father and longs to commune with us and reveal his love for us, how should that affect our self-worth? Read Psalm 139:13 and 119:73.

8. The value of anything is the price someone is willing to pay for it. What was the price God was willing to pay for us? Read John 3:16.

Lesson 5
Angels

In our last lesson, we talked about God and how in the beginning he was everything that existed and that all things were created by and for him. As we move along our timeline of eternity, we find that angels were the first creative act of God. They were the first and highest order of created beings. They play an important role in the Bible, as they are mentioned in thirty-four books for a total of 273 times (108 times in the Old Testament and 165 in the New Testament).

We read in Col. 1:16-17, "For by him (Christ), all things were created; things in heaven and on earth, visible and invisible, whether thrones or powers or rulers or authorities; all things were created by and for him. He is before all things, and in him, all things hold together."

Both the Greek word *angelos* and the Hebrew word *mal'ak* (translated "angel") literally mean "messenger." We find them over 230 times in the Bible fulfilling the assignment that their names suggests were the purpose of their creation. Like man, angels were created by a special act of God. They did not evolve into being. They are immortal, infinite, spiritual beings that are not subject to death.

Psalm 148:2, 5-6 tells us, "Praise the Lord, all his angels, praise him, all his heavenly host.... Let them praise the name of the Lord, for he commanded and they were created. He set them in place forever and ever; he gave a decree that will never pass away."

They are not capable of reproduction as you see in humans and other living creations. Jesus tells us that in Matthew 22:30 when the Sadducees questioned him about what life would be like after the resurrection for a woman who had married more than one man. The question proposed to him was, who would be her husband in heaven? Jesus replied: "At the resurrection they neither marry, nor be given in marriage, but are as the angels of God in Heaven." Therefore, we have to assume angels were created simultaneously by a special act of God and did not evolve into being by reproduction, and that their numbers will remain the same throughout eternity.

How many angels God created we cannot know. We read figures such as "ten thousand times ten thousand" (Rev. 5:11), "an innumerable company" (Hebrews 12:22), "a multitude" (Luke 2:13), "legions" (Matthew 26:53). The exact number is known only to God, and they are presented to man as innumerable and uncountable.

John refers to their numerical gathering as a host when he is telling about the angel who appeared at the time of the birth of Jesus. Luke 2:13-15 says, "Suddenly a great company of the heavenly host appeared with the angel, praising God and saying, glory to God in the highest, and on earth peace to men on whom his favor rests. When the angels had left them and gone to heaven..."

This leads us to the question as to where the angels reside. Verse 15 tells us they left and returned to heaven. Several other places in the Bible we read of them ascending and descending into heaven. Therefore we have to assume they have access to heaven and earth.

Psalm 103:19-21 tells us "The Lord has established his throne in heaven, and his kingdom rules over all. Praise the Lord, you his angels, you mighty ones who do his bidding, who obey his Word. Praise the Lord, all his heavenly hosts, you his servants who do his will." Here we see that they were created to reside with God in heaven, and for the purpose of being his servants and messengers to carry out his desires.

Where is heaven? In Hebrew, "heaven" is in the plural form, "heavens," which helps us somewhat understand the fact that at least three heavens are referred to in scripture. In 2 Cor. 12:2, Paul refers to knowing a man who was caught up to "the third heaven" which naturally gives us the assumption that there is a first and a second. It is generally accepted that he was referring to the "heaven of heavens," where God and the angels abide. It is important to review this because this is the location they were created to live (clothed with God's light and glory,) throughout eternity.

Like man though, rebellious pride entered the heart of one of the angelic beings (Lucifer) and he led a rebellion to try to overthrow the structure of heaven. Interestingly, there seems to be a justice system with rank and order much like the one we live and abide by. Lucifer, for instance, was the brightest and highest angel in heaven. He had been endowed with beauty and wisdom like none other. It was his high position of power and authority that caused him to try to overthrow God and the power structure of heaven.

Revelation 12:7-9 gives us a birds eye view of this upheaval. "And there was war in the heavens. Michael and his angels fought against the dragon (Lucifer, Satan), and the dragon and his angels fought back. But he was not strong enough, and they lost their place in heaven. The great dragon was hurled down - that ancient serpent called the devil, or Satan, who leads the whole world astray. He was hurled to the earth, and his angels with him." We read in Rev. 12:3-4 that he took one-third of the angels with him (they are referred to as *stars* in this passage).

Now we have the faithful angels who reside with God in the heaven of heavens. Then we see the fallen angels, who lost their right to have residence there, stripped of their position, cast onto the earth with Lucifer, and now are referred to as demons because they are now under the authority of the devil, going about doing his will and causing havoc for all mankind.

When the Bible starts to unfold in Genesis 1:1, we see that God had created the heavens (plural) and the earth. When we come in, apparently earth was already the residence of Satan and the fallen angels. That might explain the condition we find the earth in Gen. 1:2 "Now the earth was formless and empty, darkness was over the surface of the deep, and the Spirit of God was hovering over the waters." I can just see God hovering over the dark, desolate earth and deciding to introduce light and create a masterpiece out of it, making it the home and inheritance of the children he was going to create in his image.

When he created Adam, the first thing he did was give him authority over the earth and everything in it, including the fallen angels who moved about there. Man was a slap in the face of Satan (Lucifer). Lucifer had been the highest and brightest of all the created beings up until this point. (Ezekiel 28:12-15 - Satan was referred to here as the king of Tyre.) He had enjoyed a position of authority and power with God. Because he used that power to try to usurp God and lost his position, power, and relationship with the Almighty, the ultimate insult was to be made subservient to an even greater creation of God. A creation made in the very likeness and image of God, which had the very life of God breathed into his being (Gen. 2:7).

To sum up the answer as to where the angels reside, we would have to say, the ones who have remained obedient to God still reside with him in the third heaven, fulfilling the purpose for which they were created.

The second heaven we recognize is the starry or stellar heavens. This heaven that is above the earth and not within the gravitational force field that gives the earth its movement and function. It encompasses the sun, moon, stars, and planets. There is no capacity of life there (outside of an astronaut's suit which simulates our atmosphere). It is referred to in Gen. 26:4, Genesis 1:16-17, and Psalm 19:1.

Here we find a portion of the fallen angels residing in this aerial region as we see it referred to in Ephesians 6:12, "For we do not wrestle against flesh and blood, but against principalities, against powers, against the rulers of the darkness of this age, against spiritual hosts of wickedness in the heavenly places."

The first heaven is the atmosphere that we call skies. It is the atmospheric heaven that surrounds us. We see this heaven referred to in Matt. 24:30 "the clouds of the heaven," Matt. 8:20, the "birds of the air," Gen.7:11 talks about the "windows of heaven" referring to the burst of rain that came forth at the time of the flood.

As we mentioned earlier, there seems to be a definite structure with rank and order representing governmental authority, or supremacy, among the angelic hosts. We see it mentioned in Colossians 1:11-16, namely: thrones, dominions, principalities, authorities, and powers.

Another order of exalted celestial beings is mentioned, apart from those of rank and authority listed above, namely: Cherubim and Seraphim. Many scholars believe that these names refer to exalted spirit-beings of the angelic order closely related to the throne and heart of God.

Cherubim: We find the first appearance of cherubim in the Garden of Eden, where God had dispatched them to guard the way of "The Tree of Life" from fallen Adam (Genesis 3:24), for fear he would eat of it and be doomed to live in his now sinful state forever. We also see upon the Ark of the Covenant, golden replicas of cherubim, with the Mercy Seat in the Holy of Holies, where God dwelt in the midst of His people. Exodus 25:18-20 and Psalm 80:1 "...thou that dwellest between the cherubim." Exodus 26:1 and 2 Chronicles 3:14 talk about the curtains of the Tabernacle and the veil of the temple being embroidered with a pattern of cherubim. I Kings 6:23-35 describes the walls, doors, and the sanctuary being decorated with carved cherubim overlaid with gold.

Many Bible scholars agree that the significant meaning of the word "cherub" is "to cover, guard, protect." The cherubim guarded the way in Eden. Lucifer was appointed the "covering" cherub (evidently belonging to the order of cherubim). Theirs was definitely a high and holy position as the carved symbols of their presence, with outstretched wings, in the Holy of Holies suggest. Their position would indicate that they were in attendance and ready to be dispatched from the Throne of God as "guardians," "coverers," and "defenders" of his absolute holiness.

Seraphim: The Hebrew word for seraphim means, "burning ones," and probably speaks of the burning devotion to God on the part of these angelic beings. These beings are mentioned only once in the Bible; we see this in Isaiah when he is convicted of his sin and the sin of the nation of Israel. He is ministered to by one of the seraphim, who flew over to the heavenly altar and, with a pair of tongs, picked out a burning coal. He then touched Isaiah's lips with it and said: "Lo, this hath touched thy lips, and thine iniquity is taken away, and thy sin purged," Isaiah 6:7.

Only three angels are mentioned by name in the Bible. Lucifer ("son of the morning"), Michael ("who is like God"), and Gabriel ("mighty one.")

Lucifer: as we mentioned earlier, was the most exalted of the angels. By creation and appointment, he occupied a place of prominence in the Scriptures, second only to the Godhead. By his sin, the first created being to cross the will, the word, and the purpose of the creator, he became the devil. He appears about forty times throughout the Scriptures under different titles.

Michael: This divine angel is named five times (Daniel 10:13, 21; 12:1; Jude 9; Revelation 12:7). He is referred to as "standing" for Daniel's people. Therefore, he is regarded as the heavenly patron of Israel and the watchful guardian of God's people against both earthly and satanic foes. In Daniel 10:13, Michael is called "one of the chief princes." Other angels, who were referred to as princes, were the "Prince of Persia" and the "Prince of Grecia." These two were part of the rebellion led by Lucifer and now are fallen angels and subservient to Satan, who is called "the prince of demons, the prince of the power of the air."

It is Michael who opposes Satan in a dispute concerning the body of Moses (Jude 9). It is Michael who leads the angelic army in heaven against "that old serpent, called the Devil," and his angels (Revelation 12:7). In Jude 9, Michael is called "the archangel" (the scriptures do not speak of the plural, "archangels"). The rank of archangel is mentioned only twice and is only applied to the mighty prince of angels, Michael. It is generally believed that the unnamed archangel whose voice will be heard when Christ descends from heaven to meet His raptured saints, is referring to Michael (1 Thess. 4:16.)

Gabriel is named four times (Daniel 8:16; 9:21; Luke1:19; 1:26). He is not identified as an archangel, although the meaning of his name is "the mighty one." While Michael appears to be the messenger of law and judgment, Gabriel is the messenger of mercy and promise. It was Gabriel who brought the message to Zacharias announcing the birth of John the Baptist, the forerunner of the Messiah (Luke 1:19). It was Gabriel who brought the annunciation of the Savior's birth to the Virgin Mary, and it was Gabriel who was dispatched by God with the answer to the fervent prayer of Daniel the prophet, disclosing to him a summary of what was to come to his people.

Angels were part of God's plan from the beginning of time. He manifested them in whatever form needed for the task. They are always in attendance in heaven, and often sent to approach the sphere of human life. This does not prove, though, that they were made of material substance, as we know it, since these appearances were directed by God's will and purpose as a means to communicate with mankind. He did so by making angels visible and understandable to the senses of man.

This brings up the question: What do angels look like? The question of whether angels are purely unseen spirits, or clothed in an indescribably refined fabric or a material of nature unknown to us, will only be answered when we get to heaven. We do know that the Apostle Paul speaks of "celestial bodies" and "terrestrial bodies." We also know the glorified saints, upon their arrival in heaven, will have "a spiritual body;" therefore, it would appear that "spirits" have a determined form which is adapted to the law of their being.

When Jesus said, "...a spirit hath not flesh and bones, as ye see that I have," He did not imply that spirits have no form at all, but rather that in whatever form they are in, it is different from the form his disciples were looking at - His own glorified humanity (Luke 24:37-39.) This was after he had died and been resurrected. He was visible to the disciples in some approachable, physical form. He even asked Thomas, when he doubted it was really the resurrected Lord, to put his hands in his scars as proof (John 20:27.) He asked the disciples when he appeared to them after his resurrection if they had anything to eat, and they gave him a piece of fish, and he ate it (Luke24:41-42.) He was also able to walk through closed doors as we read of him doing in John 20:19.

How humanity and spirit blend after we die, we do not know, but the scripture does give us some insight into their general appearance by the way they are referred to in the following passages. Mark 16:5 - "And entering into the sepulcher, they saw a young man sitting on the right side, clothed in a long white garment; and they were amazed." Matthew 28:3 - "His countenance was like lightning, and his clothes white as snow." Luke 24:4 - "And it came to pass, as they were much perplexed about this, behold, two men, stood by them, in shining garments." Rev. 10:1 - "And I saw another mighty angel come down from heaven, clothed with a cloud; and a rainbow was upon his head, and his face was as though it were the sun and his feet like pillars of fire." Rev. 15:6 – "And the seven angels came out of the temple, having the seven plagues, clothed in pure and white linen, and having their breast girded with golden girdles." Rev. 18:1 - "And after these things I saw another angel come down from heaven, having great power, and the earth was made bright with his glory."

By anyone's standards, it is obvious that angels are represented by light, shining garments, dazzling with the brightness of God's glory. Possibly they wear the same garments we will wear when we go to heaven to become a glorified resident there. Adam and Eve were clothed with the glory of God when they were walking in the fullness of his love and glory in the garden. We do not know what that looked like, but we do know that when they disobeyed God and allowed sin to enter their world, that the glory of God left them. They lost their covering when they lost the glory of God's presence in their life. Suddenly they were naked and ashamed. I tend to believe that whatever Adam and Eve were clothed in the garden when they were in perfect harmony with God, will be the same covering I will have with some day when I lay down my physical body and go to live with him.

What are the activities of the angels in both Old and New Testaments?

A. They worship God. Rev. 4:8 "...day and night they never stop saying: "Holy, holy, holy is the Lord God Almighty, who was, and is, and is to come.""

B. They rejoiced in the works of God. His works of creation (Job 38:7; Rev. 4:11.) His works of redemption (1 Tim. 3:16; Rev. 5:11, 12).

C. They perform the will of God (Gen. 28:12; Dan. 7:10.)

D. They are messengers for God. We read of many places in both the Old and New Testaments where God sent angels to deliver messages to His people.

We read in Luke 1:26-33 where an angel appeared to Mary to tell her she was going to be impregnated by the Holy Spirit and given the honor of giving birth to the Son of God. In Matt. 1:20 we read how the angel appeared to Joseph in a dream to tell him not to be afraid of marrying Mary because she was pregnant. Then he appeared to the shepherds in Luke 2:9-12 to inform them of the birth.

An angel also foretold the birth of John the Baptist by appearing to Zechariah and informing him that his wife Elizabeth would bear a child who would be a forerunner of the Son of God. Other personalities who were visited by an angel to perform the will of God were:

John (Revelation 17:1; 21:9),	The Apostles (Acts 1:10, 11)
Cornelius (Acts 10:3-6)	Woman at the tomb (Luke 24:4-7)
Philip (Acts 8:26)	Daniel (Daniel 7:16; 10:5, 11)

E. They protect. Psalm 34:7 "The angel of the Lord encampeth round about them that fear him, and delivereth them." Psalm 91:11 "For he shall give his angels charge over thee, to keep thee in all thy ways." They protected Lot from the Sodomites (Gen 19:10-11). They protected Elisha from the Syrians (2 Kings 6:15-17.)

F. They comfort. 1 Kings 19:5 "And as he (Elijah) lay and slept under a juniper tree, he beheld an angel touching him, and said unto him, arise and eat." Acts 27:23-24 "For there stood by me (Paul), this night an angel of God, whose I am, and whom I serve, saying, Fear not, Paul."

G. They deliver. Acts 5:19 "But an angel of the Lord by night opened the prison doors, and brought them (the apostles) forth." Acts 12:7 "And behold, an angel of the Lord came upon him, and a light shone in the prison; and he smote Peter on the side, and raised him up, saying, "Arise quickly," and his chains fell off from his hands."

H. They assist the believer at the moment of death. Luke 16:22 "And it came to pass that the beggar died, and was carried by angels into Abraham's bosom."

We see the angels in the Old Testament busy during creation, rejoicing in its beauty. In the Fall of Man, we see them guarding and protecting man from partaking from the tree of life and being eternally doomed. In the establishment of the Old Covenant, angels appear to Abraham and Sarah and tell them God's plan for their descendants.

Over and over we see angels protecting their descendants for the plan of redemption and genealogy of Jesus. Then they attended to our Lord during his earth walk. They announced his birth, protecting him from Herod. They ministered to him in the wilderness when he was being tempted by Satan. They were there to comfort him in the garden during his greatest time of agony when he prayed all night before going to the cross. They were there to roll away the stone from his grave. They announced his resurrection. They predicted his Second Coming. And finally, they will accompany him on his return.

There is no disputing the importance of the role angels have played in the history of the Bible, and in the lives of mankind up until this point. However, when reading the accounts in Revelation of the coming judgments during end times, they still have a great deal of work left to do. They will judge the earth during the tribulation. These are a few of the tasks they have been assigned by God to do.

1. They hold back the four winds of heaven (Revelation. 7:1)
2. They pronounce the seven trumpet judgments (Revelation. 8:2)
3. They cast Satan and his angels out of heaven (Revelation.12:7, 8)
4. They announce the eternal hell awaiting all unbelievers (Revelation.14:10)
5. They pour out the seven vial judgments (Revelation. 15:1)
6. They announce Armageddon (which is the last world battle). (Revelation. 19:17)
7. They gather the unsaved for eternal hell (Matthew.13:39-43)
8. They bind Satan in the bottomless pit (Rev. 20:1)
9. They accompany Christ at his second coming (2 Thessalonians. 1:7)

Although there are many unanswered questions about the celestial beings we know as angels, we can be sure that they not only have been an active part of our history but also are today an active part of the protecting and loving grace of God in our lives. How ever-present they are we do not know, but let me sum it up by quoting this verse in Hebrews 13:2 - "Do not forget to entertain strangers, for by so doing some people have entertained angels without knowing it."

Discussion Questions:

1. What was your understanding of angels before this lesson, and how has your perspective changed now, if any?

2. Why do you think God created man when He already had so many angels to accompany Him and do His bidding?

3. Do you now have a better understanding of the meaning of Heaven and the three levels? Explain.

4. Can you describe two orders of angels? Lucifer belongs to which order?

Lesson 6
Genesis 1-3
Adam

In our last lesson, we discussed angels and the fact that they were God's first created beings. However, they were not the crowning glory of God's heart. As we talked about in a previous lesson, God wanted a being that he could love and respond to that was made in his image with the capacity to love and return his love. Man was created for fellowship with God. That is an important fact to keep in mind as we go about our day trying to find our purpose in so many things. Read Gen 1:26-27 and highlight "after our likeness" and "in His own image."

God first made Adam from the same element that the earth he created for them to live in. At that point, man was nothing more than a mud pie much like we made as children. However, after forming every detail to allow man to function, God bowed down over his physical creation and breathed into him his very breath. At that point man became a living soul.

This goes back to the illustration we had earlier about a car being assembled in a factory with everything it needs to function, but it will rust and be worthless until the charge is put in the battery. That charge gives life to the car and allows it to operate. The same is true of man. The spark that gives us life is our spirit and is dictated by our soul. The battery becomes alive when the spark or charge is put in it. The battery compares to our soul, and the spark is the very life of God - his very breath that can and will never die. Read Genesis 2:7 and highlight the part that tells us that God breathed his very breath into us. Read Isaiah 42:5 and highlight the words "breath" and "spirit."

So now we see man was created in God's image and placed in a garden of God's own planting, called Eden. He had everything good and wonderful he could possibly want.

God wanted man to have companionship and be able to reproduce himself, so he caused him to go into a deep sleep and took a part of him (one of his ribs,) and created Eve. Note that he did not start from scratch and make a new being, but used a part of Adam to create his companion. Just like God breathed a part of himself into man when he was created. Any parent can tell you the awe and wonder when you see a child born that was created from the very sperm or egg of your own being. There is something unexplainable that happens inside you - a feeling of instant union and belonging. You know at that instant that you would give your very life to protect that child. That is the union God created Adam to have with Eve, one of belonging and companionship. Like the union, he created us to have with himself. Read Gen 2: 21-24 and highlight why Eve was called woman. Read Gen: 3:20 and highlight why he named her Eve.

Now we see man placed in the garden and given the instruction to replenish the earth. He was given instructions not to live idly, but to care for the garden, exercising his body, mind, and soul having full fellowship with his creator. God told Adam and Eve to subdue and have dominion over the animal creation and to care for the paradise they had been placed in.

They were to eat freely of the fruit of every tree with the exception of one. God gave them the ability to choose to love and obey him by placing the tree in the garden and giving them very clear instructions. "Of every tree in the garden you may freely eat, but of the tree of the knowledge of good and evil, thou shalt not eat of it: for in the day that thou eatest thereof thou shall surely die." Read Gen. 2:16-17.

Obeying in this simple test would ensure Adam and his seed of perfect and perpetual happiness, paradise, and life immortal. With access to the tree in the midst of the garden (tree of life,) we are told in Gen 3:22-24, he would live forever. On the other hand, the penalty of disobedience of eating of the tree of knowledge of good and evil was death.

We know that evil already existed in the universe. There was already a company of fallen intelligences, of which Satan was the head, possessing that mysterious power we call temptation, or trying to influence others to transgress God's will. Eve gave in to that temptation and Adam followed. In that day, just as God had warned, both physical and spiritual death became their doom. The body became subject to physical death, and the soul in a like manner lost his communion with God. Read Gen 3:1-5 and highlight the words that Satan used to tempt Eve.

Immediately, Adam and Eve felt shame, a feeling they were never intended to experience. They were suddenly ashamed of their bodies and hid from God (Gen: 3:8-10.) God graciously clothed them in clothes of skin, a sacrificial covering (Gen 3:21.) Because he is a God of justice and cannot lie, he stood by his word and sent them from the garden and all the wonderful blessings that had been given to them there.

He set Cherubim and a flaming sword to guard the tree of life. I believe the tree of life was the very essence of Jesus. He is called the tree of life and we are told to eat of him and live forever. This tells me that Jesus was here from the very beginning with all we need to possess eternal life. In the New Testament, we read so many passages where Jesus says, "Come to me all you who are burdened and heavy laden and I will give you rest." He also says, "I am the way, the truth, and the life."

We could spend pages verifying verses assuring us that Jesus is the tree of life but for the purpose of this study, we will not exhaust them. Because of the choices Adam and Eve made, God put a curse or punishment on them, but with it a promise of a savior, who would redeem mankind from the curse of sin, and its eternal consequences. Read about the curses or punishments, given to man as a result of his disobedience in Gen 3: 14-19. Highlight in your Bible the curses put upon the serpent, Adam, and mankind, Eve and women to follow after her.

The good news comes in Gen 3:15 - "I will put enmity between thee and the woman, and between thy seed and her seed; it (the seed of woman, which was Jesus coming to earth through the birth through a woman, Mary) shall bruise thy head, and thou shall bruise his heel." This is saying that Jesus is coming to crush the serpent's head and repair the damage of man's fall. Then man can have communion once again with his creator and be placed back in the garden with communion and fellowship with him. That is basically the entire story of the Bible. The first few verses in the Bible tell us of the problem of man and how it happened, but the rest of the book is about the plot (or plan) to redeem and restore man back to the position he was intended to have with his creator.

So, as we look at Adam, we are looking at our spiritual ancestry. It explains why we struggle with sin and temptation, and why we need a redeemer. Jesus is called the new Adam, and he was called the firstborn from the dead. When he came to earth, a new creation was released on the earth, and anyone who acknowledged that he had taken the punishment for their sins became a new creation and was given a number. If Jesus was number 1, I can't wait until I get to Heaven and see what my number is.

II Corinthians 5:17 tells us that if we are in Christ, meaning we have accepted that he paid the price for our sin nature, then we are a new creation. We are numbered along with Jesus. The disciples and Mary Magdalene might have had numbers 2 through 15. There were 120 in the upper room who were filled with the Holy Spirit, then they told others, and 3000 were added. The number has been climbing for 2000 years, so our number is probably a high one. One day when I meet Jesus, and I call him number 1, he very likely will respond with "Hello number 986000000."

Even though Adam made a bad choice, we have been given a chance to make the right choice for ourselves because of what Jesus did on the cross for us.

Discussion Questions:

1. Are you sure you have received Jesus as your savior?

2. Tell about that experience and how it has affected your life.

3. Are you comfortable sharing your salvation experience with others?

4. In Gen 3:1-5, Satan tempted Eve. How does he use the same tactic with us today? Read II Corinthians 11:3.

Lesson 7
Cain Seth Abel

In our last lesson, we discussed God's creation of man and his desire for him to love and obey him and walk-in oneness and fellowship with him. To test their loyalty and obedience, God put a tree in the garden that would reveal to them all the evil present in this world they had been created in. Up until that time, they had been protected from knowing anything but God's love and provision for their well being. They lived and existed in the very presence and word of God.

In Genesis 3:1-5 we see that Satan, being present on this earth, embodied a serpent and contradicted the word of God and said to them, "Hath God said, you shall not eat of every tree in the garden?" Eve responded, "Yes, all but the tree in the midst of the garden for if we do we shall die." The serpent then said to her, "You shall not die. God, knows that in the day you eat of it your eyes will be opened, and you shall be as gods, knowing good from evil."

That was the time when Eve had to make a choice. Will I obey my creator or listen to a rogue spirit and maybe be as God? Notice that the first thing she was tempted with was her physical appetite, looking at the fruit. Then when she was tempted to look at it and desire it, Satan moved on into her soul where he started messing with her mind and getting her to doubt God's intention to provide the best for her. He told her that God had lied to her and that if she just ate of the tree (disobeyed), she would be a god herself. Isn't that the teaching and draw of the new age movement that is so prevalent today? The teaching that we are all gods and that we don't need to believe in a God who created us but to connect to the earth and the things he created. Those who fall prey to that thinking are being deceived just as Eve was. Paul even mentioned this in II Corinthians when warning the church. He says in 11:3, "I am afraid that just as Eve was deceived by the serpent's cunning, your minds may somehow be led astray from your sincere and pure devotion to Christ."

The moment Adam and Eve sinned, they no longer felt the presence of God and his love and protection, so much so that they hid from him. God called out to them, "Where are you?" They answered, "We heard your voice in the garden, but we were afraid because we were naked" (Genesis 3:8-10).

God clothed them physically and promised that he would make preparations for them to be once again clothed spiritually, once again restored to the oneness they had before they disobeyed. However, because God is a God of justice, they could no longer stay in the garden and were driven from the garden and angels were placed at the entrance of the garden with flaming swords. Read Genesis 3:22-24 of this account and highlight what the angels were protecting with their flaming swords.

As stated earlier, it is my personal belief that the tree of life in the garden was the physical presence of Jesus. He represents eternal life. He says that anyone who partakes of me will live forever. God could not take a chance that Adam and Eve would partake of this tree and live forever in a state of sin.

Beginning in Genesis 3:14, we see the judgments (curses) put on all who partook of this disobedience. Read these curses and highlight each one and write down the repercussions that each still has in our lives today.

Serpent:
Eve:
Ground:

It is important to review these curses because the New Testament tells us how Jesus became the curse for us and redeemed us from all feelings of guilt and condemnation that the fall of man and the ensuing curse brought. It was, and still is, a choice just as it was in the garden.

God has always given his people a choice to choose to love him and live in the blessings he has provided for us or live under the curse. Read Deuteronomy 11:26-28 and see what God was telling the children of Israel as they were about to enter the Promised Land. It sounds like the same message given in the garden, doesn't it? God's laws, and his desire for us to love and obey him, never change. Read Deuteronomy 11:13-19 to get a better picture of this and record any thoughts regarding your struggle with this today.

The promise in Genesis 3:15 gave the hope of a personal redeemer who would contend with Satan and overcome him. The prophecy also implied that there would be perpetual enmity between the opposing seeds in the world, the seed of the serpent, and the seed, or redeemed spiritual children. These seeds would be in continuing conflict, those who chose to obey God's commandments and those who chose to go their own way.

We start to see this with Cain and Abel, the first sons born to Adam and Eve. They represent these opposing seeds. Abel, we read "was righteous" while Cain "was of the wicked one" (Hebrews 11:4) and (1 John 3:12).

No doubt Adam, their father, as priest of the family had told them the story of the fall and its tragic consequences, and of the sacrificial covering that God had provided for them in their guilt. He had shed the blood of an animal and made clothes to cover their shame. This was setting up the way of atonement for the shedding of the blood of the Messiah. We see it played out throughout the Old Testament, where animals were sacrificed to atone for the sins of man until all the factors had been put in place for the coming of the redeemer.

Both Abel and Cain knew this instruction that had been set in place to appease God. Abel was of the spirit of obedience and brought an animal sacrifice of atonement, while Cain offered a token of his crops. Without shed blood, there is no remission of sin. God was pleased with Abel's sacrifice (read Genesis 4:1-16.)

We see that because God was not pleased with Cain's sacrifice and he was pleased with Abel's obedience, jealousy set in and Cain killed his brother. This is the first sign of the sin of jealousy in the Bible. However, we see it unfold throughout the entire Old Testament, and it always had devastating results.

Can you imagine the pain Eve must have endured watching jealousy consume her family? She must have thought back on her own wrong choice in the garden that set it all in motion. However, God honored his promise to provide a righteous seed and we read of Eve's account of the birth of another son, Seth. Read Genesis 4:25. In Genesis 5:3, we read that Adam begat a son in his own likeness, after his image. The righteous seed had been renewed in Seth, and Abel had a like-minded successor who walked by faith.

We see this seed also continuing with the birth of Seth's son, Enos. Genesis 4:26 tell us, "And to Seth, to him was born a son; and he called his name Enos; then began men to call upon the name of the Lord." The seed continues through the following 8 generations from Adam to Noah:

> Adam lived 930 years
> Seth lived 912 years
> Enos lived 905 years
> Cainan lived 910 years
> Mahalaleel lived 895 years
> Jared lived 962 years
> Enoch (translated) lived 365 years
> Methuselah lived 969 years
> Lamech lived 777 years
> Noah lived 950 years

Much of the population of these generations went the way of the seed of Cain, and sin ran rampant on the earth, and it grieved the heart of God. Read Genesis 6:1-12.

Just think how God's heart was grieved because of the choice man continued to make to turn away from him. This lesson just gives us a glimpse of the love he had for us as he continued to extend patience and grace until a plan was put in place to bring the Redeemer into the world. I've heard it said that the value of something is the price someone is willing to pay for it. In this context, we cannot help but feel valued and loved by our creator.

Discussion Questions

1. Has this lesson on the beginning of our history and heritage helped you understand why we have so many obstacles as we walk out our daily life? Cain tried to shortcut obedience by doing it his own way instead of the plan God put forth. Have you tried that in your life and what lesson did you learn from it?

2. Can you think of times in your life when you seemingly had everything, just like Adam and Eve, but made a bad choice that ended in your losing something of great importance to you?

3. Spend time this week meditating on God's incredible love for you and the value he placed on you by giving his only son to restore you to a oneness with himself.

Lesson 8
Genesis 3-11
Noah

As we talked about in our last lesson, corruption had become so great in the line of Cain that the evil influence had spread over the whole earth. The wickedness of man was almost inconceivable; every wicked imagination of the heart was practiced.

God saw the corruption and was grieved to the point of wanting to destroy the very man he had created in his own image. He determined to destroy the world and its corruption with a flood. Read about this in Genesis 6:13-17.

Among the universal wickedness, however, God found one righteous man. He had made a promise to Adam to preserve a righteous seed and redeem mankind, and the Bible tells us that "Noah found grace in the eyes of the Lord. Noah was a just man and perfect in his generations, and Noah walked with God."

To this righteous man, God announced his purpose to destroy the corrupt world and commanded Noah to build an ark, for the preservation of his family, and through him the righteous seed.

God laid out instructions exactly how it should be made. He told Noah the ark was to be made of Gopher wood, rooms should be included in it and that he should pitch it within and without. (Remember, man had never seen rain up until this time, and Noah would have had no idea of what was needed to preserve the ark from the waters.) God told him to make it 525 feet long, 87 ½ feet wide and 52 ½ feet high - very exact measurements.

During the building of the ark Noah called men to repentance but in vain, and when all was ready, Noah with his wife, his three sons, and their wives, the animals for the perpetuation of their species and for sacrifice, were all gathered into the ark. The door was then shut by the hand of God. I find it interesting that I had always thought of there being two of each species but never really noticed that God also made provisions for animals for sacrifice when they once again found dry ground. Can you imagine the ridicule that he must have endured as he was building this strange-looking thing in his yard and telling the people "The sky is falling," as Chicken Little would say?

Also, I am sure Noah's wife and sons were subject to the ridicule. I cannot even imagine what the pain the family must have felt as they saw the waters start to rise and their friends and extended family being drowned and crying for help.

The experience lasted one year and ten days. There were seven months from the time that Noah entered the ark, and its grounding on Mt. Ararat, then five months and ten days before the patriarch received the instruction to leave it.

You might remember that he sent forth a dove to go out and see if it was safe for them to leave. I personally believe that the dove was a picture of Jesus, just as the tree of life was in the garden.

The dove went out from the ark and brought back a sign of new life after the destruction of the flood. Jesus was sent into a world of destruction and brought us a sign of new life just as the dove had.

The first thing that Noah did upon leaving the ark was to offer a burnt offering unto the Lord. Remember that this was the provision God had made for men to be covered until the time he brought Jesus into the world to be the ultimate sacrifice. Genesis tells us that the fragrance and spirit of the offering pleased God, and he made a covenant with Noah that he would never destroy the earth with a flood again. He also told him, just as he had Adam, that all things would be subject to him. Also, like Adam, he was instructed with his family gene pool to go and replenish the earth.

For the first time, the flesh of animals with their lifeblood in it was not permitted for food, and the sacredness of life was established by the institution of capital punishment. Those who shed the blood of man, by man their blood would be required. Read and highlight this in Genesis 9:2-6.

As a pledge of his covenant promises God set a rainbow in the heavens, a token of his covenant for all generations to come. I never see a rainbow that I am not blessed with remembering this. Highlight the passage showing that God was not only giving a promise to Noah and his family to come but also, he made a covenant with the earth. Genesis 9:9-15.

Now the race had a new start. With the institution of human government, man was responsible to govern the world for God.

The sons of Noah, through whom the world was to be re-populated started on their appointed commission. They now knew God as a punisher of the wicked, and a savior of those who believe. They had seen both sin and grace working in the world to deepen their fear and faith, and their obligation to serve, worship and obey God. Yet it was not long before they once again saw wickedness abounding, and men and nations at renewed enmity with God. Noah's three sons were Ham, Shem, and Japheth. According to Gen. 9:18-19 "the whole earth was overspread," or re-peopled.

You would think they would live happily ever after with a heart of thankfulness for being the only family spared. But it is not long before we see trouble brewing in the family and the pattern of sinful man once again emerging.

In Genesis 9:20-27 we see that Noah had started planting vineyards and had too much to drink and was in his tent sleeping it off and was naked. Ham saw his father's nakedness and told his two brothers who were outside the tent. The other two, Shem and Japheth, took a garment and walked in backward to keep from seeing their father's nakedness and covered him up.

When Noah awoke he said, "Cursed be Canaan, a servant of servants shall he be unto his brethren." (You will note that in verse Genesis 9:20, Noah refers to Ham as the father of Canaan, interesting that he refers to him in terms of being the father of one of his sons' here.) We are not sure what the sin of observing his father's nakedness means. Whatever it was, it was viewed by Noah as a violation worthy of punishment, and Ham was cursed, and from that day forward he and his genealogy would be servants to his brothers.

In the spirit of prophecy, Noah assigns to his three sons, and their respective descendants, the rewards, and punishments of their respective deeds and character. Ham would be a servile race. The descendants of Shem were to be blessed; God was to dwell in their tents, and the Canaanites (Ham's kids) were to become their servants. Enlargement was to be the portion of Japheth.

God had intended for them to disperse themselves throughout the earth and repopulate it for God had made the earth to be inhabited. However, men will once again override God's intended purpose. They became prideful and refused to disperse as God had instructed them to do. They gathered in the plain of Shinar and conspired to build a city and a great tower and to make for themselves a name. They wanted to band together and not be subjected to the trials of pioneering new territory. Going against God's will, they were establishing headquarters and starting to build one great city with a great tower to make for themselves a name.

Up until this time, they had all spoken one language. God had to do something to get them to be obedient to His plan, so he confused their language. This is why it is called the tower of Babel. They were suddenly not able to understand the babbling of the other families. This compelled them to separate from each other and the speakers of each different tongue naturally departed with the others that understood them. God had to once again intervene in the lives of his people to fulfill His plan and purpose.

The principal nations which sprang from the descendants of Ham (Cush, Mizraim, Phut, Canaan), were the African nations, Ethiopians, Egyptians, Libyans, and Canaanites. Think about the slaves who were brought over from Africa and how the entire black population stemmed from Ham. This fulfills the prophecy of Noah and the curse he placed on Ham. They had that curse attached to their descendants, but we will find that the grace of the new covenant broke that curse for all mankind.

Shem's sons were Elam, Asshur, Arphaxad, Lud, and Aram. This was the line that God would choose to be the chosen genealogy to work through. They settled in Assyria, Syria, Persia, Northern Arabia, and Mesopotamia. As we think back through history you can see the favor that has been brought on them. The Hebrew nation sprang through the genealogy of Shem.

Japheth's sons were Gomer, Magog, Madai, Javan, Tubal, Meshech, and Tiras. These are the nations that we as Americans came from. They settled in Asia Minor, Armenia, Caucasus, and Europe. These became the Russians, Germans and British. Most of us whose ancestors came from a European descent would be in the family line of Japheth. We can actually trace our ancestors back in history to the scattering from the ark.

Discussion Questions:

1. What does this lesson tell us is the reason God chose Noah for this monumental task?

2. If God asks you to do something so absurd as building an ark, would you have the courage and faith to do it? What would you say to those who questioned you?

Lesson 9
Genesis 12-23
Abraham

In the last lesson, we discussed the disobedience of the descendants of Noah to spread out and replenish the earth. God confused their language to force them to scatter and repopulate the earth.

You would think they would get the message and obey God but wherever the descendants of men went, they forsook the worship of the true God and invented religious practices and gods of their own.

Idolatry was fast spreading over the earth, dishonoring God and debasing man. In consequence, God chose to separate a family from all the families of the earth so in them, he might preserve a pure and undefiled religion and the knowledge and worship of himself as the one true God.

The one chosen was Abram whose birthplace was Ur. The people of his day and place were idolaters, even his own father, Terah, was tainted with the curse. The city of Ur is believed to have been devoted to the worship of a moon-god.

Abram was commanded by God to leave his country and kindred and go to a place that would be shown to him. The command was accompanied by a promise and a covenant. He would become a great nation, and the land of Canaan would be the everlasting possession of his seed, and through him, all the families of the earth would be blessed.

God tells Abram in Genesis 17: 4-7,, "Behold my covenant is with thee, and thou shalt be a father of many nations…neither shall thy name any more be called Abram, but…Abraham; for a father of many nations have I made thee…and I will make thee exceedingly fruitful, and I will make nations of thee and kings shall come out of thee. And I will establish my covenant between me and thee and thy seed after thee in their generations for an everlasting covenant, to be a God unto thee, and to thy seed after thee." That is a covenant we read about in the New Testament several times because it is a covenant that is still in effect today. God's promises are eternal.

All this was a new start for the Kingdom of God. With the call of Abram, God began to put the world in line for the promised Redeemer with "the seed of a woman."

God appeared to Abram, when he was 99 years old and made this covenant with him. He told him that he would no longer be called Abram but his name would be Abraham because he would be the father of many nations. He confirmed the covenant and told Abraham that it would last throughout all his generations to come. He instructed him to circumcise every male as a sign that they were part of that covenant household. This would continue as a sign of the family set apart to bring the Redeemer into the world. When Jesus died on the cross, his blood completed the need for circumcision, and we read in the New Testament that God now gives us a circumcision of the heart. God has taken up residence inside us.

At this time, God also changed Abraham's wife name from Sarai to Sarah because she was to become the mother of many nations.

Although God had promised that Abraham's seed would be innumerable, years passed without any sign of an offspring. Impatient with the years of waiting, Sarah decided to "help God along" as she was not getting pregnant, and asked Abram to sleep with her handmaiden, Hagar. Hagar conceived and after she was pregnant, Sarah began to be jealous and started to despise her.

Sarah talked to Abraham about it and he told her to do with her as she wished. Then Sarah started mistreating Hagar so badly that Hagar ran away. The angel of the Lord found her near a spring in the desert and told her to go back to her mistress and submit to her. He also told her she was having a son and to name him Ishmael. He told her that he would be like a wild donkey of a man and that his hand would be against everyone and everyone's hand would be against him. He also told her that he would live in hostility toward all his brothers. Ishmael's descendants became the Muslims we know today.

Recently we were in Egypt, and the tour guide took us to the tomb of Hagar and the monument where she was ministered to by the angel. I asked them about Sarah and Isaac, and they replied that she was just a jealous woman and that Ishmael was the intended first-born God had chosen. Even today, the wars fought in the Middle East stem from this disagreement. In Jerusalem, the mosque on the temple mound stands as a symbol of the dispute. The Jews think this is where Abraham took Isaac to be sacrificed, and the Muslims built a mosque on it to symbolize their faith. It is and will always be a point of contention in Jerusalem. So, you can see that our greatest threat as a Christian nation today goes back to this very event in biblical history.

Later, after God did bless Sarah with the child, he had promised her, she became jealous of the son of her handmaiden. She insisted that Abraham send her away. This must have been hard for Abraham, but God instructed him to listen to Sarah, and he did. He gave them food and water and sent them off into the desert. After the water was gone, it looked as if they would die and Genesis 21:15-17 tells us that she put him under a bush to die. She went to sit under a tree nearby because she said she could not bear to watch. The boy began to cry, and God heard him, and the angel of God called to Hagar from heaven and said to her, "What is the matter, Hagar? Do not be afraid. God has heard the boy crying as he lies there. Lift the boy up and take him by the hand, for I will make him into a great nation."

Then God opened her eyes and she saw a well of water. So, she went and filled the skin with water and gave Ishmael a drink. God was with him as he grew up. He lived in the desert and became an archer. While he was living there, his mother got a wife for him in Egypt.

Isaac, the son of promise, was miraculously born. Isaac inherited his father's faith and obtained a renewal of the covenant that God had made with Abraham. God wants our complete obedience, and Abraham's faith was tested with his most treasured possession, his son. Genesis 22 tells us Abraham heard God's voice calling him and he answered, "Here I am." Then God said, "Take your son, your only son, whom you love -Isaac- and go to the region of Moriah. Sacrifice him there as a burnt offering on a mountain I will show you."

Early the next morning Abraham got up and loaded his donkey. He took with him two of his servants and his son Isaac. When he saw the place God had shown him, he told his servants to wait while he and Isaac went up the mountain. He took wood for the offering but told the servants _we_ will worship and _we_ will be back down. As they were going up the mountain, Isaac asked his father, "The fire and the wood are here, but where is the lamb for the burnt offering?" Abraham replied, "God himself will provide the burnt offering, my son."

When they arrived, Abraham built an altar and bound his son and laid him on the wood. He raised the knife to sacrifice him, and an angel of the Lord called out to him from Heaven, "Abraham, Abraham, do not lay a hand on the boy. Now I know that you fear God because you have not withheld from me your son, your only son." Then Abraham saw a ram caught by the horns in the thicket, and he took the ram and sacrificed it as an offering instead of his son. Abraham named the place "The Lord Will Provide."

Can you see the complete faith Abraham had in God's provision? He told his servants, _we_ will return. He told Isaac that God would provide the sacrifice. Is it any wonder that Abraham is called the father of faith? Again, also note that this was a symbol of what was to come when God gave his son, his only son, to be sacrificed for us.

Discussion Questions:

1. Waiting on God can be one of the hardest things we are asked to do, especially when time has gone by and we don't see an answer right away. What can we learn from the example of Sarah and Hagar?

2. Can you see the unnecessary pain and suffering it caused when Sarah took matters into her own hands? Has there been a time when you have done that and what was the outcome and lesson you learned?

3. Abraham obeyed God and took the thing he loved most and was willing to give it to God as a sacrifice. He found out that God did not want the sacrifice but the obedience of being willing to offer it. Have you ever been asked to give up something of value to be obedient to God's call on your life? Give an example.

4. Recall an event that is still going on today that is a result of Sarah's rush to help God along in producing an heir and fulfilling his promise to Abraham?

Lesson 10
Genesis 24-25
Isaac

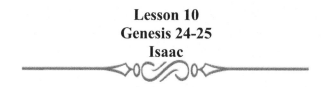

The last lesson we saw Abraham proving his faith by being willing to sacrifice his long-awaited son to God to prove his complete obedience. God was so pleased with his full commitment to him that he sent an angel to tell him, "I swear by myself, declares the Lord, that because you have done this and have not withheld your son, your only son, I will surely bless you and make your descendants as numerous as the stars in the sky and as the sand on the seashore. Your descendants will take possession of the cities of their enemies, and through your offspring, all nations on earth will be blessed, because you have obeyed me." Abraham had started a new genealogy for God to work through to fulfill his plan to bring a redeemer into the world. At last, there would once again be peace and harmony between God and man.

After giving birth to her long-awaited son Isaac, Sarah lived to a ripe old age of one hundred and twenty-seven years. Abraham buried her in Hebron. There is a monument to her that still stands there today.

Abraham himself was now very old and the Lord had blessed him in every way according to his promise. As he knew he was not going to live much longer, he told his trusted servant to swear to him that he would not let Isaac marry one of the Canaanite women where he was living at the time, but that his servant would go to the country where his people were and choose a wife from among them.

His servant asked him, "What if I go and find a wife and she is unwilling to come back with me to this land? Shall I take Isaac to the country you came from?" Abraham told him not to take Isaac back because God had promised to give this land to his descendants. He then told the servant to go and the Lord would send an angel to go before him to prepare a wife for him to bring back.

The servant took off on his journey. Abraham had sent him with ten camels loaded with good things. When he got to the land Abraham had sent him to, he had his camels kneel down near the well outside the town. It was near evening when the women go out to draw water. When he saw the women coming, he asked the Lord for help in choosing the right wife for Isaac. He asked the Lord, "May it be that when I say to a young woman, please let down your jar that I may have a drink, and she says drink, and I'll water your camels too, let her be the one you have chosen."

Before he had finished praying, Rebekah came out with her jar on her shoulder. She was very beautiful, a virgin, and of the family line of Abraham. When she filled her jar and came up again, the servant hurried to meet her and said, "Please give me a little water from your jar." After she had given him a drink, she said, "I'll draw water for your camel as well." After she had drawn enough for all the camels, the servant watched her carefully. Feeling sure she was the one God had chosen, he took out a gold nose ring and two gold bracelets. He asked her who her family was and after she told him, she invited him to come and spend the night with her family.

She ran home and told her family about the stranger and when her brother, Laban, saw the ring and bracelets and heard the story, he ran to the spring and found the servant still by the well. He said to him, "You are blessed by the Lord, why are you standing out here? I have prepared the house and a place for your camels."

The servant went with him and they put food before him to eat. He told them he could not eat until he told them the story about why he was there. He told them who his master was and the desires for him to find a wife for his son from among his own people. He explained how he had sought the Lord's guidance and how even before he was finished praying that Rebekah had come to the well.

After hearing this both her brother and her father, Bethuel, answered, "This is from the Lord, take Rebekah and go, let her become the wife of your master's son as the Lord has directed." He showered Rebekah and her family with gifts and spent the night with them.

The next morning, Rebekah went with the servant on the journey to meet her new husband. As they approached his home, they saw him in a field and when she saw him, she asked the servant who that man in the field was. He told her and she took her veil and covered herself. After the servant told Isaac what he had done, he brought her into the tent of his mother, Sarah, and married her. She became his wife and he loved her very much.

Meantime, Abraham had taken another wife after Sarah's death and had other children, but he left everything to his son Isaac because he was the one God had provided. He gave gifts to the other offspring but sent them to live in the East away from Isaac. He always knew Isaac was to be set apart for a greater purpose. Abraham died at the age of one hundred and seventy-five. His sons Isaac and Ishmael buried him near the grave of Sarah in the Hebron Valley.

Isaac was forty years old when he married Rebekah. She remained childless until Isaac prayed to the Lord on behalf of his wife. The Lord answered his prayer and she became pregnant with twins. She felt the twins jostling inside her and inquired of the Lord, "Why is this happening to me?" The Lord answered and said to her, "Two nations are in your womb, and two peoples from within you will be separated; one people will be stronger than the other; and the older will serve the younger." When they came out, the first was red, and his whole body was like a hairy garment; so they named him Esau. After this, his brother came out with his hand grasping his brother's heel; so he was named Jacob.

Isn't it amazing how God provided for every detail of Abraham's life? He went before him and prepared a wife for his son in a miraculous way. I also find it interesting that both Sarah and Rebekah were childless until God intervened. Isaac married Rebekah at age forty but his sons were not born until he was sixty. We know that Abraham was one hundred when Isaac was born and that so much time had passed that Sarah tried to intervene to help God's plan.

This is a great lesson on patience and waiting on God to provide his best for us. The lives of Isaac and Rebekah make such a beautiful love story that only God could have written.

Discussion Questions:

1. Do you have the patience to wait for God to provide his best for you? Why or why not?

2. Have you ever asked God to give you a sign as the servant did as to who he had chosen for Isaac? We see all through the Bible that God gave signs to encourage or give direction to his people. Can you share a time when God

3. How does the story of Isaac and Rebekah strengthen your faith?

Lesson 11
Genesis 25-43
Jacob

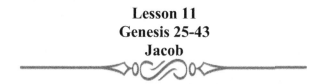

Isaac was forty years old when he took Rebekah to be his wife. They had two sons, Esau and Jacob. They were twins and the Lord told Jacob, "Two nations are in thy womb and the one people shall be stronger than the other people and the elder shall serve the younger." Then we read that the first one came out red all over and covered in hair like a hairy garment. They called his name Esau. And after that came his brother, and his hand took hold of Esau's heel, and his name was Jacob.

We see the first sign of favoritism of a child in Rebekah. She greatly favored Jacob and even though Esau was the first to be born, and was the rightful heir as the firstborn son, she plotted with Jacob to rob him of his birthright. Not only did she help her son deceive his brother, but she deceived her husband as well.

Esau was a hunter and came in from the fields one day so starved that the Bible says he was faint. He asked Jacob for some of the stew he had made, and Jacob told him he would trade him some stew for his birthright. In a moment of weakness, Esau agreed. Then Rebekah kicked into gear to get Jacob to wrap himself in the skin of an animal to make Isaac believe he was Esau and give him his blessing. Obviously, Isaac was not in good health and his eyesight was waning.

He blessed Jacob with the firstborn blessing, and this started a life-long strife that fulfilled the prophecy that the elder will serve the younger. There was constant strife between the two brothers, which perpetuated throughout the history of the chosen people. Esau was the father of the Edomites who were a constant source of trouble to the Israelites, the descendants of Jacob. You can read about this in Genesis 25.

Jacob's name was eventually changed to Israel, "A prince with God." He had twelve sons known as the children of Israel. They are Simeon, Asher, Naphtali, Dan, Gad, Issachar, Reuben, Levi, Joseph, Benjamin, Judah & Zebulon.

It is an interesting love story to read about the story of Leah and Rachel who were the two wives of Jacob. You can read of this in Genesis 29. Isaac told Jacob to not marry a Canaanite woman but to go to the house of his mother's people and choose a wife from the daughters of Laban, his mother's brother. He did as his father instructed, and as he neared where they lived, he stopped and asked some shepherds if they knew Laban. They said yes, in fact, that is his daughter Rachel now with his sheep.

Genesis 29:10, tells us of the beginning of one of the most romantic love stories in the Bible. Jacob went to her and rolled the stone away from the well for her so she could water the sheep. In verse 11 we read he then kissed her and wept aloud. He told her he was a relative of her father and a son of Rebekah. So she ran and told her father.

Laban ran to meet him and greeted him and took him to his home where he stayed for a month. Laban then told Jacob, "Just because you are a relative you should not work for me for nothing, tell me what your wages should be." Laban had two daughters Leah and Rachel. Leah was the older one and the Bible tells us "she had weak eyes but Rachel had a lovely figure and was beautiful." Jacob was in love with Rachel and told her father that he would work for him for seven years in return for Rachel to become his wife. Her father agreed and he fulfilled his seven-year commitment. Verse 20 tells us that it seemed like only a few days because he loved her so much and anticipated their being together.

The big day came and Laban brought together all the people and had a great feast. But when evening came, Laban brought to Jacob his eldest daughter Leah and Jacob made love to her. I'm not sure how he did not know that it was Leah and not Rachel, but he seemed surprised the next morning when he realized what had happened. He approached Laban and asked, "Why have you deceived me?" Laban replied, "It is not the custom here to give the younger daughter in marriage before the older one. Finish the bridal week and I will give you the younger one also in return for another seven years of work."

Jacob did as Laban instructed and after the bridal week was over, Laban gave Rachel to Jacob to be his wife. As was customary, Laban gave each of his daughters an attendant. Leah was given Zilpah, and Rachel was given Bilhah.

Jacob made love to both wives but his true love was Rachel. When the Lord saw that Leah was not loved, he enabled her to conceive while Rachel remained childless. Leah gave birth to Reuben, then another son Simeon and yet another son Levi, and then Judah.

When Rachel saw that she was not bearing Jacob any children, she became jealous of her sister and told Jacob, "Give me children or I will die." Jacob became angry and said, "Am I in the place of God, who has kept you from having children?" Then she said to him, "Here is Bilhah, my servant, sleep with her so she can bear children for me." Bilhah became pregnant and had a son they named Dan, then another they named Naphtali.

When Leah saw that she had stopped having children, she took her servant Zilpah and gave her to Jacob to have more children for her. She got pregnant and had a son they named Gad, then another they named Asher. Then once again when Leah slept with Jacob, she became pregnant and bore a son, Issachar, and then another named Zebulun. She also gave birth to a daughter she named Dinah.

Finally, the Lord remembered Rachel and enabled her to conceive. She named her son Joseph. After Jacob had taken his wives and children from the home of their father, Rachel became pregnant again and was having great difficulty with the birth. Shortly after the midwife told her of the birth of her son and with her dying breath, she named him Benjamin.

What a tangled love story. It reads much like our modern-day soap operas!

At one point in Jacob's life, he was alone and there came to him a man that was actually an angel (the angel of the covenant) and wrestled with him all night until the breaking of the day. Genesis 32 tells us that by daybreak, the hollow of Jacob's thigh was out of joint after wrestling with him all night. The angel pleaded with him to let him go and Jacob told him he would not let him go until he blessed him. At that point, the angel said, "Thy name shall be called no more Jacob, but Israel, for as a prince has thou power with God and with men, and hast prevailed. And then he blessed him there." So from this point on we no longer hear the name Jacob but he is referred to as Israel.

Then his children are the children of Israel that we read so much about in the Bible. As they each started families they were referred to as tribes. So when the Bible talks about the tribes of Israel, they are just referring to Jacob's sons and their offspring.

Jacob (Israel)

Simeon….Asher….Naphtali….(**Judah**)….Dan….Gad
Reuben….Issachar….Levi….Joseph…Benjamin…. Zebulon

Each of them has a story. But Judah was the one that God chose to be the lineage of the messiah. They were each chosen for a particular purpose. We know that Levi was the one whom God choose to be the caretakers of the temple. Joseph was a key player because his brothers, in a fit of jealously sold him into slavery, and that is how they ended up in Egypt and needed a deliverer.

We watch their evolution from their birth through the two wives of Jacob and their maidservants, through the Egyptian bondage and then their dramatic deliverance by the parting of the Red Sea. Then we follow them forty years of wandering around in the desert and struggling to remain true to God's laws.

On and on it goes, but knowing some of the facts about the people in the timeline of the Bible seems to make it more enjoyable, puts things in perspective, and helps us to relate to those who have gone before us in history.

Discussion Questions:

1. Can you see how the deceit of Laban followed in the lives of his children?

2. Can you see a parallel of the love story of God's love for us and the love story of Jacob's love for Rachel?

3. Has there ever been a time in your life when you thought you had been visited by an angel to teach you something important, like the angel appearing to Jacob in this lesson?

4. Spend some time this week asking God to show you the significance of his purpose and plan for you and ways you might better fulfill that plan.

Lesson 12
Genesis 36-47
Judah

Although when we talk about the twelve children or tribes of Jacob (Israel), we know that the genealogy of Jesus tracks through the line of Judah. The main character most talked about is Joseph. We know from history that Joseph was Jacob's favorite child, the child of his old age and he was not timid about showing his favoritism. He made him a beautiful coat with many colors that set him apart from his brothers.

Joseph was a dreamer. At one point Joseph told them of a dream he had that they were binding sheaves and that one sheaf rose and stood upright, representing himself, and the other sheaves gathered around his and bowed to it. This was the final straw. The brothers plotted to kill him and threw him in a pit to die, but when they saw a caravan coming, they decided they could make some easy money and just sell him to them as a slave.

They knew they had to come up with a story to explain to their father what happened, so they took the coat he had made for Joseph and tore it and soaked it in the blood of an animal. They told their father they had found it and apparently a wild animal had killed his favorite son. Jacob mourned so intensely that he would not be comforted, and he determined he would mourn until he joined Joseph in the grave.

The caravan of Midianites that bought Joseph sold him to Potiphar, who was one of Pharaoh's officials. The Lord continued to be with him and he ended up living in the house with his master. When his master saw that the Lord was blessing him, he put him in charge of his household and entrusted him to be in charge of everything he owned.

Joseph was well built and handsome, and after a while, his master's wife took notice of him. She tried to seduce him and when he refused her, she told her husband he had seduced her and Joseph was thrown in prison. While there, he connected with the other prisoners and one of them happened to be the cupbearer for the king. The king started having terrible dreams that troubled him so much that he sent for his magicians but they could offer him no help. After all had failed, the cupbearer remembered Joseph had interrupted dreams while he was a cellmate with him in prison. He told the king and the king sent for him.

When the king told Joseph his dream, God gave him the wisdom to interrupt it. He told the king that there were going to be seven years of prosperity and then seven years of drought. He told the king to store up supplies in the good years to be able to survive the bad ones to come. The king did as Joseph had said and actually made Joseph the ruler over the project. During this time Joseph developed great power and favor with the king.

Just as Joseph had predicted, after the seven years of surplus, the drought hit and people outside of Egypt were starving because of it. One of the families that were hard hit was the family of Jacob. Jacob sent his sons to Egypt to see if they could get some supplies. When they came before Joseph to ask for provisions, Joseph recognized them as his brothers. He then put a plan in place to once again see his father and his full brother, Benjamin. He insisted the brothers bring the family to Egypt as part of the provision for help.

My father used to tell me an old proverb, "What goes around, comes around." In this case, it certainly was true. Joseph held steadfast to his faith in God and God honored it by allowing him to be the savior of his family. What a story of forgiveness. Joseph's mind must have gone back to the day when his brothers threw him in the pit as a young man and then sold him into slavery. There must have been a temptation to repay their cruelty with revenge, but had he done so, history would have been written differently and the incredible lesson on forgiveness would have been lost.

We are told in Genesis 46 that God spoke to Jacob and told him to not fear to go into Egypt because he was going to make of him a great nation. So they went and after a grand reunion with his father and family, Joseph settled his family in Egypt to start a new life near him so he could be their advocate. There were seventy family members in all.

Joseph was thirty when he became in charge of the affairs of Egypt. He lived with his family there until he was one hundred and ten years old.

Although this lesson is about Judah, the story of Joseph explains so much that is to come in the history of the children of Israel and how they ended up in Egypt in slavery.

Before Jacob (Israel) died, he blessed each of his sons. You can read about the blessings of each in Genesis 49. When he blessed Judah, he said, "The scepter will not depart from Judah, nor the ruler's staff from between his feet, until he to whom it belongs (meaning Jesus) shall come and the obedience of the nations shall be his."

It is Judah who we find in the Genealogy of Jesus. We find the account of this in the first chapter of Matthew. "Abraham was the father of Isaac, Isaac the father of Jacob, Jacob the father of Judah, Judah the father of Perez, whose mother was Tamar."

This brings up another interesting story in the Bible, much like the script of another soap opera. Judah had left his brothers and gone to stay with a man named Hirah. While there, he met and married a woman named Shua. She gave birth to three sons. The first was named Er. As was the tradition, Judah found a wife for his firstborn son and her name was Tamar. However, Er was a wicked man and found no favor with the Lord and the Lord put him to death.

After the death of Er, Judah told his other son, Onan to sleep with Tamar and fulfill his duty as a brother-in-law to raise offsprings for his brother who had died. However, he knew that the child would never be his so whenever he slept with her, the Bible tells us that he would spill his semen on the ground to keep her from getting pregnant. The Lord knew what he was doing and put him to death as well.

Judah had only one other son who was still young, so he told his daughter-in-law, Tamar, "Live as a widow in your father's household until my son Shelah grows up." Time passed and Shelah grew up, but Judah did not give him to Tamar to be her husband. Tamar became concerned that she would not be able to bear an off spring from the family of her late husband, so she devised a plan to trick her father-in-law into sleeping with her.

By this time Judah's wife, Shua, had died and he had recovered from his grief. Tamar found out that he would be traveling on a certain road to shear his sheep, so she put a veil over her face to disguise herself so he would not recognize her as she sat by the gate he would enter.

When Judah saw her, he thought she was a prostitute and told her to come sleep with him. She said, "What will you give me?" He told her he would send her a goat. She said, "Will you give me something as a pledge till you send it?" He asked what she wanted, and she replied, "Your seal and its cord and the staff in your hand." So he gave those things to her and slept with her. She became pregnant by him.

After she had slept with him, she took off her veil and put on her widow's clothes again. When Judah sent a friend to give her the goat and get his seal and staff back, she could not be found. The friend inquired of the locals as to where the prostitute who had been at the gate might be and they replied there was no prostitute there. When he returned, Judah told his friend, "Let her keep what she has, or we will become a laughing stock."

About three months later Judah was told that his daughter-in-law Tamar is guilty of prostitution, and as a result, was pregnant. He told them, "Bring her out and have her burned to death!" As she was being brought out, she sent a message to her father-in-law. "I am pregnant by the man who owns these. See if you recognize whose seal and cord and staff these are." Judah replied, "She is more righteous than I since I wouldn't give her to my son, Shelah."

When the time came for the birth, she had twin boys. The first-born was named Perez. You will find him in the line of Jesus as well. Tamar is given a bad rap in the Bible for her deceit, but she was only fulfilling her responsibility of producing a son for her husband who had died. That son would need to be from the family line of Judah. It is easy to see that even through all the bizarre circumstances, God did preserve that seed.

In the next lesson, we will start examining the plight of the children of Israel. After Joseph died, they found themselves being persecuted for their very existence.

Discussion Questions:

1. What lessons can we learn about forgiveness and patience from Joseph?

2. As you look at Judah's life you can see how not fulfilling his promise caused him to be deceived as well. Has there been a time in your life when you were deceitful what lesson did you learn?

3. What insights do you have about the power of tradition? Do you think Tamar was wrong to deceive to fulfill the rule of her husband's family heritage? Explain

4. God gave Joseph wisdom to interpret the king's dream because he was obedient and patient. Has He ever asked that of you and how did you respond?

Lesson 13
Exodus 2-34
Moses

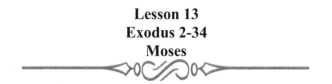

By this time Joseph, his brothers, and that entire generation had died but God continued to bless their descendants. Exodus 1: 6-7 says "the Israelites were exceedingly fruitful; they multiplied greatly, increased in number and became so numerous that the land was filled with them."

A king was raised up in Egypt who "knew not Joseph." Alarmed at the growth of the Hebrew people, he determined to crush them by cruel oppression making them slaves. The more they were oppressed, the more they multiplied and spread.

The king became alarmed and told the Hebrew midwives, whose names were Shiphrah and Puah, "When you are helping the Hebrew women during childbirth on the delivery stool, if you see the baby is a boy, kill him." The midwives, however, feared God and did not do what the king of Egypt had told them to do. When the king asked them about it, they replied, "Hebrew women are not like Egyptian women; they are vigorous and give birth before the midwives arrive." It must have been a hard decision for them to go against the king and be obedient to God. But Exodus 1:21 tells us that because the midwives feared God, he gave them families of their own.

At this point, Pharaoh gave this order to all his people: "Every Hebrew boy that is born must be thrown into the Nile."

It was during this time a baby was born to a Hebrew woman who was destined to deliver the enslaved nation. His mother decided to put him in a basket among the reeds of the river and did so for three months. She had his sister watching over him. One day the daughter of Pharaoh was bathing in the Nile and found the baby. He was crying and she felt sorry for him and wanted to take him home with her.

At that time, his sister came forth and asked her if she would like for her to get a Hebrew woman to nurse him and care for him until he was older. She agreed and she took him to his mother and she was able to care for him till he was old, at which time he was taken to Pharaoh's daughter where he was raised in the palace. She called his name Moses and claimed him as her son. Moses lived in the court of Pharaoh for forty years.

At this age, he renounced the pleasures of Egypt, and reclaimed his true inheritance as a Hebrew and set out to deliver them from the slavery and bondage they had been living in. He saw the abuse they were under and it weighed heavily on him. Once when he saw one of Pharaoh's men beating one of the Hebrew men, he jumped in and came to his rescue and killed the Egyptian. He was afraid of what would happen when Pharaoh found out and he fled to the desert and was there for forty years. God was watching over him and appeared to him in the form of a burning bush and told him to return to Pharaoh and convince him to let the Hebrew people go.

In Exodus 3:7 we read, "And the Lord said, I have surely seen the affliction of my people which are in Egypt…and I am come down to deliver them, and to bring them unto a good land…flowing with milk and honey…I will send thee unto Pharaoh, that thou should bring forth my people out of Egypt.

The king of Egypt will not let you go, but I will stretch out my hand and smite Egypt with all my wonders…and after that he will let you go."

That is exactly what happened. Because Pharaoh would not listen, God sent plagues: turned the water to blood, frogs, lice, flies, all the cattle of Egypt died, boils, hail, locust, and darkness. Even after all this devastation, Pharaoh's heart was hardened, and he still would not let the enslaved Israelites go. You can read more about these plagues in Exodus 7-10.

Finally, the Lord spoke to Moses and said," I will pass through the land of Egypt this night and will smite all the firstborn. God instructed Moses to tell the Hebrew people to kill a lamb and put the blood over the door of their homes, and the angel of death would pass over their families. They did as they were instructed, and their sons were protected while the Egyptian sons died. This event became an important celebration for the years to follow and is what we call Passover, meaning the time the angel of death *passed over* the Hebrew families. It is still celebrated today as a time to remember God's provision for his people.

This was also a foreshadowing of Jesus coming and shedding his blood to save us from spiritual death. That is one of the most fascinating things to me about studying the Old Testament. It is like connecting the dots of a blueprint for God's master plan. The Old Testament lays out the plan and the New Testament brings it to life. Jesus even compares himself to standing at the door of our hearts and knocking in Revelation 3:20, "*Here I am! I stand at the door and knock. If anyone hears my voice and opens the door, I will come in.*" But just as the Hebrew people had to obey by applying the blood, we have to answer the door and accept the fact that he shed his blood so we would be spared spiritual death.

At this last plague, Pharaoh told Moses to take his people and go. At this point, the Egyptians feared after all the plagues they had lived through that if these people did not leave soon, they would all die.

The Hebrew people started preparing to leave but decided since the Egyptians were so anxious for them to leave that they would just ask them for gold, silver, and clothing, which the Egyptians willingly gave. So not only did the Hebrews get their freedom, but they were able to leave with the wealth of the Egyptians, as well.

Now after 430 years of being in Egypt, we see 600,000 men, not counting the women and children, all leaving on foot led by Moses.

God wanted them to remember this time of deliverance and told Moses to institute the first Passover meal. One of the restrictions was that no one could celebrate it that was not circumcised. Remember circumcision was to set the genealogy of Abraham's seed apart from the rest of the population.

Part of the Passover meal was to eat unleavened bread or bread without yeast in it. The reason was when they left Egypt, they did not have time to bake bread for the journey by letting the yeast rise, and so they just wrapped their dough and carried it with them. Therefore, they ate unleavened bread. So to commemorate this time, for one week they were to eat bread without yeast and on the seventh day to have a festival to celebrate. This was to be done each year on the month they had left Egypt. We still eat unleavened bread because of this when we take communion and when Passover is celebrated.

Another thing instituted by God was to offer the firstborn of every womb to him. Every firstborn son was to be redeemed by sacrificing a lamb. (Can you see how this was foreshadowing God's plan to bring redemption by his only son?) We, as sons of God, are redeemed because Jesus became the sacrificial lamb for us. God told them to set aside this tradition for generations to come, so they would remember how the mighty hand of God brought them out of Egypt. God was setting up the pattern that Jesus' entrance into the world would follow.

As you progress through the Bible you will see this tradition is a vital part of our history. Mary and Joseph were to celebrate Passover when it was time for her to deliver Jesus. Also, Jesus was angry when he went to the temple and found men profiting from selling animals to be used for the Passover offering. I have Gentile friends who celebrate the Passover meal just before Easter as a way to teach their children about their spiritual heritage.

I think it is interesting to note the navigational system God used to direct the children of Israel on their journey. There were a million people wandering in the desert needing direction. God had to be very creative to provide a way for them all to know where he was leading. Exodus 13:21-22 tells us that "By day the Lord went ahead of them in a pillar of cloud to guide them on their way and by night by a pillar of fire to give them light so they could travel by day or night. Neither the pillar of cloud nor the pillar of fire left its place in front of the people."

When they got to the Red Sea, Exodus 14:19 tells us that "the angel of God, who had been traveling in front of Israel's army, withdrew and went behind them. The pillar of cloud also moved from in front and stood behind them, coming between the armies of Egypt and Israel. Throughout the night the cloud brought darkness to one side and light to the other side; so neither went near the other, all night long."

This tells us that God had sent an angel to lead them and that he directed the pillar of cloud and pillar of fire. I love the fact that not only did the cloud and fire hover over them to lead them, but they actually moved when needed to stand between them and the enemy to protect them. It is amazing that they could have ever doubted God's love and protection after witnessing that.

We all know how God parted the Red Sea for them to cross when the enemy was closing in behind them. Can you imagine having the sea in front of you and the enemy approaching and not seeing a way out? Once again God spoke to Moses and told him to put his rod in the water and when he did, the sea separated, and the waters rolled back and allowed the children of Israel to cross. After they were safely on the other side, the waters rolled back over the Egyptian army and drowned them.

Now that they were safely on the other side of the Red Sea, they started a 40-year journey in the desert. They murmured and complained about just about everything. First, the water was bitter and God turned it into sweet water. Then they grumbled because they wanted meat to eat. So God sent manna (bread) from heaven for them to eat in the morning and meat (quail) to eat in the evening. He told them to gather just enough for that day until the sixth day, and on that day to get enough for the Sabbath. You see God following the pattern of creation. Six days he created and on the seventh, he rested. I love the consistency God follows throughout the Bible even in all things like this.

They encountered many obstacles on their journey. At one point the Amalekites attacked them. Moses told Joshua to take some of his men and to fight them. He said." I will stand at the top of the hill with the staff of God raised in my hand."

Joshua and his men fought diligently and as long as Moses' arms were held up, they would win. As he began to get tired, Aaron and Hur held his arms up until the battle was won. God told Moses to write this event on a tablet so it will be remembered and to be sure Joshua sees it. (Interesting that God knew Joshua would be the one to lead the Children of Israel into the Promised Land. Remember all the spies that went in to scout out the land were afraid of the giants that lived there, but Joshua had seen how God had delivered them from the Amalekites, and this gave him the courage to lead the charge and take what God had promised.) This one event was probably key in giving him the courage to be the one to finish the journey into the Promised Land after Moses died.

Although we see the children of Israel freed from bondage of Egypt, we still see them in bondage to their fears and lack of trust in God's provisions.

One of the huge life lessons to glean from this lesson is the fact that it was not the distance they had to travel to get to their destination, but their lack of obedience to God that kept them wandering in the desert for 40 years. In fact, it was only a fourteen-day walk from Egypt to the Promised Land God had promised them. However, because of their unbelief and complaining, God kept them going round and round the mountain for all of those years.

Discussion Questions:

1. What lessons can we learn from Moses burning bush experience? Have you ever had God use a type of burning bush in your life to get your attention?

2. As we reflect on the way we saw God leading the Israelites with a cloud by day and fire by night, what are some ways God leads you personally in your every day life?

3. God honored Joshua in his war efforts as long as Moses's hands were raised. Aaron came and lifted them up for him when he was weary. Has anyone done a similar thing for you and how did that encourage you?

Lesson 14
Exodus 18 - Leviticus 27
Children of Israel Part One

We left our last lesson with Moses having led the charge of deliverance for the children of Israel from the bondage put on them by the Pharaoh of Egypt. After the crossing of the Red Sea and three months into the journey, they camped at Sinai and remained there for a year.

As you can imagine, moving this many people across the desert was no easy task, and God knew there had to be some form of order and organization to complete the journey and establish order as they settled in the land he had promised them.

Now we see Moses having successfully delivered them from the bondage of Egypt and having the task of caring for all these people. As you can imagine, many arguments and disagreements happened, and Moses was exhausting himself trying to settle all the disputes himself and seeking God's will in each case.

Interestingly enough, his father-in-law, Jethro, came up with a solution for him. Apparently, Moses had left his wife Zipporah and his sons to live with her parents while he led the charge to lead the children of Israel out of Egypt.

After they had settled at Sinai, he brought them to Moses, and when he saw how Moses was serving as the judge from morning until evening, he gave him some fatherly advice. Exodus 18:18 says, "What you are doing is not good. You and these people who come to you will only wear yourself out. The work is too heavy for you; you cannot handle it alone. Listen to me now and I will give you some advice, and may God be with you. You must be the people's representative before God and bring their disputes to him. Teach them his decrees and instructions and show them the way they are to live and how they are to behave. Select capable men from all the people – men who fear God, trustworthy men who hate dishonest gain and appoint them as officials over thousands, hundreds, fifties and tens. Have them serve as judges for the people at all times but have them bring the difficult cases to you; the simple cases they can decide themselves."

Sound familiar? This was the beginning of our justice system, as we know it today. City, county, state, national, and then the Supreme Court decides the difficult cases. As I have mentioned earlier, the Bible is the first place to go to understand the origin of life and why it functions the way it does in every area of our lives.

The children of Israel had camped near the foot of Mt. Sinai, and that is where Moses met with God and sought instructions to give the people. God wanted Moses to be validated before the people and told him to have them come near the mountain, so they could see God's presence speaking to him. In Exodus 19:18 it tells us, "Mount Sinai was covered with smoke because the Lord descended upon it in fire. The smoke billowed up from it like smoke from a furnace, and the whole mountain trembled violently."

Then we are told that the Lord went to the top of the mountain and called Moses to the top. There he gave instructions for the way the people were to live. Those instructions were called the Ten Commandments.

God had established a law, or a standard, for the people to live by and be judged by. In addition to that, he gave specific instructions on matters of social justice, laws of mercy concerning the treatment of others, laws concerning the Sabbath and protection of property. You can read about these in Exodus 20-23.

Another provision God made was He sent an angel to prepare the way for them. Exodus 23:20 tells us, "See, I am sending an angel ahead of you to guard you along the way and to bring you into the place I have prepared." Verse 22 states, "If you listen carefully to what he says and do all that I say, I will be an enemy to your enemies and will oppose those who oppose you." Remember, angels were one of the ways God communicated to men during the Old Testament times.

Then God told Moses to make a sanctuary for Himself, and He would dwell with them. He told him to make this tabernacle and all its furnishings exactly like the pattern He would show him. You can read about the details given for the tabernacle and all its furnishings down to the last detail of what the robes the priests are to wear in Exodus 25-30. Each article had a particular purpose and provision.

God appointed Aaron, Moses' brother, along with his four sons to serve as priests. God instructed him to make sacred garments to give him dignity and honor. Like the tabernacle, God gave explicit instructions on every detail of the garments to be made. They were to be made with gold, blue, purple and scarlet yarn and made with fine linen. Further instructions were given as to the shoulder pieces, waistband, and instructions to take two onyx stones and engrave on them the names of the sons of Israel in the order of their birth – six names on one stone and the remaining six on the other. These were to be worn by Aaron as a memorial before the Lord.

For the breastplate, he was to wear a plate of fine linen nine inches square. On it was to be mounted four rows of precious stones, each representing the twelve tribes (which were the children and descendants) of Jacob now called Israel. Another interesting instruction was for the hem of the robe to have pomegranates made of blue, purple and scarlet yarn and alternated around the hem with bells. The sound of the bells would be heard when the priest entered the Holy Place and when he left so he would not die. I list all these details, so you will see how God had every detail planned down to the color of yarn to be used. Interesting that he does the same for us. The Bible tells us we were fearfully and wonderfully made and that he knows the number of hairs on our heads.

God's instructions were just as detailed concerning the construction of the tabernacle where his presence would rest. It would have an outer court and an inner court. A curtain made of blue, purple and scarlet yarn and finely twisted linen with cherubim woven into it, was to be hung to separate the Holy Place from the Most Holy Place.

In the Most Holy Place was to be placed the Ark of the Covenant. It was to have an atonement covering over the ark made of pure gold and two cherubim that are over the ark also made of hammered gold at the ends of the covering. They were to be facing each other with their wings spread upward. God told Moses that was where he would meet with the priest and give instructions for the Israelites.

Just outside the Most Holy of Holies, God instructed them to place a table overlaid with gold to be for the bread of his presence that was to be before Him at all times. All the plates and pitchers on it were also to be made of pure gold. Another article in the court was the golden lampstand. Specific instructions were given for it as well. One of the duties of the priest was to keep the fire in the lampstand burning at all times.

Then there was the altar of incense, which again was overlaid with pure gold. It was for the sacred anointing oil and the pure fragrant incense. The total amount of the gold used was 29 talents and 730 shekels, which was a little over a ton. The altar of burnt offerings was overlaid with bronze and everything pertaining to it as well. This is where the animal was slain and offered for the sins of the people.

Just after the priest offered the sacrifice, he went in and washed his hands in the basin made of bronze as well. Interesting that the items that represented sin were made of bronze because it was an impure metal, but after the washing of the priest's hands from that time forward all was made of pure gold signifying the purity of having had a sacrifice offered for their sins.

Exodus 40 tells us that Moses set up the tabernacle just as God had instructed. The interesting thing about this was that everything in the tabernacle points to the coming Messiah and as you look at the layout, it makes a cross:

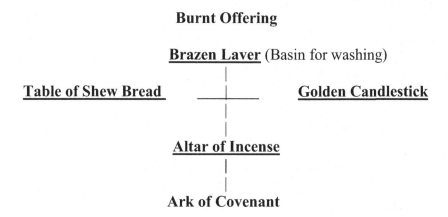

Burnt Offering

Brazen Laver (Basin for washing)

Table of Shew Bread   **Golden Candlestick**

Altar of Incense

Ark of Covenant

As we look at each piece individually, we see Jesus in every single piece. Jesus was our sin substitute offered for us as the burnt offering. He is called a river of life that washes away the sins of the world – Brazen Laver. He is called the bread of life and our substance to sustain us every day – Table of Shew Bread. He is called the light of the world – Golden Candlestick. He offered us up as a fragrance to God – Altar of Incense.

He became our mercy seat in the Holy of Holies, and when he died on the cross, the curtain was torn from top to bottom to show that God had accepted his offering and we no longer had to have a priest to intercede for us but that He had become our high priest. Now we each, like the priest in the tabernacle, could now enter into the Most Holy of Holies where his presence resides.

Because Jesus became our high priest, we now only have to come to Him and know that he ever intercedes for us with the Father. This intercessory role was played out in the Old Testament priest to give us a visual of what was to come when Jesus came and became the sacrificial lamb paying the price for our sins. As we accept him and the fact that He died for each of us, he now fills the role the Old Testament priest did. Through him, we have direct access to God.

Hebrews 7:24 tells us, "But this man (Jesus) because he continueth ever, hath an unchangeable priesthood." This tells us that the priesthood of Jesus will never change. We acknowledge Him as the sacrificial lamb. He carries his blood into the Most Holy of Holies for us once and for all times. The symbolic tearing the curtain from top to bottom (which only God could do) shows us we now have direct access to the Father.

We have been redeemed, restored to the oneness He created us to have with Him when he created Adam and Eve in the garden. Genesis 3:8 tells us that they heard him walking in the garden in the cool of the day. God wants to be just that near to us, that we can feel his presence as if he were walking beside us. He is just that close at all times.

After the tabernacle was finished and all the pieces were put in place, a cloud cover came, and the glory of the Lord filled the tabernacle. From then on whenever the cloud moved, the children of Israel moved, but as long as it was over the tabernacle, they stayed in place. As they traveled, the cloud was there by day, and a fire was in the cloud by night so they could see the presence of the Lord.

God instructed Moses to have the tribes to be camped around the tabernacle as follows: Three tribes to the north, three tribes to the south, three tribes to the east and three tribes to the west. This position ensured that they could all see the presence of God with them at all times.

Even with all they had witnessed and His presence in sight, God knew it would be easy for the people to forget Him and go their own way. So He established many remembrances in the form of feasts and offerings that would be a constant reminder of who he was and to keep the remembrance of their deliverance in front of their minds.

The offerings were:

Burnt Offering – optional offering but could be offered as a further commitment to God.

Meal Offering – voluntary offering of thanksgiving.

Peace Offering – offering to remind them of the peace God offered them by their deliverance. They would roast a lamb and have family and friends to partake of it with them as a symbol of peace.

Sin Offering and Trespass Offering – not optional as they were the offerings that they brought to cover their sins and trespasses.

And there were seven feast days to be celebrated:

Passover – Feast observed in their homes for all to participate by killing a lamb and remembering when the death angel was to kill the firstborn and God instructed them to put blood over their doorpost, and the death angel would ***pass over*** them.

Unleavened Bread – For seven days no leaven was permitted in the house of the Israelites. Leaven is a symbol of corruption. That is why Paul told the church at Corinth to purge out the leaven, meaning to get rid of sinful men. Jesus is said to be without spot and without sin; He had no leaven.

First Fruits – This observance involved the bringing of the first sheaves of grain to the priest who would wave it before the Lord. It symbolized that the whole harvest belongs to the Lord. Jesus is the first fruit of a new creation. He is called the firstborn from the dead. If you have accepted the sacrifice he made on your behalf, you have a number as well.

Pentecost – This was to prepare the way for the Holy Spirit. This feast was marked by offering of raised bread such as we eat daily, and the priest waved it before the Lord. This symbolized Jesus becoming our sin and ascending into Heaven and sending the Holy Spirit at Pentecost to always abide with us.

Trumpets – The time when they would blow the trumpets to symbolize the voice of God. This is symbolic of the day when the great trumpet will blow at the return of Jesus Christ.

Day of Atonement - This day was extremely important. It was nine days after the Hebrew New Year and was the most solemn day of all. It was a day of fasting – a day of humbling oneself before God for all Israel. Israel was a separated people to bring Jesus into the world. Of course, Jesus was our atonement.

Tabernacles – Two weeks after the Day of Atonement, the Israelites began a weeklong celebration known as the Feast of Tabernacles. During this time, the people dwelt in tents or (tabernacles) to celebrate the fact that God had brought them out of the wilderness. Jesus now lives in us, and we are called the tabernacle for his presence.

God wanted to be sure the family line he had set apart did not forget him or the purpose he had called them to. We know that was not always the case, but God provided the offerings and sacrifices for them until the time the ultimate sacrifice (Jesus), could be brought into the world, and once and for all, cleanse us of all unrighteousness.

This is a longer lesson, but I feel it is important to see how God has always provided a plan and the provisions for his people. I love seeing the plans outlined by God for even the smallest detail of everything down to the color thread to be used in the priest's robe. It is amazing that even though Jesus had not come yet, we see him like a thread woven throughout the whole Old Testament.

Discussion Questions:

1. Did you realize that the very basis of our justice system originated with God giving a way for Moses to manage the children of Israel as they moved toward the Promised Land? How can you use this system in managing aspects of your life today? Example: Sometimes it is hard to delegate work because we think we are the only ones who can get things done right.

2. Moses was willing to listen to his father-in-law when he saw a blind spot in Moses life. Has there been a time you can recall when someone gave you advice about something you might need to change your ways? Did you receive it, and if so, how did it give you more freedom?

3. If God gave attention to the small details such as what color thread was to be used in the tabernacle for the children of Israel, how much more do you think he is concerned about every detail of your life as his earthly tabernacle? Reflect on the things that concern you now and how God cares about each and every one. Share any thoughts you have on this.

4. God made sure every tribe could see his presence. Why do you think that was important? What ways can we see His presence today in our lives?

5. God gave them feasts and offerings to not forget the provisions he had made and to keep his promises before their eyes. Which of these would be most meaningful to you today?

6. As you look at the layout of the temple and see the comparison to our walk into the presence of God today, at which article in the temple might you get stuck? Example: Laver – knowing he has washed away your sins, or table of shewbread – knowing he will provide for your daily needs, etc. Explain.

7. Knowing you have the high priest Jesus living in you and giving you direct access to God, how does that make you feel?

Lesson 15
Numbers 1-36
Children of Israel Part Two

The children of Israel had now been camped in Sinai for a year. While there, they were organized into a nation. They were given laws to live by and had appointed judges to uphold them. God had also given them rituals to follow in the form of feasts and offerings to keep His name and provisions at the forefront of their mind.

Before they continued any further, they had a census to determine how many people were in each tribe. Then, later on, they had another numbering for the purpose of war and land allotment. The total men twenty years old or more and able to serve in the army was 603,550. God had spoken to Moses and told him to exclude the tribe of Levi from this numbering because they had been set aside to care for the tabernacle and have priestly duties.

After they numbered the people and arranged the tribes, they moved towards the occupation of the Promised Land. It was a distance of about 150 - 200 miles. When the time came for them to move, the cloud lifted from over the tabernacle.

In Numbers 10-11, Aaron steps out and says: "The Lord bless thee and keep thee: The Lord make his face shine upon thee and be gracious unto thee: The Lord lift up his countenance upon thee, and give thee peace." I have quoted this in church and sung it in hymns but did not realize its origin until now. This was a blessing he put on the people before they were to move. He was giving them the divine signal that when the trumpet blew, they would begin the march forward.

Moses went into the Holy of Holies and covered the Ark of the Covenant. Aaron and his sons went in and covered up every one of the holy things in a prescribed way. The tribes of Levi took charge of the curtains and on and on it went. Each had a responsibility for moving different parts of the tabernacle. As they moved, four men carried the Ark, and Moses and Aaron followed with trumpets blowing. The Ark was kept under the cloud that led them.

Judah, Issachar, and Zebulon, who were camped to the east of the tabernacle, followed with 186,000 armored men. Then the trumpets blew a second time and the tribes of Reuben, Gad, and Simeon who were camped west moved out with an army of 151,450. The third trumpet blew and the tribes of Ephraim, Manasseh, and Benjamin who were camped on the south moved with a total of 108,600 men. The last trumpet blew and the tribes to the north consisting of Dan, Naphtali, and Asher followed.

When they reached their place of encampment, they assumed the same positions appointed to them around the tabernacle as before. They stayed in the desert for 38 years. There they grumbled and complained, and Moses continually had to go before the Lord on their behalf.

At one point they began grumbling against Moses and Aaron. Korah, a descendent of Levi, challenged Moses' leadership, claiming that Moses had exalted himself above all the people. He gathered 250 well-respected men who had been appointed as councilmen (Numbers 16:2) to question Aaron's authority as serving as priest. They wanted the same priestly rights as Aaron. God was so angry for their rebellion that He wanted to come down and put an end to them.

Moses and Aaron fell on their faces and cried out, "Oh God, the God who gives breath to all living things, will you be angry with the entire assembly when only one man sins?" God heard their prayer and told them to tell the assembly to step away from the tents of the men who followed Korah in the rebellion. Moses then told them, "This is how you will know God has appointed Aaron to the priestly role. If the earth swallows them up you will know God has validated his instructions to me concerning Aaron. Numbers 16:31 tells us that as soon as he finished saying all these things, the ground underneath them split apart and opened its mouth and swallowed Korah, his men and their households, and all those associated with Korah, together with their possessions. They went down alive and the earth closed over them."

Moses' patience must have been worn thin by this point, but God gave him another way to show them that Aaron was the one appointed to serve as priest before God. He had the leader of each tribe bring their staff (which was a symbol of their leadership and power as leader of their tribe). He told them to write their names on their own staffs. He told them on the staff of Levi to write Aaron's name. Then they were placed in front of the Ark of the Covenant. He said the staff of the one God had appointed to be the priest would sprout. In the morning Aaron's rod had not only sprouted, it had blossomed and produced almonds. God continued to prove himself to the people that he was their God and not to be questioned because His ways were higher than their ways.

Even Moses disobeyed God and was forbidden to enter the promise land because of it. They were camped at the Desert of Zin and again the people grumbled about being brought into this desert where there was no water. Moses and Aaron fell facedown before the Lord, and God's presence appeared to them, and he spoke in Numbers 20:8, "Take the staff and you and your brother Aaron gather the assembly together. Speak to that rock before their eyes and it will pour out its water. You will bring water out of the rock for them and their livestock as well."

So Moses did as God instructed and brought them all together and said to them," Listen you rebels, must we bring you water out of this rock?" Then instead of speaking to the rock as God had told him, he struck it two times and water came gushing out and the people saw once again God's provision for them, but the Lord told Moses, "Because you did not trust in me enough to honor me as holy in the sight of the Israelites, you will not bring this people into the land I give them."

Next, we see them camped at the border of Edom. While there, God told Moses to take Aaron up on Mt. Hor because he was going to die. He told Moses that because he and Aaron rebelled against his instruction by striking the rock back in Meribah, Aaron would not be allowed to enter the Promised Land either. God instructed him to take his son Eleazar up with him to the top of the mountain and there remove Aaron's priestly garment and put it on Eleazar to succeed his father as priest.

Again, we see the people grumbling and complaining and God sent snakes among them; they bit the people and many died. They knew they had sinned against God. They once again came to Moses and he sought the Lord on their behalf. I love this part! God told Moses in Numbers 21:8, "Make a snake and put it up on a pole; anyone who is bitten can look upon it and live." So Moses made a bronze snake (remember when we were talking about the things put in the tabernacle, that the altar and laver were made of bronze because they represented sin) once again we see Moses making a snake out of bronze, an impure metal, and the people were saved who looked upon it.

Now this is the good part. In John 3:14-15, it tells us, talking about Jesus, "Even as Moses lifted up the serpent in the wilderness, even so must the son of man be lifted up." This was foreshadowing Jesus' death on the cross. Just as Moses lifted up the symbol of sin that the people had to look at to be saved from their sin, Jesus would have to come and be put on a tree and become sin, but anyone who came to look upon him will be saved. This is then followed by the most famous passage in the Bible that almost every child memorized. John 3:16, "For God so loved the world that He gave his only begotten son that whosoever believeth in him shall not perish but have eternal life."

I love how relevant the Old Testament is to our lives today. Again, we see the foreshadowing of what was to come by the serpent (remember Satan came to Eve as a serpent representing sin) being lifted up as a symbol of what was to come in the New Testament by Jesus being lifted up on a cross representing our sin. We still have to look upon Jesus as the solution to ridding ourselves of the old serpent, the devil and his influence in our lives. This is just another way it shows how important it is to study both the Old and New Testament. I heard it said once that the Old Testament is the New Testament concealed and the New Testament is the Old Testament revealed.

The children of Israel had many more adventures as they crossed the desert because they came across resistance with every territory they crossed.

One incident I find interesting is an encounter with the King of Moab. As they were about to cross to Jericho they came to the land of the Moabites. Their king, Balak, had heard of how they had defeated the Amorites before coming to their land. He decided to take some preventive measures before he had to confront them. He sent for Balaam who was a prophet that he thought was able to put curses on people. He told him in Numbers 22:6 "A people has come out of Egypt; they cover the face of the land and have settled next to me. Now come and put a curse on them because they are too powerful for me. Perhaps then I will be able to defeat them and drive them out of the land because I know whatever you bless is blessed and whatever you curse is cursed."

The king's men went to Balaam and took the fee charged for divination to give him. Balaam told them to stay the night and he would seek the Lord to see what God instructed him to do. He went before the Lord and was told not to curse them because the Israelites were His people and they were blessed. He told the elders and they went back and told the king. This infuriated him and he sent them back again to tell him that he would pay him handsomely if he would do this. Balaam sought the Lord again and got the same message. You can't curse what God has blessed. God had already spoken to Balaam, but the temptation was so great that he sought God again. That night God came to Balaam and said, "Since these men have come to summon you, go with them and do only what I tell you."

The next morning, Balaam got up, saddled his donkey and went with them. As Balaam went on his way, an angel of the Lord appeared to the donkey. The angel was holding a sword and standing in the middle of the road. The donkey was frightened and turned off the road into a field. Balaam beat the donkey and got him back on the road. Again, the angel of the Lord appeared in a narrow road of a vineyard and the donkey was fearful and pressed close to the wall on the side of the road crushing Balaam's foot. So he beat the donkey again and got back on his journey. The third time the angel of the Lord appeared on the road, there was nowhere for the donkey to lie down with Balaam on his back, and he beat him again.

Now, God did a unique thing, He opened the donkey's mouth and he spoke to Balaam, "What have I done to you to make you beat me three times? Am I not your own donkey, which you have always ridden to this day? Have I been in the habit of doing this to you?" It was as if the donkey was questioning their relationship.

Balaam answered him no; you are not in the habit of acting like this. That must have been a shock to Balaam to have his donkey talking to him. Just then God opened Balaam's eyes and he saw the angel of the Lord standing in the road with his sword drawn. So he fell face down on the ground. He knew he had displeased God by not listening to him the first time and sending them away.

The angel asked him, "Why have you beaten our donkey these three times? I have appeared to him to protect you because you are going down a wrong path." Balaam repented and told the angel he would turn around and go back. The angel told him not to turn back but to continue to go with the men sent by the king but to say only what he was instructed to say.

King Balak came and he took him up on a mountain overlooking the Israelites camp. Balaam had him build altars and offer sacrifices. But when he tried to curse God's people, only blessings came out. Balak continued to take him to another mountain trying to get another location thinking it would make a difference, but Balaam continued to bless the people. When Balak grew angry with him, he replied, "I can't curse what God has blessed." Those words are still true today. We are God's chosen people and he has blessed us with amazing blessings. As long as we walk in his way, no curse can come against us.

Moses continued to lead them through the land defeating the people who tried to oppose them. They not only defeated them but took the spoils of their land as well. You can read about the amount of their bounty in Numbers 31:32.

In spite of Gods' deliverance and provisions along the way for almost 40 years, the children of Israel continued to grumble and complain and it greatly displeased God. In numbers 10 it tells us, "The Lord spoke unto Moses, saying, send out men, that they may search the land of Canaan to see how it is. They brought back an evil report of the land and all the people murmured against Moses and Aaron…And the Lord spoke unto Moses, saying, "How long shall I bear with this evil congregation which has murmured against me? Say unto them, your carcasses shall fall in the wilderness. And your children shall wander in the wilderness forty years." So now not only will Moses and Aaron not be able to enter the promised land but the ones who came out of Egypt as well. It would be the next generation that would enjoy the land promised to their ancestors.

We read in Deut. 34 that before Moses died he climbed Mt Nebo, and from there God showed him the whole land that each of the tribes would inherit when they arrived. Then the Lord said to him, "This is the land I promised in an oath to Abraham, Isaac, and Jacob when I said, I will give it to your descendants. I have let you see it with your eyes, but you will not cross over into it."

At the age of one hundred twenty years, Moses died and we are told his eyes were not weak nor his strength gone. God kept him in good health and when it was time for his death, we are told, "Moses, a servant of the Lord died in the land of Moab…and he (the Lord) buried him in a valley, and no man knows of his sepulcher unto this day." So God himself buried Moses in a place known only to him.

Before he died, Moses gave many farewell speeches, recapping the history of the Israelites, and warning them against further mistakes. His main encouragement was for them to "love the Lord your God with all your heart and with all your strength to be able to enjoy all God's blessings." These sermons and life instructions comprise most of the book of Deuteronomy.

Before Moses died, he laid his hand on Joshua and passed the mantle to him to bring the people into the much-awaited promise land.

I found it important to spend some time on the details of the journey in the wilderness as God taught so many lessons on obedience, and it lays the foundation for so much of the rest of the Bible.

Discussion Questions:

1. How would you compare your life journey with the children of Israel? Are there any similarities?

2. When you feel like you are being bitten by the serpents of sin, have you experienced freedom by looking at the cross and letting Jesus cleanse you of that feeling of guilt? Share an experience.

3. The children of Israel were not allowed to go into the Promised Land because of their constant disobedience and lack of faith in Gods' provision. Is there anything in your life that might be keeping you from the best God has for you?

4. What lessons can we learn from the story of the Balaam and the donkey? Has God ever spoken to you in an unusual way?

5. None of the original tribes were allowed to enter the land they were promised because of their grumbling and complaining which represented their lack of trust in God. Are there areas of your life that you struggle to give over to him? Explain.

Lesson 16
Joshua 1-24
Joshua

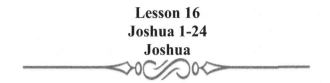

In our last lesson, we said goodbye to Moses, and we see in Deuteronomy 34 that Joshua succeeded him. Joshua was from the tribe of Ephraim and was a general and minister to Moses. We saw him referred to many times as God was preparing him to lead the charge to take the children of Israel into the Promised Land. You might remember in our study in Exodus that during the battle with Amalek, God told Moses to be sure Joshua saw the victory. He was building up Joshua's faith in preparation for this time.

You remember he was among the spies who were sent to check out the land, and when the others said they could not enter in because the men were giants and they looked like grasshoppers beside them, Joshua stood firm in God's ability to deliver the enemy into their hands. It reminds me of David and Goliath. When Saul's army saw a giant, David saw the God who would fight for him.

In the beginning of the book of Joshua, we see where the Lord is now giving the assurance of his presence and guidance to Joshua. He says in Joshua 1:2, "Moses my servant is dead. Now then, you and all these people, get ready to cross the Jordan River into the land I am about to give to them – to the Israelites. I will give you every place where you set your foot, as I promised Moses." In verses 5-6 he says, "No one will be able to stand up against you all the days of your life. As I was with Moses, so I will be with you; I will never leave you or forsake you. Be strong and courageous because you will lead these people to inherit the land I swore to give to your forefathers."

Joshua told the tribes to prepare to continue the journey, which would mean conquering the town of Jericho. He first sent two spies to get an idea of how difficult this was going to be. They went and ended up staying at the house of a prostitute named Rahab.

Rumors of them being there got back to the king and he sent messengers to find them. He sent this message to Rahab, "Bring out the men who came to you and entered your house because they have come to spy out the whole land." But she had hidden them on her roof under some flax and told the messengers that they had left when the city gates were closed. She told them to hurry and maybe they could catch them.

As soon as they left, she went up to the spies and told them how fearful everyone was of the Israelites because they had heard the stories of how the Red Sea had dried up for them, and how the Lord had delivered the other cities into their hands. She pleads with them in verses 2:12-13, "Now then, please swear to me by the Lord that you will show kindness to my family because I have shown kindness to you. Give me a sure sign that you will spare the lives of my father and mother, my brothers and sisters, and all who belong to them, and that you will save us from death."

They assured her they would spare her family's lives because she had spared theirs if she did not tell anyone about the plan they were putting together. She then opened a window and let them down by a rope because she lived on a wall. She told them to go to the hills and hide for three days until the pursuers had returned to the city. They told her the sign would be to tie a scarlet cord in the window through which she let them down, and she and her family would be spared.

The spies did exactly as she said and took the report to Joshua that the Lord would deliver Jericho into their hands because they were all in such fear of them. So early the next morning, Joshua and all the Israelites set out and arrived first at the River Jordan. God spoke to Joshua and told him, "Today I will begin to exalt you in the eyes of all Israel, so they may know that I am with you as I was with Moses. "

He gave instructions to the priest to bring the Ark of the Covenant out and instructed the tribes to follow it. He told them to keep a distance of about one thousand yards and not to go near it. He then told them that as soon as the priest set foot in the Jordan, its waters flowing downstream will be cut off and stand up in a heap. Sound familiar? God is giving another validation of stopping the river to allow them to cross just as he did for Moses with the Red Sea.

The priest stepped in the water and the waters piled up in a heap a great distance away at the town called Adam. I think this is another symbol of Jesus coming. Jesus came and brought salvation to his people back from the time of his death until the time of Adam. He delivered us from the sinful past that Adam brought on mankind and now we see him rolling back the waters all the way back to the town of Adam. The Bible is full of prophecies, if you keep your eyes open to see them.

Just as Joshua had said when the priest stepped in the water, the waters parted. The priest then stood in the middle of the river holding up the ark and all the people passed by. Then God did a unique thing. He told Joshua to choose twelve men, one from each tribe and have each choose a stone from the middle of the river where the priest stood. Then he told them to take the stones with them to the place where they would be camping that night and to place them there as a memorial for future generations. Joshua 4:6 tells us, "When your children ask you, 'What do these stones mean?' tell them that the flow of the Jordan was cut off before the ark of the covenant of the Lord." God has always left memorial stones for future generations.

When they had crossed over the Jordan, God gave Joshua the instruction to circumcise those who were entering the promise land. Remember God had told Moses to mark the family line that was to be called His people by circumcision. Now that generation had died and a new generation was to enter in, and God wanted them circumcised as part of the covenant family. It tells us in 5:2, "The Lord said to Joshua, 'Make flint knives and circumcise the Israelites again.' So Joshua made flint knives and circumcised the Israelites at Gibeath Haaraloth." Then in 5:8, it tells us that they stayed there until all the men were healed.

On the fourteenth day they celebrated Passover and the very next day they ate produce of the land. Remember up until that time they had been eating the manna God had provided for them. After that, the manna stopped appearing. They had now reached the land of milk and honey God had promised their ancestors all those years ago when they were delivered out of the bondage in Egypt.

However, they still had to conquer the city of Jericho. An angel of the Lord appeared to Joshua and he asked him what message God had for him. The angel responded with a famous quote, "Take off your sandals because you are standing on holy ground." The angel assured him that Jericho would be delivered into his hands.

God gave very specific instructions as to the means of deliverance. He told Joshua to march around the city with all his armed men one time for six days. He told him to carry the ark having the priest carrying trumpets of rams' horns in front of it.

On the seventh day, they were to march around the city seven times with the priest blowing the trumpets. With the loud blast of the trumpets, all the people were to give a loud shout; then the wall of the city would collapse. They did just as instructed, and the city fell and they went in and killed every living thing including animals.

Joshua remembered Rahab and sent the two spies she had hidden to get her and her family. They put them in a place just outside their camp and then burned the city. From that time on her and her family lived among the Israelites, and the thing I find so fascinating is the fact that she married one of the spies, Salmon, and is in the genealogy of Jesus. God always honors our obedience with things greater than anything we could ever imagine.

They continued their conquest of the land promised them and soon arrived at Mt. Ebal. There Joshua renewed God's covenant with his people. He built an altar and offered burnt sacrifices. Then in the presence of the Israelites, copied on stones the laws of Moses. There in the valley between Mt. Gerizim and Mt. Ebal he read all the law, which included the blessings and the curses that had been handed down so all the people would hear them.

He sends them reminders as well as warnings. Joshua 23:14, "You know with all your heart and soul that not one of all the good promises the Lord your God gave you has failed. Every promise has been fulfilled; not one has failed. But just as every good promise of the Lord your God has come true, so the Lord will bring on you all the evil he has threatened, until he has destroyed you from the good land he has given you." So although they were continuing to conquer the remaining territories, Joshua wanted to be sure before he died that they understood the provisions of the blessings they were to receive. As they conquered lands, allotments were given for each tribe to settle in.

At the age of one hundred and ten, Joshua died and was buried in the land of his inheritance. Israel served the Lord throughout the lifetime of Joshua and of the elders in his generations who outlived him.

Discussion Questions:

1. As you think of Rahab, what lessons can we learn from her example of obedience even in such a scary circumstance?

2. As you think of the spies who were sent out earlier to give a report on Jericho, what set the two spies, Joshua and Caleb, apart?

3. What are some of the memorial stones in your life that have been left by the generation before you, and what stones are you leaving for future generations?

4. What lessons can we learn about obedience from the warning Joshua gave before he died?

Lesson 17
Judges 1-21
Judges

While Joshua and the elders lived, the people served the Lord, but after their death, there was a gradual backsliding of the nation. The condition is summed up in the words, "Israel did evil in the sight of the Lord, and the Lord sold them into the hand of their oppressors." As long as they were obeying God, they lived under his protection, but when they forgot Him and started worshiping idols, he punished them by sending neighboring nations to fight and rule over them.

At this critical period, God raised up men from the tribes through whom he could govern and execute his judgments. These officers were called Judges. A total of fifteen judges are recorded as serving in this leadership capacity. The best known among them are Deborah, Gideon, and Samson.

Deborah was one of the few female judges. Chapter four tells us, "Deborah, a prophetess, was leading Israel and she held court under the Palm of Deborah between Ramah and Bethel in the hill country of Ephraim, and the Israelites came to her to have their disputes decided."

At one point she sent for Barak, one of the military leaders, and told him that the Lord had commanded him to take ten thousand men and lead the way to Mount Talbot. She said she would lure Sisera, the commander of the opposing army to the Kishon River and deliver him into their hands. Barak told her he would not go unless she went with him. I love how she responds in Judges 4:9, "Very well, I will go with you. But because of the way you are going about this, the honor will not be yours, for the Lord will hand Sisera over to a woman."

As they approached the opposing army led by Sisera, the Lord went before them and allowed them to be victorious. However, Sisera ran away on foot and escaped the slaughter. He came to the tent of Jael, who was the wife of one of Moses' descendants, and thought she would be a safe haven for him because there had been peace between their families. I will quote exactly from the Bible what happened next, "Come, my Lord, come right in, don't be afraid." So, he (Sisera) entered her tent, and she put a covering over him. "I'm thirsty," he said. "Please give me some water." She opened a skin of milk, gave him a drink, and covered him up again. "Stand in the doorway of the tent," he told her. "If someone comes by and asks you if anyone is here, say no."

But she picked up a tent peg and a hammer and went quietly to him while he lay fast asleep, exhausted. She drove the peg through his temple into the ground, and he died.

Barak came by in pursuit of Sisera, and Jael went out to meet him. "Come," she said, "I will show you the man you're looking for." So, he went into the tent with her and found Sisera, dead with the tent peg through his temple. Interesting how bold and relevant the women were during this time.

After that, the land had peace for forty years while Deborah was a judge.

Soon the Israelites did evil in the sight of the Lord again. The Lord took his hand of protection from them, and for seven years he gave them into the hands of the Midianites.

Once again we find them calling out to God to save them. One day the angel of the Lord came and sat down under an oak tree where a young man named Gideon was threshing wheat. The angel said to him, "The Lord is with you, mighty warrior." "But sir," Gideon replied, "If the Lord is with us, why has all this happened to us? Where are all his wonders that our fathers told us about when they said, 'did not the Lord bring us up out of Egypt?' But now the Lord has abandoned us and put us into the hands of Midian."

The Lord turned to him and said, "Go in the strength you have and save Israel out of Midian's hand." Gideon replied, "But Lord, how can I save Israel? My clan is the weakest in Manasseh, and I am the least in my family." (Sounds familiar to the story of David.)

The Lord told him He would be with him and he would be successful in conquering the Midianites. Gideon felt so weak and unqualified for the job that he asked the Lord for a sign.

Now during this time, the men of the town, including his father, had started worshiping Baal, and God instructed him to go and demolish the altar of Baal and build a proper altar to God. Gideon was afraid and did it, but he did it at night when no one could see him. When they discovered their altar broken down and found out Gideon did it, they went to his father and demanded he be put to death. His father told them that if Baal was real, he could fight for himself. "Let Baal contend with him," he said. From that day on they called him Jerubaal as a mocking gesture.

Gideon continued to send messengers throughout the camps to gather an army. He found out that other eastern people had united with the Midianites and crossed over the Jordan and were waiting for them. Gideon was still fearful and asked God for a sign that he could do this. He said to God, "I will place a wool fleece on the threshing floor. If there is dew only on the fleece and all the ground is dry, then I will know that you will save Israel by my hand." That is exactly what happened. He arose the next morning and wrung a bowl full of water from the fleece.

Still fearful, he said to God, "Do not be angry with me, let me make just one more request. Allow me one more test with the fleece. This time make the fleece dry and the ground covered with dew." That night God did so and Gideon was encouraged.

Early the next morning he gathered his army of men, and as they camped near a spring called Harod, God spoke to him and said, "You have too many men for me to deliver the Midianites into your hands. In order that Israel may not boast against me that her own strength has saved her, announce now to the people, 'Anyone who trembles with fear may turn back and leave.'" So, twenty-two thousand men left, while ten thousand remained.

But the Lord said to Gideon, "There are still too many men. Take them down to the water, and I will sift them for you there." Then the Lord said to him, "Separate those who lap the water with their tongues like a dog from those who kneel down to drink." Three hundred men lapped with their hands to their mouths. All the others got down on their knees to drink, and God told him to send them home.

Now Gideon was left with only three hundred men to go against the vast army camped nearby. God knew Gideon's fearful heart and told him, I am going to deliver them into your hands but if you are still afraid, take your servant, Purah and sneak down to their camp and listen to what they are saying. As they approached, they saw the Midianites, the Amalekites and all the other eastern people settled in the valley and thick as locusts. Judges 7:12 tells us "The camels could no more be counted than the sand on the seashore." All that is to say that Gideon and his men were grossly outnumbered.

Gideon did as the Lord had told him and as he arrived at the outskirts of the camp, he overheard one of the soldiers telling a friend of his dream. He said, "A round loaf of barley bread came tumbling into the Midianite camp. It struck the tent with such force that the tent overturned and collapsed." His friend responded, "This can be nothing but the sword of Gideon. God has given the Midianites and the whole camp over into his hands."

God did deliver the Midianites into their hands, and Gideon's faith was renewed. I love the story of Gideon because it is such an example of my life. So many times, when I feel God is calling me to do something and I feel so unqualified to do it. But God knows my fears and insecurities and always allows me to have a sign that when He asks me to do something, the battle is his. I am only to be the instrument he wants to use to do his work on earth.

After that Gideon went back to his people and they asked him, his sons and grandsons, to rule over them since he had saved them from the Midianites. He refused and said only God will rule over you. During his lifetime, the land enjoyed peace for forty years.

He had seventy sons because he had many wives, and his concubine also bore him a son named Abimelech, who later convinced the people to make him the single ruler over Schehem. He led a revolt against Gideon's other sons and killed all seventy of them except for the youngest named Jothan. Jothan warned the people about the evils of Abimelech, and then fled and hid for fear he would be murdered like his brothers. After Abimelech had ruled three years, God sent an evil spirit between him and the people. Other tribes rose up against him as well, and he murdered many and burned their cities.

Animelech'ss demise came when he besieged and captured the city of Thebes. Inside the city was a strong tower to which the men and women fled. They locked themselves on the tower roof for protection against Abimelech. When he went in to storm it an interesting thing happened. A woman dropped a millstone on his head and cracked his skull. Hurriedly he called to his armor-bearer, "Draw your sword and kill me so that they can't say, 'A woman killed him.'" His pride carried him all the way to his deathbed.

It's interesting that a woman did what all the armies could not do, and his greatest concern was that it would be said he fell by the hands of a woman. Seriously, this sounds like something out of a Hollywood movie, but you can read about it in Judges 9:53.

God repaid the wickedness that Abimelech had done to his father, Gideon, by murdering his brothers. All the things the younger brother, Jothan, had told them about Abimelech had come true.

After Gideon, many more judges served the Israelites.   One of the more famous ones is my favorite. His name was Samson. This is a love story of deceit, betrayal and God's faithfulness.

The Israelites continually did evil in the sight of the Lord, and at this time, the Lord had delivered them into the hands of the Philistines for forty years. This is the time Samson came on the scene.

He was set apart from his birth to be a deliverer of Israel. His father, Manoah, was from the tribe of Dan. He and his wife had not been able to have children because she was sterile. The angel of the Lord appeared to her and said, "You are sterile and childless, but you are going to conceive and have a son. Now see to it that you drink no wine and that you eat nothing unclean because you will give birth to a son. No razor may be used on his head, because the boy is to be a Naziriite, set apart to God from birth, and he will begin the deliverance of Israel from the hands of the Philistines."

She gave birth and named him Samson. Judges 13:24 tell us, "...He grew, and the Lord blessed him, and the spirit of the Lord began to stir him..."

When he grew older, he saw a beautiful Philistine woman who caught his eye. He told his father and mother, to get her for his wife. They asked him if he could not find a woman among their people and not go to the uncircumcised Philistines for a wife. But he told them he knew she was the right one for him and convinced them to go with him to get her. As they were on their way, a young lion came roaring toward Samson. The spirit of the Lord came on him in power, and he killed the lion with his bare hands. He did not tell his father or mother about it.

Later as they were coming back for the wedding, Samson passed the spot where he had killed the lion and went to see if the carcass was still there. It was and in it was a swarm of bees and some honey. He scooped some out and ate it as he traveled along the road. He even gave some to his parents but still did not tell them where it came from.

The wedding festivities began, and Samson gave the attending Philistines a riddle to answer. He said, "If you give me the answer within the seven days of the feast, I will give you thirty linen garments and thirty sets of clothes." Then he gave them the riddle. "Out of the eater out of the strong, something sweet, something to eat."

They could not figure it out, and on the fourth day, they came to his new wife and asked her to coax him into telling her the answer and then threatened to burn her and her father's house down and put them to death. Samson refused, and she cried the entire seven days of their wedding celebration. Finally, worn out with her crying, he told her the answer and she, in turn, told the Philistines.

When they told him the answer, he responded, "If you had not plowed with my heifer, you would not have solved my riddle." How would you like to be referred to as your husband's heifer?

He honored his word and went down to Ashkelon and struck down thirty men and stripped them of their clothes and gave them to the men who had answered the riddle. He may have honored his word, but he was burning with anger and to top it all off, when he went back home and was told that his wife had been given to his best man. Not an ideal honeymoon.

He persevered and took a young goat and some fresh grain (the equivalent of chocolate and roses in our day) and went to her father's house and told him he was going to his wife's room. Her father would not let him go in and explained. "I was so sure you thoroughly hated her that I gave her to your friend. Isn't her younger sister more attractive? Take her instead."

This really ticked Samson off and he went out to get revenge on the Philistines for tricking him. He came up with a clever idea. He caught three hundred foxes and tied their tails together. Then he set them on fire and turned them loose in the fields. The fire destroyed all their crops of grain as well as the vineyards and olive groves.

When the Philistines found out Samson had done this, they asked why and when told it was because his father in law had given his wife to his friend, they took revenge and went up and burned her and her father to death.

As you can imagine, Samson was furious and said in Judges 15:7, "Since you have acted like this, I won't stop until I get my revenge on you." Then he attacked them viciously and slaughtered many of them. Then Samson took refuge in a cave to rest.

The Philistines came after him and camped near the tribe of Judah. Judah asked them what they wanted and they told them they were pursuing Samson and told them what he had done. Judah took three thousand men and went to the cave where Samson was and asked him what he was thinking. In Judges 15:11 they confront him, "Don't you realize that the Philistines are rulers over us? What have you done to us?" He answered, "I merely did to them what they did to me."

They promised Samson they would not kill him but would allow them to tie him up and hand him over to them. They bound him with new ropes and as they approached the Philistines, the spirit of the Lord came on him and the ropes fell off and he picked up a jawbone of a donkey and killed a thousand men. After that, he was tired and thirsty. He told God he was thirsty and God opened up a hollow place in the Lehi and water came out to quench his thirst. The spring that God brought forth on his behalf is still there today. It is obvious Samson was under God's protective hand. After that Samson led Israel for twenty years.

One day he was in a town called Gaza and saw a prostitute. He went in to spend the night with her. The Philistines heard he was there and decided to wait at the city gate and when he tried to leave and come out the locked gate, they would attack him. Samson decided to leave in the middle of the night and the fact that the city gates were locked did not bother him. He took hold of the city gate along with the two posts and tore them loose, bar and all. He then lifted them to his shoulders and carried them to the top of the hill. You can see why the Philistines were intimidated by him and constantly trying to find a way to conquer him.

So often is the case that a man's demise is for the love of the wrong woman. He fell in love with a woman named Delilah. When the rulers of Philistine realized this, they went to her and offered her eleven hundred shekels of silver if she could entice him to tell her the secret of his strength. He first played along and told her if he was tied up with seven fresh limbs that had never been dried, that he would become as weak as any other man. She got the fresh limbs and with the Philistines hiding in the room, she told him they were coming for him. He snapped the limbs off and she realized he had lied to her.

She cried and said he had made a fool of her and begged him to tell her the real secret of his strength. He again gave her a story that if he was tied up with new ropes that had never been used he could not be taken. Then he told her that if she tied his hair up in pins, etc. Finally, she brought out the big gun. "If you really loved me, you would tell me the secret to your great strength." After nagging him day after day, he finally told her, "No razor has ever been used on my head because I have been a Naziriite set apart by God since birth. If my head were shaved, my strength would leave me, and I would become as weak as any man."

When she realized he had told her the truth, she called the Philistines and they brought her the silver she had been promised. She lured him to sleep in her lap and cut his hair off.

When the Philistines came to take him, he jumped up and was going to show his strength, but the spirit of the Lord had left him. They captured him and gouged out his eyes and took him down to Gaza and put him in prison where he was forced to do hard work the rest of his life. However, his hair was continuing to grow all this time.

They had a great festival to worship their gods and especially for delivering Samson into their hands. They sent for Samson to be brought out into the temple so they could ridicule him and make a spectacle of him, humiliating him and making him perform for them. The temple was crowded with all the rulers of the Philistines and as many as three thousand men and women were watching from the roof.

Samson asked the guard who was leading him to take him to the pillar of the temple so he could lean on it. As he put his arms around it, he prayed, "Oh Sovereign Lord, remember me. Oh God, please strengthen me just once more, and let me with one blow get revenge on the Philistines for my two eyes." Then he took hold of one of the pillars with his right hand and the other with his left. He said, "Let me die with the Philistines." With that proclamation, he pushed with all his might, and down came the temple on the rulers and others in the temple. He killed more when he died than when he lived. His brothers and father came and got his body and buried it in his family grave.

God had called Samson, and like Joseph and so many others in the Bible, it seemed at times that God had deserted them, but in the end, he returned and restored all that had been taken from them.

Discussion Questions:

1. As you look at the prophets, we discussed in this lesson, which one can you most identify with and why? Example...Gideon struggled with fear that could hinder him being able to be used byGod.

2. Have you asked God for a sign to show you that he is working something out in your life like Gideon and the fleece?

3. Samson had been set apart by God for a purpose as we each are. Are there ways you can relate to him in wanting to take revenge?

4. Have you ever done something that disappointed God only to find him ready to renew your strength when you came to him like Samson?

5. I think it is interesting that in the story of Deborah when the armies could not capture Sisera that a woman was at the right place to bring about an enemy's doom. Even though we read more stories of brave men in the Bible, does this show you that God has a plan for all of us? Have you ever felt God had placed you in a unique position like this?

Lesson 18
Ruth 1-4
Ruth

The story of Ruth is a true love story of faithfulness and loyalty. It begins when famine had struck the land during the time the judges were in charge of the Israelites.

There was a man named Elimelech who took his wife Naomi and their two sons to live in Moab for a while. Elimelech died and left Naomi with her two sons who ended up marrying Moabite women. One of the wives was named Orpah and the other Ruth. After about ten years both her sons died and she was left with only her two daughters-in-laws.

Food was scarce and she decided to go back to Judah where she had lived before when she heard the Lord was providing food there. She kissed her daughters-in-laws goodbye and told them to go back to their mother's home. She prayed that God would show kindness to them and that they would find rest in the home of another husband.

Orpah kissed her mother-in-law goodbye but Ruth clung to her. Naomi said to Ruth, "Look, your sister-in-law is going back to her people and her gods, go back with her." She went on to explain that she was old and would not be able to find another husband and did not want them to be burdened with her.

Then we see a famous passage in Ruth 1:16. Ruth says to Naomi, "Don't urge me to leave you or turn my back on you. Where you go, I will go, and where you stay, I will stay. Your people will be my people and your God, my God. Where you die, I will die and there I will be buried. May the Lord deal with me, be it ever so severely if anything but death separates you and me." Wow, you don't hear many talk that way about their mothers-in-law!

After that, Naomi gave up trying to urge her to leave. They went back to Bethlehem, and when Naomi's friends saw her, they were shocked to see her and to have with her a Moabite daughter-in-law.

They welcomed her, but Naomi had become bitter and told her friends in Ruth 1:20, "Don't call me Naomi, call me Mara because the Almighty has made my life very bitter." As I thought about her negative attitude, I was a bit judgmental but when I put myself in her place and thought of her leaving her home and following her husband to a strange land, then having her husband and two sons die, I began to wonder how she endured. Remember, she had only sons and now she was left far from her home with two daughters-in-laws who were from the Moabite race that would not be received well by her Hebrew family.

Now that they were settled back in Bethlehem they found themselves needing to find a way to survive since all the men in the family had died. Ruth volunteered to go out to glean in the grain fields. She would walk behind the men who cut the wheat and pick up any that was left on the ground.

Now in that time, there was a man named Boaz who was very successful and in whose field she was gleaning. As it turns out, he was in the family line of Elimelech, who also was Naomi's husband's family line. That turns out to be a very important part of the story.

It is easy to see that Boaz was a good man who loved God. It tells us in Ruth 2:4 that when he arrived at his fields that he greeted his harvester workers by saying, "The Lord be with you!" They called back, "The Lord bless you."

As he glanced around the fields, he noticed Ruth and asked his foreman, "Whose young woman is that?" The foreman replied, "She is the Moabitess who came back from Moab with Naomi." Then he told him that she was following the harvesters and picking up any leftover grain.

Boaz went over and said to Ruth, "My daughter, listen to me. Don't go and glean in another field and don't go away from here. Stay here with my servant girls. Watch the field where the men are harvesting, and follow along with the girls, I have told the men not to touch you. And whenever you are thirsty, go and get a drink from the water jars the men have filled." Obviously, he was smitten from the very sight of her because he was insistent that she did not go glean in anyone else's field, and he instructed his men to leave her alone. Apparently, the men would sometimes take advantage of the women who were gleaning in the field.

Ruth asked him, "Why have I found such favor in your eyes that you notice me, a foreigner?" Boaz replied, "I've been told all about what you have done for your mother-in-law since the death of your husband - how you left your father and mother and your homeland and came to live with people you did not know before. May the Lord repay you for what you have done. May you be richly rewarded by the Lord, God of Israel, under whose wings you have come to take refuge."

I think the last sentence is of considerable significance. It points out that even though Ruth came to be with Naomi, she had accepted her God. Remember her response to Naomi when she said, "Your God will be my God." Boaz recognized her loyalty not only to Naomi but her willingness to turn her back on the god of her people and come to worship the God of his people, the God of Israel.

When he spoke these things to her, she replied, "May I find favor in your eyes, my Lord. You have given me comfort and have spoken kindly to your servant - though I do not have the standing of one of your servant girls." I guess you could say his next move was to ask her to have lunch with him. He invited her to eat with him. He said in Ruth 2:13, "Come over here, have some bread and dip it in the wine vinegar." Then offered her some roasted grain. She ate all she wanted and had some leftover.

Boaz then gave orders to his men, "Even if she gathers among the sheaves, don't embarrass her. Rather pull out some stalks for her from your bundles and leave for her to pick up, and don't rebuke her." Not only was he providing for her physically but also, he wanted to protect her from any humiliation that the other servant girls might endure.

When she finished her day's work, she went back to Naomi and took the grain she had gathered and also the leftovers from her lunch. Naomi asked, "Where did you glean today? Blessed be the man who took notice of you."

Ruth continued to tell her it was in the field of Boaz, and Naomi was pleased and told her he was a close relative and one of our kinsman-redeemers. This meant that he was in line to redeem Elimelech's family by marrying the next of the kin. That would redeem the family line and restore life in the family after death had interrupted it. It was a big thing then to restore the family line after a man's death. Remember

Tamar, when we studied the process she was willing to go through to redeem a child through her brothers-in-law after her husband died?

So now we find Ruth having caught the eye of a wealthy landowner who was part of the genealogy of her dead husband. She continued to work in his fields until harvest was finished.

Naomi was becoming concerned for the future of Ruth and told her in Ruth 3:1, "My daughter, should I not try to find a home for you, where you will be well provided for? Is not Boaz, with whose servant girls you have been, a kinsman of ours? Tonight, he will be winnowing barley on the threshing floor. Wash and perfume yourself and put on your best clothes. Then go down to the threshing floor, but don't let him know you are there until he has finished eating and drinking. When he lies down, note the place where he is lying. Then go and uncover his feet and lie down. He will tell you what to do."

Ruth did exactly as she was told and after Boaz was finished eating and drinking (verse 7 tells us he was in good spirits, which probably meant he had enough to drink to lighten his mood), he went over to lie down at the far end of the grain pile. Ruth quietly slipped in and uncovered his feet and lay down. In the middle of the night, something startled Boaz and he turned and discovered a woman at his feet. "Who are you?" he asked. "I am your servant Ruth. Spread the corner of your garment over me, since you are a kinsman-redeemer." Basically, she was proposing to him.

Boaz was flattered and told her, "This kindness is greater than that which you showed earlier: you have not run after the younger men, whether rich or poor. And now, don't be afraid, I will do all that you ask. All the fellow townsmen know you are a woman of noble character. Although it is true I am near of kin, there is a kinsman-redeemer nearer than I. Stay here the night and in the morning if he wants to redeem, good; let him redeem. But as surely as the Lord lives, I will do it. Lie here until morning."

So she lay at his feet until morning, but got up and left before anyone could recognize her. Before she left Boaz told her to take the shawl off, she was wearing and spread it out. She did as he asked, and he filled it with barley to take back to her mother-in-law. It was symbolic of the grain offering that we read about in the book of Leviticus. It was a way of showing his good intentions. He was offering himself to redeem Naomi's dead son. This is such a beautiful picture of Jesus. He presented himself to be the offering that was given to redeem us. I love the fact that even before Boaz knew he could have Ruth as his own, he wanted to provide for her. As we look at the entire Old Testament, we see God doing just that, providing for his children.

Boaz quickly acted on his word to Ruth and went into town and waited until the one first in line as the kinsman redeemer came along. He asked him to come and sit with him and also asked ten of the elders to sit in on the conversation as well. He explained that Naomi was selling a piece of land that belonged to their brother Elimelech. He said he wanted to bring the matter to his attention since he was the next in line to be able to buy it. He added, "No one has a right to do it except you, and I am next in line." To Boaz' disappointment, he replied that yes, he would buy it.

Boaz went on to tell him, "On the day you buy the land from Naomi and Ruth, you will acquire the dead man's widow, in order to maintain the name for the dead with his property." At this, the kinsman-redeemer said, "Then I cannot redeem it because I might endanger my own estate. You redeem it yourself. I cannot do it." This must have been music to Boaz' ears. Then the kinsman took off his sandal and gave it to Boaz. (This was in accordance with the laws of redemption and transfer of property to become final as had been set forth earlier among the Israelites. One party took off his sandal and gave it to the other as a sign that the deal was final.)

You can refer back to Deuteronomy 25:5, where Moses was instructing the Israelites before his death. "If brothers are living together and one of them dies without a son, his widow must not marry outside the family. Her husband's brother shall take her and marry her and fulfill the duty of a brother-in-law to her. The first son she bears shall carry on the name of the dead brother so that his name will not be blotted out from Israel. However, if a man does not want to marry his brother's wife, she shall go to the elders at the town gate and say, my husband's brother refuses to carry on his brother's name in Israel. He will not fulfill the duty of a brother-in-law to me."

If he persists in saying he does not want to marry her, his brother's widow shall go up to him in the presence of the elders and take off one of his sandals, spit in his face and say, "This is what is done to the man who will not build up his brother's line. That man's line shall be known in Israel as, The Family of the Unsandaled." In other words, this lack of taking responsibility will reflect on the entire family as being disobedient to God's laws.

So now Boaz has obtained his right to marry Ruth. He turns to the elders and witnesses and says, "Today I have bought from Naomi all the property of Elimelech, Kilion, and Mahlon. I have also acquired Ruth the Moabitess, Mahlon's widow, as my wife, in order to maintain the name of the dead with the property, so that his name will not disappear from among his family or from the town records. Today you are witnesses."

The elders had an interesting response, "May the Lord make the woman who is coming into your home like Rachel and Leah, who together built up the house of Israel." Remember they, along with their servant girls, gave birth to the twelve children of (Jacob) Israel who became the twelve tribes God brought out of Egypt and lead into the Promised Land.

They went on to refer to Tamar who had been through similar circumstance by redeeming her dead husband through a family member. They said to Boaz, "Through your offspring, the Lord gives you by this young woman, may your family be like that of Perez, whom Tamar bore to Judah."

So it was, and Ruth was blessed with a son by Boaz and they named him Obed. Naomi had lost her sons but now felt redeemed as well. Ruth 4:16 tells us, "Naomi took the child, laid him in her lap and cared for him. The women living there said, "Naomi has a son." Obed became the father of Jesse, who gave birth to a son named David. So, Ruth became the great-grandmother of David and is found in the genealogy of Jesus.

So many lessons to be learned about obedience, loyalty, and honor in the story of Ruth.

Discussion Questions:

1. Can you compare times in your own life when you have been in a situation like Ruth where you have seemingly lost everything and had to dig deep to do the right thing?

2. What was the outcome of your obedience?

3. How do you see the story of Ruth reflecting the story of Jesus?

I Samuel
I Samuel 1-31

I Samuel establishes Israel's first monarchy, about 1050 BC. Samuel led Israel for many years in roles of prophet, priest, and judge. The book of Samuel opens with a family history of his birth, which is a fascinating story.

The story opens telling us about his father, Elkanah, who lived in the town of Ramah.   Elkanah had two wives. One named Peninnah and one named Hannah. Peninnah had given him children, but Hannah had been unable to conceive. Hannah was what we might call his true love, and he showed favor to her as it mentions in I Samuel 1:5. "When Elkanah had gone up to Shiloh to offer his sacrifice, he had given a portion to his wife Peninnah and her sons and daughters, but he loved Hannah and gave her a double portion, but Jehovah had shut up her womb."

I am sure Peninnah sensed this, and out of jealousy taunted her with the fact that she could not bear Elkanah any children. This went on year after year and was almost more than Hannah could bear. One day Elkanah saw her crying and said, "Why do you weep, why is your heart sad and you do not eat, am I not more to you than ten sons?" He obviously could not understand her need to have children of her own, and that he could not fill that place of emptiness she felt.

On one occasion, they had gone up to present their annual offerings in Shiloh. Hannah and the others had finished eating and drinking, and Hannah was overcome with sadness and began to weep bitterly and prayed silently to herself concerning her inability to conceive. She prayed as recorded in I Samuel 1:11, "O Lord of hosts if you will indeed look on the affliction of your servant and remember me and not forget your servant, but will give to your servant a son, then I will give him to the Lord all the days of his life, and no razor shall touch his head."

Eli, the priest, was sitting by the doorpost of the temple and observed how emotional she was and that her mouth was moving, but no words were coming out. He thought she was drunk. He said to her, "How long will you go on being drunk? Put your wine away from you." But Hannah answered, "No my lord, I am a woman troubled in spirit. I have drunk neither wine nor strong drink, but I have been pouring out my soul to the Lord. Do not regard your servant as a worthless woman, for all along I have been speaking out of my great anxiety and vexation."

After Eli heard her heart, he told her to go in peace and that the God of Israel would grant her petition. She felt very comforted and went away with a newfound joy.

The next day they returned home, and God remembered Hannah's prayer. She conceived and bore a son and appropriately named him Samuel, for she said, "I have asked for him from the Lord."

The next year when it was time to go for the annual sacrifice, Hannah told her husband that she did not want to take her son until he was weaned and then she would fulfill her promise to the Lord to give him to serve Him all his life. She stood true to her word, and when he was weaned, verse 24 tells us, "She took him up along with a three-year-old bull, an ephah of flour, and a skin of wine, and she brought him to the house of the Lord at Shiloh." Then they slaughtered the bull and brought the child to Eli, the priest.

She presented him to the Lord with these words, "Oh, my Lord! As you live, my lord, I am the woman who was standing here in your presence, praying to the Lord. For this child, I prayed, and the Lord has granted me my petition. Therefore, I have lent him to the Lord. As long as he lives, he is lent to the Lord." Even though the boy was young, he was worshiping and ministering to the Lord in the presence of Eli, the priest. It was evident at this young age God had set him aside as well.

Read Chapter 2:1-10 and read Hannah's prayer. It is a beautiful song of praise and admiration for the Lord. She must have had mixed emotions as a mother to leave this young child that she had longed for so long in the temple to be raised by Eli, the priest. She must have treasured those annual visits when they went up to make their offerings to the Lord, and she got to see him. We read that she made him a little robe and took one up to him each year. God honored her obedience, and she conceived and had three more sons and two daughters.

Eli, the priest, was growing older and his sons were doing evil in the sight of the Lord. He tried to talk to them and reason with them. He tells them in 2:24-25, "No, my sons; it is no good report that I hear the people of the Lord spreading abroad. If someone sins against a man, God will mediate for him, but if someone sins against the Lord, who can intercede for him?" They would not listen to their father, and verse 25 tells us it was the will of the Lord to put them to death.

Meantime, the boy Samuel continued to grow both in stature and in favor with the Lord and also with man. Eli was old, and his eyesight had begun to grow dim. One day he heard Samuel coming to him and saying, "Here I am, you called me?" Eli told him he had not called him and to go back to bed.

Once again Samuel heard someone call his name and he ran to Eli again. After the third time this happened, Eli perceived that the Lord was calling to Samuel and told him, "Go, lie down, and if he calls you, you shall say, 'Speak, Lord, for your servant hears." So Samuel went and lay down in his place.

Again the Lord came and stood, calling Samuel as at other times. Samuel responded as Eli had told him, and the Lord began speaking to him: "Behold, I am about to do a thing in Israel at which the two ears of everyone who hears it will tingle." He went on to tell him that he was going to punish Eli's house for the disobedience of his sons and for the fact that Eli failed to correct them. He said that the iniquity of Eli's house could not be atoned for by sacrifice or offering forever.

The next day when Samuel went to the house of the Lord, he was afraid to tell Eli the vision God had given him. Eli encouraged him to tell him saying," If you don't tell me what the Lord said to you, he will do worse to you." So Samuel told Eli all that God had shown him. Eli responded, "It is the Lord. Let him do what seems good to him."

Samuel grew, and the Lord was with him. All of Israel knew he had been established as a prophet of the Lord. Shiloh once again experienced the presence of the Lord in a greater way because of Samuel.

At one-point Israel found itself in a battle with the Philistines and was being slaughtered. The elders of Israel asked, "Why has the Lord defeated us today before the Philistines? Let us bring the ark of the covenant of the Lord here from Shiloh that it may come among us and save us from the power of our enemies." So they sent for the ark to be brought into battle. However, the Philistines not only won the battle but also captured the ark. (It was in this battle that the prophecy of the death of Eli's sons came true because they died during this battle.)

When news came back to Eli, he fell over backward off the side of the gate and broke his neck and died. He was ninety-eight years old and had judged Israel for forty years.

The Philistines had captured the ark but was unsure what to do with it. It was brought from Ebenezer to Ashdod, then taken to be put in the house of Dagon. They set it up beside their idol god, Dagon, and when they awakened the next day, the idol had fallen face downward on the ground before the ark of the Lord. They set it back up in its place, and when they arose the next morning, Dagon had fallen face downward, and his head and both hands were cut off on the floor.

God dealt severely with the Philistines for taking the ark, and the people became afflicted with tumors. They were afraid and called all the lords of the Philistines and said, "What shall we do with the ark of the God of Israel?" They agreed to send it from Ashdod to the city of Gath.

Again the wrath of God brought panic and tumors on the residents of Gath, so they moved it to Ekron. They passed it around from city to city for seven months. Fear spread throughout the land, and the elders of the Philistines were requested to return it lest it kill all their people. The men who did not die were struck with tumors.

Anxious to get it back in the hands of the Israelites, they summoned the priest and asked how they should return it. The priest told them not to send it back empty but to send it full of golden tumors and five golden mice, according to the number of the lords of the Philistine, for the same plague was on all of them.

They were then told to take two milk cows and place a yoke on them and a cart. Place the ark on the cart with the guilt offering and then let them go, and watch to see which way they go. They said if the ark goes straight back to the Israelites, we will know it was the Lord that did us great harm. The cows did head straight to Beth-shemesh and stopped there. When the Israelite people who were harvesting in the fields saw it they began rejoicing.

When the leaders received it, they split up the wood from the cart and offered the cows as a burnt offering to the Lord for its return. They took the golden images they had made and put them up on a large stone. That stone is a witness to this day there in the field of Joshua of Beth-shemesh.

The ark stayed there for the next twenty years, and Eleazer was put in charge of watching over it.

Samuel warned the people, "If you are returning to the Lord with all your heart, then put away your idols." From that time on when the Philistines tried to attack them in their territory, God confused them, and Israel was able to take back all the cities the Philistines had taken from them.

Samuel judged Israel all the days of his life. When he was old, he made his sons judges over Israel. However, they did not have the heart of their father. They turned aside after gain. They took bribes and perverted justice. So the elders came together and came to Samuel and said to him, "Behold, you are old, and your sons do not walk in your ways. Now appoint us a king to judge us like all the nations."

God told him to obey the voice of the people but to warn them about having a king that would reign over them. He told them how they would become servants to the king and lose the freedoms they now had. They refused to listen and told them they wanted to be like the other nations who were ruled by a king. Peer pressure has always been with us!

Discussion Questions:

1. What lessons can we learn from Hannah's life?

2. Samuel heard God's voice and thought it was Eli. Have you heard God's voice speaking to you and if so did you respond as Samuel did?

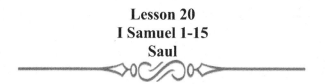

Lesson 20
I Samuel 1-15
Saul

In our last lesson, we find Israel demanding a king even though God had spoken to Samuel and gave him warnings against it. Read I Samuel 8:10-18 and hear the warnings given to the people. But the people refused to obey the voice of Samuel. They said, "No! But there will be a king over us, that we also may be like all the nations, and that our king may judge us and go out before us and fight our battles."

Samuel went to the Lord with their demands and was told to obey their voice and give them a king. God told Samuel he would show him the man he had chosen. The story of how he found that man goes like this.

There was a man from the tribe of Benjamin, named Saul, who was an impressive young man and a head taller than any of the others. One day his father, Kish, had lost his donkeys and sent young Saul and some of his servants to find them. They looked for days with no luck. Finally, they came to the land where Samuel was, and one of the servants said to him, there is a seer (that is what they called the judge God had appointed), so let's ask him if he can tell us where our donkeys are.

As Saul approached him, God spoke to Samuel and told him this was the man he had chosen to be the king over the people.

When Saul asked Samuel about the whereabouts of his donkeys, Samuel told him not to worry about them because they had been found. Then he told him, "And to whom is all the desire of Israel turned, if not to you and all your father's family?"

Saul was astonished and replied, "But am not I from the smallest tribe of Israel, and is not my clan the least of all the clans of the tribe of Benjamin?" (This sounds a lot like Gideon whom we studied in Lesson 17.

Samuel invited Saul and the thirty others who had gone up with him to stay and eat with him. Saul was then seated at the place of honor and given the best portion of meat. The next day Samuel told Saul to send his servants back to tell his father where he was, but he was to stay with him so he could tell him the things God had shown him about his future.

Saul did stay and spent time with Samuel, and at one point Samuel anointed Saul's head with oil and kissed him, saying, "The Lord has anointed you leader over his inheritance." Then he told him to go on his way and that at the spot of Rachel's tomb, he would meet two men and they will say to him that his father's donkeys have been found, but he is worried about him. Interesting that this was Saul's grandmother's tomb as if he were validating to Rachel that a descendent of the child she had longed for was going to rule over Israel.

Then Saul was told to go on to a particular tree and three men who would be carrying three young goats, bread and wine would meet him there. Next, he was instructed to go to another place where he would be met by a procession of prophets playing instruments and prophesying. He was told there the spirit of the

Lord would come upon him in power and he would prophesy with them, and that he would be changed into a different person. After that happened, he was to go and do whatever his hand found to do, and God would be with him.

Saul did as he was told and all the signs were fulfilled just as Samuel had said. God changed Saul's heart that day, and he began prophesying as the spirit of God came upon him.

Samuel brought all the tribes together and told them Saul was the king God had chosen for them. Before he announced him though, he gave a warning, "This is what the Lord God of Israel says: 'I brought Israel up out of Egypt, and I delivered you from the power of Egypt and all the kingdoms that oppressed you. But you have rejected your God, who saves you out of all your calamities and distresses. And you have said, 'No, set a king over us.''

Samuel said, "God has granted your request even though it is not his will for you", and Saul was presented to them as their first king. They all responded, "Long live the King." Do you ever think about that saying which is still in use today as coming from the Bible? Then Samuel explained to the people the regulation of the kingship and sent them all back to their homes.

Samuel realized his age and gave a farewell speech to the people. He reminded them how they had continually forsaken God even after he continued to deliver them out of the hands of their enemies. He warned them again in I Samuel 12:12-13, "When you saw the Ammonites moving against you, you said to me, 'No, we want a king to rule over us, even though the Lord your God is your king. Now here is the king you have chosen, the one you asked for; see the Lord has set a king before you." Then he warned them to continue to obey the Lord, or both they and their king would be swept away.

Saul was thirty years old when he became king and reigned over Israel for forty-two years. Unfortunately, Saul did not keep the command of the Lord and his reign ended in disgrace.

Saul had three sons named Ishvi, Malki-Shua, and Jonathan. He also had two daughters named Merab and Michal. Our story continues around the life of his son, Jonathan. He fought alongside his father in battle. At one point when Saul had not been successful in winning the battle with the Philistines, Jonathan slipped away and decided to fight the Philistines on his own. The Lord was with Jonathan, and he rescued the Israelites. He had rebelled against his fathers' commands, and his father had set a rule that anyone who rebelled against him would be put to death. The people intervened after seeing what Jonathan had done to save them, and his life was spared. Jonathan will play a key role later in the story.

All the time Saul was in power, there was bitter war. At one-point God sent a message through Samuel to Saul to destroy the Amalekites because they had waylaid the Israelites when they came out of Egypt.

One point of interest: God had Saul to tell the Kenites to leave before the attack so they would be saved, (Remember Rahab and her family were Kenites and had shown favor to the spies and allowed them to take Jericho.) God did not forget his promise to Rahab to protect her and her family even after they fled from Jericho and had settled in the land. God is always true to his Word.

Saul did attack the Amalekites, and even though God told him to destroy everything, even the animals, Saul disobeyed God and spared the king of the Amalekites and took the best of their animals. After the battle, Saul went up to Mt. Carmel and made a monument to himself.

God came to Samuel and told him how disappointed he was that he had made Saul king. Samuel went to Saul and told him what the Lord had said. Saul tried to talk to Samuel, but Samuel gave him this reply in I Samuel 13:13, "You have not kept the command of the Lord your God gave you; if you had, he would have established your kingdom over Israel for all time. But now your kingdom will not endure; the Lord has sought out a man after his own heart and appointed him leader of his people because you have not kept the Lord's command."

Samuel grieved for Saul for a long time until one day the Lord came to him and said, "How long will you mourn for Saul since I have rejected him as king over Israel? Fill your horn with oil and be on your way; I am sending you to Jesse of Bethlehem. I have chosen one of his sons to be king."

This is a sad ending to the reign of the first king over Israel. The lesson I think we can learn from this story of Saul is the fact that God has a plan for each of us, and the heart of God is for us to obey and enjoy the blessings that come with that obedience. Saul could have been a hero in the eyes of history if he had not decided to go his own way and disobey God.

Discussion Questions:

1. We see Saul going from being humble and thinking he may not be fit to be king to becoming so arrogant and full of himself that God could not use him. What character traits might be in your life that would keep God from using you?

2. What does the fact that God continued to watch over Rahab's family mean to us as we reflect on the promises God has made to us?

3. Saul could have had it all and left a legacy of integrity as the first king of Israel. What was his downfall?

Lesson 21
I Samuel 16-31
David Part 1

We saw in our last lesson that Saul's character was marked by impulsiveness and self-will and that God told Samuel he had chosen a new king and to go to the house of Jessie because he had chosen one of his sons to be the new king.

Samuel obeyed God and went to Bethlehem where Jesse lived and asked to see his sons. God told Samuel that he would show him which of the son he had chosen. Jesse proudly paraded his sons before Samuel who was impressed. In I Samuel 16:6, Samuel says of his son Eliab, "Surely the Lord's anointed stands here before the Lord. But the Lord says, do not consider his appearance or height because I have rejected him. The Lord does not look at the things man looks at. Man looks at the outward appearance, but the Lord looks at the heart."

On and on it went until they all had been rejected. Samuel was a little confused and asked Jesse if he had other sons. Jesse explained that he had a young son who was tending the sheep and Samuel told him to send for him. We read in verse 12 that "he was ruddy; with a fine appearance and handsome features." When he came in, God told Samuel, "Rise and anoint him; he is the one." Samuel anointed him in the presence of his brothers, and the spirit of the Lord came upon him in power.

However, the spirit of the Lord had left Saul, and an evil spirit began to torment him. He asked his servant to find someone who could play the harp because he thought it would make the evil spirit go away and make him feel better. His servant thought of David and sent word to Jesse to allow him to come to play for him. Saul was very pleased with David. When he played the harp, the evil spirit would leave.

He sent word to Jesse that he wanted David to enter his service. David remained with Saul and became one of Saul's armor-bearers and played his harp for him when he was tormented by an evil spirit.

The Philistines were archenemies of the Israelites and had gathered their forces for war against Saul's army. Each side was armed and camped on opposing mountains. Then a huge soldier named Goliath came out and presented a challenge. He said, "Choose a man and have him come down to me. If he is able to fight and kill me, we will become your subjects; but if I overcome him and kill him, you will become our subjects and serve us."

At the sight of him, Saul and his army were terrified. Goliath is described in chapter 17 as "over nine feet tall, wearing a bronze helmet, heavy bronze coat of armor, on his legs he wore bronze greaves, and a bronze javelin was slung on his back. His spear shaft was like a weaver's rod, and the iron point weighed fifteen pounds." He also had a shield-bearer that went ahead of him.

Goliath came out and taunted them every day for forty days morning and evening. Imagine both armies lined up on opposing mountains and this huge giant coming out twice a day with this challenge.

Three of the soldiers in Saul's army were sons of Jesse. Jesse told his youngest son David to go where his brothers were camped and take them some roasted grain and cheese. He told David to see how his brothers were and bring back some assurance to him that they were all right.

Early in the morning David left the flock of sheep and loaded up and set out as his father had directed. He reached the camp as the men were going out to assume their battle positions. He left their supplies and just as he went out to greet his brothers, Goliath stepped out of the line of the Philistine army and shouted his defiance.

Saul's men trembled in fear and stated that the king had offered to give great wealth to the man who kills this giant. Also he had offered his daughter in marriage and would exempt his father's family from paying taxes. David overheard this and said, "Who is this uncircumcised Philistine that he should defy the armies of the living God?"

David's older brother, Eliab, heard him talking to the men and burned with anger at him and asked him, "Why have you come down here? And with whom did you leave those few sheep in the desert? I know how conceited you are and how wicked your heart is; you came down only to watch the battle." David replied, "Now what have I done? Can't I even speak?" This gives you an idea of how insignificant he was in the family and how jealous his brothers were of him being anointed as the future king.

David again approached another soldier and brought about the same point, and someone reported it to Saul, and he sent for David to be brought to him. David said to Saul, "Let no one lose heart on account of this Philistine; your servant will go and fight him." Saul replied, "You are not able to go against this Philistine and fight him, you are only a boy, and he has been a fighting man from his youth."

David replied, "Your servant has been keeping his father's sheep. When a lion or bear came and carried off a sheep, I went after it and struck it and rescued the sheep from its mouth. When it turned on me, I seized it by its hair, struck it and killed it. Your servant has killed both the lion and the bear; this uncircumcised Philistine will be like one of them because he has defied the armies of the living God. The Lord who delivered me from the paw of the lion and the paw of the bear will deliver me from the hand of this Philistine." When hearing this Saul told him, "Go, and the Lord will be with you."

The first thing Saul did was fit him in a helmet and armor. David told him he could not wear the armor, so he took it all off and took his staff in his hand, chose five smooth stones from the stream, put them in a pouch of his shepherd's bag and with his sling in his hand, approached Goliath.

Meanwhile, Goliath with his shield-bearer in front of him kept coming closer to David. He looked him over and saw he was only a boy and he was insulted. He said, "Am I a dog, that you come at me with sticks?" Then he started to curse him. He taunted David by saying, "Come here and I'll give your flesh to the birds of the air and the beasts of the field!"

David came to Goliath and said, "You come against me with sword and spear and javelin, but I come against you in the name of the Lord Almighty, the God of the armies of Israel, whom you have defied. This day the Lord will hand you over to me, and I'll strike you down and cut off our head. Today I will give the carcasses of the Philistine army to the birds of the air and the beasts of the earth, and the whole world will know that there is a God in Israel. All those gathered here will know that it is not by sword or spear that the Lord saves; for the battle is the Lord's, and he will give all of you into our hands."

At that Goliath moved closer to attack him and David ran quickly to meet him. He reached into his bag, took out a stone, and slung it and struck the Philistine on the forehead. The stone sank deep into his forehead, and he fell face down on the ground. David quickly drew Goliath's sword and cut off his head.

When the Philistines saw that their hero was dead, they turned and ran. The army of Israel then pursued them and defeated them. David took Goliath's head to Jerusalem, and when Saul saw what he had done, he asked his servant to bring him and find out whose son he was. David came to Saul still holding the head of Goliath and told him he was the son of Jesse of Bethlehem.

From that day on Saul kept David with him and did not let him return to his father's house in Bethlehem. He made him a high-ranking officer in the army. However, jealousy began to grow as David won the favor of the people. The women were singing and dancing in the streets after David had killed Goliath, "Saul has slain his thousands, and David his tens of thousands." This angered Saul, and he kept a jealous eye on David from that time on.

One day an evil spirit came upon Saul, and as David was playing the harp for him, Saul hurled a spear at him saying he would pin David to the wall. David eluded him twice. Saul could see that God was with David, and everything he did was successful. He sent him away to lead military campaigns, but David came back the victor and all of Israel loved him because the Lord was with him.

Saul became fearful of David and decided to honor his vow to give him his daughter. But David said to Saul, "Who am I, and what is my family or my father's clan in Israel that I should become the king's son-in-law?" So Saul gave his oldest daughter to someone else.

However, Saul had another daughter named Michal who was in love with David, and when Saul heard about it, he was pleased because he thought she would be a snare to him. He went to David and told him he had a second chance to become his son-in-law. He even sent his servants to try to talk him into it. Finally, he had his servants tell him that he could pay a price of a hundred Philistine foreskins. Saul thought that the Philistines would kill David, and that would be the end of it, but David and his men brought the foreskins as payment. So he took Michal as his wife.

With David's success, Saul was more fearful of him because he knew the Lord was with him. He ordered him killed but David and Saul's son, Jonathan had become best friends, and in fact, Jonathan made a covenant of friendship with him because he loved him as himself. When his father set out to kill David, Jonathan came to David and warned him. Saul made several attempts on David's life.

At one point, Saul sent his men to David's house and told them to watch his house all night and kill him in the morning. Michal heard about this and warned her husband. She let him down through a window, and he fled and escaped. Michal then laid idols in the bed under the covers with goat's hair to look like David was asleep in the bed. When the men came in the morning, she told them he was ill. Saul was angry with his daughter for allowing him to escape.

Saul continued to pursue David and he went from town to town to evade Saul's attempt on his life. Jonathan was there to protect him whenever he could. You can read of the pursuit in I Samuel 19 - 23.

At one point David and his men had Saul trapped in a cave. David came so close to him that he was able to cut off a corner of Saul's robe. However, he spared his life and went out of the cave and said to Saul, "My Lord, and the king!"

When Saul looked behind him, David bowed down and prostrated himself with his face to the ground. He said to Saul, "Why do you listen to men that I am out to harm you? This day you have seen with your own eyes how the Lord delivered you into my hands in the cave. Some urged me to kill you, but I spared you; I said, 'I will not lift a hand against my master because he is the Lord's anointed.' See, look at this piece of your robe in my hand. I cut off the corner of your robe but did not kill you. Now understand that I am not guilty of wrongdoing or rebellion. I have not wronged you, but you are hunting me down to take my life. May the Lord Judge between you and me. May the Lord avenge the wrongs you have done to me, but my hand will not touch you."

When David finished saying this, Saul asked, "Is that your voice, David? And he wept aloud. "You are more righteous than I, you have treated me well, but I have treated you badly. You have just now told me of the good you did to me; the Lord delivered me into your hands, and you did not kill me. May the Lord reward you well for the way you treated me today. I know that you will surely be king and that the kingdom of Israel will be established in your hands." Then Saul asked him to swear an oath he would not wipe out his name or the descendants of his father's family. David did so, and Saul returned home. David settled with his family in the Desert of Maon.

There was a wealthy man named Nabal there who had a wife named Abigail. She was described as an intelligent and beautiful woman. Nabal had a thousand goats and three thousand sheep. When David was in the area, he sent ten of his young men to him to give them a blessing and to ask for some supplies. David and his men protected his flock and did not take even one of them. Nabal was an evil man and responded, "Who is this David? Who is this son of Jesse? Why should I take my bread and water, and the meat I have slaughtered and given it to men coming from who knows where?"

The men went back to David and told him what Nabal had said. He told them to put on their swords, and they would go down and take what they needed, and not one man would be left alive who belonged to Nabal.

One of the servants overheard this and went to Abigail and told her what was about to happen. She gathered bread, wine, meat, raisins, and figs, and loaded them on her donkey and met David and his men as they were coming down a ravine. She got off her donkey and bowed down before him and told him to let the blame be on her alone. She asked him to pay no attention to her husband Nabal, for he was an evil man and a fool. She pleaded with him to accept the gifts she had brought and begged him not to have unnecessary bloodshed on his hands.

David said to her, "Praise be to the Lord who sent you today to meet me. May you be rewarded today for your good judgment, and for keeping me from bloodshed this day, and from avenging myself." He accepted her gifts, and she returned home. She found Nabal drunk when she got there and decided to wait until morning to tell him what she had done. The Lord struck him, and he died ten days later.

When David heard Nabal was dead, he sent word to Abigail asking her to be his wife. She accepted the proposal and quickly got on her donkey and went to him. David also had a wife named Jezreel. (Michal, Saul's daughter that had been given to him after slaying Goliath, had been given to another man, Paltiel, who was from Gallim.) In that day, fathers who did not approve of a marriage could take back their daughters and give them to another man.

You would think by now that Saul would have given up, but he heard where David was and took three thousand men to find him. When David heard that Saul had followed him, he sent out scouts to find out where he was camped. That night David took one of his men and went into the tent where Saul slept. Saul had his spear stuck in the ground near his head. Abishai who had accompanied David said that the Lord had delivered Saul into his hands and wanted to pin him to the ground. But David replied, "No, as surely as the Lord lives, the Lord himself will strike him; either his time will come and he will die, or he will go into battle and perish, but the Lord forbid that I lay a hand on the Lord's anointed." They took his spear and his water jug and left.

The next day David called to the chief officer of Saul and chided him saying, "As surely as the Lord lives, you and your men deserve to die, because you did not guard your master, the Lord's anointed. Look around you. Where are the king's spear and water jug that were near his head?"

Saul recognized David's voice and said, "Is that your voice, David, my son?" David replied, "Yes it is, my lord and king. Why is my lord pursuing his servant? What have I done and what wrong am I guilty of?" Saul, realizing David had once again spared his life said to him, "Because you have considered my life precious today, I will not try to harm you again. Surely I have acted like a fool and have erred greatly." Then Saul gave him the king's spear saying, "May you be blessed my son David; you will do great things and surely triumph."

David settled in a land of the Philistines because he thought Saul would not give up searching for him, but would never look for him there. David found favor with the king and his son, and they asked him to stay in the royal city with them, but David asked if he would assign him one of the country towns to settle in. Achish, son of the king, did give him the town called Ziklag. He, along with his two wives and the families of his men, lived there a year and four months. It has belonged to the kings of Judah ever since.

The Philistines decided to fight against the Israelites. Saul heard of this and sought the Lord, but the Lord did not answer him. So he sent for a medium, and his servant found a witch who lived in Endor.

Saul disguised himself and went to her to ask for advice. He told her he wanted to consult the spirit of Samuel because Samuel had died much earlier. Then when she brought up the spirit of Samuel, she began crying at the top of her lungs. "Why have you deceived me? You are Saul!" Saul told her not to be afraid but to tell him what she saw. She said she saw a spirit coming up from the ground. Saul asked her what he looked like and she told him that it was an old man wearing a robe. Then Saul knew it was Samuel. Then Samuel said, "Why have you disturbed me by bringing me up?" Saul told Samuel that he was in great distress because the Philistines were fighting against him and God has turned away from him. He told him that God no longer spoke to him in dreams or by prophets. He said he did not know what to do so he came to him for advice.

Samuel said, "Why do you consult me? The Lord has turned away from you and become your enemy? The Lord has done what he predicted through me. The Lord has torn the kingdom out of your hands and given it to David. Tomorrow you will be given over to the hands of the Philistines."

David, who had been living with the Philistines and was the right-hand man of the king, went along with the army. But some of the men were afraid that he would not be loyal to them when they fought the Israelites. So he and his men were sent back home to Ziklag. When they arrived, they found that while they were gone, the Amalekites had raided their town and burned it to the ground. They had taken captive their wives and sons and daughters. David and his men wept aloud until they had no more strength to weep.

Then he sought the Lord and asked if he should pursue them and the Lord told him they would be delivered into his hands. David took four hundred men and fought from morning until night and recovered everything they had taken from them. David sent some of the plunder to the elders of Judah, and all other places he and his men had roamed.

Meantime, the Philistines killed Saul's sons, and Saul was gravely injured. He told one of his servants to take his sword and finish him off so the Philistines would not abuse him, but the servant would not kill his king. Saul then fell on his own sword and died.

Discussion Questions:

1. What lessons can we learn about revenge from David's relationship with Saul?

2. David was considered unworthy by his father to be considered as the next king, but God knew his heart and exalted him above his seemingly better-qualified brothers. Have you ever experienced a time when God gave you favor when others seemed more qualified?

3. What lessons can we learn from David and Jonathan about friendship?

4. What lesson can we learn from the actions of Abigail?

5. Have you ever had to choose whether to take things into your own hands to get revenge or listen to God's when dealing with an issue in your life? If so, how did it turn out?

Lesson 22
II Samuel
David Part 2

We left our last lesson with Saul falling on his own sword and killing himself. David was very distressed when he got the report of Jonathan's death, as well. One of the men who escaped from the Israelite camp came to him with the report that he had come upon Saul and he was not completely dead and Saul had asked him to finish him off. The young man said he did, and after he was dead, he took his crown and the band on his arm and brought them straight to David.

David and his men were so distraught that they tore their clothes and mourned by weeping and fasting until evening. David, during his mourning for Saul and his best friend Jonathan, wrote a lament for them and insisted that the men of Judah be taught it. You can read it in II Samuel 1:29.

Now David inquired of the Lord as to what he was to do now. He asked the Lord where he should go and the Lord told him to go to Hebron. So David went up there with his two wives, Ahinoam and Abigail. He also took his men and their families to settle there. When he got there, the men of Judah came to anoint David king over the house of Judah.

Meantime, Abner was the commander of the army under Saul and the most powerful man in Israel after the death of King Saul. He decided to crown Saul's son Ishbosheth as king, and he reigned in Mahanaim for two years while David reigned in Hebron as King of Judah. The loyalties of the Israelite people were divided. Many battles and deaths occurred during the next seven years that David was king over Judah.

It had become clear that David would not be without opposition, but in the end, a settlement was reached, and David was to become the king. One thing David demanded in the settlement was for his wife Michal be given back to him. Remember she was the daughter of Saul that was gifted to him for killing Goliath. Somewhere in the mix, she was given to someone else named Paltiel. At his request, she was returned as his wife again.

During the seven years, he was in Hebron as king of Judah, he took several wives and had several sons born to him. The oldest was Amnon, born to his wife, Ahinoam. His second son, Chileab, was born to Abigail. The third was Absalom, son of Maacah. The fourth was Adonijah, born to Haggith. Then Shephatiah was born to Abital, and Itheam was born to Eglah.

David was thirty years old when the elders of Israel came to him and made him king over all Israel. The first thing he did was to go and capture Jerusalem from the Jebusites who lived there. He took up a fortress there and named it the city of David. He started to expand and build up the city and before long the king of Tyre sent supplies and stonemasons and built a palace for David to reside. David now knew the Lord had established him as king over Israel and would exalt his kingdom.

He still had some opposition from the Philistines who heard he had been anointed king and decided to come against him. David inquired of the Lord, and the Lord delivered them into his hand. I suppose they still were holding a grudge over him killing Goliath who was a Philistine!

David sent messages out to the tribes throughout the land and said, "Since you think I should be your king and since the Lord has given his approval, let us send messages to our brothers throughout the land of Israel, including the priest and Levites, inviting them to join us. And let us bring back the Ark of our God. We have been neglecting it since ever since Saul became King."

There was unanimous consent, so David summoned people from across the nation so they could be present when the Ark of God was brought from Kiriathjearim. Then David and all of Israel went to bring back the Ark. It was taken from the house of Abinadab on a new cart. Uzzah and Ahio drove the oxen. David and all the people danced before the Lord with great enthusiasm, accompanied by singing and instruments playing.

At one point the oxen stumbled, and Uzzah put out his hand to steady the ark. The anger of the Lord flared against him, and he was killed for doing this. David now asked, "How can I ever bring the Ark home? He became afraid of the Lord and took it aside to the home of Obededom. It remained there three months, and while there, God blessed him and his entire household. When David heard of the household being blessed, he was no longer afraid and decided to bring the Ark on to Jerusalem where he had a tent prepared for it.

David issued these instructions: "When we transfer the ark to its new home, no one except the Levites may carry it, for God has chosen them for this purpose." Then David summoned all Israel to Jerusalem to celebrate the bringing of the ark into the new tabernacle.

The priest and Levites underwent ceremonies of sanctification, and then the Levites carried the Ark on their shoulders with carrying poles, just as the Lord had instructed Moses. David appointed certain Levites to minister before the Ark by giving constant praise and thanks to the Lord.

The Ark was accompanied by a great celebration with singing and dancing. David was in the middle of it all. He offered sacrifices and gave blessings on the people, but when he returned home to bless his household, his wife Michal, daughter of Saul, had looked out the window and saw David dancing in the streets, and despised him. She mocked him saying, in II Samuel 6:20, "How the king of Israel has distinguished himself today, disrobing in the sight of the slave girls of his servants as any vulgar fellow would!"

David replied, "I was dancing before the Lord, who chose me rather than your father or anyone from his house when he appointed me ruler over the Lord's people of Israel. I will celebrate when I want to before the Lord. I will become more undignified than this, and I will be humiliated in my own eyes. But by these slave girls you spoke of, I will be held in honor." He put her in her place, and she was never able to bear him children.

David built several palaces for himself and at one point called Nathan, the prophet and said, "Here I am living in a palace of cedar while the Ark of God remains in a tent."

Nathan sought God, and you can read God's response to him in II Samuel 7:5-10. He told Nathan to tell David, "I have been with you wherever you have gone, and I have cut off your enemies from before you, now I will make your name great, like the names of the greatest men on earth…..I will raise up your offspring to succeed you who will come from your own body, and I will establish his kingdom. He will be the one who will build a house for my name, and I will establish the throne of his kingdom forever. I will be his father, and he will be my son…when he does wrong, I will punish him, but my love will never be taken from him as I took it away from Saul, whom I removed from before you. Your house and your kingdom will endure forever before me; your throne will be established forever."

When Nathan told David these things, he went before the Lord and offered a beautiful prayer that you can read in II Samuel 7:18-29.

Now David was established as king, but there were still many enemies to contend with. God assured David he would go before him and deliver them into his hands, which He did.

David became famous among the people and did what was just and right for all the people. At one point he asked if there was anyone left from the house of Saul to whom he could show kindness for Jonathan's sake. Remember he and Jonathan, Saul's son, had made a covenant of friendship. He was told that Jonathan had a son who was crippled in both feet. He sent for him to be brought to the palace. When he arrived, he bowed down before the king afraid. David said to him, "Don't be afraid for I will surely show you kindness for the sake of your father, Jonathan. I will restore to you all the land that belonged to your grandfather, Saul, and you will always eat at my table." He did come to live in the palace with David and was treated as his own son. David had made a vow to his father, Jonathan, and kept it through giving favor to his son.

The following spring, the season when the wars usually began, Joab led the Israelite army in successful attacks against their enemies. David however, had stayed behind in Jerusalem. One night he couldn't sleep and went for a stroll on the roof of the palace. As he looked over the city, he noticed a woman of unusual beauty taking her evening bath. He went to find out who she was and was told that she was Bathsheba, the wife of Uriah.

David sent for her and when she came, he slept with her and then she returned home. When she found that he had gotten her pregnant, she sent a message to inform him. So David sent a message to Joab, his military commander to send her husband home. When Uriah arrived, David asked him how the army was getting along, and then told him to go home and relax.

Uriah did not feel that was right since his fellow men were out fighting and stayed with the servants at the palace that night. David heard of this and asked him why he did not go home and sleep with his wife. He told him, and David sent him back into battle but sent a letter to Joab to put him on the front lines and pull the other men back so he would be killed. The news came back to David that he had been killed and Bathsheba mourned for him. After the mourning period was over David brought her to the palace to be one of his wives, and she gave birth to their son.

The Lord was furious with David and sent Nathan to him to tell him a story. "There were two men, one very rich, owning many flocks of sheep and goats, and the other very poor, owning nothing but a little lamb he had managed to buy. It was his children's pet, and he even fed it from his own plate at the table and let it drink from his cup. He cuddled it in his arms like a little baby. Recently, a guest arrived at the home of the man. Instead of killing a lamb from his own flock for food for the traveler, he took the poor man's lamb and roasted it and served it."

David was furious. "Any man who would do a thing like that should be put to death; he shall repay four lambs to the poor man for the one he stole and for having no pity."

Then Nathan told him, "You are that rich man! The Lord God says, 'I made you king over Israel and saved you from the power of Saul. I gave you his palace and the kingdoms of Israel and Judah; and if that had not been enough, I would have given you more. Why, then, have you despised the laws of God and done this horrible deed? You have murdered Uriah and stolen his wife. Therefore, murder shall be a constant threat in your family. Because of what you have done, I will cause your own household to rebel against you. You did it secretly, but I will do this to you in the sight of all Israel.'"

"I have sinned against the Lord," David confessed. Nathan replied, "Yes, but the Lord has forgiven you, and you won't die for your sin."

The Lord made Bathsheba's baby deathly sick. David begged God to spare his life and went without food. Leaders of the nation pleaded with him to eat, but he refused. On the seventh day, the baby died. David got up washed, changed his clothes, and went into the tabernacle and worshiped the Lord. Then he returned to the palace and ate.

His servants were puzzled and asked why when his baby was alive he did not eat, but now that he is dead he was breaking his fast. He said he was fasting to ask the Lord to spare his son's life. But there was no reason to fast since he was dead. "Can I bring him back again? I shall go to him, but he shall not return to me."

He comforted his wife, Bathsheba, and had sexual relations with her, and she bore him another son they named Solomon.

Meantime, the soap opera continued with one of David's sons, Prince Amnon, who fell in love with his half-sister Tamar. She was the full sister of Prince Absalom. One day Amnon was sad looking, and his cousin asked him what was wrong, and he told him he was in love with his half-sister. His cousin was crafty and devised a plan for him to pretend to be ill and when King David came to check on him, ask him to send in Tamar to prepare some bread for him. King David did, and after she had made the bread and given it to him, he raped her.

She was shamed, and when her brother Absalom found out, he devised a plan to kill Amnon to take revenge for what he had done to his sister. He had his father send all the brothers to a party and then he told the servants that when Amnon was drunk to kill him, which they did. King David was so sad and hurt that Absalom fled to live with a nearby king for three years but David eventually did forgive him and welcomed him back into the kingdom. However, we are told for the first two years he did not see King David's face. Absalom sent for Joab, the king's right-hand man, and asked him to tell the king he wanted to see him, but Joab would not come. Finally, Absalom had his servants set his fields on fire and that got his attention. He came to see Absalom and arranged for him to see his father. Absalom bowed down on the ground before him and King David kissed him.

You would think all was well; however, Absalom had a plan of his own. He turned many of the people against David and devised a plot to set himself up as king. He went to Hebron, and while there, word got back to David what he was up to, and David became afraid and left Jerusalem. Eventually, a battle was fought between the men who had gone with Absalom and David's army. Even though Absalom had set out to destroy David, a father's love was more powerful than the hurt afflicted on him by his son. He gave instructions that even in battle Absalom was not to be killed. Absalom died in a strange way. He was fleeing on his mule and when the mule went under a tree branch, Absolam's hair got caught and the mule went on. He was left dangling from the tree. David's men came upon him but would not kill him because he was the king's son and because of the order he had given. Joab knew Absalom would not stop and wanted to protect his king and so he took three javelins and plunged them into Absalom's heart. Then he blew the trumpet putting a halt to the fighting. David mourned his son's death and returned to Jerusalem.

David had a census taken to number the fighting men. God had not instructed him to do so, and David went before the Lord and asked forgiveness. God gave him a choice of three punishments: Three years of famine, three months of fleeing his enemies while they pursued him, or three days of plague on his land. He chose the plague and 70,000 people died. When David saw what was happening, he told the Lord to stop the punishment on the people and let it be on him and his family. The angel of the Lord who was giving the punishment stood at the threshing floor of a man named Araunah when God stopped the slaughter.

David built an altar at that site and it has special significance because it is the site the great temple of Solomon will be constructed later. On this sacred spot, today stands the dome of the rock, a Muslim mosque. It is a galling thing to the Jews to have this sacred place in the hands of the Muslims. It is also believed to be the site where Abraham built an altar to sacrifice Isaac.

David had his faults. He did much that was very wrong, but he kept his nation from going into idolatry. Although his private sins were grievous, he stood like a rock for Jehovah. He sinned, but he repented and gave God a chance to forgive and cleanse him. He was called a man after God's own heart. He took a chaotic nation and established a dynasty that was to last to the time of captivity, a period of over 450 years. There never was a greater warrior or statesman than David. He made Israel the dominant power in western Asia.

As you understand the life of David, it gives you a better understanding of the Psalms he wrote expressing his plight in life, his sorrows, his joys and his love for God.

Discussion Questions:

1. As you look back over the story of David and the ups and downs he had, why do you think God continued to use him in his service even after he had sinned?

2. God had pronounced as a punishment for David's sin that his household would turn against him. We saw that happen with his son, Absalom. Can you see how far-reaching sin can be? Jesus died to forgive our sins and take the curse on himself. Can you pause for a moment and just thank him?

3. What lessons can we learn from David's life?

Lesson 23
I Kings 1-11
Solomon

As we saw in our last lesson, David was ending his reign after forty years. Although he was only seventy years old, he was not in good health. Interestingly enough, we find in the first chapter of I Kings that he was old and could not keep warm. The solution that his servants came up with was, "Let us find a young virgin to attend to the king and take care of him. She can lie beside him so that our lord the king may keep warm." They were successful in finding a beautiful young girl Abishag, and she came and cared for the king until he died. That is not exactly the protocol we today would follow, especially since he already had so many wives and concubines.

It was clear that a successor was needed to follow in his footsteps. Adonijah was the oldest son and would be the most logical successor. However, David saw that Solomon was the most fit to succeed him. Solomon was only nineteen at the time. More importantly, he was also God's choice.

Adonijah started to assume his throne without David's blessing. When it was known of Adonijah's intent, Bathsheba went to David to remind him that he had promised her son Solomon would be king. We read about it in I Kings 1:17. Bathsheba went in to the king and knelt before him. "What do you want?" the king asked. She said to him, "My Lord, you yourself swore to me, your servant by the Lord your God: 'Solomon your son shall be king after me, and he will sit on my throne.' But now Adonijah has become king, and you, my lord, do not even know about it." She went on to explain how Adonijah had sacrificed many animals and invited all the king's sons except Solomon. People were chanting, "Long live King Adonijah."

Bathsheba pleaded with David and said, "My Lord the king, the eyes of all Israel are on you to learn from you who will sit on the throne of my lord the king after him. Otherwise, as soon as my lord the king is laid to rest, my son Solomon and I will be treated as criminals."

Nathan, the prophet came in to see the king and asked of his intentions and he had him call for Bathsheba. He told her, "As surely as the Lord lives, who has delivered me out of every trouble, I will surely carry out today what I swore to you by the Lord, the God of Israel: Solomon, your son, shall be king after me, and he will sit on my throne in my place."

He then told the priest to take his own donkey and sit Solomon on it and sound the trumpet. Then they were instructed to sit Solomon on the throne and declare that Solomon is the newly appointed king. At this Adonijah realized his efforts were in vain and pleaded for Solomon to not kill him for his actions.

In I Kings 2: 1-12, we read of David's charge to Solomon before he died. He instructs, "Be strong and show yourself a man and observe what the Lord your God requires: Walk in his ways, and keep his decrees and commands, his laws and requirements, as written in the Law of Moses, so that you may prosper in all you do and wherever you go, and that the Lord may keep his promise to me: 'If your descendants watch how they live, and if they walk faithfully before me with all their heart and soul, you will never fail to have a man on the throne of Israel.'"

I am struck again by the influence of Bathsheba. Had she not interceded, Solomon might not have become king. King David honored his oath to her concerning Solomon.

After Solomon became king, Adonijah approached Bathsheba to ask a favor of the king. He wanted Abishag, the young virgin that had attended his father, as his wife. She agreed and went to her son to ask this favor. We read in verse 19, "When she enters the king bowed down to her and sat down on his throne. He had a throne brought for the king's mother and she sat at his right hand." Interesting that he gives her such a place of prominence and then in Proverbs 31, he refers to her as the woman all women are to imitate. The scripture goes on to say that Solomon was furious that Adonijah had made such an insulting request and had him killed.

One of the first things we see Solomon do is make an alliance with Pharaoh, king of Egypt, to marry his daughter. He brought her to Jerusalem and she was with him while he built the temple, palace and a wall surrounding Jerusalem.

Solomon walked in the footsteps of his father and desired to please the Lord. At one point God appeared to him in a dream and said, "Ask for whatever you want and I will give it to you." Solomon replied, "You have made your servant king in place of my father, David. But I am just a child and do not know how to carry out my duties…Give your servant a discerning heart to govern your people and to distinguish between right and wrong."

God was pleased and told him, "Since you have asked for this and not long life or wealth for yourself, nor have asked for the death of your enemies but for discernment in administering justice, I will do what you have asked. I will give you a wise and discerning heart so that there will never have been anyone like you nor will there ever be. Moreover, I will give you what you have not asked for - both riches and honor - so that in your lifetime you will have no equal."

God was true to his Word and Solomon was given great wisdom in the profound and simple things brought before him.

At one point two women came to him and one of them said, "My Lord, this woman and I live in the same house. I had a baby while she was there with me. The third day after my child was born, she also had a baby. During the night, her son died because she lay on him. She came in the night and got my son and put him at her breast and put her dead son in the bed with me. When I woke up to nurse my son the next morning and looked at him closely, I realized what she had done."

The other one said, "No! The living one is my son; the dead one is hers." They argued before the king and Solomon asked them to bring the baby to him. He lifted a sword and said he would cut the baby in two and give half to one mother and half to the other. One replied, "Please my Lord, give her the living baby! Don't kill him." Then Solomon knew who the birth mother was and gave her baby back to her.

All of Israel and the surrounding areas were amazed at the way God was blessing him with prosperity and wisdom beyond measure. Men of all nations came to listen to his wisdom, sent by all the kings of the world.

At one point, the king of Tyre sent a message to Solomon as a sign of respect for his father David offering his services. When Solomon received it, he sent word back that he wanted to build a temple and asked him to send his skilled men to help. The king agreed and with his help and supplies, the temple construction began.

The work began with thirty thousand workers. Solomon gave detailed blueprints of every minute detail. You can read the details of it in I Kings 6: 1-13. One part of his instruction was to partition off twenty cubits in the rear of the temple with cedar boards from floor to ceiling to form an inner sanctuary. It was called The Most Holy Place. Within it was placed the Ark of the Covenant of the Lord. He overlaid everything with pure gold, including the altar.

The temple took seven years to build. When it was finished, Solomon summoned all the elders of Israel and leaders of the tribes to bring up the ark to be placed in the temple. The priest and Levites put everything in their place. After placing the ark in the Most Holy Place, a cloud filled the temple. Solomon knew it was the glory of the Lord and that He was pleased. Solomon also built for himself a palace that took thirteen years to complete. His fame and fortune seemed to be endless. At one point the Queen of Sheba heard about the fame of Solomon and his relationship to the Lord and came to test him with hard questions. He successfully answered them all and she was in awe saying the half has not been told of Solomon's wisdom. She gave him gold, spices, and precious stones before returning to her country.

Solomon continued to prosper and the whole world sought an audience with him to hear the wisdom God had put in his heart. As so often is the case, women became his downfall. He had seven hundred wives of royal birth and three hundred concubines. As he grew older, he began to listen to his wives and allowed his heart to be turned to other gods. His heart was not fully devoted to the Lord as his father David's heart had been.

God held true to his Word and spoke to Solomon, "Since this is your attitude and you have not kept my covenant and my decrees, which I commanded you, I will most certainly tear the kingdom away from you and give it to one of your subordinates. However, for the sake of David, your father, I will not do it during your lifetime. I will tear it out of the hand of your son."

During this time, Jeroboam, who was Solomon's most trusted leader and captain of his army, was traveling down the road one day and was met by a prophet named Ahijah. The prophet was wearing a new cloak. He took it off and tore it in twelve pieces. Then he told Jeroboam, "Take ten pieces for yourself, for this is what the Lord, the God of Israel, says: 'See, I am going to tear the kingdom out of Solomon's hand and give you ten tribes. ...However, I will not take the whole kingdom out of Solomon's hand; I have made him ruler all the days of his life for the sake of David, my servant whom I chose, and who observed my commands and statues. ...I will give the other tribes to his son (Rehoboam) so that David will always have a lamp before me in Jerusalem.'"

We will see that is exactly how it happened in our next lesson. Just as the prophet had said, the kingdom was divided and the destruction of what David had started began its decline.

Solomon ruled for forty years over Israel and his accomplishments were vast. He built the temple, palaces and the great wall around Jerusalem. He was also famous for his literary attainments. He wrote 3000 proverbs, 1005 songs, and scientific works in botany and zoology. He wrote three of the books of the Bible: Proverbs, Ecclesiastes, and Song of Solomon.
Psalms, Proverbs, Ecclesiastes, and Song of Solomon will make more sense as you read with this background on David and Solomon. The issues and heartbreaks they were encountering lead to the saga we will read about in Ecclesiastes.

Discussion Questions:

1. As you look at the life of Solomon and ask yourself how you would answer the question God asked him about what he wanted above all else, what do you think would be your answer?

2. What lessons can we learn from Solomon's life?

3. Why do you think he set his mother up as the Proverbs 31 woman, the woman every woman was to imitate?

Lesson 24
I Kings 12-22
Divided Kingdom

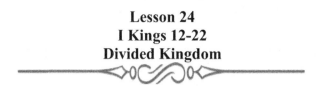

We ended our last lesson with the end of the reign of Solomon. Near the end of his death he found out about the prophet visiting Jeroboam and telling him that ten tribes would be delivered to him and he would reign over Israel. He sent orders to have him killed to prevent this from happening, but Jeroboam fled to Egypt. He stayed there until after Solomon's death.

Meantime, Rehoboam succeeded his father as king. He continued to put a heavy burden on the people, and they were beginning to rebel. When Jeroboam heard of this, he returned from Egypt and led the people in a rally to meet with the king to try to get him to lighten up the yoke his father had put on them.

Rehoboam heard their pleas and told them to go away for three days while he consulted his elders. His elders advised him to lighten the loads and serve the people with a new level of respect, but he refused, and it tells us in I Kings 12:14, "My father made your yoke heavy; I will make it even heavier. My father scourged you with whips; I will scourge you with scorpions."

The people replied, "What share do we have in David, what part in Jesse's son? To your tents, O Israel! Look after your own house, O David!"

That began the kingdom division. The people raised up against Rehoboam and made Jeroboam their king, all except the house of Benjamin and Judah.

When Rehoboam realized the extent of the revolt, he gathered an army of 180,000 subjects to his father's dynasty and set out to regain the divided kingdom. But God intervened by sending a prophet to restrain him, telling him not to fight against his own people. When he realized this was of God, he disbanded his army.

Now that the Kingdom of David had reached its end, the two tribes who were followers of Rehoboam were now called the Kingdom of Judah. Their capital remained in Jerusalem. The ten tribes who were followers of Jeroboam were called the Kingdom of Israel. Their capital was Samaria. This division and disruption was the beginning of the end of Israel's national glory.

Jeroboam began his reign by showing disregard for God as the source of protection, provision, and blessing to the people. His first plan was to destroy the religious unity of the people of the two kingdoms. He feared when they went back to Jerusalem for their annual sacrifices, they might be influenced back to their old allegiance to the house of David. So he erected two golden calves for them to worship and tells them, "It is too much for you to go up to Jerusalem. Here are your gods, O Israel, who brought you up out of Egypt." This began the worship of idols among the people.

Jeroboam established priests and festivals of his own. At one point, he was beginning to offer a sacrifice on the altar, and God sent a prophet to warn him of his disobedience. He reached out his hand to tell his men to seize him but the hand he stretched out shriveled up, and he could not pull it back. The altar also was split in half just as the prophet had warned. The king pleaded with him to intercede for him with God to restore his hand, and the prophet did, and his hand was restored.

It is amazing how oblivious he was to these extreme warnings God sent to him. He did not heed them and continued to set up idols and shrines against God's will.

At one point his son became seriously ill, and he told his wife to disguise herself and go to the prophet that had met him on the road many years before and given him the prophecy about becoming the king of the ten tribes. She was to ask him what was to happen to his sick son. He knew it could not be known she was his wife. She obeyed and went and found the prophet. However; the Lord had gone before her and already warned the prophet of her coming. He was old and blind at this point, but when he heard the knock on the door, he said, "Come in wife of Jeroboam. Why this pretense?" Then he went on to give her the word the Lord had given him for Jeroboam.

You can read it in I Kings 14:7-16. It was a strict reprimand for his disobedience and a prophecy of the destruction of all he had established. Regarding his son, his wife was told that as soon as she set foot in her city again, that her son would die. That is exactly what happened.

In all, Jeroboam reigned for twenty-two years and was buried with his father. His son Nadab succeeded him and followed in his footsteps. After a short reign of two years, he was murdered.

The Kingdom of Israel that Jeroboam had set up lasted 250 years, and not one of the nineteen kings was a godly man in spite of the pleadings of the prophets of God. The story of Elijah in chapter eighteen stands out as a prime example of the extent God went to for his people to return to him.

During this time God sent many prophets to minister to them. Among them that we are most familiar with are Jonah, Elisha, Elijah, Hosea, and Amos.

Meantime, Rehoboam was the king over the house of David, called Judah. He reigned 17 years, and during that time Judah also did evil in the sight of the Lord. They also began to set up idols and even had male shrine prostitutes, and chapter 14 tells us they engaged in all kinds of evil practices.

In the fifth year of Rehoboam's reign, the king of Egypt attacked and carried off all the treasures of the temple of the Lord and the treasure of the palace.

The kingdom lasted four hundred years after separating from the other ten tribes. During this time they were governed by 19 kings and one queen. The queen was Athaliah who was the only woman to ever sit upon the Throne of David.

While Athaliah was on the throne, many massacres culminated in the slaughter of all the royal seed of Judah by the wicked queen. She reduced the descendants of David until only one representative was left– the little prince, Joash, who was hidden with his nurse in the house of the Lord during one of the massacres. At the age of seven, he was brought out of hiding and proclaimed King of Judah. Queen Athaliah was slaughtered and the Davidic dynasty made a fresh start under this young king.

Some of the kings of Judah were godly men and others were not. However, all were descendants of King David, confirming the covenant God had made with David that his kingdom throne would last forever.

God continued with them as he had with Jeroboam's tribes to bring them back to obedience to him. He sent prophets to minister to them. We read their story in the Bible under many of their names. They were Isaiah, Micah, Jeremiah, Ezekiel, Daniel, Haggai, Zachariah, and Malachi. We will take a look at some of their stories in the following lessons.

Discussions Question:

1. God was faithful to send prophets to the tribes even though they were rebelling. In looking back at your life, can you see how God has remained with you in times even when you were not walking in obedience?

Lesson 25
I Kings 17-19
Elijah

As we talked about in our last lesson, the Kingdom of David had now been divided between the son of Solomon, Rehoboam, and the military leader, Jeroboam. The kingdom established by Jeroboam showed utter disregard for God and the plan He had laid out for his people. The nine different dynasties practiced idolatry and were in constant war. The prevailing practice was creating plots against the reigning king and the murder of his entire household.

After Jeroboam died, he left his throne to his son, Nadad, who followed the bad example of his father. After a short reign of two years, he was murdered, the throne was overthrown, and the line continued with gross idolatry, murder, and rebellion against God. However, God was faithful to send prophets to show them His love and His power to save them.

One of the more interesting stories came during the reign of King Ahab. He had married the daughter of the King of Sidon whose name was Jezebel. He began worshiping Baal and even built an altar to Baal in the capital city of Samaria. God sent his prophet Elijah to give the king a message: "As surely as the Lord God of Israel lives - there won't be any dew or rain for several years until I say the word."

Then the Lord told Elijah to go to a certain brook and wait there. He told him to drink water from the brook and eat the food that the ravens would bring him because God had commanded the birds to do so. Amazing how God used the animals to serve his purposes. Remember the talking donkey just a few lessons ago?

Elijah did as the Lord told him, but eventually, the brook dried up. God then told him to go and live in Zarephath and that a widow would feed him. God told him he had already given her the instructions to do so.

As he arrived at the gates of the city, he saw a widow gathering sticks and asked her for a cup of water. As she was going to get it, he called to her to bring him a piece of bread also. She replied, "I swear by the Lord your God that I haven't a single piece of bread in the house and I have only a handful of flour and a little cooking oil. I was gathering a few sticks of wood so I could cook this last meal, then my son and I must die of starvation."

Elijah told her, "Don't be afraid! Cook that last meal but bake me a little loaf of bread first, and afterward, there will be enough food for you and your son because God said there will always be plenty of flour and oil in your containers until the Lord sends rain and the crops grow again." She did as Elijah said, and she and Elijah and her son continued to eat from her supply of flour and oil as long as it was needed. No matter how much they used, there was always plenty left in the container.

It was three years later that the Lord told Elijah to go and tell King Ahab that he would soon send rain again. So Elijah went to tell the king what God had spoken.

The man in charge of Ahab's household was Obadiah, a devoted follower of the Lord. Once when Queen Jezebel had tried to kill all of the Lord's prophets, Obadiah had hidden one hundred of them in caves and had fed them with bread and water.

One day, while Elijah was on his way to see King Ahab, the king said to Obadiah, "We must check every stream to see if we can find enough grass to save at least some of the horses and mules. You go one way and I'll go another."

So they did. Suddenly Obadiah saw Elijah coming toward him. Obadiah fell to the ground. "Is it really you, Elijah?" he asked. "It is," Elijah replied. "Go and tell the king I am here." Obadiah went to tell Ahab, and Ahab went out to meet him. "So it's you - the man who bought disaster upon Israel!" Ahab exclaimed.

"You're talking about yourself," Elijah answered. "For you and your family have refused to obey the Lord and have worshiped Baal instead. Now bring all the people of Israel to Mt. Carmel, with all 450 prophets of Baal and the 400 prophets of Asherah who are supported by Jezebel."

So Ahab summoned all the prophets and people to Mount Carmel, and Elijah talked to them. "How long are you going to waver between two opinions? If the Lord is God, follow him. But if Baal is God, then follow him."

"Now bring two young bulls. The prophets of Baal may choose whichever one they wish and cut it into pieces and lay it on the wood of their altar, without putting any fire under the wood. I will prepare the other young bull and lay it on the wood of the Lord's altar, with no fire under it. Then pray to your god, and I will pray to my God and the one who answers by sending fire to light the wood is the true God!"

All the people agreed to this test. Then Elijah turned to the prophets of Baal. "Choose one of the bulls and prepare it and call on your God." They prepared one of the young bulls and placed it on the altar, and they called to Baal all morning shouting to Baal to hear them but there was no reply. Then they began to dance around the altar. By noon Elijah began to mock them saying maybe they needed to shout louder because their God might be asleep or maybe he was away on a trip. They shouted louder and even began to cut themselves with knives until time for the evening sacrifice.

Then Elijah called to the people, "Come over here." They all crowded around the altar of the Lord which had been torn down. He took twelve stones, one to represent each tribe of Israel and used the stones to build the altar. (Sounds like the altar the children made by taking twelve stones from the Jordan River after they had crossed over.) Then he dug a trench around the altar, he piled wood on the altar and cut up the young bull and laid it on the wood.

Then he told them to get four barrels of water and pour over the carcass and the wood. Then after they did he told them to do it again. When they did the water overflowed off the altar and filled the trench.

At the customary time for offering the evening sacrifice, Elijah walked up to the altar and prayed, "Oh Lord God of Abraham, Isaac, and Israel, prove today that you are the God of Israel and that I am your servant; prove that I have done this at your command."

Suddenly fire flashed down from heaven and burned up the young bull, the wood, and the stones to dust and even evaporated all the water in the ditch. When the people saw this they fell to their faces on the ground shouting, "Jehovah is God!" Then Elijah told them to grab the prophets of Baal. They did and Elijah took them to the Kishon Brook and killed them.

When Ahab told Queen Jezebel what Elijah had done, she sent this message to Elijah: "You killed my prophets and now I swear that I am going to kill you by this time tomorrow night."

Elijah fled for his life into the wilderness and stayed all day and all night. He rested under a tree and was so frightened that he prayed to die, saying to God, "I have had enough. I have to die sometime, it might as well be now." Then he lay down and slept. As he was sleeping, an angel touched him and told him to get up and eat. He looked around and saw some bread baking on the hot stones, and a jar of water. He ate and drank and then continued his rest.

Then the angel came again and said, "Get up and eat some more, for there is a long journey ahead of you." He obeyed the angel and gained enough strength to travel forty days to Mount Horeb, the mountain of God where he lived in a cave. Isn't it amazing that he had such faith and boldness to challenge the king and prophets of Baal but went weak-kneed at the threat of a woman?

The Lord said to him, "What are you doing here Elijah?" He replied, "I have worked very hard and all the other prophets but me have been killed, and now they are trying to kill me." The Lord told him, "Go out and stand before me on the mountain."

As Elijah stood there the Lord passed by, and a mighty windstorm hit the mountain. Then there was an earthquake and then a fire. But God was not in any of them. But after the fire, there was the sound of a gentle whisper. "Why are you here, Elijah?"

He replied again, "I have been working very hard for the God of Heaven, but the people have torn down your altars and killed all your prophets but me. Now they are seeking me to kill as well." Then the Lord told him, "Go back and anoint Jehu to be king of Israel, and anoint Elisha to replace you as my prophet. And incidentally, there are 7,000 men in Israel who have not bowed down to Baal."

Elijah went out and found Elisha and placed his coat around him, anointing him as a prophet of God.

The time came for God to take Elijah to heaven. Elijah said to Elisha, "Please stay here for the Lord has sent me to the Jordan River." Elisha replied, "I will not leave you." So the two of them went to the edge of the Jordan River. Elijah folded his cloak together and struck the river with it and the river divided and they went across on dry land.

On the other side, Elijah asked Elisha, "What wish shall I grant you before I am taken away?" Elisha told him, "Please grant me twice as much prophetic power as you have had." Elijah replied, "You have asked a hard thing. If you see me when I am taken from you, then you will get your request. But if not, then you won't."

As they were walking along talking suddenly a chariot of fire drawn by horses of fire appeared and drove between them, separating them, and Elijah was carried by a whirlwind into Heaven. Elisha picked up Elijah's coat and returned to the bank of the river. He struck it as Elijah had and cried out, "Where is the Lord God of Elijah?" Suddenly the waters parted and he went across. When the young prophets saw this, they knew that now the spirit of Elijah was now on Elisha.

Discussion Questions:

1. What lesson can we learn from the widow who fed Elijah the last of her food supply?

2. Why do you think he was so frightened and ran away from Jezebel?

3. When God spoke to Elijah on the mountain, he demonstrated many natural occurrences before he spoke to him in a still whisper. Can you think of a time that you were seeking God in ways that were not reaching Him, only to find Him in the whispers of your life?

4. Name one thing that you learned from this lesson that you did not know before.

Lesson 26
I Kings 19- II Kings 13
Elisha

In our last lesson, we saw Elisha take the place of Elijah as a prophet. However, this was not the last time Elijah is seen in history. He appears again at the transfiguration of Jesus in the New Testament. He supernaturally was taken to heaven and supernaturally reappeared when Jesus was taken to heaven to sit at the right hand of his father.

He was the prophet during the time of King Ahab, who was the absolute worst king over Israel. This was partly due to his wife Jezebel whom we talked about in our last lesson. She was yet one more of the strong, evil women in the Bible who took matters into her own hands and usurped the power of her husband.

An example of this is found in I Kings 21. Her husband, King Ahab, approached his neighbor, Naboth about acquiring his land that joined the property of his palace. He wanted it for a vegetable garden. Naboth refused, saying, "The Lord forbid that I should give you the inheritance of my fathers." King Ahab was so angry that he went home and pouted. The Bible says "sulking" but today we would also call it pouting. He even refused to eat. Seems a little childish for a king but that is what it says.

His wife, Jezebel, came in and asked him why he was pouting and not eating. He told her and she chided him by saying, "Is this any way for a king to act? Get up and eat, I will take care of things and get you your vineyard."

She devised a plan by writing letters, signing her husband's name on them and placing the seal of the king on them as well. She sent these to the elders and nobles who lived near Naboth. Her instructions were to invite him to a feast and seat him in a prominent place. On either side, she had them seat scoundrels who would give a false testimony claiming that Naboth had cursed both God and the king. They did as they were told, and Naboth was taken out and stoned. As soon as she heard that her plan had worked and Naboth was dead, she went into the king and told him to get up and eat and take possession of the land he wanted so badly.

The king went to walk over the land, and the Lord had told Elijah to go to him and tell him, "This is what the Lord says: Have you not murdered a man and seized his property? Then in the place where dogs licked up Naboth's blood, dogs will lick up your blood." He went on to say that because he had done evil in the sight of the Lord that he would bring disaster on him and that he would cut off every living male from his family line.

"Furthermore, concerning your wife, Jezebel, dogs will devour her at the wall of Jezreel." We see that is exactly what happened. As for Ahab, he was killed in battle when a sword pierced him and he bled all over the chariot. After he had been buried, they took his chariot to wash at a pool in Samaria and the dogs licked up his blood, just as the prophet had said would happen.

We read in II Kings 9, that after her husband's death, Jezebel's son, Joram, became the king of Israel. But the Lord had sent word to the prophet Elisha to go and secretly anoint Jehu as the king. He further instructed him, "Destroy the family of Ahab; you will avenge the murder of my prophets and of all the other people who were killed by Jezebel."

Elisha went to the town of Jezreel where the king lived and killed both Ahaziah and Joram. When Jezebel heard that he was coming into the city, she painted her eyelids and fixed her hair and sat at a window. When Jehu entered the gates, she shouted, "You murderer!" When he looked up and saw her he instructed two men standing near her to throw her out the window. They did, and her blood splattered against the wall, and she was trampled by horses. This fulfilled the prophecy given earlier that dogs would lick her blood from the walls of Jezreel.

When Athaliah, the mother of King Ahaziah of Judah, learned that her son was dead, she proceeded to destroy the entire royal family. It is hard to imagine killing all your children and grandchildren, but it only goes to show you how evil she was. She wanted to destroy the family dynasty except for herself.

However, Jehosheba, Ahaziah's sister, took his small son and hid him away in the temple for six years while Athaliah was on the throne. At the age of seven years, he was presented as the rightful king. When Athaliah heard that he had been crowned, she went to the temple and yelled treason, but the priest ordered her to be taken out and murdered in the street. After her death, peace and quiet once again returned to Judah.

Elisha was given the anointing that had been on Elijah and God did many miraculous things through him. After Elijah had been taken to Heaven supernaturally, word was out that Elisha had been given the anointing that had been on Elijah. At one point the king of Syria had heard about Elisha and sent his commander-in-chief, Naaman to him to be healed of leprosy. The king had written a letter of introduction for him and when he arrived at his house, Elisha did not even come out but just sent a messenger to tell him to go wash in the Jordan River seven times and he would be healed. He was instantly healed and his skin became as new.

At one point, Elisha warned the king of Israel that the Syrians were planning to attack and where they were to be assembling. The king sent out a scout and found Elisha was right and they were saved from disaster. This happened many times. The king of Syria was confused and thought there must be a spy in his camp who kept telling Israel their plans.

Finally, he realized that it was Elisha who was telling the king of Israel their plans and he sent troops to seize him. They found out that he was in the city of Dothan, so the king sent a great army with many chariots and horses to surround the city. When the prophet's servant got up early the next morning and went outside, there were troops, horses, and chariots everywhere. "Alas, my master, what shall we do now?" he cried out to Elisha. "Don't be afraid!" Elisha told him. "For our army is bigger than theirs."

Then Elisha prayed, "Lord, open his eyes and let him see!" So the Lord opened the eyes of the servant and he could see horses of fire and chariots of fire everywhere upon the mountain. As the Syrian army advanced upon them, Elisha prayed, "Lord, please make them blind." And he did.

Then Elisha went out and told them, "You've come the wrong way! This isn't the right city! Follow me and I will take you to the man you're looking for." And he led them to Samaria! As soon as they arrived Elisha prayed, "Now open their eyes Lord and let them see." And the Lord did and they discovered they were in Samaria, the capital of Israel. When the king of Israel saw this he shouted to Elisha, "Shall I kill them?" "Of course not!" Elisha told him. "Do we kill prisoners of war? Give them food and drink and send them home again." So he prepared a great feast for them and sent them home to their king. After that, the Syrian raiders stayed away from Israel.

It is so interesting how God used the prophets to show his power but at times like this, he allowed the enemy to be spared and showed mercy and grace.

Another time, the men of the city came to Elisha and said, "Look, this town is well situated, as you can see, but the water is bad and the land is unproductive." Elisha told them to bring him a bowl and put salt in it." They did as he told them. Then Elisha took the bowl and went out to the spring that fed the water supply and threw it in it saying, "This is what the Lord says: 'I have healed this water. Never again will it cause death or make the land unproductive.'" The water has remained wholesome until this day according to the word of Elisha.

Then Elisha was walking up to Bethel. As he was walking along the road, some youths came out of the town and jeered at him. "Go on up, you baldhead!" He turned around, looked at them and called down a curse on them in the name of the Lord. Then two bears came out of the woods and mauled forty-two of the youths.

Another time, the king of Judah, the king of Israel, and the king of Edom were attacking the king of Moab. After seven days of marching, they had no more water for themselves or their animals. The king of Israel said, "Has the Lord called we three kings together to hand us over to Moab?" Then Jehoshaphat remembered Elisha, and they went down to inquire of him what to do. Elisha told them to bring him a harpist and while the harpist was playing, the Lord spoke to Elisha saying, "Tell them to make this valley full of ditches. You will see neither wind nor rain, yet this valley will be filled with water, and you, your cattle and your other animals will drink. The Lord will also hand Moab over to you. You will overthrow every fortified city and every major town. You will cut down every good tree, stop up all the springs, and ruin every good field with stones."

The next morning water began to flow and filled the ditches with water. The Moabites started their march to destroy them. It was early morning and the sun was shining on the water. To the Moabites, it looked like blood and they said, "Those kings have slaughtered each other. Now us go in and plunder their land." But when the Moabites got to the camp of Israel, the Israelites rose up and fought them until they fled. They then invaded their towns, stopped up their wells, cut down every tree and filled their land with stones just as Elisha had prophesied.

Then there is the story of the widow's oil. The wife of one of the prophets came to Elisha and told him that her husband was dead and the creditors were coming to take her two sons as slaves. Elisha responded, "How can I help you? Tell me, what do you have in your house?" She replied, "Your servant has nothing there at all, except a little oil." Elisha told her to go and gather all the containers she could find. He told her to even go and borrow some from her neighbors. Then he told her to go in her house and close the door behind her and her sons. He told her then to start pouring the little oil she had into the containers until they were all full. She did as he said and filled all the containers until they were full. Elisha then told her to go and sell the oil and pay her debtors.

One day when Elisha was traveling to Shunem, he met a wealthy woman who invited him for a meal. From then on when he was in town, he would stop by and have a meal with her and her family. She asked her husband one day that since he is a holy man of God could they make a room for him on the roof with a bed, table, chair, and lamp. He agreed and Elisha was so pleased that he asked what he could do for them. He found out they could not have children so he called her and told her, "This time next year you will hold a son in your arms." She said to him, "Don't get my hopes up." She had obviously been through many disappointments trying to have a child.

Sure enough, she got pregnant and at the same time, the next year had a son. The boy grew but got very sick and died. His mother took him on the roof and laid him on the bed that had been prepared for Elisha. Then she told her servant to get a donkey and take her to Mount Carmel where Elisha was. When they arrived she fell at his feet and said, "Didn't I tell you not to raise my hopes?" She was probably thinking how much easier it would have been to not have had a child than to experience the pain of this loss.

Elisha told her servant to go quickly and take his staff and lay it on the boy's face. Then Elisha and the mother started to the place where the boy lay dead. When Elisha got there, he went into the room with the boy and shut the door. He prayed to the Lord then laid on top of the boy's body, mouth-to-mouth, eyes to eyes, hands to hands. All of a sudden, the boy's body began to get warm. He walked back and forth in the room and then stretched out on the boy's body once more. The boy sneezed seven times and opened his eyes. Elisha called his mother and handed him to her.

We often see foreshadows of Jesus in the prophets of old. One such story was when a man brought twenty loaves of barley to Elisha. He told the man to feed the people with it. "How can I feed one hundred men with this?" Elisha said, "Give it to the people to eat. For this is what the Lord says: "They will eat and there will be food left over.'" Then they set the bread before the crowd and they ate and there was plenty for everyone and there was even some leftover. Sounds like when Jesus feeds the five thousand with the loaves and fishes.

There are many amazing stories of how God's spirit worked through the prophets. One of the most unusual was when the prophets said to Elisha that the place where they met was too small, and they wanted to go to the Jordan and build a place for them each to live. While working, an ax head flew off the handle of one of the prophets and landed in the river. He was upset and told Elisha it was borrowed. Elisha asked where in the river it landed and he showed him. Elisha cut a stick and threw it in the river in that place and the ax head floated to the top and the prophet retrieved it.

Discussion Questions:

1. King Ahab wanted property that did not belong to him and his wife devised a way to take it by using lies and deceit. They were punished by a cruel death. What lessons can we learn from this story about honesty?

2. The prophets worked many miracles and were tuned in to listen to God's voice. Compare what they did with the works of Jesus and share what they have in common.

3. After Jesus came, he anointed his disciples to do the same kind of works he did and then told them that when he was gone, they would do even greater work. What do you think he meant?

4. The widow who had little oil was obedient to God's prophet, acted on faith and God rewarded her. Have you ever been asked to step out on faith and how did you respond?

Amos 1-9, Hosea 1-14
Amos & Hosea

In previous lessons, we talked about two of the prophets that God sent to call the people back to him. Even though they continued to disobey, God never forsook them.

He sent a list of prophets to the northern kingdoms:

Ahij
Elijah
Micaiah
Elisha
Hosea
Jonah
Amos
Oded

We have studied Elijah and Elisha and will touch on the other more well-known prophets.

Amos was a prophet who does not have a large place in the Bible but was given a beautiful vision warning the people of what was to come. He was a herdsman living in the village of Tekoa. While he sat watching sheep, God appeared to him in a vision and told him some of the things that were going to happen to his nation. God actually spoke to him in a series of five visions. He came on the scene when Israel was in a time of great riches and wealth. He warned about the behavior of turning away from God, being cruel to the poor and living selfishly.

The visions warned both Israel and Judah. The vision was as follows: The Lord says, "The people of Israel have sinned again and again. This is your doom! It is spoken by the Lord against both Israel and Judah – against the entire family brought out from Egypt. Of all the people of the earth, I have chosen you. That is why I must punish you the more for your sins. For how can we walk together with your sins between us? I, the Lord, am sending disaster into your land. But always, first of all, I warn you through my prophets. This I now have done."

"My people have forgotten what it means to do right. Their homes are full of the loot from their thefts and banditry. Therefore an enemy is coming…I sent you hunger, but it did no good…. I sent blight and mildew on your farms and vineyards; locust ate your figs and olive trees.

"I destroyed some of your cities, as I did Sodom and Gomorrah; those left are half-burned and still you won't return to me. Therefore, prepare to meet your God in judgment, Israel. For you are dealing with the one who formed the mountains and made the winds, and knows your every thought; Jehovah the Lord, the God of Hosts is his name."

The Lord says to the people of Israel, "Seek me - and live. Don't seek the idols of Bethel, for the people of Bethel shall surely come to grief."

Amos urged the people to "seek him who created the seven stars and the constellation Orion, who turns darkness into morning, and day into night, who calls forth the water from the oceans and pours it out as rain upon the land. The Lord, Jehovah, is his name. Be good, flee evil and live! Then the Lord will truly be your helper, as you have claimed he is. Hate evil and love the good; remodel your courts into true halls of justice. Perhaps even yet the Lord God of Hosts will have mercy on his people who remain."

He tells them, "You lie on ivory beds surrounded with luxury, eating the meat of the tenderest lambs and the choicest calves. You sing idle songs to the sound of the harp and fancy yourselves as great musicians as King David was. You drink wine by bucketful and perfume yourself with sweet ointments, caring nothing at all that your brothers need your help. Therefore, you will be the first to be taken over as slaves; suddenly your revelry will end."

Jehovah the Lord of Hosts has sworn by his own name, "I despise the pride and false glory of Israel, and hate her beautiful homes. I will turn over this city and everything in it to her enemies. O Israel, I will bring against you a nation that will bitterly oppress you from your northern boundary to your southern tip. The eyes of the Lord are watching Israel, and I will root her up and scatter her across the world. Yet this rooting out will not be permanent. For I have commanded that Israel will be sifted in a sieve, yet not one true kernel will be lost. Then I will rebuild the City of David, and return it to its former glory." So the Lord, who plans it all, has said.

I think this is such a beautiful prophecy about what was about to come, and as we know from history, the things absolutely came true. It was not long after this prophecy that Babylon captured them and all the things prophesied came true. We can take this prophecy for today as well. It is both a prophecy and a promise.

He prophesies about how, when we do not obey God, he chastises us. He is trying to preserve us for the best He has for us. I love where he says not one true kernel will be lost. Of course, he is talking about Israel, but it equally applies to us. It reminds me of a parent who warns a child not to go near the stove that is hot or they will be burned. If they do, the parent might swat their hand as punishment, but it is an act of love so they will learn to not get burned. Understanding that God is love and everything that comes from Him is an act of love, helps us accept the trials we encounter. His ways are not our ways and we must trust that He has our best interest at heart like the parent who is protecting his child. I am sure the child who gets his hand slapped when he goes near the stove does not understand the love behind it, but a parent would be negligent if he did not teach this lesson.

Hosea was a prophet sent during the reigns of the following kings: Uzziah, Jotham, Ahaz, and Hezekiah. The story of Hosea is a beautiful love story of forgiveness and mercy. It seems strange, but God seems to be using Hosea as a visual for the people to learn a lesson. In Hosea 1:2, when the Lord began to speak through Hosea, the Lord said to him "Go, take to yourself an adulterous wife and children of unfaithfulness, because the land is guilty of the vilest adultery in departing from the Lord."

Hosea was obedient and married a woman named Gomer. She conceived and God told him to name his firstborn son Jezreel because he would punish those responsible for the massacre at Jezreel we talked about in previous lessons.

Then she conceived again and had a daughter. God told him to name her Lo-Ruhamah. Her named meant "not loved." This represented the fact that he would no longer show love to the house of Israel for their rebellion.

Gomer gave birth to another son and the Lord instructed Hosea to name him Lo-Ammi, which means "not my people." This is showing God's frustration with the people, but during the same prophesy he says, "Yet the Israelites will be like the sand on the seashore, which cannot be measured or counted. In the same place it was said, 'you are not my people; they will be called sons of the living God. The people of Israel and the people of Judah shall be reunited, and they will appoint one leader and will come up out of the land, for great will be the day of Jezreel.'"

While Amos prophesied about the capture of the people by Babylon, Hosea told about the restoration of Israel as a nation after the capture.

On one hand, in the second chapter we see God's punishment in verse 3 and 4, "I will make her like a desert, turn her into a parched land and slay her with thirst. I will not show my love to her children, because they are the children of adultery."

Then, on the other hand, He says in verse 14, "Therefore I am going to allure her; I will lead her into the desert and speak tenderly to her. There I will give her back her vineyards and will make the Valley of Achor a door of hope. There she will sing as in days of her youth, as in the day she came up out of Egypt." (Interesting note that in the next verse the Lord says, "In that day you will call me husband; you will no longer call me master...I will betroth you in righteousness and justice, in love and compassion. I will betroth you in faithfulness, and you will acknowledge the Lord...I will plant her for myself in the land; I will show my love to the one I called 'not my loved one.' I will say to those called 'Not my people' and say, 'You are my people, and they will say, 'You are my God.'"

This is such a powerful prophecy because this is saying that when Christ came, we could become covenant partners with him and no longer see Him as a master but as a husband.

We often play this out in weddings where the bride and groom each light a candle and then join their flames into one unity candle that symbolizes they are no longer two individuals walking beside each other, but they have chosen to become one as husband and wife. The Church (that is you if you have accepted Christ) is called the bride of Christ in Revelation 19. This means we have taken our light and joined with him who is called the light of the world and become one.

Few have ever grasped that concept, but Jesus says that in John 14:2, "On that day (the day we accept him and his death on the cross on our behalf), you will realize that I am in my Father, and you are in me, and I am in you." We are restored to the state Adam and Eve were in the garden where they were one with God and sin had not been introduced.

Jesus himself says this in Revelation 19:14, "Blessed are those who wash their robes, that they may have the right to the tree of life and may go through the gates into the city. Outside are the dogs, the sexually immoral, the murderers, the idolaters and everyone who loves and practices falsehood."

We are born into a world with our robes (our spirits) having the DNA of sin due to the fall in the garden. When we accept the fact that Jesus became our sin by shedding his blood on the cross, we are restored to righteousness or right standing with God! We are said to have put on robes of righteousness. In Revelation 19:13, it even tells us Jesus comes dressed in a robe dipped in his own blood. His robe was dipped in his blood so our robes would be clean and white as snow. Isaiah 1:18 tells us just that, "Though your sins were as scarlet, they shall be white as snow."

You may ask why then do we not walk as residents of the garden? The answer is that we are still living in a fallen, sin-filled world and until we go to heaven, we will be constantly drawn to walk in disobedience, just like the children of Israel. But like Adam and Eve, it is a choice. Jesus goes on in chapter 15 and tells us about this new relationship. "I am the vine; you are the branches. If a man remains in me and I in him, he will bear much fruit; apart from me, you can do nothing. If anyone does not remain in me, he is like a branch that is thrown away and withers; such branches are picked up, thrown into the fire and burned. If you remain in me and my words remain in you, ask what you wish, and it will be given you."

This verifies what Solomon spoke many years before in Proverbs 11:30, "The fruit of righteousness is a tree of life."

As you can see, prophecies are not just for the saints of old but are still being lived out in our lives today to help and guide us to understand the future and ourselves.

Hosea's call to forgive his adulterous wife is a visual of what God did for us by sending Jesus. He tells Hosea to go and show love to his wife, and even though she is loved by another and is an adulteress, he is to go and love her as God loved Israel. He talks about paying the price of redemption in Hosea 3:2, "So I bought her for 15 shekels of silver and about a homer and a lethek of barley."

Just like Hosea, Jesus paid the price of redemption for us. Can you see how all these Old Testament prophecies were shadows of what was to come? Many people miss out on the blessings of studying the prophets, thinking that was just for Israel, but it gives us a beautiful picture of our lives today as we walk in God's forgiveness for our own lives.

Discussion Questions:

1. God sent warnings through the profit Amos. How can those same warnings be true for us today?

2. Does seeing the visual of Hosea's life help you understand what Jesus did for us?

3. What lesson can we learn about forgiveness from the story of Hosea?

Lesson 28
Jonah 1-4, Isaiah 1-66
Jonah & Isaiah

Jonah is one of the more popular stories in the Bible because of the unusual circumstances involved. He was a prophet whom God called to preach to a particular foreign city called Nineveh. "Go to the great city of Nineveh and give them this announcement from the Lord: 'I am going to destroy you, for your wickedness smells to the highest heaven.'" I guess that is where we get the phrase something smells to the high heavens.

But Jonah was afraid to go and ran away. He went down to the seacoast to the port of Joppa where he found a ship leaving for Tarshish. He bought a ticket, went on board and climbed down into the dark hold of the ship to hide from the Lord.

As the ship was sailing along, the Lord flung a terrific wind over the sea, causing a great storm that threatened to send them to the bottom. Fearing for their lives, the sailors shouted to their gods for help and threw the cargo overboard to lighten the ship. All this time Jonah was sound asleep down in the hold.

The Captain went down after him. "What do you mean," he roared, "sleeping at a time like this? Get up and cry to your God and see if he will have mercy and save us!" Then the crew decided to draw straws and see which of them had offended the gods and caused this terrible storm. Jonah drew the short straw.

"What have you done," they asked, "to bring this awful storm upon us? What is your nationality?" He said, "I am a Jew; and I worship Jehovah, the God of Heaven, who made the earth and the sea." Then he told them he was running away from the Lord.

The men were frightened. "Why did you do it?" they shouted. "What shall we do to stop the storm?" "Throw me into the sea and the seas will become calm," Jonah answered.

They tried to row the boat ashore, but couldn't make it. Then they shouted out a prayer to Jonah's God: "Oh Jehovah, don't make us die for this man's sin, and don't hold us responsible for his death, for you have sent this storm upon him for your own good reason."

Then they picked up Jonah and threw him into the raging sea and the storm stopped. The men stood in awe before Jehovah, and sacrificed to him and vowed to serve him.

The Lord had arranged for a great fish to swallow Jonah. And Jonah was inside the fish three days and three nights before praying to God to deliver him. He prayed, "You threw me into the ocean depths, I was covered by wild and stormy waves. You have rejected me; how shall I ever again see your holy temple? I went down to the bottoms of the mountains that rise from off the ocean floor. I was locked out of life and imprisoned in the land of death. Those who worship false gods have turned their backs on all the mercies waiting for them from the Lord! I will never worship anyone but you! I will surely fulfill my promises."

The Lord heard his prayer and ordered the fish to spit up Jonah on the beach. Then the Lord spoke to Jonah again: "Go to that great city, Nineveh, and warn them of their doom as I told you before."

The very first day Jonah went to Nineveh, a city so big it would take three days to walk around it. The very first day Jonah entered the city and began to preach, the people repented. Jonah shouted to the crowds who gathered around him to listen to him: "Forty days from now Nineveh will be destroyed unless you repent!!" he shouted. The people believed him and declared a fast; from the king on down, everyone put on sackcloth - the rough, coarse garments worn at times of mourning.

The king and his nobles sent this message throughout the city: "Everyone must cry mightily to God, and let everyone turn from his evil ways. Who can tell, perhaps God will decide to let us live and will hold back his fierce anger." When God saw that they had put a stop to their evil, he abandoned his plan to destroy them.

Interestingly, this change of plan made Jonah angry. He complained to the Lord about it: "This is exactly what I thought you would do, for I knew you were a gracious God, merciful, slow to get angry, and full of kindness."

Jonah went out and sat sulking on the east side of the city. The Lord arranged for a vine to grow up quickly and spread its leaves over Jonah's head to shade him. This made him comfortable and very grateful. But God also prepared a worm! The worm ate through the stem of the plant so that it withered away and died.

When the sun was hot, God ordered a scorching east wind to blow on Jonah, and the sun beat down upon his head until he grew faint and wished to die. He said, "Death would be better than this!" Then God said to Jonah, "Is it right for you to be angry because the plant died?" "Yes," Jonah said, "it is right for me to be angry enough to die!"

The Lord said, "You feel sorry for yourself when your shelter is destroyed, though you did no work to put it there, and it is at best short-lived. And why shouldn't I feel sorry for a great city like Nineveh with its one hundred and twenty thousand people in spiritual darkness?"

God reprimanded Jonah for his selfish attitude of wanting to disobey God when he had an assignment to go and warn an entire city, which could save them from destruction. When he still had a bad attitude and pouted about God saving them, God gave him a personal visual of himself. He brought the vine to comfort him with shade and then allowed it to be taken away. When his anger and rebellious spirit once again rose up, God asked him, "Do you have a right to be angry with a vine?" Jonah said he did. The Lord said, "You have been concerned about this vine, though you did not tend it or make it grow. It sprang up overnight and died overnight. But Nineveh has a hundred and twenty thousand people who cannot tell their right hand from their left, and many cattle as well. Should I not be concerned about that great city?"

Jesus references the story of Jonah in Matthew 12:39-41, "A wicked and adulterous generation asks for a miraculous sign! But none will be given it except for the sign of the prophet Jonah. For as Jonah was three days and three nights in the belly of a huge fish, so the Son of Man will be three days and three nights in the heart of the earth (talking about the three days Jesus had to go to the pits of hell to defeat Satan. This happened before Jesus was resurrected from the dead.) The men of Nineveh will stand up at the judgment with this generation and condemn it; for they repented at the preaching of Jonah, and now one greater than

Jonah is here." He was speaking of himself as he was now on the earth to bring redemption to mankind as Jonah had brought the message to Nineveh that they needed to turn back to God.

Now let's look at some of the prophets God sent to the two tribes of the southern kingdom whose capital was Judah:

Shemaiah
Iddo
Azariah
Hanani
Jehu
Eliezer
Jahaziel
Zechariah
Isaiah
Micah
Nahum
Joel
Jeremiah
Habakakhuk
Zephaniah
Ezekiel
Daniel
Obadiah

We will cover the highlighted prophets, starting with one of my favorite prophets, _Isaiah_. He was a prophet during the time the Northern Kingdom was destroyed by the Assyrians. He lived during the reign of Uzziah, Jotham, Ahaz, and Hezekiah. In fact, his father was the brother of King Uzziah and grandson of King Joash, so he himself had a royal bloodline.

He had great literary skills and wrote many historical works about the kings of both Israel and Judah. In the New Testament, he is quoted more than any other prophet. He was known for his great mind and experts have said that many of his works of poetry and expression are unequaled even by Shakespeare or the equivalent of our day.

On one occasion, he wrote about seeing the Lord. You could say this was the time of his commission and acceptance of his task as a prophet. He tells us in chapter 6, "In the year that King Uzziah died, I saw the Lord seated on a throne, high and exalted, and the train of his robe filled the temple. Above him were seraphs, each with six wings: With two wings they covered their faces, with two they covered their feet, and with two they were flying. And they were calling to one another "Holy, holy, holy is the Lord God Almighty; the whole earth is full of His glory."

At the sound of their voices, the doorposts and thresholds shook and the temple was filled with smoke. "Woe to me!" Isaiah cried, "I am ruined! For I am a man of unclean lips, and my eyes have seen the King, the Lord Almighty."

He goes on: "Then one of the Seraphs flew to me with a live coal in his hand, which he had taken with tongs from the altar. With it he touched my mouth and said, 'See, this has touched your lips, your guilt is taken away and your sin atoned for.' Then I heard the voice of the Lord saying, 'Whom shall I send: And who will go for us?' And I said, 'Here am I, Send me!' "This was a prophecy for the nation of Israel, but also for the future coming of the Messiah when our guilt would be atoned for.

Isaiah lived during the time that Assyria captured the Southern Kingdom, and during his lifetime saw his own kingdom taken into captivity, all but Jerusalem. In a miraculous act of God, in answer to his prayer and advice to the king, the armies were stopped outside the walls of Jerusalem by an angel of God.

All other cities had been captured, and when King Hezekiah heard that a large army was now coming to destroy Jerusalem, he sent his administrators to find Isaiah to pray to God for the small remnant to survive, and for Jerusalem to be spared. Isaiah did intercede and gave word to the king. When the army came, an angel of the Lord went out and put to death a hundred and eighty-five thousand men in the Assyrian camp. When the residents of Jerusalem got up the following morning the dead bodies were all that was left of the powerful army.

After that, Hezekiah became ill and was at the point of death. Isaiah went to him and told him the Lord said he should get his house in order because he was going to die. Hezekiah turned his face to the wall and prayed to the Lord. "Remember, O Lord, how I have walked before you with wholehearted devotion and have done what is good in your eyes." Then he wept bitterly.

Then God spoke to Isaiah saying, "Go and tell Hezekiah, I have heard your prayer and seen your tears. I will add fifteen years to your life." Then Isaiah said, "This is the Lord's sign to you that he will do what he has promised: ' I will make the shadow cast by the sun go back the ten steps it has gone down on the stairway of Ahaz.'" So the sunlight went back the ten steps it had gone down.

After Hezekiah was well again, the king of Babylon sent a letter and a gift to Hezekiah because he had heard of his illness and recovery. Hezekiah gladly receives him and his envoy to visit the palace. He showed the envoy the entire palace and all his storehouse of treasures.

After they left, Isaiah came to Hezekiah and asked what he had shown them and when he told him he had shown them everything, Isaiah prophesied to the king saying, "Hear the word of the Lord Almighty. The time will surely come when everything in your palace and all that your fathers have stored up until this day will be carried off to Babylon. Nothing will be left, says the Lord. And some of your descendants, your own flesh and blood who will be born to you, will be taken away, and they will become eunuchs in the palace of the king of Babylon."

We know that is exactly what happened, but Isaiah was not only a prophet of doom but was known as a prophet of hope. We see him give great comfort in chapter forty. It is a beautiful prophecy of the faithfulness and power of God. It is well worth taking the time to read it now and be strengthened in your faith as you hear Isaiah tell of the all-powerful God we serve.

One of my favorite parts of the chapter is found in verse 29, "To whom will you compare me? Or who is my equal?" says the Holy One. "Lift your eyes and look to the heavens: Who created all these? He who brings out the starry host one by one, and calls them by name because of his great power and mighty strength, not one of them is missing."

Have you ever thought about the fact that God has a name for every star and knows just where each one is it at all times? This gives us just a glimpse of the almighty God who likewise knows how many hairs are on our heads at any given time. Jesus tells us that in Matthew 10:30, "And even the very hairs of your head are all numbered. So don't be afraid, you are worth more than many sparrows." He was just talking about how valuable even a little sparrow is in the verse before.

During the time of King Ahaz, the king of Syria and the king of Israel were planning an attack on Judah. The Lord told King Ahaz to ask for a sign to calm his fears. He refused, saying he would not put the Lord to the test. Then Isaiah said, "Hear now, you house of David! Is it not enough to try the patience of men? Will you try the patience of my God also? Therefore the Lord himself will give you a sign: The virgin will be with child and will give birth to a son, and will call him Immanuel. He will eat curds and honey when he knows enough to reject the wrong and choose the right. But before the boy knows enough to reject the wrong and choose the right, the land of the two kings you dread will be laid to waste."

Isaiah was again giving a glimpse of hope by prophesying the future coming of the Messiah who would bring light into a world that would seem to be in utter darkness. The familiar passage we read at Christmas each year was from the lips of Isaiah, "For to us a child is born, to us a son is given, and the government will be on his shoulders. He will be called Wonderful Counselor, Mighty God, Everlasting Father, Prince of Peace."

Later on, in chapter 40, he tells us, "The Lord is an everlasting God, the Creator of the ends of the earth. He will not grow tired or weary, and his understanding no one can fathom. He gives strength to the weary and increases the power of the weak. Even youths grow tired and weary, and young men stumble and fall, but those who hope in the Lord will renew their strength. They will soar on wings like eagles; they will walk and not be faint." Such a beautiful description of our God and his unbelievable love for us!

Discussion Questions:

1. How can we learn from Jonah's disobedience?

2. Isaiah tells us that God knows the name of every star in heaven. If God knows the names of the stars, do you have any doubt that he knows your name and the things that concern you? How does this encourage your faith?

3. What three things stood out to you in this lesson?

Lesson 29
Jeremiah 1-52
Jeremiah

We saw in our last lesson that Isaiah was prophesying about the destruction of Judah. *Jeremiah* lived about one hundred years after Isaiah.

While we saw Isaiah saving Jerusalem from Assyria, we see Jeremiah trying to save it from Babylon. Jeremiah repeatedly warned the king and predicted the kingdom's coming doom. He also foretold that the period of captivity would be seventy years (Jeremiah 25:11).

His call to be a prophet is found in Jeremiah 1:4 and is a beautiful and familiar theme we find in many other people God called for a particular time and purpose. "Before I formed you in the womb I knew you, before you were born I set you apart; I appointed you as a prophet to the nations."

Jeremiah responded, "Ah, Sovereign Lord, I do not know how to speak, I am only a child." The Lord said to him, "Do not say, I am only a child, you must go to everyone I send you to and say whatever I command you. Do not be afraid of them, for I am with you and will rescue you."

Then the Lord reached out his hand and touched his mouth and said to him, "Now, I have put my words in your mouth. See today I appoint you over nations and kingdoms to uproot and tear down, to destroy and overthrow, to build and to plant."

Then he told him of his plan to allow Jerusalem to be overtaken by Babylon if they did not repent and turn from their evil ways. He warned him that the kings would not receive him but he gave him a new identity and confidence by telling him, "I have made you a fortified city, an iron pillar and a bronze wall to stand against the whole land against the kings of Judah, its officials, its priests and the people of the land. They will fight against you but will not overcome you, for I am with you and will rescue you."

With this assurance, Jeremiah started prophesying to Jerusalem obeying the Word of the Lord, "They have forsaken me, the spring of living water, and have dug their own cisterns, broken down cisterns that will not hold water."

You can hear the sadness in the heart of the Lord that his people have deserted him. "I had planted you like a choice vine of sound and reliable stock. How then did you turn against me into a corrupt, wild vine? Although you wash yourself with soda and use an abundance of soap, the stain of your guilt is still before me," declares the Lord.

"Does a maiden forget her jewelry, a bride her wedding ornaments? Yet my people have forgotten me, days without number."

Then the Lord completes his sadness in Jeremiah 3:19, "How gladly would I treat you like sons and give you a desirable land, the most beautiful inheritance of any nation. I thought you would call me Father and not turn away from following me. But like a woman unfaithful to her husband, so you have been unfaithful to me, O house of Israel."

This is the message Jeremiah was prophesying to bring Jerusalem back to God to be spared being taken captive.

Although God was showing his disappointment and sadness because the people had forsaken Him, He always gives hope and in Jeremiah 17:7, He expresses that. "Blessed is the man who trusts in the Lord, whose confidence is in him. He will be like a tree planted by the water that sends out its roots by the stream. It does not fear when heat comes, its leaves are always green. It has no worries in a year of drought and never fails to bear fruit."

Perhaps the most famous prophecy given by Jeremiah is found in chapter 18. This is the word that came to Jeremiah from the Lord. "Go down to the potter's house and there I will give you my message." So I went down to the potter's house, and I saw him working at the wheel. But the pot he was shaping from the clay was marred in his hands, so the potter formed it into another pot, shaping it as seemed best to him.

Then the Word of the Lord came to me: 'O house of Israel, can I not do with you as this potter does? Like clay in the hands of the potter, so are you in my hands house of Israel. If at any time I announce that nation or kingdom is to be uprooted, torn down and destroyed, and if that nation repents of its evil, then I will relent and not inflict on it the disaster I had planned."

Even though they did not repent, and it was prophesied that they would be taken captive for seventy years, the Lord gave a prophecy of hope for their future. Jeremiah 29:10-11, "When seventy years are completed for Babylon, I will come to you and fulfill my gracious promise to bring you back to this place. For I know the plans I have for you," declares the Lord, "plans to prosper you and not to harm you, plans to give hope and a future."

It would be during these seventy years of Babylonian captivity that events now so familiar to us such as Daniel in the lion's den, the story of Queen Esther, Nebuchadnezzar's forgotten dream, the handwriting on the wall, and the fall of Babylon made spiritual history.

Like Isaiah, Jeremiah gives a glimpse of the future coming of Jesus. Chapter 23, "The days are coming," declares the Lord, "When I will raise up to David a righteous branch, a King who will reign wisely and do what is just and right in the land. In his days Judah will be saved and Israel will live in safety. This is the name by which he will be called: The Lord of Our Righteousness."

Jeremiah was sometimes known as the weeping prophet because of his sorrow for what was to come to Judah. He moved about them day and night begging, pleading, and trying to persuade them to turn to the Lord and repent. He tells us in chapter 9, "Oh, that my head were a spring of water and my eyes a fountain of tears! I would weep day and night for the slain of my people." An entire book of the Bible is devoted to his lamentations during this time. The book Lamentations is a funeral song because Jeremiah was grieving over the death of Jerusalem.

Unlike Isaiah and Hosea who were married, the Lord instructed Jeremiah to not marry. Chapter 16 says, "Then the Word of the Lord came to me: 'You must not marry and have sons and daughters in this place.'" The reason given him was that the impending doom that was to come would not be fair to his children. He said they would die of deadly diseases or perish by sword or famine.

Jeremiah was bold enough to wear a yoke around his neck like that of oxen and march around the city saying that Babylon would put a similar yoke on them if they did not repent. He was put in prison for presenting the message given to him.

After 23 years of prophesying, Jeremiah was instructed to gather the people together and write a book that could be read to everyone and be preserved. It took a year to write and it made a profound impression on some of the princes, but the king defiantly burned it. Jeremiah, with a spirit of determination to be obedient to the Lord, wrote it again.

The place and manner of Jeremiah's death are not known. One tradition has it that he was stoned to death in Egypt. It is thought that he fled to Egypt with a remnant to avoid being taken captive. Whatever the case, his life taught us many lessons on obedience and God's incredible love for us.

Discussion Questions:

1. Can you identify with the feeling of unworthiness that Jeremiah felt when he was called upon to be an ambassador for God? I love the fact that God changed his idea of himself as just a child to being a fortified city, iron pillar and bronze wall. What insecurities do you have that you might respond with when called upon to serve him?

2. As you think back over Jeremiah's life, what lesson can we learn from the visit to the potter's house?

3. Jeremiah 17:7 tells us we are like a tree planted by the water when we trust in the Lord. What does that mean to you in your walk with Him?

Lesson 30
Ezekiel 1-48, Daniel 1-12
Ezekiel / Daniel

Ezekiel was a prophet of the captivity. He was carried to Babylon in 595 BC, eleven years before Jerusalem was destroyed. The name Ezekiel means, "God is strong." He was born in 623 BC to a priestly family and grew up in the surroundings of the temple in Jerusalem. In 597 BC he was included in the exile to Babylon. Four years later he was called by God to be a prophet to those that had been taken into captivity.

During the first part of his ministry, Ezekiel proclaimed basically the same message given by Jeremiah, that Jerusalem and the temple were doomed to destruction because of the sinfulness and idolatry of the people.

After the news reached Babylon that Jerusalem had been destroyed, Ezekiel proclaimed a new message that was one of hope and restoration. He told the people that God would gather the Israelites from the ends of the earth and re-establish them in their own land. The nations who challenged Israel's return would be defeated and judged.

Ezekiel seemed to be explaining the actions of God in causing or permitting Israel's captivity. Although other nations who had committed abominations against God had been destroyed, Israel would be restored and by their punishment would come to know that their God is the only God. Coming to understand this seemed to have cured them of their idolatry. Up until then, they had continued to worship other gods but from that day until this, they have not practiced idolatry.

When God called Ezekiel, he called him "Son of man" and referred to him as such ninety different times. Interestingly it is the name Jesus called himself.

He was warned at the beginning that he was being called to a life of hardship and persecution. As a symbol of identification with the plight of the city and those being taken captive, he imposed an act of famine. Ezekiel lived on loathsome bread. Throughout the siege, he lay on one side, either continuously or for the greater part of each day. It was a time of famine in the land, and his diet meant great discomfort.

After the seized ended, as a symbol of the fate of Jerusalem's inhabitants, he shaved off his hair, burned part of it and scattered the rest into the wind.

Ezekiel was given great prophetic visions and at one point was transported, in rapture to Jerusalem to see the idolatries being practiced in the temple.

The Lord went to great extremes with Ezekiel to get his point across to the people. In chapter 24, the Word of the Lord came to him: "Son of man, with one blow I am about to take away from you the delight of your eyes. Yet do not lament or weep or shed any tears. Groan quietly; do not mourn for the dead. Keep your turban fastened and your sandals on your feet; do not cover the lower part of your face or eat the customary food of mourners."

So he spoke to the people in the morning, and in the evening his wife died. The next morning, he did as he was commanded. The people asked what this had to do with them and Ezekiel replied, "The Lord says he is about to desecrate my sanctuary - the stronghold in which you take pride, the delight of your eyes, the object of your affection. The sons and daughters you left behind will fall by the sword. And you will do as I have done. You will not cover the lower part of your face or eat the food of the mourners. You will not mourn or weep, but groan among yourselves. Ezekiel will be a sign to you; you will do just as he has done. When this happens, you will know that I am the Lord."

Ezekiel's visions were colorful and relevant. They included a parable of the vine, which was a tree showing that in the state Israel was in, they were useless for fruit or as wood. They were fit only for fuel, so Jerusalem was useful for nothing but burning. This is found in chapter 15.

The allegory of the unfaithful wife shows how Israel was the beloved of her husband, who made her a queen, and lavished upon her silks and every beautiful thing. She then made herself a prostitute to every man who came by. This is found in chapter 16.

In the *parable of the two eagles,* the first was the king of Babylon who carried off some of the nobility and would be punished. The other was the king of Egypt. In this prophecy, he speaks of a twig being taken and planted to restore the house of David. That was fulfilled in Jesus.

A boiling cauldron symbolizes the destruction of Jerusalem found in chapter 24.

The shepherds and sheep accuse the shepherds of Israel who only took care of themselves and did not look after their sheep. Then he gives a beautiful description of himself as a shepherd. Ezekiel 34:11-16, "I myself will search for my sheep and look after them. As a shepherd looks after his scattered flock when he is with them, so will I look after my sheep. I will rescue them from all the places where they were scattered on a day of clouds and darkness. I will bring them out from the nations and gather them from the countries, and I will bring them into their own land. I will pasture them on the mountains of Israel. I will tend them in a good pasture, and the mountain heights of Israel will be their grazing land. They will lie down in good grazing land, and there they will feed in a rich pasture of the mountains of Israel. I myself will tend my sheep and have them lie down, declares the Lord. I will search for the lost and bring back the strays. I will bind up the injured and strengthen the weak." This reminds me of the 23rd Psalm.

The vision of dry bones was a prediction of scattered Israel. It showed a return to their land, and the re-uniting of Judah and Israel under the reign of an everlasting king found in chapter 37.

Then during Passover, 14 years after the destruction of Jerusalem, Ezekiel received his second vision-journey to Jerusalem, 19 years after he was transported to Jerusalem. He said the Lord set him on a high mountain and told him to pay attention to everything his eyes would see and ears would hear. The vision was of the rebuilding of the temple with exact measurements and very similar to the Temple of David. It is thought to be a prophecy of the Messianic Age. Many have studied Ezekiel to look for signs of the second coming of the Lord. After he gave the description of the temple and the other details to be put in place, he told us that the glory of the Lord filled it, and the Lord told him that he would remain there with the house of Israel forever.

One thing that the Lord told Ezekiel was that the Eastern gate was to be shut on the six working days, but on the Sabbath day and on the day of the New Moon it was to be opened. The prince is to enter from the outside through the portico of the gateway and stand by the gatepost. This was to be a prophecy of the second coming of the Lord. Having been to Jerusalem many times, it is interesting to see all the gates surrounding the city open except the Eastern gate that is closed with blocks and mortar. Many are also researching the significance of the new moon in the anticipation of the second coming of the Lord. These are very interesting days to be alive as so many of the prophecies are being fulfilled.

God sent Ezekiel and the other prophets to help prepare his people of the coming events and to warn them of the consequences of their disobedience. At the same time, God rose up those to take a stand of faith to fulfill his plan.

Daniel was another prophet who was taken into captivity in 606 BC when Nebuchandezar of Babylon was king. The king took some of the temple vessels and chose a company of certain captives. Those included several of the young and godly princes, among them, were Daniel and the three Hebrew children whose names were later changed to Shadrach, Meshach, and Abendnego.

The king instructed the chief of his council to teach the young men the language and literature of the Babylonians. He assigned them the best of food and wine from his own kitchen during a three-year training period. They were being trained to serve in the king's palace.

Daniel, knowing the food he was given had probably been sacrificed to idols, refused to eat the extravagant meals put before him. When he asked permission to not eat it, the superintendent replied that he was afraid he would grow pale and thin and the king would behead him for allowing that to happen.

Daniel suggested that they be given a ten-day diet of only vegetables and water and at the end of the ten days he would compare them to the others who had eaten the rich food from the king's table.

He agreed and at the end of the ten days, Daniel and his three friends looked healthier and better nourished than the young men eating from the king's table. So they were allowed to eat a diet of vegetables and water from then on.

God gave these four young men great abilities to learn and they soon mastered the literature and science of the time. God gave Daniel a special ability in understanding the meaning of dreams and visions.

One-night King Nebuchadnezzar had a nightmare and awoke trembling with fear. To make matters worse, he could not remember his dream! He immediately called in his magicians, sorcerers, and astrologers, and demanded that they tell him what his dream was. He told them that if they would not tell him what it means, he would have them torn from limb to limb and their houses would become heaps of rubble! But if they could give him the answer, they would receive wonderful gifts and honors.

They replied, "How can we tell you what it means if you don't remember the dream?" The king was furious and told them they were stalling for time and hoping the calamity that the dream foretold would happen to him. They told him, "There is not a man alive who can tell you what you dreamed and not a king in the world that would ask such a thing. Only the gods can tell you your dream and they are not here to help."

The king ordered them to execute all the wise men of Babylon, and Daniel and his three friends were rounded up with the others to be killed. When the executioner came to kill them Daniel asked, "Why is the king so angry?' When he was told what had happened, he asked to see the king.

Daniel went home and told his three friends, and they began to pray for God to reveal this secret so they would not die. God heard their prayers and that night revealed to Daniel the dream of the king. Then he asked the steward to take him to the king. The steward told the king that one of his Hebrew captives said he could interpret his dream. The king called for Daniel and asked if it was true, and Daniel replied, "No wise man, astrologer, magician or wizard can tell the king such things, but there is a God in Heaven who reveals secrets, and he has told you in your dream what will happen in the future."

Then Daniel told the king his dream. "You saw a huge and powerful statue of a man, shining brilliantly, frightening and terrible. The head of the statue was made of purest gold, its chest and arms were made of silver, and its belly and thighs of brass, its legs of iron, its feet of part iron and part clay. But as you watched, a rock was cut from the mountainside by supernatural means. It came hurtling toward the statue and crushed the feet of iron and clay, smashing them to bits. Then the whole statue collapsed into a heap of iron, clay, brass, silver, and gold, its pieces were crushed as small as chaff, and the wind blew them all away. But the rock that knocked the statue down became a great mountain that covered the whole earth"

Then Daniel said to the King, "Your Majesty, you are a king over many kings, for the God of heaven has given you your kingdom, power, and glory. You rule the farthest provinces; you are that head of gold. But after your kingdom has come to an end, another world power will arise and take your place. This empire will be inferior to yours. After that kingdom has fallen, yet a third great power will be represented by the bronze belly of the statue will rise to rule the world. Following that the fourth kingdom will be strong as iron smashing, bruising and conquering. The feet and toes you saw-part iron and part clay-show that later on this kingdom will be divided. Some parts of it will be strong as iron and some as weak as clay. This mixture shows that these kingdoms will try to strengthen themselves by forming an alliance with each other, but this will not succeed because iron and clay do not mix."

He went on, "During the reigns of those kings, the God of heaven will set up a kingdom that will never be destroyed, and no one will ever conquer it. It will shatter all these kingdoms into nothingness, but it shall stand forever, indestructible. That is the meaning of the rock cut from the mountain without human hands. Thus the great God has shown what will happen in the future, and this interpretation of your dream is as certain as my description of it."

Nebuchadnezzar fell to the ground before Daniel and worshiped him, and commanded his people to offer sacrifices before him. "Truly Daniel," the king said, "Your God is the God of gods, ruler of kings, the revealer of mysteries because he has told you this secret."

The king made Daniel very great and gave him expensive gifts and appointed him ruler over the whole province of Babylon and made him ruler over all the wise men. Daniel asked the king for permission to take Shadrach, Meshach, and Abednego as his assistants.

At one point during the time Daniel was serving the king in the palace, Nebuchadnezzar made an image of gold ninety feet high and nine feet wide and set it upon a plain and gave orders for all in his service to bow down and worship it at the sound of the horn. He gave the proclamation that anyone who disobeyed his orders would be thrown into a blazing furnace.

At the sound of the horn, all bowed down except the three Hebrews; Shadrach, Meshach, and Abednego. The king was told of this and was furious with rage. He summoned them and asked if it was true and gave them another chance to fall down and worship the golden image. He warned them that if not they would be thrown into the blazing furnace and burned to death. They told the king, "We are not worried about that because our God is able to deliver us, but if He doesn't we will never under any circumstances serve your God or bow down to your golden image."

The king became furious and commanded that the furnace be heated seven times hotter than usual. Then he had them bound and thrown into the fire. The flames were so intense, they killed even the soldiers who threw them in the fire.

Then the best part of all: Nebuchadnezzar watched and said to his advisors, "Didn't we throw three men into the furnace?" They assured him they did. He said, "But I see four men unbound, walking around in the fire, and the fourth looks like a god!" He yelled down to the three to come out. As all watched, they came out unburned and did not even have the smell of smoke on their bodies.

Then Nebuchadnezzar said "Blessed is the God of Shadrach, Meshach, and Abednego, for he sent his angel to deliver his servants when they were willing to die, rather than serve any god except their own. Therefore I have made a decree that any person, nation, or religion speaks against the God of Shadrach, Meshach, and Abednego will be torn from limb to limb. For no other God could do what he did." Then he gave them a promotion and they prospered greatly after that in his service.

Meantime Daniel was summoned after the king had another troubling dream. In his dream, a very tall tree grew taller and taller until it was so high everyone in the world could see it. It was full of fruit and animals rested under it. Then an angel came and shouted to cut down the tree, scatter its branches, but leave the stump and roots in the ground barred by iron and brass. Let the dew of heaven drench him and let him eat grass with the animals for seven years."

Daniel sat silent for an hour and finally told the king, "Oh that the events foretold in his dream would happen to your enemies and not to you." He explained that he was the tree and that he would be cut down for seven years and live as an animal in the fields. Twelve months after the dream, it became a reality.

Belshazzar became king and at one point had invited a thousand of his officers to a great feast where the wine flowed freely. He ordered the sacred cups that had been taken from the temple in Jerusalem to be brought to him. He along with his wives, concubines, and princes began to drink a toast from them. Suddenly they saw a finger of a man's handwriting in the plaster of the wall. The king became so fearful his knees were knocking. He screamed for the magicians and astrologers to be brought to him to tell him what the writing said. None of them could understand it. He became hysterical and his stewards told him to calm down that there was a man in the kingdom with the spirit of God in him and told him how he had interpreted the dreams of King Nebuchadnezzar.

He sent for Daniel and told him that if he could tell him what this meant he would make him the third ruler over the kingdom. Daniel told him and warned him of following in the footsteps of his predecessor. Afterward, Daniel was given a purple robe and a golden chain announcing his new authority in the kingdom. That very night Belshazzar was killed and Darius came to the throne.

Darius divided the kingdom into 120 provinces and placed a governor over each one, of which Daniel was one. Daniel proved himself more capable than the others and the king began considering making him over the others. This made the other governors jealous and they began a plot to destroy him. They got together and took a decree for the king to sign saying that any man who asks a favor of their god or prayed for the next thirty days would be thrown to the lions. They coaxed the king to sign it and to be sure it was irrevocable.

Daniel knew about it but went home and knelt as usual in his bedroom, with its windows open toward Jerusalem and prayed three times a day, just as he always had. His enemies watched and when they saw him praying they rushed to the king and told him. The king was furious that he had signed the law, but they reminded him that it was irrevocable.

The king gave the order for Daniel to be thrown into the lions' den. He said to Daniel, "May your God whom you worship continually deliver you." After Daniel was bound and thrown into the den with the lions, the king returned to the palace and went to bed without dinner. He didn't sleep all night. Very early the next morning he rushed to the lions' den and called, "Daniel, servant of the living God, was your God able to deliver you from the lions?"

Daniel called back to him, "Your Majesty, my God has sent his angel to shut the lions' mouths so they can't touch me." The king had him lifted out of the den and sent for the men who had accused him and had them thrown into the den. The lions leaped upon them and tore them apart.

Afterward, Darius wrote this message to his empire: "Greetings, I decree that everyone shall fear the God of Daniel in every part of my kingdom. His God is the living, unchanging God whose kingdom shall never be destroyed and whose power shall never end."

Daniel went on to prophesy about the future coming events leading up to the end times. He said there will be a time of trouble like has never been seen and that many would run to and fro, and that knowledge shall be increased. Think of the problems we have seen in our lifetime, and how the internet has increased the knowledge of all ages beyond anything our ancestors could have even imagined. Daniel and the three Hebrews gave us a great example of faith in action.

Discussion Questions:

1. What lessons can we learn from Ezekiel and Daniel?

2. Do you think you would be able to continue to pray openly like Daniel even if it meant death?

3. Share a time you felt like you were in the fiery furnace and felt God was walking beside you.

Lesson 31
(Ezra 1-10, Nehemiah 1-14, Haggai 1-2, Zechariah 1-14, Malachi 1-4)
Haggai / Zechariah / Malachi

In our last lesson, we found Daniel winning great favor with King Nebuchadnezzar because of his ability to interpret his dream. He quickly rose to be third in command in the kingdom.

When the new ruler, Cyrus, came into power, Daniel met with him and asked about his future and the future of his people. He reminded him of a prophecy written more than 160 years before stating that "one who knew not God" would be the instrument for setting God's people (the Hebrews) free from their Babylonian captivity. Cyrus must have been startled to find himself mentioned by name in the old Hebrew scroll over a century before he was born. This is found in Isaiah 44:28, "That saith of Cyrus, he is my shepherd, and shall perform all my pleasures: even saying to Jerusalem thou shall be built, and to the temple, thy foundation shall be laid."

Daniel also showed him the fulfillment of the prophecy up until that time. Deeply moved by that evidence, Cyrus issued a proclamation: "Who is there among you of all his people? His God be with him, and let him go up to Jerusalem…and build the house of the Lord God of Israel…." He not only consented to their return but also provided them with money and material for the rebuilding of the Temple. He also gave them 5,400 gold and silver vessels that Nebuchadnezzar had taken from the temple when Jerusalem was destroyed. He made it a written decree that was known as the decree of Cyrus, which ended the period of captivity for the Hebrew nation.

The return was made in three expeditions. The first was led by Zerubbabel, a prince of Judah, and consisted of less than fifty thousand men, women, and children. Because the ones returning were from the tribe of Judah, they were called Jews and that name continues with the Hebrew people until this day. It took them four months to travel the seven hundred miles back to their homeland.

The work began, but the people who had settled there after the captivity of the tribes hindered the work. Their vindictiveness brought it to a halt, but after a period of sixteen years, the prophets Haggai and Zechariah stirred the people and obtained a confirmation of the decree of Cyrus, and the work was resumed. The fact that it was a written decree was of great importance at this time to convince the locals it had been ordered by the king. After four years of building, it was finally completed fulfilling the prophecy found in Isaiah 44:28.

The second expedition was led by Ezra, a scribe, about 78 years after Zerubbabel's return. He returned with a dedicated band of about six or seven thousand exiles. They carried a large number of gold and silver vessels belonging to the temple. After a long four-month journey, he was saddened to find that the ones who had come before and rebuilt the temple had "mingled their holy seed" with the old enemies of the land. After three months of appealing to the consciences of the people and praying and weeping before God, the people assembled and spiritual awakening and reformation of the returned Jews came about. Ezra is credited with re-establishing the laws of Moses and instilling an order of worship in the temple.

The third expedition was led by Nehemiah. It had now been 94 years since the first expedition had returned. Nehemiah had gotten word that although the temple was rebuilt, the walls of the city were still broken down and the gates that had been burned with fire had never been replaced, which left the city unprotected. This grieved him so much that he returned to oversee the rebuilding of the wall. Although he came against much opposition, he and his band of followers continued with enthusiasm, prayer, and faith, and finished the task in fifty-two days.

Together Ezra and Nehemiah labored. The forgotten Feast of Tabernacles was restored, the people separated themselves from their foreign and idolatrous entanglements, and they stood up when the book of the law was opened, marking a new reverence for the Word of God. They promised to not intermarry with unbelievers and not to buy and sell on the Sabbath. They promised to bring their tithe into the storehouse and not to forsake the house of God. With determined hearts, they renewed, signed and sealed the sure covenant. A spiritual awakening had once again come upon the children of Israel.

Nehemiah returned after twelve years to his home in Shushan. Not that long afterward he returned to find the people once again in spiritual chaos. The record ends with Nehemiah being "sorely grieved" and rebuking the people for violating the Sabbath, neglecting their tithes and forsaking the house of worship. They also had returned to their old sin of intermarriage with the heathen so that their children could not even speak the Hebrew language (Nehemiah 13:6-3).

This is the ending of the story of the return of the Jews to their land. The same pattern continued of turning from the Lord even after He had showered them with blessings and provisions. The prophets were God's mouthpieces to bring them through until the time of redemption.

During this time the prophets God sent to instruct and encourage his people were:
> Haggai
> Zechariah
> Malachi

Haggai was born in Babylon during the captivity and accompanied the returning remnant under Zerubbabel.

Zechariah also appears to have been one of the returning pilgrims with Zerubbabel; he was co-laborer with Haggai, exhorting, prophesying and encouraging the people in the work of restoration. Zechariah was sent to reprove the people for delaying to build the Temple. Malachi was sent to reprove them for neglecting it after it was built.

Zechariah prophesied about 520 B.C. His prophecies began two months after Haggai's first message. The people had just begun building the temple. His message was for them to listen to God's message through the prophets and to keep a close relationship with their God so there would be no further judgment.

His messages were followed by visions that offered encouragement to the builders at a time when they were ready to give up. He comforted them by telling them that God had a long-range plan for Israel. He also spoke about the coming Messiah, the last judgment and the final kingdom.

Malachi was sent to the Jews after they had completed the temple, but once again had turned away from obeying God. They were marrying foreign women and neglecting the act of worship. Malachi felt they were dishonoring to God and called for them to return to him before he called judgment on them. However, he gives great hope to those who revere and hold fast to their faith. I love the passage in Malachi 4:2, "But for you who revere my name, the son of righteousness will rise with healing in his wings. And you will go out and leap like calves released from the stall."

God also gives us a glimpse of his character in Malachi 3:1: "I the Lord do not change." That is reassuring to us as we base our faith and life on his Word. He is like an anchor in the water that we can always go to and not wonder if it has moved. We are all desperate for stability in our lives and this one quote from God should empower us to fully put our trust in Him in all things.

The next sentence in that passage shows us his redemptive love. "Ever since the time of your forefathers you have turned away from my decrees and have not kept them. Return to me and I will return to you," says the Lord Almighty.

Malachi chastises them by telling them that they have been robbing Him by not giving of their tithes and offerings. He basically tells them it is not about the money because God does not need their money. But he wants them to walk in obedience and allow God to shower them with blessings. He even goes so far as to suggest to them that they test the Lord. Malachi 3:10 says "Bring the whole tithe into the storehouse, that there may be food in my house. Test me in this, says the Lord Almighty, and see if I will not throw open the floodgates of heaven and pour out so much blessing that you will not have room enough for it. I will prevent pests from devouring your crops, and the vines in your fields will not cease their fruit… Then all the nations will call you blessed, for yours will be a delightful land,'" says the Lord Almighty.

God, like every parent, has a desire to bless his children with everything possible. But those blessings come with responsibility. The intent of any parent is to prepare their children to function well in the world. God set this pattern in place in the garden. Obey the rules, and life will go well for you. Rebel and disobey, and you will be punished. Not punished for the purpose of pain, but like the children of Israel, punishment is for the purpose of getting back on the right track to be in a place to have all God intended.

God has not changed, and his plan and rules of conduct are written in bold letters for us to follow. The promise is the same.

With these prophets, the Old Testament comes to close. It has laid out our creation, purpose, and fall from God's perfect plan. It reveals the heart of a loving father who immediately sets a plan in motion to redeem and win back the love and devotion of his creation.

The span of 4000 years covered in the Old Testament is a history of covenants, promises, and fulfillments, despite the rebellious nations and individuals God had to work through to bring about the crowning glory of what is next to come.

Discussion Questions:

1. Has the study of some of the Old Testament prophets helped you understand how God never left his children alone, even though many years of captivity?

2. As you look back over our study of the Old Testament, can you name some of the things that you have been particularly touched by and learned from? How has this study helped you have a better understanding of God and how he has always dealt with his people?

3. Compare the children of Israel and your life in your daily walk as you purpose to be obedient to God's laws. Can you see a comparison of your own struggle to be obedient?

Lesson 32
The Gap

As we ended the last lesson, the Jews were freed from captivity and returned to Jerusalem, rebuilding the temple and re-establishing an order of worship.

There is a great chasm of 400 years between the ending of the Old Testament writings and the beginning of the New Testament writings. During this time, there were no prophets or inspired writers among the Jews. Most of our knowledge of what took place during these centuries, of which the Bible is silent, is derived mainly from the Jewish historian Josephus, from parts of the Apocrypha, and from many Greek and Roman writers.

Great historical events took place during these 400-year span. Malachi closes with the world under Persian rule. Matthew opens with the world under Roman rule. Many things happened during this time in world history that affected the climate and culture of the beginning of the New Testament during the time of Christ.

During these 400 years, the Persian Empire of Malachi's day was overthrown by the Grecian Empire. The Greeks, in turn, were overthrown by the Roman conquerors. It was at this particular God-appointed time in world history that Christ and Christianity appeared.

To get a better understanding of the times, let's go back to the time of Malachi and what was taking place. At the end of the book of Malachi, we find the Jews restored to their homeland and practicing a period of peace. It was short-lived, and the Jews once again found themselves being persecuted by those who conquered them.

The climax came under the cruel invader named Antiochus Epiphanes. This tyrant invaded Jerusalem, slaughtered 40,000 Jews in three days, forced his way into the Holy of Holies, set up an idol altar and sacrificed a sow as a burnt offering. This was foretold in Daniel 1:31 when Daniel prophesied that armed men would come forth and pollute the sanctuary and set up "the abomination that maketh desolate."

It is important also because it is part of a future abomination that is described when the anti-Christ, of whom this blasphemous tyrant is a pre-figure, shall again desecrate the temple in the end times.

This is mentioned in the New Testament by our Lord as his disciples asked him what would be the sign of the end times, referring to Daniel's prophecy. He responded, "When, ye therefore, shall see the abomination of desolation, spoken of by Daniel the prophet, stand in the Holy Place."

Antichus Ephiphanes was so evil that the Jewish people he did not kill, he sold into slavery. He also made it his mission to destroy all known copies of scripture that could be found. He sent out a decree that anyone known to be in possession of a copy of the scriptures would be slaughtered. He resorted to every conceivable form of torture to force Jews to renounce their religion. This led to what is called the Maccabean revolt.

Infuriated at the attempt of Antiochus Epiphanes to destroy the Jews and their religion, a courageous priest, Mattathias Maccabee gathered a band of loyal Jews and started a revolt. He had five brave and warlike sons join him: Judas, Jonathan, Simon, John, and Eleazar were the valiant leaders of the great fight for Jewish independence.

In less than a year, the old warrior died, and his son Judas succeeded him in the struggle. Under his inspiring leadership, and restored faith in God, every army that was sent out against them was defeated, until at last, Judas Maccabee was successful in defeating the invaders and establishing independence for the long-oppressed Jews.

The Maccabean family governed for a period of one hundred years. They re-opened, cleansed, and re-dedicated the Temple, and some of the splendor of the old days of the kingdom was restored.

The Maccabean leadership, however, became selfish and ambitious. Greed for position and material things overcame their patriotism, and party divisions weakened their cause. It was this loss of loyalty that gave rise to two great parties of the New Testament history, the Pharisees, and Sadducees.

This is interesting as we approach the New Testament because much is said about these sects in the story of Jesus. It is interesting to learn how they came about and the role they played in New Testament history.

Let's look at the role they played. The Pharisees were a group formed after the Maccabean wars. During this period, the Greek dominion was strong, and the effort to dominate Jewish culture was strong. The rise of the Pharisees was a reaction and protest against this tendency among their fellow-countrymen. Their aim was to preserve their national integrity and strict conformity to the Mosaic Law.

They later developed into a self-righteous and hypocritical group. Jesus himself refers to this in Matthew 23: "Then Jesus says to his disciples, 'the teachers of the law and the Pharisees sit in Moses' seat. So you must obey them and do everything they tell you. But do not do what they do, for they do not practice what they preach.'" He goes on to outline their hypocrisy throughout the chapter.

In verse 27 of that chapter he sums it all up, "Woe to you, teachers of the law and Pharisees, you hypocrites! You are like whitewashed tombs, which look beautiful on the outside but on the inside, are full of dead men's bones and everything unclean. In the same way, on the outside you appear to people as righteous but on the inside you are full of hypocrisy and wickedness."

The Sadducees were a sect that originated about the same time and unlike the Pharisees, they were in favor of adopting the Greek custom. They took no part in the Maccabean struggle for their nation's liberty. They were a priestly clique, and though they were the religious officials of their nation, they were themselves irreligious. They were not numerous but were wealthy and influential. To a great extent, they controlled the Sanhedrin. The Sanhedrin was the recognized headship of the Jewish people that continued during the time of Christ.

The successors of Antiochus continued the fight against Jewish dominion. They continued to invade the land with a large army determined to destroy the Jews. Finally, after hardship, discouragement, and confusion, Judas Maccabee made an alliance with Rome. Rome was fast becoming a dominant world power, and although the alliance seemed likely to ensure peace for Israel, the Jews were destined to find Rome, to be a persecutor beyond them all.

The end of the struggle came when the Roman army under Pompey besieged the city, storming the walls, utterly destroying the temple, and ruthlessly slaying all the young and old. Henceforth, Judea was declared a Roman Province.

Julius Caesar followed Pompey. Caesar appointed Antipator as ruler over Judea. Antipator appointed his two sons to authority, Phasel over Galilee and Herod over Jerusalem. Herod was about twenty years of age when his father appointed him governor over Judea, and after a few years of cruel events, he was appointed king of Judea and the Jews. It was during his notorious reign that Jesus was born.

There were now three great national groups involved in world affairs: the Romans, the Greeks, and the Jew. They were each in their own way preparing the world for the planting of the Gospel seed in the hearts of men everywhere.

First, the rise and worldwide influence of the Grecian Empire gave the world a universally understood language; the Greek tongue becoming generally known throughout the world. Thus, the New Testament scripture was written in Greek.

Secondly, the rise of the Roman Empire, which established political and judicial unity in its far-reaching dominion, built magnificent roads, making all of the territories of their conquest accessible. It was a great contributing factor in preparing the world to hear and to receive the message of the coming of the Messiah. On the same roads that carried marching armies and banners of world-dominion, there followed, in God's appointed time, the marching arm of Christian witnesses.

With this, we bring a close to the study of the Old Testament and the 400-year-span between the end of Malachi and the beginning of Matthew, which begins the story of the long-awaited Messiah to finally redeem the Jewish people and bring them back into an intimate relationship with God.

The Old Testament was the preparation of what was about to happen. Hardship, trials, and suffering prepared the way for the Messiah. Sadly, the Jews did not recognize him. The gospel of Jesus has been preached and will continue until he returns again for his church (the bride) to live eternally with him in oneness of spirit as the Father intended from the beginning.

I personally do not think it is possible to truly understand and appreciate the story of redemption in the New Testament without the background, history and understanding the Old Testament gives us. Now as we look to the New Testament, we will find the beginning of a new era with the birth of Christ and the early days of the church.

Discussion Questions:

1. Why do you think there seems to be 400-year silence between the Old and New Testament? What are some of the significant things that took place during this time?

2. What were the three national groups involved in world affairs at the end of the 400-year gap? What role did each of them play in preparing for Jesus' birth and the gospel to be spread?

3. We read in this lesson that the Pharisees were compared to whitewashed tombs. What practice did they have that caused them to get this name? Have you observed whitewashed tomb Christians in the world today? Explain.

New Testament

Birth of Jesus
^
Escape to Egypt
^
Growing up in Nazareth
^
Age 12 went to Temple
^
Baptized by John the Baptist age 30
^
Tempted in Dessert by Devil
^
Called Disciples
^
Worked miracles-Healed sick-Cast out demons-Raised the dead
^
Preached in Synagogues, Sea of Galilee, Mt. of Beatitudes
^
Taught Disciples The Lord's Prayer, Principles of Kingdom of God
^
Leaders plot to kill him/ Entered Jerusalem on a donkey
^
Last Supper with Disciples
^
Garden of Gethsemane/ Betrayal by Judas/Crucifixion
^
3 Days in Hell/Resurrection/40 Days on Earth
^
120 in Upper Room receive Holy Spirit/Birth of Church
^
Prophesies Fulfilled/Antichrist/Battle of Armageddon
^
Jesus Returns/ Satan Bound/Christ Reigns on Earth

Lesson 33
Luke 1
New Testament

Last time we talked about the 400-year gap between the Old Testament and the New Testament. Remember the word testament means sharing of details of an event or events. We testify in court to tell what happened in a particular situation. When someone dies, they leave their last will and testament. Webster defines testament or testify as:

> *1. Part relating to one's personal property.*
> *2. Something that serves as a sign and evidence of fact or events.*
> *3. From the original English translated from Latin; a covenant or dispensation.*

Looking at these definitions, it is easy to see how all three speak of what the Old Testament and New Testaments are about.

1. *Relating to one's property*: This is in fact what the entire Bible is about as we talked about at the beginning of this study. We are the creation and property of God. The entire Old Testament is the extent He was willing to go to reclaim His property that had been taken from Him.
2. *Something that serves as a sign and evidence of fact or events*: This is the entire story of the Old Testament; telling the story of the facts and events that took place. All of the prophecies we have read about were for evidence for those to come and be able to see God had put this entire plan in place. He had it recorded so there would be no question of its validity and that it was from Him.
3. *Covenant or dispensation*: We have studied about how the entire plan of the Bible is about how the Bible is a history of the covenant God made with man to redeem or restore him back to a oneness with himself. He made specific covenants with Adam, Abraham, etc. to bring about His plan.

I point this out as it is so important to keep in mind the big picture, and to break down words that we don't often use (like testament) can help us keep that in mind.

It is important to remember that the Old and the New Testament are not separate, opposing books: they both are about redemption and a Savior who is the Alpha and Omega, the Beginning and the End. As stated before, "The Old Testament is the New Testament concealed, and the New Testament is the Old Testament revealed."

The Old Testament dealt almost exclusively with Israel. This was the preparation stage, but now we are coming to the climax of the story. The Jews were the people set apart to bring about this coup, but now the New Testament is about sharing the news of what was to take place with all mankind because of it.

There were four distinctively different thoughts and influences in the known world at this time; the Roman, the Jew, the Greek, and those who were embracing the Christian faith, or (those who were following this new Messiah who had been presented to the world.) They each had their views of the ills of the world, but neither the power of the Romans, the culture of the Greeks, nor the Rabbinical Law of the Jews, satisfied the heart. The world was ready for its Spiritual King.

The Jews were looking for a long-promised Deliverer down through the ages as we saw in the pages of the Old Testament study. Now that He has arrived, the rulers among the Jews refused to accept Him largely because both He and the method of his coming were extremely different from their traditional ideas of what the Messiah was to be.

This brings us to the opening pages of the New Testament.

It starts with four gospels. The word gospel means good news. The good news is that the Savior of the world had finally arrived. You may ask why four and not just one account of His arrival. You know if you ask four people about a vacation they had all been on together, you would get four different perspectives. Because of hearing the story from four different people, you would get a more complete picture of the details of the trip. They would all be true and detailed but from the perspective, of the one who drew out the things that they felt were important. The same is true of Matthew, Mark, Luke, and John.

Although presenting an all-sufficient Savior and a complete plan of truth to a sinful world, Matthew's gospel is written primarily to convince the Jews that Jesus of Nazareth is the Messiah, the King of Israel, promised in their Old Testament scriptures. The writer uses about sixty references to Jewish prophecies and traces the genealogy of Jesus back through David to Abraham. The Jews would consider no one claiming the throne of Israel outside of "the Covenant line of Promise" given to their father, Abraham.

The message of Mark was primarily written to converts from among both Romans and Greeks. He gives no genealogy of Jesus; for it would be of little importance to prospective Gentile converts. He explains the Hebrew and Aramaic names and customs, which would have been familiar to Jews. The Gentile converts would not be interested in Jewish prophecies but in the immediate claims of Christ; therefore, Mark stresses the "doings" of Jesus more than the "sayings." For instance, he records nineteen miracles while only four parables.

The message of Luke, although written to both Jew and Gentile, undoubtedly has the Greek primarily in mind. Power and authority was the ideology of the Romans, but to the Greek, culture was pre-eminent. The Greek philosophy was to elevate and perfect humanity by culture, wisdom, and beauty. Therefore, Luke presents Jesus as the embodiment of perfection as "Son of Man" and "the Son of God" who was interested in all men, both the cultured and the uncultured. Luke traces the genealogy of Jesus back to Adam, the progenitor of the whole race of which Jesus is the perfect Savior who has come to seek and save those who are lost.

The message of John is for all. The genealogy of Jesus is traced immediately to God. John's gospel is the gospel of eternity. It begins with the mystery of the new birth and has as its focus the fact that all must believe that Jesus is the Christ, the Son of God and that if we believe in Him, we have life eternal through his name. This means that when we accept that Jesus is the Messiah and that he came and died in our place, that we now can use his name as being part of his family.

When I married my husband, I took his name and from that point on, everything I did was a reflection of his family. If I was hanging off a bar stool drunk as can be and someone who recognized me came along, they might say, "isn't that Ronnie's wife?" I was no longer just an individual; I belonged to him and carried his name. I also carried the burdens and responsibilities that came with being a part of his family, as well as, the inheritance and blessings. Ronnie and I entered into a covenant to share one another's burdens and reap the benefits of our union. Remember the marriage vows, "for better or worse, richer or poor?" The difference in our covenant with Jesus is that it is all better and there is no worse. We are instantly made richer in the spiritual realm where it counts. That emptiness in our heart is filled with his love and we are restored to the relationship we were created to have with our father from the beginning. It seems that John is all about the restoration of this relationship.

Let's look at the authors of the gospels. One thing I love is the fact that God used ordinary people like me to share His story. Matthew was a publican, Luke a physician and John a fisherman. It is not stated what Mark's profession was. Matthew and John were companions of Jesus. Mark was a companion of Peter. His gospel tells what he had heard Peter say over and over again.

Luke was a companion of Paul. His gospel contained what he had heard Paul preach from one end of the Roman Empire to the other, verified by his own investigations.

We see this in Luke 1:1-4, "Many have undertaken to draw up an account of the things that have been fulfilled among us, just as they were handed down to us by those who from the first were eyewitnesses and servants of the Word. Therefore, since I have carefully investigated everything from the beginning, it seemed good also to me to write an orderly account for you, so that you may know the certainty of the things you have been taught."

They all told the same story. They traveled far and wide. They often went together. John and Peter were intimate companions. Mark was associated with both Peter and Paul. Luke and Mark were in Rome together between 61 A.D. and 63 A.D. (Colossians 4:10, 14).

We don't know if they made many copies of the gospels for different churches or individuals, or if they were a collection of writings of the apostles and their helpers recounting stories they had heard about Jesus. But we do know that God in his providence watched over and preserved the writings as being sufficient to convey his Word to all future generations.

Both Luke and Matthew give the genealogy of the Messiah. Interesting, Matthew goes back to Abraham and Luke to Adam. The commonly accepted view is that Matthew gives Joseph's line showing Jesus to be the legal heir to the promise going back to Abraham and David, while Luke focuses on Mary's line showing legitimate blood descent as talked about in Romans 1:3, "Son of David according to the flesh."

It is not clear about the father of Joseph as it is contradicted in Matthew and Luke. Matthew states in the genealogy, "and Jacob, father of Joseph the husband of Mary, of whom was born Jesus, who is called Christ." This would lead you to believe Jacob would be the father of Joseph.

However; in Luke 3:23 we read, "Now Jesus himself was about thirty years old when he began his ministry. He was the son, so it was thought, of Joseph, the son of Heli." My personal opinion is that because it says "so it was thought" coupled with the fact that Luke is establishing the bloodline of Mary, that Joseph is referred to here as Heli's son but actually he was his son-in-law. You could also put in the phrase, "as far as anyone knew, Joseph was his father. Mary's father's name is not given anywhere else in the Bible.

Now to start the story of the life of Jesus, we have to go to the story about Elizabeth and Zachariah. This is because we often think of God sending an angel to Mary, but before that ever happened, God was preparing one to come before him, an advance man if you will, to prepare the way for people to receive him. It too is a story of a miraculous birth.

Zechariah was a Jewish priest when Herod was king of Judea. He and his wife, Elizabeth, were both descendants of Aaron. They were careful to obey God's law in spirit as well as to the letter. They had no children, for Elizabeth was barren, and now they were both very old.

One day Zechariah was going about his work in the temple, going into the inner sanctuary to burn incense before the Lord. In the sanctuary, an angel suddenly appeared to the right of the altar of incense. Zechariah was terrified. The angel told him, "Do not be afraid for God has heard your prayer, and you are going to have a son. Name him John, and he will be a great man of God. He must never touch wine or liquor, and he will be filled with the Holy Spirit before his birth. He will be a man of rugged spirit like Elijah, the prophet of old, and he will precede the coming of the Messiah."

Zachariah replied, "This is impossible! I'm an old man and my wife is also well along in years." The angel said, "I am Gabriel! I stand in the very presence of God. He sent me to you with this good news! Because you have not believed me, you will be stricken silent until the child is born. My Words will come true at the proper time."

When he came out of the temple, the people realized he could not speak and thought he had seen a vision. Soon after he returned home, Elizabeth became pregnant and was delighted. She says in Luke 1:25, "the Lord has done this for me. In these days, he has shown me his favor and taken away my disgrace among the people."

She remained in seclusion for the first five months. In her sixth month, her cousin, Mary, came for a visit because an angel had informed her that she was chosen to carry the Messiah and that her cousin Elizabeth was in her sixth month of pregnancy as well. When Elizabeth greeted Mary, John leaped in her womb and Elizabeth was filled with the Holy Spirit. I think this is so interesting because Mary was impregnated with the Holy Spirit and now Elizabeth would be the second one to be filled with the Holy Spirit. I love the fact that even though they were in the womb, the very presence of Jesus caused John to jump for joy. If there is any question about the validity of an unborn child being a real person, this alone should put that to rest.

Now let's back up and pick up Mary's story. The story opens with a young teenager who was engaged to be married. Her name is Mary and one day she was approached by an angel who gave her this message, "Greetings, you who are highly favored! The Lord is with you." As most of us would be, she was greatly troubled and wondered what kind of greeting this was. Then the angel said to her, "Mary, do not be afraid, you have won favor with God. You will be with child and give birth to a son, and you are to give him the name of Jesus. He will be great and will be called the Son of the Most High. The Lord will give him the throne of his father David, and he will reign over the house of Jacob forever; His kingdom will never end." "Mary replied, "How can this be since I am a virgin?" The angel answered, "The Holy Spirit will come upon you and the power of the Most High will overshadow you. So the one to be born will be called the Son of God. Even Elizabeth, your relative, is going to have a child in her old age, and she who was said to be barren is in her sixth month of pregnancy, for nothing is impossible with God."

I love the fact that God kept it in the family. He showed Mary that even though this seemed impossible that he had already done an impossible thing in her cousin Elizabeth. This must have given her comfort. Now she had Elizabeth, who was immediately filled with the Holy Spirit when Mary came to visit, to talk to about this miraculous thing that was happening to them both. They were both part of the miracle story and were carrying men of God.

The time came for Elizabeth to have her baby and it was a boy just as the angel had prophesied. On the eighth day, it was time for him to be circumcised and given a name. Elizabeth obeyed the voice of the angel and said his name was to be John. The neighbors and friends were shocked because that was not a family name and so they asked Zechariah. Since he could not speak, he asked for a tablet and wrote the name, John. Immediately his speech was restored and he was filled with the Holy Spirit and praised God.

Luke 1:80 tells us "John grew and became strong in spirit and lived in the desert until he appeared publicly to Israel."

The stage is now set. God had everything in place for the entrance of His Son into the world. John was in place to start telling the people that the Messiah was soon coming and to prepare their hearts with anticipation to be ready to receive Him.

It had taken God 2000 years in preparation to set the stage. The greatest coup the world would ever know was about to take place. Jesus was hidden inside a young virgin girl until now and then quietly raised in the remote town of Nazareth. The next question was to be, how will the world receive him?

I think that is a question we all have to ask ourselves. Do I truly receive Him as my savior? Not the savior of the world but as my personal savior.

Discussion Questions:

1. What does it mean to you to have a personal relationship with God?

2. Put in Mary or Elizabeth's position, how do you think you would respond? Are there times in your life that you have had to trust God to do what seems impossible? Share a time that God has asked you to trust Him even against all odds.

3. This lesson tells us of the first people to be filled with the Holy Spirit, Mary, Elizabeth, John and then Zachariah. They each received much joy and revelation. What does it mean to you to be filled with the Holy Spirit?

4. How has that experience changed your life?

Lesson 34
Luke 1-3
Jesus

In our last lesson, we left Mary pregnant and her cousin Elizabeth had given birth to John the Baptist, who was to be the forerunner of Jesus.

Now let's back up and look at the experience of Mary's preparation to be the mother of the Messiah.

The stage was set and time had come for God to choose a woman to incubate and bring forth his son into the world. God choose Mary, a young virgin from Nazareth. The story is all too familiar to us as we relive it every Christmas when we celebrate the birth of Jesus.

We will recap a few things of interest though to tie the Old and New Testaments together.

We read in Genesis 3:15 where God is talking to the devil after he enticed Eve to sin, "I will put enmity between you and the woman, and between your offspring and hers." Then in the next verse, he speaks to Eve and says, "I will increase your pains in childbearing; with pain, you will give birth to children."

Interesting that part of the curse on women concerned childbearing in the Old Testament and to bring in the New Testament, God is asking a young virgin to enter into childbearing for his sake and the sake of mankind.

1 Corinthians 15:22, tells us, "For as in Adam all die, so in Christ, all will be made alive."

Isaiah and other prophets in the Old Testament show us that this birth about to happen is the culmination of the past 2000 years.

The angel speaking to Joseph tells him in Matthew 1:22, "All this will take place to fulfill what the Lord had said to the prophet Isaiah (750 years earlier) the virgin will be with child and give birth to a son and they will call him Immanuel, which means, God with us."

So here we are at this pivotal point in time and history. It split the calendar of time right down the middle. Before the birth of Christ (B.C.) and after the birth of Christ (A.D.) Isn't it amazing that an unbelieving world acknowledges his birth and adjusts its timetable of affairs by what happened in the stable, in what must have seemed uneventful to the world at the time to everyone except Mary and Joseph.

I can only imagine the excitement and confusion that Mary felt as the angel came to her and told her she was to become impregnated with the Son of God. After all, she was a virgin and engaged to be married. One of the first thoughts she must have had after she realized the magnitude of what was about to happen was how would she ever explain this to Joseph? But God had every detail planned and sent an angel to inform Joseph of His plan.

Overwhelmed with the reality of what was about to happen, Mary broke out in song to express her joy. You can read it in Luke 1:46-55.

I thought it was interesting to note what Elizabeth said to Mary when she came for a visit after she conceived Jesus. Luke 1:45, "Blessed is she who has believed that what the Lord has said to her will be accomplished." In essence, she is saying that it was because Mary *believed* what the angel said to her was from the Lord and that God knew he could entrust her with this great assignment.

Mary was not boastful of this position but stated in her response, "My soul glorifies the Lord and my spirit rejoices in God my Savior, for He has been mindful of the *humble state of his servant.*" I believe the reason God choose her was because she was humble and had a pure heart. That is the same thing he is looking for in each of us today. Remember when Jesus was teaching the Beatitudes, he told those following him seeking His wisdom, "Blessed are the pure in heart for they shall see God."

Mary came to understand that this was not going to be another supernatural birth like Sarah or Elizabeth, who had experienced a miracle by being able to conceive long after childbearing years, but this was different. It could only be described as a virgin birth because a part of God Himself was entering into the world through her body.

In Luke 1:26, the angel is talking to Mary and refers to Jesus as being "that Holy Thing which shall be born of thee." There had to be a distinction made that this was not germinated from the same stock of the race but that the origin of the body of Jesus is ascribed to God.

In Hebrews 10:5 refers to this, "Therefore when Christ came into the world, he said: "Sacrifice and offering you did not desire, but a body you prepared for me." This was not the origin of a new being never before existing, as in all natural generations, but the mystery of a pre-existing, divine being implanted in a person (humanity) is the mystic union of divinity and humanity, going through the successive periods of natural gestation. Mary went through a normal pregnancy as any other woman would. She is referred to as "*being great with child...the days were accomplished that she should deliver...she brought forth her firstborn.*" These are expressions used for a normal pregnancy.

As I stated earlier, the New Testament opens under Roman rule. During the reign of Caesar Augustus, a decree was issued that required all people to enroll in their own cities for taxation purposes. This decree brought Joseph and Mary to Bethlehem, the city of their fathers, for both of them were descendants of the house of David. This meant that Jesus would be born there fulfilling prophecy in Micah 5:2: "...out of Bethlehem shall he come forth unto me that is to be the ruler in Israel..."

We have all heard the story of how crowded the city was at this time and how Mary and Joseph had to seek shelter in a stable because there were no rooms available in the hotels in town.

Mary gave birth to Jesus in a stable, wrapped him in a blanket and laid him in a manger. Not the grand entrance you would expect for the King of Kings who would save mankind. But remember, Jesus was being secretly placed here to live as an ordinary man so he could be as Adam, only without sin.

It was important that he be able to grow up as an ordinary boy, going through the same stages of other boys to reach manhood. He had to be tempted with all things a normal boy would so he could prove to be able to withstand the temptation to sin before the time came for him to redeem the sinful state of man. Only he could do this because he was conceived by the Holy Spirit from above. Jesus did not have the tainted blood of sin running though his veins as all other people on the earth but was conceived through the lineage of Adam after the fall.

Although his birth was not the grand entrance of glamour, God did provide validation of the event by appearing to shepherds. They were minding their own business of watching over their sheep when an angel appeared, and the landscape around them changed with a great light in the sky. They were obviously frightened, but the angel reassured them that he was bringing good news that the much-awaited Savior had arrived and where they could go to find him. Then a host of angels appeared singing, "Glory to God in the highest heaven, and peace on earth for all those pleasing Him."

The shepherds decided they needed to go and check this out and they found Mary, Joseph, and baby Jesus just as they had been told. They rejoiced at being chosen to witness this and told others who were astonished, as well.

We also know the story of the wise men that saw the star in the east. When Herod heard their story, he tried to trick them into showing him where the baby was, but when they found him they did not report back to Herod and instead took an alternate route home. While they were there, they were able to present the baby with valuable gifts that no doubt financed the happy couple for quite a while.

God's hand of protection was on the new parents. He sent an angel to Joseph to tell him not to go home but to take the baby to Egypt until Herod had died because he was so desperate to find and destroy the proclaimed Messiah that he ordered all babies under the age of two killed.

Mary and Joseph followed the law in all respects. As was the custom, on the eighth day the baby was taken to the temple and circumcised and publicly given the name Jesus just as the angel had instructed his parents earlier.

Interestingly, in the New Testament, the name Jesus is recorded over six hundred times. As strange as it may be, never once was our Lord addressed directly as Jesus, except on two occasions, and then by demons (Matthew 1:24 and Mark 5:7). The names Messiah and Christ were names, which represented his office as the anointed one, but Jesus was given as his personal name.

Forty days after Jesus birth, Mary presented herself before the priest at the temple. It was the custom after giving birth that a woman present herself along with an offering of atonement and cleansing, and to present the baby to the Lord. When she arrived at the temple, a devout man named Simeon and an aged prophetess named Anna were there.

Simeon was said to be a righteous and devout man. Luke 2:25 tells us, "The Holy Spirit was upon him." The Holy Spirit had revealed to him that he would not see death until he had seen the promised Messiah. On this day, moved by the Holy Spirit, he went to the temple, and when he saw the infant Jesus, he took him in his arms and began to sing a song of adoration, which stated that now he could depart in peace because he had seen the Messiah. He blessed Joseph and Mary and gave prophecies about their newborn baby.

Anna was a prophetess from the tribe of Asher. She was eighty-four years old and a widow. She never left the temple, but stayed and worshiped night and day, fasting and praying. She, too, gave thanks for she recognized the significance of who he was.

When they had done everything required by the law, and felt it was safe, they returned to Galilee to their hometown of Nazareth. There Jesus grew and lived probably a normal life for a boy of his day.

Only one other time is he mentioned during these formative years. At the age of twelve, he accompanied his parents to Jerusalem to the Passover Feast. They missed him and found him in the temple sitting and listening and asking questions of the teacher of the law. When His mother reproached him, we hear the first recorded words of Jesus. "How is it that ye sought me? Wist ye not that I must be about my Father's business?" This tells us that he was very much aware of his divine heritage and purpose. Yet he submitted to growing up in the same fashion as any other boy at each stage. Luke 2:41 tells us" he grew in wisdom and stature, and in favor with God and man."

Not much more information is given of Jesus' years growing up until his baptism and when his ministry began at the age of thirty.

Discussion Questions:

1. Have you ever been put in a place where God asked you to believe and do something that seemed impossible like Mary? How did you respond?

2. As we look at the birth of Jesus and his early years, how did God provide everything Mary and Joseph needed to protect and care for Jesus?

3. We are told that Jesus was left behind in Jerusalem and that he was found in the temple learning and sharing words of wisdom with the teachers of the day. What do you think he meant his response to his parents that he must be about his Fathers' business?

4. What lessons can we learn from the way Mary and Joseph continued to obey the customs of the day even though they realized they had been entrusted with the long awaited Messiah?

Lesson 35
Luke 3, Mark 1, Matthew 1-4
Jesus the Man

Our last lesson left Jesus at the age of 12. This is the last time he is referred to directly until he becomes an adult and is ready to start his ministry to fulfill the mission he was sent to accomplish.

In the fifteenth year of Emperor Tiberius Caesar, a message came from God to John as he was living in the desert, informing him that time was drawing near for the arrival of the long-awaited Messiah for whom he had been sent to be the advance man.

John was, as you remember, a different sort of man. We know he lived in the desert, probably much as a hermit, and we are told in Mark 1:6, "He wore clothes made of camel's hair, with a leather belt around his waist, and he ate locusts and wild honey." Not the typical Jewish man of the times, but he had been set apart by God for this time. He, no doubt, was always aware of that because when Mary, who was carrying Jesus in her womb, approached his mother Elizabeth, we are told that he leaped inside his mother's womb. There was a spiritual connection between the Lord Jesus and John the Baptist (as he is called) before they were born. His mission, like that of Jesus, began before he had taken his first breath.

His message was as the prophet Isaiah describes him, "A voice shouting from the wilderness: 'Prepare a way for the Lord, make straight paths for him.'"

When people heard his message, they began coming from Jerusalem, all over the Jordan Valley, and Judea listening to him preach. Many confessed their sins, and he baptized them in the Jordan River.

Many of the Sadducees and Pharisees came to hear him, and he immediately called them out, Matthew 3:7, "You brood of vipers! Who warned you to flee from the coming wrath? Produce fruit in keeping with repentance. And do not think you can say to yourselves, 'We have Abraham as our father.' I tell you that out of these stones God can raise up children of Abraham. The ax is already at the tree, and every tree that does not produce good fruit will be cut down and thrown into the fire." He is saying to them that the heritage of being a Jewish leader and descendant of Abraham is not enough to get into the kingdom of God. The kingdom that Jesus is coming to establish is based on repentance, not the law.

One point of interest is the phrase where John announces that the ax is already at the tree. We know that in the Garden of Eden the Tree of Life is a symbol of Jesus. Then Isaiah refers to Jesus in Isaiah 53:2, "He grew up before him like a tender shoot, and like a root out of dry ground." Jesus also refers to himself as the Root and Offspring of David in Revelation 22:16. I think what John is saying here is the tree of life has come and the ax is already sharpened to cut him down to pay the price for all humanity. He was not announcing he was coming, but that he was here and the plan was already in play. The curse that had been put on humanity because of the sin of Adam was about to be removed. Galatians 3:13 tells us just that, "Christ redeemed us from the curse of the law by becoming a curse for us, for it is written: 'Cursed is everyone who is hung on the tree.'"

The religious leaders questioned John saying, "Why then do you baptize if you are not the Christ, nor Elijah, nor the Prophet." He tells them, "I baptize with water, but among you stands one you do not know. He comes after me, the thongs of whose sandals I am not worthy to untie. He will baptize you with Holy Spirit and fire. His winnowing fork is in his hand, and he will clear his threshing floor, gathering his wheat into the barn and burning up the chaff with unquenchable fire." This must have confused them even more. They were getting anxious as the people were following this man who proclaims the long-awaited Messiah is here, and people are following him, upsetting their Jewish traditions.

All this took place in Bethany where John baptized people in the Jordan River. The very next day, John saw Jesus coming toward him and cried, "Look, the Lamb of God who takes away the sin of the world! This is the one I meant when I said, 'A man who comes after me has surpassed me because he was before me.' I myself did not know him, but the reason I came baptizing with water is that he might be revealed to Israel."

I find it interesting that John did not recognize Jesus in the flesh, as they would have been cousins. In John 1:32 he says, "I saw the Spirit come down from heaven as a dove and remain on him. I would not have known him, except for that one who sent me to baptize with water told me, 'The man on whom you see the Spirit come down and remain, is he who will baptize with the Holy Spirit.' I have seen, and I testify that this is the Son of God." It makes you wonder if he felt the same spiritual connection when he saw Jesus coming that he did when he leaped in his mother's womb 30 years earlier.

Luke tells us in chapter 1:10, "As Jesus was coming out of the water, he saw heaven being torn open and the Spirit descending on Him like a dove. And a voice came from Heaven: 'You are my son, whom I love; with you I am well pleased."

It is hard not to ask the question, why should the sinless Son of God be baptized unto repentance? Jesus himself reveals the answer. He says in Matthew 3:15, "Let it be so now; it is proper for us to do this to fulfill all righteousness." In submitting to baptism, he formally identified Himself with man, entering by the same gateway as those who would follow Him. It was in this act of identification that God opened up Heaven and announced to the world who he was.

Luke also tells us that at once the Spirit sent him out into the desert, and he was there forty days, being tempted by the devil. It seems that as soon as God announced his son was here, it was game on. Remember how Satan had worked through Herod to try to find and kill Jesus before he could grow up. He had all the baby boys under two killed just to destroy any possibility he could come to the earth and take away his hold on humanity. Had God not protected him by sending an angel to warn Joseph to flee to Egypt, he might have been successful. But now he was here and without the tainted blood of sin running in his veins. The only chance the devil had to conquer him was to work through fleshy weakness and get him to give over his authority just as Adam had in the garden.

Jesus was aware of the magnitude of the task to which he stood committed, and conscious of a new inner power (being "full of the Holy Spirit"). He no doubt had a need to go away to spend time with his Father, to meditate upon the way he would spend the next three years of preparation.

Satan, now being aware of his identity, appealed to every aspect of his humanity to try to get him to relinquish his power and plan to him.

Matthew 4:1-11 tells us "Then was Jesus led up of the spirit into the wilderness to be tempted of the devil. And when he had fasted forty days Jesus was afterward hungry." Satan first appealed to his physical appetite. The long fast left Jesus with gnawing pangs of hunger and Satan approached him to get him to turn stones to bread. It was aimed to get Jesus to exercise the power given him in an ungodly way to satisfy his own physical appetite, much like Eve in the garden by appealing to her physical senses and how delicious the forbidden fruit looked. Remember, the Holy Spirit led Jesus into the desert to be tempted as an ordinary man would but unlike Adam and Eve, the temptation was immediately met with the word of His Father-God. He quoted Deuteronomy 8:3 "Man shall not live by bread alone but by every word that comes from the mouth of the Lord."

When Satan was not successful at that, he took Jesus to the temple in Jerusalem and dared him to jump off. It was presumed to be about 250 feet. Satan even quoted scripture to him. Psalm 91:12, "For he will command his angels concerning you to guard you in all your ways; they will lift you up in their hands, so that you will not strike your foot against a stone." This would have been an easy and convincing way to show he was the Messiah to the crowd below, an act of advertisement self-display. Again Jesus quoted the Word, Deuteronomy 6:18, "You shall not tempt the Lord your God…"

Next, Satan offered him world dominion, offering him the prospect of regaining his kingdom on the earth in an easier way than the way of the cross. All Jesus had to do was give him one act of homage, because Satan knew that one act would upset all that for which Jesus had come into the world.. Notice Jesus did not challenge the Devil's claim to the kingdoms of this world, because his mission on earth was to reclaim it from him. But instead of bowing down to Satan, Jesus simply quoted the Word, "Thou shalt worship the Lord thy God, and Him only shalt thou serve." At this Satan left him and the angels attended him.

We have talked before in previous lessons about the trinity of man as compared to the trinity of the Godhead. It is a note of interest that Satan must have been aware of that as he appealed to each aspect of man in his temptations of Jesus. He appealed to him *physically* by using hunger, he appealed to his *soul* by using emotions and tempting him to use his will, and he appealed to his *spirit* in an attempt to gel him to give spiritual authority to him. Satan still tries to usurp God's authority in our lives in the very same way. We must use the same method Jesus did to resist him, the Word of God. That is why it is so very important to know the Word of God.

Once Jesus was successful in regaining authority, the battle did not end. Unless we hold true to God's Word, the devil is waiting to regain the territory he lost in your life. We read this in many passages in the Bible.

1 Peter 5:8, "Be self-controlled and alert. Your enemy, the devil prowls around like a roaring lion looking for someone to devour." We can never be complacent thinking we are above temptations.

Ephesians 4:27, "In anger, do not sin. Do not let the sun go down while you are still angry, and do not give the devil a foothold." It is the subtle things that give the devil a slight foothold in our lives and giving into false beliefs that the harmful things (and bad behavior) that we have no control are really okay.

1 John 3:8, "He who does what is sinful is of the devil because the devil has been sinning from the beginning. The reason the Son of God appeared was to destroy the devil's work." John is warning us here that the devil is here and has been tempting man to sin from the beginning.

Ephesians 6:10, "Be strong in the Lord and in his mighty power. Put on the full armor of God that you can take your stand against the devil's schemes."

When we accept the fact that Jesus came and reclaimed us as his own, Satan's hold on us is broken. We have authority over him now, but just like Adam and Eve, we can so easily be seduced by the things of this world. Remember, there is still a snake in the garden.

We talked earlier in this lesson about the tree representing Jesus. He tells us in John 15:5, "I am the vine and you are the branches. If a man abides in me and I in him, he will bear much fruit (fruit of the spirit, love, joy, peace, etc.), apart from me you can do nothing." The branch of a tree draws its life from the vine. I recently was looking at a tree in my front yard that had been damaged from high winds. Some branches were broken off and completely dead. They were just resting on the other branches for support. Some of the branches had partially been broken but there were still signs of green new growth. They were not stable but still somewhat attached to the tree. It was such a perfect picture of what Jesus is saying here. When we are not fully attached to Him, we become shaky in our walk. We may still have signs of spiritual life but now are constantly struggling to stay attached.

The Old Testament speaks of it as well. Psalm 1:2-3, "He who delights in the law of the Lord and meditates on it day and night is like a tree planted by the streams of water, which yields its fruit in season and whose leaf does not wither. Whatever he does prospers."

Discussion Questions:

1. Looking at the Words of Jesus about the vine and branches, how secure are you that you are drawing all the life from his vine that was appropriated for you on the cross?

2. What lessons can we learn from John and his devotion to his mission?

3. What lessons can we learn from Jesus' temptations in the desert? Which one can you most easily identify with?

Lesson 36
Jesus Ministry-Miracles

As we start our study of Jesus' ministry, it is important to remember that even though he was about to embark on moving in the supernatural, he was also fully man. He felt love, pain, sadness, etc. just as we would. He needed sleep, exercise and a healthy diet just as we do.

Faithful High Priest in the service of God, to make expiation for the sins of the people. For because he himself has suffered and been tempted, he is able to help those who are tempted." (Hebrews 2:17-18)

"For we have not a High Priest who is unable to sympathize with our weaknesses, but one who in every respect has been tempted as we are, yet without sin." (Hebrews 4:15)

Jesus Christ, as a human, was *completely human.* He could not have been killed, and been *completely dead* for 3 days and 3 nights, and *resurrected from the dead* otherwise. During His human lifetime, He knew hunger, thirst, weariness, joy, grief, and temptation. The only difference was that He *never sinned.*

"In the morning, as He was returning to the city, he was *hungry."* (Matthew 21:18)

"Jacob's well was there, and so Jesus, *wearied* as he was with His journey, sat down beside the well." (John 4:6)

And behold, there arose a great storm on the sea, so that the boat was being swamped by the waves; but he was *asleep.* And they went and woke Him, saying, "Save us, Lord; *we* are perishing." (Matthew 8:24-25)

"When Jesus saw her weeping, and the Jews who came with her also weeping, he was deeply moved in Spirit and troubled; and He said, "Where have you laid him?" They said to Him, "Lord, come and see." *Jesus wept."* (John 11:33-35)

"And being in an *agony,* he prayed more earnestly: and his sweat was as it were great drops of blood falling to the ground." (Luke22: 44)

These are just a few of the verses that show the emotional and physical side of Jesus.

How did Jesus Christ live a life completely free of sin? How did he perform the miracles that he did? You have to ask yourself, where did he get his power?

"And when Jesus was baptized, he went up immediately from the water, and behold, the heavens were opened and he saw the Spirit of God descending like a dove, and rested on him; and lo, a voice from heaven, saying, "This is my beloved Son, with whom I am well pleased." (Matthew 3:16-17)

"And Jesus, full of the Holy Spirit, returned from the Jordan, and was led by the Spirit"
(Luke 4:1)

"And Jesus returned in the Power of the Spirit into Galilee, and a report concerning him went out through all the surrounding country" (Luke 4:14)

"…By the Spirit of God that I cast out demons" (Matthew 12:28)

"Jesus said to them, "Truly, truly, I say to you, the Son can do nothing of his own accord" (John 5:19)

"And Jesus answered them, "Truly, I say to you, if you have faith and never doubt, you will not only do what has been done to the fig tree, but if you say to this mountain, 'Be taken up and cast into the sea,' it will be done. And whatever you ask in prayer, you will receive, if you have faith." (Matthew 21:21-22)

"Truly, truly, I say to you, he who believes in me will also do the works that I do and greater works than these will he do, because I go to the Father. Whatever you ask in my name, I will do it, that the Father may be glorified in the Son" (John 14:12-13)

"In that same hour, he rejoiced in the Holy Spirit and said, "I thank Thee, Father, Lord of heaven and earth, that Thou hast hidden these things from the wise and understanding and revealed them to babes; yea, Father, for such was Thy gracious will. All things have been delivered to me by my Father; and no one knows who the Son is except the Father, or who the Father is except the Son and anyone to whom the Son chooses to reveal Him." Then turning to the disciples, he said privately, "Blessed are the eyes which see what you see!" (Luke 10:21-23)

We see in these verses the unity of Jesus' manhood and the presence of the Holy Spirit. When he was baptized, the Holy Spirit came upon him, and then he went out in the power of doing supernatural miracles.

He was no doubt aware of his heritage before because you remember at the temple at age twelve, he told his mother, "Don't you know I have to be about my Father's business?" But it was not until he was 30 years old that the appointed time came for him to be introduced to the world at large. Remember there were a few like Simeon and Anna in the temple, the wise men, and shepherds who had been given divine knowledge of him as a babe, but from then until he was 30 years old he had lived an obscure life in Nazareth as the son of a carpenter.

After his baptism when the Holy Spirit came upon him, the Bible tells us he was led away by the same Holy Spirit into the desert to be tempted by the devil. It was as if God was saying, 'Go ahead and face the enemy head on and put him behind you, then go and tell the others who you are and the reason for your coming into the world."

Although he was fully human filled with the Holy Spirit, he was always quick to point out his oneness with the Father as well. "I only do the things I see my Father do." "If you see me you see the Father." He had to establish now that he was indeed the Messiah sent from God to redeem them.

To do this he began performing miracles, sometimes called signs and wonders. You know when you see a sign it gives you information, points you in a direction. When Jesus started performing supernatural miracles it made them wonder, could this be the Messiah we have waited for so long?

At one point after he went out to the mountainside to pray, he gathered a group of disciples around him as he traveled throughout the countryside. The word disciple means "learner." The Pharisees, Sadducees, and Scribes, for example, had disciples. In fact, John the Baptist had disciples. Jesus entrusted his disciples with the mission of getting the message out that the Messiah had come and was walking among them. There were no specific qualifications or background required for them to be disciples. They were tax collectors, fishermen, etc.   The same thing was required of them as was of Mary when the Holy Spirit called upon her to bring the messenger into the world: a willing and obedient heart.

They were: Simon (whom he named Peter), his brother Andrew, James, John, Philip, Bartholomew, Matthew, Thomas, James son of Alpheus Simon who was called the Zealot, Judas son of James, and Judas Iscariot, who became a traitor.

Each played an important part in spreading the news as Jesus went through the towns and villages, teaching in their synagogues, preaching the good news of the kingdom, and healing every disease and sickness. Jesus also gave His disciples power to perform signs and wonders so the people would believe the message they were delivering as well.

Now Jesus had a following and a group of men to help him spread the Word. Crowds began to follow him everywhere he went and he always had compassion on them his miracles ranged from healings to casting out demons from those who had been taken captive by the devil.

Each miracle shows a different side to Jesus story. He always used the miracle to teach a lesson on kingdom principles. Below are the miracles Jesus performed.

- Jesus changed water into wine (John 2:1-11).
- Jesus cured the nobleman's son (John 4:46-47).
- The great haul of fishes (Luke 5:1-11).
- Jesus cast out an unclean spirit (Mark 1:23-28).
- Jesus cured Peter's mother-in-law of a fever (Mark 1:30-31).
- Jesus healed a leper (Mark 1:40-45).
- Jesus healed the centurion's servant (Matthew 8:5-13).
- Jesus raised the widow's son from the dead (Luke 7:11-18).
- Jesus stilled the storm (Matthew 8:23-27).
- Jesus cured two demoniacs (Matthew 8:28-34).
- Jesus cured the paralytic (Matthew 9:1-8).
- Jesus raised the ruler's daughter from the dead (Matthew 9:18-26).
- Jesus cured a woman of an issue of blood (Luke 8:43-48).
- Jesus opened the eyes of two blind men (Matthew 9:27-31).
- Jesus loosened the tongue of a man who could not speak (Matthew 9:32-33).
- Jesus healed an invalid man at the pool called Bethesda (John 5:1-9).
- Jesus restored a withered hand (Matthew 12:10-13).
- Jesus cured a demon-possessed man (Matthew 12:22).
- Jesus fed at least five thousand people (Matthew 14:15-21).
- Jesus healed a woman of Canaan (Matthew 15:22-28).

- Jesus cured a deaf and mute man (Mark 7:31-37).
- Jesus fed at least four thousand people (Matthew 15:32-39).
- Jesus opened the eyes of a blind man (Mark 8:22-26).
- Jesus cured a boy who was plagued by a demon (Matthew 17:14-21).
- Jesus opened the eyes of a man born blind (John 9:1-38)
- Jesus cured a woman who had been afflicted eighteen years (Luke 17:11-17).
- Jesus cured a man of dropsy (Luke 14:1-4).
- Jesus cleansed ten lepers (Luke 17:11-19).
- Jesus raised Lazarus from the dead (John 11:1-46).
- Jesus opened the eyes of two blind men (Matthew 20:30-34).
- Jesus caused the fig tree to wither (Matthew 21:18-22).
- Jesus restored the ear of the high priest's servant (Luke 22:50-51).
- Jesus rose from the dead (Luke 24:5-6).
- The second great haul of fishes (John 21:1-14).

Discussion Questions:

1. Look up three of the miracles and tell what lesson they teach about Jesus.

2. Do you consider yourself a disciple of Jesus and what does that mean to you?

Lesson 37
Jesus (Beatitudes 1)

In our last lesson, we talked about the miracles Jesus went about doing to prove that he was the Messiah sent by God to redeem the world. People were amazed at his power to do miracles and did believe what he was preaching. One important element of his teaching was also to prepare those who would be left behind how to live when he returned to his Father.

He gathered his disciples together on the north shore of the Sea of Galilee where the land is gently sloped and is sparsely covered by trees, leaving large grassy areas. It was a place of quiet serenity. They sat down on the slopes and before long were joined by the multitudes, which had become a familiar sight wherever Jesus went.

Each of the three times I have been to Israel, we have taken the trip to this very place, and it is always moving. Not only the thought that our Savior stood on that very hill giving instructions on how to live but also the view from the slopes is one of looking over the Sea of Galilee where multitudes of stories took place.

Looking out over the Sea of Galilee I could see the remains of the town of Capernaum where we later visited the synagogue where Jesus preached and went in the remains of the home of His disciple, Peter. It was here in this very house that Jesus healed Peter's mother-in-law.

He started the preaching by offering eight blessings to the crowd.

These blessings, or beatitudes, can be found in Matthew 5:3-12.

Blessed are the poor in spirit, for theirs is the kingdom of Heaven.

Blessed are those who mourn, for they shall be comforted.

Blessed are the meek, for they shall inherit the earth.

Blessed are those who hunger and thirst for righteousness, for they shall be filled.

Blessed are the merciful, for they shall obtain mercy.

Blessed are the pure in heart, for they shall see God.

Blessed are the peacemakers, for they shall be called sons of God.

Blessed are those who are persecuted for righteousness sake for theirs is the kingdom of Heaven.

Blessed are you when they revile and persecute you, and say all kinds of evil against you falsely for My sake. Rejoice and be exceedingly glad, for great is your reward in heaven, for so they persecuted the prophets who were before you.

These are words that form the very basis of all righteousness. They form the rock on which any believer's efforts are built. And most importantly, they were attributes, which Christ had demonstrated in his life. Christ was trying, through this preaching, to draw men to life and light and away from the darkness of human ambition and death.

And he said after he had spoken of the blessings:

"Be ye therefore perfect, even as your Father which is in heaven is perfect." Matthew 5:48.

The ideas Jesus mentions in these blessings should not be ideas that we think about in our quiet time when we are meditating but ignored in the rush of our daily lives. They are things which form part of our lives all of the time. Jesus was teaching the disciples through these blessings how to live life on the same high level he was on.

1.   Blessed are the poor in spirit

Christ is telling us with this blessing the way we should view ourselves in light of his love and provision. Being poor in spirit means lowering our egos to nothing and putting ourselves completely in the hands of God. We are to live in a kingdom mentality on earth as it is in Heaven. I think that is something we all desire, but it goes against the dictates of this world we live in.

So often we judge ourselves, and others, by accomplishments and abilities of what we can do in our own endeavors. It is easy to let our self-esteem increase by such things as our superior education, social status, or physical beauty. More often than not that leads to an inflated ego, and God's hands are tied in accomplishing his purpose in our lives. But 2 Chronicles 16:9 tells us his eyes are roaming throughout the earth seeking to whom he might make himself strong. Note the key phrase in that verse is "that he might make **himself** strong." His heart's desire is to find men and women who will be so abandoned to themselves that he can accomplish his will and purpose through them.

Mary is a perfect example of this. When the angel came to her and told her that God wanted to use her life and body to be impregnated with his son, her response shows that humble spirit He is looking for. She simply replied, "let it be done to me thy servant." She did not argue with him about how it would affect her reputation, engagement, or what it would cost her physically to be the one to bring his life into the world.

We see this all throughout the Old and New Testament. Gideon was a good example. He was asked to lead the charge to save his people. At first, when the angel came to him with this assignment, he said: "O my Lord, how can I save Israel? Indeed my clan is the weakest in Manasseh, and I am the least in my father's house." Judges 6:15. God could have just moved on and found someone with more confidence and stamina, but that was not what he was looking for. He wanted someone that he knew would not let their ego interrupt his plans for Israel. After some encouraging events, Gideon led the charge and won a great battle.

When God sent Samuel to the house of Jessie to anoint one of his sons to be the one chosen to be king, Jessie paraded all his sons before him telling of the great virtues they each had. You can read about it in 1 Samuel 16:6-13. But Samuel says no to each of the seemingly most qualified sons. When Samuel asked Jessie if he did not have other sons, he admitted that his youngest son was tending sheep. Not even one in the eyes of his father to be considered, but God had his eyes on David, and we read that when Samuel meets David, the Lord says, "Rise and anoint him; he is the one." He also later states that David was a man after **his** own heart.

With many other examples in the Bible, God shows us he wants a man of poor spirit like the time he said through his prophet Isaiah in Isaiah 66, "This is the one I esteem, he who is humble and contrite in spirit and trembles at my word."

Another verse that I have meditated on many times. Psalm 51:17. "The sacrifices of God now for this generation is a broken and contrite heart." So often we still want to offer him a golden calf, or monetary sacrifice to appease him, but he is saying, "All I want is you, just like I wanted Adam and Eve in the garden. "

The Lord is still looking for that man or woman who recognizes how poor they are spiritually without being abandoned to God. Mother Teresa is a good modern-day example. In the eyes of the world this small, frail nun seemed an unlikely candidate to leave the legacy of love she gave to the world. Her recognition of being poor in spirit allowed God to do wondrous things with her life.

2.   Blessed are they that mourn

The word "blessed" means happy. So it seems strange that Jesus should be saying here "happy are they that mourn." This seems to contradict itself. How can someone be happy when he mourns?

I think what God is saying here is when we reach a place of recognizing the depravity of our existence and mourn over the state we are in, we will ultimately come to him and be comforted by receiving the salvation and fruits of the spirit that was purchased on the cross.

Jesus showed his deep compassion for those who are bereaved when he mourned over Lazarus' death, and he was comforted by his resurrection. It was because of the mourning of his heart that led him to work a miracle of raising Lazarus from the dead.

It is the awareness and mourning for our sinful state that we come to him and are comforted by the assurance of our salvation. The verse that speaks to me often is, "The Spirit of life in Christ Jesus has made me free from the spirit of sin and death." The spirit of sin that led to the death of the oneness Adam and Eve had in the garden with their Father and creator. The good news here is that the Spirit of life in Christ Jesus has set us free from the mentality that seeks self and the things that oppose God. The things that ultimately lead us to mourn over the emptiness in our life.

It is the mourning for a lost world that leads us to be in intercessory prayer for others, and we feel the pleasure and comfort of the Lord as we are moved to share the gospel.

What comfort then is there, for those that mourn? The answer to this can be found in Luke's version of this blessing: "Blessed are you who weep now, for you shall laugh." Luke 6:21

Jesus and his apostles experienced mourning and yet were joyful.

"Beloved, do not think it strange concerning the fiery trial which is to try you, as though some strange thing happened to you; but rejoice to the extent that you partake of Christ's sufferings, that when his glory is revealed, you may also be glad with exceeding joy." 1 Peter 4:12-13

James told his readers to: "Lament and mourn and weep! Let your laughter be turned to mourning and your joy to gloom. Humble yourselves in the sight of the Lord, and He will lift you up." James 4:9-10

Paul himself mourned or lamented over his own unworthiness by exclaiming in Romans: "O wretched man that I am! Who will deliver me from this body of death?" Romans 7:24

If Paul laments over such things, then surely we must do the same. And when a man is bowed down with depression at his own spiritual condition, there is hope for him. When he suffers from a heavy heart, Jesus says, "Come unto me all who are heavy laden, and I will give you rest."

It is comforting to know that as we face trials and temptations while on this earth, that Jesus faced the same trials and continually looked to his Father for comfort. One of my favorite verses about Jesus alludes to this. Remember in the garden he was in so much anguish that He sweat drops of blood, but in Hebrews 12:2, we are told "He endured the cross for the joy set before him." He was mourning his trial but was comforted by the joy of what it would accomplish.

I was talking to a mother recently who had a son on drugs and she was rejoicing that he had hit bottom and was living under a bridge. I was confused as to why she was rejoicing, but she explained that it was a sign that he had hit bottom and would see his need for help and could find restoration. They had tried to help him in their own efforts but now realized that he had to reach a place of deprivation to seek it for himself.

3. Blessed are the meek

To be meek means recognizing your true worth before God and then applying this attitude of mind in the situations of everyday life. I remember reading that Jesus was meek. In my mind that had always meant one who was not outgoing or a mover and shaker. No one wanted anyone to describe him or her as meek. But after studying the meaning of the word, I came to understand that it means, "a quiet confidence." I then thought of Jesus when he was in the desert being teased and tempted by the devil. He did not argue, yell or belittle him. He simply stated with a quiet confidence the word of His Father. By doing so, as this blessing states, he inherited the earth.

So being meek means taking an attitude something like that which is described in one of the Psalms where it says:

> Rest in the LORD, and wait patiently for him; do not fret…Cease from anger, and forsake wrath; do not fret—it only causes harm. Psalm 37:7-8

> Another one of my favorite verses is, Psalm 46:10, "Be still and know that I am Lord."

When we know our standing with our Heavenly Father, we can enjoy a quiet confidence that he alone can give. I always think of Mother Teresa as a quiet, meek person, but a person that through her meekness won the hearts of the world and accomplished so much for the kingdom. I would say she inherited the earth, as it would be hard to find anyone on this earth who has not heard of her and holds her in high regard as one to be imitated.

Meekness is not a weakness, as it seems to the world, but through the words of Jesus, the disciples realized that it was a quality to be found only in the bravest and strongest characters. For it requires a high degree of courage and self-control to achieve a proper meekness before God, and we are told that if we are meek we shall inherit the earth, so by a strange paradox, by forsaking the world we inherit the earth.

4. Blessed are they which do hunger and thirst after righteousness, for they shall be filled.

Christ here is telling us that blessed is the man who is continually trying to change himself or improve himself. No believer in Christ could possibly be completely satisfied or content with his or her lacking spiritual position. We should always be striving to make ourselves more Christ-like. We should be always hungering and thirsting after godliness, and this is made easier by the fact that we know that one day our hunger will be satisfied and that we will be filled, as it says in the last part of verse six:

> Blessed are those who hunger and thirst for righteousness for they shall be filled. Matthew 5:6

Consider some of the verses in the Psalms and how the Psalmist looks for God, and thirsts and hungers after him:

> My soul longs, yes, even faints for the courts of the LORD, my heart and my flesh cry out for the living God. Psalm 84:2

> O God, you are my God; early will I seek you; my soul thirsts for you; my flesh longs for you in a dry and thirsty land where there is no water. Psalm 63:1

For me, that is all we need to be concerned with on this earth. On the cross, there was a great exchange. He took my sin and I took his righteousness. If you want to do something enlightening, go through your Bible and look at all it says about the righteous.

Psalm 34:15 says, "The eyes of the Lord are on the righteous."

When we are told to put on the full armor of God, we are told to put on the breastplate of righteousness. That is what is going to protect the heart when the enemy tries to come in and defeat us by getting us into anger, jealousy, envy, etc. Knowing who we are in Christ and that he gave us his righteousness allows us to look beyond ourselves when struggling with these issues.

I love this passage from Psalm 85:10. "Love and faithfulness meet together; righteousness and peace kiss each other." When we truly understand our place of being in right standing with God, it is like an affectionate kiss that always leads to peace.

Then in Psalm 89:14, "Righteousness and justice are the foundation of your throne; love and faithfulness go before you." This tells us that God's kingdom is established in justice and righteousness. Can you imagine what would happen to our nation if we operated our government with these principles?

This is the verse that our government was based upon. The principle of establishing a justice system whereby laws would be obeyed and a bill of rights that the freedoms were given to us would be upheld.

This is even quoted in Proverbs 14:34, "Righteousness exalts a nation, but sin is a disgrace to any people."

Then bringing the importance of righteousness a little closer to home, Psalm 3:33, "The Lord's curse is on the house of the wicked, but he blesses the home of the righteous." If we want our homes and families to be blessed, we need to be focusing on what it means to be righteous.

I spent two years studying righteousness, and it was only when I quit trying to find a way to deserve it and realize it was simply a gift from the one who created me that I could live in the freedom it gives.

Discussion Questions:

1. Which of the Beatitudes do you relate to the most?

2. Which one do you struggle with most?

Lesson 38
Beatitudes (2)

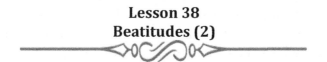

In our last lesson, we talked about the first four of the Beatitudes, and in this lesson, we will finish our study of them.

5.   Blessed are the merciful, for they will be shown mercy

The word mercy means compassionate, helpful, kind; giving towards the weak, sick and the poor.

Being merciful is an action-based emotion. You cannot truly be merciful or compassionate to someone unless you do something about it. It is not merely feeling bad about someone's situation. It is an emotion, which prompts one to act.

Today most of us would agree that it is good to be merciful to others. Likewise, it was true of the audience listening to Jesus on the side of the hill at the time he was teaching these principles.

The Romans despised pity. Being merciful was an exception. The Pharisees were very judgmental to others and showed no mercy. Jesus even chastised them for it in Matthew 23:23, "Woe to you, teachers of law and Pharisees, you hypocrites! You give a tenth of your spices of dill and cumin. But you have neglected the more important matters of the law justice, mercy, and faithfulness."

Jesus is now bringing a ministry of compassion, love, and care to the less fortunate of the world. He is exposing the traditions of the law that are not of God. He has come to be a visual of God's love to the world and is telling them how the Father would have them live. Luke 6:36 "Be merciful, just as your Father is merciful."

We read in Colossians 3:12, "Therefore, as God's chosen people, holy and dearly loved, clothe yourself with compassion."

Jesus has come to show us the mercy of God and mercy comes first from the realization that you have received mercy.

It brings to mind the parable found in Matthew 18 where Jesus is telling about a king who wanted to settle his accounts with his servants. Verse 24-35. "As he began the settlement, a man who owed him ten thousand talents was brought to him. Since he was not able to pay, the master ordered that he and his wife and his children and all that he had be sold to repay the debt. The servant fell on his knees before him, 'Be patient with me,' he begged, 'and I will pay back everything.' The servant's master took pity on him, canceled his debt and let him go. But when the servant went out, he found one of his fellow servants who owed him a hundred denarii. He grabbed him and began to choke him, 'Pay back what you owe me!' he demanded. His fellow servant fell to his knees and begged him, 'be patient with me and I will pay you back.' But he refused and went off and had the man thrown into prison until he could pay the debt. When the other servants saw what had happened, they were greatly distressed and told the master everything that had happened. The master was furious and called his servant in and rebuked him, 'You wicked servant,' he said, I canceled all that debt of yours because you begged me to. Shouldn't you have had mercy on your fellow servant just as I had on you?' In anger, his master turned him over to the jailers to be tortured until he paid back all he owed. This is how your heavenly Father will treat each of you unless you forgive your brother from the heart."

I wonder how often we forget just how much Jesus showed mercy to us as he was being tortured and nailed to the cross for our sins. He did not deserve it but extended us the gift of mercy that we might not have to endure the punishment that sin had caused. His spirit now lives in us as we accept the price he paid. He wants us to extend that same mercy to others. We are to imitate his life and be his hands and feet on this earth.

One of the ways we know we have the spirit of God living in us is observing the way we live our life. We find kindness listed in Gal 5:22 as one of the fruits of the Spirit. "The fruit of the Spirit is love, joy, peace, patience, <u>kindness</u>, goodness, faithfulness, gentleness, and self-control."

Jesus summarized it in a wonderful manner in Matthew 25:35-40, "For I was hungry and you gave me something to eat, I was thirsty and you gave me something to drink, I was a stranger and you invited me in, I needed clothes and you clothed me, I was sick and you looked after me, I was in prison and you came to visit me.' Then the righteous will answer him, 'Lord, when did we see you hungry and feed you, or thirsty and give you something to drink? When did we see you a stranger and invite you in, or needing clothes and clothe you? When did we see you sick or in prison and go to visit you?' The King will reply, 'I tell you the truth, whatever you did for one of the least of these brothers of mine, you did for me.''

I have never felt closer to God than when I was taking my children to the nursing home. They learned more lessons of life there than anything I could have taught them. The only reward they got from the time spent with the people there was the joy of feeling God's pleasure. It blesses my heart to see them living that out in their lives today.

6. Blessed are the pure in heart, for they shall see God.

What does it mean to be pure in heart? The "*heart*" spoken of in the Bible is the very core of our soul, our mind, our will, and our emotions. When we accept Jesus as our Savior, we are given a new heart, his heart. It is from that heart we are to live as he did.

Our heart is that place where the awareness of Jesus resides. The disciples referred to this in Luke 24:32 when Jesus appeared to them as they were walking on the road to Emmaus, "They asked each other, 'Were not our <u>*hearts*</u> burning within us while He (Jesus) talked with us on the road and opened the scriptures to us?" They were speaking of the awareness of His presence. I know each of us who have accepted Him as our Savior has experienced that same burning of His presence.

2 Corinthians 1:21-22 assures us of this, "…He anointed us and set his seal of ownership on us, and put his Spirit in our *hearts* as a deposit guaranteeing what is to come."

So we find that we have been given a pure heart as a gift of God, but the problem comes when we try to maintain that purity in the world we live in. How do we do that? Hebrews 3:8 tells us not to harden our hearts and to live as children of light, and not as the Gentiles who had not received Jesus. We are told in Ephesians 4:18, "They are darkened in their understanding and separated from the life of God because of the ignorance that is in them due to the hardening of their *hearts,* having lost all sensitivity, they have given themselves over to sensuality so as to indulge in every kind of impurity, with a continual lust for more."

The question we have to ask ourselves is, do I want to please God and feel his pleasure in my life more than I want the pleasures of this world? And if I do, how can I accomplish that? The key is found in Colossians 3:1-3, "Since then, you have been raised with Christ, set your *hearts* on things above, where Christ is seated at the right hand of God. Set your minds on things above, not on earthly things. For you died and your life is now hidden with Christ in God."

That is why it is so important to spend time in prayer communicating with God, reading the scriptures to hear his message and to be diligent to associate with others who will encourage you in your desire to remain pure.

The rewards are greater than you can ever imagine. **You will see** God working in your life, and you will experience his pleasure. It is the only way to have true joy and peace. You will see and sense him in the very depths of your soul.

For now, we have to see God through a heart of faith. For in the flesh the Bible says that no one has ever seen God (Exod. 33:18-23; 1 Tim. 6:16). People have seen appearances of the Lord in various forms, like Moses on Mount Sinai seeing the hem of the garment (Exod. 33), or the Israelite leaders eating with the Lord and seeing the God of Israel in the form of the revealed presence (Exod. 24), or Isaiah (Isa. 6) or John (Rev. 1).

Here on earth, the carnal vision of God is denied to us. Ephesians 3:17 tell us that God dwells in our hearts through faith. But one day when heaven will be opened he will be visible to our transfigured eyes. As Job said, "I know that my Redeemer lives and that in the end, he will stand upon the earth. And after my skin has been destroyed, yet in my flesh, I will see God; I myself will see him with my own eyes--I and not another. How my heart yearns within me" (Job 19:25-27).

7. Blessed are the peacemakers for they shall be called sons of God.

To understand peacemakers, I think you have to understand peace. Webster defines it as freedom from disturbance, quiet and tranquility.

As we look at peace with this definition, we realize that we were born into a world of disturbance and Jesus came to restore the peace that Adam and Eve had in the garden before they sinned. Genesis tells us they walked in the cool of the evening with God. That sounds like a life of quiet and tranquility to me.

We know that when sin entered the world that peace was disturbed. We have since longed for peace in every aspect of our lives. Proverbs 14:30, tells us, "A heart at peace gives life to the body."

God is a God of peace; His whole plan of redemption is to provide peace for those who were formerly alienated from him, and ultimately bring peace to the entire world. We see in Isaiah 9:6, he is actually called the Prince of Peace.

Unfortunately, in the world we live in there is strife and conflict and what seems like little hope for lasting peace and unity. The peace that God brings is not just cessation of hostilities, intolerance, or wars. It is what the Bible calls "peace that passes understanding." It is a peace that calls for a complete change of nature. And only God can give this kind of peace. It is a peace that the world does not understand. In John 14:27, Jesus says, "Peace I leave with you, my peace I give you. I do not give to you as the world gives. Do not let your hearts be troubled and do not be afraid."

Those who are peacemakers are first and foremost people who understand what true peace is. True peace comes with being in right relationship with God, our creator. When we are operating from a place of peace we will naturally strive to live at peace with others. In other words, the true peacemakers are those who promote the kingdom of God. Their lives are given to working on promoting the kingdom of God, reconciling adversaries, quenching hatred, uniting those who are divided, and fostering true understanding and spiritual love.

And the promise we have is when we walk in His peace we shall be called the sons of God. We are no longer slaves, but sons and daughters with his very nature.

In the Old Testament "sons of God" is a description of angels, and rarely is such language used for salvation. But in the New Testament sonship is a powerful expression for salvation. It means that believers have been born into the family of God by the Holy Spirit and that those so designated have a personal relationship with the Father through Christ the Son, that they are joint-heirs with him, and that they have a place in their heavenly home by birthright. Not yet in the full sense, but truly in the certainty of the promise can believers say, "We are called the children of God" (see John 1:12, 13 and 1 John 3:1).

8. Blessed are they who suffer persecution for justice sake, for theirs is the kingdom of heaven.

In this beatitude, Christ pronounces a blessing on those who are being persecuted. But the persecution that they are suffering is not for evil acts or crimes they have done, but their persecution is for being righteous.

They are persecuted for godly conversation and Godly actions which in turn brings upon them the hatred and enmity of the men of the world. For by living righteously the believers separate themselves from the world and profess themselves not to belong to the world. I think this is confusing to those who don't understand the peace that I described earlier as followers of Jesus have.

There is much evidence that proves that more Christians around the world have been martyred for their faith in this century alone, than in the combined previous nineteen centuries of the church's history. In many countries today it is a crime to be a Christian. If you live in the United States, you may think that the idea of persecution of Christians is not very relevant today. Even though we are not experiencing any real persecution here in this country, as you look around you can't help but see many great evil inroads that have been made into destroying anything having to do with Jesus Christ, the Bible, or the laws of God. The greatest assault on Christianity has been the many laws that have been passed recently, all with the idea of suppressing Christianity in all areas of society.

Much of the persecution that we experience in our country is verbal language or the looks of disgust when you take a stand on biblical principles. If you doubt this then tell a group of your friends what the Word of God says about a lifestyle they may be living that contradicts what the Bible says is right. Try to defend the freedoms and rights that are laid out in the Constitution and Declaration of Independence that do not support the beliefs that have become so accepted. Our nation was founded on Christian principles and at the very core of everything our founding fathers did they inserted such phrases that we are one nation under God, and put on our coins, in God we trust. It is getting harder and harder to stand up for those values as so many others have come in and tried to make our nation politically correct. Those of us who take a stand for those values are often met with ridicule and feelings of being alienated.

But why is there such persecution in the world, and why is the Word of God so offensive to so many? I think it is because it is a stumbling block to ungodly people. They take pleasure in their sin and the conviction that comes with the Word makes them uncomfortable. God placed a conscience inside every man's spirit so even though man can disregard the Word, there is always an awareness of the void that only God can fill.

The unbelieving sinner feels guilty and doesn't like that feeling, so it is easy for him to lash out at the believers of God, blaming them for making him feel bad. That is why the things of God and the beliefs of God are constantly being ridiculed and made fun of. The unbelievers are attempting to destroy anything that has to do with God in a desperate attempt to do away with the source of their feeling bad. Throughout human history blaming someone else for their troubles has always been an easy way out for a great many groups. So the sinner is an enemy of God, and he is trying to fight back against God. And since the sinner can't get at God, he does the next best thing - he goes after those that follow God. Jesus told us in **John 3:20** that, "Everyone who does evil hates the light," and in **John 7:7** he declared, "The world hates me because I testify that what it does is evil." This can all be summed up by another verse in the Book of John. **John 15:20** "If they persecuted me, they will also persecute you."

The world hates Jesus because he is light, righteousness, and truth. They hate him because he reveals the wickedness of the people of the world, and they hate him because he exposes their evil. Jesus also told his disciples that they were his servants, and he told them just as he is telling us, that if the master is hated, then the servants of the master will also be hated. The great thing is that if Jesus truly lives in you, your position is clear and you take a stand against wrong even when it makes you uncomfortable. When others ridicule us or give us looks of disgust, we can know that we are identifying with our Savior and what we have the world can't buy.

So this brings us to the question if I am not being persecuted, why not? And the answer just may be that you are not taking a stand for Christ. In **Luke 6:26** Jesus said, "**Woe to you when all men speak well of you**, for that is how their fathers treated the false prophets." When the world applauds, appreciates, and commends you, be aware that you may be allowing your lack of faith in God to keep you from being the witness he wants you to be.

It is easy to think that severe persecution is a thing of the past, but right now in Iraq, we have thousands stranded on a mountaintop having been displaced from their homes and villages by radical Isis whose sole intent is to destroy Christians, and that includes the United States that calls itself a Christian nation. That is true of so many places in the world, and we should pray daily for our brothers and sisters in Christ who are truly being persecuted in ways we cannot even perceive.

Discussion Questions:

1. Have you ever experienced persecution for taking a stand for what is right?

2. What in your life might be keeping you from being pure in heart as you stand before God?

3. Can you tell a time that you experienced being a peacemaker and how the peace of God directed you?

4. What does it mean to you to show mercy to another? Can you think of a time you extended mercy to another even when they may not have deserved it?

Lesson 39
Jesus and Mary Magdalene/Nicodemus

Mary Magdalene

As we look at the people in Jesus' earthly walk, Mary Magdalene stands out as one of his closest companions.

She was sometimes referred to as, "The Magdalene," which identifies her with her place of birth, just as Jesus was called "The Nazarene" because he grew up in Nazareth.

Magdala was a thriving town on the coast of Galilee about three miles from Caperna in the time of Christ. Dye works and productive textile factories added to the wealth of the community. It may be that "The Magdalene" was connected with the industry of the town, for it would seem as if she was not without means, enabling her to serve the Lord with her substance.

We have no record of Mary's parents, her marital status, or her age. That she was free to follow Jesus in his journeys would suggest that she had no home obligations.

She is mentioned fourteen times in the gospels, and from references to her, we can see clearly what she did and how she did it. A striking feature in eight of the fourteen passages is that Mary is named in connection with other women, but she always heads the list, implying that she occupied the place at the front of service. In the five times where she is mentioned alone, the connection is with the death and resurrection of Christ (Mark 16:9; John 20:1, 11, 16, 18).

Although Mary was a woman of high standing and in comfortable circumstances, the first thing we read about her is that she was possessed with seven demons. She became one of Jesus' most trusted companions, but when he first saw her she must have been revolting to look at with her disheveled hair, glaring eyes, and sunken cheeks.

Luke links Mary with Joanna and Susanna and "many others" as those healed of evil spirits and infirmities by Jesus. As Mary is referred to as having "seven demons" her condition must have been worse than the rest. But the moment Jesus' compassionate eyes saw the wild-eyed and cringing woman of Magdala, he looked beyond the appearance of evil that had possessed her and saw a woman who would be a blessing to his own heart and to many others. In his authoritative voice, he commanded the tormenting demons to come out of her and stay out of her. "Back! Back! To your native hell, ye foul spirits of the pit!" and the miracle happened. Her deranged and troubled mind became as tranquil as the troubled lake Jesus calmed.

Sanity returned, the rosy tint was restored to her cheeks, and she was made whole. Now, "clothed and in her right mind," she was ready to become a devoted disciple of Jesus to whom she owed so much. That she was deeply grateful for physical and mental healing, is shown by what she endeavored to do for him and his cause. Saved from the terrible power of hell, she gave of the best she had to her deliverer. Her deliverance was obvious to others. Our deliverance is often not visible to the outside world, but there is never a question in our own hearts when Jesus sets our hearts free.

Now that Mary was freed from satanic bondage she, along with the other women who had been healed, greatly aided Jesus in His missionary activities as he went from place to place preaching and teaching his message.

Grateful, these women became generous, ministering unto Him of their substance. Mary left her home in Magdala to follow Jesus. Constantly on the move as Jesus and His disciples were, there were many details in connection with their personal comfort and wellbeing requiring attention to which these women could see. Quietly and effectively Mary would do what she knew needed to be done. Further, money was necessary for the Master's campaign work. We never read of Him or His disciples asking for money, yet funds were necessary. Much of it we can assume came from Mary and others like her who had been so richly blessed by Him.

Mary helped Jesus to evangelize as she willingly gave of herself and her substance to help meet his needs. She went with her Lord into the shadows and is thus represented as being among those who followed Jesus on His last sad journey from Galilee to Jerusalem. And as they followed, they still "ministered unto him." Mary was present with the other holy women at the mock trial of Jesus. No longer is he on the road with crowds gathering and hanging on his words. He is now arrested and tried for his life. Some of his intimate friends deserted him, but Mary and her band of women did not forsake him.

She was present in Pilate's Hall and saw and heard the religious leaders clamoring for the blood of him who was so precious to her heart. She listened as Pontius Pilate pronounced his death sentence of crucifixion although he had found no fault in him. She witnessed and wept as Jesus left the hall to be spat upon and ill-treated by the crowd thirsting for his blood. Then she saw him led out to Calvary's fatal mount to be nailed to a tree.

Mary was one of the sorrowing group of holy women who stood as near as they could to comfort Jesus by their presence in the closing agonies of the crucifixion (Luke 23:49). Mary listened with a broken heart to his bitter cries and watched through those dreaded hours until at last the Roman soldier thrust his spear into the Savior's side and declared him dead.

No sooner had Jesus dismissed his spirit than the question arose among the women at the cross, "How could they secure that bloodstained body, and prepare it for burial?" Joseph of Arimathea and Nicodemus came and saved the day for they had come for that very purpose. They prepared his body and placed it in a new tomb in the garden. Mary Magdalene remained "sitting over against the sepulcher" until Joseph had laid the Lord's body away (Matthew 27:61; Mark 15:47; Luke 23:55).

She was last at the cross and the first at the garden tomb to witness the most important event in world history, and this pivotal point of Christianity -- namely the Resurrection of Jesus Christ.

What a great honor God conferred upon the faithful Mary Magdalene in permitting her to be the first witness of that Resurrection! She was at the tomb early on that first Easter morning, and as the light of day came across Jerusalem, she looked into the cave. Seeing it was empty, she wept. She rushed to Peter and John, and most excitedly said, "They have taken away the Lord out of the sepulcher, and we know not where they have laid him." The disciples returned with Mary Magdalene to the tomb and when they saw that what she had told them was true, they departed to their own homes. But not Mary! She stood at the door of the tomb weeping and as she wept, two angels appeared, one at the head and the other at the feet where the body of Jesus had lain. Seeing her distressed and afraid, they tenderly asked, "Woman, why weepest thou?" Trembling, she replied, "Because they have taken away my Lord, and I know not where they have lain him."

Then one word from the voice she recognized uttered her name, "Mary"! That old familiar tone must have gripped her heart, and instantly she cried "Rabboni!" This word in English means teacher. This must have been a response of shock mixed with both love and relief. I am sure her first response was to bow before him and then embrace him, but he said, Matthew 20:17, "Do not hold on to me, for I have not yet returned to the Father, Go instead to my brothers and tell them. I am returning to my Father and your Father, to my God and your God." In this instance, Mary knew he was telling her to release the earthly bond and to receive the spiritual oneness she now would have with Him. I think his emphasis on referring to Father as her father as well as his, reflects this new relationship that had just taken place.

Then Jesus commissioned Mary to become the first one to tell of his resurrection. She had to go and announce the greatest news ever proclaimed. We can imagine with what speed Mary ran back through the gates of Jerusalem to tell the disciples that their Lord who had died was alive forevermore.

Mary had stayed near to Christ in his journeys and had cared for many of his human needs until his corpse was laid in the tomb. He now rewarded her with a closer knowledge of things divine, and she was given an honor that cannot be taken away from her, namely, that of being the first among men or women to see the Risen Lord and to receive the first message from his lips (John 20:18).

Although this is the last glimpse we have of Mary Magdalene, we have no hesitation in assuming that she was present with the women (Acts 1:14) who assembled with the apostles in the upper chamber for prayer and supplication, and to await the coming of the promised Spirit at Pentecost. Mary must have been caught up by his power and made an effective witness of her risen and now ascended Lord.

Mary Magdalene's life is an example of what the power of Jesus can do in our troubled souls by transforming even the most tormented and afflicted individual into a valued and devoted follower.

Nicodemus

Nicodemus was a Pharisee and a leader of the Jewish people. He was also a member of the Sanhedrin, the high court in Israel. He had heard the teachings of Jesus and saw the miracles. He became curious, and not wanting to ruin his reputation to seek out the truth, he came to Jesus at night. John 3:1-4, he approached Jesus and said, "Rabbi, we know you are a teacher who has come from God. For no one could perform the miraculous signs you are doing if God were not with him." Jesus replied, "I tell you the truth, no one can see the kingdom of God unless he is born again." This sounded very confusing to Nicodemus and he questioned Jesus further. "How can a man be born again when he is old? Surely he cannot enter a second time into his mother's womb."

Jesus answered him by saying, "I tell you the truth, no one can enter the kingdom of God unless he is born of water and the Spirit. Flesh gives birth to flesh, but the Spirit gives birth to spirit. You must not be surprised when I say you must be born again. The wind blows wherever it pleases. You hear its sound, but you cannot tell where it comes from or where it is going. So it is with everyone born of the Spirit."

Jesus is telling Nicodemus that to acquire the Kingdom of God is much deeper than just believing in the miracles he did. He is telling Nicodemus that this is drastic, like birth. The change has to be total. You must become a new creation.

Remember, the Jews and the Pharisees were all anticipating the coming kingdom. Their problem was that they thought that mere physical lineage and keeping of religious externals qualified them for entrance into the kingdom, rather than the needed spiritual transformation Jesus emphasized.

Then Jesus tells Nicodemus, "I say unto thee, except a man be born of water and of the Spirit, he cannot enter into the kingdom of God." Jesus wasn't referring to literal water here but to the need for "cleansing."

Ezekiel 36:24-27 tells us: "For I will take you from among the heathen, and gather you out of all countries, and will bring you into your own land. Then will I sprinkle clean water upon you, and ye shall be clean from all your filthiness, and from all your idols, will I cleanse you. A new heart also will I give you, and a new spirit will I put within you: and I will take away the stony heart out of your flesh, and I will give you a heart of flesh. And I will put my spirit within you, and cause you to walk in my statutes, and ye shall keep my judgments, and do them."

There are arguments about baptism and even the methods of baptism, and these are distractions from the real message Jesus was trying to make. As I pointed out with the Ezekiel passage, baptism is an outward pronouncement to the world by a physical act of what has happened inside. When we baptize at our church the pastor says the person is "buried with Christ and risen with him to a new life." That new life is a life of following Jesus and walking away from the dictates of our old selfish way of life.

If there has not been a baptism of our heart changing us from an old flesh creature to a brand-new Spirit being, we can be outwardly baptized a hundred times, and it will not mean anything.

Jesus says, "That which is born of the flesh is flesh, and that which is born of the Spirit is spirit." The spirit of a man is what he is. Our flesh or our spirit rules over us. We cannot serve two masters. Those who live in the flesh, lust after the things of the flesh. The flesh is not in tune with God. When we are born of the flesh, we are consumed by the lusts for the things of the world.

Jesus picked up that Nicodemus was still trying to figure out this mystery, so he reassures him again in John 3:7, "Marvel not that I said unto thee, ye must be born again."

Nicodemus was an educated man of the law and all this seems so strange to him. Jesus tells him not to wonder at it but just accept it. Jesus makes sure Nicodemus knows what He is saying because He says it again, "Ye must be born again of the Spirit to inherit the kingdom."

Then Jesus gives him a visual in verse 8, "The wind bloweth where it listeth, and thou hearest the sound thereof, but canst not tell whence it cometh, and whither it goeth: so is everyone that is born of the Spirit."

You cannot see the wind or the Spirit. To try to say where the wind came from or where it is going would be pure presumption. This is like the new birth in the Spirit. You know it is there, you feel the effects, but it is impossible to explain in natural terms. The wind comes through and rearranges leaves when it comes through; the same is true with the Spirit. It has a way of rearranging lives. After a windstorm, you see the results. After a new birth in the Spirit, you see the results as well.

So the point that Jesus was making was that just as the wind cannot be controlled or understood by human beings but its effects can be witnessed, so also it is with the Holy Spirit. He cannot be controlled or understood, but the proof of His work is apparent. Where the Spirit works, there is undeniable and unmistakable evidence. That is when a person's whole outlook on life changes.

As we said at the very beginning of this study, Nicodemus was a logical man. He analyzed everything all the time, but this he could not understand. He kept asking Jesus how this was possible.

"Jesus answered and said unto him, Art thou a master of Israel, and knowest not these things?"

This is not quite a reprimand, but perhaps a caution. Jesus is telling him, you are a man of the law and you don't know this. It seems that Nicodemus must have held a prominent position because he is called here master of Israel. Nicodemus should have known more about what the Old Testament Scriptures taught.

Jesus' reply emphasized the spiritual bankruptcy of the nation at that time since even one of the greatest of Jewish teachers did not recognize this teaching on spiritual cleansing and transformation based clearly in the Old Testament.

Jesus continues, "Verily, verily, I say unto thee, we speak that we do know, and testify that we have seen; and ye receive not our witness."

Nicodemus believed the miracles, but he could not turn loose of his affluent life and become a new creature. He wasn't ready to give up friends and family (that's why he came to find Jesus at night). Nicodemus did not really want a total change; he was trying to understand how far he had to go to get this new life.

He didn't want to be a new creature with the old passed away. He liked his old way as master of Israel. He wanted it all and continued to question. Jesus tells him, we are giving you our firsthand knowledge, and you don't believe us.

When Nicodemus presses him for more information, Jesus replies, "If I have told you earthly things, and ye believe not, how shall ye believe, if I tell you of heavenly things?"

Jesus says to Nicodemus here, "The example I gave you was of earthly things that you are acquainted with, and you do not understand. What makes you think you would understand heavenly things of which you know nothing? " He goes on to say, "No one has ever gone into heaven except the one who came from heaven-the Son of God." Saying basically it is by faith that we believe because we have not been given access to heaven where all these things are made clear.

It was to Nicodemus that Jesus responded with the most famous verse in the Bible. John 3:16, "For God so loved the world that he gave his only begotten son, that whosoever believeth in him should not perish but have everlasting life."

We know that later Nicodemus stood up for Jesus when the Pharisees were conspiring against him: Nicodemus, who had gone to Jesus earlier and who was one of their own, asked, "Does our law 'condemn a man without first hearing him to find out what he has been doing?" (John 7:50-51)

We also see him helping Joseph of Arimathea take Jesus' body down from the cross and lay it in a tomb, at great risk to his safety and reputation. He defied the Sanhedrin and Pharisees by treating Jesus' body with dignity and assuring that he received a proper burial.

He also donated 75 pounds of expensive myrrh and aloes to anoint Jesus' body after he died.

Nicodemus would not rest until he found the truth. He wanted badly to understand, and continued to seek truth and his life was eternally changed.

Discussion Questions:

1. As you look at Mary's life, can you find any parallels with your own?

2. Jesus delivered Mary from the issues that were tormenting her soul. Can you share a time when Jesus delivered you from an anxious time in your life?

3. As you look at Nicodemus' life and how he sought truth, can you relate to the time in your life that you were seeking to understand the supernatural process of rebirth and how you discovered it for yourself?

4. What lesson can we learn from Nicodemus' life?

Lesson 40

Mary/Martha/Lazarus

The Bible tells us little about Lazarus or his two sisters' history. There is no mention of Lazarus having a wife but we can assume Martha and Mary were widowed or single because they lived with their brother.

They lived in Bethany, a village about two miles from Jerusalem on the Mount of Olives. The Bible tells us in Luke 10:38, "As Jesus and his disciples were on their way, he came to a village where a woman named Martha opened her home to him." This indicates that perhaps it was Martha's home that they lived. She also was the one who felt the need to show hospitality and be the hostess that indicates it may have been her home.

The gospels record that Jesus felt comfortable in their home. The four weren't just acquaintances, they were close friends. They were like family. John 11:5, tells us, "Jesus loved Martha and her sister and Lazarus." Even though we know that Jesus loved all mankind, this is one of the few times he pointed out his love for another by name during his three years of his ministry.

They were confident in his love because, in verse 3, it tells us, "Therefore his sisters sent unto him, saying, Lord, behold, he whom thou lovest is sick." They spoke to Jesus as if he were a part of their immediate family. Jesus was so troubled by their anguish over their brother's death that he was moved to tears before raising Lazarus to life again.

Their home might have been considered Jesus' home away from home. We see the story of Lazarus opening with word being sent to Jesus that his friend Lazarus was very sick and that he should come immediately. However, he decides to delay going to him until it appears it is too late.

However, as the scriptures tell us, God's ways are higher than our ways and Jesus points this out to his disciples when he is given this message. John 11:4 tell us, "This sickness will not end in death. No, it is for God's glory so that God's Son may be glorified through it." Then in verse 11, he tells his disciples, "Our friend Lazarus has fallen asleep, but I am going there to wake him up."

It is obvious that Jesus had determined to make this a teaching opportunity to teach his ability and power over death. He goes on in verse 14 and tells them, "Lazarus is dead, and for your sake, I am glad I was not there, so that you may believe. But let us go to him."

His disciples had warned him that he should not go back there because the Jews had tried to stone him when he was there before. After Jesus tells them he is going back, Thomas tells the other disciples, "Let us also go, that we may die with him." This shows the devotion of these men who had committed to follow him even if it meant death. (These are the same ones who later would deny that they had ever known him.)

As they approached Bethany, Martha ran to meet Jesus, but Mary remained at home. Martha told him that she knew that if he had come when he had first heard about his illness that her brother would not have died. However; she says, "I know that even now, that God will give you whatever you ask." She is expressing disappointment and hope. Then Jesus tells her, "Your brother will rise again." She replies, "I know he will rise again in the resurrection at the last day." She obviously was well versed in prophecy and what was to come.

Jesus speaks straight to her heart. "I am the resurrection and the life. He who believes in me will live, even though he dies; and whosoever lives and believes in me will never die. Do you believe this?" He is asking her whether she believes he is who he says he is. She replies, "Yes, Lord, I believe that you are the Christ, the Son of God, who was to come into the world."

They are still outside of town where Martha had run to meet him, and now she turns and runs home and tells Mary that Jesus is here and that he is asking to see her. Mary immediately got up and ran to meet him. The visiting Jews who had come to visit and comfort her followed her thinking she was going to the tomb to mourn.

When she approached Jesus, she said, "Lord, if you had been here, my brother would not have died." When Jesus saw her sadness and those who were with her, He was deeply moved and wept with them.

Then he asked, "Where have you laid him?" The Jews saw this emotion in Jesus and pointed out, "See how much he loved Lazarus." This points out how evident the richness of the relationship Jesus had with this family. But they quickly began to question his ability. "Could not he who opened the eyes of the blind man have kept this man from dying?"

Upon arriving at the tomb, Jesus commanded them to take away the stone of the grave. Martha, being the practical one, questions Jesus as if he did not know what he was doing. "Lord, by now there will be a bad odor because he has been dead for four days." Then once again Jesus tells her, "Did I not tell you, (probably just a few minutes before when she ran to meet him on the road) that if you believed, you would see the glory of God?"

Jesus then looked up into Heaven and said, "Father, I thank you that you have heard me. I knew that you always hear me, but I said this for the benefit of the people standing here, that they may believe that you sent me." Then he called in a loud voice, "Lazarus, come out." At that command, Lazarus came out of the grave with his hands and feet wrapped with strips of linen, and a cloth on his face. Jesus said to them, "Take off the grave clothes and let him go."

Seeing this, many Jews who were there to comfort Mary and Martha, put their faith in Jesus and believed. However, some went back and reported to the Pharisees what had happened. They immediately called a meeting of the Sanhedrin and began plotting to kill him.

After this Jesus no longer moved about publicly among the Jews but stayed in an area called Ephraim with his disciples because word had gotten out that if anyone knew where he was, they were to report it so he could be arrested.

Six days before Passover Jesus and his disciples were on their way to Jerusalem and stopped at the home of Lazarus, Mary, and Martha about mealtime. Luke gives a detailed description of the tone of the evening where Martha calls into question the fact that she is doing all the work and Mary is just sitting at the feet of Jesus hanging on every word.

Notice the exchange between Jesus and Martha in Luke 10:39, "She [Martha] had a sister called Mary, who also sat at Jesus' feet and heard His word. But Martha was distracted with much serving, and she approached him and said, 'Lord, do you not care that my sister has left me to serve alone? Therefore tell her to help me.' And Jesus answered and said to her, 'Martha, Martha, you are worried and troubled about many things. But one thing is needed, and Mary has chosen that good part, which will not be taken from her.'"

Martha appears to be the leader and the more hospitable and social of the two. Her outlook on life was quite different from Mary's. It is possible that Martha was the older sister and that her age figured into her personality and perspective. Martha's words and actions depict her as the more ambitious and responsible one. The one who felt the responsibility to see to it that there was food for the guests and that the house was picked up.

Martha was the one who did not wait at the house but went out to meet Jesus when Lazarus had died. On both occasions, she was confrontational wanting answers. She would be the type A personality that today we would call high justice.

I can personally imagine the scene and the frustrations she felt. We are also told that Lazarus was reclining at the table with Jesus and his disciples. Martha must have felt like the only one who cared enough to attend to these guests (and remember Jesus had twelve disciples). I'm not sure if others were there or not, but this was before microwave ovens and take-out.

Mary may have been more of an introvert naturally, but I suspect that Martha was extremely efficient and Mary was the deep psychological thinker.

I'm sure Jesus appreciated the hospitality and care that Martha was showing but wanted to teach the lesson that what is spiritual is of more value than having enough food or the proper placement of the napkin and silverware at the table. After all, he had already shown that he could multiply a small loaf of bread and a few fish to feed five thousand if needed.

You must also realize the setting of what Jesus knew was about to take place. I think part of his frustration with Martha was wanting her to grasp the importance of spiritual understanding knowing the time was coming soon that everyone's faith and loyalty would be tested. He wanted to be sure she understood the value of the spiritual truths versus the things the world would say about Him.

To better understand Mary's actions, let's read details in John's account of that same visit. "Then, six days before the Passover, Jesus [and the disciples] came to Bethany, where Lazarus was who had been dead, whom he had raised from the dead. There they made him supper, and Martha served, but Lazarus was one of those who sat at the table with him. Then Mary took a pound of very costly oil of spikenard, anointed the feet of Jesus, and wiped his feet with her hair. And the house was filled with the fragrance of the oil" (John: 12:1-3).

Judas even questioned her using such expensive perfume for this purpose when it could have been sold and helped the poor. Jesus replied, "Leave her alone, it was intended that she should save this perfume for the day of my burial. You will always have the poor among you, but you will not always have me."

John emphasizes here that Mary was so humble, convicted and dedicated to Jesus and his teachings that no expense or personal act was too high. Little did she know that she was actually being used as part of the preparation for his death and burial.

Jesus made a point to notice that Mary made a conscious decision between two alternatives: She chose to listen to Jesus over doing what seemed important in our everyday lives. People are asked to make choices all the time. It is a part of life. The Bible speaks of these choices from the beginning to the end.

Moses declared: "I call heaven and earth as witnesses today against you that I have set before you life and death, blessing and cursing; therefore choose life that both you and your descendants may live" (Deuteronomy: 30:19).

Jesus tells us our highest priority in life should be to "seek first the kingdom of God and His righteousness . . ." (Matthew: 6:33).

He tells us this in the New Testament, Luke 4:4: "Man shall not live by bread alone, but by every word of God."

That was almost identical to Deuteronomy 8:3 in the Old Testament: "And he humbled thee, and suffered you to hunger, and fed thee with manna, which thou knew not, neither did thy fathers know; that he might make thee know that man doth not live by bread only, but by every word that proceeds out of the mouth of the LORD doth man end."

John 6:63 tells us the importance of Jesus' words as well, "It is the spirit that quickeneth; the flesh profiteth nothing: the words that I speak unto you, they are spirit, and they are life."

The book of Hebrews tells us the importance of hearing and heeding the words of life: "Therefore we must give the more earnest heed to the things we have heard, lest we drift away. For if the word spoken through angels proved steadfast, and every transgression and disobedience received a just reward, how shall we escape if we neglect so great a salvation, which at the first began to be spoken by the Lord, and was confirmed to us by those who heard Him" (Hebrews 2:1-3).

God's truth and laws will abide forever. Our bodies won't last forever, for they must be replaced with spirit bodies. The spiritual knowledge we accumulate in this life will be ours forever, never taken away from us. But we must not allow physical needs and duties to consume us.

We read in Revelation 14:12, "Here is the patience of the saints; here are those who keep the commandments of God and the faith of Jesus." This verse is comparing those who worship the idols of the time and those who have been found faithful until the end and as they are presented to God the Father.

Like Mary, we need patient faith as we live in a world destined to destruction. A world that is filled with false ideas and trappings that come with lust, greed and a desire to think we can be happy apart from God. Jesus came as an image of our creator and withstood all these trappings while on earth in physical form. He experienced all the emotions and issues we do today.

He revealed his compassion for people through a genuine display of emotion. Even though he knew that Lazarus would live, he was still moved to weep with the ones he loved. Jesus cared about their sorrow. He was not timid to show emotion, and we should not be ashamed to express our true feelings to God. Like Martha and Mary, we can be transparent with God because he cares for us.

Jesus waited to travel to Bethany to raise Lazarus from the dead, so he could perform an amazing miracle there. Sometimes we pray and get anxious as to why God does not act sooner on our behalf. But he is asking us, like he did Martha, do you believe? Believe that his plan and purpose will be done. Can we trust that he knows more of what we need than we ourselves know? When it seems all is lost, he has a greater plan waiting for us.

Discussion Questions:

1. Who do you relate more to, Mary or Martha in the story?

2. Do you struggle to be the one listening at Jesus feet instead of trying to make things work in your way and timing?

3. Are you comfortable coming to Jesus with your questions, struggles, and pain? Do you really know he is there, and when you weep, he weeps with you?

4. What did you learn from studying this lesson?

Lesson 41
Jesus' Parables

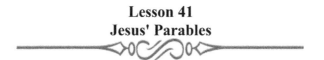

"He began to teach them many things in parables." (Mark 4:2)

As we look at the way Jesus conducted his mission during the three years of ministry, we see first of all that he got the attention of the people by working signs and wonders. We examined them in an earlier lesson. But when they became followers, he had many lessons to teach about this new life he was calling them into. One of the ways he taught significant lessons was through the telling of parables.

What is a parable? A parable is a word picture, which uses an image or story to illustrate a truth or lesson. It creates a mini-drama in picture language that describes the reality being illustrated. It shows a likeness between the image of an illustration and the object being portrayed. It defines the unknown by using the known. It helps the listener to discover the deeper meaning and underlying truth of the reality being portrayed. It can be a figure of speech or comparison such as "the kingdom of God is like a mustard seed or like yeast" (Luke 13:19, 21). More commonly it is a short story told to bring out a lesson or moral. Jesus used simple stories or images to convey important truths about God and his kingdom, and lessons pertaining to the way of life and happiness, which God has for us. They commonly feature examples or illustrations from daily life in ancient Palestine, such as mustard seeds and fig trees, wineskins and oil lamps, money and treasure, stewards, workers, judges, and homemakers, wedding parties and children's games. Jesus' audience would be very familiar with these illustrations from everyday life.

Jesus' parables have a double meaning. First, there is the literal meaning, apparent to anyone who has experience with the subject matter. But beyond the literal meaning lies a deeper meaning – a beneath-the-surface lesson about God's truth and his kingdom. For example, the parable of the leaven found in Matthew 13:33, describes the simple transformation of dough into bread by the inclusion of the yeast. In like manner, we are transformed by God's kingdom when we allow his Word and Spirit to take root in our hearts. And in turn, we are called to be leaven that transforms the society in which we live and work.

Jesus' parables often involve an element of surprise or an unexpected twist. We are taken off guard by the progression of the story. The parable moves from the very familiar and understandable aspects of experience to a sudden turn of events or a remarkable comparison, which challenges the hearer and invites further reflection. For example, why should a shepherd go through a lot of bother and even risk his life to find one lost sheep when ninety-nine are in his safe keeping? The shepherd's concern for one lost sheep and his willingness to risk his own life for it tells us a lot about God's concern for his children who go astray.

Jesus told his disciples that not everyone would understand his parables. "To you, it has been given to know the secrets of the kingdom of God; but for others they are in parables, so that seeing they may not see, and hearing they may not hear" (Luke 8:10). Did Jesus mean to say that he was deliberately confusing his listeners? No, Jesus was speaking from experience. He was aware that some who heard his parables refused to understand them. It was not that they could not intellectually understand them, but rather, their hearts were closed to what Jesus was saying. They had already made up their minds to not believe. God can only reveal the secrets of his kingdom to the humble and trusting person who acknowledges the need for God and for his truth. The parables of Jesus will enlighten us if we approach them with an open mind and heart, ready to let them challenge us. If we approach them with the conviction that we already know the answer we may look but not see, and listen but not hear or understand.

When reading the parables it is important not to get bogged down in the details of the story. The main point is what counts. Very often the details are clear enough, but some are obscure (for example, why would a rich man allow his dishonest steward to take care of his inventory? (Luke 16:1-8). Look for the main point and don't get bogged down in the details. In addition, Jesus often throws in a surprise or unexpected twist. These challenge the hearer and invite us to reflect. Jesus meant for his parables to provoke a response. If we listen with faith and humility we will understand what Jesus wishes to speak to our hearts.

PARABLES FROM NATURE

- The Sower and the Seeds (Mark 4:3-9; Matthew 13:3-9; Luke 8:5-8)
- The Grain of Wheat (John 12:24)
- The Weeds in the Grain or the Tares (Matthew 13:24-30)
- The Net (Matthew 13:47-50)
- The Seed Growing Secretly (Spontaneously) or The Patient Husbandman (Mark 4:26-29)
- The Mustard Seed (Matthew13:31; Mark 4:30-32; Luke 13:18.)
- The Leaven (Matthew 13:33; Luke 13:20)
- The Budding Fig Tree (Matthew 24:32; Mark 13:28; Luke 21:19-31)
- The Barren Fig Tree (Luke 1Matthew3:6-9)
- The Birds of Heaven (Matthew 6:26; Luke 12:24)
- The Flowers of the Field (Matthew 6:28-30; Luke 12:27f.)
- The Vultures & the Carcass (Matthew 24:28; Luke 17:37)
- The Tree and its Fruits (Matthew 7:16; Luke 6:43-49)
- The Weather Signs (Luke 12:54-56; Matthew 26:2; Mark 8:11-13)

WORK AND WAGES

- Master and Servant (Luke 17:7-10)
- The Servant Entrusted with Authority or The Faithful and Unfaithful Servants (Matt. 24:45-51; Luke 12:42-46)
- The Waiting Servants (Luke 12:35-38; Mark 13:33-37)
- The Laborers in the Vineyard or The Generous Employer (Matthew 20:1-16)
- The Money in Trust or The Talents (Matthew 25:14-30; Luke 19:12-27)
- The Lamp (Matt 5:14-16; Mark 4:21; Luke 8:16, 11:31) and The City Set on a Hill (Matt. 5:14b)
- The Body's Lamp (Matthew 6:22 ; Luke 11:34-36)
- The Discarded Salt (Matthew 5:13; Mark 9:50; Luke 14:34 f.)
- The Patch and the Wineskins (Matthew 9:16; Mark 2:21; Luke 5:36-39)
- The Householder's Treasure (Matthew 13:52)
- The Dishonest Steward (Luke 16:1-12)
- The Defendant (Luke 12:58; Matthew 5:25.)
- The Unforgiving Official or The Unmerciful Servant (Matthew 18:23-35)
- The Rich Fool (Luke 12:16-21)
- The Wicked Vinedressers (Matthew 21:33-41; Mark 12:1-9; Luke 20:9-16)
- The Two Builders (Matthew 7:24-27; Luke 6:47-49)

- The Two Debtors (Luke 7:41-43)
- The Hidden Treasure (Matthew 13:44)
- The Pearl of Great Price (Matthew 13:45)

OPEN & CLOSED DOORS

- The Closed Door (Luke 13:24-30)
- The Doorkeeper (Mark 13:33-37 Matthew 24:42);
- The Thief in the Night and the Faithful Servants (Matthew 24:42-51; Luke 12:32-48.)
- The Strong Man Bound (Matthew 12:29; Mark 3:27; Luke 11:21)
- The Divided Realm (Mark 3:24-26; Luke 11:17-20)
- The Unoccupied House or The Demon's Invasion (Matthew 12:43-45; Luke 11:24-26)
- The Importunate Neighbor (Luke 11:5-8)
- The Son's Request (Matthew 7:9-11; Luke 11:11-13)
- The Unjust Judge or The Importunate Widow (Luke 18:1-8)
- The Pharisee and the Publican (Luke 18:9-14)

WEDDINGS AND FEASTS

- The Sulking Children or The Children in the Marketplace (Matthew 11:16-19; Luke 7:31-35)
- The Arrogant Guest (Luke 14:7-11)
- The Bridegroom's Friend (John 3:28)
- The Bridegroom's Attendants (Matthew 9:15a; Mark 2:18 f.; Luke 5:34)
- The Bride's Girlfriends or Ten Virgins (Matthew 25:1-13)
- The Tower Builder and The Warring King (Luke 14:28-32)
- The Wedding Feast or The Unwilling Guests (Matthew 22:1-10; Luke 14:16-24)
- The Wedding Garment (Matthew 22:11-14)
- The Rich Man and Lazarus (Luke 16:19-31)

LOST AND FOUND, FATHER AND SON

- The Good Samaritan (Luke 10:25-37)
- The Prodigal Son or The Loving er (Luke 15:11-32)
- The Two Sons, The Apprentice Son, and The Slave and Son (Matthew 21:28-32; John 5:19)
- The Lost Coin (Luke 15:8-10)
- The Lost Sheep (Matthew 28:12-14; Luke 15:4-7)
- The Shepherd, the Thief, and the Doorkeeper (John 10:1-18)
- The Doctor and the Sick (Matthew 9:12; Mark 2:17; Luke 5: 31 f.)
- The Sheep and the Goats (Matthew 25:31-46)

Discussion Questions:

1. Pick out three parables and read the scripture that tells about it and write the summary of the lesson you think Jesus is trying to teach.

2. Which parable spoke to a life lesson you needed to learn?

Lesson 42
Jesus Life Lessons

In past lessons, we have looked at Jesus coming into the world and being the long-awaited Messiah. We have seen prophecies about his coming, looked at John the Baptist who was preparing the way for his coming, and the actual birth and ministry of his time on earth.

Before we leave the ministry part of his life, let's pause and summarize his life before we move on to the death and resurrection. This is important because it shows us the purpose and plan that his death was meant for.

Purpose

To Demonstrate God's Love "For God loved the world so much that he gave His only begotten Son, that whosoever believes in him should not die, but have eternal life." (John 3:16)

To Bring Good News 'The Spirit of the Lord is upon me because he has chosen me to bring good news to the poor. He has sent me to proclaim liberty to the captives and recovery of sight to the blind, to set free the oppressed and announce that the time has come when the Lord will save his people.' (Jesus describing himself by quoting Isaiah, as recorded in Luke 4:18.)

To Sacrifice Himself for Others "The Son of Man did not come to be served but to serve, and to give his life as a ransom for many" (Matthew 20:28)

To Be a Source of Abundant Life "I came that they may have life and may have it abundantly." (John 10:10)

To Help People Understand the Kingdom of God "I must preach the kingdom of God to the other cities also, for I was sent for this purpose." (Luke 4:43)

Although Jesus' chief purpose was to redeem man from the sinful state he was born into, he taught many life lessons to his followers during the three years of ministry on the earth.

Love

The main focus of his life lessons was based on the importance of love. We learned in our study of the Old Testament that God _is_ love and as such, Jesus had many lessons to teach us about how to love both the Father as well as each other.

"If anyone loves me, he will keep my Word; and My Father will love him, and we will come to him, and make our abode (home) with him." (John 14:23)

This is very humbling as Jesus is saying here that a test of our love is by keeping his Word.

"He who has My commandments and keeps them, he it is who loves Me; and he who loves Me shall be loved by My Father, and I will love him and will disclose Myself to him." (John 14:21) Here he is telling us that if we want God to disclose Himself to us, we must know and keep his commandments. My heart's desire is to know God better and understand Him and His will for my life. He is telling us here that He will disclose himself to us as we draw near to him and do His will. It is not enough to go to church and do a daily Bible reading to be in a place to receive from Him. He wants our whole heart. He wants us to be as passionate about learning of him as he is about every detail of our life.

"For God so loved the world that he gave his only begotten Son, that whoever believes in him should not perish, but have eternal life." (John 3:16) Here we see the ultimate expression of love. I wonder how many of us would be willing to give our life for him.

"Just as the Father has loved me, I have also loved you; abide in my love." (John 15:9) It is sometimes easy to think we are abiding in his love, but the word "abide" here means steadfast. How steadfast and consistent are you in walking in a love relationship with him? I walk in a steadfast relationship with my husband. That means that even when I am not with him, I feel his love and know that he is there for me. I know I can call him at any time to just talk or tell him my troubles and ask for his advice. It is an ever-present feeling that is a part of me. I don't tell him goodbye in the morning and not feel that we are in relationship until we reconnect when he gets home. He is a part of my very fabric and I am a part of his. Every decision I make I consider how it will affect him or our relationship. That is an example of the type of relationship God wants us to have with Him. Having an awareness of his presence and provision for us at all times and letting that be a comfort as we go through the many joys and trials we encounter in life.

John 4:21 says, "And He has given us this commandment, whoever loves God must love his brother." The question you may be asking is how we love our brother. The only way we can love as Jesus did is because he gave us the example to follow. 1 John 4:19, "We love because he first loved us. Then in 1 John 3:1, he gives us the knowhow, "Let us not love with words or tongue but with actions and truth. So often we talk about loving others but how often do we act on it? What if Jesus said, he loved mankind enough to die on the cross and suffer the ultimate humiliation but he never acted on it. It was a decision that was so painful that we are told that he asked his Father if there was any other way this mission could be accomplished. It was so painful for him that he actually sweats drops of blood while in the Garden of Gethsemane praying about acting on his love for us. Had he not acted on that love, we would still be living in a world of sin without hope of ever being restored to oneness with God. I like the saying that asks that "if we were convicted for being a Christian, would there be enough evidence to convict us." I am afraid many of us would have a hung jury if our actions were on trial.

Kingdom

Another of the important teachings Jesus left with his disciples was the principle of the kingdom of God. He speaks almost as much of it as He does about love.

He tells his disciples in John 18:36, "My kingdom is not of this world. If it were, my servants would fight to prevent my arrest by the Jews. But now my kingdom is from another place."

Then we read in the Lord's Prayer, "thy kingdom come, thy will be done on earth as it is in Heaven". He is trying to get them to adopt a kingdom mentality.

In a kingdom, there is a king and protection for all those in the kingdom where the king reigns. Jesus is called the King of kings and he wants all those who follow him to be a part of the kingdom he came to prepare for them.

He gave it such priority that he said in Matt 6:33, "Seek ye first the kingdom of God and his righteousness, and all these things will be given to you as well. Therefore do not worry about tomorrow, for tomorrow will worry about itself. Each day has enough trouble of its own." Jesus wants us to feel a part of his kingdom here on earth as we deal with earthly issues the same way he will have us deal with them when we get to heaven.

The disciples were confused, and Jesus used many different metaphors to try to explain what the kingdom was like.

Matthew 13:24, "The kingdom of heaven is like a man who sowed good seed in his field. But while everyone was sleeping, his enemy came and sowed weeds among the wheat and went away." Jesus gives this parable to explain the weeds that grow up will be bundled up and burned at harvest time, but the wheat will be brought into his kingdom.

Matthew 13:31 states, "The kingdom of heaven is like a mustard seed, which a man took and planted in his field. Though it is the smallest of all seeds; yet when it grows, it is the largest of garden plants and becomes a tree, so that the birds of the air come and perch in its branches." Jesus uses the mustard seed in another place in His teachings to explain that if we just had the faith of a mustard seed, we could say to the mountain, be cast into the sea and it would have to obey us. The point he is making is that even the smallest, or least, in the kingdom will inherit great rewards. Our job is to believe and act on our faith and he will produce our growth.

Matthew 13:33, "The kingdom of heaven is like yeast that a woman took and mixed into a large amount of flour until it worked all through the dough." When yeast is first mixed into bread dough, it is not very noticeable, but a small amount eventually produces a large result. The kingdom begins small and inconspicuous, but it grows quickly.

Matthew 13:44, "The kingdom of heaven is like a treasure hidden in a field. When a man found it, he hid it again, and then in his joy went and sold all he had and bought that field." Again, the story begins with the kingdom small and hidden—but it does not remain hidden. The traditional interpretation of these parables is that when we hear the message of the kingdom, we should be so full of joy that we are willing to give up everything else. We can never "buy" the kingdom or earn our salvation. Rather, in this parable it may be that *Jesus* is the main character. He is the one who sees hidden treasure in his people (the field), and gives everything he has to purchase the prize. The value may not be evident right now, but it is there. The same is true of the next parable.

Matthew 13:45, "The kingdom of heaven is like a merchant looking for fine pearls when he found one of great price, he went away and sold everything he had and bought it."

Matthew 13: 47, "The kingdom of heaven is like a net that was let down into the lake and caught all kinds of fish. When it was full, the fishermen pulled it up onshore. Then they sat down and collected the good fish in the basket, but threw the bad away." He goes on to explain in verse 49, "This is how it will be at the end of the age. The angels will come and separate the wicked from the righteous and throw them into the fiery furnace, where there will be weeping and gnashing of teeth." The kingdom of God captures both good and bad people. The message is given to both. They live together and are given a chance to change and grow. Eventually, the time comes when judgment is made, and God keeps the good.

The lessons on love and being a part of the kingdom lets us move in our next lesson to the way Jesus acted on his love for us. Each of the lessons he taught the disciples are just as relevant to us today as they were when he spoke them.

The last thing Jesus taught his followers was how to pray. He gives them a model prayer to look to for guidance.

Prayer

Our Father, who art in heaven…acknowledges that God is our Father and is in heaven awaiting our communion with Him.

Hallowed be thy name…this gives him the place of respect, honor, and authority in our lives.

Thy kingdom come, thy will be done on earth as it is in heaven…When we accept Jesus as our Lord, we are part of His kingdom and He wants us to live on earth with the same benefits that we will have in Heaven. Living in love, joy and peace.

Give us this day our daily bread…He wants us to know that he will supply our needs daily. Just as he did by giving the children of Israel manna each day.

Forgive us our trespasses as we forgive others who trespass against us... God wants us to walk in a state of forgiveness always remembering how he has forgiven us.

Lead us not into temptation but deliver us from evil…He is telling us to ask for deliverance from the times we are going to be tempted and to keep us from evil.

For thine is the kingdom, the power, and the glory forever and ever…Here we are to acknowledge that God is the kingdom, he has the power and his glory (presence) will be with us forever and ever. Amen…(so be it)

Discussion Questions:

1. As you look at the awareness Jesus had of his purpose, do you ever wonder what your purpose is on this earth? Do you feel like you are living out that purpose?

2. Looking at the teachings that Jesus gave on the importance of love, how have you responded to these verses? Do you love your neighbor as yourself? How does that change your life?

3. Thinking of the importance Jesus gave to teaching about the kingdom, have you ever considered yourself a part of an earthly kingdom that has its headquarters in heaven? If so, how does this affect the way you live your life?

4. What part of the Lord's Prayer most impacts your life?

Lesson 43
Jesus the Final Days

We have spent several lessons exploring Jesus' ministry during the three years he ministered on earth. This started at the age of thirty when John the Baptist baptized him in the Jordan River, and God spoke from heaven announcing that this was indeed his son who had been sent to restore the broken relationship between Himself and mankind.

We saw Jesus teaching, working miracles, and healing the sick everywhere he went to prove to those who would listen that he was indeed the Messiah.

His message to the crowd is found in Mark 8:34: "If anyone would come after me, he must deny himself and take up his cross and follow me. For whoever wants to save his life will lose it, but whoever loses his life for me and for the gospel will save it. What good is it for a man to gain the whole world, yet forfeit his soul? Or what can a man give in exchange for his soul? If anyone is ashamed of me and my words in this adulterous and sinful generation, the Son of Man will be ashamed of him when he comes in his Father's glory with the holy angels."

This was his message, and we see the disciples setting an example by obeying and doing just that. As they left everything and followed him, they saw many miraculous things. At one point Jesus took Peter, James, and John with him and led them up on a high mountain, where they were all alone. Then he was transfigured before them. His clothes became dazzling white, whiter than anyone in the world could bleach them. And there appeared before them Elijah and Moses, who were talking with Jesus. Then a cloud appeared and enveloped them, and a voice came from the cloud: "This is my son, whom I love. Listen to Him." Can you imagine going up on a mountain with Jesus and he becomes translucent and then you hear God speak to you? The Bible tells us in Mark 9:6, "They were so frightened they did not know what to say." As they were coming down the mountain, Jesus gave them orders not to tell anyone what they had seen.

Even though they were privy to supernatural things like this, they were still human. At one point Jesus had heard them arguing on the road while they were traveling and when they got to Capernaum to the house where they were staying, he asked them what they were arguing about. Mark 9:34 tells us, "But they kept quiet because on the way they had argued about who was the greatest." Jesus knew what the conversation was about and called them together and said; "If anyone wants to be first, he must be the very last, and the servant of it all."

Later on, we see in Mark 10:35 that James and John came to Jesus and said, "Teacher, we want you to do for us whatever we ask." Jesus responds, "What do you want me to do for you?" They replied, "Let one of us sit at your right hand and the other at your left in your glory." Jesus replies, "You will drink the cup I drink and be baptized with the baptism I am baptized with, but to sit at my right or left is not for me to grant. These places belong to those for whom they have been prepared."
He then began to teach them that he would suffer many things and be rejected by the chief priests and the elders. He told them that he must be killed and after three days rise again from the dead. This must have

been very confusing to them as they were rejoicing in the knowledge the long-awaited Messiah was walking among them and now he was talking about being killed and taken away.

We saw in a previous lesson where Jesus had come to raise Lazarus from the dead, and at that time there were many Jewish leaders there to comfort Mary and Martha. After they saw the miracle of Jesus commanding Lazarus to come out of the tomb and seeing this miracle, many of them put their faith in Jesus. Some of them, however, went to the Pharisees and told them about the miracle and how people were starting to become followers of Jesus. The chief priests and Pharisees got very concerned and called a meeting of the Sanhedrin. We read about their concerns in John 11:47: "What are we accomplishing?' they asked. "Here is this man performing many miraculous signs. If we let him go on like this, everyone will believe in him, and then the Romans will come and take away both our place and our nation."

After this meeting, they sent out an order that if anyone knew where Jesus was, they should report it so they could arrest him. When Jesus heard of this, he no longer moved about publicly but stayed in a desert region with his disciples until the time came for the Jewish Passover.

About six days before the Passover, Jesus, and his disciples came to Bethany to the home of his dear friends, Mary, Martha, and Lazarus. They gave a dinner in his honor, and as usual, we see Martha serving and we read that Lazarus was reclining at the table with Jesus. Mary took an expensive perfume and poured it on Jesus' feet and wiped his feet with her hair. We are told the house was filled with the fragrance. One of the disciples, Judas Iscariot, objected saying the costly perfume could have been sold and helped the poor. Jesus replied to him in John 12:7 saying, "Leave her alone, it was intended that she should save this perfume for the day of my burial. You will always have the poor among you, but you will not always have me."

The word got out that Jesus was there and a large crowd of Jews came, not only because of Jesus but also to see Lazarus whom he had raised from the dead. The chief priest made plans to kill Lazarus as well because it was because of him that many Jews were beginning to follow Jesus.

Time was drawing near for Jesus to make his final entry to Jerusalem and he told two of his disciples, "Go to the village ahead of you, and at once you will find a donkey tied there, with her colt by her. Untie them and bring them to me. If anyone says anything to you, tell them that the Lord needs them, and he will send them right away." (It had been prophesied in Isaiah 62:11 that He would come into Jerusalem riding on a donkey.)

The next day Jesus rode the donkey into the city, and the crowd that had come for the feast took palm branches and went out to meet him, shouting, "Hosanna! Blessed is he who comes in the name of the Lord! Blessed is the King of Israel!"

Jesus went to the temple and found that people were buying and selling in the temple and it infuriated him. He overturned the tables and drove them out saying, "It is written, My house will be called a house of prayer, but you are making it a den of robbers." While he was there the blind and the lame came to him and he healed them. When the chief priest and teachers of the law saw this and heard the praise going up from the children saying "Hosanna to the son of David, they were indignant. They asked Jesus, "Do you hear what they are saying?" Jesus asked them, "Yes, have you never read, 'from the lips of children and infants you have ordained praise?" He then left them and went back to Bethany to spend the night.

Early in the morning, as he was on his way back to the city, he was hungry. Seeing a fig tree by the road, he went up to it but found nothing on it except leaves. Then he said to it, "May you never bear fruit again!" Immediately the tree withered. The disciples were amazed and asked how the fig tree withered so quickly. Jesus took this opportunity to teach them about faith. He said, "I tell you the truth, if you have faith and do not doubt not only can you do what was done to the fig tree, but also you can say to this mountain, 'Go throw yourself into the sea, and it will be done if you believe, you will receive whatever you ask for in prayer."

Jesus entered the temple courts and began to teach. The chief priest and elders came to him, "By what authority are you doing these things? They asked. "And who gave you this authority?"
Jesus replied, "I will also ask you one question. If you answer me, I will tell you by what authority I am doing these things. John's baptism-where did it come from: Was it from heaven or from men?" They discussed it and said we don't know. Then Jesus told them, "Neither will I tell you by what authority I am doing these things." It almost seems like Jesus is messing with them, trying to force their hand.)

Jesus went on to teach many parables, and they tried to trap Him. One of the parables found in Mark 12:1-12, was about a man who planted a vineyard and put a wall around it, dug a pit and built a watchtower. Then he rented the vineyard and left. At harvest, he sent a servant to the tenants to collect from them some of the fruit of the vineyard. But they seized him, beat him and sent him away empty-handed. Then he sent another servant to them, and they did the same thing to him. He sent another and that one they killed. He sent many others and some they beat, and some they killed. He had one left to send, his son whom he loved. He sent him last of all, saying, 'They will respect my son.' But the tenants said to one another, "This is the heir. Come, and let's kill him and the inheritance will be ours." So they took him and killed him and threw him out of the vineyard. What then do you think the owner of the vineyard will do? He will come and kill those tenants and give the vineyard to others. Haven't you read this scripture: The stone the builders rejected, has become the capstone; the Lord has done this, and it is marvelous in our eyes." His enemies looked for a way to arrest him because they knew he had spoken the parable against them. But they were afraid of the crowd; so they left him and went away. Again, it seems that Jesus is taunting them with messages about what is to come.

Then they tried another tactic to trap him. They sent some Pharisees and others to try to catch him in his words. They came to him and said, "Teacher, we know you are a man of integrity. You aren't swayed by men because you pay no attention to who they are; but you teach the way of truth. Is it right to pay taxes to Caesar or not? Should we pay or shouldn't we?" Jesus knew their hypocrisy and asked them, "Why are you trying to trap me? Bring me a denarius and let me look at it." They brought the coin, and he asked them, "Whose portrait is this? And whose inscription?" Caesar's portrait was on the coin they replied. Then Jesus said to them, "Give to Caesar what is Caesar's and to God what is God's." Once again they had failed in their attempt to find some reason for his arrest.

The Sadducees, who say there is no resurrection, came to him with a question. "Teacher," they said, "Moses wrote for us that if a man's brother dies and leaves a wife but no children, the man must marry the widow and have children for his brother. Now there were seven brothers, the first one married and died without leaving any children. The second one married the widow, but he also died, leaving no child. It was the same with the third. In fact, none of the seven left any children. The last woman died too. At the resurrection whose wife will she be, since the seven were married to her?" Jesus replied, "Are you not in error because you do not know the scriptures or the power of God? When the dead rise, they will neither marry nor be given in marriage; they will be like the angels in heaven." Once again Jesus did not fall for the trap set for him for his time had not yet come.

One of the teachers of the law came to him and asked him, "Of all the commandments, which is the most important?" Jesus answered, "The most important one is this: Love the Lord your God with all your heart and with all your soul and with all your mind and with all your strength. The second is this: Love your neighbor as yourself. There is no commandment greater than these." The teacher who had asked the question responded wisely by agreeing, and Jesus said to him, "You are not far from the kingdom of God." We are told that from then on, no one dared to ask him any more questions.

One day Jesus was sitting opposite the place where the offerings were brought and he watched the crowd putting their money into the temple offering box. Many rich people threw in large amounts. But a poor widow came and put in two very small copper coins, worth only a fraction of a penny. Calling his disciples to him, he said, "I tell you the truth, this poor widow has put more into the treasury than all the others. They all gave out of their wealth; but she, out of her poverty, put in everything she had to live on." This is a great lesson on finances and the value God puts on our obedience versus our treasures.

Jesus had taken his last days to teach lessons that his disciples would need to know when he was no longer with them. The disciples asked him about the coming times of his return and the end of the age. Read the account of what Jesus told them in Mark 13. The message was simple, be alert, on guard, be aware of false prophets, and always be ready because we are told in verse 32 that no one knows the day or hour, not even the angels in heaven, nor the Son, but only the Father.

Jesus had done all he could to prepare them for what was to come. Now it was time for his final hours leading up to his death. It was only two days till Passover and the chief priest and teachers of the law were looking for some sly way to arrest Jesus and kill him. While he was in Bethany, a woman came with an alabaster jar of perfume. She broke it and poured the perfume on his head. Again, some of the ones present complained that this was a waste. Jesus told them, "Leave her alone; she has done a beautiful thing to me. The poor will always be with you but you will not always have me. She did what she could. She poured perfume on my body beforehand to prepare for my burial. I tell you the truth, whenever the gospel is preached throughout the world, what she has done will also be told, in memory of her."

Then Judas Iscariot, one of the twelve, went to the chief priest to offer to betray Jesus in exchange for 30 pieces of silver. They were delighted to hear this and took him up on his offer. Now he only had to watch to find an opportune time to turn him over to them. The plan was that he would tell them where Jesus was and then he would be there and give them a sign by kissing Jesus to let them know for sure which one he was.

It was now time for the first day of the Feast of Unleavened Bread, which was customary to sacrifice the Passover lamb. His disciples asked him where they should go to make preparations to eat the Passover. Jesus told them, "Go into the city and a man carrying a jar of water will meet you. Follow him. Say to the owner of the house he enters, 'the teacher asks: Where is my guest room, where I may eat the Passover with my disciples?' He will show you a large upper room, furnished and ready. Make preparations there."

When evening came, Jesus arrived with his disciples. While they were reclining at the table eating, he said, "I tell you the truth, one of you will betray me-one who is eating with me." They were saddened and said one by one, "Surely not I?" Jesus replied, "It is one of the twelve, one who dips bread into the bowl with me. ...... But woe to that man who betrays the Son of Man! It would be better for him that he had never been born." We know that was true and that Judas ended up committing suicide by hanging himself because of the shame of what he had done.

They finally asked him which one he meant would betray him, "It is the one to whom I will give this piece of bread when I have dipped it into the dish." Then dipping the piece of bread, he gave it to Judas Iscariot. As soon as Judas took the bread, Satan entered into him. Jesus told him, "What you are about to do, do quickly." The disciples did not understand but thought that since he was the treasurer, he was going to buy what was needed for the feast.

After he was gone, Jesus talked to his disciples, "My children, I will be with you only a little longer. You will look for me and just as I told the Jews, so I tell you now: Where I am going, you cannot come. A new command I give you: Love one another. As I have loved you, so you must love one another. By this, all men will know you are my disciples if you love one another."

While they were eating, Jesus took bread, gave thanks and broke it, and gave it to his disciples, saying, "Take it; this is my body." Then he took the cup, gave thanks and offered it to them, and they all drank from it. "This is my blood of the covenant, which is poured out for many, I tell you the truth, I will not drink again of the fruit of the vine until that day when I drink it anew in the kingdom of God."

His disciples assure him that they are steadfast and will never leave him or deny him. Peter tells him in Luke 22:33, "Lord, I am ready to go with you to prison or to death." Jesus tells him, "I tell you Peter, before the rooster crows today, you will deny three times that you ever knew me." We know that is exactly what happened and my question to you is in what ways do we deny him in our lives?

Discussion Questions:

1. What do you think Jesus meant when he talked about losing one's soul?

2. Looking at the passage in Mark, what do you think he means when he says if we want to be his disciples, we must take up our cross and follow him?

3. What lesson can we learn from the fig tree, the parable about the tenant farmer and the widow who gave out of her poverty?

4. Why do you think Jesus said the greatest commandment was to love God and love your neighbor as yourself?

Lesson 44
Rejection and Betrayal

We saw Jesus taking his last supper with his disciples in our last lesson. He was preparing them for the coming events of his betrayal, death and return to the Father.

He tells them in John 13:33, "My children, I will be with you only a little longer. You will look for me, but just as I told the Jews, so I tell you now. Where I go, you cannot come." Then in the next verse, he tells them, "A new command I give you: Love one another. As I have loved you, so you must love one another. By this, all men will know that you are my disciples."

Confused and trying to figure out the mystery of what he was saying, Peter asked, "Lord, where are you going?" Jesus replied, "Where I am going you cannot follow now, but you will follow later."

He goes on to comfort them in John 14, "Do not let your hearts be troubled. Trust in God and trust also in me. In my Father's house are many rooms; if it were not so, I would have told you. I am going away to prepare a place for you. And if I go and prepare a place for you, I will come back and take you to be with me that you also may be where I am. You know the way to the place that I am going."

Thomas speaks up and says, "Lord, we don't know where you are going, so how can we know the way?" Jesus replies, "I am the way and the truth and the life. No one comes to the Father except through me. If you really knew me, you would know my Father as well. From now on you do know him and have seen him."

Then Phillip chimes in, "Lord, show us the Father and that will be enough for us." Jesus answers him saying, "Don't you know me, Phillip, even after I have been among you such a long time? Anyone who has seen me has seen the Father. How can you say, 'Show us the Father?' Don't you believe that I am in the Father and that the Father is in me? The words I say to you are not just my own. Rather, it is the Father, living in me, who is doing his work. Believe me when I say I am in the Father and the Father is in me, or at least believe on the evidence of the miracles themselves. I tell you the truth; anyone who has faith in me will do what I have been doing. He will do even greater things than these because I am going to the Father. And I will do whatever you ask in my name, so that the Son may bring glory to the Father. You may ask anything in my name, and I will give it."

Then he goes on to tell them that they will not be left alone to figure this all out. He tells them about the gift that he is going to ask his Father to give them. Then in verse 16, he says, "I will ask the Father, and he will give you another counselor to be with you forever-the Spirit of Truth. The world cannot accept him because it neither sees him nor knows him. But you know him, for he lives with you and will live in you. I will not leave you as orphans; I will come to you. Before long, the world will not see me anymore, but you will see me. Because I live, you also will live. On that day you will realize that I am in the Father, and you are in me, and I am in you."

Wow, that is quite a lesson on identification. He is telling the disciples (and us), that what is about to happen is going to restore us back to the Father. That the entire Godhead will be involved in our restoration, and just as they are one, we will be one with them. We will be placed back to the original state that Adam and Eve were in when they were in perfect harmony with their creator in the garden before the fall.

Now Judas speaks up, (not Judas Iscariot), "Lord, why do you intend to show yourself to us and not to the world?" Jesus replies, "If anyone loves me, he will obey my teaching. My Father will love him, and we will come to him and make our home with him." Then he goes on to say, "All this I have spoken while still with you. But the Counselor, the Holy Spirit whom the Father will send in my name, will teach you all things and will remind you of everything I have said to you."

Then he comforts them again with these words, "Peace I leave with you; my peace I give you, I do not give to you as the world gives. Do not let your hearts be troubled and do not be afraid."

Jesus goes on to give a simple visual aid to help them understand what must have seemed to them to be a very complex and complicated lesson. He says, "Now let's compare this to a tree, something you observe every day. Let's say I am the vine and you are the branches, and my Father is the gardener. His job is to prune any branch that is not producing fruit so that it can produce more fruit once the dead areas have been removed. This is done so that every branch will be as productive as it was created to be."

Then he tells them how simple this is in John 15: 4, "Remain in me, and I will remain in you. No branch can produce fruit by itself; it must remain in the vine." I love this visual because I have a tree in my yard that has luscious green leaves and flowers in the spring. This past year, I noticed a branch that was just hanging there and had turned brown and had no leaves or blooms. I looked closer and found it had broken off, probably from the ice in the winter, from the main base (or vine as Jesus puts it here) and died. It had died because it had no source of nourishment. The tree trunk (or vine) is deeply rooted in the solid ground where the necessary nutrients and minerals are that sustain life. Every branch attached to it then sucks up that life. They, in turn, produce the beautiful leaves, flowers or fruit that it was created to produce. Jesus is telling them that the only way they can sustain a vital spiritual life once he is gone, is to allow the Holy Spirit to graft them into his life-giving body.

Another comparison is of a pregnant mother with a baby attached to her by an umbilical cord during the nine months of development. Without this connection, the baby cannot sustain life because all the nourishment comes from this connection to the mother. Once the umbilical cord is cut, the child must find nourishment from an outside source. Jesus tells us that he came and sent the Holy Spirit to be the umbilical cord that again allows us to freely eat of the tree of life. We were cut off from the tree of life when sin caused man to have to leave the beautiful garden God had prepared for him. Jesus now represents that tree of life that allows us to live eternally with him.

Jesus, knowing he has so little time to prepare them for what is to come, is trying to pack in every life lesson they will need to know. I think every parent who has ever sent his child off into the world can understand Jesus frustration as to all the things he wants to tell them to prepare them for the world they are entering. How much more they need to know to face all the trials that will come their way. Jesus finally says in John 16:12, "I have much more to say to you, more than you can now bear. But when he, the Spirit of Truth, comes, he will guide you into all truth. He will not speak on his own, he will speak only what he hears, and he will tell what is yet to come…" He goes on to say, "In a little while you will see me no more, and then after a little while you will see me."

John 16:17 says, "Some of the disciples said to one another, 'What does he mean by saying, In a little while you will see me no more, and then in a little while you will see me because I am going to the Father?.' They kept asking, 'what does he mean by a little while? We don't understand what he is saying.'"

Jesus saw that they wanted to ask him about this, so he said to them, "Are you asking one another what I meant when I said, "In a little while you will see me no more, and then after a little while you will see me?" (I love how Jesus always seems to know what was on their minds.) He goes on to explain to them, "I tell you the truth, you will weep and mourn while the world rejoices. You will grieve, but your grief will turn to joy." Again, he gives them a visual aid of real-life experience to help them understand. "A woman giving birth has pain because her time has come; but when her baby is born, she forgets the anguish because of her joy that a child is born into the world. So it is with you, now is your time to grieve, but I will see you again, and you will rejoice, and no one will take away your joy."

Jesus goes on in verse 25 to say, "Though I have been speaking figuratively, a time is coming when I will no longer use this kind of language but will tell you plainly about my Father. In that day you will ask in my name. I am not saying that I will ask the Father on your behalf. No, the Father himself loves you because you have loved me and have believed that I came from God. I came from the Father and entered the world; now I am leaving the world and going back to the Father."

The disciples responded, "Now we can see that you know all things and that you do not even need to have anyone ask you questions. This makes us believe that you came from God. "

Jesus responded, "You believe at last!" But a time is coming and has come, when you will be scattered, each to his own home. You will leave me all alone. Yet I am not alone, for my Father is with me."

We see that is exactly what happened. We know Judas Iscariot betrayed him for a few pieces of silver.

Questions have been brought up as to why Judas? It is interesting to note that there is evidence to point to the fact that he may not have believed that Jesus was the true Messiah. Unlike the other disciples who called him Lord, Judas never used this title for Jesus but instead referred to him as Rabbi, which acknowledged Jesus as nothing more than a teacher.

While other disciples at times made great professions of faith and loyalty (John 6:68; 11:16), Judas never did so and appeared to have remained silent.

Another point of interest found in Matthew 10:2-4; Mark 3:16-19; Luke 6:14-16, where the disciples are listed. The general order is believed to indicate the relative closeness of their personal relationship with Jesus. Despite the variations, Peter and the brothers James and John are always listed first, which is consistent with their relationships with Jesus. Judas is always listed last, which may indicate his relative lack of a personal relationship with Christ. Also, the only documented dialogue between Jesus and Judas involves Judas being rebuked by Jesus after his greed-motivated remark to Mary (John 12:1-8), Judas' denial of his betrayal (Matthew 26:25), and the betrayal itself (Luke 22:48).

There are a few Old Testament verses that point to the betrayal, some more specifically than others. Here are two:

"Even my close friend, whom I trusted, he who shared my bread, has lifted up his heel against me." (Psalm

41:9. We see where this was fulfilled in Matthew 26:14, 48-49). .

Also, "I told them, 'If you think it best, give me my pay; but if not, keep it.' So they paid me thirty pieces of silver. And the LORD said to me, 'Throw it to the potter'—the handsome price at which they priced me!' So I took the thirty pieces of silver and threw them into the house of the LORD to the potter" (Zechariah 11:12-13, Matthew 27:3-5 for the fulfillment of the Zechariah prophecies).

Even though it was foreknown by God, Judas rejection must have been hurtful to Jesus as Judas had been one of his followers, and no doubt Jesus considered him his friend and had even trusted him with handling the finances.

The rejection was part of the price of the redemption story. We read in John 7:5, "For even his own brothers did not believe in him."

Then there is Peter. He was incensed that Jesus thought he would ever betray him. He told Jesus in John 13:37, "I will lay down my life for you." But Jesus looked him straight in the eye and said, "Will you really lay down your life for me? I tell you the truth before the rooster crows, you will disown me three times!" We know that is exactly what happened.

After Jesus was arrested and led away by the soldiers, Peter followed them into the courtyard of the high priest. He took a seat near some of the guards and waited to see what would happen with Jesus. A servant walked up to Peter and asked him if he was with Jesus. Peter said, "I don't know what you're talking about."

Peter then got up and went outside of a gateway where another person saw him and identified him as a follower of Jesus. Peter again denied knowing Jesus. Other people then identified Peter as being a follower of Jesus, and again Peter denied knowing Jesus. In all, Peter had denied knowing Jesus three times before dawn, just as Jesus had predicted.

When Peter remembered that Jesus had predicted his denials, he began to weep because he realized Jesus had been right in his statement and that he had just denied knowing the one he proclaimed he loved and trusted in.

It seems Jesus had always had to prove even to his disciples that he was who he said he was, even after seeing incredible miracles. Remember when the crowds were following Jesus and had nothing to eat. Jesus took the few fish and loaves and multiplied them to feed five thousand. Afterward, Jesus went to the other side of the lake and his disciples came looking for him. You would think this incredible miracle would be proof enough for them to believe, but Jesus knowing their hearts and minds addresses them in John 6: 26, "I tell you the truth, you are looking for me, not because you saw miraculous signs but because you ate the loaves and had your fill. Do not work for food that spoils, but for food that endures to eternal life, which the Son of Man will give you. On him, God the Father has placed his approval." Then they asked him, "What must we do to do the works God requires?" Jesus answered, "The work of God is this: to believe in the one he has sent."

Jesus sums it all up in that phrase. It seems so often we are trying to find that magic bullet to find out the plan and how we can work to accomplish it, but Jesus simplifies it so beautifully in this verse. Our work is to simply believe. We are much like the disciples many times wanting more evidence or thinking this is too simple. After he had told them this, they asked him, "What miraculous sign then will you give that we may see it and believe you? What will you do? Our forefathers ate the manna in the desert; as it is

written: 'He gave the bread from heaven to eat.'" (John 6:30)
Jesus replies to them by saying, "I tell you the truth, it is not Moses who has given you the bread from heaven, but it is my Father who gives you the true bread from heaven. For the bread of God is he who comes down from heaven and gives life in the world."

Then they replied, "Give us this bread." Then Jesus is able to get to the point of his entire ministry, "I am the bread of life. He who comes to me will never go hungry, and he who believes in me will never be thirsty. But as I have told you, you have seen me, and still, you do not believe. All that the Father gives to me will come to me and whoever comes to me I will never drive away… For my Father's will is that everyone who looks to the Son and believes in him shall have eternal life and I will raise him up at the last day."

Jesus is telling them he is the bread of life and goes on in verse 48 to tell them again, "I am the bread of life, your forefathers ate the manna in the desert, yet they died. But here is the bread that comes down from heaven, which a man may eat and not die. I am the living bread that came down from heaven. If any man eats of this bread, he will live forever. This bread is my flesh, which I will give for the life of the world."

We read in John 6:60, after this teaching many of his disciples deserted him by saying, "This is a hard teaching. Who can accept this?"

Jesus responds to them, "Does this offend you? What if you see the Son of Man ascend to where he was before! The spirit gives life; the flesh counts for nothing. The words I have spoken to you are spirit, and they are life. Yet there are some of you who do not believe." Jesus had known from the beginning which of them did not believe and who would betray him. He went on to say, "This is why I told you that no one can come to me unless the Father has enabled him."

Seeing some of the followers turn back and no longer follow him, he turned to the twelve and asked, "You don't want to leave me too, do you?" Simon Peter answered him, "Lord, to whom will we go? You have the words of eternal life. We believe and know that you are the Holy One of God." Then Jesus replied, "Have I not chosen you, the twelve? Yet one of you is a devil!" Of course, he meant Judas Iscariot, who later would betray him for 30 pieces of silver.

Jesus withstood rejection not only by the Jews and religious leaders of the day but even from those he loved and trusted to be his closest followers. He did so to fulfill his mission and get the message to the world that he had come to offer life to anyone who would believe that he was who he said he was. The message was that he was sent from God to restore spiritual oneness with God his Father.

It is one thing to deny Jesus with our words, but Titus has some very strong words about that. Titus 1:15, "They (meaning we who claim to be followers of Jesus) claim to know God, but by their actions they deny him. They are detestable, disobedient and unfit for doing anything good."

Discussion Questions:

1. Thinking about the words from Titus, in what ways might your actions deny that you are a follower of Jesus?

2. Thinking of Jesus comparing himself as the vine and us as the branches that draw from him, are there times that you feel you are drawing more strength from him than others? What do you think makes those times different?

3. When issues that conflict with the Bible come up in conversation, am I embarrassed to take a stand for what God's Word says against those of my peers or do I deny the truth by my silence?

4. What did Jesus tell his disciples was the work of God? Why do we try to put so much more effort into doing other works?

5. If you were convicted for being a follower of Jesus and taken to court, do you think there would be enough evidence to convict you?

Lesson 45
The Sacrifice

In previous lessons, we have discussed the rejection and betrayal of Jesus, and we find him having his final supper with his disciples.

Before the actual betrayal by Judas, as the meal was ending, Jesus did a curious thing. In John 13, we read he got up from the meal, took off his outer clothing, and wrapped a towel around his waist. After that he poured water into a basin and began to wash his disciples' feet, drying them with the towel that was around him. He came to Simon Peter who said to him, "Lord, are you going to wash my feet?" Jesus replied, "You do not know now what I am doing, but later you will understand." Peter replied, "No, you shall never wash my feet." Jesus answered, "Unless I wash you, you have no part with me."

When he had finished washing their feet, he put on his clothes and returned to his place. "Do you understand what I have done for you?" He asked them. "You call me Teacher and Lord, and rightly so, for that is what I am. Now that I, your Lord and Teacher have washed your feet, you should wash one another's feet. I have set you an example that you should do as I have done for you. I tell you the truth, no servant is greater than his master, nor is a messenger greater than the one who sent him. Now that you know these things, you will be blessed if you do them."

I think we all would react with the same response as Peter, that Jesus should not be washing our feet, but that we should be washing his to show our love and adoration for him.

Remember that travel in those days was mostly on foot and they wore sandals, so the act of washing the dirt off their feet was a humbling act. The message he is trying to get across to them, and also to us today, is the fact that in God's family we are as one.

That goes along with his teaching earlier where Jesus tells us that when we do something to the very least of his children, that it is like doing it to him. There are no big shots in heaven. He is taking the place of a servant here by washing the feet of his followers. Little did they know he was preparing himself and them for the ultimate act of humility and service by submitting to being beaten, spat upon, stripped naked and nailed to a cross for their sins.

As a young girl in the church we attended, I observed that often before Communion, the women would go in one classroom and the men in the other. The women would sit in a circle and one by one they would take the towel and wrap it around their waist, as Jesus did, and wash the feet of the woman sitting next to them. Then it was passed around the circle until everyone had a turn having their feet washed as an act of humility and fellowship with one another. I remember that even though I was probably the youngest, and there were many older and wiser women in the circle, I felt like an equal part of their fellowship by participating. That image will go with me forever as I meet people in different walks of life and different stages of their walk with the Lord. The message was if God could look beyond their differences and minister to them, how could I dare not do the same?

After some encouraging and comforting words to his disciples, Jesus prays for himself. It is a beautiful passage found in John 17. We are told that he looked toward heaven and said, "Father, the time has come. Glorify your Son that your Son may glorify you. For you granted Him authority over all people that he might give eternal life to all those you have given Him. Now, this is eternal life; that they may know you, the only true God, and Jesus Christ, whom you have sent. I have brought you glory on earth by completing the work you gave me to do. And now, Father, glorify me in your presence with the glory I had with you before the world began."

How wonderful to get to listen in on this conversation as Jesus is winding up the mission he had been sent to accomplish. He is stating to his Father that eternal life would soon be back in reach of all he had been given authority over. Considering all the rejection and betrayal he had just experienced, I can only imagine the feeling of comfort and accomplishment to know it was coming to an end and he had fulfilled the work his Father had sent him to do.

More than once he had heard his Father speak from heaven saying, "This is my son in whom I am well pleased." He was about to bring to a close the greatest coup the world would ever see. All those years of secrecy were coming to an end. Many times, we read that his heart was weary as he desperately tried to get his message across only to find that humanity scoffed at hm.

It must have been especially hard for him to realize the very ones who had been put in positions of power to instruct and teach the way of redemption and the preparation of his coming again were the very ones who were opposing him and calling for his death. You can hear the almost anxious tone in his voice that he would soon be back in the presence of his Father like he had been before the world began.

Next, he prayed for his disciples. He tells the Father that he has revealed the truth about himself, his mission, their relationship, and they had believed and obeyed. Then in Chapter 17, he expresses his love and concern for them to his Father. "I will remain in the world no longer, but they are still in the world, and I am coming to you. Holy Father protect them by the power of your name-the name you gave me-so that they may be one as we are one. While I was with them, I protected them and kept them safe by that name you gave me. None has been lost except the one doomed to destruction that scripture would be fulfilled. I say these things to you now while I am still in the world, so that they may have the full measure of my joy within them. My prayer is not that you take them out of the world but that you protect them from the evil one... Sanctify them by the truth; your Word is truth. As you sent me into the world, I have sent them into the world." You can feel the love and compassion in that prayer. Much like the prayer, we as parents pray over our children.

Then we, as future followers, are included in his prayer. He prays in verse 22: "Father, my prayer is not for them alone. I also pray for those who will believe in me through their message, that all of them may be one. Father, just as you are in me and I in you. May they also be in us so that the world may believe that you sent me."

Before he was arrested, he went with his disciples to a place called Gethsemane, and he said to them, "Sit over here while I go over there and pray." He took Peter, James, and John with him, and he began to be sorrowful and troubled. Then he said to them, "My soul is overwhelmed with sorrow to the point of death. Stay here and keep watch with me." He went a little further, and with his face to the ground he prayed, "My Father, if it is possible, may this cup be taken from me, yet not my will but your will be done."

Then he returned to his disciples and found them sleeping. "Could you men not keep watch with me one hour?" Then he said to Peter, "Watch and pray so that you will not fall into temptation. The spirit is willing, but the body is weak."

I can only imagine the disappointment he must have felt at this crucial and painful time when he found his trusted disciples asleep after he had asked them to please just watch while he went into the garden to pray. Apparently, the first time was very short because he asked them if they could not even stay awake one hour for him.

Again, he went away a second time and prayed, "My Father, if it is not possible for this cup to be taken away unless I drink it, may your will be done."

When he came back, he again found them sleeping. So he left them and went once more and prayed a third time, saying the same thing. Then he returned to the disciples and said to them, "Are you still sleeping and resting? Look, the hour is near, and the Son of Man is betrayed into the hands of sinners. "Rise, let us go! Here come my betrayers."

I have visited the Garden of Gethsemane several times, and every time I go, my heart is overwhelmed with grief and joy. I could almost hear his prayer and feel the pain as we are told it was so intense that he sweat drops of blood. There is now a church over a large rock that they assume might have been the place where he prayed. The olive trees that are there are from the same root as when Jesus himself was there. I can honestly say nothing has touched me as deeply as being in the garden and thinking of the decision that was made on my behalf that day. Tears flowed uncontrollably as I stood there realizing the painful decisions Jesus made on my behalf at this very place. I realized this was the place of no turning back. The place where he could have said no, Nina is not worth all this, Father. The time when his humanity was backed up against doing his Father's will at great cost physically, emotionally and spiritually. It is still impossible to think about without an overwhelming feeling of awe and gratitude beyond anything I have ever experienced.

Now that he has his disciples awake, he starts to walk away and is met by Judas, and with him are soldiers and a crowd sent from the chief priests, the teachers of the law and the elders. Soldiers ready to arrest this one who was causing the unrest and claiming to be the Messiah. Jesus meets them head on and John 18:4 tells us he went up to them and asked, "Who do you want?" "Jesus of Nazareth they replied." Jesus replies, "I am he." At that, they drew back and fell to the ground. Again he asked them, "Who is it you want?" Again they answered, "Jesus of Nazareth." "I told you that I am he, if you are looking for me, then let these men go." Meaning his disciples who were with him, but at that, Peter took out his sword and cut off the ear of the high priest servant whose name was Malchus. Luke's account of this tells us that Jesus said, "No more of this," and touched the man's ear and healed it.

Jesus commanded Peter, "Put your sword away! Shall I not drink the cup the Father has given me?" We see Peter at this point still ready to identify with and even fight for Jesus. We know that was short-term and in only a few short hours he would deny he had ever even known him.

After Jesus had confronted Peter, it was time for the plan of deceit to take place. Judas had told his accomplices that he would signal which one was Jesus by going up to him and kissing Him. At the right time Judas goes over to Jesus and greets him by saying, "Rabbi." Then gives him the fateful kiss that leads to his arrest. They arrested him much like a hunted criminal, and Jesus responds by saying. "Am I leading a rebellion that you have come out with swords and clubs to capture me? Every day I was with you, teaching in the temple courts, and you did not arrest me. But the scripture must be fulfilled." At that, everyone deserted him and fled.

I find it a bit humorous to think of this band of soldiers, armed to the hilt and followed by a crowd of people going on this big manhunt and coming to a group of men and telling them they are looking for a man named Jesus. At that Jesus speaks up and says, "That would be me." They ask again, and he says, "That would be me." They proceed to arrest him like a dangerous criminal and he simply says, "I have been among you all along, even teaching in your temple." This must have been a little unsettling for the soldiers because this was not their usual arrest. He was essentially telling them, " I am willingly being taken, even pointing myself out to you, you don't need the swords and weapons to arrest me. "

At this, the disciples all fled and now Jesus was truly alone. It was at this point Peter and the others denied they had ever known him for fear of what would happen to them if they admitted their loyalty to him.

According to historical accounts, it was Friday, April 15th, between 1:30 and 3:30 in the late afternoon when Jesus was taken to the place where the Sanhedrin chief priests were gathered. They were looking for evidence to put him to death but could find none. Many testified falsely against him, but their statements did not agree. One testified that he had heard him say he would destroy this man-made temple and in three days would build another not made by man. Then the high priest stood up before them and asked Jesus, "Are you not going to answer? What is this testimony that these men are bringing against you?" But Jesus remained silent and did not answer.

Again the high priest asked him, "Are you the Christ, the Son of the Blessed One?" Jesus responded, "I am, and you will see the Son of Man sitting at the right hand of the Mighty One and coming on the clouds of heaven." At this, the high priest tore his clothes, "Why do we need any more witnesses? You have heard the blasphemy." At that, they all condemned him worthy of death. Then some began to spit at him. They blindfolded him and began to beat him with their fists, and the guards took him and beat him." Mark 14:61 -65.

John's account tells us more detail by providing a conversation between Jesus and the high priest when Jesus was asked about his disciples and his teaching. In John 18:20, we read Jesus response. "I have spoken openly to the world; I always taught in synagogues or at the temple, where all the Jews come together. I said nothing in secret. Why question me? Ask those who heard me. Surely they know what I said." When Jesus said this, one of the guards nearby struck him in the face. "Is this the way you answer the high priest?" he demanded. Jesus replied, "If I said something wrong, testify as to what is wrong, but if I spoke the truth, why did you strike me?"

At this Jesus was led to the palace of the Roman governor. By now it was early morning, and to avoid ceremonial uncleanness, the Jews did not enter the palace; they wanted to be able to eat the Passover. So Pilate came out to them and asked what charges were being brought against Jesus. They responded by saying, "If he were not a criminal, we would not have handed him over to you." Pilate said, "Take him yourselves and judge him by your own law. "The Jews responded," But we have no right to execute anyone."

Pilate then went into the palace and summoned Jesus to come to him and he asked him, "Are you the king of the Jews?" Jesus responded by saying, "Is that your idea, or did others talk to you about me?" Pilate seemed a little confused and asked Jesus, "Am I a Jew? It was your people and your chief priests who handed you over to me. What is it you have done?" Jesus responded, "My kingdom is not of this world, if it were, my servants would fight to prevent my arrest by the Jews.

But now my kingdom is from another place." "You are a king then!" said Pilate. Jesus answered, "You are right in saying I am a king. In fact, for this reason, I was born, and for this I came into the world, to testify to the truth. Everyone on the side of truth listens to me.

By this time Pilate was getting very frustrated and asked, "What is the truth?" He immediately went out again to the Jews who had brought Jesus to him and said, "I find no basis for a charge against him. But it is your custom for me to release to you one prisoner at the time of Passover. Do you want me to release the king of the Jews?" The Jews replied, "No, give us another prisoner named Barabbas!"

Then Pilate took Jesus and had him flogged. The soldiers twisted together a crown of thorns and put it on his head. They went up to him, again and again, mocking saying, "Hail, king of the Jews!" As they did this, they struck him in the face.

Again Pilate came out to them and said to the Jews, "Look, I am bringing him out to you to let you know that I find no basis for a charge against him." When Jesus came out wearing the crown of thorns and the mocking purple robe, Pilate finally said, "Here he is." The chief priests and their officials saw him and started shouting, "Crucify! Crucify!"

Again, Pilate answered them, "You take him and crucify him. As for me, I find no basis for a charge against him. The Jews insisted, "We have a law that says he must die because he claims to be the Son of God."

With this Pilate was even more afraid and went back in the house and asked Jesus, "Where do you come from? But Jesus gave him no answer. "Do you refuse to speak to me?" Pilate asked. "Don't you realize I have the power either to free you or to crucify you?" Jesus then answers, "You would have no power over me if it were not given to you from above. Therefore, the one who handed me over to you is guilty of a greater sin."

From then on Pilate tried to set Jesus free, but the Jews kept shouting, "If you let this man go, you are no friend of Caesar. Anyone who claims to be a king opposes Caesar." At this Pilate brought Jesus out and sat on the judge's seat and said to the Jews, "Here is your king?" But they shouted,

"Take him away! Crucify him." Pilate said, "Shall I crucify your king?" They replied to him that they had no king but Caesar. Finally, Pilate handed him over and sentenced him to be crucified.

You can see the reluctance and the pain that Pilate was in as he was forced to make this decision. At one point he had even sent him to Herod because he had heard that Jesus was a Galilean and was under Herod's jurisdiction. Herod and his men were the ones who mocked him and put a purple robe on him, but he was ultimately sent back to Pilate. Even Pilate's wife had asked her husband to have nothing to do with him because of a dream she had. But Pilate had no choice, as he was the only one with authority to give the sentence of execution that the chief priest and leaders were demanding. Even though Pilate believed in Jesus innocence, he ultimately had to betray him as so many others had.

We read that Judas felt so much remorse at his betrayal that he went to the chief priest and gave the money back and then hanged himself.

Then there is Peter who was so devoted that he swore to never leave him. He even drew his sword and cut off the ear of one of the arresting soldiers when they came to arrest Jesus. But ultimately he did deny Him just as Jesus had predicted. Jesus had told him when he was giving him his unfailing loyalty speech that he would deny him three times before the rooster crowed in the morning. We read in Mark 14:72 that after his third denial, he heard the rooster crow and broke down and wept.

Jesus had loved and trusted these men, yet in his time of need, they forsook him.

Discussion Questions:

1. As we look back at the scene where Jesus is washing his disciples' feet, how do you think you would react if Jesus came to earth today and asked to wash your feet? What was the message he was trying to teach them by this act?

2. We can see how the disciples fell asleep physically when Jesus was in the garden praying. What are some ways you also might have fallen asleep when he asked you to be the guardian of his Word and showing his love to the world?

3. It is easy in times of peace to stand up for Jesus, but have you ever knowingly denied your faith in Christ for the sake of your reputation?

4. Can you identify personally with Pilate's dilemma? He had to choose between taking a stand politically and acting on his belief about Jesus. In what way are we personally, and as a country (claiming to be founded on the values of Jesus beliefs as a Christian nation), being asked to do the same thing?

5. Has this lesson given you a better appreciation of the turmoil Jesus went through for your salvation?

Lesson 46
Crucifixion

We left with the arrest of Jesus in our last lesson. We ended with the struggle of Pilate to pronounce sentence on him because he was not sure he was not who he said he was; the long-awaited Messiah the Jews had been waiting for. In fact, we read in John 19:19, "Pilate had a notice prepared and fastened to the cross. It read: JESUS OF NAZARETH, THE KING OF THE JEWS. Many of the Jews read the sign, for the place where Jesus was crucified was near the city, and the sign written in Aramaic, Latin, and Greek. The chief priests of the Jews protested to Pilate, "Do not write The King of the Jews, but that this man claimed to be king of the Jews." Pilate answered, "What I have written, I have written."

Despite anything that might try to prevent the crucifixion of Jesus, it had been prophesied and would take place just as God had planned. We read it clothed in prophecy from the beginning of Genesis to the end of Revelation.

Jesus is spoken of in the book of Revelation as the "Lamb slain before the foundation of the world." And Peter writes, "You know that you were ransomed from the futile ways inherited from your fathers, not with perishable things such as silver or gold, but with the precious blood of Christ, like that of a lamb without blemish or spot. He was destined before the foundation of the world but was made manifest at the end of the times for your sake." (1 Peter 1:18-20)

The prophet Isaiah gives us a beautiful prophecy of what God had planned for the redemption of man. The detail of Jesus entrance and subsequent death is amazing. This is proof that God had the plan set in place from the beginning.

Note the following, Isaiah 52-53; "Behold, my servant shall prosper, he shall be exalted and lifted up, and shall be very high. As many were astonished at him---his appearance was so marred beyond human semblance, and his form beyond that of the sons of men---so shall he startle many nations; kings shall shut their mouths because of him; for that which has not been told them they shall see, and that which they have not heard they shall understand."

"Who has believed what we have heard? And to whom has the arm of the LORD been revealed? For he grew up before him like a young plant, and like a root out of dry ground; he had no form or comeliness that we should look at him, and no beauty that we should desire him. He was despised and rejected by men; a man of sorrows and acquainted with grief; and as one from whom men hide their faces he was despised, and we esteemed him not. Surely he has borne our grief and carried our sorrows; yet we esteemed him stricken, smitten by God, and afflicted. But he was wounded for our transgressions, he was bruised for our iniquities; upon him was the chastisement that made us whole, and with his stripes we are healed."

"All we like sheep have gone astray; we have turned every one to his own way, and the LORD has laid on him the iniquity of us all. He was oppressed, and he was afflicted, yet he opened not his mouth; like a lamb that is led to the slaughter; and like a sheep that before its shearers is dumb, so he opened not his mouth. By oppression and judgments he was taken away; and as for his generation, who considered that he was cut off out of the land of the living, stricken for the transgression of my people?"

"And they made his grave with the wicked and with a rich man in his death, although he had done no violence, and there was no deceit in his mouth. Yet it was the will of the LORD to bruise him; he has put him to grief; when he makes himself an offering for sin, he shall see his offspring, he shall prolong his days; the will of the LORD will prosper in his hand; he shall see the fruit of the travail of his soul and be satisfied; by his knowledge shall the Righteous One, My Servant, make many to be accounted righteous; and he shall bear their iniquities."

"Therefore I will divide him a portion with the great, and he shall divide the spoil with the strong; because he poured out his soul to death, and was numbered with the transgressors; yet he bore the sin of many, and made intercession for the transgressors."

It is always fascinating to me to see how beautifully the Old and New Testament validate each other.

We read this passage written in Isaiah's time, and then we hear Jesus himself prophesying as to his death and resurrection using an Old Testament prophet, (Jonah's adventure in the belly of a whale), as a visual of what was to come. Matthew 12:40; "For as Jonah was three days and three nights in the whale's belly; so shall the Son of man be three days and three nights in the heart of the earth."

Then we see him almost taunting the religious leaders as they are trying to trap him with a riddle in John 2:19, "Destroy this temple, [of His body], and in three days I will raise it up." They all would have known stories of the destruction of the temple and of all the events and many years that it took to have it restored. Little did they know he was talking about himself being the temple of God on earth at this time.

As we read the accounts of the feast and festivals God put in place in the Old Testament, we can see how they were a type and shadow of the events that were to take place in the future. As they observed these rituals, they were being prepared to understand what was to take place in the death of Jesus.

In Exodus 12:46 we read about the Passover lamb that was to be slain and the extent of the detail and how it compares to the actual for-ordained death of Jesus crucifixion.

You remember that the origin of Passover was when Moses was told to take the children of Israel out from under the bondage of Egypt. In an attempt to get Pharaoh to let them go, God was sending an angel of death to kill the firstborn of every household. To protect the children of Israel from being a part of this plague, he told the children of Israel to slay a lamb and put the blood over their doorpost, and the angel of death would pass over their home. We know that is what happened and every year they were to observe a ritual that celebrated that deliverance by celebrating Passover.

The ritual was that each family was to take a lamb that was without blemish and have it live with the family inside the house for several days before the slaughter. You can imagine how sweet a little lamb was, and that no doubt an attachment was made. Then they were to slaughter it and eat it, but the fascinating part for me is the detail that was spoken of in verse 46, "…do not break any of the bones."

As we fast forward to the time of Jesus crucifixion and he is referred to as our Passover lamb, even this small detail is fulfilled. We know that the Jews did not want the bodies left on the cross because it was to be a special Sabbath, so they asked Pilate if they could go ahead and break the bones of the three hanging there. The nailing of hands and feet forced the victim to push up against the weight of his own body to take a single breath. In the hot sun, terrible thirst ensued, and death came in most cases from suffocation amidst great pain, so by breaking their legs, they could no longer prolong their death, and they could take their bodies down.

We read in John 19: 32, "The soldiers therefore came and broke the legs of the first who had been crucified with Jesus and then the other. But when they came to Jesus they found that he was already dead, they did not break his legs. Instead, one of the soldiers pierced Jesus side with a spear, bringing a sudden flow of blood and water." Verse 36 says, "These things happened so that the scripture would be fulfilled: "Not one of his bones will be broken," and, as another scripture says, "They will look to the one they have pierced." As the old saying is that the proof is in the detail, this is just one of many seemingly small details that validate his death as being for-ordained by God.

As we look back at the crucifixion, the gospel narratives concerning the death of Jesus will show that he was nailed to the cross at 9 o'clock in the morning and was dead by 3 in the afternoon. His terrible ordeal, it would seem, was over in a mere six hours.

The agony in the Garden of Gethsemane the night before had been an ordeal in prayer to his Father that must have left him emotionally and spiritually exhausted.

Then, too, Jesus had been up the rest of the night without sleep enduring beating, cruel mockery and unspeakable brutality. The next morning, the Romans scourged him… (Mark 15:15, John 19:1). Jesus was already greatly weakened when he carried his cross, stumbling, to the place of crucifixion alongside the main public highway, probably just outside the Damascus Gate.

Now we see Jesus hanging naked, wearing a crown of thorns and experiencing more pain than we can imagine. He had been beaten so badly that it is said he was unrecognizable as a man. At the foot of the cross, the soldiers are mocking him and gambling for his clothes.

In Luke 23 we read, "One of the criminals who hung there hurled insults at him: Aren't you the Christ." Save yourself and us!" But the other criminal rebuked him, "Don't you fear God since you are under the same sentence? We are punished justly, for we're getting what our deeds deserve, but this man has done nothing wrong." Then he said, "Jesus, remember me when you come into your kingdom." Jesus responded, "I tell you the truth, today you will be with me in paradise."

At the foot of the cross also we see three Mary's: his mother, Mary Magdalene, and his aunt who was also named Mary.

John 19:26 says, "When Jesus saw his mother there, and the disciple whom he loved nearby (John), he said to his mother, 'Dear woman, here is your son,' and to his disciple, he said, 'here is your mother.'" From that time on John took her into his home. I love the fact that even in his darkest hour he provided for his mother. This also shows his trust and love for John that he would choose him to look after her.

At the sixth hour, darkness came over the whole land until the ninth hour. And at the ninth hour Jesus cried out with a loud voice, "My God, My God, why has thou forsaken me?" This was no doubt the greatest point of his human pain.

Knowing now that all was completed and scripture was fulfilled, Jesus said, "I am thirsty." They put a sponge of vinegar to his lips. He looked up into the heavens and said, "It is finished. Father, into your hands, I commit my spirit." At that, the curtain of the temple was torn from top to bottom. The earth shook and the rocks split. The tombs broke open and the bodies of the many holy people who had died were raised. They came out of the tombs, and after Jesus' resurrection, they went into the holy city and appeared to many people.

Several things are important to note: One, that the curtain in the temple was torn from top to bottom, which meant that only God could have done it. This signified that God's presence was no longer veiled from mankind and no longer did the Jews need to come every year to offer a lamb for sacrifice for their sins. Jesus had come as the sacrificial lamb for all mankind, and no longer did there need to be a priest to intercede for them because Jesus is our high priest who has access to the Holy of Holies in heaven where the presence of God dwells. Hebrews 8:1 tells us, "We have a high priest who sat down at the right hand of the throne of the Majesty in heaven, and who serves in the sanctuary, the true tabernacle set up by the Lord, not by man." Hebrews 9:24 says, "Christ did not enter a man-made sanctuary that was only a copy of the true one; he entered heaven itself, now to appear for us in God's presence."

 Second was the phrase, "It is finished." What was finished was the old covenant and all the provisions had been met. Now God was going to make a new covenant with man, having provided a way for man to once again be reunited with him. Hebrews 9:15 says, "Christ is the mediator of a new covenant, that those who are called may receive the promised eternal inheritance-now that he has died as a ransom to set them free from the sins committed under the first covenant. "

Third was the fact that he gave up his spirit. No man could have taken it from him, but he willingly endured the cross and the suffering for us. At any time in the garden, being beaten, mocked and crucified he could have said we were not worth the price he was paying. Hebrews 12:2 says, "Let us fix our eyes on Jesus, the author, and perfector of our faith, who for the joy set before him endured the cross, scorning its shame and sat down at the right hand of the throne of God." He willingly endured the cross for us. The joy set before him was the redemption of each one of us. This compares to a mother who suffers labor pains, but the joy of the new life she is bringing into the world makes it worth it.

I can only imagine the fear that gripped the hearts of all who were witness to the darkness and events that followed Jesus death. Matthew 27 tells us that when the centurion and those with him who were guarding Jesus saw the earthquake, they were terrified, and exclaimed, "Surely he was the Son of God."

Discussion Questions:

1. Every time you take communion, you are celebrating the ultimate Passover celebration. Compare the meaning of communion we take today with the Passover feast in Old Testament.

2. What aspect of Jesus suffering from the garden to the final words of "It is finished" impact you most?

3. What thoughts do you have about Jesus being our high priest?

Lesson 47
The Resurrection

In our last lesson, we left Jesus suffering on the cross, and now we find him having been placed in the tomb of Joseph of Arimathea. Although Joseph was a member of the council, he did not consent to their decision and their actions concerning Jesus. He went to Pilate and asked for Jesus body. Pilate consented, and he took the body of Jesus down from the cross and laid it in his tomb that was cut out of rock and where no one had even been laid.

The women who had come with Jesus from Galilee (Mary Magdalene, Jesus' mother, and Salome) followed Joseph and saw the tomb and how the body was laid in it. They immediately went home and prepared spices and perfumes to prepare the body properly. They did not go back the next day since it was the Sabbath and they were commanded to rest according to Jewish law.

Early in the morning on the first day of the week, they took their spices and headed to the tomb. On the way, they were concerned as to how they would roll the heavy stone away from the mouth of the tomb. But as they arrived, they were astonished to find the stone had already been moved and the entrance to the tomb was open. They entered the tomb and saw that the body of Jesus was gone. A young man dressed in a white robe was sitting on the right side of where Jesus' body had laid, and they were afraid. In Mark 16:6-7, we see the man talking to them, "Don't be alarmed." He said, "You are looking for Jesus the Nazarene, who was crucified, He has risen! He is not here. See the place where they laid him. Go and tell his disciples and Peter, He is going ahead of you into Galilee. There you will see him just as he told you." The women were afraid and went trembling and confused and ran from the tomb and ran to tell the others.

John's account tells us that Mary Magdalene went running to tell Simon Peter and John, "They have taken the Lord out of the tomb, and we don't know where they have put him!" So Peter and John were running as fast as they could to see what she was talking about. Peter ran faster than John and arrived first. Seeing the tomb was empty, he bent over and looked at the strips of linen lying there but did not go in.

Then Peter arrived and went inside. He also saw the linen strips lying there along with the burial cloth that had been around Jesus's head. The cloth was folded up by itself, separate from the linen. A note of interest is the fact that it was a custom in those days to fold the napkin at the end of the meal if you were coming back and leave it beside your plate. I actually experienced this while visiting friends in Michigan a few years ago. When we finished the meal, the hostess said to all those who would be having breakfast the next day to please fold their napkin beside the plate and those who were not returning the next day to leave the napkins on their chair and it would be taken to the laundry. I thought of the fact that Jesus had told his disciples he would come again and he folded the napkin and placed it separate as if to leave that message once more in the way of tradition that they would understand. We are told in John 20:8 that when John saw this he understood and believed Jesus had risen just as he said he would.

Afterward, the two disciples went back to their homes, but Mary stood outside the tomb crying. As she wept, she bent over to look into the tomb and saw two angels in white, one seated at the head and one at the feet of where Jesus body was. They asked her, "Woman, why are you crying?" "They have taken my Lord away, and I don't know where they have put him." At that, she turned around and saw Jesus standing there, although she did not realize it was he. He spoke to her saying, "Why are you crying? Who is it you are looking for?" Thinking he was another gardener, she replied, "Sir, if you have carried him away, tell me where you have put him, and I will get him." Then he called her by name, "Mary." She immediately recognized that familiar voice and responded in Aramaic, "Rabboni," which means teacher.

She probably tried to wrap her arms around him in excitement, but Jesus said, "Do not hold on to me, for I have not yet returned to the Father. Go instead to my brothers and tell them. I am returning to my Father and your Father, to my God and your God." I find it so interesting that his first words to his disciples were pointing out that his Father was their Father and his God was their God. The work of redemption had been done.

Mary did as he told her and went to the disciples and told them what had just happened and gave them the message Jesus had sent them. I am sure some were skeptical of what they were hearing Mary say thinking that maybe her grief was talking because she so wanted to find her Lord.

That same day, two of Jesus disciples were walking along the road going to a village called Emmaus, about seven miles from Jerusalem. They were talking with each other about everything that had happened. All of a sudden, they realized someone was walking beside them and it was Jesus himself, but they were kept from recognizing him. He asked them, "What are you discussing together as you walk along?" They stood still with their faces downcast. One of them named Cleopas, asked him, "Are you only a visitor to Jerusalem and do not know the things that have happened there?" Jesus asked as if not to know, "What things?" They went on to tell him the story adding how they had hoped he was the one who would redeem Israel. After hearing them recount the events, Jesus said to them, "How foolish you are, and how slow of heart to believe all that the prophets have spoken! Did not the Christ have to suffer these things and then enter his glory?"

Then Jesus went on to explain all the prophecies concerning him beginning with Moses. As they approached the village where they were going, Jesus acted as if he were going farther. But they urged him to stay with them as it was almost evening, so he went in and stayed with them.

When they were sitting at the table, Jesus took bread, gave thanks, broke it and began to give it to them. Then their eyes were opened, and they recognized him, and he disappeared from their sight. They commented to each other, "Were not our hearts burning within us while he talked with us on the road and opened the scriptures to us?"

They got up immediately and returned to Jerusalem. There they found the eleven and others gathered and they were saying, "It is true that the Lord has risen and appeared to Simon Peter." Then the two told about their experience on the road to Emmaus and how they had recognized him when he broke bread with them.

While they were still talking, Jesus himself appeared before them. They were astonished because they had locked the doors, as they were still fearful of the Jews. Jesus said to them, "Peace be with you." They were frightened thinking they were seeing a ghost. Jesus said, "Why are you troubled, and why do doubts arise in your minds? Look at my hands and my feet. It is I myself! Touch me and see; a ghost does not have flesh and bones, as you see I have."

When he had said this, he showed them his hands and feet. And while they were still shocked and in awe, he asked them, "Do you have anything here to eat?" They gave him a piece of broiled fish, and he took it and ate it in their presence.

He said to them, "This is what I told you while I was still with you: Everything must be fulfilled that is written about me in the Law of Moses, the prophets, and the Psalms."

Then he opened their minds so they could understand the scriptures, He told them, "This is what is written: The Christ will suffer and rise from the dead on the third day, and repentance and forgiveness of sins will be preached in his name to all nations, beginning at Jerusalem. You are witnesses to these things. I am going to send you what my Father has promised, but stay in the city until you have been clothed with power from on high."

He was preparing them for the mission they were about to receive. He follows up with, "As the Father has sent me, so I am sending you," Receive the Holy Spirit."

Thomas was not with the other disciples when Jesus came. When they told him all they had witnessed, he told them, "Unless I see the nail marks in his hands and put my finger where the nails were, and put my hand into his side, I will not believe it." A week later the disciples were all together again with the door locked again, and Jesus came and stood among them and said, "Peace be with you!" Then he said to Thomas, "Put your finger here; see my hands. Reach out your hand and put it into my side. Stop doubting and believe." Thomas exclaimed, "My Lord and my God." Then Jesus told him, "Because you have seen me, you have believed; blessed are those who have not seen and yet have believed."

Jesus appeared many times to his disciples and did many miracles. At one point he appeared standing on the shore while they were out in the boat fishing. They did not know who he was when he called out to them, "Friends, have you caught any fish?" No, they answered. He said, "Throw your net on the right side of the boat, and you will find some." When they did, they were not able to pull in the net because there were so many fish in it. John looked at Peter and said, "It is the Lord!" At this Peter jumped into the water and swam to Jesus. The other disciples followed in the boat.

When they came to shore they saw that Jesus had a fire going with burning coals with fish on it, and some bread. Jesus said to them, "Bring some of the fish you have just caught." They no doubt enjoyed a meal with Jesus on the shore and as they talked, Jesus said to Peter, "Do you truly love me more than these?" "Yes Lord," he said, "you know that I love you." Jesus said, "Feed my lambs." Again Jesus said, "Peter, do you truly love me?" Once again Peter replied, "Yes Lord, you know I love you." Jesus replied, "Take care of my sheep." Then the third time he asked Peter the same question, "Do you love me?" Peter was hurt that Jesus was still asking the same question and responded, "Lord, you know all things, you know I love you." Jesus then told him, "Feed my sheep."

I can just imagine how anxious Peter was when he saw Jesus on the shore. So anxious that he could not wait for the boat to get there, he jumped in and swam to him. I think it is interesting that Peter was the one who denied Jesus three times and now that Jesus was here, he must have wanted to be alone with him to apologize and ask his forgiveness. But we see Jesus taking the initiative and asking him three times if he loves him. Once for each time he had denied him. Jesus is telling him here that the way to prove his love for him is to go and tell others the plan of salvation.

We see that was the theme of every encounter Jesus had with his disciples. Mark 16:15-18 states, "Go into all the world and preach the good news to all creation. Whoever believes and is baptized will be saved, but whoever does not believe will be condemned. And these signs will accompany those who believe: In my name they shall cast out demons; they will speak in new tongues; they will pick up snakes with their hands and when they drink deadly poison, it will not hurt them at all; they will place their hands on sick people, and they will get well."

Matthew 28:18, tells us that Jesus had asked his disciples to come to the area of Galilee to a certain place on the mountain and there Jesus gave them what is called the great commission. Jesus told them, "All authority in heaven and on earth has been given to me. Therefore go and make disciples of all nations, baptizing them in the name of the Father and of the Son and of the Holy Spirit, and teaching them to obey everything I have commanded you. And surely I am with you always, to the very end of the age."

Jesus had been with them forty days and had worked many miracles and did many things to prove that all power had been given to him and that he was passing that on to them. He instructs them to go into Jerusalem and stay there until the Holy Spirit comes upon them to bathe them with the same power he had.

With that he led them out to the vicinity of Bethany, he lifted up his hands and blessed them. While he was blessing them, he left them and was taken up into heaven. There he is seated at the right hand of God. Then the disciples went out and preached everywhere, and the Lord worked with them and confirmed his Word by the signs that accompanied it.

When we read about the resurrection, we know that Jesus was the firstborn from the dead. You could say he was #1. Somewhere down the line is your number if you have received the truth that he was the Messiah, the Son of God who came and redeemed mankind to himself.

Discussion Questions:

1. When Mary was standing at the entrance of the empty tomb, what questions might be going through her mind? At first, she had mistaken him for the gardener, but when he called her name, she immediately knew who he was. Have there been times Jesus has been standing beside you, and you did not recognize who he was? Share a time you can look back on when he was with you in your life circumstance even though you did not realize it.

2. If you were one of the disciples when Jesus came through a locked door and began talking to you, do you think you would accept that he was who he said he was, or would you be more like Thomas needing proof? As you look at your faith today, are you one who takes Jesus at his word or do you continually need proof?

3. Why do you think Jesus continued to ask Peter the same question three times? Has there been a time in your life that like Peter you may have turned from Jesus only to find that he was there waiting for your return with only one question, "Do you love me?"

4. What was the way Jesus told Peter to prove his love? Do you follow that example? If so give an example.

5. When Jesus was walking beside the two disciples on the road to Emmaus, they did not recognize him until he broke bread with them. How can we compare this to our taking of communion?

6. Is it hard for you to accept the words of Jesus that all power had been given to him in heaven and earth and that now he wants to give us that same power? That gives new light to the phrase in the Lord's Prayer, "Thy will be done on earth as it is in heaven." What are your thoughts on our being able to work miracles today using his name and authority?

Lesson 48
Pentecost

When we finished our last lesson, Jesus had risen from the dead and was making appearances in many places to his followers. He wanted to give them evidence that he truly had been resurrected from the dead. He walked through closed doors and allowed them to touch the nail scars in his hands. He then spent the next forty days with his disciples, continuing to prepare them for the time when he shortly will return to Heaven and take his place sitting at the right hand of his Father. He tells them in John 20:21, "As the Father has sent me, I am sending you." He is sending them out into the world to be His ambassadors to spread the news that the long-awaited Messiah has come.

One of his last instructions, before he lifted his hands and ascended to Heaven, is found in Mark 16:15-18: "Go into all the world and preach the good news to all creation. Whoever believes and is baptized will be saved, but whoever does not believe will be condemned. And these signs will accompany those who believe. In my name they will drive out demons; they will speak in new tongues; they will pick up snakes with their hands; and when they drink deadly poison, it will not hurt them at all; they will place their hands on sick people, and they will get well."

The good news is the familiar passage found in John 3:16-17; "For God so loved the world, that He gave his only begotten Son that whosoever believeth in him will not perish but have eternal life. For he sent not his son into the world to condemn the world but that the world through him would be saved."

Jesus spends a lot of time emphasizing the point that the things he is teaching them are to be spiritually understood. He tells Nicodemus in John 3:6, "Flesh gives life to flesh, but the Spirit gives birth to spirit."

We read in John 4:24, where Jesus is talking to the Samaritan woman, "God is spirit and those who worship Him must worship Him in spirit and in truth."

Then we read in John 6:63, where Jesus is talking to his disciples, "The Spirit gives life; the flesh counts for nothing. The words I am speaking to you are spirit, and they are life."

As the disciples listen to these words about an unseen world, it must have seemed like a daunting task to be able to bring this message to mankind. But Jesus reassures them that he is not leaving them to figure it all out alone, but in fact as soon as he goes back to heaven to be with his Father, the third person of the Trinity will come and dwell not only among them as he has, but actually dwell in them. John 14:15 says, "If you love me, you will keep what I command. And I will ask the Father, and he will give you another Counselor to be with you forever-the Spirit of truth. The world cannot accept him because it neither sees him nor knows him. But you know him, for he lives with you and will be in you. I will not leave you as orphans; I will come to you. On that day you will realize that I am in my Father, and you are in me, and I am in you."

Jesus again tells them in John 16: 7, "I tell you the truth: It is for your good that I am going away. Unless I go away, the Counselor will not come to you; but if I go, I will send him to you."

Then he refers to the Holy Spirit as a gift. Acts 1:4-5 says, "Do not leave Jerusalem, but wait for the **gift** my Father promised, which you have heard me speak about. For John baptized with water, but in a few days you will be baptized with the Holy Spirit." This he goes on to say, "You will receive power when the Holy Spirit comes on you, and you will be my witnesses in Jerusalem, and in all Judea and Samaria, and to the ends of the earth."

Being obedient, they went to a chamber where they had been instructed to go and waited for the presence of the Holy Spirit, not being sure what to expect. Along with the disciples were many followers of Jesus and his mother, Mary, as well as, his brothers. We are told there were one hundred and twenty in all. They all joined together in prayer constantly we are told in Acts 1:14.

Then the time came. Suddenly a sound like the blowing of a violent wind came from heaven and filled the whole house where they were sitting. They saw what seemed to be tongues of fire that separated and came to rest on each of them. All of them were filled with the Holy Spirit and they began to speak in other tongues as the Spirit enabled them.

The crowd outside heard all that was going on and was confused as to what was happening. They wanted to know why these people were speaking this new language, but they all understood it in their own language although they were from Rome, Egypt, Judea, Mesopotamia, Libya, etc. We read about their reaction in Acts 2:7 "Utterly amazed, they asked: 'Are not all these men who are speaking Galileans?'" With this evidence, many believed, but some made fun of them saying they had too much to drink.

Peter addressed the crowd, "Fellow Jews and all of you who live in Jerusalem, let me explain this to you; listen carefully to what I say. These men are not drunk, as you suppose. It is only nine in the morning! No, this is what was spoken by the prophet Joel: 'In the last days, God says, I will pour out my Spirit on all people."

Then he continues to tell them, "Men of Israel, Jesus of Nazareth was a man accredited by God to you by miracles, wonders, and signs, which God did among you through him, as you yourselves know. He was handed over to you by God's set purpose and foreknowledge; and you, with the help of wicked men, put him to death by nailing him to the cross. God raised him from the dead, freeing him from the agony of death because it was impossible for death to keep its hold on him." He then validates it by saying that he and the apostles, who were standing with him, had witnessed all this. He goes on to explain that what was happening now was that Jesus had gone back to heaven and just as he had promised, he had sent the Holy Spirit to come and indwell them.

When the people heard this, they were cut to the heart and said to Peter and the other apostles, "Brothers, what shall we do?" Peter replied, "Repent and be baptized every one of you in the name of Jesus Christ for the forgiveness of your sins. And you will receive the **gift** of the Holy Spirit. This promise is for you, your children and for all who are far off." Those far off are those of us who are yet to be born, but will hear and obey the gospel just as Peter had spoken it that day.

After they heard this message, about three thousand were baptized and added to that number that day. Jesus is called the firstborn from the dead. You could say the 120 were added and now there are 121. Now we have 3,121. I can't wait to see what my number is when I get to heaven.

We are told that the new converts devoted themselves to the apostle's teaching, fellowship and prayer and that they had everything in common meeting the needs of each other. During this time, the apostles did many miraculous signs, and we are told the Lord added to their number daily.

There was such a sense of community that there were no needy among them because those who had property would sell it to care for the needs of those less fortunate. At one point a man named Ananias had sold a piece of property and with his wife's full knowledge, had kept back some of the money for himself and lied to Peter about it. Peter asked him how he had allowed Satan to fill his heart so much that he would lie to the Holy Spirit. Upon hearing this, Ananias fell to the ground and died. They carried his body out and buried him. About three hours later his wife, Sapphira, came in and Peter asked her if this was the full amount they had gotten for the property. She also lied and immediately fell dead. A reverence for truth must have filled the hearts of all who heard of these events.

One day Peter and John were going up to the temple to pray and they noticed a crippled man who was begging at the gate to the temple. He saw them coming and asked them for money. Peter looked straight at him, as did John, and said, "Look at us!" So the man gave them his attention, expecting to get something from them. Then Peter said, "Silver or gold I do not have, but what I have I give you. In the name of Jesus Christ of Nazareth, walk." Taking him by the right hand, he helped him up and instantly the man's feet, and ankles became strong, and he jumped to his feet and began to jump. He went with them to the temple, and as the people who knew him saw him jumping and praising God, we are told they were filled with wonder and amazement.

Peter took this chance to minister and said, "Men of Israel, why does this surprise you? Why do you stare at us as if by our power or godliness we had made this man walk? … By faith in the name of Jesus, this man whom you see and know was made strong. It is Jesus' name and the faith that comes through him that has given this complete healing to him, as you can all see." Then he encourages them, "Repent, then and turn to God, so that your sins may be wiped out, that times of refreshing may come from the Lord and that he may send Christ, who has been appointed for **you**-even Jesus." He is making it personal by telling them that Christ was appointed for each of them.

The priest, captain of the temple guard, and Sadducees came to Peter and John while they were speaking to the people and were greatly disturbed because they were telling of Jesus' resurrection from the dead. They put Peter and John in jail, but many that had heard them teach now believed. We are told that the number of men grew to about five thousand.

The next day the rulers met and discussed what was to be done with them. They brought both Peter and John in for questioning. "By what power or what name did you do this?" Peter stepped up and responded, "Are we being called to account today for an act of kindness shown to a cripple and are you asking how he was healed? Then know this, you and all the people of Israel: It is by the name of Jesus Christ of Nazareth, whom you crucified but whom God raised from the dead, that this man stands before you healed."

When they saw the courage of these two disciples, they noted that they were unschooled and ordinary men, and they were astonished but did take note that they had been with Jesus. Now they had a problem because there was no denying that this forty-year-old man who had been lame since birth was standing before them healed.

The leaders were unsure how to punish them, as everyone in Jerusalem would have heard about this miracle, so they brought them in and warned them not to speak or teach in the name of Jesus anymore. Peter and John were not intimidated. They told them they had rather obey God than them and they could not help but speak what they had seen and heard.

The apostles continued to teach and minister to the people and worked many miracles and healed many who were sick. Many more became believers and as a result, would bring the sick and lay them in the streets on mats so that Peter's shadow might fall on them as he passed by. Crowds began to gather from other towns bringing those who were sick and also those who were tormented by evil spirits and **all** of them were healed.

This caused great jealousy among the leadership of the Sadducees, so they arrested the apostles and put them in jail so they could not teach about Jesus and influence the people. They posted guards at the door of their cell so they could not escape. But during the night an angel of the Lord opened the door of the jail and brought them out with the instruction to go and stand in the temple courts and continue to share the message of the gospel.

At daybreak, they did as the angel had told them. Meantime the Sanhedrin and the full assembly of Israel had arrived at the jail only to find the prisoners were gone, but the strange thing was that the door was still securely locked, and the guards were still there standing watch. They seized the apostles again and brought them before the high priest to be questioned. They were asked why they had disobeyed the orders not to preach in Jesus' name and they replied that they must obey God rather than man. They went on to point out in Acts 5:30, "The God of our fathers raised Jesus from the dead – whom you killed by hanging him on a tree. God exalted him to his own right hand as Prince and Savior that he might give repentance and forgiveness of sins to Israel. We are witnesses to this as is the Holy Spirit, whom God has given to those who obey him."

When they heard this, they were furious and wanted to put them to death but a man named Gamaliel, a teacher of the law and honored by all the people, convinced them to let it run its course. He told them that if their activity were of human origin, it would fail. But if it is of God, they would not be able to stop them and they would only find themselves fighting against God. He convinced them, and they had the apostles brought in and flogged and released once again, warning them to quit teaching in the name of Jesus. The disciples continued to teach the same gospel in the temple courts and going from house to house to get the message out.

The church, being the body of believers, was being born and the numbers were growing fast. There were grumblings that some of the widows were being overlooked in the distribution of food and other matters that concerned the body of believers. The apostles were unable to keep up with all the responsibilities and devised a plan to have the people choose seven men that were known to be full of the Spirit and wisdom, and have them take care of these personal matters so they would not have to neglect their time of prayer and ministry of the Word.

They chose Stephen, among others who were full of faith and the Holy Spirit. The apostles prayed and laid hands on them, and their ministry to the people began. Stephen worked many miraculous things among the people and came against great opposition. At one point, he was brought before the leaders to try to intimidate him into stopping the work he was doing, but upon being questioned, they could not stand up to his wisdom, or the Spirit by which he spoke.

They had to figure out another way to stop him, so they secretly persuaded some men to say that he had spoken words of blasphemy against Moses and against God. When he was brought before the Sanhedrin, the accusers gave their false testimony, but as the members looked at him, we are told they saw that his face was like that of an angel. When the high priest asked him if the charges were true, he replied with a history lesson of the Old Testament prophets, reminding them of the deliverance by Moses of their people and how they had killed the prophets who had predicted Jesus coming. After a lengthy speech, he referred to them as stiff-necked people with uncircumcised hearts and reminded them that they had murdered the true Messiah.

They became furious and gnashed their teeth at him, but we are told that Stephen, full of the Holy Spirit, looked up to heaven and saw the glory of God and Jesus standing at the right hand of God. "Look," he said, "I see heaven open and the Son of Man standing at the right hand of God." At this, they rushed at him, dragged him out of the city and began to stone him. While they were stoning him, Stephen prayed, "Lord Jesus, receive my spirit." Then he fell to his knees and cried out, "Lord, do not hold this sin against them." With that, we are told he died. I am struck with by the comparison of the words of Jesus on the cross as he released his spirit to God with those of Stephen who asked for forgiveness of his persecutors.

Godly men buried Stephen, but this started great persecution against the church at Jerusalem, and all were scattered except the apostles. A man named Saul began to try to destroy the church. He went house-to-house and dragged off men and women and put them in prison. But this did not stop the spreading of the gospel because everywhere the believers went, they preached about the resurrected Christ. Phillip went to Samaria and not only preached but worked miracles and delivered many from demons. A great revival broke out and when Peter and John heard that Samaria had accepted the Word of God. They went there and prayed for the Holy Spirit to come upon them and shared the gospel to other villages in Samaria on their way back to Jerusalem.

One day as Phillip was walking along; an angel appeared to him with a message to go south to the desert road that goes down from Jerusalem to Gaza. He obeyed and came upon an Ethiopian eunuch who was a prominent official in charge of all the treasury of Candance, the queen of Ethiopia. He was returning from Jerusalem where he had gone to worship and had stopped alongside the road and was sitting there reading the book of Isaiah. The Spirit told Phillip to go to the Chariot where he was, and when he heard him reading writings of the prophet Isaiah, he asked him, "Sir, do you understand what you are reading?" "How can I unless someone explains it to me?" he responded. So he invited Phillip to join him in the carriage. Phillip noticed he was reading the passage, "He was led like a sheep to the slaughter, and as a lamb, before the shearer is silent, so he did not open his mouth. In his humiliation, he was deprived of justice." He asked Phillip who Isaiah was talking about and Phillip was quick to tell him the good news of Jesus. As they were traveling along, they came to a body of water, and the eunuch asked him to baptize him. When they came out of the water, the Spirit of the Lord suddenly took Philip away. We are told that he appeared at Azotus and continued to travel and preach the gospels in towns all the way to Caesarea. It is interesting to hear that he was taken away and appeared somewhere else. That just goes to show that there is no time and space with God. He was not the first that had experienced a supernatural form of travel. Remember we read in 2 Kings 2:11-12, that Elijah was taken to heaven in a whirlwind, and then appeared with Moses at the transfiguration of Jesus. How exciting to know that our God has dominion over, not only the time and space we live in but all space in all eternity.

Speaking of the supernatural, we will go back to the story of Saul that we talked about earlier who was persecuting the church and giving murderous threats against the disciples. On one occasion when he was traveling on the road to Damascus, suddenly a light from heaven flashed around him. He fell to the ground and heard a voice say to him, "Saul, Saul, why do you persecute me?" Saul asked, "Who are you, Lord?" The Lord said, "I am Jesus, whom you are persecuting. Now get up and go into the city, and you will be told what to do." The men traveling with Saul stood there speechless; they heard the sound but did not see anyone. Saul got up from the ground, but when he opened his eyes he could see nothing. So the men led him by the hand into Damascus. For three days he was blind and did not eat or drink anything.

In Damascus, there was a man named Ananias. The Lord called to him in a vision and told him to go to the house of Judas on Straight Street and ask for a man from Tarsus named Saul. He told him that he would find him praying and that he had been given a vision that a man named Ananias would come and place his hands on him to restore his sight. Ananias was shocked and responded with, "Lord, I have heard many reports about this man and all the harm he has done to your saints in Jerusalem. And he has the authority from the chief priest to arrest all who call on your name." But the Lord said to Ananias, "Go! This man is my chosen instrument to carry my name before the Gentiles and their kings and before the people of Israel. I will show him how much he must suffer for my name."

Ananias obeyed and went where he had been told he would find Saul. He told him, "Brother Saul, the Lord-Jesus, who appeared to you on the road as you were coming home-has sent me so that you may see again and be filled with the Holy Spirit." Immediately, something like scales fell from Saul's eyes, and he could see again. He got up and was baptized and starting eating and regained his strength. He spent several days with the disciples in Damascus and started preaching in the synagogues that Jesus is the Son of God. All those who heard him were astonished and asked, "Isn't he the man who raised havoc in Jerusalem, persecuting those who call on Jesus name, and hasn't he come to Damascus to take prisoners to the chief priest?" Yet Saul grew more and more powerful and baffled the Jews living in Damascus by proving that Jesus is the Christ.

The chief priests conspired to kill him, but Saul learned of their plan and went to Jerusalem. At first, the disciples were reluctant to accept that he had truly changed. Barnabas stood up for him and took him to the disciples and witnessed the change and the things he had preached in Damascus. From then on he stayed with them and moved about freely in Jerusalem. There he openly debated with the Grecian Jews, and they tried to kill him. When the disciples heard of this, they sent him off to Tarsus.

Then the church throughout Judea, Galilee, and Samaria enjoyed a time of peace. It was strengthened and encouraged by the Holy Spirit as it grew in numbers.

Discussion Questions:

1. Why did Jesus say the Holy Spirit could not come unless he went to heaven to be with the Father?

2. Jesus refers to the Holy Spirit as a gift that had to be received. He also separates it from believing and being baptized. Have you received this gift and if so, what evidence do you have?

3. Seeing how the early believers shared all they had with each other, do you think we have missed the mark today by not caring more for those in need?

4. When Peter was asked by the crippled man for something, he responded by saying, "Silver and gold I don't have, but a greater gift I give you." Then he healed him. Do you look for ways of sharing this gift of the gospel with others?

5. Considering the fate of Ananias and his wife, do you think it is ever smart to lie to God or any way try to deceive him?

6. Before Stephen was stoned, he looked up and saw the heavens open and he saw Jesus at the right hand of God. Do you think this happens today? (I have heard of people who had an after death experience and saw Jesus and other loved ones there.)

7. Saul had a blinding experience that led to his salvation. Share your salvation experience and how you knew it was real.

8. Why do you think God choose Saul to be his instrument for the building of the church?

Lesson 49
Peter the Rock

You may remember that Jesus had said of Peter, "Upon this rock, I will build my church."

In Acts 9, we begin to travel along with Peter as he spreads the good news that the long-awaited Messiah had come. He traveled from town to town telling everyone who would listen to him that all they had to do was to believe and confess that Jesus died on the cross for them, and they would be restored to oneness with the heavenly Father who created them.

Word had gotten out about the power of the Holy Spirit coming upon the believers who were gathered in the upper room in Jerusalem. We know that 3,000 were added to the body of believers that very day and the news was spreading throughout the countryside.

Peter went to visit a church in Lydia. There he found a man named Aeneas, a paralytic who had been bedridden for eight years. Peter spoke to him and said, "Aeneas, Jesus Christ heals you, take up your bed." Immediately Aeneas got up. All those who saw this man walk became believers.

Next, we see Peter traveling to a town named Joppa, after having been summoned by two of the disciples to come at once because there was a disciple named Tabitha, (also translated Dorcas), who had gotten sick and died. She was a well-respected woman who was known for doing well and helping the poor. Her body had been washed and placed in an upstairs room. When Peter arrived, he was taken upstairs where her body had been placed. All the widows stood around her body, and they were crying and showing Peter the beautiful robes and clothing she had made for them.

Peter sent them out of the room and got down on his knees and said as he turned toward her, "Tabitha, get up." She opened her eyes and seeing Peter she sat up. He took her by the hand and helped her to her feet. Then he called the believers and the widows and presented her to them alive. This became known all over the city of Joppa and many, after seeing this miracle, became believers. Peter stayed in Joppa for a while and stayed with a man named Simon who was a tanner.

In the town of Caesarea, there was a man named Cornelius, who was a centurion in what was known as the Italian Regiment. He was a good, God-fearing man, prayed regularly and helped those in need when he could. God sent an angel to him in a vision and said, "Cornelius." Cornelius stared at him in fear. "What is it Lord?" he asked. The angel answered, "Your prayers and gifts to the poor have come up as a memorial offering before God. Now send men to Joppa to bring back a man named Peter. He is staying in the house of Simon the tanner, whose house is by the sea." When the angel who spoke to him was gone, Cornelius called two of his servants and a devout soldier who was one of his attendants and told them everything that had happened and sent them to Joppa.

About noon the following day as they were on their journey and approaching the city, Peter had gone up on the roof to pray. He became hungry and wanted something to eat, and while the meal was being prepared, he fell into a trance. He saw heaven opened and something like a large sheet being let down to earth by its four corners. It contained all kinds of four-footed animals, as well as reptiles of the earth and birds of the air. Then a voice told him, "Get up, Peter, kill and eat." "Surely not Lord," Peter replied. "I have never eaten anything impure or unclean." The voice spoke to him a second time, "Do not call anything impure that God has made clean." This happened three times, and immediately the sheet was taken back to heaven. God was telling him many of the things that had been pronounced unclean under the Old Testament laws were no longer forbidden. A message that all things and everyone was included in the work of redemption on the cross.

While Peter was wondering about the meaning of the vision, the men sent by Cornelius found out where Simon's house was and stopped at the gate. They called out, asking if Peter was staying there. About that same time, the Spirit said to Peter, "There are three men looking for you. So get up and go downstairs. Do not hesitate to go with them, for I have sent them."

Peter went downstairs and said, "I am the one you are looking for. Why have you come?" The men went on to tell him that they had been sent by Cornelius, the centurion and affirmed that he was a righteous and God-fearing man, who was respected by all the Jewish people. They went on to tell him that an angel had appeared to him and told him to send for you so he could hear what you have to say. Peter invited them in, and they spent the night and the following day Peter went with them back to Caesarea. Some of the believers from Joppa went along as well.

When he arrived, Cornelius was expecting him and had called together some relatives and close friends. As Peter entered the house, Cornelius met him and fell at his feet in reverence. But Peter made him get up. "Stand up, for I am only a man myself." He saw the people who had gathered there and told them, "You are well aware that it is against our law for a Jew to associate with a Gentile or visit with him. But God has shown me that I should not call any man impure or unclean. So when I was sent for, I came without any objections. May I ask why you sent for me?" Cornelius told him about the vision and said to him, "Now we are all here in the presence of God to listen to everything the Lord has commanded you to tell us."

Peter told them, "I now realize that God does not show favoritism but accepts men from every nation who fear him and do what is right. You know the message God sent to the people of Israel, telling the good news of Jesus Christ who is Lord of all. You know what has happened throughout Judea, beginning in Galilee after the baptism that John preached-how God anointed Jesus of Nazareth with the Holy Spirit and power, and how he went around doing good and healing all who were under the power of the devil because God was with them." He goes on to tell them that he was one who witnessed all that had happened in Jerusalem and that, indeed they had killed him by hanging him on a tree, and how God had raised him from the dead on the third day. He caused him to be seen by some who were chosen before, so they could testify to his resurrection. In fact, he had actually shared a meal with him and walked with him.

Peter continued to tell them that Jesus had given them the instructions to go and spread the news that he was appointed by God, and while he was still speaking, the Holy Spirit came on all who heard the message. The believers who had accompanied Peter were astonished that the gift of the Holy Spirit had been poured out even on the Gentiles, for they heard them speaking in tongues and praising God. Peter gave instructions for them all to be baptized with water signifying they were fellow believers.

When he gets back to Jerusalem, the word had gotten out that Peter was ministering to the Gentiles and they criticized him saying, "You went into the house of uncircumcised men and ate with them." Peter explained about the vision and then told them how the Holy Spirit had fallen on them just as it had on them at the beginning. Then he said, remember what the Lord had said, "John baptized with water, but you will be baptized with the Holy Spirit." After reminding them of this, he said, "If God gave them the same gift he gave us, who believe in the Lord Jesus Christ, who was I, to oppose God?" When they heard this, they had no more objections and praised God that he had granted even the Gentiles repentance unto life.

Because of the spreading of this new gospel, King Herod decided to try to stop it by killing the apostles who were the apparent leaders. He first had James, brother of John, put to death by a sword and when he saw how this pleased the Jews. He had Peter arrested and put in prison and intended to bring him out for a public trial during the Passover. Herod had him guarded by four squads of four soldiers to be sure he could not escape. In the meantime, the church was praying to God on his behalf. The night before Herod was going to bring him to trial, Peter was sleeping between two soldiers and bound with chains. Suddenly an angel of the Lord appeared, and a light shone in his cell. The angel struck Peter in the side to wake him and told him to get up quickly and immediately the chains fell off him. Then the angel told him, "Put on your clothes and sandals, wrap your cloak around you and follow me. Peter did as the angel instructed and they passed the first and second guards and came to the iron gates leading to the city. When they approached, the gates opened by themselves. After they had gone the length of one street the angel left.

At first, Peter thought this was not real and he was observing a vision, but when he came to himself and realized what God had done, he said, "Now I know that God sent that angel to rescue me from Herod's clutches and what the Jewish people had planned for me." He immediately went to the house of Mary, mother of John, where many were still gathered praying. When he knocked at the door, a young servant girl named Rhoda went to answer it. She asked who was there and when she heard Peter's voice, she got so excited that she did not open the door but ran and told the others that Peter was at the door. They told her she was out of her mind and told her it must have been Peter's angel. But Peter kept on knocking until they finally opened the door. They were astonished, and Peter motioned with his hands for them to be quiet and told them how the angel had rescued him. He told them to go and tell James and the others about this, and then he left to go to another place.

When Herod found out what had happened in the jail, he had an extensive search done and then cross-examined the guards and ordered them all executed. After that Herod went to spend some time in Caesarea, and when the people heard he was in town, they asked for an audience with him. They wanted to ask for peace because they were dependent on the king's bounty for their food supply. He agreed and on the appointed day, he sat on his throne wearing his royal robe, he gave an address to the people. Afterward, the people recognized his evil heart and shouted that he had the voice of a god and not of a man. Immediately, because Herod would not praise God, an angel of the Lord struck him down, and he died and was eaten by worms. And that was the end of him.

The church, of which Peter was the first to preach on the day of Pentecost, had now been formed and the Holy Spirit had indeed come to dwell in those who would believe as Jesus had promised.

Jesus had proclaimed that Peter would be the rock that would be the foundation he would build upon and even changed his name from, Simon, to Peter which means "rock".

Peter's beginnings were certainly humble in origin. He was born about 1 B.C. and died sometime around A.D. 67. He was a Galilean fisherman and was the brother of Andrew. The brothers came from the village of Bethsaida. He was also a follower of John the Baptist. He was perhaps the very first disciple that Jesus called along with His brother, Andrew.

He was one of the boldest apostles of all. He willingly suffered persecution, imprisonment, beatings, and even rejoiced, at the fact that he was worthy to suffer disgrace for the Lords sake (Acts 5:41).

Peter was an eyewitness to the many miracles that Jesus did, and also was chosen to be one of the disciples to witness the Shekinah glory along with John and James at the transfiguration.

Peter was no doubt the right-hand man of Jesus. I think Jesus saw his boldness as was demonstrated when the disciples saw Jesus walking on the water in the storm and Peter was the only one who challenged Jesus to allow him to walk on top of the water to him supernaturally. He quickly learned the lesson that many of us still struggle with today; that when you take your eyes off Jesus you will start to sink in life's struggles, but as long as you keep your eyes on him, you can defy nature and do miraculous things.

Then one day when the disciples were out in their boat fishing they saw Jesus on the shore of the Sea of Galilee. Peter jumped in the water to swim to be the first to embrace him, and we know that is when Jesus first gave him the instruction to go and spread the gospel. Jesus asked Peter if he loved him three times and when he replied yes, Jesus told him the way he could prove it would be to feed his sheep. (I personally think he asked him three times to validate his forgiveness of Peter for the three times he denied him.)

That is what we see him doing from that day on. Besides the ministry we talked about earlier in this lesson in Jerusalem, Joppa, and Caesarea, we read that he preached to the churches in Pontus, Galatia, Cappadocia, Asia, and Bithynia. These sermons, or instructions, are written in the books of 1 Peter and 2 Peter.

In 1 Peter, he encourages believers in their faith and instructs them in the living of a holy life. In 2 Peter he warns them of false teachers and encourages them to continue to strengthen their knowledge so they will be strong and not fall prey to the schemes of the enemy.

At some point, Peter left Jerusalem and traveled to Rome, and tradition says that is where he died having been martyred by Nero on an inverted cross when he protested that he was not worthy to die in the same way that Jesus died. In the days leading up to Peter's death, almost all of the apostles had been martyred.

From an arrogant, cocky, man of thunder, he became a humble, willing, obedient servant of the Lord even to death. He rejoiced in the day of his death, knowing that he would be reunited with his beloved Savior. This was a lifetime of 65 years – of which his last forty would be devoted to proclaiming the gospel of Jesus Christ.

The fisherman became a mighty fisher of men – and one that changed and shaped the world forever and is still proclaiming the Gospel of Jesus Christ through his gospel written in the book of Acts, and through the epistles of 1and 2 Peter.

Discussion Questions:

1. As you look at Peter's history, do you find similarities in your own walk with the Lord?

2. At one point in his ministry, Jesus showed him that he does not have favorites and that the gospel was for all. How can you see the ways we might be denying that by our separate doctrines and beliefs that God has favorites?

3. Peter says that he was surprised that the Gentiles were filled with the Holy Spirit and speaking in tongues. Have you ever thought your church was the main way God channeled his gospel and been surprised when you see him working in the lives of those who don't share your doctrinal beliefs?

4. Why do you think it was important for him to have the grieving people leave the room when he raised the widow, Dorcas, from her deathbed?

5. What do you think Jesus saw in Peter that set him apart from the others to be named a rock and told his church would be built on that name?

Lesson 50
Paul's 1st Missionary Journey

The Word of God and the church continued to increase and spread. In the last lesson, we focused on Peter, but God dramatically called another man to be at the center of his plan. Paul, as you may remember, had a wake-up call by God while traveling along the road to Damascus when he was struck by a blinding light that transformed him from being a persecutor of the church to being the one chosen to lead the spreading of the gospel. The account says that "he [Saul] fell to the earth, and heard a voice saying unto him, 'Saul, Saul, why persecutes thou me?' Saul replied, 'Who art thou, Lord?' And the Lord said I am Jesus whom thou persecutest." According to the biblical account, he was blinded for three days and had to be led into Damascus by the hand. During these three days, Saul took no food or water and spent his time in prayer to God. After that, Paul knew that God had a call on his life and began to fulfill his destiny as one who would proclaim the gospel.

Some additional facts about Paul: He was likely born between the years of 5 B.C. and 5 A.D. The Book of Acts indicates that Paul was a Roman citizen by birth because he describes his father as such. Paul referred to himself as being of the stock of Israel, of the tribe of Benjamin, a Hebrew and a Pharisee.

He was part of a Jewish family in the city of Tarsus—one of the largest trade centers on the Mediterranean coast. It had been in existence several hundred years before his birth. He used his status as both a Jew and a Roman citizen to his advantage in ministering to both Jewish and Roman audiences.

Approximately half of the book of Acts deals with Paul's life and works. Fourteen of the twenty-seven books in the New Testament have traditionally been attributed to Paul. Seven of the epistles are undisputed by scholars as being authentic, with varying degrees of argument about the remainder.

The other six are believed by some scholars to have come from followers writing in his name, using material from Paul's surviving letters and letters written by him.

For reasons known only to God, he was chosen to be a key figure to tell the story of salvation. We began the journey in Acts 12:25, where Barnabas, Paul, and John Mark were at the church in Antioch. While there the prophets and teachers were in a time of worshiping and fasting, and the Holy Spirit spoke to them and said, "Set apart for me Barnabas and Saul for the work to which I have called them." After hearing the voice of God that they had been set apart for this purpose, they laid hands of them and sent them off.

This became known as Paul's first missionary journey. The time was late Spring 44 A.D. They first went down to Seleucia, sailed from there to Salamis, which was the main city and seaport of Cyprus. While there they preached in Jewish synagogues and traveled through the whole island spreading the good news.

Then they went on foot to Paphos. While there, the Roman Governor, sent for them because he wanted to hear the gospel they were preaching.

There was a sorcerer, or magician, named Elymas who tried to oppose them witnessing to the governor. When Paul saw him, he looked him straight in the eye and said, "You are a child of the devil and an enemy of everything that is right! You have perverted everything that is right, and now you will be blind." Immediately, darkness came over him, and he was blinded. As the governor saw what had happened, he believed and was amazed at their teaching of the gospel.

From Paphos, Paul and his companions sailed to Perga, and it was there that John Mark left them and returned to Jerusalem. They continued their journey to Antioch, and on the Sabbath, they entered the synagogue and sat down. After the reading of the law and the prophets, the rulers sent word to them, "Brothers, if you have a word of encouragement for the people, please speak."

They took the opportunity to give them a history lesson of where they had come from and how God had provided protection and blessings on the plan set in place to bring forth the Messiah. We read in Acts: 13:16-31xd, "Standing up, Paul motioned with his hand and said: 'Men of Israel and you Gentiles who worship God, listen to me! The God of the people of Israel chose our fathers; he made the people prosper during their stay in Egypt, and with mighty power, he led them out of that country. He endured their conduct for about forty years in the desert, he overthrew seven nations in Canaan and gave their land to his people as their inheritance. All this took about 450 years.

After this God gave them judges until the time of Samuel, the prophet. Then the people asked for a king, and he gave them Saul, son of Kish, of the tribe of Benjamin, who ruled forty years. After removing Saul, he made David their king. He testified concerning him that he was a man after his own heart.

From this man's descendants, God brought to Israel the Savior Jesus, as he promised. Before the coming of Jesus, John preached repentance and baptism to all the people of Israel. As John was completing his work, he said: 'Who do you think I am: I am not that one. No, but he is coming after me, whose sandals I am not worthy to untie.'

Brothers, children of Abraham, and you God-fearing Gentiles, it is to us that this message of salvation has been sent. The people of Jerusalem and their rulers did not recognize Jesus, yet in condemning him they fulfilled the words of the prophets that are read every Sabbath. Though they found no proper ground for a death sentence, they asked Pilate to have him executed. When they had carried out all that was written about him, they took him down from the tree and laid him in a tomb. But God raised him from the dead, and for many days he was seen by those who had traveled with him from Galilee to Jerusalem. They are now his witnesses to our people."

He continued, "We tell you the good news: What God promised our fathers long ago, he has fulfilled for us, their children, by raising up Jesus."

We can refer back to the study in Psalms: "You are my son; today I have become your Father. I will give you the sure and holy blessings promised to David."

Then the fact it was written long ago that God would raise Jesus from the dead never to see decay is stated in Psalm 16, "God raised Him from the dead, never to decay. For when David had served God's purpose in his own generation, he fell asleep; he was buried with his fathers, and his body decayed. But the one whom God raised from the dead did not see decay. Therefore, brothers, I want you to know that through Jesus the forgiveness of sins is proclaimed to you. Through him, everyone who believes is justified from everything you could not be justified from by the Law of Moses."

As Paul and Barnabas were leaving the synagogue, the people invited them to speak further about these things on the next Sabbath. On the next Sabbath, almost the whole city gathered to hear the word of the Lord that Paul preached. When the Jews saw the crowds, they were filled with jealousy and stirred up persecution against Paul and Barnabas and expelled them from teaching there. However, they had presented the gospel and it had spread throughout the whole region. We are told in Acts 13: 52 that "after that, they shook the dust off their feet and left, but left filled with joy and the Holy Spirit."

From there they went to Iconium where they spoke again in the Jewish synagogue. After a great many Jews and Gentiles believed, jealousy again erupted among the Jewish leaders. But they continued to preach boldly, and the Holy Spirit enabled them to work miraculous signs and wonders. They found out that a plot was being formed to have them stoned and they fled to the nearby city of Lystra.

In Lystra, there sat a man crippled in his feet, who was lame from birth and had never walked. He listened to Paul as he was speaking. Paul looked directly at him, saw that he had faith to be healed and called out to him, "Stand up on your feet!" At that, the man jumped up and began to walk.

When the crowd saw this, they thought their gods, Zeus and Hermes, who were mythical Greek gods, had sent spokesmen in human form and began to worship them. Paul and Barnabas were so distraught that they tore their clothes and rushed into the crowd shouting, "Men, why are you doing this? We are just human like you. We are bringing you good news, telling you to turn from these gods and worship the true and living God who made heaven and earth and everything in them."

But even with these words, they had difficulty keeping the crowd from sacrificing to them. Then some Jewish leaders came and convinced the crowd that they were of the devil and they took Paul and stoned him and dragged him outside the city thinking he was dead. But after the disciples gathered around him, he got up and went back into the city. However, they realized it was time to move on and the next day he and Barnabas left for the city of Derbe. While they were there, they won large numbers of people to become disciples.

Paul and Barnabas then returned to the cities of Lystra, Iconium, and Antioch where they had established churches. They went to strengthen and encourage them to remain true to the faith. While they were there, they appointed elders. With prayer and fasting, they committed them to the Lord. This started a tradition that we still hold today in most churches.

They continued their journey and preached the Word in Perga and then went down to Attalia where they caught a ship back to Antioch. There they reported all God had done through them and how he had opened the door of faith to the Gentiles. They stayed there almost three years with the other disciples.

Paul and Barnabas heard that some men from Judea had come down to Antioch and were teaching the new Gentile believers that they must be circumcised according to the Law of Moses. This angered them, and they went up to Jerusalem to address this with the apostles and elders. They explained how the Gentiles had received the message of the gospel and what God had done on their journey. All were glad except a few Pharisees who protested. Peter got up and addressed them, "Brothers, God who knows the heart, showed that he accepted them by giving the Holy Spirit to them, just as he did to us. He made no distinction between them and us for He purified their hearts by faith. Now then, why do you try to test God by putting on the necks of the disciples a yoke that neither our fathers nor we have been able to bear? No! We believe it is through the grace of our Lord Jesus that we are saved, just as they are."

James spoke up and said all that had been said agreed with the prophets of old, and that they should not make it harder for the Gentiles who were turning to God. Rather, he said, that they should write a letter and send it to them saying they should abstain from food polluted by idols, from sexual immorality, and from the meat of strangled animals and from their blood.

They chose two leaders of the church, Silas, and Judas, to go with Paul and Barnabas and take the letter. After they read it to the churches in Antioch both Silas and Judas spent time encouraging the believers there. Then they returned home. Paul and Barnabas stayed for a while to continue to be an encouragement to the church. The message that prevailed was not just the message of the gospel, but that the gospel was for Gentiles as well as Jews.

Discussion Questions:

1. As you reflect on Paul's life and ministry, what about his life stands out most to you?

2. What qualities do you think Paul had that caused God to choose him to record the majority of the New Testament for all future generations to learn from?

3. What qualities could God find in you that would make you a candidate for this job?

4. Coming from a place of persecuting the church, how do you think Paul dealt with guilt over the persecution he had caused?

5. Why do you think he gave a history lesson to the church of Antioch?

Lesson 51
Paul's 2ⁿᵈ Missionary Journey

Paul's second journey began on a rather unfortunate circumstance. Barnabas wanted to take John, also called Mark, with them, but Paul did not think it wise to do that because he had deserted them in Pamphylia and had not continued with them in the work. They had such a sharp disagreement that they parted company. Barnabas took Mark and sailed for Cyprus, but Paul chose Silas and left.

Although Paul and Barnabas apparently never again traveled together, there was no lasting animosity between them - Paul later spoke highly of Barnabas. Paul also made up with Mark, who later was with him during Paul's imprisonment in Rome (Colossians 4:10, 2 Timothy 4:11).

Paul's second missionary journey began about 49 AD, and as the first journey, it was no 10-day excursion. He would not return for about 3 years.

The previous journey began by sailing to Cyprus, but this time he set out overland through Syria and Cilicia, to revisit the churches he had earlier established in Asia, including those at Derbe, and then at Lystra where a disciple named Timothy joined him.

From there they continued northward through Phrygia and Galatia. Paul remained in Galatia for some time due to an unspecified illness. We read about it in Galatians 4:13-14, where he refers to his first visit to the church there. "As you know it was because of an illness that I first preached the gospel to you. Even though my illness was a trial to you, you did not treat me with contempt or scorn. Instead, you welcomed me as if I were an angel of God or Jesus Christ himself."

From Galatia, Paul then intended to travel northeastward through Bithynia, a region on the shore of the Black Sea, however "they tried to enter Bithynia, but The Spirit of Jesus would not allow them to."

So they passed by Mysia and went down to Troas. Isn't it interesting that it says that the Spirit of Jesus Christ was directing them where He wanted them to go? Fortunately, they were obedient and waited for instructions.

During the night Paul had a vision of a man of Macedonia standing and begging him, "Come over to Macedonia and help us." Paul realized that the vision was a message from the Lord, so the very next day he sailed across the Dardanelles, which separated him from Europe where he thought he would be preaching. This turn of travel plans opened up a new region to the gospel.

They sailed straight for Samothrace, then on to Neapolis. From there they arrived at Philippi, a Roman colony and the leading city of the district of Macedonia, where they stayed several days.

While there, on the Sabbath day he then went outside the city gate to the river where they expected to find a place of prayer. They sat down and began to speak to the women who had gathered there. One of those listening was a woman named Lydia, a dealer in purple cloth from the city of Thyatira, who was a worshiper of God. The Lord opened her heart to respond to Paul's message. When she and the members of her house were baptized, she invited them to her home. She said to them, "If you consider me a believer in the Lord, come and stay at my house." So they stayed with her while they were ministering there.

Once when they were on the way to the place of prayer, they met a slave girl who had a spirit by which she predicted the future. She earned a great deal of money for her owners by fortune-telling. This girl followed Paul and the rest of the disciples shouting, "These men are servants of the Most High God who are telling you the way to be saved." She kept this up for several days, and finally, Paul became so troubled that he turned around and said to the spirit, "In the name of Jesus Christ I command you to come out of her!" At that moment the spirit left her.

When the owners of the slave girl realized that their hope of making money by using her was gone, they seized Paul and Silas and dragged them into the marketplace to face the authorities. They brought them before the magistrates and said, "These men are Jews and are throwing our city into an uproar by advocating customs unlawful for us Romans to accept or practice."

The crowd joined in the attack against Paul and Silas, and the magistrates ordered them to be stripped and beaten. After they had been severely flogged, they were thrown into prison, and the jailer was commanded to guard them carefully. Upon receiving such orders, he put them in the inner cell and fastened their feet in the stocks. About midnight Paul and Silas were praying and singing hymns to God, and the other prisoners were listening to them.

Suddenly there was such a violent earthquake; the foundations of the prison were shaken. At once all the prison doors flew open and the prisoners' chains came loose. The jailer woke up, and when he saw the prison door open, he drew his sword and was about to kill himself because he thought the prisoners had escaped. But Paul shouted, "Don't harm yourself! We are all here!"

The jailer called for the lights, rushed in and fell trembling before Paul and Silas. He then brought them out and said, "Sirs, what must I do to be saved?" They replied, "Believe in the Lord Jesus, and you will be saved-you and your household." Then they spoke the Word of the Lord to him and the others in his house. At that hour of the night the jailer washed their wounds, then immediately he and all his family were baptized.

When it was daylight, the magistrates sent their officers to the jailer with the order, "Release those men." The jailer told Paul, "The magistrates have ordered that you and Silas be released. Now you can leave. Go in peace." But Paul said to the officers; "They beat us publicly without a trial, even though we are Roman citizens, and threw us into prison. And now do they want to get rid of us quietly? No! Let them come themselves and escort us out."

The officers reported this to the magistrates, and when they heard that Paul and Silas were Roman citizens, they were alarmed. They came to appease them and escorted them from the prison, requesting them to leave the city. After Paul and Silas came out of the prison, they went to Lydia's house where they met with the brothers and encouraged them in their faith before they left town.

Next, they went to Thessalonica where they went to the synagogue as they usually did when they entered a city. They proclaimed that Jesus was the Christ and some of the Jews were persuaded and joined Paul and Silas, as did a large number of Greeks.

The Jews were jealous and rounded up some bad characters from the market place, formed a mob and started a riot in the city. They went to the house of a man named Jason where they thought Paul and Silas had been staying. When they did not find them there, they dragged Jason and some of the other brothers who had become believers before city officials saying, "These men who have caused trouble all over the world have come here and Jason has welcomed them into his house. They are all defying Caesar's decrees saying that there is another king, one called, Jesus." The city officials and the people in the town were thrown into turmoil, so they made Jason and the others post bond and let them go.

As soon as it was nightfall, the brothers sent Paul and Silas away to Berea. There they preached in the synagogue and found the people there were of more noble character than the Thessalonians, for they received the message with great eagerness, and examined the Scriptures every day to see if what Paul was saying was true. Many became believers, but when the Jews in Thessalonica learned that Paul was preaching the Word of God at Berea, they went and agitated the crowds against them. The brothers immediately sent Paul to the coast, but Silas and Timothy stayed at Berea. They took Paul to Athens with instructions that Silas and Timothy would join him as soon as possible.

It was while Paul was in Athens that he was distressed to see that the city was so full of idols. Paul was greatly troubled by this and spoke boldly to them, "Men of Athens! I see that in every way you are very religious. For as I walked around and looked carefully at your objects of worship, I even found an altar with this inscription: To an unknown God. Now what you worship as something unknown I am going to proclaim to you. The God who made the world and everything in it is the Lord of heaven and earth and does not live in temples built by hands. He is not served by human hands as if he needed anything because he gives all men life and breath and everything else. From one man he made everything else. From one man he made every nation of men that they should inhabit the whole earth, and he determined the times set for them and the exact places where they should live. God did this so that men would seek him and perhaps reach out for him and find him, though he is not far from each one of us. For in him we live and move and have our being."

He goes on. "Therefore since we are God's offspring, we should not think that the divine being is like gold or silver or stone-an image made by man's design and skill. In the past, God overlooked such ignorance, but now he commands all people everywhere to repent. For he has set a day when he will judge the world with justice by the man he has appointed. He has given proof of this to all men by raising Him from the dead." When they heard about the resurrection of the dead, some of them sneered, but others believed.

After this, Paul left Athens and went to Corinth. There he met a Jew named Aquila, a native of Pontus, who had recently come from Italy with his wife, Priscilla because Claudius had ordered all the Jews to leave Rome. Paul went to see them, and because he was a tentmaker as they were, he stayed and worked with them. Every Sabbath he went to the synagogue trying to persuade Jews and Greeks of the message he had been sent to give.

Not long after, Silas and Timothy arrived from Macedonia, and Paul then devoted himself exclusively to preaching, testifying to the Jews but when they began to oppose him and become abusive, he shook out his clothes in protest and said to them, "Your blood be on your own head! I am clear of my responsibility. From now on I will go to the Gentiles." Paul then went to live among the believers and continued to preach, and many were baptized.

The Lord must have known that Paul was getting discouraged because one night he came to Paul in a vision about Corinth. "Do not be afraid; keep on speaking, do not be silent. For I am with you and no one is going to attack you or harm you because I have many believers in this city." So Paul stayed a year and half teaching them the Word.

After leaving Corinth he sailed to Syria and was accompanied by Priscilla and Aquila. Before he sailed, he had his hair cut off at Cenchrea because of a vow he had made.

(Note as to why he cut his hair: Paul had assumed a Nazarite vow (see Numbers 6:1-21) which was an Old Testament act of thanksgiving or dedication to God. During the period of the vow, the devotee allowed his hair to grow uncut, and at the end of the period, he cut his hair. As he came to Cenchrea, the eastern port of Corinth, on his way to Syria and Palestine, the time of his vow elapsed, and he, therefore, cut his hair.)

They arrived at Ephesus, where Paul left Priscilla and Aquila. When he went into the synagogue to preach, they asked him to spend more time with them, but he declined. But as he left he promised, "I will come back if it is God's will." Then he set sail from Ephesus headed to Caesarea where he greeted the church there and then went down to Antioch.

After numerous other spiritually profitable visits throughout the region, Paul then began making his homeward journey because he wanted to observe Pentecost at Jerusalem.

Discussion Questions:

1. What do you think gave Paul such confidence to continue in the faith even after such persecution?

2. When Paul was in Athens, he was amazed at the many false gods they worshiped. What are some of the gods we worship today instead of putting our complete trust in the true God?

3. I underlined a phrase, (In him we live and move and have our being), do you think that is what your life exemplifies? What might you be putting your trust in other than God?

4. When Paul was in prison, and God caused an earthquake to come and open the prison doors, it appeared God had given him a way of escape. Why do you think he choose not to take it?

5. While in Macedonia, a fortune teller was following them proclaiming what they were saying was true, why do you think Paul cast a spirit out of her?

7. Are there any things, (idols) today that you are intrigued with that might be keeping you from putting your full trust in God's Word alone?

Lesson 52
Paul's 3rd Missionary Journey

We are continuing our travels with Paul as we watch the church being spread through the known world at this time. In our last lesson, we left Paul going to Jerusalem to celebrate Passover. He then left Jerusalem and went to Antioch. After spending some time there, he set sail and traveled from place to place throughout the region of Galatia and Phrygia, encouraging and strengthening the believers in the region.

Meanwhile, others who had been followers of John were sharing the gospel, as they knew it as well. A Jew named Apollos came to Ephesus. He was a learned man, with a thorough knowledge of the Scriptures. He spoke with great fervor and taught about Jesus accurately, though he knew only the baptism of John. (Remember John preached of Jesus coming and being the Messiah and He baptized people who would believe and repent.) Although they believed, they knew nothing of the Holy Spirit.

When Apollos began to speak boldly in the synagogue, a couple named Priscilla and Aquila, heard him and invited him to their home to explain to them the gospel more deeply, as he was eager to learn more. Apollos was so enthusiastic about all he had learned that he wanted to go to Achaia to share the gospel there. The believers there encouraged him and wrote a letter to the disciples there to welcome him with open arms. When he arrived, he was a great help to those who by grace had believed because he vigorously refuted his Jewish opponents in public debate, proving from the scriptures that Jesus was the Messiah. He continued to be a great asset in helping to evangelize the region.

Paul begins his third missionary journey really by revisiting the churches in Galatia to follow-up on the epistle he wrote to them in late spring, (book of Galatians). He continues to visit brethren in the Phrygia province to strengthen and encourage them in their faith before going on to Ephesus where he stays a little more than three years. The time is now autumn 54 A.D.

It is while he was there in the late winter of 56 A.D. that he writes the book of 1 Corinthians. Then he follows up with writing the book of 2 Corinthians in the late summer of 57 A.D. We call them books but they were actually letters or instructions and encouragement to the churches given to him by inspiration of the Holy Spirit.

While in Ephesus he discovers other believers, who like Apollos, were baptized as a sign of repentance by John the Baptist, but did not as yet have God's spirit living in them. He then is able to share the full gospel with them and the coming of the Holy Spirit. (Acts 19:1-7)

Paul continues to preach boldly about the gospel for three months in a local synagogue. Some however who did not believe what he was teaching began to speak evil of Paul and those who believed the gospel left the synagogue.

One day seven sons of a Jewish priest named Sceva arrive in Ephesus. The sons are Jewish exorcists who travel from place to place and pretend to cast demons out of people. They witness Paul casting out demons and decide to try his method for themselves. They run into someone possessed of an evil spirit and attempt to cast it out of the person the way Paul did. The response they receive is totally unexpected! As the sons learn, merely using the name of Jesus does not guarantee the ability to access His power because one time when they tried it, the evil spirit replied, "I know Jesus, and I know Paul, but who are you?" Then the man with the evil spirit leaped on them, overpowered them, and attacked them with such violence that they fled from the house naked and battered. After this happened, many who practiced magic repented of their deeds and burned their books of spells and other evil-related practices. (Acts 19:18-19)

In the early winter of 57 A.D. an Ephesian silversmith named Demetrius, who makes a significant profit creating small replicas of the pagan goddess Diana and her temple, becomes concerned about the recent loss of business. The preaching of Paul in the area has persuaded many people to stop purchasing and using idols and to abandon the worship of false gods like Diana.

The goddess Diana is zealously worshipped in Ephesus and in other places around the empire. The city of Ephesus is famous for possessing the Temple of Diana (Artemis), which in modern times is considered one of the seven wonders of the ancient world. Demetrius, the silversmith, organizes a meeting of fellow tradesmen to discuss the drop in idol sales.

During the meeting, a riot breaks out. The crowd finds and seizes two of Paul's traveling companions. When Paul wants to talk to the mob some disciples stop him from doing so, as it would jeopardize his life. A clerk quiets the crowd by reminding them that the worship of Diana is so well known and universally accepted that there was no danger of it being destroyed by the evangelist and what he taught. The clerk chides the crowd for their unreasonable fears and warns them there are consequences if they continue being disorderly! The riot soon disperses. At this point, Paul decides to leave the city and journey to Macedonia.

During his three-month stay in the region, he visits Corinth, and it is there he writes his letter to the Romans.

It is now 58 A.D, and Paul and his companions travel back through Macedonia to Troas, where they keep the Feast of Unleavened Bread. On his last day at Troas, he preaches and teaches until late in the night. Listening to him is a young man sitting in a window. The man soon goes into a deep sleep and dies when he falls out the window to the street below. The evangelist immediately goes to the young man, embraces him, and he comes back to life!

Meantime, Luke and a few others sail from Philippi and meet Paul in Troas. Although Luke and several others decide to sail from Troas to Assos, Paul chooses to walk to the city. In Assos the entire group takes a ship to Mitylene, sail past the islands of Chios and Samos, and eventually arrive at Miletus, which was a seaport town located about 36 miles from Ephesus.

While there he requests that the elders in the Ephesian church visit him. When they arrive, he warns them about the coming apostasy in the church; which is a warning that many will abandon their religious beliefs.

He tells them that he is compelled by the Spirit to go to Jerusalem, not knowing what will happen to him there, but knowing that in every city, the Holy Spirit warns him that prison and hardship are facing him.

He then tells them the line that has been quoted many times from pulpits; Paul says, "My life is worth nothing to me if only I can finish the race and complete the task Jesus Christ has given me of testifying to the gospel of his grace." He goes on to tell them to help the weak, reminding them of the words of Jesus, "It is more blessed to give than to receive." Afterward, he knelt down with all of them and prayed. They all wept as he embraced them knowing they would never see him again. They followed him all the way to the ship to say goodbye.

Paul boards a ship and sails to the islands of Cos and Rhodes where he eventually arrives at Patara. There he boards another boat bound for the city of Tyre in Phoenicia. Landing at Tyre, he stays with fellow believers in the area for one week then sails to Ptolemais where he visits other believers for a day.

He again boards a boat and arrives at Caesarea. Phillip, the evangelist, who lives in Caesarea, has him stay in his home for many days. While at Phillip's house a prophet from Judea named Agabus comes to see him. He takes Paul's belt and binds his own hands and feet, and says, "The Holy Spirit says, in this way the Jews in Jerusalem will bind the owner of this belt and will hand him over to the Gentiles." After this prophecy, those with him pleaded with him not to go to Jerusalem. He responds to them by saying, "Why are you weeping and breaking my heart? I am ready not only to be bound but to die in Jerusalem for the name of the Lord Jesus."

Some of the disciples accompanied him to Jerusalem and took him to the home of Mnason who was an early believer from Cyprus. Paul arrived in Jerusalem around late spring of 58 A.D., possibly near the time of the Feast of Pentecost. (Acts 21:17) This ends Paul's third missionary journey, but Paul has a lot to go through before he finishes his ministry.

Discussion Questions:

1. At the beginning of the lesson, we refer to a man named Apollos who was a learned man and was going about fervently sharing the gospel, as he knew it. Aquila and Priscilla took him home and gave him the complete gospel. Has there been a time in your life that you were fervent about the gospel only to find you were not aware of key elements? If so, explain an example.

2. Paul is known for not only sharing the gospel but also for being an encourager. He continues to write letters and send others out when he could not go to teach. He wanted to be sure they were solid in their faith as followers of Jesus. Have you continued to encourage and help those God has put in your life? Explain.

Lesson 53
Paul's Arrest and Trial

In our last lesson, we left Paul going back to Jerusalem despite numerous warnings that he would suffer persecution if he returned.

After entering Jerusalem, he went to see James and some of the elders. He told him of the great results he had sharing the gospel with the Gentiles and they all rejoiced and praised God. Then they said to Paul, "You see, brother, how many thousands of Jews have believed, and all of them jealous for the law. They have been informed that you teach all Jews who live among the Gentiles to turn away from Moses, telling them not to circumcise their children or live according to our customs. What shall we do? They will certainly hear that you have come."

Then they told Paul, "There are four men with us who have made a vow. Take these men and join in their purification and pay their expenses so they can have their heads shaved. Then everyone will know there is no truth in these reports about you, but you yourself are living in obedience of the law." Paul did as they said and the next day went to the temple to give notice of the date when the days of purification would end and the offering would be made for each of them. Paul did this as a way of proving that he was not separating himself from the law but was willing to show, by committing to be set apart for a time of purification, that he was truly one of God's prophets.

When the seven days were nearly over, some Jews from the province of Asia saw Paul at the temple. They stirred up the crowd and seized him, shouting, "Fellow Israelites, help us! This is a man who teaches everyone everywhere against our people and our law. And besides, he has brought Greeks into the temple and defiled this holy place."

People came running from every direction and seized Paul and dragged him from the temple, and immediately the gates were shut. While they were trying to kill him, the commander of the Roman troops heard that the city was in an uproar and immediately took soldiers to see what was going on. When the rioters saw the soldiers, they quit beating Paul. The commander had him arrested and bound with two chains. When he inquired as to what Paul had done, some shouted one thing and some another. Since he could not get an accurate answer, he had Paul taken into the barracks. The violence of the mob was so great that the soldiers had to carry Paul as the crowd shouted, "Get rid of him!"

As the soldiers were about to take Paul into the barracks, he asked the commander, "May I say something to you? Do you speak Greek?" He replied, "Aren't you the Egyptian who started a revolt and led four thousand terrorists out into the wilderness some time ago?" Paul answered, "I am a Jew, from Tarsus in Cilicia, a citizen of no ordinary city. Please let me speak to the people." After receiving the commander's permission, Paul stood on the steps and motioned to the crowd. When they were all silent, he said to them in Aramaic, "Brothers and fathers, listen now to my defense." The crowd became very quiet once they heard Paul speak to them in Aramaic.

Then Paul said: "I am a Jew, born in Tarsus of Cilicia, but brought up in this city. I studied under Gamaliel and was thoroughly trained in the law of our ancestors. I was just as zealous for God as any of you are today. I persecuted the followers of this way to their death, arresting both men and women and throwing them into prison, as the high priest and all the Council can, themselves, testify. I even obtained letters from them to their associates in Damascus, and went there to bring these people, as prisoners, to Jerusalem to be punished. About noon, as I came near Damascus suddenly a bright light from heaven flashed around me. I fell to the ground and heard a voice say to me, 'Saul! Saul! Why do you persecute me?' 'Who are you, Lord?' I asked. 'I am Jesus of Nazareth, whom you are persecuting,' he replied. My companions saw the light, but they did not understand the voice of Him who was speaking to me. 'What shall I do, Lord?' I asked. 'Get up,' the Lord said, 'and go into Damascus. There you will be told all that you have been assigned to do.'"

"My companions led me by the hand into Damascus, because the brilliance of the light had blinded me. A man named Ananias came to see me. He was a devout observer of the law and highly respected by all the Jews living there. He stood beside me and said, 'Brother Saul, receive your sight!' And at that very moment I could see him." Then he said: 'The God of our ancestors has chosen you to know His will and to see the Righteous One and to hear words from His mouth. You will be his witness to all people of what you have seen and heard. And now what are you waiting for? Get up, be baptized and wash your sins away, calling on his name.' When I returned to Jerusalem, and was praying at the temple, I fell into a trance and saw the Lord speaking to me. 'Quick!' He said, 'Leave Jerusalem immediately, because the people here will not accept your testimony about Me.' I replied, 'Lord, these people know that I went from one synagogue to another to throw them in prison, and I beat those who believe in you. And when the blood of your martyr Stephen was shed, I stood there giving my approval and guarding the clothes of those who were killing him.' Then the Lord said to me, 'Go; I will send you far away to the Gentiles.'"

The crowd listened to Paul as he said this. Then they raised their voices and shouted, "Rid the earth of him! He's not fit to live!" As they were shouting, and throwing off their cloaks and flinging dust into the air, the commander ordered that Paul be taken back into the barracks. He directed that Paul be flogged and interrogated to find out why the people were shouting at him like this. As they stretched him out to flog him, Paul said to the centurion standing there, "Is it legal for you to flog a Roman citizen who hasn't even been found guilty?" When the centurion heard this, he went to the commander and reported it. "What are you going to do?" He asked the centurion, "This man is a Roman citizen." The commander went to Paul and demanded, "Tell me, are you a Roman citizen?" "Yes, I am," Paul conceded. Then the commander said, "I had to pay a lot of money for my citizenship." "But I was born a citizen," Paul replied. Those who were about to interrogate him withdrew immediately. The commander himself was alarmed when he realized that he had put Paul, a Roman citizen, in chains.

The commander wanted to find out exactly why Paul was being accused by the Jews. So, the next day Paul was released, and the commander ordered the chief priests and all the members of the Sanhedrin to assemble. He brought Paul in and had him stand before them. Paul looked straight at the Sanhedrin and said, "My brothers, I have fulfilled my duty to God in all good conscience to this day."

At this, the high priest, Ananias, ordered those standing near Paul to strike him on the mouth. Then Paul said to him, "God will strike you, you whitewashed wall! You sit there to judge me according to the law, yet you yourself violate the law by commanding that I be struck!" Those who were standing near Paul exclaimed, "How dare you insult God's high priest!" Paul replied, "Brothers, I did not realize that he was the high priest; for it is written: 'Do not speak evil about the ruler of your people.'"

Then Paul, knowing that some of them were Sadducees and the others Pharisees, called out in the Sanhedrin, "My brothers, I am a Pharisee, descended from Pharisees. I stand on trial because of the hope of the resurrection of the dead." When he said this, a dispute broke out between the Pharisees and the Sadducees, and the assembly was divided. (The Sadducees believed there is no resurrection, and that there are neither angels nor spirits, but the Pharisees believed all these things.) There was a great uproar and some of the teachers of the law who, were Pharisees stood up and argued vigorously. "We find nothing wrong with this man," said the Pharisees. "What if a spirit or an angel has spoken to him?" The dispute became so violent that the commander was afraid Paul would be torn to pieces by them. He ordered the troops to go down and take Paul away.

But when the son of Paul's sister heard of this plot, he went into the barracks and told Paul. Then Paul called one of the centurions and said, "Take this young man to the commander; he has something to tell him." So the centurion then took him to the commander. The centurion said, "Paul, the prisoner, sent for me and asked me to bring this young man to you because he has something to tell you." The commander took the young man by the hand, drew him aside, and asked, "What is it you want to tell me?" The young man went on to explain, "Some Jews have agreed to ask you to bring Paul before the Sanhedrin tomorrow on the pretext of wanting more accurate information about him. Don't give in to them, because more than forty of them are waiting in ambush for him. They have taken an oath not to eat or drink until they have killed him. They are ready now, waiting for your consent to their request." The commander dismissed the young man with this warning: "Don't tell anyone that you have reported this to me."

Immediately, the commander called two of his centurions and ordered them, "Get ready a detachment of two hundred soldiers, seventy horsemen, and two hundred spearmen to go to Caesarea at nine tonight. Provide a horse for Paul so that he may be taken safely to Governor Felix." He wrote a letter as follows: "Claudius Lysias, To His Excellency, Governor Felix: Greetings. The Jews seized this man and they were about to kill him, but I came with my troops and rescued him, for I had learned that he is a Roman citizen. I wanted to know why they were accusing him, so I brought him to their Sanhedrin. I found that the accusation had to do with questions about their law, but there was no charge against him that deserved either death or imprisonment. When I was informed of a plot to be carried out against the man, I sent him to you at once. I also ordered his accusers to present to you their case against him."

So, the soldiers, carrying out their orders, took Paul with them during the night and brought him as far as Antipatris. The next day they let the cavalry go on with him, while they returned to the barracks. When the cavalry arrived in Caesarea, they delivered the letter to the governor and handed Paul over to him. The governor read the letter and asked what province he was from. Learning that Paul was from Cilicia, he said, "I will hear your case when your accusers get here." The governor then ordered that Paul be kept under guard in Herod's palace.

Five days later, the high priest, Ananias, went down to Caesarea with some of the elders and a lawyer named Tertullus to bring their charges against Paul before the governor. When Paul was called in, Tertullus presented his case before Felix: "We have enjoyed a long period of peace under you, and your foresight has brought about reforms in this nation. Everywhere, and in every way, most excellent Felix, we acknowledge this with profound gratitude. But in order not to weary you further, I would request that you be kind enough to hear us briefly." "We have found this man to be a troublemaker, stirring up riots among the Jews all over the world. He is a ringleader of the Nazarene sect and even tried to desecrate the temple; so, we seized him. By examining him yourself you will be able to learn the truth about all these charges we are bringing against him." The other Jews joined in the accusation, asserting that these things were true.

When the governor motioned for him to speak, Paul replied: "I know that for a number of years you have been a judge over this nation; so, I gladly make my defense. You can easily verify that no more than twelve days ago, I went up to Jerusalem to worship. My accusers did not find me arguing with anyone at the temple, or stirring up a crowd in the synagogues or anywhere else in the city. Neither can they prove to you the charges they are now making against me. However, I admit that I worship the God of our ancestors, as a follower of the Way, which they call a sect. I believe everything that is in accordance with the Law and that is written in the Prophets, and I have the same hope in God as these men themselves have: that there will be a resurrection of both the righteous and the wicked. Therefore, I strive always to keep my conscience clear before God and man. After an absence of several years, I came to Jerusalem to bring my people gifts for the poor and to present offerings. I was ceremonially clean when they found me in the temple courts doing this. There was no crowd with me, nor was I involved in any disturbance. But there are some Jews from the province of Asia, who ought to be here before you and bring charges if they have anything against me. These who are here should state what crime they found in me when I stood before the Sanhedrin—unless it was this one thing I shouted as I stood in their presence: It is concerning the resurrection of the dead that I am on trial before you today."

Then Felix, who was well acquainted with the Way, adjourned the proceedings. "When Lysias the commander comes," he said, "I will decide your case." Felix then ordered the centurion to keep Paul under guard but to give him some freedom and permit his friends to take care of his needs.

Several days later, Felix came with his wife Drusilla, who was Jewish. He sent for Paul and listened to him as he spoke about faith in Christ Jesus. As Paul spoke about righteousness, self-control and the judgment to come, Felix was afraid and said, "That's enough for now! You may leave. When I find it convenient, I will send for you." At the same time, he was hoping that Paul would offer him a bribe, so he sent for Paul frequently and talked with him. When two years had passed, Felix was succeeded by Porcius Festus. However, because Felix wanted to grant a favor to the Jews, he left Paul in prison.

Three days after arriving in the province, Festus went up from Caesarea to Jerusalem, where the chief priests and the Jewish leaders appeared before him and presented the charges against Paul. They requested Festus, as a favor to them, to have Paul transferred to Jerusalem, for they were preparing an ambush to kill him along the way. Festus declared, "Paul is being held at Caesarea, and I myself am going there soon. Let some of your leaders come with me, and if the man has done anything wrong, they can press charges against him there."

After spending eight or ten days with them, Festus went down to Caesarea. The next day he convened the court and ordered that Paul be brought before him. When Paul came in, the Jews, who had come down from Jerusalem, stood around him. There were many serious charges alleged against Paul; however, none could be proven. In turn, Paul made his defense: "I have done nothing wrong against the Jewish law or against the temple or against Caesar." Festus, wishing to do the Jews a favor, said to Paul, "Are you willing to go up to Jerusalem and stand trial before me on these charges?" Paul countered: "I am now standing before Caesar's court, where I ought to be tried. I have not done any wrong to the Jews, as you yourself know very well. However, if I am guilty of doing anything deserving death, I do not refuse to die. But if the charges, brought against me by these Jews, are not true, no one has the right to hand me over to them. I appeal to Caesar!" After conferring with council, Festus proclaimed: "You have appealed to Caesar. To Caesar, you will go!"

A few days later King Agrippa and Bernice arrived at Caesarea to pay their respects to Festus. Since they were spending many days there, Festus discussed Paul's case with the king. He said, "There is a man here whom Felix left as a prisoner. When I went to Jerusalem, the chief priests and the elders of the Jews brought charges against him and asked that he be condemned." "I told them that it is not the Roman custom to hand over anyone before they have faced their accusers and have had an opportunity to defend themselves against the charges. When they came here with me, I did not delay the case, but convened the court the next day and ordered the man to be brought in. When his accusers got up to speak, they did not charge him with any of the crimes I had expected. Instead, they had some points of dispute with him about their own religion and about a dead man named Jesus, who Paul claimed was alive. I was at a loss how to investigate such matters; so, I asked if he would be willing to go to Jerusalem and stand trial there on these charges. But when Paul made his appeal, to be held over for the Emperor's decision, I ordered him held until I could send him to Caesar." Then Agrippa said to Festus, "I would like to hear this man myself." "Tomorrow you will hear him," Festus replied.

The next day Agrippa and Bernice came and entered the audience room with the high-ranking military officers and the prominent men of the city. At the command of Festus, Paul was brought in. Festus said, "King Agrippa, and all who are present with us, you see this man! The whole Jewish community has petitioned me about him in Jerusalem, and here in Caesarea, shouting that he ought not to live any longer. I found he had done nothing deserving of death, but because he made his appeal to the Emperor, I decided to send him to Rome. But I have nothing definitive to write to His Majesty about him. Therefore, I have brought him before all of you, and especially before you, King Agrippa, so that because of this investigation I may have something to write. For I think it is unreasonable to send a prisoner on to Rome without specifying the charges against him."

Then Agrippa said to Paul, "You have permission to speak for yourself." Paul then motioned with his hand and began his defense: "King Agrippa, I consider myself fortunate to stand before you today, as I make my defense against all the accusations of the Jews, and especially so because you are well acquainted with all the Jewish customs and controversies. Therefore, I beg you to listen to me patiently. The Jewish people all know the way I have lived ever since I was a child, from the beginning of my life in my own country, and in Jerusalem. They have known me for a long time and can testify, if they are willing, that I conformed to the strictest sect of our religion, living as a Pharisee. And it is now because of my hope in what God has promised our ancestors that I am on trial today.

"This is the promise our twelve tribes are hoping to see fulfilled as they earnestly serve God day and night. King Agrippa, it is because of this hope that these Jews are accusing me. Why should any of you consider it incredible that God raises the dead I too was convinced that I ought to do all that was possible to oppose the name of Jesus of Nazareth; therefore, that is just what I did in Jerusalem. On the authority of the chief priests, I put many of the Lord's people in prison, and, when they were put to death, I cast my vote against them. Many a time I went from one synagogue to another to have them punished, and I tried to force them to blaspheme.

"I was so obsessed with persecuting them that I even hunted them down in foreign cities. On one of these journeys I was going to Damascus, with the authority and commission of the chief priests, and around noon, King Agrippa, as I was on the road, I saw a light from heaven, brighter than the sun, blazing around me and my companions. We all fell to the ground, and I heard a voice saying to me in Aramaic, 'Saul, Saul, why do you persecute me? It is hard for you to kick against the goads.' Then I asked, 'Who are you, Lord?' The Lord replied. 'I am Jesus, whom you are persecuting, now get up and stand on your feet. I have appeared to you to appoint you as a servant and as a witness of what you have seen and will see of me. I will rescue you from your own people and from the Gentiles.

I am sending you to them to open their eyes and turn them from darkness to light, and from the power of Satan to God, so that they may receive forgiveness of sins and a place among those who are sanctified by faith in Me.'

"So then, King Agrippa, I was not disobedient to the vision from Heaven. First to those in Damascus, then to those in Jerusalem and in all Judea, and then to the Gentiles, I preached that they should repent and turn to God and demonstrate their repentance by their deeds. That is why some Jews seized me in the temple courts and tried to kill me. But God has helped me to this very day; so I stand here and testify to small and great alike. I am saying nothing beyond what the prophets and Moses said would happen—that the Messiah would suffer and, as the first to rise from the dead, would bring the message of light to His own people and to the Gentiles."

At this point, Festus interrupted Paul's defense. "You are out of your mind, Paul!" he shouted. "Your great learning is driving you insane." Paul answered him, "I am not insane, most excellent Festus. What I am saying is true and reasonable. The king is familiar with these things, and I can speak freely to him. I am convinced that none of this has escaped his notice, because it was not done in a corner. King Agrippa, do you believe the prophets? I know you do." Then Agrippa said to Paul, "Do you think that in such a short time you can persuade me to be a Christian?" Paul replied, "Short time or long—I pray to God that not only you but all who are listening to me today may become what I am, except for these chains." Then rose the king, along with the governor and Bernice and those sitting with them. After they left the room, they began saying to one another, "This man is not doing anything that deserves death or imprisonment." Agrippa then informed Festus, "This man could have been set free if he had not appealed to Caesar."

Discussion Questions:

1. Paul had the boldness to proclaim his faith despite possible retribution. Do you have that same boldness when faced with an unbelieving one, or do you shy away from the subject?

2. Paul spoke boldly about hearing directly from Jesus and hearing him give him instructions on how to proceed. Have you had a time when you heard Jesus speak to you directly about something and, if so, what did you do about it?

3. Paul was accused of breaking the Jewish law and was willing to go the extra mile of going through a consecration at the temple to prove his loyalty to God's tradition. Have you ever had your faith questioned? If so, how did you respond?

4. Paul went through all the false accusations and God always gave him a way out by appealing to another court. Have you ever been in a place where you felt hopeless and God gave you an escape?

Lesson 54
Paul's Ending Journey

We left Paul in our last lesson being questioned by King Agrippa and Festus. The general consensus was that he had done nothing wrong and would have been set free if he had not appealed to Caesar.

It was decided that Paul and some other prisoners would set sail for Italy. It would be handed over to a centurion named Julius who belonged to the Imperial Regiment who had heard Paul speech. They set sail hoping to reach Phoenix and winter there.

They were sailing along the shore of Crete when suddenly a wind of hurricane force, called the Northeaster, swept down from the island. The ship was caught by the storm and could not head into the wind. They were hardly able to make the lifeboat secure so the men hoisted it aboard. Then they passed ropes under the ship itself to hold it together. Because they were afraid they would run aground on the sandbars of Syrtis, they lowered the sea anchor and let the ship be driven along by the storm.

They took such a violent battering from the storm that the next day they began to throw the cargo overboard. On the third day, they threw the ship's tackle overboard with their own hands. When neither sun nor stars appeared for many days and the storm continued raging, they finally gave up all hope of being saved. After they had gone a long time without food, Paul stood up before them and said: "Men, you should have taken my advice not to sail from Crete so you would have spared yourselves this damage and loss. But now I urge you to keep up your courage because not one of you will be lost; only the ship will be destroyed. Last night an angel of the God to whom I belong and whom I serve, stood beside me and said, 'Do not be afraid, Paul. You must stand trial before Caesar; and God has graciously given you the lives of all who sail with you.' So keep up your courage men, for I have faith in God that it will happen just as he told me. Nevertheless, we must run aground on some island."

On the fourteenth night, they were still being driven across the Adriatic Sea, when, about midnight, the sailors sensed they were approaching land. Just before dawn, Paul urged them all to eat. "For the last fourteen days," he said, "you have been in constant suspense and have gone without food—you haven't eaten anything. Now I urge you to take some food. You need it to survive. Not one of you will lose a single hair from his head." After he said this, he took some bread and gave thanks to God in front of them all. Then he broke it and began to eat. They were all encouraged and ate some food themselves. Altogether there were 276 on board. When they had eaten as much as they wanted, they lightened the ship by throwing the grain into the sea.

When daylight came, they did not recognize the land, but they saw a bay with a sandy beach, where they decided to run the ship aground if they could. Cutting loose the anchors, they left them in the sea and at the same time untied the ropes that held the rudders. Then they hoisted the foresail to the wind and made for the beach. But the ship struck a sandbar and ran aground. The bow stuck fast and would not move, and the stern was broken to pieces by the pounding of the surf. The soldiers planned to kill the prisoners to prevent any of them from swimming away and escaping. But the centurion wanted to spare Paul's life and kept them from carrying out their plan. He ordered those who could swim to jump overboard first and get to land. The rest were to get there on planks or on other pieces of the ship. In this way, everyone reached land safely.

Once safely on shore, they found out that the island was called Malta. Paul wrote, "The islanders showed us unusual kindness. They built a fire and welcomed us all because it was raining and cold." Paul gathered a pile of brushwood and, as he put it on the fire, a viper, driven out by the heat, fastened itself on his hand. When the islanders saw the snake hanging from his hand, they said to each other, "This man must be a murderer; for though he escaped from the sea, the goddess Justice has not allowed him to live." But Paul shook the snake off into the fire and suffered no ill effects. The people expected him to swell up or suddenly fall dead; but after waiting a long time and seeing nothing unusual happen to him, they changed their minds and said he must be a god.

There was an estate nearby that belonged to Publius, the chief official of the island. He welcomed them to his home and showed generous hospitality for three days. His father was sick in bed, suffering from fever and dysentery. Paul went in to see him and, praying, placed his hands on him and he was healed. After word of this got out, the rest of the sick on the island came and were healed as well. They treated the men with honor and respect and when they were ready to sail, they furnished them with the supplies they needed.

Paul wrote, "After three months we put out to sea in a ship that had wintered on the island—it was an Alexandrian ship with the figurehead of the twin gods Castor and Pollux. They put in at Syracuse and stayed there for three days. From there we set sail and arrived at Rhegium. The next day the south wind came up, and on the following day, we reached Puteoli. There we found some brothers and sisters who invited us to spend a week with them and then to Rome. The brothers and sisters there had heard that they were coming, and they traveled as far as the Forum of Appius and the Three Taverns to meet us." At the sight of these people, Paul thanked God and was encouraged. After arriving in Rome, Paul was allowed to live by himself, with a soldier to guard him.

Three days later he called together the local Jewish leaders. When they had assembled, Paul said to them: "My brothers, although I have done nothing against our people or against the customs of our ancestors, I was arrested in Jerusalem and handed over to the Romans. They examined me and wanted to release me because I was not guilty of any crime deserving death. The Jews objected, so I was compelled to make an appeal to Caesar. I certainly did not intend to bring any charge against my own people. For this reason, I have asked to see you and talk with you. It is because of the hope of Israel that I am bound with this chain."

They replied, "We have not received any letters from Judea concerning you, and none of our people who have come from there have reported or said anything bad about you. But we want to hear what your views are, for we know that people everywhere are talking against this sect."

They arranged to meet Paul on a certain day and came in even larger numbers to the place where he was staying. He witnessed to them from morning till evening, explaining about the kingdom of God, and from the Law of Moses and from the prophets, he tried to persuade them about Jesus. Some were convinced by what he said, but others would not believe. They disagreed among themselves and began to leave after Paul had made this final statement: "The Holy Spirit spoke the truth to your ancestors when He said through Isaiah the prophet, 'Go to this people and say, you will be ever hearing but never understanding; you will be ever seeing but never perceiving." Paul realized the profound truth in the words of the prophet because he said, "For this people's heart has become calloused; they hardly hear with their ears, and they have closed their eyes. Otherwise, they might see with their eyes, hear with their ears and understand with their hearts and I would heal them." He added, "However, I want you to know that God's salvation has been sent to the Gentiles and they listened."

For two whole years, Paul stayed there in his own rented house and welcomed all who came to see him. He proclaimed the kingdom of God and taught about the Lord Jesus Christ—with all boldness and without hindrance!

We know that Paul had further journeys after he was released from the prison in Rome in 63 AD. After his release, he wrote the epistles of Titus, 1 Timothy, and 2 Timothy, and possibly Hebrews. They were not however necessarily in that order, although 2 Timothy was apparently his last. This took place after the events recorded in Acts, so all our information comes from various statements that Paul makes in his letters.

In them are clues that Paul may have traveled to some or all following places: Colosse, Spain, Corinth, Miletus, Troas, Crete, Nicopolis, Philippi, Italy, Judea, Ephesus, and Macedonia. This allows for the possibility that Paul traveled to about as many diverse places as all of his previous journeys combined. There are probably several possible ways that one could reconstruct the sequence of these travels, which would not disagree with scripture.

The references below are not intended to be chronological, although they all occurred after Paul's release from prison in 63 AD.

In Philemon 2:2, Paul foresaw his release and tells those in Colosse to prepare him lodging. We know that Philemon was written to the Colossians. (Colossians 4:17). Also, while in prison in Rome, Paul wrote to those in Philippi that he might be coming to visit them (Philippians 1:26).

In Romans 1:10, 15:24 and 28, and 16:1, 3, and 5 Paul speaks of aspirations of eventually going to Spain. Did he ever do this in his final years? The Bible does not say.

We read that Paul leaves Titus in Crete so his journey must have taken him there and it would have been during a period of liberty after Paul's imprisonment in Rome ended in 63 AD. Paul did not go there during the first 3 journeys. There is no mention of Titus or of any preaching on Crete in Acts 27:7-13, on the voyage to Rome. Paul says he will send Artemas or Tychism to Titus. He tells Titus to come to Nicopolis where Paul has determined to winter (Titus 3:12). The letter to **Titus** was probably written around 64-65 AD. There are three cities called Nicopolis: (1) in Achaia (southern Greece), most likely the one to which Paul was referring, (2) 15 miles west of Jerusalem, and (3) in the area that is now Romania.

The book of Hebrews was supposedly written from Italy (Hebrews 13:24). Timothy had been released from prison (Hebrews 13:23) and was coming to Paul. Paul was apparently at liberty as well, since they planned to then go to visit the Hebrews. This could have been in Judea, as Paul says, "... *ye had compassion for me in my bonds* ..." (Hebrews 10:34). This must have been about Paul's imprisonment in Caesarea.

Paul had told Timothy to stay and teach in Ephesus while Paul went to Macedonia (1 Timothy 1:3). During the third journey, Paul had done the opposite, staying in Ephesus himself, and sending Timothy with Erastus to Macedonia (Acts 19:22). So, 1 Timothy was written around 64-65 AD during a period of liberty after Paul's Roman imprisonment of 61-63 AD. Paul said he was hoping to come to Timothy in Ephesus shortly, but may have to tarry long (1 Timothy 3:14-15). Timothy was in Ephesus where he received both 1 Timothy and 2 Timothy (1 Timothy 1:3, 2 Timothy 1:16-18, 4:14, 4:19, Acts 19:33, and 1 Timothy 1:20).

2 Timothy was apparently written from prison (2 Timothy 1:8) with Paul ready to die (2 Timothy 4:6-8),

possibly about 66 AD. Yet he asks Timothy to come to him before winter (2 Timothy 4:9 and 21). Paul was probably martyred sometime around 67 AD.

The Bible does not say how the apostle Paul died. We see him writing in 2 Timothy 4: 6–8 that he seems to be anticipating his soon demise: "For I am already being poured out as a drink offering, and the time of my departure has come. I have fought the good fight, I have finished the race, I have kept the faith. Henceforth there is laid up for me the crown of righteousness, which the Lord, the righteous judge, will award to me on that Day, and not only to me but also to all who have loved his appearing."

There are a few different Christian traditions as to how Paul died, but the most commonly accepted one comes from the writings of Eusebius, an early church historian. Eusebius claimed that Paul was beheaded at the order of the Roman emperor, Nero, or one of his subordinates. Paul's martyrdom occurred shortly after much of Rome burned in a fire—an event that Nero blamed on the Christians.

It is possible that the apostle Peter was martyred around the same time, during this period of the early persecution of Christians. The tradition is that Peter was crucified upside down and that Paul was beheaded since Paul was a Roman citizen (Acts 22:28), and Roman citizens were normally exempt from crucifixion. Since the Bible does not record exactly how Paul died, there is no way to be certain regarding the exact circumstances of his death We know he was ready to die for Chris and he died for his faith. (Acts 21:13), and Jesus had prophesized that Paul would suffer much for the name of Christ (Acts 9:16). Based on what the Book of Acts records of Paul's life, we can assume he died declaring the gospel of Christ, spending his last breath as a witness to the truth that sets men free (John 8:32).

The following is a summary of where Paul wrote the books of the New Testament:

52 AD	1 & 2 Thessalonians written from Corinth
56 AD	1 Corinthians written from Ephesus
57 AD	Romans, Galatians, 2 Corinthians written from Macedonia
61-63 AD	Ephesians, Colossians, Philippians, Philemon, possibly Hebrews (Written during his two-year imprisonment)
63-64AD	1Timothy & Titus written from Corinth
65-66AD	Probably wrote 2 Timothy from prison in Rome
67AD	Died in Rome

Discussion Questions:

1. Reflecting on Paul's life, what do you think gave him the strength to endure all the hardships he encountered and yet keep the faith?

2. When shipwrecked on an island, and a poisonous snake attached to Paul's hand, the people felt he would soon die but God spared him as a witness. Have you ever felt God spared you for a purpose to be a witness for him?

3. Why do you think Paul believed it was important to keep visiting and writing to the churches that were established?

4. In what way has our study of Paul's journeys impacted your life?

Lesson 55
I Thessalonians

This is the first letter to the Thessalonians and was probably the first of Paul's letters, and written by the end of 52 AD, making it the first written book in the New Testament.

Thessalonica was formerly the metropolis of Macedonia; it is now called Salonichi and is the most populated and one of the best towns for commerce. The apostle Paul, being diverted from going into the provinces of Asia, was directed to preach the gospel in Macedonia (Acts 16:9, 10).

For the most part, the letter is personal with only the final two chapters spent addressing issues of doctrine, almost as an aside. Paul's main purpose in writing is to encourage and reassure the believers there. Paul urged them to go on working while waiting in hope for the return of Christ.

Paul claimed the title of the "Apostle to the Gentiles," and established gentile churches in several important cities in the Roman Empire. The Thessalonians to whom this letter is addressed were mainly made up of Gentile Christians although some were converted Jews. This reflects the ethnic and religious makeup of the congregation in Thessalonica, and is supported by Paul's brief remark in 1:9 that they "turned to God from idols." It was Gentiles, not Jews, who stopped worshiping idols. The Jews as a body fiercely opposed Paul's work there.

This brings up a point of interest as to the very first words Paul used to address the Christians: "Grace and peace to you." The usual apostolic benediction, "Grace" is the Greek and "peace" is the Jewish form of salutation. The Greeks commenced their epistles with wishing grace for those to whom they wrote, and the usual form of salutation among the Jews was Shalom or "peace." The apostle combines them, thus intimating that both Greeks and Jews are one in Christ Jesus.

He also begins with great words of validation and encouragement, "For we know, brothers loved by God, that he has chosen you, because our gospel came to you not simply with words, but also with power, with the Holy Spirit, and with deep conviction." He wanted to reassure their confidence in the things they had been taught and that the power of the Holy Spirit was with them.

He was concerned because of the infancy of the church. He had spent only a few weeks with them before leaving for Athens. Because of his concern, he had sent his delegate, Timothy, to visit the Thessalonians and to return with a report. While on the whole the news was encouraging, it also showed that serious misunderstandings existed concerning Paul's teaching of Christianity. Paul devotes part of the letter to correct these errors and then urges them to live a life of purity, reminding them that it was God's will for their lives.

Paul, speaking for himself and Silas and Timothy gave thanks for the good news about their faith and love. He reminds them of the kind of life he had lived while he was with them and stresses how honorably he conducted himself, reminding them that he had worked to earn his keep, taking great pains not to burden anyone. He did this, he says, even though he could have used his status as an apostle to impose upon them. This may seem like he was bragging, but I think he was saying that he understood some of the struggles they faced. While he was there he had helped them with their problems, which validated his commitment to them.

He continually reminded them how much he wanted to be with them. It almost reads like a love letter. "But brothers, when we were torn away from you for a short time (in person, not in thought), out of our intense longing we made every effort to see you. Night and day we pray most earnestly that we may see you again and supply what is lacking in your faith. May the Lord make your love increase and overflow for each other and everyone else, just as ours does for you."

Then Paul gives them advice, much like a parent would when sending his child off into the world, "Make it your ambition to lead a quiet life, to mind your own business and to work with your hands, just as we told you, so that your daily life may win the respect of outsiders and so that you will not be dependent on anyone."

Paul goes on to answer some concerns that had arisen in the church. Notably, there was some confusion regarding the fate of those who die before the arrival of the new kingdom. Many seem to have believed that an afterlife would be available only to those who lived to see the kingdom. Paul addresses this and explains that the dead will be resurrected and dealt with before those still living who will greet the Lord in the air.   You can read this account in 4: 13-18. Thus, he assures, there is no reason to mourn the death of fellow Christians, and to do so is to show a lack of faith.

Then he tells them not to worry about the dates of the coming of the Lord. In 5:2, he says the Lord will come like a thief in the night. He says people will be talking about peace and safety, and destruction will come on them suddenly, and then compared it to labor pains of a woman.

However, he tells them that will be for those who still live in darkness, but that they are sons of light and should stay alert and self-controlled. He gives them a visual by saying in 5: 8, "Since you belong to the day, let us be self-controlled, putting on faith and love as a breastplate and the hope of salvation as a helmet. God did not appoint us to suffer wrath but to receive salvation through our Lord Jesus Christ. He died for us so that, whether we are awake or asleep, we may live together with him."

He ends with final words of instructions starting in 5:12, "But we appeal to you, brothers and sisters, to respect those who work hard among you, and have charge of you in the Lord and admonish you; esteem them highly in love because of their work. Live at peace with each other. And we urge you, brothers, to warn those who are idle, encourage the faint-hearted, help the weak, be patient with all of them. See that none of you repays evil for evil, but always seek to do good to one another and all. Be joyful always, giving thanks in all circumstances, for this is God's will for you in Christ Jesus.

 "Pray without ceasing, give thanks in all circumstances, for this is the will of God in Christ Jesus for you. Do not put out the Spirit's fire; do not treat prophecies with contempt. Test everything and hold on to the good. Avoid every kind of evil. May God himself, the God of peace sanctify you through and through. May your whole spirit and soul and body be kept blameless at the coming of our Lord Jesus Christ, the one who calls you is faithful, and he will do this."

Then he ends by asking for their prayers. "Beloved, pray for us. Greet all the brothers and sisters with a holy kiss. I solemnly command you by the Lord that this letter is read to all. The grace of our Lord Jesus Christ be with you."

Unlike all other of Paul's epistles, 1 Thessalonians does not focus on justification by faith or questions of Jewish–gentile relations themes that are covered in all other letters.

Discussion Questions:

1. Paul obviously sends his love and encouragement to them in a way that would help them stay focused on the true gospel and not be led astray. Have you had those in your life who have been there to help keep you encouraged? If so, how?

2. In 4:11, he encourages them to live a quiet life and mind their own business so they would win the respect of those around them and that they might be won to the Lord. Share how your life does or does not reflect this.

3. Paul's answer to the church when questioned about the time of the coming of the Lord was not to worry but to be alert and self-controlled. He tells them that it is only those walking in darkness who need to be concerned. Who are those described as walking in darkness?

4. Paul tells them to keep their whole spirit, soul, and body blameless until the coming of the Lord. How would you distinguish between these three areas of our lives and which one do you struggle with most?

5. Paul's final words to the church were to live at peace, help the fainthearted, help the weak, etc. Which of those apply most to your life today?

Lesson 56
II Thessalonians

2 Thessalonians was written from Corinth probably no later than a few months after the first letter. This would have been around 52 AD.

Paul and his friends received news from Thessalonica that the church there still needed more instruction, as they had not fully understood some of what was in the first letter. So, the purpose of the second letter was to clarify those issues.

One of the topics they misunderstood was the timing of Jesus return. They thought He was coming just any day and in fact, they had stopped working and were just waiting for Jesus. So in this second letter, Paul describes to them again what the second coming of Jesus would be like. He urges them to continue working and to use their time wisely.

Like 1 Thessalonians, this letter is from Paul, Silas, and Timothy. The writer of this letter used the same style as 1 Thessalonians and other letters that Paul wrote. This shows that Paul was the main author. Silas and Timothy are included in the greeting. In many verses, he states, "we write." This shows that all three of them agreed. The handwriting was not Paul's since he wrote just the final greeting and prayer (2 Thessalonians 3:17). It seems that Paul dictated the letter, maybe to Timothy or Silas.

Paul starts his greeting to them with the greeting of grace and peace from God the Father and the Lord Jesus Christ. This shows the awareness that Paul had that he was truly an ambassador of God and that his words would be as if God himself were speaking truth.

I love the fact that before he straightens them out on the confused issues, he builds them up by saying, "We always thank God for you, bothers, and rightly so, because your faith is growing more and more, and the love every one of you has for each other is increasing. Therefore, among God's churches, we boast about your faith and perseverance…" Paul must have had some psychology classes because he uses this classic technique to address the churches throughout the New Testament.

Paul then goes on to acknowledge the trials they are going through and tells them that they will be rewarded and counted worthy of the kingdom of God because they are enduring persecutions. Then he points out one of the attributes of God in verse 6 telling them that God is just. They must have felt the same confusion that we do sometimes when we are doing everything right and things are just not working out the way we think they should.

He goes on in verse 6 and says, "God will pay back trouble to those who trouble you and give relief to you who are troubled, and to us as well. This will happen when the Lord Jesus is revealed from heaven in blazing fire with his powerful angels." No wonder they wanted Jesus to return soon.

Paul continues, "He will punish those who do not know God and do not obey the gospel of our Lord Jesus. They will be punished with everlasting destruction and be shut out from the presence of the Lord and from the majesty of his power on the day he comes to be glorified in his holy people and to be marveled at among all those who have believed. This includes you because you believed our testimony to you."

This must have been as hard a concept for them as it is for us to comprehend. They must have had loved ones or friends who did not believe in the testimony about Jesus, and here Paul is saying they will experience everlasting destruction and be shut out of the presence of God. This alone must have given them a reason to not only live right themselves but to be sure all those they come in contact know this wonderful truth.

Remember Jesus' instruction to Peter when he came to him at the lake and asked if he loved him. Peter said, yes he loved him. Jesus replied, "If you love me, feed my sheep." His message was always the same, John 3:16, "For God so loved the world that he gave his only begotten son that whosoever believeth in him shall not perish but have everlasting life."

Then we are left with the question, what happens to those who do not believe the gospel? Is it God's will that some are condemned to everlasting destruction? The next verse after John 3:16 answers that question, "For God sent not his Son into the world to condemn the world but that the world through him might be saved." That is why Jesus sent the disciples out with the message in Matthew 9:37, "The harvest is plentiful but the workers are few." That is why we send missionaries around the world and are expanding the gospel television stations via satellite now to almost every nation in the world.

Paul continues after telling them he understands it is hard but tells them that he and the others are constantly praying that God would find them worthy of their calling. Then he says he will pray that in God's power they fulfill every good purpose of theirs and every act prompted by their faith. I thought this was an interesting phrase, "that God would fulfill every act prompted by their faith."

As we look back through the Bible we see how it was indeed the act of faith that prompted people to do things that were impossible. Just read Hebrews 11 for a record of these events. It reads like a hero journal of the Bible. All were on this list because of their faith. By faith Noah built an ark, by faith, Abraham, Isaac, Jacob, Joseph, Moses, Rehab, and on, and on, and on…. Then in the New Testament the woman with the issue of blood was healed because of her faith, and Jesus said of the Centurion that he had never seen so great a faith because he understood the authority of Jesus just to say the word and his servant would be healed. So Paul realizes that they will need to have faith to undergo the trials they will have to face.

Paul goes on in chapter 2 to address their concerns of Jesus coming. He tells them not to be alarmed at prophecy. He goes on to explain that many things have to be set in place before Jesus' return. One of them being the coming of what is referred to as the man of lawlessness. This is another name for the antichrist. He goes on to explain how he will come and set himself up as powerful and will proclaim himself to be God. Then in 2:8, Paul goes on to say, "Then the lawless one will be revealed, whom the Lord Jesus will overthrow with the breath of his mouth and destroy by the splendor of his coming."

With this Paul encourages them to stand firm and hold fast to the teachings that had been given to them. He ends by telling them, "May the Lord Jesus Christ himself and God our Father, who loved us and by his grace gave us eternal encouragement and good hope, encourage your hearts and strengthen you in every good deed and word."

Then Paul asked for their prayers as well. "Pray for us that the message of the Lord may spread rapidly and be honored, just as it was with you. And pray that we may be delivered from wicked and evil men, for not everyone has faith."   Again, he ends with encouragement and prayer for them, "May the Lord direct your hearts into God's love and Christ's perseverance."

His last instruction to them in this letter was a warning to avoid men who are idle. He encourages them to follow the example they gave them when they were with them, "We were not idle when we were with you, nor did we eat anyone's food without paying for it. On the contrary, we worked night and day, laboring and toiling so that we would not be a burden to any of you. We did this, not because we do not have the right to such help, but in order to make ourselves a model for you to follow. For when we were with you, we gave you this rule saying if a man will not work, he shall not eat!"

He goes on to tell them, "Be aware of those who are not busy but are busybodies. He tells them to take special note of them and do not associate with them, in order that they may feel ashamed. Yet do not regard him as an enemy, but warn him as a brother."

Paul ends by saying, "May the Lord of peace himself give you peace at all times and in every way. The Lord be with all of you."

Discussion Questions:

1. After Paul's first letter we see confusion about the teaching of Jesus' return Have you ever felt confused about the teaching that you had heard about the gospel?

2. I think Paul set an example of building up those he ministered too in an effort to keep them encouraged. Have you experienced this from a fellow believer and if so, how did it build up your faith?

3. We pointed out the importance that Paul put on encouraging them to act on their faith. In what ways are we asked to act on our faith? Give an example from your own life.

4. At the end, he instructs them to not be lazy but to work and follow the example he set for them. How can we live out that example in our lives today?

5. Paul shows humility by not only praying for them but by asking for their prayers as well. Are you hesitant to ask for the prayers of others and do you offer to hold others up in prayer?

Lesson 57
Galatians

Galatians was written in late Spring 53 AD in Antioch, (Syria) just before Paul set out on his third missionary journey.

Paul wrote this letter to the Christian churches in the Roman province of Galatia. These churches were being confused by false teachers called Judaizers, who were teaching the Gentile Christians that they were not really saved unless they obeyed all the Jewish laws-such as circumcision, eating special foods, and celebrating the Jewish feast days. This group also said that Paul did not have God's authority and therefore was not to be listened to.

Paul starts his letter correcting this and telling them what gospel it is that he preaches and that indeed his authority is from God. The gospel he was telling them was that they couldn't be saved from their sins by obeying the law; we are saved only by believing in Jesus Christ. He adds Christians are free to live by the law of love, not the Law of Moses. Faith, says Paul must be shown in love and believers must live by the Spirit.

He starts with his usual greeting of, "Grace and peace be to you from our God and Father and the Lord Jesus Christ who gave himself for our sins."

He quickly addresses the things he has heard about their confusion. 1:7-8 states, "I am astonished that you are so quickly deserting the one who called you by the grace of Christ and are turning to a different gospel-which is really no gospel at all." From there he gets very direct with them. "Even if we or an angel from heaven should preach a gospel other than the one we preached to you, let him be eternally condemned!"

Paul is disappointed that in such a short time they had turned to something other than what he had taught them. He goes on in verse 11-12, "I want you to know, brothers that the gospel I preached is not something that man made up. I did not receive it from any man, nor was I taught it; rather I received it by revelation from Jesus Christ."

He then goes on to remind them of where he had come from, reminding them that he used to persecute the Jews and how he was advancing in Jewish law beyond many Jews his own age and how jealous he was to learn about the traditions of his fathers.

In 1:15 he tells them that God had set him apart from birth, and called him to reveal his son to him that he might preach to the Gentiles. He reminds them that he did not consult with any man, nor go to Jerusalem to see those who were apostles before he was taught this revelation from God himself.

He goes on to tell them that after three years he went to Jerusalem to get acquainted with Peter and stayed with him fifteen days. He says he only saw James, the brother of Jesus, while there and none of the other apostles. He wanted them to know that his revelation was not because he had spent time learning from the apostles, but that God himself had taught him.

His next trip to Jerusalem was fourteen years later. He took Barnabas and Titus and met with those who seem to be the leaders. He had gotten word that some false brothers had infiltrated their ranks to spy on them and the freedom they had in Christ Jesus and wanted to once again make them slaves of the law.

Paul tells them whatever they were saying or doing makes no difference because God does not judge by external appearance. They were trying to teach them that they had to obey outward traditions to please God while Paul was teaching Jesus came to fulfill the law.

He refuted the things they were being told and tells them that he had indeed been sent to preach the gospel to the Gentiles just as Peter had been sent to preach to the Jews.

Likewise, he said, James, Peter and John, those reputed to be the pillars, gave us the right hand of fellowship when they recognized the grace given to us by God. They encouraged us to continue our work with the gentiles and then to the Jews but asked one thing and that was that we would remember the poor and that was what we were eager to do anyway.

Paul stood strong on obedience and faith even though some gave way to peer pressure. At one point Paul opposes Peter when he came to Antioch because he was being a hypocrite. Peter would eat with the Gentiles until certain men came and when they arrived, he began to draw back and separate himself from the Gentiles. He was afraid of the group who preached the importance following the law of circumcision still. Jesus said that the circumcision he wanted under the New Covenant was the circumcision of the heart. But many Jews followed in this hypocrisy and even Barnabas was led in that direction.

Paul confronts him in front of the others and asks him how he can force gentiles to follow Jewish customs. He goes on to tell him in verse 15, "We who are Jews by birth and not Gentile sinners, know that a man is not justified by observing the law, but by faith in Jesus Christ. For through the law I died to the law so that I might live for God. I have been crucified with Christ and I no longer live, but Christ lives in me. The life I live in the body, I live by faith in the Son of God, who loved me and gave himself for me. I do not set aside the grace of God for if righteousness could be gained through the law, Christ died for nothing."

He goes on in chapter three, by asking them the question, "Did you receive the spirit by observing the law or by believing what you heard. Are you so foolish? After beginning with the spirit, are you now trying to attain your goal by human effort? Does God give you his Spirit and work miracles among you because you observe the law, or because you believed what you have heard?"

He then refers back to the Old Testament and the story of Abraham, "Consider Abraham: he believed God, and it was credited to him as righteousness. Understand then that those who believe are children of Abraham. The scripture foresaw that God would justify the Gentiles by faith, and announced in advance to Abraham, all nations will be blessed through you. So those who have faith are blessed along with Abraham, the man of faith."

He tells them that all who rely on observing the law are under a curse, for it is written: "Cursed is everyone who does not continue to do everything written in the Book of the Law. Clearly, no one is justified before God by the law, because the righteous will live by faith. The law is not based on faith." He continues, "Christ redeemed us from the curse of the law by becoming a curse for us. For it is written: Cursed is everyone who hung on a tree. He redeemed us in order that the blessing given to Abraham might come to the Gentiles through Christ Jesus so that by faith we might receive the promise of the Spirit."

The promises or blessings given to Abraham were given to Abraham and his seed. It does not say seeds but means one person, Jesus Christ. Paul makes the point that the law, introduced 430 years later, does not set aside the covenant previously established by God and does not do away with the promise. If the inheritance depends on the law, then it no longer depends on a promise, but God in his grace gave it to Abraham in a promise. He promised him that if he would step out on faith and go where God asked him to go that his people would be set apart for the line that the long-awaited Messiah would come through.

We know as we looked in the story of Abraham's life that God tested his faith and he proved to God he could be trusted with this awesome responsibility. Up until this time, man had earned God's favor by obeying the law, observing the feast, offering sacrifices, etc. Abraham believed God and set a new plan in motion.

Paul then answers the question, what was the purpose of the law? He tells us in 3:19 that it was added because of transgressions until the Seed to whom the promise referred had come. "Before this faith came, we were held prisoners by the law, locked up until faith should be revealed. So the law was put in charge to lead us to Christ that we might be justified by faith. Now that faith has come, we are no longer under the supervision of the law."

This is such a freedom letter from Paul because he shows that God is no respecter of persons. He tells us we are all sons of God if we believe in Christ Jesus and that he came and died for us. He says in 3:28, "There is neither Jew nor Greek, slave nor free, male nor female, for you are all one in Christ Jesus. If you belong to Christ, then you are Abraham's seed and heirs according to the promise."

He goes on to compare an heir to a slave by saying there were no differences even though one owns the whole estate. He points out that guardians and trustees are there to manage what is done until the appointed time that has been set before he can claim his inheritance. Likewise, at the appointed time, God sent his Son, born of a woman, born under the law, to redeem those under law that we might receive the full right of sons. "Because you are his sons, God sent the Spirit of his Son into our hearts, the Spirit. So you are no longer a slave, but a son; and since you are a son, God has made you also an heir." (4:6)

He warns them again about listening to those who would have them fall away from the teaching. He uses the story of Sarah and Hagar. "Abraham had two sons, one by the slave woman and the other by the free woman. His son by the slave woman was born in the ordinary way; but his son by the free woman was born as the result of a promise. …Now you brothers, like Isaac, are children of promise. At times the son born in the ordinary way persecuted the son born by the power of the Spirit. It is the same now. Abraham had to get rid of the slave woman and her son, for the slave woman's son will never share in the inheritance with the free woman's son. Therefore, brothers, we are not sons of the slave woman, but of the free woman." This is a great visual because no doubt everyone had studied and knew the story of Abraham, Sarah, and Hagar. They knew what had happened when Abraham tried to take things into his own hands and not walk in faith and obedience to what God had said. The lessons are still being played out today as we see the different religions resulting from these two brothers are still at war with each other.

He ends with encouragement saying that it is for freedom that Christ set us free. Then a warning, "Stand firm and do not let yourselves be burdened again by a yoke of slavery. He is talking about being put back under laws of tradition to please God.

He addresses the issue that seems to have been such a hot topic and that is circumcision. "For in Christ Jesus circumcision has no value. The only thing that counts is faith expressing itself through love. Side note as to how strongly Paul feels about those who are trying to convince the people they still are to live under the law and be circumcised, "As for those agitators, I wish they would go the whole way and emasculate themselves!" Wow! He does not mince words as to how strongly he feels about this.

He ends by telling them again they were called to be free and that the entire law could be summed up in a single command, "Love your neighbor as yourself. If you keep on biting and devouring each other, watch out or you will be destroyed by each other."

His final thoughts were to encourage them to embrace the Spirit that was within them and live by the dictates of the Spirit. "So I say, live by the Spirit, and you will not gratify the desires of the sinful nature, for the sinful nature desires what is contrary to the spirit, and the Spirit what is contrary to the sinful nature."

He then tells the things that are the desires of the sinful nature and warns that those who live by them will not inherit the kingdom of God. He goes on to tell the fruits of those who walk by the Spirit: love, joy peace, patience, kindness, goodness, faithfulness, gentleness, and self-control. He tells them to keep in step with the Spirit. I like that because it is easy to fall back, but as long as you are keeping in step with the Spirit, it will be hard to fall away.

Another phrase we have heard all our life comes from this passage, 6:7-9: "Do not be deceived: God cannot be mocked. A man reaps what he sows. The one who sows to please his sinful nature will reap destruction; the one who sows to please the Spirit, from the Spirit will reap eternal life. Let us not become weary in doing good, for at the proper time we will reap a harvest if we do not give up."

Discussion Questions:

1. One of the things Paul points out is that he was chosen before birth to be a follower of Jesus. The truth is we are all chosen before birth for this purpose. Do you ever feel you have been called for a particular reason for His service because of the way you are wired?

2. The frustrating thing Paul was wrestling with was how they wanted to go back under the law by doing religious things. What are some of the ways you might be tempted to fall into a pattern of trying to please God on the outside and not from the heart?

3. Paul has to confront Peter, and I am sure it was a huge disappointment to see Peter giving in to pressure to keep the Jewish traditions. Have you ever been disappointed in a spiritual leader, and how does it affect your faith?

4. Had you ever thought how the comparison of Hagar and Sarah applies to our lives today? One was a result of obedience and the other out of disobedience. Waiting for God to act on prayer sometimes takes a lot of patience. What are some ways to build patience?

5. Which of the fruits of the spirit flow freely through your life? Which may take a little more work?

6. Paul also says God cannot be mocked and we will reap what we sow. What are some ways God is mocked?

7. What do you think Paul means when he says to keep in step with the Holy Spirit?

Lesson 58
I Corinthians

Paul wrote this letter to the church in Corinth, probably in the winter of 55 A.D. It was while he was in Ephesus that he sent this letter in response to a letter from the Corinthian church.

Located on the Mediterranean, the city of Corinth was a wealthy trading center. It was also a wicked city and was known for that throughout the Roman world.

Because the church there was new, it was hard for them not to act like their neighbors, so the church had some problems. They began to take sides against each other, and a spirit of division was taking hold. Some of them, in fact, were living very sinful lives. Paul wrote this letter to scold them and teach them how Christians should act. He laid out practical lessons about the Christian life so that people in Corinth would know right from wrong.

He starts out the letter, "To those sanctified in Christ Jesus and called to be holy, together with all those everywhere who call on the name of our Lord Jesus Christ-their Lord and ours." He is setting the stage for the letter by saying this letter is to those who are called to be holy since that is the issues he is going to address.

He uses his usual greeting to them and starts with words of encouragement. "I always thank God for you because of this grace given you in Christ Jesus. For in him you have been enriched in every way—in all your speaking and in all your knowledge---because our testimony about Christ was confirmed in you. Therefore, you do not lack any spiritual gift as you eagerly wait for our Lord Jesus Christ to be revealed. He will keep you strong to the end so that you will be blameless on the day of our Lord Jesus Christ."

After a few words of encouragement he gets to the heart of the letter by telling them, "I appeal to you, brothers, in the name of our Lord Jesus Christ, that all of you agree with one another so that there may be no divisions among you and that you may be perfectly united in mind and thought.

Then he proceeds to tell them who told on them, "Some from Chloe's household have informed me that there are quarrels among you." Then he addresses the thing that seems to be dividing them. Some were saying they followed Paul, some Apollos, another Cephas, and still another saying they follow Christ.

Paul says to them, "Is Christ divided? Was Paul crucified for you? Were you baptized into the name of Paul? I am thankful that I did not baptize any of you except Crispus and Gaius, so no one can say that you were baptized into my name." He goes on to say, "Christ did not send me to baptize, but to preach the gospel-not with words of human wisdom, lest the cross of Christ is emptied of its power."

The real message here was that the message of the cross is something that is only accessed through faith and belief in Jesus. Paul continues, "The message of the cross is foolishness to those who are perishing, but to us who are being saved, it is the power of God. For it is written: I will destroy the wisdom of the wise; the intelligence of the intelligent I will frustrate."

This is the beauty of the way God chose to redeem mankind from a sinful state. John 3:16 states, "For God so loved the world that He gave his only begotten son that whosoever believeth in Him shall not perish but have everlasting life." This has been the roadblock for so many because it includes everyone and does not give an advantage to the wise scholars or philosophers of the day.

1 Corinthians 1:21 states, "For since the wisdom of God the world through its wisdom did not know him, God was pleased through the foolishness of what was preached to save those who believe. Jews demand miraculous signs, and Greeks look for wisdom, but we preach Christ crucified: a stumbling block to the Jews and foolishness to Gentiles, but to those whom God has called, both Jews and Greeks, Christ the power of God and the wisdom of God. For the foolishness of God is wiser than man's wisdom, and the weakness of God is stronger than man's strength."

Then he reminds them of what God has done for them. "Brothers, think of what you were when you were called. Not many of you were wise by human standards; not many were influential; not many were of noble birth. But God chose to shame the wise; God chose the weak things of the world to shame the strong. He chose the lowly things of this world the things that are not—to nullify the things that are, so that no one may boast before him. "

Paul goes on to tell them that he did not come to speak as a wise man of great knowledge, but that he came with fear and trembling. He said he did not have wise and persuasive words, but he came with a demonstration of the Spirit's power so that their faith would not rest on him but God's power.

He goes on to speak to those who are spiritually more mature. "We speak a message of wisdom among the mature, but not the wisdom of this age or of the rulers of this age who are coming to nothing. No, we speak of God's secret wisdom, wisdom that has been hidden and that God destined for our glory before time began. None of the rulers of this age understand it, for if they had, they would not have crucified the Lord of glory."

Then comes one of my favorite and most amazing promises in the Bible. "For it is written: No eye has seen, no ear has heard, no mind has conceived what God has prepared for those who love him. But God has revealed it to us by his Spirit. The Spirit searches all things, even the deep things of God. For who among men know the thought of a man except for the man's spirit within him. In the same way, no one knows the thought of God except the Spirit of God. We have not received the spirit of the world but the Spirit who is from God, that we may understand what God has freely given him."

Then he explains why so many are confused about the gospel and refuse to believe the truths in it. "The man without the Spirit does not accept the things that come from the Spirit of God, for they are foolishness to him, and he cannot understand them because they are spiritually discerned." Then he warns about judging the spiritual man saying that we as believers have the mind of Christ. That is an amazing statement. If we could only wrap our heads around that so much of our life would be different.

After Paul makes his point of the power of the presence of the Spirit, he goes on to tell them he is disappointed that they have not grown in their faith. He then scolds them by telling them that they are like infants who still need the milk of the Word and are not ready to be fed solid food. He wants to tell them so many deeper truths about the gospel but says that since there is jealousy and quarreling among them that they are still worldly.

He makes another point of their immaturity by saying they are mere men when they start comparing who they are following. He tells them that he and Apollos are only servants who were sent and each assigned a task. He says, "I planted the seed, Apollos watered it, but God made it grow. So he who plants nor he who waters is anything, but only God, who makes things grow."

Then he uses the comparison of a building. He says that he lays the foundation, but someone else comes and builds upon it. He warns not to build on anything but Jesus Christ. He says that each man's work will be shown for what it is and if it is not built on Jesus Christ, it will be burned up. Then he makes the point that we are God's temple and that God's Spirit lives in each of that and us if anyone destroys God's temple, he will be destroyed, for God's temple is sacred. Have you ever thought of your body as the sacred dwelling place of God on earth?

What an awesome thought to dwell on. God chose to set up housekeeping inside of you. In the Old Testament, He had a temple built to house the Holy of Holies where His presence dwelt. But when Jesus was crucified the curtain was torn from top to bottom to show that God's presence no longer dwelt on earth because when Jesus was crucified, the Holy Spirit went back to the Father.

Remember at the cross when Jesus exclaimed, "I give up my spirit?" He had to be as a man then to go to hell and defeat Satan, so the Holy Spirit had to leave Him. But after three days and three nights, the price for man's sin was paid, and the Holy Spirit joined His body, and he came out of the tomb. He told his followers to wait until he returned to his Father to take care of some details of redemption, and then the presence of God would come live inside those who believed and accepted the truth of what had just happened. They waited in the upper room, and the Holy Spirit came on them like tongues of fire. So here Paul is using these things to tell them to value themselves as well as their fellow brothers as having possessing the same Holy Spirit.

Paul warns against judging people and tells them when the Lord comes, he will bring to light what is hidden in darkness and will expose the motives of men's hearts.

He tells them that he is sending them Timothy, who is his son in the Lord, and that he will teach those more about how to live. He also tells them he will come himself as soon as he can, to find out who these arrogant people are who are living immoral lives. He goes on to say that it has been reported that there is sexual immorality among them and that it is of a kind that is not even practiced among pagans. "A man has his father's wife. And you were proud! Shouldn't you rather have been filled with grief and have put out of your fellowship the man who did this? Even though I am not physically present, I am with you in spirit. And I have already passed judgment on the one who did this, just as if I were present. When you are assembled in the name of our Lord Jesus, and I am with you in spirit, and the power of our Lord Jesus is present, hand this man over to Satan so that the sinful nature may be destroyed and his spirit saved on the day of the Lord."

He warns against allowing immorality to exist in the church and compares it to having a little yeast in a bread bowl and how it spreads throughout the whole batch of dough. He compares the yeast to malice and wickedness and the bread without yeast to sincerity and truth. He is very firm on this issue and says to not even associate with anyone who calls himself a brother but is sexually immoral or greedy, an idolater, slanderer, drunkard or a swindler. He says to expel such a person from among your fellowship. He says, "Do not be deceived: Neither the sexually immoral nor idolaters, nor adulterers, nor male prostitutes, nor homosexual offenders, nor thieves, nor the greedy, nor drunkards, nor slanderers, nor swindlers, will inherit the kingdom of God."

Even though he is harsh on other offenses, he is especially harsh on sexual immorality. He says all other sins a man commits are outside his body, but he who sins sexually, sins against his own body. He says in 6:19-20, "Do you not know that your body is a temple of the Holy Spirit, who is in you, whom you have received from God? You are not your own; you were bought with a price. Therefore, honor God with your body."

He addresses the issue of marriage. Paul himself was not married and says that it is good for a man not to marry, but since there is so much immorality, each man should have his own wife, and each woman her own husband. He says a wife and husband are to fulfill their marital duty and that their body is not their own any longer.

"As for the unmarried and the widows I say: It is good for them to stay unmarried as I am. But if they cannot control themselves, they should marry, for it is better to marry than to burn with passion." To the married, "a wife must not separate from her husband. But if she does, she must remain unmarried or else be reconciled to her husband. And a husband must not divorce his wife."

Then he addresses those men and women who live with an unbelieving spouse. He says that if the unbelieving spouse is willing to live with them that they should remain, but if they leave to let him do so, and that a believing man or woman is not bound in such circumstances because he says God has called us to live in peace. He has much more advice concerning relationships of a man and woman that can be found in chapter 7.

On the subject of sacrificing to idols, Paul says that we believers have the knowledge that there is only one God, and although it is not a problem for us, we should be conscious of our brothers who are weaker in the faith and not do anything that would hinder them. So if a brother sees us eating or drinking something that they think is wrong, we should abstain from it so as not to discourage them from growing until they are stronger in their faith.

Paul goes on to talk about how he is willing to become as others to win them to the Lord. He says, "To the weak, I have become weak to win the weak. I will become all things to all people so that by all possible means I might save some."

He tells them that as apostles they have the right to reap a harvest along with those who walk beside them but he does not use that right and boasts that he is compelled to preach the gospel because he has been called to do so. He says in 9:15, "I have not used any of these rights. And I am not writing this in the hope that you will do such things for me. I would rather die than have anyone deprive me of this boast. When I preach the gospel, I cannot boast, for I am compelled to preach. Woe to me if I do not preach the gospel."

He addresses propriety in worship saying that the head of every man is Christ and that the head of the woman is the man, and the head of Christ is God. He says a man who worships with his head covered dishonors God, and a woman who worships God without her head covered dishonors her head, saying it is just as though her head was shaved. He goes on to explain. A man should not cover his head since he is the image and glory of God, but the woman is the glory of man. For man did not come from woman but woman from man (Adam and Eve). For this reason, a woman should have a sign of authority on her head. We as women could get pretty hung up on this, but he goes on to say, "In the Lord, however, a woman is not independent of man, nor is man independent of woman. For as woman came from man, so also man is born of woman, but everything comes from God."

Paul also gives instructions concerning the Lord's Supper. He says that anyone who eats or drinks in an unworthy manner sins against the body and blood of the Lord. The meaning here is that everyone should examine himself or herself before partaking of communion, the remembrance of the death of Jesus.

Concerning the Spiritual gifts. He says, "There are different gifts but one Spirit. There are different kinds of service but the same Lord. There are different kinds of workings, but the same God works all of them in all men." He says each one is for the common good of all. He lists the different gifts as knowledge, wisdom, faith, healing, miraculous powers, prophecy, distinguishing between spirits, speaking in tongues and the interpretation of tongues (the speaking and interpreting a spiritual unknown tongue). He says all these are the working of the same Spirit, and God gives to each person, just as he determines.

Paul compares it to our body. "The body is one unit, though it is made up of many parts; and though all its parts are many, they form one body. So it is with Christ. For we were all baptized into one Spirit into one body—whether Jew or Greeks, slave or free, and we were all given the one Spirit to drink." He goes on to make it even simpler to understand. "Now the body is not made up of one part but of many. If the foot should say because I am not a hand, I do not belong to the body; it would for that reason not cease to be part of the body. And if the ear should say because I am not an eye, I do not belong to the body; it would not for that reason cease to be part of the body. If the whole body were an eye, where would the sense of hearing be? If the whole body were an ear, where would the sense of smell be? But in fact, God has arranged the parts in the body, every one of them, just as HE would have them to be. "I think you get the picture as to why God created us all so different and gave us each different gifts.

He goes on in the next verses saying that because of this that none of the parts can say they do not need the other parts. He even says that the parts we think are less honorable we treat with special honor. Also, the parts that are not presentable are treated with special modesty, while our presentable parts need no special treatment. He says he does this so there will be no division in the body and that all parts are equal. He goes on to say that because of that if one part suffers that every part suffers with it and if one part is honored we all rejoice in it. Can you imagine what kind of world we would live in if every person understood those simple concepts and lived by them?

Paul goes on to say a lot about love. In chapter 13 he starts by saying, "Now I will show you the most excellent way." He is speaking of the power of love. He describes love as being patient, kind, does not boast, is not proud, not rude, nor self-seeking, not easily angered and keeps no records of wrongs. Does not delight in evil but rejoices with the truth. It always protects, always trusts, always hopes, and always perseveres. Love never fails."

He then says that if he is the greatest in prophecy, has enough faith to move mountains, has all knowledge, but has not love, that he is only a sounding gong or a clanging cymbal. He tells us that all these things will pass away, but three things will remain: faith, hope, and love. But the greatest of these is love.

Paul addresses the gift of speaking in tongues, and orderly worship and then talks about the resurrection of Christ. He emphasizes the importance of holding on to the gospel they had heard and that had been their salvation. He reminds them that Christ died for their sins, was buried, and was raised on the third day." He appeared to Peter, then the twelve and after that, he appeared to more than five hundred at one time, and most of who were still living witnesses. Jesus appeared to James, then the apostles, and last of all he appeared to me also, as to one abnormally born." Paul admits his past failures of persecuting the church and says that he does not deserve to be called an apostle, but that the grace of God prevailed in his life. Interesting that he states he was abnormally born. Maybe he felt that he now understood that he was born to fulfill the special task of building the church, and God had that in mind when he was first conceived.

Paul ends his letter by addressing the resurrection and the importance of embracing the truth of not only the resurrection of Christ but also the future resurrection of our bodies. He tells us in chapter 15 that if Christ was not raised from the dead, then our faith is futile and we are still living in our sinful state, and that those who have fallen asleep in this life are without hope and to be pitied. However, he goes on to re-emphasize that Christ was indeed raised from the dead and that he was the firstfruit of those who have fallen asleep. He says in verse 26, "For as in Adam all die, so in Christ, all will be made alive. But each in his turn: Christ, the first fruits; then, when he comes, those who belong to him. Then the end will come when he hands over the kingdom to God the Father after he has destroyed all dominion, authority, and power. For he must reign until he has put all his enemies under his feet."

He reminds them that they should not question what kind of body they will have after they are resurrected, as it will be a spiritual body. He compares it to a seed being sown and bringing forth a new kind of fruit. "The body that is sown is perishable; it is raised imperishable; it is sown in dishonor, it is raised in glory; it is sown in weakness, it is raised in power; it is raised a spiritual body. If there is a natural body, there is a spiritual body. So it is written: The first man Adam became a living being, the last Adam, a life-giving spirit. The spiritual did not come first, but the natural, and after that the spiritual. The first man was of the dust of the earth, the second man from heaven."

He goes on to say concerning of the time of the resurrection, "Listen, I tell you a mystery: We will not all sleep, but we will all be changed in a flash, in the twinkling of an eye, at the last trumpet. For the trumpet will sound, the dead will be raised imperishable, and we will be changed." He is telling us here that not all will have died when Jesus returns, but we will all be changed instantly to be imperishable and in the likeness of Christ.

After some personal messages about when he will come and about Timothy and Apollos, he leaves them with this powerful message. "Be on your guard; stand firm in the faith; be men of courage; be strong. Do everything in love."

Discussion Questions:

1. As you read this lesson about the failings of the church in Corinth, which of these weaknesses do you find yourself struggling with today?

2. At one point Paul finds the believers at Corinth following false leaders instead of only following Christ. Can you think of a time when you put your trust in a human leader and paid more attention to his words and instruction than the actual Word of God?

3. Paul puts great emphasis on honoring our body. Why do you think he put so much emphasis on sexual immorality? And why do you think if we take communion without examining our lives that we are sinning against our body?

4. As you look at your gifting, does this lesson give you a feeling of being more important in the body? What do you think your gifting is? Can you look at our life and see how you have been able to use this gift for his kingdom.

Lesson 59
II Corinthians

Paul's second letter to the church at Corinth seems to have been written a few months after the first letter. The divisions and problems that we read about in 1st Corinthians were still in the church at Corinth. Paul himself may have taken a quick trip to Corinth, but left rather quickly because some of the members of the church there refused to change or believe that Paul was an apostle of God.

After returning to Macedonia, Paul felt much better when Titus brought him the good news that the people in the Corinthian church had seen their problems and sins and were willing to change. It was at this time that Paul wrote his second letter to the Corinthians.

The first part of this letter tells how happy and thankful Paul was when he heard that the Corinthians were sorry for the way they had acted and were now trying to live the way God wanted them to.

In the second part of the letter, Paul defends himself against the people who were angry with him and who were saying untrue things about him.

He starts the letter with his usual greeting of grace and peace from God our Father and the Lord Jesus Christ. I find it interesting that he uses the intro as if he were speaking for God himself. He continues with "Praise be to the God and Father of our Lord Jesus Christ, the Father of compassion and the God of all comfort, who comforts us in our troubles so that we can comfort those in any trouble with the comfort we ourselves have received from God. For just as the sufferings of Christ flow over into our lives, so also through Christ our comfort overflows. If we are distressed, it is for your comfort, which produces in you patient endurance of the same sufferings we suffer. And our hope for you is firm because we know that just as you share in our sufferings, so also you share in our comfort."

It seems that Paul is trying here to bring the body to an awareness of unity. He wants them to feel like one body that extends comfort and suffers with each other as they go through trials. This is much like we do when a member of our family is hurting, we all hurt for them because of the bond of love we have. He goes on to tell them of the sufferings that he has received while in the province of Asia. He tells them that he was under more pressure than he was able to endure except for the comfort and grace of God. He tells them that those things happened to him so that he might not depend on himself but on God's provision for him.

Paul assures them that God's promises are always true and that his answer is always yes to fulfill his Word if they stand firm in Christ. He tells them that God anointed them by sending his Spirit into their hearts as a deposit guaranteeing what was to come. That is so reassuring to us as the same body of Christ (you and I as believers) to know that the Holy Spirit was given to us as a deposit of more to come from God. When you put a deposit down on something, it means you are investing something to assure that what is coming will be yours and will be done. Recently I had some construction work done, and they said that I would need to put down a deposit as a promissory note that I would follow through with payment when they were done. The promissory note God gave us was the Holy Spirit. What an awesome down payment that we have living inside us.

I love the intense way Paul expresses himself when he is telling them about the stress endured. "I wrote you out of great distress and anguish of heart and with many tears, not to grieve you but to let you know the depth of my love for you." He goes on to say that if someone grieves part of the body that everyone is grieved, but they should forgive, comfort, and reaffirm their love for him. He tells them that as the one who has been put in charge over them that if they forgive anyone their wrongdoings that he himself would forgive them. And that all is done in the sight of Christ and so that Satan might not outwit them for he says they are not aware of the schemes he has. We read that same thing in 1 Peter 5:8, "Be self-controlled and alert. Your enemy, the devil, roams around like a roaring lion, seeking whom he may devour." The lesson here is to live in a spirit of Christ's love so that Satan will not have a root of bitterness, jealousy, envy, etc. to get us to stray from God's best for us and lead us down a path of sin.

He then says in 2:14-16, "Thanks be to God, who always leads us in triumphal procession in Christ, and through us spreads everywhere the fragrance of the knowledge of him. For we are to God the aroma of Christ, among those who are being saved and those who are perishing. To the one, we are the smell of death, to the other, the fragrance of life. "What a powerful statement. Comparing the knowledge, we have of Christ as being a fragrance we can spray on others and that we are to live giving off an aroma of his love. This reminded me of a time when my daughter was about eight years old and came home from school, and as soon as she walked through the door, she said Granny had been here. I asked her how she knew and she said, I can still smell the fragrance of the perfume she always wears.

This is a good analogy of the way we are to live; leaving a fragrance of Christ's love behind us so that people would know a representative of him had just been there. The greatest compliment I can get is when a guest in my home says, "I sense the Holy Spirit here." That happens often, and my heart is always overwhelmed with a spirit of gratitude for being able to represent Christ in a spirit of love that would overflow on others. This happened last week as a young woman came to talk about an issue she was dealing with, and as soon as she walked in the front door, she stopped and said, "Jesus is here, I can sense his peace." We truly are His hands and feet on this earth and should be aware of that everywhere we go, and I think this is the message Paul wanted to get across to the body in Corinth.

As he continues, he tells them that they themselves are like letters in that they are giving forth information about Christ, but he tells them that the letter they represent is a letter written on the heart and not with ink on paper. He tells them that they "are ministers of a new covenant not of the letter but of the Spirit; for the letter kills, but the Spirit gives life." He is referring to the covenant given to Moses when he went up into the mountain and met with God. He was given a tablet of laws for them to live by and if they were not obeyed, often resulted in death. "Now if the ministry that brought death, which was engraved in letters on stone, came with glory, so that the Israelites could not look steadily at the face of Moses because of its glory, fading though it was, will not the ministry of the Spirit be even more glorious? If the ministry that condemns men is glorious, how much more glorious is the ministry that brings righteousness."

He goes on to say that Moses had to put a veil over his face to keep them from gazing as the radiance was fading away and how their minds were so quickly made dull. He says that the same veil remains to this day when the Law of Moses is read because it was written before there was freedom found in Christ and that when anyone turns to the Lord, the veil is taken away.

One of my favorite passages comes into play at this point in the letter 3:14-18. It states, "Now the Lord is the Spirit and where the Spirit of the Lord is, there is freedom. And we, who with unveiled faces all reflect the Lord's glory, are being transformed into his likeness with ever-increasing glory, which comes from the Lord who is the Spirit." The Bible phrase, "Where the Spirit of the Lord is, there is freedom" says that when I have not been experiencing freedom, I can always find that I have moved away from his promises and tried to do life my way.

2 Corinthians, 4:3-7 states, "The god of this age blinds the minds of unbelievers so that they cannot see the light of the gospel of the glory of Christ, who is the image of God. For we do not preach ourselves, but Jesus Christ as Lord, and ourselves as your servants for Jesus' sake. For God, who said, "Let light shine out of darkness, made his light shine in our hearts to give us the light of the knowledge of the glory of God in the face of Christ. But we have this treasure in jars of clay to show that this all-surpassing power is from God and not from us." In verses 10-11 he makes a profound statement that we each need to meditate on, "We always carry around in our body the death of Jesus, so that the life of Jesus may also be revealed in our body. For we who are alive are always being given over to death for Jesus sake, so that his life may be revealed in our mortal body." He goes on to emphasize that we are living for an eternity that is to come. "Though outwardly we are wasting away, yet inwardly we are being renewed day by day…so we fix our eyes not on what is seen but what is unseen. For what is seen is temporary, but what is unseen is eternal."

Earlier we hear Paul refer to his body as an earthen jar, and then refer to it in chapter 5 as an earthly tent. He writes that God has for us an eternal house in heaven, not built by human hands. Then he talks about a time we will all appear before the judgment seat of Christ, that each one will receive what is due him for the things done while in the body, whether good or bad. That can be very convicting as we go through each day knowing that at some point we will be standing before Christ being held accountable for our behavior while on earth.

Then Paul talks to them about the ministry of reconciliation. He emphasizes that the whole point of their new life is because Jesus came to reconcile us back to God and we are no longer the same. Paul tells them that if anyone is in Christ, he is a new creation; the old has gone, the new has come and that God has now given us the ministry of reconciliation. He says in 5:20, "We are therefore God's ambassadors, as though God makes an appeal through us." He is encouraging them to be reconciled to God as well as each other. We have that same responsibility.

Another point he made was to be careful to whom they attached themselves. "Do not be yoked together with unbelievers. For what do righteousness and wickedness have in common? Or what fellowship can light have with darkness? …What agreement is there between the temple of God and idols? For we are the temple of the living God." Many couples have had to wrestle with this question as they consider marriage. The question is whether to marry someone who is not a believer. The same thing is true in becoming partners in business, or anytime there is a covenant or contract binding one to another. Paul tells them to purify themselves from everything that contaminates the body and spirit, perfecting holiness in reverence for God.

Concerning the matter of giving, he starts with comparing what Jesus did for them. "For you know the grace of our Lord Jesus Christ that though he was rich, yet for your sakes, he became poor so that you through his poverty might become rich." He is encouraging them to support each other and all brethren everywhere. His famous saying sums it up, "Remember this: Whoever sows sparingly will also reap sparingly, and whoever sows generously will also reap generously."

Paul makes an appeal to them about his visit and gives a glimpse into his personality. He tells them that although he is bold when writing letters to them that he is actually timid when he comes face to face and encourages them to understand and not expect him to act boldly. He tells them that although they live in the world that they do not wage war as the world does because on the contrary, they have divine powers to demolish strongholds and every pretension that sets itself up against the knowledge of God, and to take captive every thought to make it obedient to Christ.

He tells them that he appreciates them putting up with his foolishness but that he is jealous for them with a godly jealousy. He says he wants to present them to one husband who is Christ, and he wants them to be virgins to him. He readily admits though in 11:3, "I am afraid that just as Eve was deceived by the serpent's cunning, your minds may somehow be led astray from your sincere and pure devotion to Christ."

He warns that there are false prophets who will preach a gospel other than the gospel of Christ and that they will be appealing, but they are from a different spirit. He goes on to say that such men are false apostles masquerading as apostles of Christ and even warns that Satan masquerades as an angel of light. He says then that it is not surprising that his servants masquerade as servants of righteousness. We don't have to look far to find our world bombarded with false prophets who encourage us to worship everything from the universe to idols of every possible sort.

One of the most seductive is the new age movement that calls on us to be meditative, peaceful and seek ways of higher consciousness. They take a grain of truth from God's Word and distort it just enough to entice followers. They encourage followers to channel from a deceased spirit saying we can tap into a higher understanding. The only higher consciousness we need to be meditating on is the one who created us. That was what tripped up Eve in the garden. Satan appealed to her desire to know more of the immortal things of life and disobeyed God, which is what he himself did. That did not work out so well for him, and he is trying to bring as many down with him as possible.

Paul not only refers to himself as timid as we said before but also as a fool who boasts. He adds in 11:17, "In this self-confident boasting, I am not talking as the Lord would, but as a fool. Since many are boasting in the way the world does, I too will boast." I think this makes Paul more human and most of us can identify with him for exposing his weakness. I love the way he puts this, "What anyone else dares to boast about-I am speaking as a fool-I also dare to boast. Are they Hebrew, So am I. Are they Israelites? So am I. Are they Abraham's descendants? So am I. Are they servants of Christ? (I am out of my mind to talk like this.) I am more. I have worked much harder, been in prison more frequently, been flogged more severely, and been exposed to death again and again. Five times I received from the Jews the forty lashes minus one. Three times I was beaten with rods, once I was stoned, three times I was shipwrecked, I spent a night and a day in the open sea, I have constantly been on the move. I have been in danger from rivers, in danger from bandits, in danger from my own countrymen, in danger from Gentiles; in danger in the city, in danger in the country, in danger at sea; and in danger from false brothers. I have toiled and labored and often gone without sleep; I have known hunger and thirst and have often gone without food; I have been cold and naked. Besides everything else, I feel daily the pressure of my concern for all the churches." Wow! Even through all that, Paul says, "If I must boast, I will boast of the things that show my weakness," and he declares that he will go on boasting even though it will gain him nothing.

He refers to having visions and revelation from the Lord. He says he knows a man in Christ who fourteen years ago was caught up to the third heaven. Whether it was in the body or out of the body, he says only God knows. He was caught up to paradise. He heard inexpressible things; things that man is not permitted to tell. Then Paul goes on to say that he will boast about things like that but not about himself. However, he said to keep him from becoming conceited because of these surpassingly great revelations, there was given to him a thorn in his flesh.

Much has been said about what his thorn was, but he clearly says in verse 7 that it was a messenger of Satan sent to torment him. He says he pleaded with the Lord three times to take it away, but he said to him, "My grace is sufficient for you, for my power is made perfect in weakness." Therefore, Paul says he will boast all the more gladly about his weaknesses so that Christ's power may rest on him. He proclaims he will boast more now about his hardships because when he is weak he is strong, and God's grace will always see him through. He points out that Jesus was crucified in weakness yet reigns in power.

He gives a final warning to them to examine themselves and be diligent to keep the faith, assuring them that he is praying for them during his absence. He leaves them with the final greeting to aim for perfection, to be of one mind, and live in peace.

Discussion Questions:

1. As you look at Paul's life, do you see any comparisons to your spiritual struggles?

2. As you look at Paul's thorn in the flesh and how God dealt with him, what would you say your own personal thorn is? How have you seen God deal with you concerning it?

3. Paul makes a point to not be yoked with unbelievers. Have you ever considered that in making a covenant type agreement with someone? What was the outcome of not heeding Paul's message?

4. Paul talks about the fragrance of Christ that we should leave behind us. What fragrance do you think people have of you after you have left them?

Lesson 60
Romans

Paul wrote this letter as he was finishing his third missionary journey. He wrote it in preparation of going to Rome for a visit. He had never been there but had expressed a desire to do so while in Ephesus planning his itinerary. Acts 19:21 states that Paul "decided to go to Jerusalem, passing through Macedonia and Achaia, after that, I must go to Rome."

The letter was written while he was still in the Greek city of Corinth, just three years after the 16-year-old Nero had ascended to the throne as Emperor of Rome. The political situation in the capital had not yet deteriorated for the Roman Christians as Nero wouldn't begin his persecution of them until he made them scapegoats after the great Roman fire in AD 64. Therefore, Paul wrote to a church that was experiencing a time of relative peace, but it was a church that he felt needed a strong dose of basic gospel doctrine.

Again, I am impressed with Paul's greeting, "To all in Rome who are loved by God and called to be saints. Grace and Peace to you from God our Father and from the Lord Jesus Christ." He speaks with much authority as an ambassador representing God and Jesus. Then in true Paul fashion, he builds them up by saying, "I thank my God through Jesus for all of you, because your faith is being reported all over the world." He goes on to tell them how he had longed to visit them before but had been prevented from doing so, and tells them now the way has opened for him to come.

He starts by telling them how eager he is to preach the gospel to them. "For I am not ashamed of the gospel, for it is the power of God for salvation to everyone who believes, to the Jew first and also to the Greek. For in it the righteousness of God is revealed, a righteousness that is by faith from first to last, it is written; the righteous man shall live by faith."

In the letter he greeted twenty-six different people by name, personalizing the letter from a man who would have been a personal stranger to most of the recipients. No doubt they had heard of Paul and would have been honored by the letter, but Paul always took opportunities to personally connect with his audience so that the message of the gospel might be better received.

We see the central theme throughout the book is righteousness and the importance of faith and belief in the gospel. He tells them that the wrath of God is being revealed to the wicked since the facts about God have been made plain to them. "For since the creation of the world God's invisible qualities–his eternal power and divine nature have been clearly seen, being understood from what has been made, so that men are without excuse. For although they knew God, they neither glorified him as God nor gave thanks to him, but their thinking became futile, and their foolish hearts were darkened. Although they claim to be wise, they became fools and exchanged the glory of the immortal God for images made to look like mortal man and birds and animals and reptiles." Paul is saying they have no excuse and God has handed them over to the sinful desires of their hearts.

Paul lays it out in very simple terms: "To those who by persistence in doing good seek glory, honor, and immortality, he will give eternal life. But for those who are self-seeking and who reject the truth and follow evil, there will be wrath and anger."

He warns them about being judgmental and feeling superior because they have been circumcised as a Jew. "A man is a Jew if he is one inwardly; and circumcision is circumcision of the heart, by the Spirit, not by the written code. Such a man's praise is not from men, but from God." Paul is trying to level the playing field between the Jews and the Gentiles by explaining that the gospel gives equally for anyone, and the circumcision that matters is the circumcision of the heart when the truth of the gospel is embraced.

Paul makes a good point in 3:20, "No one will be declared righteous in his sight by observing the law; rather through the law, we become conscious of sin." If you remember when the laws were made, it was to give the children of Israel a standard of right living. They were wandering in the desert with no guidance, and God was establishing a precedent for the righteousness to come. They had to learn obedience and honor to be ready to receive the Messiah in future generations.

Remember one of God's attributes is justice and that requires a standard to live by. However, He always gives man free will to choose just as he did Adam and Eve in the garden. That was the first justice system set in motion. Remember, God told them they could eat of every tree in the garden, but he set a rule, (law) for them not to eat of the tree of knowledge of good and evil. God's ways never change and are consistent throughout the Bible. Obey and we obtain favor and righteousness with God; disobey and we will reap the harvest of God's wrath. The good news here is found in 5:17, "But if by the trespass of the one man, death reigned through that one man, how much more will those who receive God's abundant provision of grace and the gift of righteousness reign in life through the one man, Jesus Christ."

Paul reminds them to remember Abraham and his faith that set him apart even before he was circumcised. "He is also the father of the circumcised who not only are circumcised but who also walk in the footsteps of the faith that our father Abraham had before he was circumcised. It was not through law that Abraham and his offspring received the promise that they would be heirs of the world, but through the righteousness that comes by faith."

He goes on in chapter 5 to tell them that since we have been justified through faith that we now have peace with God. That came through the incredible love of God for us even though we were still living in a sinful state. Romans 5:6-8 states, "You see, at just the right time when we were still powerless, Christ died for the ungodly. Very rarely will anyone die for an unrighteous man, but for a good man someone might possibly die. God demonstrates his love for us in this: While we were still sinners, Christ died for us."

He tells them that as surely as we were united with Jesus in his death, that we will also be united with him in his resurrection. "Now if we died with Christ, we believe that we will also live with him. For we know that since Christ was raised from the dead, he cannot die again; death no longer has mastery over him. 6:11 states, "In the same way, count yourselves dead to sin but alive to God in Christ Jesus. Do not let sin reign in your mortal body so that you obey its evil desires. Do not offer the parts of your body to sin, as instruments of wickedness but rather offer yourselves to God, as those who have been brought from death to life and offer the parts of your body to Him as instruments of righteousness. For sin shall not be your master because you are not under law, but under grace."

Paul spends a good part of the letter warning them that they will still have to fight the battle of sin in their bodies but to be ever mindful of the spirit of Christ who lives in them. "Those who live according to their sinful nature have their minds set on what that nature desires, but those who live in accordance with the Spirit have their minds set on what the spirit desires. The mind of sinful man is death but the mind controlled by the Spirit is life and peace."

Another point he makes is one that thrills my heart to think about. "For you did not receive a spirit that makes you a slave again to fear, but you received the Spirit of sonship. And by him, we cry Abba, Father. The Spirit himself testifies with our spirit that we are God's children. Now if we are children, then we are heirs of God and co-heirs with Christ." That is an amazing thing to meditate on, that we are actually part of the family of God and a co-equal sibling with Jesus.

He tells them that Jesus, having gone back to Heaven, is seated at the right hand of the Father and is interceding for us. What a comforting thought. I know on the few occasions in my life that someone has taken it upon himself to intercede on my behalf, how loved and blessed I felt. The thought that Jesus is always there standing up for me is so comforting.

I love the way he ties in the stories in the Old Testament that they no doubt had heard, with what he is teaching them now. He goes back to the story of the children of Abraham to make the point of the difference in the natural children and the children that are of God's promise. Hagar's son was a natural child conceived out of God's will, but Isaac is the child of God's promise and the one that the seed of Christ will come through. So it is with those who are sons of God's promise at this point versus those who are still under the law. He also talks about Rebekah's children, being Jacob and Esau and how one was despised and the other honored. How Pharaoh was placed in the time he lived and how God hardened his heart for his purposes. He even talks about the prophecy of Isaiah.

He warns them that unless they accept Jesus as Lord, they will not be saved. Then he tells them how, "If you confess Jesus as Lord, and believe in your heart that God raised him from the dead, you will be saved. Anyone who trusts in him will never be put to shame. For there is no difference between Jew and Gentile-the same Lord is Lord of all and richly blesses all who call on him for everyone who calls on the name of the Lord will be saved."

Paul addresses the concerns about those who were Israelites. "I ask then, did God reject his people? By no means! I am an Israelite myself, a descendant of Abraham, from the tribe of Benjamin. God did not reject his people, whom he foreknew." He used the words of Elijah when he was appealing to God to go against Israel because they were killing the prophets and tearing down altars. God's reply to him was, "I have reserved a remnant of those who have not chosen to bow the knee to Baal." So today there is a remnant chosen by grace. We have heard much lately about the remnant returning to Jerusalem in preparation for the coming of Christ. I am not sure if this is the remnant they are talking about or not, but it is a point of interest.

Asked again about this, Paul uses Jesus' example of the vine and the branches. Paul answers, "Did they stumble so as to fall beyond recovery? Not at all! Rather, because of their transgression, salvation has come to the Gentiles to make Israel envious. If the root is holy, so are the branches. If some of the branches have been broken off, and you, though a wild olive shoot, have been grafted in among the others and now share in the nourishing sap from the olive root, do not boast over those branches. If you do, consider this: You do not support the root, but the root supports you. You will say then, 'Branches were broken off so that I could be grafted in.' Granted, but they were broken off because of unbelief, and you stand by faith." He goes on later in the chapter saying, "If they do not persist in unbelief they will be grafted in, for God is able to graft them in again. After all, if you were cut out of an olive tree that is wild to nature, and contrary to nature were grafted into a cultivated olive tree, how much more readily will these, the natural branches, be grafted into their own olive tree!" He is telling us that if the Gentiles could be grafted in who were not of the natural descent of Abraham, how much more the Jews can be grafted in.

Then he urges them to offer their bodies as living sacrifices that will be pleasing to God and no longer conform to the pattern of this world but to be transformed by renewing their minds to the things of God that they can know his good and perfect will. He goes on to make the point that they are all different parts of one body and to encourage each part to use the gift given them and not be judgmental of others whose gifts are different. He lists some of the gifts as teaching, serving, encouraging, contributing to the needs of others, leadership and showing mercy.

Then the portion on love is the most humbling. "Love must be sincere. Hate evil, cling to what is good. Be devoted to one another in brotherly love. Honor one another above yourselves. Never be lacking in zeal, but keep your spiritual fervor, serving the Lord. Be joyful in hope, patient in affliction, faithful in prayer. Share with God's people who are in need. Practice hospitality. Bless those who persecute you; bless and do not curse. Rejoice with those who rejoice; mourn with those who mourn. Live in harmony with one another. Do not be proud, but be willing to associate with people of low position. Do not be conceited. Do not repay anyone evil for evil. Be careful to do what is right in the eyes of everybody. If it is possible, as far as it depends on you, live at peace with everyone. Do not take revenge, but leave room for God's wrath, for it is written: It is mine to repay, says the Lord. If your enemy is hungry, feed him; if he is thirsty, give him something to drink. In doing this, you will heap burning coals on his head. Do not be overcome by evil but overcome evil with good."

He addresses those that have been put in authority over us. He tells them that God placed those in authority and that they should respect the position they are in and do what is right and they will have no problems with them. He uses very strong words in 13:4-7, "For he is God's servant to do you good. But if you do wrong, be afraid, for he does not bear the sword for nothing. He is God's servant, an agent of wrath to bring punishment on the wrongdoer. Therefore, it is necessary to submit to authorities, not only because of possible punishment but also because of conscience." He goes on, "This is also why you pay taxes, for the authorities are God's servants, who give their full time to governing. Give everyone what you owe him; If you owe taxes pay taxes; if revenue then revenue; if respect then respect; if honor then honor."

Concerning the commandments, Paul says you can sum them all up with this one commandment, "Love your neighbor as yourself." Can you imagine how we could discontinue most of the law enforcement agencies if we all adopted this policy? He continues on that theme by telling them to accept those whose faith is still weak in some matters and not to pass judgment on them. He is encouraging them to function as one body and he states that in 15:5, "May the God who gives endurance and encouragement give you a spirit of unity among yourselves as you follow Christ Jesus, so that with one heart and mouth you may glorify the God and Father of our Lord Jesus Christ."

He then builds them up with encouragement by saying, "I myself am convinced, my brothers, that you yourselves are full of goodness, complete in knowledge and competent to instruct one another."

He gives them a beautiful final farewell, "May the God of hope fill you with all joy and peace as you trust in him, so that you may overflow with hope by the power of the Holy Spirit."

Romans is the most complete presentation of the doctrine of Christ and is most often used in sharing the plan of salvation. He points the way of salvation, buts gives guidelines as to how to walk it out every day.

Discussion Questions:

1. The central theme of the book of Romans is righteousness. How would you describe righteousness and how do you know if you have it?

2. Make the comparison of physical circumcision and spiritual circumcision according to Paul's teaching.

3. In chapter 5 Paul tells us that if we have been justified that we have peace with God. How has that played out in your life? Did you automatically feel that peace after making a profession of faith?

4. Paul talks about being grafted from the root which is Jesus, and that we draw life from the root and that the root does not draw from the branches. Have you experienced a time in your life that you tried to be in charge and get God to fit into your plans?

Lesson 61
Ephesians

Ephesians is one of four letters written by Paul while he was in prison in Rome. The time was between 61-63 AD.

One letter was written to the congregation at Ephesus, which was the capital of Asia at that time. It was located about a mile from the seacoast and was the great religious, commercial and political center of the country. It was noteworthy because of two notable structures there. First, the great theatre, which had a seating capacity of 50,000 people, and second the temple of Diana, which was one of the seven wonders of the ancient world. It was 342 feet long and 164 feet wide, made of shining marble, supported by a forest of columns 56 feet high, and was 220 years in building. This made it the center of the influence of Diana worship, of which we read in Acts 19:23-41. The statue with its many breasts represented the fertility of nature.

Next, to Rome, Ephesus was the most important city visited by Paul. It has been called the third capital of Christianity being the center of work in Asia through which were founded all the churches, of Asia, especially the seven churches to which Jesus sent the messages found n the book of Revelation. Jerusalem, the birthplace of power is the first, and Antioch the center of mission work, is the second capital.

Paul had spent well over two years with the Christians there. There is an impersonal tone to the writing for a community with which Paul was so intimately acquainted. There are no personal greetings.

The book of Ephesians is the great Pauline letter about the church. It deals, however, not so much with a congregation in the city of Ephesus in Asia Minor, as with the worldwide church, the head of which is Christ. The purpose of the church was to be the instrument for making God's plan of salvation known throughout the world.

The central theme of the letter is unity and God's plan to bring all things together in heaven and on earth under one head, which is Christ. As such, Paul is saying they should act as one big family and act with love toward one another. The letter is, therefore, instructions on the relationship between a wife and husband, parent and child, and slave-master.

He starts out the letter by telling them that they were chosen to be with the Lord before the creation of the world, and to be holy and blameless. We know that did not work out as planned, but because God is a loving Father, he redeemed us with his blood and gave us a path to be restored to fellowship. "In Him, we have redemption through his blood, the forgiveness of sins, in accordance with the riches of God's grace that he lavished on us with all wisdom and understanding. And he made known to us the mystery of his will according to his good pleasure, which he purposed in Christ, to be put into effect when the times will have reached their fulfillment, to bring all things in heaven and on earth together under one head, even Christ."

Paul goes on to tell them that they were predestined to be with him and are marked with a seal, the Holy Spirit, who is a deposit guaranteeing our inheritance in him.

He tells them how happy he was to hear about their faith and the love they show for each other. He also says that he prays for them to have a spirit of wisdom and revelation so they can continue to know Christ better.

A prayer I have prayed for many years for those I love is found in 1:18-23, "I pray that the eyes of your heart may be enlightened in order that you may know the hope to which he has called you, the riches of his glorious inheritance in the saints, and his incomparably great power for us who believe. That power is like the working of his mighty strength, which he exerted in Christ when he raised him from the dead and seated him at his right hand in the heavenly realms, far above all rule and authority, power and dominion, and every name that can be given, not only in the present age but in the one to come." This tells me that there is no end to the enlightenment of the power and knowledge he has for us. It is only to the degree that I allow myself to be enlightened that I can receive it. That is why it is so important that we know the Word and believe it is inspired by God to instruct us and show us the mysteries of this world and the one we will someday inherit.

He expresses the importance of God's grace and mercy. He says in 2:4, "Because of the great love for us, God, who is rich in mercy, made us alive with Christ even when we were dead in transgressions-it is by grace you have been saved." He goes on to say, "for it is by grace you have been saved through faith-and this not from yourselves, it is the gift of God-not by works, so that no one can boast. For we are God's workmanship, created in Christ Jesus to do good works, which God prepared in advance for us to do."

I love the thought of being a product of God's workmanship. I have been to craft shows and art exhibits and people would ask, "Whose work is this?" Then they would tell the one who came up with the design and brought it into being. To think that God created the design for me, (not like anyone else) is so amazing and gives me such a sense of value.

Then Paul talks about the Gentiles being able to come into the fellowship of believers and how through Christ we are all made one. He uses the example of a building that has a cornerstone that joins both sides together to become one building, and that cornerstone is Jesus. "In Him, the whole building is being joined together and rises to become a holy temple in the Lord. In Him, you two are being built together to become a dwelling in which God lives by his Spirit." He tells them that they have been given the knowledge of mysteries that have been given to him that previous generations did not have. "This mystery is that through the gospel the Gentiles are heirs together with Israel, members together with one body, and sharers together in the promise of Christ Jesus."

Paul tells them not to be discouraged because of his sufferings, (being in prison and persecuted for being a Christian), but to know that now since they are in Christ, they have the freedom to approach God with freedom and confidence.

He tells them how he prays for them. "I kneel before the Father and pray that out of his glorious riches he may strengthen you with power through his Spirit in your inner being, so that Christ may dwell in your hearts through faith. And I pray that you, being rooted and established in love, may have power with all the saints, to grasp how wide and long and high and deep is the love of Christ, and to know this love that surpasses knowledge, that you may be filled to the measure of all fullness of God."

Then he adds to this beautiful prayer. This is one of my favorite promises from the Bible, "Now to him who is able to do immeasurably more than all we ask or imagine, according to his power that is at work within us, to him be glory in the church and in Christ Jesus throughout all generations, forever and ever." I love this passage because it tells me that God can and will do more than we can even think to ask him for or even imagine because I am his creation and he had a plan in mind when he created me. We read in Psalm 40:5, "Many, O Lord my God, are the wonders you have done. The things you planned for us no one can recount to you; were I to speak and tell them, they would be too many to declare."

The phrase, according to this power that is at work within us, is a key to understanding how God operates in our life. We were given free will (choice) to give God first place in all of our life or to go our own way and visit him on Sundays. The more we spend time living from the spirit within us, the more we understand who God is and who we are in relationship to him. The more we understand the power of prayer and meditation, which in actuality is connecting with the power of the supernatural mind of God, the more we access that power.

Knowledge is power! God understood that when he placed Adam and Eve in the garden and gave them more than they could have asked or imagined. But he gave them the ability to stay connected to him and have all the power that was within him, or to compromise that connection by acquiring the knowledge of the world. They made a bad choice, and we can read their story and think how dumb to not just stay as close to the one who created them as possible and live in that protected place, but every day we are being asked to make the same decision they had to make.

Paul uses this to encourage them to stay connected to God and each other as well. He tells them to live in peace; building each other up accepting the diversity of gifts God has given to each one. He says to some he gave the gift of being apostles, some prophets, some evangelists and some pastors and teachers. He says God gave all these gifts so that everyone could be reached and attain the fullness of all God has to offer.

He expresses it this way in 4:14-16, "Then we will no longer be infants, tossed back and forth by the waves, and blown here and there by every wind of teaching and by the cunning and craftiness of men in their deceitful scheming. Instead, speak the truth in love; we will in all things grow up into him who is the Head, that is, Christ. From Him, the whole body joined and held together by every supporting ligament, grows and builds itself up in love, as each part does its work."

Paul then gives them keys to walking this out in their everyday lives:

"In anger do not sin. Do not let the sun go down while you are still angry and do not give the devil a foothold." This tells us that when we continue in anger, we are allowing the devil to start messing with our mind and are more subject to losing our oneness with God.

He tells those who have stolen to quit stealing and work so that they have something to give to those in need.

"Do not let unwholesome talk come out of your mouth, but only what is helpful in building up others and benefit those who hear you." Now that is convicting but it's also a good reminder of how we can affect others with our speech.

He writes, "Do not grieve the Holy Spirit." Then he tells things that might contribute to that: bitterness, rage, anger, brawling and slander, every form of malice. He then tells the counterpart to that. Be kind and compassionate to one another, forgiving each other, just as God forgave you.

He says in 5:3, "But among you, there must not be even a hint of sexual immorality, or of any kind of impurity, or greed, because these are improper for God's holy people. Nor should there be obscenity, foolish talk or coarse joking, which are out of place, but rather thanksgiving."

He sums it up with, "Be very careful, then, how you live-not as unwise but as wise making the most of every opportunity because the days are evil. Therefore do not be foolish, but understand what the Lord's will is."

He gives further instructions to husbands and wives. He tells wives to submit to their husbands and husbands to love their wives as Christ loved the church. A lot has been said about this subject, but in reality, it is a structure set forth for our protection. Christ is head of the church and husband's head of the household. The same model is set forth in the church. We have a pastor who looks over his congregation, not in a superior way but in the way of guidance and protection. Can you imagine a church where there was no structure? The pastor or priest has no more authority under God as we all are one, but he has been put there for our benefit. So is the family structure. If we get hung up on the submission part, we miss the point.

He instructs children to obey their parents and for fathers to not exasperate their children, but to bring them up in the training and instruction of the Lord.

Slaves are told to obey their earthly masters with fear, respect, and sincerity of heart, just as they are to obey Christ. They are encouraged to serve wholeheartedly and as if they were serving Christ because Christ will reward everyone whether he is slave or free. Then he tells the masters, treat your slaves in the same way. Do not threaten them, since you know that he who is both their Master and yours is in heaven, and there is no favoritism with him.

His final words have become the bedrock for instruction on faith and Godly living. "Finally, be strong in the Lord and his mighty power. Put on the full armor of God so that you may take a stand against the devil's schemes. For our struggle is not with flesh and blood, but against the rulers, against the authorities, against the powers of this dark world and against the spiritual forces of evil in the heavenly realms."

Paul then gives instructions to stand their ground and tells them what the armor of God is. "Stand firm then, with the belt of truth buckled around your waist, with the breastplate of righteousness in place, and with your feet fitted with the readiness that comes from the gospel of peace. In addition to all this, take up the shield of faith, with which you can extinguish all the flaming arrows of the evil one. Take the helmet of salvation and the sword of the Spirit, which is the Word of God."

He ends by asking them to pray for him. "Pray also for me, that whenever I open my mouth, words may be given me so that I will fearlessly make known the mystery of the gospel, for which I am an ambassador in chains." He is referring to being in chains while in prison when he wrote this letter.

Discussion Questions:

1. Have you ever considered the fact that you are God's workmanship? How does this one fact affect your self-esteem?

2. What do you think the works are we are suppose to be doing?

3. Had you ever thought about the fact of predestination and how you were chosen for a particular reason? How does this fact play out in your life?

4. Paul tells us to not grieve the Holy Spirit. What in your life might be grieving him?

6. Which of the armor that Paul talks about at the end of the chapter do you struggle with wearing as you go about your day?

Lesson 62
Colossians/Philippians/Philemon
(Letters written from prison in Rome)

This letter was written to the small congregation at Colossae located about 100 miles east of Ephesus and was part of what was known as Asia Minor.

It was one of three cities located in the Lycus Valley (Colossae, Hierapolis, and Laodicea) that formed an important trade route, a virtual meeting point between east and west. At one time Colossae had been a large and populous city, but when Paul wrote to the Colossian church, it had become just a small town in contrast to its nearest neighbors, Hierapolis and Laodicea.

Though small, Colossae of Paul's day was still a cosmopolitan city with different cultural and religious elements that were mingled together. Since God's concern for His own is never based on human distinctions like size, the Colossian church was still close to the heart of God. He obviously thought it important enough to lay it on the heart of the apostle Paul. Significantly, the letter to this small group of believers became one of the letters of the canon of the New Testament and one of the most important because of what it teaches us regarding the person and work of Jesus Christ. For the most part, the inhabitants of the area were Gentiles, but there was a considerable quantity of Jews among them. It has been estimated the Jewish population may have been as high as 50,000 people.

Colossians is the third letter written while Paul was imprisoned in Rome. It was written in response to a visit from a follower named Epaphras whom Paul called a faithful minister of Christ. He reported that there had been false teachers in Colossae who were telling people the Christian faith was incomplete. They were teaching them to worship angels and follow different rules and ceremonies.

Paul sent this letter, along with letters to Philemon and the Ephesians, with Tychism who was a coworker of Paul who would have been able to help the Colossian believers understand and apply the apostle's teachings in the letter. We read in Colossians 4:7, "Tychism will tell you all the news about me. He is a dear brother, a faithful minister and fellow servant of the Lord. I am sending him to you for the express purpose that you may know about our circumstances and that he may encourage your hearts. He is coming with Onesimus, our faithful and dear brother who is one of you. They will tell you everything that is happening here."

Though Paul had never been to the church itself, he addressed the issues head-on. The nature of Jesus Christ as Creator and Redeemer was being questioned, and Paul was straightening them out about the certainty of this truth.

He starts the letter by telling them that he had heard of their love of the gospel and that he had not stopped praying for them and asking God to fill them with knowledge of his will through spiritual wisdom and understanding. Then he tells them his hope for them. "We pray this in order that you may live a life worthy of the Lord and may please him in every way: bearing fruit in every good work, growing in the knowledge of God, being strengthened with all power according to his glorious might so that you may have great endurance and patience, and joyfully giving thanks to the Father, who has qualified you to share in the inheritance of the saints in the kingdom of light."

Then he gets to the heart of his message, and that is the supremacy of Christ. He elaborates on this in 1:15, "He is the image of the invisible God, the firstborn over all creation. For by him all things were created: things in heaven and on earth, visible and invisible, whether thrones or powers or rulers or authorities; all things were created by him and for him. He is before all things, and in Him, all things hold together. And he is the head of the body, the church; he is the beginning and the firstborn from among the dead so that in everything he might have the supremacy. For God was pleased to have all his fullness dwell in him, and through him to reconcile to himself all things, whether things on earth or things in heaven, by making peace through his blood shed on the cross."

That sums up the gospel as well as anything that could be said. He goes on to tell them that because of Jesus' death they have been presented holy without blemish and free from any accusations, and to make an effort to remain holy and steadfast in their faith.

He tells them that he is pleased to present to them the Word of God in its fullness-the mystery that had been kept hidden for ages and generations but was now being delivered to them and the other believers. Then he tells them in 1:27, "To them God has chosen to make known among the Gentiles the glorious riches of this mystery, which is Christ in you, the hope of glory." What an incredible gift to be the generation alive to have the mystery revealed to them. Remember they had no doubt heard their ancestors speak of what was to come through the teachings of prophets of old all their life, but Paul is reminding them that they are the generation to have the fulfillment of prophecy and this mystery revealed.

Paul continues with this theme by repeating it in the letter in 2:2: "My purpose is that you may be encouraged in heart and united in love, so that you may have the full riches of complete understanding, in order that they may know the mystery of God, namely Christ, in whom are hidden all the treasures of wisdom and knowledge." Then he addresses the main purpose of the letter, "I tell you this so that no one may deceive you by fine-sounding arguments." He goes on to say, "See to it that no one takes you captive through hollow and deceptive philosophy, which depends on human tradition and the basic principles of this world rather than on Christ."

He addresses the fact that they were circumcised not by human hands, but by Christ having their sinful nature buried in him in baptism, and raised with him through their faith in the power of God who raised Jesus from the dead.

He goes on to address the old law by saying that this new freedom they have cancels the old law given them in the past. "Having canceled the written code, with its regulations, that was against us, and that stood opposed to us; he took it away, nailing it to the cross. And having disarmed the powers and authorities, he made a public spectacle of them triumphing over them by the cross."

Paul warns them about letting anyone judge them about what they do or do not do because of the past laws. He tells them that those things were only a shadow of things to come and that now they are circumcised into fellowship with Jesus and have a new nature with the ability to discern truth for themselves.

Then we see a warning that we need to heed today as we are bombarded with spiritual imitations. We are told in 2:18, "Do not let anyone who delights in false humility and the worship of angels disqualify you for the prize. Such a person goes into great detail about what he has seen, and his unspiritual mind puffs him up with idle notions." Don't we see that every way we turn today? There are many religions and cults where man has become the central figure, Buddha, Mohammad, Gandhi, as well as all the new age spiritualists. I love the direct approach Paul takes in verse 21. "Do not handle! Do not taste! Do not touch! These are all destined to perish with use because they are based on human commands and teachings."

Then as before in his letters, he warns them against allowing their minds to be set on earthly things. "Set your minds on things above, not on earthly things. For you died, and your life is now hidden with Christ in God." He goes on to emphasize that they must rid themselves of the things of the old self-such as anger, rage, malice, slander and filthy language, and to clothe themselves with compassion, kindness, humility, gentleness, and patience.

He tells them to view themselves as one body. "Let the peace of Christ rule in your hearts, since as members of one body you were called to peace." He speaks of the importance of forgiveness and calls on them to forgive their brothers as Christ forgave them.

After admonishing them in these things, he sums it up in 3:14, "And over all these virtues put on love, which binds them all together in perfect unity." As I meditated on this verse, the awareness of the power of love was made more real to me. As I think of those I love, I don't have to worry about so many of these behaviors because of my love for them. I not only don't want to treat them in an ungodly way but I will fight like a mother lion if I see others doing so. So if I can concentrate more on viewing others as a unique child of God, and a member of the same family, it is much easier not to be caught up in anger, unforgiveness, jealousy, etc. This does not come naturally to our carnal nature that is always trying to vindicate the flesh. That is why Paul urges us in 2 Corinthians 10: 5 to take captive every thought to make it obedient to Christ.

As in the letters to the Corinthians, he gives specific instructions on how to conduct relationships between husband and wives, parents and children, and slaves and masters.

His final instructions are for them to devote themselves to prayer, being ever watchful and thankful. He asked for their prayers that God will open doors for them to proclaim the mystery of Christ.

He ends with what is a beautiful lesson on how to live. "Be wise in the way you act toward outsiders; make the most of every opportunity. Let your conversation be always full of grace, seasoned with salt, so that you may know how to answer everyone."

I wondered why he spoke of being seasoned with salt, but as I reflected on it, I thought of the purpose of salt. It is used to preserve things as in preserving hams, etc., but it also is used to bring out the natural flavor of anything. I can remember someone giving me a recipe and telling me to be sure and add a little salt, as it will enhance the taste. I always thought that was strange especially when it was a cake or something that was supposed to be sweet. It seems you always add a pinch of salt. I think the message here is much the same. Act out of a grace-filled life and by so doing you will bring out the best in others and possibly preserve the gospel that has been planted in them.

Philippians/Philemon

Philippians was written while Paul was in prison in Rome as well. The church had sent Epaphroditus to Rome to see Paul and bring him a gift. While he was there, he became sick, and after he had recovered, Paul sent him back with this letter.

He has his usual greeting of grace and peace and encourages them by saying he is confident that they will continue the good work that had been started there. He tells them how he prays for them to be strong and filled with the fruits of righteousness.

Then Paul tells them that the fact that he is in prison has advanced the gospel. "Now I want you to know, brothers, that what has happened to me has really served to advance the gospel. As a result, it has become clear throughout the whole palace guard and to everyone else that I am in chains for Christ. Because of my chains, most of the brothers in the Lord have been encouraged to speak the Word of God more courageously and fearlessly."

He shows how committed he is to his calling by saying that he wants Christ to be exalted in his body whether by life or death. "For to me, to live is Christ and to die is gain. If I am to go on living in the body, this will mean fruitful labor for me. Yet what shall I choose? I do not know! I am torn between the two: I desire to depart and be with Christ, which is better by far; but it is more necessary for you that I remain in the body." The lesson we can learn from Paul here is to live with a perspective that we are already living in eternity. Whether we stay in the body and move around on earth is one thing, but to live with Jesus in heaven would be a better deal. However, like Paul, we wait for God's timing.

In a Word of encouragement, he talks about how Christ died for them and how God exalted him to the highest place. And gave him a name above every name and that at the name of Jesus every knee should bow, in heaven and on earth and under the earth, and every tongue confess that Jesus Christ is Lord. This is so powerful to know that we have the power of using the name of Jesus and at his name, every other name that comes against it will have to bow. Jesus himself tells us that in John 12:23, "In that day (after he is resurrected and seated at the right hand of God) you will no longer ask me anything. I tell you the truth; my Father will give you whatever you ask in my name."

He compares them to shining stars in the universe as they hold fast to the gospel and encourages them to have no confidence in the flesh but to worship by the spirit. He goes on once again to tell of all he is and has done. He follows up with the Words that he compares all these things as loss compared to the surpassing greatness of knowing Christ Jesus and not holding to a righteousness of his own that comes from the law but that which is from faith in Christ.

Although he says he has attained this place of righteousness, he tells them that he continually presses on to take hold of that for which Christ took hold of him. Then he gives advice as to how he lives this life: "This one thing I do: Forgetting what is behind and straining toward what is ahead." He is telling us here to keep our eyes on the eternal and heavenly things, always remembering that at some point our flesh with all its desires will become dust, but if we keep our eyes on Jesus Christ he will transform our bodies to be like his glorious body and we will live eternally with him.

His last words of wisdom to them are to rejoice in the Lord always. He continues to tell them that the Lord is near and to lean on him. "Let your gentleness be evident to all. The Lord is near. Do not be anxious for anything, but in everything, by prayer and petition, with thanksgiving, present your request to

God. And the peace of God, which transcends all understanding, will guard your hearts and your minds in Christ Jesus. Finally, brothers, whatever is true, whatever is noble, whatever is right, whatever is pure, whatever is lovely, whatever is admirable-whatever is praiseworthy-think about such things."

These are such beautiful gems of wisdom to show us how to live.

He leaves them with the secret of contentment. "I have learned the secret of being content in any and every situation, whether well fed or hungry, whether living in plenty or in want. I can do everything through him who gives me strength."

There was one more letter written from his prison time in Rome, and that was the book of Philemon. It is significant only in the respect that it teaches about forgiveness. Philemon was a leader of the church of Colossae and a friend of Paul's. The story goes that Philemon's slave Onesimus had stolen money from him and had run away to Rome. While he was there, he met Paul and became a Christian. Paul sends him back to Philemon with this letter asking Philemon to forgive him. He encourages him to receive him back as a brother and not a slave. He even goes so far as to say that he will pay the debt he owes to him. Paul tells him to please welcome him back the same way he would if he were coming himself.

That is a good example of being a peacemaker. The parallel is interesting as to what Christ did for us. He interceded for us with the Father and was willing to pay our debt. He tells us also that we are no longer to be slaves but brothers because of our life in Christ.

Discussion Questions:

1. In the first part of this lesson, we find Paul explaining the supremacy of God to the church. Why do you think he felt the church was to be the central theme of his message?

2. How could understanding this help them from being led astray by false teachers? Have you ever found yourself questioning that God is supreme over everything in your life, and how did you resolve it?

3. Paul talks a lot about the mystery being revealed to them in their generation. What was this mystery and do you think our generation has an understanding of it?

4. Paul puts a lot of emphasis on the importance of love overriding everything else in our lives. Have you found that to be true when you have given it a priority? Explain.

5. Paul says he has found the secret to contentment. That is something the world is looking for. What is that secret, and have you been able to apply this to your life?

6. What are some ways you can become a peacemaker in your family and all those God puts in your life?

Lesson 63
Hebrews

In our last few lessons, we have found Paul writing from prison in Rome. We know that he had further journeys after his release in 63 AD.

From various statements that Paul makes in his letters, we see clues that Paul may have traveled to some or all of the following places: Colossae, Spain, Corinth, Miletus, Troas, Crete, Nicopolis, Philippi, Italy, Judea, Ephesus, and Macedonia. This allows for the possibility that Paul traveled to about as many diverse places after prison as in all of his previous journeys combined.

During this time, he is thought to have written the epistles of Hebrews, Titus, First Timothy, and Second Timothy, not necessarily in that order, although Second Timothy was apparently his last.

The author of Hebrews is thought to be Paul because of the timing and different clues given throughout the other letters, but there is no address or greetings to identify it as such.

This letter was most likely written to the Jewish Christians in either Palestine or Rome who were ready to give up their faith and return to Jewish faith because of persecution from outsiders, as well as, getting weary with the demands of Christian life.

Hebrews was apparently written from Italy as we find in the final verse, 13:24, "Greet all your leaders and all God's people. Those from Italy send their greetings."

The theme of this letter is to convince them that the Christian faith is in every way better than the Jewish faith they had grown up with. He starts the letter by saying, "In the past, God spoke to our forefathers through the prophets at many times and in various ways, but in these last days, he has spoken to us by his Son, whom he appointed heir of all things, and through whom he made the universe. The Son is the radiance of God's glory and the exact representation of his being, sustaining all things by his powerful Word."

He is trying to differentiate between the times the prophets lived and the present new life they have in Christ. He did this by emphasizing the superiority of Jesus. He begins by comparing him to the angels since in the past others had begun to worship angels and other false deities. "He became as much superior to the angels as the name he has inherited is superior to theirs. For to which of the angels did God ever say, you are my Son; today I have become your Father.... And again, when God brings his firstborn into the world, he says, let all God's angels worship him."

Then in verse 1:13-14, he says, "To which of the angels did God ever say, "Sit at my right hand until I make your enemies a footstool for your feet. Are not all angels ministering spirits sent to serve those who will inherit salvation?"

We then see him setting man apart by saying in 2:5, "It is not to angels that he has subjected the world to come, about which we are speaking." He leaves nothing to doubt about the position of man as compared to the angels who reside in heaven with God.

He continually points to Jesus whom he says is the author of their salvation through his suffering. Then I love the connection he makes with us in verse 2:11, "Both the one who makes men holy and those who are made holy are of the same family. So Jesus is not ashamed to call them (us) brothers (sisters)."

That is such a wonderful confirmation of our standing in the family of God. Just to think that Jesus is proud to call me his sister and we have the same Father. It is hard for us to even comprehend that we have equality with Jesus in God's eyes, but that is exactly what he is saying here and throughout the New Testament. That is something to meditate on and absorb in our thinking as we go about our day, not allowing the cares of this world to rob us of our inheritance of love, joy, and peace because we are part of the family of God.

He explains a little more in 2:14-18, "Since the children have flesh and blood, he too shared in their humanity so that by his death he might destroy him who holds the power of death-that is, the devil-and free those who all their lives were held in slavery by their fear of death. For surely it is not angels he helps, but Abraham's descendants. For this reason, he had to be made like his brothers (and sisters) in every way, in order that he may become a merciful and faithful high priest in service to God, and that he might make atonement for the sins of people. Because He Himself suffered when he was tempted, he is able to help those who are being tempted."

That gives us such comfort as we struggle with temptation. To know that Jesus came and became flesh and blood to become like me in every way and go through the same temptations that I go through gives me confidence that I can identify with him and overcome just as he did. He even compares our endurance to that of a house. "Christ is faithful as a son over God's house. And we are his house if we hold on to our courage and the hope of which we boast."

This is followed by a warning referring to the children of Israel in the desert. "So the Holy Spirit says: Today, if you hear his voice, do not harden your hearts as you did in the rebellion, during the time of testing in the desert, where your fathers tested and tried me for forty years and saw what I did. That is why I was angry with that generation, and I said, "Their hearts are always going astray, and they have not known my ways. So I declared an oath in my anger; they shall never enter my rest."

We know that entire generation died in the desert because they hardened their hearts against God. That is so hard for us to understand since they had just been freed from slavery in Egypt, left with the treasure of their enemies, saw the Red Sea part so they could escape and then drown the enemy army that was chasing them, and being fed supernaturally from heaven, etc. Yet we have been freed from the same type of captivity and how easy it is for us to go our own way and forget the will of the one who died and paid the ultimate price for us to experience the Promised Land he has for us.

His will for us is to abide in his rest. In 4:1, he tells us, "Therefore, since the promise of entering his rest still stands, let us be careful that none of you be found to have fallen short of it. For we also have had the gospel preached to us, just as they did; but the message they heard was of no value to them, because those who heard did not combine it with faith." Interesting that the missing component was faith. They heard and were willing to receive the freedom it provided for a season but when they could not see with their eyes, the promised land God was leading them into, they began murmuring and complaining and ended up spending 40 years trapped in a desert when the best God had for them was only a 14-day walk. I think the message here is not the distance of our journey on earth but our confidence that we will walk it out trusting in the one who planned our itinerary. Paul even says that in 3:14, "We have come to share in Christ (all he has for us) if we hold firmly till the end the confidence we had at first..."

The question you may ask is, how do I enter the rest of God and how do I stay there? Most likely if you are doing this study, you have accepted Jesus' gift of eternal life and are going down the path of your life much like the children of Israel were when they first experienced the freedom from Egypt. They must have given a great sigh of relief when they realized they were no longer in bondage and God had sent them a deliverer to give them a safe place to live. They could rest from the burdens that had been put on them while in slavery.

We saw earlier that where they had failed was by not walking by faith. Faith in what? Faith in the Word given to them through Moses who was called up into a mountain to obtain a structure of living that would ensure they lived in peace and harmony. Not only did they not obey Moses' instruction to wait while he communed with God for these instructions, but they also started melting down gold and silver and making an idol to worship. They wanted a visual of something other than God to put their trust in.

In 4:11, we are given a warning as relevant today as it was then. "Let us, therefore, make every effort to enter that rest, so that no one will fall by following their example of disobedience. For the Word of God is sharper than any two-edged sword, it penetrates even to dividing soul and spirit, joints and marrow; it judges the thoughts and attitudes of the heart. Nothing in all creation is hidden from God's sight. Everything is uncovered and laid bare before the eyes of him to whom we must give account."

The message here is not only to enter the rest, but also to remain in rest by having faith in knowing and obeying his Word. He left his Word in written form and confirms it in our hearts as we commune with him. As we can see from the passage, it is not a stagnant Word. It has life and is active to bring about the things promised in it. One promise in the Bible is, "My Word will not return to me void." Meaning if you plant it in your heart, it will produce fruit. Like dew coming up from the ground and going into the clouds and producing rain that comes back and waters the plants that produce substance for our bodies. "Land that drinks in the rain often falling on it produces a crop useful to those for whom it is farmed receives the blessing of God...."

The other part of that verse is so powerful. It has the power to divide the soul from the spirit and the joints and marrow (body). When we are struggling with our soul, (mind, will, emotions), we can always go to the Word and see how to overcome those struggles. For example, if we are struggling with lack of peace, the Word says, "I give you my peace, not as the world gives but my peace." As I look to the Word and see that the way to peace is to live in forgiveness and love. I can make a decision based on the power of the Word to forgive and love even when it seems impossible. I do it by faith in the Word that if I apply the principles in it that it will not return void but will produce the fruit of peace.

The way to do that is found in 2 Corinthians 10:5, "Demolish arguments and every pretension that sets itself up against the knowledge of God, and take captive every thought to make it obedient to the Christ."

The key is found in 1 Peter 5:6, "Humble yourself, therefore, under God's mighty hand, that he may lift you up in due time. Cast all your anxiety on him because he cares for you." The next verse says to resist the devil's temptation and to stand firm in faith and the result is found in 1 Peter 5:10, "And the God of all grace, who called you to his eternal glory in Christ after you have suffered a little while, will himself restore you and make you strong, firm and steadfast."

The key to faith is to know the one you have faith in and to know that you can trust his Word and be willing to walk by them states, "Your hands made me and formed me; give me understanding to learn your commands. May those who fear you rejoice when they see me for I have put my hope in your Word."

Psalm 119:89, "Your word, O Lord is eternal; it stands firm in the heaven. If your law had not been my delight, I would have perished in my afflictions. I will never forget your precepts, for by them you have preserved my life."

Another promise from Psalms states, "Your commands make me wiser than my enemies, for they are ever with me. I have more insight than my teachers, for I meditate on your statutes. I have more understanding than the elders, for I obey your precepts. I have kept my feet from every evil path so that I might obey your word."

Then I think the one that speaks most to me is Psalm 119:129, "Your statutes are wonderful; therefore I obey them. The unfolding of your words gives light; it gives understanding to the simple." That's me! I don't have a degree from a seminary, but this passage says it will give understanding even to me.

We are also encouraged to grow and not remain infants in our faith and understanding. "By this time you ought to be teachers, you need someone to teach you the elementary truths of God's Word all over again. You need milk, not solid food! Anyone who lives on milk, being still an infant, is not acquainted with the teaching about righteousness. But solid food is for the mature who by constant use, have trained themselves to distinguish good from evil."

We are given more insight here as well to God's nature. "God is not unjust; he will not forget your work and the love you have shown him as you help his people and continue to help them."

Then we are referred back to Abraham where God made a promise to him, and we read in 6:13, "When God made his promise to Abraham, since there was no one greater for him to swear by, he swore by himself, saying 'I will surely bless you and give you many descendants.'" As I think of an oath, I always think of being in court where we are asked to take an oath that what we are saying is the truth, nothing but the truth, so help me God. And when we are asked to swear to something we always swear on something that is bigger than we are. I have often heard the phrase, "I swear to God," or "I swear on my mother's grave" Why would anyone say that? Because these are something higher and bigger than anything they could say or do. Why would you say you swear on your mother's grave? Because next to God, your mother is the one who gave you life and if she has died, that is a sacred place of remembrance you would never bring disgrace to. I find it interesting that in verse 13 God says, "Since there was no one greater for him to swear by, he swore by himself." That shows the supremacy of God over all mankind.

Jesus is then described as our high priest. Much is said in this book about the role of the earthly priest, but here we are told that they play a role in preparing us to receive Jesus as our high priest. The term priest expresses one who is an intermediary between God and us. When the veil was torn from top to bottom when Jesus was crucified, that was the sign that God was no longer veiled from direct access. That Jesus had just become our high priest and would be sitting at the right hand of God ever interceding for us. Jesus has become our high priest for all eternity.

We find in 5:6 that Jesus was said to be a priest in the order of Melchizedek. This brings up a much-debated question. Who was Melchizedek? He seems to be a mystery man. Here is what we know about him. He was of an order of priest greater than the earthly priest we read about in the Old Testament. He seemed to be of a Heavenly order, a priesthood that Jesus would be able to come through as fully man and fully God. His manhood gave him identification as a man; His godliness required him to come before a priest who was of God.

We read in chapter 5 that earthy priests were subject to sin and that is why they had to offer gifts and sacrifices for their sins to enter into the presence of God in the Holy of Holies. Verse 4 of this chapter says, "No one takes this honor upon himself; he must be called by God, just as Aaron was. So Christ also did not take upon himself the glory of becoming a high priest. But today God said to him. You are my Son; today I have become your Father, and then he says in another place, you are a priest forever, in the order of Melchizedek."

Several things we know about Melchizedek from scripture is found in Genesis 14:18, "This Melchizedek was king of Salem (Salem being Jerusalem), and priest of God Most High. This puts him in a class of his own. He was the appointed priest of God to bring Jesus through a priestly order not made of human hands. If Jesus were brought about in the order of Aaron or Levi, he would have an earthly genealogy and be subject to carnal influence.

We see the same question brought up in 7:11, "If perfection could have been attained through the Levitical priesthood, why was there a need for another priest to come-one in the order of Melchizedek."

Another point is that God told him he would be a priest forever in the order of Melchizedek, so we can assume that was a position that extended into eternity and not for a period that ended in death like the lineage of priests in the Old Testament. Hebrews 7:3 tells us, "He was without father or mother, without genealogy, without beginning of days or end of life, like the Son of God he remains a priest forever."

We first see him appear to Abraham when he was returning from the defeat of the kings. Melchizedek came to him and blessed him.

His name means king of righteousness and prince of peace. He is a shadow of Jesus in every way as a heavenly priesthood. Jesus is called the prince of peace, he is our righteousness, and the comparison to validate this is endless but very interesting to study.

Then in 7:18, "The former regulation is set aside because it was weak and useless and a better hope is introduced, by which we draw near to God. And it was not without an oath! Others became a priest without any oath, but he became a priest with an oath when God said to him: the Lord has sworn and will not change his mind: you are a priest forever."

In chapter 8 we see this expanded by saying he is the high priest of a new covenant. 8:8, "The ministry Jesus has received is superior to theirs (line of Old Testament priest), as the covenant of which he is a mediator is superior to the old one, and it is founded on better promises. For if there had been nothing wrong with that first covenant, no place would have been sought for another. He goes on to say it will not be like the covenant he made with the house of Israel but he says of this new covenant, 8:10, "This is the covenant I will make with the house of Israel after that time, declares the Lord. I will put my laws in their minds and write them on their hearts. I will be their God, and they will be my people."

He says in 8:15, "For this reason, Christ is the mediator of a new covenant, that those who are called may receive the promised eternal inheritance now that he has died as a ransom to set them free from the sins committed under the first covenant."

Then we see in 8:27 something that puts to rest the theory of reincarnation. "Just as man is destined to die once, and after that to face judgment, So Christ was sacrificed once to take away the sins of many people; and he will appear a second time, not to bear sin, but to bring salvation to those who are waiting for him."

We see a call for them to persevere. "Therefore, brothers, since we have confidence to enter the Most Holy Place by the blood of Jesus, by a new and living way opened for us through the curtain, that is his body, and since we have a great priest over the house of God, let us draw near to God with a sincere heart in full assurance of faith, having our hearts sprinkled (remember the priest had to sprinkle the people with the blood of the animal sacrifice) to cleanse us from a guilty conscience and having our bodies washed with pure water. Let us hold unswervingly to the hope we profess, for he who promised is faithful."

Two of my favorite verses are found in 10:35-36, "So do not throw away your confidence; it will be richly rewarded. You need to persevere so that when you have done the will of God, you will receive what he has promised." He goes on to say, "My righteous ones will live by faith. And if he shrinks back, I will not be pleased with him." That is quite a warning. God has proven throughout the Old Testament that he has set forth a plan, and if we choose not to follow, we will not inherit all he has for us. He states it very well in 10:16, "If we deliberately keep on sinning after we have received the knowledge of the truth, no sa1rifice for sins is left, but only a fearful expectation of judgment and of raging fire that will consume the enemies of God. That leaves nothing to the imagination, does it?

Then we come to the famous chapter on faith. Chapter 11:1, "Faith is being sure of what we hope for and certain of what we do not see." Following that we see a list of some of the ones who are in the faith hall of fame. Abel offered a better sacrifice than his brother Cain and was called a righteous man. We are told that he still speaks, even though he is dead. That alone is room for much conversation. Can those who are in heaven still speak to us?

By faith, Enoch was taken from this life and did not experience death. Before he was taken, he was commended as one who pleased God. Then the famous quote in 11:6, "Without faith, it is impossible to please God, because anyone who comes to him must believe that he exists and that he rewards those who earnestly seek him."

By faith, Noah believed God and built an ark and saved his family and generations to come and was said to be a righteous man in God's eyes.

By faith, Abraham believed God and left his homeland and went to an unknown land shown to him by God. By faith, he was able to produce a child even though his wife was barren. By faith, he offered that son Isaac as a sacrifice.

By faith Isaac, Jacob, Joseph, Moses, Rahab, and on and on it goes. In 11:32 it says, "And what more shall I say? I do not have time to tell about Gideon, Barak, Samson, Jephthah, David, Samuel, and the prophets, who through faith conquered kingdoms, administered justice; shut the mouth of lions, quenched the fury of the flames and escaped the edge of the sword; whose weakness was turned to strength; and who became powerful in battle and routed foreign armies. Women received back their dead, raised to life again." Wow, each of these stories in the Bible teaches us incredible lessons in faith and how to please God.

The writer goes on to say that some were tortured and refused to be released so that they might have a better resurrection. They were stoned, flogged, cut in two and put to death with a sword. They were destitute, persecuted and mistreated; they wandered in deserts and mountains and caves and holes in the ground. In 11:39-40 it says, "They were all commended for their faith, yet none of them received what had been promised. God had planned something better for us so that only together with us would they be made perfect."

He goes on in 12:1, "Therefore, since we are surrounded by such a great cloud of witnesses, let us throw off everything that hinders and the sin that so easily entangles, and let us run with perseverance the race marked out for us." When we look at some of the things those witnesses who came before us went through, the struggles and temptations we go through seem meaningless. I think it is important for each of us to look at what the sin that so easily entangles us is. It will be as diverse as there are people in the world. It comes from our individual heritage, as well as, experiences we have had along the way. This reminds me of the passage in Hosea that says; "My people shall know the truth, and the truth shall set them free." Sometimes we don't want to see the truth because it is painful and it may mean we give up a crutch we have been leaning on instead of trusting in Jesus.

Hebrews 12:2 tells us how to do that. "Let us fix our eyes on Jesus, the author, and perfecter of our faith, who for the joy set before him endured the cross, scorning its shame, and sat down at the right hand of the throne of God." The joy set before him was you and me. He was looking at all the saints that had come before the cross and to the ones to come to bring salvation and freedom.

Paul then refers to God as the Father of our spirits and says like a human father. He disciplines us when he sees us going astray. "No discipline seems pleasant at the time, but painful. Later on, however, it produces a harvest of righteousness and peace for those who have been trained by it."

His final exhortation to them is to "Keep on loving each other as brothers. Do not forget to entertain strangers, for by so doing some people have entertained angels without knowing it." I remember the TV show, "Touched by an Angel," and it brought home how many times things happen or are resolved in an unexplained way. It makes us wonder if perhaps we have encountered angels in the affairs of our life.

He warns us to remember to put our trust in the Lord because he tells us in 13:5, "Never will I leave you; never will forsake you." So we can say with confidence, "The Lord is my helper; I will not be afraid. What can man do to me?" That is a verse I have repeated thousands of times in my life as I have encountered trials that I was not capable of handling myself.

A final warning was not to be carried away by strange teachings. He then gives the assurance that is a comfort to us as we look for a steadfast place to establish our faith. "Jesus Christ is the same yesterday and today and forever."

Discussion Questions:

1. As you look back in this lesson where it talks about us being called brothers (and sisters) with Jesus, how does that increase your sense of self-worth?

2. We see the children of Israel wandering in the desert for forty years uselessly for not being obedient to God's loving plan for their lives. Can you point out times in your life that you were trying to circumvent God's best for you by doing it your way?

3. What will happen to us according to Hebrews 8:26, if we keep on sinning after we know the truth?

4. We read in this lesson about throwing off the sin that so easily entangles us. Have you identified that sin and what steps have you taken to throw it off and not let Satan get a stronghold in your life?

5. Is there a time that you may have entertained an angel?

6. Since the Bible says it is impossible to please God without faith, what are some ways to build up our faith?

7. What are the most encouraging words in Hebrews to you concerning God's love for you?

Lesson 64
1st & 2nd Timothy-Titus

In the last lesson, we had a good lesson on faith and how God would never leave us or forsake us. Hebrews is a tremendous lesson on the faithfulness of God in every area of our lives.

We have been looking at Paul's letters to the church, and now we are going to shift gears a little and look at a letter Paul had written specifically to one of his associates, Timothy.

Timothy was born at Lystra and had a Greek father and Jewish mother who taught him scriptures from childhood. He had come alongside Paul and helped him in his ministry and had gone with Paul on his second missionary journey. At the time Paul wrote this letter to him, he was the leader of the church at Ephesus.

Timothy was young and had a large responsibility in leading the church, and Paul wrote this letter to give him advice on how to be a man of God and warns him about the importance of false teachers who may lead him astray.

Paul starts his first letter to Timothy by addressing him as, "My true son in the faith." This tells you it is a very personal letter sent from a heart of love and concern for Timothy. He starts by telling him that there are those who will steer him away from the true gospel of love, which comes from a pure heart and a good conscience, as well as a sincere faith. He warns that there are those who just want to teach the precepts of the law but are not committed to upholding the truth of the law.

He reminds Timothy of the power of God's love and grace by reminding him of what he had done for him. "Christ Jesus our Lord, who has given me strength, that he considered me faithful, appointing me to his service. Even though I was once a blasphemer and a persecutor and a violent man, I was shown mercy because I acted in ignorance and unbelief. The grace of our Lord was poured out on me abundantly, along with the faith and love that are in Christ Jesus. Here is a trustworthy saying that deserves full acceptance: Christ Jesus came into the world to save sinners-of whom I am the worst. But for that very reason I was shown mercy so that in me the worst of sinners, Christ Jesus might display unlimited patience as an example for those who would believe on him and receive eternal life."

Then he goes on to tell Timothy why he is writing to encourage him. "Timothy, my son, I give you these instructions in keeping with the prophecies once made about you, so that by following them you may fight the good fight, holding on to faith and a good conscience. Some have rejected these and so have shipwrecked their faith." Then he gives examples of two who had done just that, Alexander and Hymenaeus. He goes on to say because of their departure from the faith, he had handed them over to Satan to be taught not to blaspheme. Wow! That is a strong message and encouragement to continue in the faith and calling you were given.

Paul encourages him to pray for everyone including kings and those in authority and that there could be peace and a sense of holiness throughout the area. He points out that God wants all men to be saved and know the truth that there is only one God and one Mediator between God and man and that is Christ Jesus.

Then he gets to the details of his instructions about the church saying that he wants men to lift up holy hands in prayer without anger or dispute. He goes on to say that he wants women to dress modestly, without braided hair, or gold, pearls or expensive clothes, but with good deeds appropriate for women who profess to worship God. This can get sticky if taken literally but I think the lesson here is for women to let their hearts and good deeds be the thing that gives them worth and not needing to flaunt worldly things to be noticed.

Then the next lesson about women is still being debated by some today because it concerns women's position in the church. "A woman should learn in quietness and full submission. I do not permit a woman to teach or to have authority over a man; she must be silent. For Adam was formed first, then Eve. And Adam wasn't the one deceived; it was the woman who was deceived and became a sinner. But women will be saved through childbearing-if they continue in faith, love, and holiness with propriety." Much could be said about this last sentence but here is my take on it. I think he was saying by referring to the fact that Eve was the one who brought sin into the world that she was the one, through childbearing, that brought the redemption of sin by being the vessel to bring Jesus into the world.

I think the phrase that she must learn in quietness and submission means that because man was created first and woman for man that God had instructed Adam, and Adam in turn instructed Eve. That was the pattern set up in the beginning. I think that is why he is referring to the garden and the fact that a woman was the one who leads man astray.

Both man and woman are equal in God's eyes, but as a measure of order and protection, God instructed man to be the one to give instructions about his plan just as Adam had taught Eve in the garden. That does not mean he is superior but was put in that position of leadership in the family and the church family as well.

Remember what God told Adam in the garden why he was putting a curse on him, the serpent, and the very ground he walked on. "Because you listened to your wife and ate from the tree about which I commanded you, 'You must not eat.' Cursed is the ground because of you; through painful toil, you will eat of it all the days of your life, by the sweat of your brow you will eat your food until you return to the ground, since from it you were taken; for dust you are and to dust you will return." Then in the next verse, it says he named his wife Eve because she would become the mother of all the living. This refers us to our statement earlier where Eve (woman) would be redeemed through childbearing.

God is a God of order, and he gave us this as a pattern to live by. Every successful business or other structure of society has to have a hierarchy of order if it is successful. Can you imagine what our schools or court system would be like if there were not superintendents, principals, teachers and then students, or a justice system without judges, lawyers, etc? To say nothing of our homes where there are no parents to instruct and train children in the way they should go. The judge, superintendent, and parent have all been put there as a means of protection and to give order and oversight. They are not superior to those they are in charge of but have been given a responsibility to aid in their process of equality and development.

The same is true of our church and what Paul is doing here is advising as to what to look for in the leaders of the church. Paul says the pastor is to be above reproach.

You can read the qualifications found in 3:1-13 he gives for pastors as well as deacons. Not only are they to be above reproach but their wives and families as well. I am not sure how many of those are in our churches today. It almost seems impossible to find such a one.

Paul warns Timothy again that some will fall away and follow deceiving spirits and things taught by demons. He advises him in 4:7, "Have nothing to do with godless myths and old wives tales; rather, train yourself to be godly.

Obviously, Timothy was young because Paul tells him in 4:12, "Don't let anyone look down on you because you are young, but set an example for the believers in speech, in life, in love, in faith, and in purity." Paul also gives him the advice in 4:16, "Watch your life and doctrine closely, and persevere in them, because if you do, you will save both yourself and your hearers."

Paul then tells him to exhort older men as if he were his father. Treat younger men as brothers, older women as mothers, and younger women as sisters, with absolute purity. He also gives the advice to care for widows and family. "If anyone does not provide for his relatives, and especially for his immediate family, he has denied the faith and is worse than an unbeliever." Very strong words and if not careful can be used to manipulate lazy family members who are not providing for themselves even though they are healthy and able to do so. God has much to say about laziness.

As far as widows, he say, "No widow is not to be put on the list of widows unless she is over sixty years of age and has been faithful to her husband, and is well known for her good deeds, such as bringing up children, showing hospitality, washing the feet of saints, helping those in trouble and devoting herself to all kinds of good deeds." He has strong words for young widows as well. "As for younger widows, do not put them on such a list. For when their sensual desires overcome their dedication to Christ, they want to marry." He goes on to say that if they are put on the list of widows to care for they often will be found to be idle and going from house to house becoming gossips and busybodies. So Paul says he advises younger widows to marry and have children so that they do not fall into the traps of Satan.

Paul says the elders of the church are to be honored, but if they sin, they are to be rebuked publicly, so that others will take warning. Then he says something that many have used in zest. "Stop drinking only water, and use a little wine because of your stomach and your frequent illnesses." This is not a license to become an alcoholic, but the medical community is now catching up with the Bible in the fact that scientists are now telling us the properties of wine, resveratrol, has many healing benefits.

He gives some advice about the dangers of the love of money. He says that some men have been robbed of the truth and may think of godliness as a means to financial gain. However, he says, 6: 6-10 "But godliness with contentment is great gain. For we brought nothing into the world and we can take nothing out of it. But if we have food and clothing, we will be content with that. People who want to get rich fall into temptation and a trap and into many foolish and harmful desires that plunge men into ruin and destruction. For the love of money is a root of all kinds of evil. Some people, eager for money, have wandered from the faith and pierced themselves with many griefs."

Then these are his final words of encouragement to Timothy. "But you, man of God, flee from all this and pursue righteousness, godliness, faith, love, endurance, and gentleness. Fight the good fight of faith. Take hold of the eternal life to which you were called when you made your good confession in the presence of many witnesses."

Then a few warnings, 6:20, "Guard what has been entrusted to your care. Turn away from godless chatter, and the opposing ideas of what is falsely called knowledge, which some have professed and in so doing have wandered from the faith."

In his second letter to Timothy, he starts by telling him that he has heard good things about his faith and how his grandmother, Lois, and his mother Eunice had as well. He encourages him to fan the gift that was given to him when he had hands laid on him to go out and preach the gospel. I find that an interesting use of words but one that is so applicable to us today. When a fire is about to go out it is losing oxygen, we fan it enough to give it more air so it will ignite and continue burning. That is what Paul is telling Timothy here, don't be idle but continue to grow and learn that your fire will stay a strong flame. Then he quotes a famous verse that blesses me every time I hear it. 2 Timothy 1:7, "For God did not give us a spirit of timidity but a spirit of power, of love and self-discipline." This tells me that I was given a gift of power and self-discipline, so when I am tempted to think I can't do something; I can refer to this verse and claim this promise.

More advice is to avoid godless chatter and to present himself as one approved by God, a workman who does not need to be ashamed and who correctly handles the Word of truth. Also to flee the evil desires of youth and pursue righteousness, faith, love, and peace.

He warns that in the last days there will be terrible times. People will be lovers of themselves, lovers of money, boastful, proud, abusive, disobedient to their parents, ungrateful, unholy, without love, unforgiving, slanderous, without self-control, brutal, not lovers of the good, treacherous, rash, conceited, lovers of pleasure rather than lovers of God-having a form of godliness but denying its power. Sounds way too familiar as we can see this playing out every night when we watch the news.

Paul reminds Timothy how he had been taught the scriptures from infancy and how studying them will make him wise. He says in 3:16, "All Scripture is God-breathed and is useful for teaching, rebuking, correcting and training in righteousness, so that the man of God may be thoroughly equipped for every good work. "

His final words, 4:1, "In the presence of God and of Christ Jesus, who will judge the living and the dead, and in view of his appearing and his kingdom, I give you this charge: Preach the Word; be prepared in season and out of season; correct, rebuke, and encourage—with great patience and careful instruction. For the time will come when men will not put up with sound doctrine. Instead, to suit their own desires, they will gather around them a great number of teachers to say what their itching ears want to hear. They will turn their ears away from the truth and turn aside to myths. But you, keep your head in all situations, endure hardship, do the work of an evangelist, discharge all the duties of your ministry."

Briefly, we look at the book of Titus. Titus was another friend and helper of Paul's. He had traveled some with Paul and was the leader of the church of Crete.

Apparently, the church in Crete was unorganized and made up of people who needed much instruction. The letter is much the same as the letters sent to Timothy. He encourages Titus to teach sound doctrine. Teach the older men to be temperate and worthy of respect, self-controlled and sound in faith, love, and endurance. To the women he says they should be reverent in the way they live, not to be slanderers or addicted too much wine but to teach what is good. Then they can and should teach the younger women.

He reminds him that at one time we all were living a life of disobedience but Jesus saved us, not because of any righteous thing we did but by the washing of rebirth and renewal by the Holy Spirit, who was poured out on us generously, thus making us heirs of eternal life.

He tells him that if he sees a person being divisive, warn him once, and then warn him a second time. After that, have nothing to do with him. You may be sure that such a person is warped and sinful; he is self-condemned.

He ends with the instruction to the people to devote themselves to doing good so that they may live productive lives.

Discussion Questions:

1. The book of Timothy speaks of fighting the good fight of faith. Why do you think Paul calls having faith something we have to fight for?

2. Paul uses as part of his testimony the fact that he was the worst of the worst. Do you think this was an effective way of encouraging Timothy, and do you ever share your story as a way of showing God's power and life-changing ability? Share what parts of your story you are comfortable with?

3. One of the phrases Paul uses to encourage Timothy is to fan the flame of his spirit. How would that look in your life. How would you go about fanning the flames in your spirit?

4. What are your thoughts concerning Paul's words about women and their place in the church?

Lesson 65
James

The book of James may be the earliest of the New Testament letters. The brother of Jesus wrote it about A.D. 48. He was a leader in the church in Jerusalem. The letter was addressed to Christians everywhere, as were the books of Jude, First and Second Peter; First, Second, and Third John, and the book of Jude. These seven books were called general letters because they were not addressing a particular church.

He starts the letter by addressing it to the twelve tribes scattered among nations. He wants to help them know that through faith they can live the life of a follower of Jesus.

He tells them to consider it joy when they face trials because the testing of their faith brings them perseverance. He goes onto say that perseverance will help them become mature and complete in their walk. He encourages them to go to God for help and that he will give them everything they need. "If any of you lacks wisdom, he should ask God, who gives generously to all without finding fault, and it will be given to him. But when he asks, he must believe and not doubt, because he who doubts is like a wave of the sea, blown and tossed by the wind. That man should not think he will receive anything from the Lord; he is a double-minded man, unstable in all he does."

He warns about the influence of money and says that the man who is in humble circumstances should consider himself in a high position. He is telling them that to be humble and dependent on God and not money or worldly possessions, is to be valued because it produces faith.

He continues to proclaim, "Blessed is the man who perseveres under trial because when he has stood the test, he will receive the crown of life that God has promised to those who love him."

He addressed something that has been debated for years about temptation. "When tempted, no one should say, God is tempting me. For God, cannot be tempted by evil, nor does he tempt anyone, but each one is tempted when, by his own evil desire, is dragged away and enticed. Then, after desire has been conceived, it gives birth to sin; and sin, when it is full-grown, gives birth to death."

I have heard people say that God tempted them with sin to make them stronger or to see if their faith could stand the test of time. James puts that reasoning to bed here and says that giving in to our own evil desires lead us into sin. We can't blame God for allowing our old sin nature to raise its ugly head and lead us astray. He even goes on to compare what God does for us by saying in the next verse that every good and perfect gift is from our Father above, and that he does not change like shifting shadows.

James 1:18 says he chooses to give us birth through the word of truth that we might be a kind of first fruits of all he created. Then in 19-21, he says, "My dear brothers, take note of this: Everyone should be quick to listen, slow to speak and slow to anger, for man's anger does not bring about the righteous life that God desires. Therefore, get rid of all moral filth and the evil that is so prevalent, and humbly accept the Word planted in you which can save you."

Then he gives a statement that I have meditated on many times. "Do not merely listen to the Word, and so deceive yourselves. Do what it says. Anyone who listens to the Word but does not do what it says is like a man who looks at his face in the mirror, and after looking at himself, goes away and immediately forgets what he looks like." How many times have I read the Word or heard it preached, and know what is right but I've gone about doing exactly what I wanted to do, not paying attention to God's instruction? Then when I get in a tight spot call I out to God to save me. Unfortunately, that is true more times than I want to admit in my life.

James goes on to say in 1:25, "But the man who looks intently into the perfect law that gives freedom, and continues to do this, not forgetting what he has heard, but doing it-he will be blessed in what he does." I can personally attest to this as truth. When I am being attentive to my prayer life and spending time in God's Word, I have more peace and life does seem to send more blessings my way. But just as it was for Adam and Eve in the garden, it is a choice I have to make every day.

We read the same story in the Old Testament when Moses was giving the same instructions to the children of Israel. Deuteronomy 30:11 "Now what I am commanding you today is not too difficult for you or beyond your reach. It is not in heaven so that you have to ask, who will ascend into heaven to get it and proclaim it to us so we may obey it? Nor is it beyond the sea, so that you have to ask, 'Who will cross the sea to get it and proclaim it to us so we may obey it?' No, the Word is very near you; it is in your mouth and in your heart so you may obey it." He is giving them no excuse not to believe and obey what they have heard. Then in verse 19, he sums it up by saying, "This day I call heaven and earth as witnesses against you that I have set before you life and death, blessings and curses. Now choose life so that you and your children may live and that you may love the Lord your God, listen to his voice, and hold fast to him." It always amazes me how often the same theme follows from Genesis to Revelation and somehow even after reading the reports of how disobedience did not work out so well in past generations, we still follow the same patterns.

James then tells them to be careful not to show favoritism. He says we should treat the poor man who comes to our church in shabby clothes the same as we treat a man wearing a gold ring and fine clothes. He says that if we discriminate we are becoming judges with evil thoughts. He points out also in 2:5 that God has chosen those who are poor in the eyes of the world to be rich in faith and to inherit the kingdom he promised those who love him. As you think back on the stories in both the Old and New Testament that seems to be true. David, for instance, was just the young shepherd boy whom his father did not even consider worthy to be one of his sons chosen to be the future king. Rahab, a prostitute and considered the least on the social ladder of that day, to be the one to help the spies conquer Jericho and ended up being in the genealogy of Jesus, or a young teenage girl from Nazareth to become the mother of the one to bring redemption into the world.

He talks a lot about keeping the law, but summarizes it by saying in 2:8, "If you really keep the royal law found in Scripture, 'Love your neighbor as yourself,' you are doing well.'" Can you imagine living in a world where this one principle was adhered to? If we treated everyone the way we wanted to be treated, we would not even have to think about obeying the law. It would all take care of itself. God's ways would naturally follow because that is the law he put in his Word and our hearts.

James talks about the importance of letting our faith be followed by deeds that show it. "What good is it, my brothers, if a man claims to have faith but has no deeds? Can such faith save him? Suppose a brother or sister is without clothes and daily food. If one of you says to him, 'Go, I wish you well; keep warm and well fed,' but does nothing about his physical needs what good is it? In the same way, faith by itself, if it is not accompanied by action is dead."

Then he uses the example of Abraham being willing to offer Isaac as a sacrifice. He points out that his faith and his actions were working together, and because of that God credited unto him righteousness and called him his friend. He points out, "You see that a person is justified by what he does and not by faith alone." Then he makes a comparison. "As the body without the spirit is dead, so faith without deeds is dead." Wow! That is convicting. It is easy to say we have faith and believe but as we examine our life would that prove out to be true. We should ask ourselves if our faith is a noun or verb in our life. If it is a verb and is active, then we will have fruit to show as a result.

Next, he addresses the power of the tongue. James 3:3-6 reads, "When we put bits into the mouths of horses to make them obey us, we can turn the whole animal. Or take ships as an example; although they are so large and are driven by strong winds, they are steered by a very small rudder wherever the pilot wants to go. Likewise, the tongue is a small part of the body, but it makes great boasts. "

Consider what a great forest is set on fire by a spark. The tongue also is a fire, a world of evil among the parts of the body. It corrupts the whole person, sets the whole course of his life on fire, and is itself set on fire by hell." He goes on to say that the same tongue that praises God, curses men and that should not be. He says that a fig tree cannot bear olives or a grapevine bear figs. I think the point he is trying to make here is how powerful our words are. Jesus spoke of that very thing in Matthew 12:34, "For out of the overflow of the heart the mouth speaks. The good man brings good things out of the good stored up in him, and the evil man brings evil things out of the evil stored up in him." Jesus is basically saying if you are a fig tree, you will produce figs. What comes out our mouth is giving others a view as to what is stored in our heart.

On the subject of wisdom, James says wisdom that comes from heaven is first of all pure, then peace loving, considerate, submissive, full of mercy and good fruit, impartial and sincere. He goes on to say that peacemakers who sow in peace raise a harvest of righteousness. I define righteousness as being in right standing with God, and isn't that what we all are striving for? James gives us advice as to how to attain that in 4:7, "Submit yourselves to God. Resist the devil, and he will flee from you. Come near to God, and he will come near to you." "Humble yourselves before the Lord, and he will lift you up."

He warns against quarreling and judging one another. Also, he tells us not to boast about our life or about what might happen tomorrow. He puts it very boldly in 4:14, "Why you do not even know what will happen tomorrow. What is your life? You are a mist that appears for a little while and then vanishes." He tells us that our emphasis should be on doing what God's will is for our lives while we are here.

We are also told to be patient when suffering like the farmer is when he plants his crops and waits for the seasons to come and bring forth a harvest. He encourages us to persevere and be faithful because the Lord's coming is near. He tells us not to swear and to be true to our word saying, "Let your yes be yes and your no be no."

Now talking about how to live, he tells us, "Is anyone of you in trouble? He should pray. Is anyone happy? Let him sing songs of praise. Is anyone of you sick? He should call the elders of the church to pray over him and anoint him with oil in the name of the Lord. And the prayer offered in faith will make the sick person well; the Lord will raise him up. If he has sinned, he will be forgiven.
Therefore confess your sins one to another and pray for each other so that you may be healed. The prayers of a righteous man are powerful and effective."

He uses Elijah as an example of this. He reminds us that Elijah prayed earnestly that it would not rain, and it did not rain for three and a half years. Then he prayed, and the heavens gave rain and produced crops. Just one of many examples of faith in the Bible to prove to us that prayer works if it is coupled with faith and a desire to do God's will.

James is a short book but is packed with instructions on ways to live according to God's intended plan and purpose for our lives.

Discussion Questions:

1. James talks about living according to the Word planted in you by God's Holy Spirit. Are you confident that the word planted in you is the true Word of God? Explain how that has changed or remained steadfast?

2. James talks about being tempted and how it is never God who tempts us, but our own carnal desires. Can you name some things that might tempt you to stray from the Lord and his Word?

3. James talks about looking into the Word and knowing what it says, but then turning away. Can you remember a time in your life when you choose to turn away even though you knew it wasn't right?

4. Do you treat others as you want them to treat you? What happens when you do this? How do they treat you in return?

5. James says a lot about the power of the tongue. If Jesus is right, and what comes out our mouth is a reflection of what is in our heart, what perception do you think people have of you as they hear you speak?

6. James tells us that faith without works is dead. Do you consider yourself a person of faith, and if so, what are some of the fruit that comes from your faith tree?

7. What does James tell us to do to overcome the wiles of the devil?

8. Why do you think he tells us to confess our sins one to another that we might be healed?

Lesson 66
First & Second Peter

Peter was one of Jesus' twelve disciples. This letter was written by him to the churches in the northern part of Asia Minor. He had heard they were being persecuted for their faith and this first letter was written to encourage them.

One of the main themes in these two letters is to remind them that Jesus suffered for them and to follow his example of trusting God to care for them. He goes on to give them instructions on how to live the life God intended them to live in a world that was not approving.

He starts the first letter by reminding them that they were God's chosen people. He elaborates on how because of the resurrection of Jesus, they have a living hope and have an inheritance that can never perish or fade. He tells them that their hope is in heaven and that it is shielded by God's power and will be revealed in the last times.

Peter emphasizes that it is through faith that we can take hold of that hope saying that the trials come so that their faith, which he says is more valuable than gold, can be proved genuine. In 1 Peter 1:8, "Though you have not seen him, you love him; and even though you do not see him now, you believe in him and are filled with an inexpressible and glorious joy, for you are receiving the goal of your faith, the salvation of your souls."

He warns them to be self-controlled; and to be sure their hope is fully set on the grace given them when Jesus Christ is revealed. 1 Peter 1:15 says, "Just as he who called you is holy, so be holy in all you do; for it is written: 'Be holy because I am holy.'" Then the next verse is an even greater warning, "Since you call on a Father who judges each man's work impartially, live your lives as strangers here in reverent fear. For you know that it was not with perishable things such as silver or gold that you were redeemed from the empty way of life handed down to you from your forefathers, but with the precious blood of Christ, a lamb without blemish or defect. He was chosen before the creation of the world but was sent in these last days for your sake." We are not often told to live in fear but the point he is making here is that we are to live on this earth as strangers in that we do not live as the world does, but always to be mindful or have a reverent fear of losing our way and being sucked into the ungodly ways of the world we live in.

Peter encourages them to love one another from their heart since they have been purified by the truth. He goes on to remind them in 1:23-25, "For you have been born again, not of perishable seed, but of imperishable, through the enduring Word of God. For all men are like grass and all their glory is like the flowers of the field; the grass withers and the flowers fall, but the Word of the Lord stands forever." What a comfort to know and be reminded that the Word of God is not a good book for a certain generation but will stand as a solid foundation for our life forever. There are not many absolutes we can trust in this life, but it is reassuring to know that the Word of God is one we can count on.

He gives further instructions for them to rid themselves of every kind of evil and to be like a newborn baby craving pure spiritual milk so that by it they will grow up in their salvation. So many times after we have heard the good news of salvation and accepted it, we don't continue in our growth process. It can be compared to a newborn baby who comes into this world a new creation but has no skills to grow and develop without effort and training. If he stays in his crib and just basks in the fact that he has been given life, he would not be able to walk, run, and find the joys of growing up. Peter is telling them here to make an effort to grow in their faith and knowledge of God and what this new life holds.

Jesus is then referred to as a living stone and a stone that was rejected by men but chosen by God and when we accept him and invite him to come and live inside our spirits, we too become living stones. He tells us in 2:5, "You also, like living stones, are being built into a spiritual house to be a holy priesthood offering spiritual sacrifices acceptable to God through Jesus Christ." Wow! We are called a holy priesthood. He elaborates more on this in verse 9, "You are a chosen people, a royal priesthood, a holy nation, a people belonging to God, that you may declare the praises of him who called you out of darkness into his wonderful light." That makes me feel so accepted and valued. We think of a priest as one who can go straight to God and just as Jesus was called our high priest, now we are adopted into that same priesthood. We no longer have to have a mediator between our Father and us since the mediator is living inside us.

We are then encouraged to submit ourselves to every authority instituted in our lives among men, kings, governors, and others who are put in a position of punishing those who do wrong. He says for us that it is God's will that by doing good we should silence the ignorant talk of foolish men. He sums it up in 2:17 "Show proper respect to everyone; Love the brotherhood of believers, fear God, honor the king."

We are encouraged to follow the example of Christ when having to suffer for doing what is right. He points out that even when they were hurling insults at Jesus, he did not retaliate or make any threats against them, but he entrusted himself to his Father. Then one of my favorite verses, 2:24 states, "He himself bore our sins in his body on the tree, so that we might die to sins and live for righteousness; by his wounds, you have been healed." Verse 6 explains the condition of man, "You were like sheep going astray, but now you have returned to the Shepherd and Overseer of our soul." What a beautiful phrase, the Shepherd, and Overseer of our soul. This reminds me of the 23rd Psalm, "The Lord is my Shepherd, I shall not want, He makes me to lie down in green pastures, he leads me beside the still waters, he restores my soul. He leads me in the path of righteousness." If we allow him to be the overseer of our souls (mind, will, and emotions), he will restore our souls and lead us into paths of the righteous ways of living.

Peter has a few things to say about marriage, encouraging wives to be submissive to their husband. I like the next phrase after that. "So that, if any of them do not believe the Word, they may be won over without words by the behavior of their wives, when they see the purity and reverence of your lives." He goes on to say that the beauty of a woman should come from a gentle and quiet spirit and not from outward adornment. I cannot tell you how many times I have heard women say that after they accepted Christ, their husbands didn't want to have anything to do with that religious stuff. The more they preached to them the more they resisted. But when they prayed and walked in a new level of peace their husbands noticed something different and began to ask questions. I think this is the point that Peter is making here more than the much talked about submissive role a woman should take, not being equal to a man.

Then to the men, he says, in the same way, to be considerate of their wives as the weaker partner (in that they were created for and from man) but to treat them as heirs alongside themselves honoring the precious gift of life. He even says he should do this so that nothing would hinder his prayers. Peter emphasizes the point that they are both heirs of God's promise and members of his family and in his family, they are all equal. Women should not be offended because the Bible states many times God has no favorites.

The end of the third chapter gives us some great insight on ways to respond to others. "Do not repay evil with evil or insult with insult, but with blessing, because to this, you were called so that you may inherit a blessing. For, whoever would love life and sees good days must keep his tongue from evil and his lips from deceitful speech. He must turn from evil and do good; he must seek peace and pursue it. For the eyes of the Lord are on the righteous, and his ears are attentive to their prayer, but the face of the Lord is against those who do evil."

The important phrase here for me was to seek peace and pursue it. If I am truly seeking peace, I will be aware of my tongue and the way I treat others. In a household of many children, it is sometimes hard to find peace, but usually, there will be one child who is the peacemaker and will try to keep order in the family. That child usually will be the one who goes on to be the most successful and sought out by others. We all are drawn to that person who seems to have the key to calm the storm. That goes along with Jesus' Sermon on the Mount when he says, "Blessed are the peacemakers, for they shall see God."

He ends with a warning; "The end of all things is near. Therefore be clear-minded and self-controlled so that you can pray. Above all, love each other deeply because love covers a multitude of sins."

Peter adds a word to the elders of the church encouraging them to walk a life of humility saying, "God opposes the proud but gives grace to the humble." In 5:6 we are told to, therefore, "Humble yourself under God's mighty hand, that he may lift you up in due time. Cast all your anxieties on him because he cares for you. Be self-controlled and alert. Your enemy, the devil, prowls around like a roaring lion looking for someone to devour. Resist him, standing firm in your faith..." I could not help but compare this verse about the devil prowling around to see whom he may devour with the verse in 2 Chronicles 16:9, "The eyes of the Lord range throughout the earth to strengthen those whose hearts are fully committed to him." What a comparison. On the one hand, we see the devil is looking for someone to devour, and at the same time, God's eyes are looking to see whom he can strengthen. God has told us he will never leave us nor forsake us, and when I stay close to him, I can feel his love making me strong, and the fact that the devil is roaming around trying to devour me is irrelevant.

2 Peter

Peter wrote this second letter to the same group as the first, but this letter is aimed more at helping them overcome the dangers of being led astray by false teachers.

He starts by assuring them that God's divine power has given them everything they need for life and godliness as they seek knowledge of him who called them by his glory and goodness. He reminds them that he gave them great and precious promises so that they could participate in the divine nature of God and escape the corruption in the world.

He tells them to believe these promises and to make every effort to add to their faith goodness; and to goodness, knowledge; and to knowledge, self-control; and to self-control, perseverance; and to perseverance, godliness and godliness, brotherly kindness, and to brotherly kindness, love. He goes on to say that if they possess these qualities, they will keep them from being ineffective and unproductive in knowing Jesus Christ.

One thing he makes clear is that he was an eyewitness to this truth and that he was not just following cleverly invented stories. In 1:17 he says, "For he received honor and glory from God the Father when the voice came to him from the Majestic Glory, saying, "This is my Son, whom I love; with him, I am well pleased." Peter goes on, "We ourselves heard this voice that came from heaven when we were with him on the sacred mountain." How great it would be to have been in that place and heard that voice make the proclamation of love from God the Father to his Son Jesus Christ. Being an eyewitness gave Peter a greater platform to preach from.

He reminds them to, "Pay attention to prophecy," and to understand that no prophecy in Scripture came through the prophet's own interpretation, for prophecy never had its origin in the will of man, but "men spoke from God as they were led by the Holy Spirit." He warns them that just as the prophets of old were instruments of God, there were false prophets who would come with made up stories to exploit and deceive them. He reminds them that God will destroy the evil that they bring but will rescue the righteous.

He uses examples of Noah and how God saved him and his family but destroyed the rest of the evil population. He reminds them of how Sodom and Gomorrah were destroyed because of the sinful lifestyle they had accepted, but how Lot was spared because he was a righteous man in God's eyes. Peter even reminds them how God did not spare the angels when they sinned but sent them to hell and put them in dungeons to be held for judgment. However, in 2:9 he says the Lord knows how to rescue godly men from trials and to hold the unrighteous for the Day of Judgment. That is so reassuring as I think back over the many times in the Old Testament and New that we see this to be true.

He continues to warn against these men who had given themselves over to false teachings and lustful lifestyles. "These men are springs without water and mists driven by a storm. Blackest darkness is reserved for them. For they mouth has empty, boastful words and, by appealing to the lustful desires of sinful human nature, they entice people who are just escaping from those who live in error. They promise them freedom, while they themselves are slaves of depravity-for a man is a slave to whatever has mastered him."

Final words were given about being prepared for the coming of our Lord Jesus Christ and telling them not to get weary in waiting. He says in 3:8, "But do not forget this one thing, dear friends: With the Lord, a day is like a thousand years, and a thousand years are like a day. The Lord is not slow in keeping his promise, as some understand slowness. He is patient with you, not wanting anyone to perish, but everyone to come to repentance. But the day of the Lord will come like a thief. The heavens will disappear with a roar; the elements will be destroyed by fire, and the earth and everything in it will be laid bare."

His last encouragement to them is to make every effort to be found spotless, blameless and at peace and to grow in the grace and knowledge of our Lord and Savior Jesus Christ.

Discussion Questions:

1. Peter is encouraging the Christians to thirst for spiritual growth and compares it to a newborn baby who thirsts for milk. Do you have this kind of thirst to grow spiritually?

2. He says that the Word is not made of perishable seed, but imperishable. As you look at your life, how much importance do you give to the things that are perishable as compared to the things that are imperishable? Explain your answer?

3. Jesus is referred to as the living stone, and that we likewise, are living stones and born into a royal priesthood. How does that give you value as you meditate on that fact? Have you ever considered yourself a priest?

4. What do you think it means when it says Jesus is to be the Shepherd of our souls? How can you apply that to your life and how you make your decisions?

5. Peter says that we are not to repay evil for evil, nor insult with insult, but to repay with a blessing. Have you ever tried doing that and if so, what were the results?

Lesson 67
John 1, 2 and 3

John, who was a close follower and apostle of Jesus, wrote these books. He was very likely the only surviving apostle at this time and may have been the only remaining eyewitness of the actual events surrounding Jesus' life on earth. He had made Jerusalem his headquarters where he cared for Jesus' mother until her death. You may remember from our previous lessons when Jesus was hanging on the cross before he died he looked down at John and his mother and asked John to care for her. John remained in Jerusalem until the destruction of the city. He then made Ephesus his home, which by this time had become the center of the Christian population. It is from here he wrote his epistles and the book of Revelation.

These letters were written sometime between A.D. 85 and 90. Jerusalem had been destroyed in A.D. 70 and Christians had been scattered throughout the region. It was not sent to a particular church but several congregations. The purpose of the letters was to reassure the Christians of their faith and to counter false teachings.

He presented God to them as light, love, and life and explained in simple terms what it means to be in fellowship with him. This was particularly important at this time as false teachers had entered among them and were diverting the truth.

He begins by validating that he was an eyewitness to this truth and affirms his fellowship with God through Jesus. He encourages them likewise to enter into the same fellowship. He says that one reason he is encouraging them is to make his own joy complete. Sounds a lot like what we read in Hebrews 12:2, "Let us fix our eyes on Jesus, the author, and perfecter of our faith, who for the joy set before him endured the cross, scorning its shame, and sat down at the right hand of the throne of God." That joy was the fact that we were going to have our fellowship restored with the Father.

He first compares God to light. "This is the message we have heard from him and declare to you: God is light; in Him, there is no darkness at all. If we claim we have fellowship with him and yet walk in the darkness, we lie and do not live out the truth. But if we walk in the light as he is in the light, we have fellowship with one another, and the blood of Jesus, his Son, purifies us from all sin."

Then he advises them on the natural state of man saying. "If we claim to be without sin, we deceive ourselves, and the truth is not in us. If we confess our sins, he is faithful and just and will forgive us our sins and purify us from all unrighteousness. If we claim we have not sinned, we make him out to be a liar, and the Word is not in us." John does not mince any words about putting everyone at ease that we all have sin in our lives, but we now have an advocate with the Father and can be forgiven.

Then he gives them the ultimate test to prove whether they truly know him or not. "We know that we have come to know him if we keep his commands. Whoever says, I know him, but does not do what he commands, is a liar and the truth is not in him." This must have seemed like a harsh statement, and they must have felt like it was not possible to attain it but then he goes on to say in verse 5, "If anyone obeys his words then the love for God is made complete in them. This is how we know we are in him: Whoever claims to live in him must live as Jesus did." Now he is telling them that it had been done and that Jesus had paved the way. We only had to follow his example.

He tells them that the darkness is passing, and the true light is already shining. Then again, he gave them a way to test if they are walking in the light. "Anyone who claims to be in the light but hates a brother or sister is still in the darkness. Anyone who loves their brother or sister lives in the light, and there is nothing in them to make them stumble. But anyone who hates a brother or sister is in the darkness. They do not know where they are going because the darkness has blinded them." This brings up the question as to whether we are experiencing the love of Jesus if we dislike someone. We live in a world of diverse people with differing thoughts and ideas of right and wrong. Sometimes we disagree on how things are to be and may dislike the behavior of a brother or sister, but that is a world apart from harboring anger and hatred that would grieve the Holy Spirit within us and distract us from experiencing God's love.

John goes on to warn them about loving the things of this world saying, if we love the world and everything in it, we will give in to the lust of the flesh, the lust of eyes and the pride of our life and that all these things are not from the Father. He points out further that all those things and their desires will pass away but whoever does the will of the Father lives forever.

Next, he writes to them about the antichrist. He tells them in 2:18, "Dear children, this is the last hour; and as you have heard that the antichrist is coming, even now many antichrists have come. This is how we know that it is the last hour. They went out from us, but they did not really belong to us. For if they had belonged to us, they would have remained with us; but their going showed that none of them belonged to us." Interesting that even then he was saying it was the last hour. It seems men have thought we were in the last days for many years because the signs of deceit and false teachers have always been with us. As long as I can remember, people have been saying we were living in the end of time on earth. Every generation seems to think they are going to be the last before the coming of Christ.

He goes on to point out that they each have an anointing that was a gift from the Holy One and that they already know the truth and then again gives them the test to know the truth. "Who is the liar? It is whoever denies that Jesus is the Christ. Such a person is the antichrist, denying the Father and the Son." I have never thought of there being more than one antichrist. We only think of the antichrist as being the one spoken of in Revelation that will appear in the end times but here he is saying that anyone who denies Christ is an antichrist. The very definition of antichrist makes that clear when you stop and think about it. So while many in the world are speculating as to who the antichrist might be, we are living with antichrists all around us every day.

John explains that he is talking to them in this way so they won't be lead astray, but he reminds them that the anointing is in them and that they do not need to listen to anyone else to teach them. He elaborates in verse 27, "But as the anointing teaches you about all things and as that anointing is real, no counterfeit-just as it has taught you, remain in him." I think John is trying to convince them that the very presence of the Holy Spirit in them will teach them the truth and warn them that there are those who are coming to them with false teachings, but they have everything they need to discern truth.

In 1 John 3:1, he writes, "See what great love the Father has lavished on us, that we should be called children of God! And that is what we are! The reason the world does not know us is that they did not know Him. We are children of God and what we will be has not been shown us, but we know that when Christ appears, we will be like him for we shall see him as he is." We are still living in a world controlled by sinful desires and behaviors and we all sin, but he is telling them (and us), that although we sin at times if we truly have the life of God living in us, we will not continue to sin and make a practice of it. I think if the Holy Spirit is in residence and we are attuned to him, our conscious will convict us of our sin and we will be miserable until we confess it and turn from it. It is the attitude of the heart that He looks at when we come to him in repentance. It is easy to say, I will do this and then repent and get away with it, but if our repentance is from our head and not our heart, he will not hear it.

He uses an example of Cain and Abel to tell them that this temptation has been from the beginning. "Do not be like Cain, who belonged to the evil one and murdered his brother. And why did he murder him? Because his own actions were evil and his brothers were righteous." Then he tells them not to be surprised if the world hates them just because they are doing right because it stands as a conviction of their own sinful ways. His big lesson here is to love your brother and once again another test, 3:14; "We know that we have passed from death to life because we love each other."

Next test is found in 3:16, "This is how we know what love is: Jesus Christ laid down his life for us. And we ought to lay down our lives for our brothers and sisters. If anyone has material possessions and sees a brother and sister in need and has no pity on them, how can the love of God be in that person?" Then the big life lesson, "Dear children, let us not love with words or speech but with actions and in truth." We can say we love all day long, but the real test is what our actions say about us. We have all heard the old saying; actions speak louder than words, well now we know it came straight from the Bible.

Next test: this is how we know we belong to the truth and how we set our hearts at rest in his presence: If our hearts condemn us, we know that God is greater than our hearts, and he knows everything. "Dear friends, if our hearts do not condemn us, we have confidence before God and receive from him anything we ask because we keep his commands and do what pleases him. The one who keeps his commands lives in him and he in them. And this is how we know that he lives in us: We know it by the Spirit he gave us." I love this verse because it verifies that in my carnal nature, I cannot keep his commands but because he gave me a spirit to commune directly with his Holy Spirit, I can know and do his will." The challenge is to live in a way that we can sense the promptings of the spirit when we need to know the truth.

John gives them an exhortation to test the spirits that come with a message. He tells them that there are many false spirits that will come and appear so good and have a message that appeals to what seems to be light, but he says the test to see if it is false or real, "This is how you can recognize the Spirit of God: Every spirit that acknowledges that Jesus Christ has come in the flesh is from God, but every spirit that does not acknowledge Jesus is not from God." He goes on to tell them that they are from God and have overcoming power over these spirits because greater is the one who is in you than the one who is in the world.

Again, he repeats the former message, "Dear friend since God so loved us, we also ought to love one another. No one has seen God, but if we love one another, God lives in us and his love is made complete in us." He goes on in 4:17, "This is how love is made complete among us so we will have confidence on the Day of Judgment; In this world, we are like Jesus. There is no fear in love. But perfect love drives out fear because fear has to do with punishment. The one who fears is not made perfect in love." Wow! That should help us deal with the fears that bother us and examine how we are walking in love.

The central theme of his letter is the love of Jesus and in 1 John 5:6; he writes that He is the one who came by water and by blood-Jesus Christ. He did not come by water only, but by water and blood. And it is the spirit who testifies because the spirit is the truth. For there are three that testify: the Spirit, the water, and the blood; the three are in agreement. We accept human testimony, but God's testimony is greater because it is the testimony of God, which he has given about his son." Many have different ideas as to what it means in this verse by water and blood. Some say it was the water baptism and the blood shed at the crucifixion. I personally believe that it is talking about that he came by the water of his mother's womb making him carnal and by the blood of the Holy Spirit, which was of God. You remember that he had to be conceived by the Holy Spirit and not by man, so he did not have the tainted blood of sin that every man since Adam had running in his veins. Then at his baptism, the Spirit of God testified that he was, in fact, His son and that he was well pleased with him. That is something we will have to wait till we get to heaven to find out for sure.

John concludes by saying in 5:13, "I write these things to you who believe in the name of the Son of God so that you may know you have eternal life." Then one of my personal favorite verses, "This is the confidence we have in approaching God: that if we ask anything according to his will, he hears us. And if we know he hears us-whatever we ask-we know that we have what we ask of him."

2 John

This book is a very short book and really is just an acknowledgment of their faithfulness. He says in 1:3, "It gave me great joy when some believers came and testified about your faithfulness to the truth and how you are walking in it." Truth is a vital theme in this epistle. The word truth appears five times in the first four verses.

Then he addresses some who are spreading what he calls malicious nonsense about him and others who are coming through. He warns them that to practice love does not mean to encourage those who are trying to distort the truth. Likewise, He assures them that he will deal with them when he comes to visit.

3 John

John wrote this epistle to Gaius, who was a convert of his. Some say he became John's scribe, but in any case, he was much loved by John and John called him beloved four times in this book. He is encouraging him to practice love but upholds truth.

John emphasizes as well in this book that it is not wrong to have temporal as well as spiritual blessings. He is pointing out that even if it is not wrong to have means and prosperity, it is important to be careful about loving the things of this world.

He gives a stern warning about false prophets in this book as well and points out Diotrephes as one of them. He sends this letter to Demetrius and another delegation to help in correcting these issues.

Jude

It is thought that the Jude that wrote this epistle was the half-brother of Jesus. (See Matthew 13:55) It was probably written about A.D. 67 to the churches in Asia Minor.

He is encouraging them to contend in their faith and not be lead astray. Apparently, news of heresy in the churches had reached him, and like John in the previous lessons, he was giving a stern warning.

He minces no words in describing them. He calls them ungodly men, says they are like Sodom, given to fortification, brute corrupt beast, trees without fruit, murmurs, complainers, mockers walking in their own lust of their flesh, and he accuses them of not having the spirit. He then warns the congregation to avoid such men.

He reminds them of how the children of Israel were delivered out of Egypt but then fell away because of disobedience. He also reminded them of the angels who were cast out of heaven when they turned on God and following his ways. He reminded them what happened to Sodom and Gomorrah and how they were destroyed because of the sexual immorality.

He also reminds them that Enoch prophesied about these men and gave them a message in Jude 1:21, "Keep yourselves in the love of God, looking for the mercy of our Lord Jesus Christ unto eternal life." Then in verse 24, "Now to Him who is able to keep you from stumbling, and to present you faultless before the presence of His glory with exceeding joy. To God, our Savior, who alone is wise, be glory and majesty, dominion and power, both now and forever." You have probably heard this quoted and not known the context it was written in.

Discussion Questions:

1. John is talking about the importance of walking in the light. What does walking in the light mean to you? What are the things that can draw you into an area of darkness?

2. John says the way we know we are walking in truth and light is if you love your brother and sister. Have you had a time in your life when you have harbored resentment in your heart for someone? If so, did it affect your sense of the presence of God?

3. John tells us perfect love cast out fear. Explain what this means.

4. John tells us if our hearts do not condemn us, we will have confidence in God. What does it mean to you to have a heart that doesn't condemn you?

5. How did John say we are to test the spirits?

6. We are told if we ask anything according to God's will that he will hear us. How do we know what his will is?

Lesson 68
Revelation: Lesson 1

Revelation is the wrap-up story in the Bible. Genesis is the seed plot of the Bible as it represents the beginning, and Revelation is the book of endings.

It is based on Christ's statements on things to come. He refers to these in his teaching in Matthew 24, Mark 13 and Luke 21.

When asked about end times by his disciples, Jesus answers in Matthew 24: 4-8, "Watch out that no one deceive you, for many will come in my name claiming they are the Christ and will deceive many. You will hear of wars and rumors of wars. but see to it that you are not alarmed. Such things must happen, but the end is still not come. Nations will rise up against nation, and kingdoms against kingdoms. There will be famines and earthquakes in various places. All these are the beginning of birth pains."

That passage goes on to say, "For false Christs and false prophets will appear and perform great signs and miracles to deceive even the elect. So I have told you ahead of time if anyone tells you, there he is, out in the desert do not go out; or here he is in in the inner rooms, do not believe it. For as lightning that comes from the east is visible even in the west, so will the coming of the Son of Man…" Immediately after the distress of those days, the sun will be darkened, and the moon will not give its light, the stars will fall from the sky, and the heavenly bodies will be shaken. At that time, the sign of the Son of Man will appear in the sky, and all the nations of the earth will mourn. They will see the Son of Man coming on clouds of the sky with power and great glory. And he will send his angels with a loud trumpet call, and they will gather his elect from the four winds, from one end of the heavens to the other."

Then Jesus uses a visual of a fig tree, "Now learn this lesson from the fig tree: As soon as its twigs get tender and its leaves come out, you know that summer is near. Even so, when you see all these things, you know that it is near, right at the door. I tell you the truth; this generation will certainly not pass away until all these things have happened. Heaven and earth will pass away, but my Word will never pass away."

Next, Jesus talks about the fact that no one will know the day or the hour. Matthew 24:36 says, "No one knows about that day or hour, not even the angels in heaven, nor the Son, but only the Father. As it was in the days of Noah, so it will be at the coming of the Son of Man. For in the days before the flood, people were eating and drinking, marrying and giving in marriage up to the day Noah entered the ark; and they knew nothing about what would happen until the flood came and took them all away. That is how it will be at the coming of the Son of Man."

Then he gives a warning in verse 42, "Therefore, keep watch because you do not know on what day your Lord will come. But understand this: If the owner of the house had known at what time of night the thief was coming, he would have kept watch and would not have let his house be broken into. So you also must be ready, because the Son of Man will come at an hour when you do not expect him."

In Luke 21, we see Jesus elaborating on what will personally happen as well, "They will lay hands on you and persecute you. They will deliver you to synagogues and prisons, and you will be brought before kings and governors, and all on account of my name. This will result in you being witnesses to them. But make up your mind not to worry beforehand how you will defend yourselves. For I will give you words and wisdom that none of your adversaries will be able to resist or contradict. You will be betrayed even by parents, brothers, relatives, and friends, and they will put some of you to death. All men will hate you because of me. But not a hair of your head will perish. By standing firm, you will gain life."

We hear Mark echoing that account in Mark 13:9, "You must be on your guard. You will be handed over to the local councils and flogged in the synagogues. On account of me, you will stand before governors and kings as witnesses to them. And the gospel must first be preached to all nations. Whenever you are arrested and brought to trial, do not worry beforehand about what to say. Just say whatever is given you at the time, for it is not you speaking, but the Holy Spirit."

I thought it was important to get a perspective of what Jesus taught directly to his disciples about the end times before we start digging into the elements given in Revelation because that is the theme and purpose of the book. Revelation 1:1, "The Revelation of Jesus Christ, which God gave unto him, to show unto his servants things which must shortly come to pass; and he sent and signified it by his angel unto his servant John." This shows the divine order of communication: God the Father gave the revelation to Jesus Christ, the son: Christ employed an angel to communicate it to John, and he was instructed to give it to the churches.

It is Jesus' personal appearance that is the subject, center, and purpose of the book. It is the revelation of Jesus in his own person, unveiled from his present invisible estate to visible estate to mortal view, when we are told, "every eye shall see him." The very name revelation, (Apokalupsis), from which our English word apocalypse is derived, conveys the idea of an appearing, an unveiling, a manifestation.

It was written in A.D. 95 while John was exiled on the Island of Patmos, which is in the Mediterranean Sea. Patmos is a rocky island about ten miles in length. I have visited the monastery of Saint John, which is on a hill overlooking the island. He was there because he had been banished during the reign of Domitian. Eighteen months later, under the reign of Nerva, he was released. It was during this time that the angel gave him the vision and revelation of what was to come.

His purpose in writing was to give hope and encouragement to those Christians who were suffering severe persecution for their faith in Jesus Christ. John is writing primarily to the seven churches in Asia, (selected churches, for there were much more in Asia) which were representative assemblies both as to church history and spirituality. The object was to show them what was to come.

The times had been harsh for the Christian community. The church was 66 years old and had suffered terrible persecution. The first being 30 years before the book of Revelation was written during the time of Nero, A.D. 64-67 when multitudes of Christians were crucified, or thrown to wild beasts or wrapped in combustible garments and burned to death while Nero laughed at the pitiful cries as they suffered.

The second persecution was instituted by Emperor Domitian A.D. 95. It was short but extremely severe. Over 40,000 Christians were tortured or slain. This was the persecution that caused John to be banished to the Island of Patmos.

Then in A.D. 98, the third persecution was that of Trajan. John had lived through the first two and was about to enter the third attempt of Rome's efforts to blot out the Christian faith. These were dark days for the church, and God gave these visions evidently to help steady the church for the awful days ahead.

These Christians needed to know that God controls whatever happens on earth and that through imagery and symbols, which may sometimes seem difficult to understand, one thing is made clear, Jesus Christ is the Lord and ruler over everyone and everything and will someday come and judge and punish that which is evil. He also will establish an everlasting kingdom with a new heaven and a new earth.

Paul alludes to this in his letter to the churches when he is talking about the importance of doing what is right, and he was telling them to know that God's judgment is always fair. God is a just God who will pay back trouble to those who cause them trouble. He gives them a visual as well in 2 Thessalonians 1: 6-10. "This will happen when the Lord Jesus is revealed in blazing fire with his powerful angels."

As it is important to look at the words of the apostles, I think, to fully understand Revelation it is important to look at the prophecies in the Old Testament, especially the book of Daniel. It is called the apocalyptic book because he was given a glimpse into the near and distant future through dreams and visions.

Nebuchadnezzar was king of Babylon during the time of Daniel's captivity there. Daniel was a godly man committed to prayer and obedience to his God. One night King Nebuchadnezzar had a dream, and none of his wise men could reveal its meaning to him. He was so furious that he ordered all the wise men in the country killed, including Daniel. With this, Daniel went to the king and asked for time that he might interpret the dream. Then he went to his friends and asked them to join him in prayer to reveal the mystery of this dream. During the night, the mystery was revealed to Daniel in a vision. He praised God and the next day went to the chief officer whom the king had appointed to execute all the wise men and asked him not to kill them until he could see the king because God had shown him the answer to his dream.

He took Daniel to the king and the king asked him if he could tell him what his dream meant. Daniel replied in Daniel 2:27, "No wise man, enchanter, magician or diviner, can explain to the king the mystery he has asked about. But there is a God in heaven who reveals mysteries. He has shown you, Nebuchadnezzar, what will happen in days to come. Your dream and the visions that passed through your mind as you lay on your bed are these." Then he proceeded to tell him the interpretation of the dream..

In his dream, Nebuchadnezzar saw an image of a beast with a head of gold, breast and arms of silver, belly and thighs of brass and legs of iron with feet of iron and clay. Daniel explained to him that the head of gold represented the Babylon Empire. Daniel 2:37-38 states, "Thou, O king art a king of kings: for the God of heaven hath given thee a kingdom, power and strength, and glory. And wherever the children of men dwell, the beasts of the field and the fowls of the heaven has he given into your hand and has made thee ruler over them all. Thou are the head of gold."

Then he explained about the breast and arms of silver. Daniel 2:39 states, "And after thee shall arise another kingdom inferior to thee." This was referring to the Medo-Persian, which was an empire of two parts, as was demonstrated by the two arms of silver. The two nations united to conquer Babylon. Today those nations are Iran and Iraq.

Next was the belly and thighs of brass. This represented the Grecian Empire. Daniel 2:39 states, "...and another third kingdom of brass, which shall bear rule over all the earth. This was telling the king that next, the Greek Empire would overcome the Medes and the Persians and later would be divided among four generals after the death of Alexander the Great. The modern-day division of the Greek Empire would be Greece, Turkey, Syria, and part of Africa.

Then he explains the legs of iron with feet of iron and clay. Daniel 2:41 states, "And the fourth kingdom shall be strong as iron: forasmuch as iron breaketh in pieces and subdueth all things: and as iron that breaketh all these, shall it break in pieces and bruise. And whereas thou saw the feet and toes, part of potter's clay, and part of iron, the kingdom shall be divided; but there shall be the strength of the iron, forasmuch as thou saw the iron mixed with miry clay."

In this fourth empire, the Roman Empire would govern with an iron rule. It would be an empire that would take up a great deal of the vision or image, because of its long legs. We see two legs, and we know that the Roman Empire was divided into the eastern and the western empires. We also know that the ten toes represent ten kingdoms. In the end times, the antichrist will rise again from the area of the old Roman Empire. Undoubtedly, he will have ten nations who give honor unto him, but in the vision, a stone crushes the image.

We know that image is Christ. Daniel 2:34-35 states, "While you were watching, a rock was cut out but not of human hands. It struck the statue on its feet of iron and clay and smashed them. Then the iron, the clay, the bronze, the silver and the gold were broken to pieces at the same time and became like chaff on a threshing floor in the summer. The wind swept them away without leaving a trace. But the rock that struck the statue became a huge mountain and filled the whole earth."

This is a picture of end times and is compatible with the book of Revelation. (By the way, after the king heard this, he honored Daniel and said, "Surely your God is the God of gods and the Lord of kings and a revealer of mysteries.) He placed Daniel in a high position and lavished many gifts on him. He made him ruler over the entire province of Babylon and placed him in charge of all its wise men. The king had some setbacks but eventually turned back to God because of Daniel's witness.

I think it is important to look at the thread that is being woven throughout from Jesus own words, as well as, the prophets and apostles, recognizing that the book of Revelation is the gathering of the threads of the Old and New Testaments, and how it weaves them into one clear and complete tapestry of the divine purpose of all creation.

There are many symbols in this book. Throughout the Bible we see symbols: We see that leaven was used as a symbol of evil in the Old Testament and used as a symbol of resurrection in the New Testament. Jesus taught in parables and used many symbols in teaching about the kingdom. Seed as a symbol of the Word of God, fowls are a symbol of the wicked one, and the ground is symbolic of the heart of man. We also see that tares are a symbol of godless people, and wheat is a symbol of godly people. Of course, we all know that the dove is the symbol of the Holy Spirit and that the bread of life refers to Jesus. So keep an open mind as we go through the pages of Revelation and unpack the meaning of the symbolism used.

We will see candlesticks and stars representing churches and messengers. We will see a woman and a man-child representing God's people and Satan pictured as a dragon. We will also see a beast and the false church pictured as a scarlet woman. Jesus Christ also appears under various names in this book.

Numbers are often used in this book and here is a quick look at their significance: one is the number of God, three represents the Trinity, four has to do with the world, (because of the four directions) and six is the number of evil, seven has to do with completeness, and ten shows specific happenings. Twelve has to do primarily with those who are redeemed.

God promises a blessing to those who read the book of Revelation. The word blessing here means happy. The book of Revelation is intended to be a source of happiness. So as we study through it, know that these promises are for you. It may seem like a hard book to understand, but God always reveals the truth to those who seek to study and learn the truth.

Discussion Questions:

1. What are your thoughts about Revelations that you brought into the study of this book?

2. Had you realized that it was all about the revealing of Jesus from the invisible to the visible? How does this impact your study of this book?

3. Are you comforted by the fact that Jesus is continually telling us not to worry, that we will be given what we need in difficult times?

4. Of the prophecies discussed in this lesson, have you seen any come to pass in your lifetime?

5. As you look at Nebuchadnezzar's dream, can you trace the history and see some of its fulfillment? What does this dream tell you about the antichrist?

---

6. Daniel stood firm in his faith, and God rewarded him with power and influence. Can you name others who did the same in the Old Testament?

7. Does it surprise you that even Jesus does not know when he is coming back?

8. Jesus is described as the rock that will come and smash all other kingdoms. We see Jesus referred to as stone in the New Testament when he is called the cornerstone of the church. He is referred to as the rock we should build our house on (as opposed to sand that is shifting). Then in Roman 9:33, Paul is talking about Israel, and he refers to Jesus as the stumbling stone. As you think about your life, is Jesus your rock of stability, or is your security based on other things?

9. Why do you think that the Bible says that those who study Revelation will be blessed? "Blessed is the one who reads the words of this prophecy, and blessed are those who hear it and take to heart what is written in it, because the time is near."

Lesson 69
Revelation: Lesson 2
(Letters to the churches)

The basic themes of this book are redemption and regeneration. Redemption means to restore to its original owner. Regeneration means to restore to its original state.

As you look back to the beginning of our study in Genesis, we began by talking about how God created man and placed him in a beautiful garden on the planet earth. You remember that all God asked of them was to be obedient and not eat of the tree of good and evil. However, man failed the test and was thrown out of the garden and lost their state of righteousness with God. This lead to a need for the redemption of our soul and body.

We read in Isaiah 51:6, "Lift up your eyes to the heavens, look at the earth beneath; the heavens will vanish like smoke, the earth will wear out like a garment, and its inhabitants die like flies. But my salvation will last forever; my righteousness will never fail." We see here Isaiah alluding to the fact that the earth is in a perpetual state of dying in wait for the time that it will be regenerated.

Then in Psalm 102:25, "In the beginning you laid the foundations of the earth, and the heavens are the work of your hands. They will perish, but you remain; they will all wear out like a garment. Like clothing, you will change them, and they will be discarded. But you remain the same, and your years will never end."

As you look at the big picture of the Bible, the stage was set in Genesis, and the fulfillment of God's promises are established in Revelation. We can see that by the very definition of revelation, which means, "the removing of the veil, unveiling, disclosure, appearing, coming, or manifestation."

We studied in the Old Testament the process of preparing the world for the time that Jesus would come and bring redemption to our souls.

Then in the New Testament, we see Peter telling the church, "In keeping with his (God) promises we are looking forward to a new heaven and a new earth, the home of righteousness." Also, Paul wrote to the church at Corinth, "Therefore do not lack any spiritual gift as you eagerly wait for our Lord Jesus Christ to be revealed." This is exactly what the book of revelation is; the revealing of Jesus Christ as we see in the very first verse, Revelation 1:1 states, "The revelation of Jesus Christ, which God gave him to show his servants what must soon take place."

This book is really divided into two parts; Chapters 1-3 talks about things that are, (that is, things which were in John's day.) This is like an introduction to the main body of the book. The rest of the book tells of things to come in the future.

John begins with a greeting to the seven churches to whom this is written. He tells them how this letter came to be in 1:9: "I, John, your brother and companion in the suffering and kingdom and patient endurance that are ours in Jesus, was on the island of Patmos because of the Word of God and the testimony of Jesus."

"On the Lord's Day I was in the Spirit, and I heard behind me a loud voice like a trumpet, which said, 'Write on a scroll what you see and send it to the seven churches to Ephesus, Smyrna, Pergamum, Thyatira, Sardis, Philadelphia, and Laodicea.' I turned around to see the voice that was speaking to me. And when I turned, I saw seven golden lampstands, and among the lampstands was someone like a son of man, dressed in a robe reaching down to his feet and with a golden sash around his chest. His head and hair were white like wool, as white as snow, and his eyes were a blazing fire. His feet were like bronze glowing in a furnace, and his voice was like the sound of rushing waters. In his right hand, he held seven stars, and out of his mouth came a sharp double-edged sword. His face was like the sun shining in all its brilliance."

"When I saw him, I fell at his feet as though dead. Then he placed his right hand on me and said, 'Do not be afraid. I am the First and the Last. I am the Living One: I was dead, and behold, I am alive forever and ever! And I hold the keys to death and Hades. Write, therefore, what you have seen, what is now, and what will take place later. The mystery of the seven stars that you saw in my right hand and of the seven golden lampstands is this: The seven stars are the angels of the seven churches, and the seven lampstands are the seven churches.'"

As we see throughout scripture when God sends a message to his people, he begins with, do not be afraid. "Fear not'" is one of the most used phrases in the entire Bible. Then he follows up with why John does not need to be afraid. He tells him that he is the first and the last. He is the totality of all that is, and then he reminds him that even though he was dead, now he is alive and will remain so forever. He follows up with the assurance that he alone holds the keys to death and Hades. He is the one with complete access to the throne of God, and he has the key to all things pertaining to life and death. That should have taken any fear away from John as he continued to record what was happening.

He explains the first mystery of the images he saw in the vision. The seven lampstands were representative of the seven churches. These churches were listed in geographical order starting with Ephesus. They were laid out in a triangle about one hundred miles to the farthest point to the north being Pergamum, and Laodicea about one hundred miles to the east.

Asia was a Roman province in the west part of what we know as Asia Minor, now a part of Turkey. Ephesus was its chief city, and Pergamum was its political capital. There were many more churches, but these were main centers in their respective districts.

One thing of interest is the fact that the book of Revelation is built around a system of the number seven. Seven letters to seven churches, seven seals and seven trumpets, seven vials, seven candlesticks, seven stars, seven angels, seven spirits, a lamb with seven horns and seven eyes, seven lamps, seven thunders, a red dragon with seven heads and seven crowns, a leopard-like beast with seven heads, a scarlet-colored beast with seven heads, seven mountains and seven kings.

Now let's look at the other places in the Bible the number seven is used. The Sabbath was on the seventh day, Jericho fell after seven priests with seven trumpets for seven days marched around the walls and blew their trumpets seven times on the seventh day. Naaman dipped in the Jordan River seven times. The Bible begins with seven days of creation and ends with a book of sevens. There are also seven blessings listed in this book, starting in verse one that says blessed is the one who reads this book.

It seems seven is a favorite number of God because there are seven days in the week, seven notes in music and seven colors of the rainbow. It is thought to represent the number of completion, a unit, fullness, and totality. Jesus sums that up well in verse eight, where he says, "I am the alpha and the omega, who is, and who was, and who is to come, The Almighty." That just about covers it all.

After he explains the meaning of the candlesticks, he explains the meaning of the stars, which are angels of the churches. Angels play a large role in the scheme and unfolding of this book. They are mentioned twenty-seven times as to the various activities they have in Revelation.

Starting in chapter one, we see the angel dictating the information to John, and ending in chapter twenty when an angel binds Satan.

John gives a beautiful description of God's appearance. "His head and his hair were white like **wool**, as white as **snow.**" This is suggestive not of age as we see it, but of wisdom from the one who is from everlasting to everlasting, and the purity of His holiness. The Psalmist David referred to snow as representing purity in Psalm 51:7, "Cleanse me with hyssop, and I will be clean; wash me, and I will be whiter than snow." Then we look at Isaiah, and he references both snow and wool. Isaiah 1:18 "Come now, let us reason together, says the Lord. Though your sins are like scarlet, they shall be white as snow; though they are red as crimson, they shall be like wool." Both of these passages are representative of what we will be like when we become like him, so to read that he appeared to John in those same terms is very exciting. I so love how the Bible threads are consistent truths throughout.

"His eyes were as a flame of **fire**." You remember the Holy Spirit came and rested over the Ark of the Covenant as a pillar of fire to give them direction and light as they were seeking the Promised Land. In Jeremiah 23:29, the Lord says, "Is not my Word like fire, declares the Lord, and like a hammer that breaks a rock in pieces." Then in 1 Corinthians, we see the church was told to build their foundation on Jesus Christ, which is a solid foundation, but the time would come when his works would be judged. "His work will be shown for what it is because the day will bring it to light. It will be revealed with fire, and the fire will test the quality of each man's work." We see in acts that the Holy Spirit descended on the believers like tongues of fire. This description shows that he is the fire that provides light that leads and directs, and lives within us, but also a fire of judgment that we all must one day stand before. One of my favorite verses in the Bible alludes to this. 2 Chronicles 16:9, "For the eyes of the Lord range throughout the earth to strengthen those whose hearts are fully committed to him." We refer to someone who has a passion as someone who has a fire in his belly. Well, here we see a passionate Father with fire in his eyes.

"His feet are like unto fine brass, as it burned in a furnace." This is a reference to a purifying fire that abolishes every place that wicked men trod. Feet are used to express good news and authority in the scripture. Psalm 10:15 states, "How beautiful are the feet of those who bring good news." Then in Psalm 110:1 it tells us, "Sit at my right hand until I make your enemies a footstool for your feet." In 1 Corinthians 15:25 this very thing is referenced, "The end will come, when he hands over the kingdom to God the Father after he has destroyed all dominion, authority, and power. For he must reign until he has put all his enemies under his feet." Here we are told his feet will be like fine brass and the churches would have known the significance of this reference.

"His voice is as the sound of **rushing waters.**" We see in Job 37:4, beginning with the voice of excellence. Then in Psalm 29, "The voice of the Lord is powerful; the voice of the Lord is full of majesty." We think of rushing waters as something that carries you away with great force, and that is exactly what is going to happen when we are caught up in the air with him one day.

Out of his mouth went a sharp **two-edged sword**. "We find a reference to this in Hebrews 4:12, "For the Word of God is living and active. Sharper than any double-edged sword, it penetrates even to dividing soul and spirit, joints and marrow; it judges the thoughts and attitudes of the heart."

"And when I saw him I fell to my feet as dead." Here we find the same John who was the beloved disciple who sat beside Jesus and laid his head on his chest, now prostrating himself as one dead in the awesome presence of the glorified Christ.

Then one by one he dictated a letter to each of the churches. It is thought that each letter consisted of the whole book with a special message to each church. In every church letter, he commanded them, condemned them, counseled them, and challenged them. Each letter had an appraisal of the spiritual standing of that assembly.

The churches are represented as candlesticks, and even though these letters are sent to a particular church, it is also true for us individually. Jesus tells us in Matthew 5:14, "You are the light of the world. A city on a hill cannot be hid. Neither do people light a lamp and put it under a bowl. Instead, they put it on its stand, and it gives light to everyone in the house. In the same way, let your light shine before men, that they may see your good deeds and praise your Father in heaven."

The churches each had a reputation. Two were very good: Smyrna and Philadelphia. Two were very bad: Sardis and Laodicea and three were part good, and part bad: Ephesus, Pergamum, and Thyatira.

The first church he addressed is the church at Ephesus. Historically Ephesus was of outstanding political importance. It was known as a free city, meaning it governed itself independent of outside influence. It was the site of the temple of Diana of the Ephesians, which was a pretentious structure, and it was the great pride of the city. It was made of 127 beautiful marble pillars, which were each, a gift from the king. Inside the shrine was a great altar with the image of Diana, which the Ephesians said fell from heaven. Their worship was wild and weird, and therefore Ephesus became a haven for criminals and fugitives.

It is today in utter ruin. I visited the site a few years ago, and all you can see are a few pillars still standing. It was devastated by the Turks and Mongols in the 14th century. The desolation is complete. Ephesus is a picture of what happens to those who leave their first love that is talked about in chapter two.

In Paul's day, this church was a tremendous testimony for Jesus Christ. It was a church that experienced outstanding miracles that we find in Acts 19:11-12. It was also a church that was persecuted for its single-minded devotion to Christ. It was the church that Paul wrote his most profound epistle, the letter of Ephesians. Before it lost its first love, Ephesus was the kind of church we need in our day. They labored patiently; they did not tolerate evil in the church, and worldly men were not allowed to hold office in the assembly. Those who sought to exalt themselves were judged and exposed.

However, over time, they became very cold. We can hear it in Paul's letter to them in Acts 20:29-31, "For I know this, that after my departing shall grievous wolves enter in among you, not sparing the flock. Also of your own selves shall men arise, speaking perverse things, to draw away disciples after them. Therefore watch, and remember, that by the space of three years, I ceased not to warn every one night and day with tears."

The beginning of the letter is one of praise for enduring hardships and having perseverance. But he says, "Yet I hold this against you: You have forsaken your first love. Remember the height from which you have fallen. Repent and do the things you did at first. If you do not repent, I will come to you and remove the lampstand from its place. He who has an ear, let him hear what the Spirit says to the churches. To him who overcomes, I will give the right to eat from the tree of life, which is in the paradise of God."

Next, he addresses the church at Smyrna. It was located about 35 miles north of Ephesus and was very pro-Roman and was one of the centers of emperor worship. It was compulsory to once a year burn incense on the altar to Caesar, for which you were given a commendation. Christians who refused to do this were imprisoned.

It was called the church of persecution. The name itself means Myrrh. Myrrh was used in the burial of Christ. It is a fragrant spice, which is beaten into fine pieces so it can give off its fragrance. It is a clear picture of the Christians we see in this town.

The persecution produced many martyrs. One was Polycarp who was a noted Christian father and bishop of Smyrna. He confessed freely that he was a Christian and was given a choice to sacrifice to Caesar or be burned. His reply was, "Eighty and six years I served Christ, and he has never done me wrong. How can I blaspheme my king who saved me." Wood was gathered, and as the flames licked his body, he prayed this prayer, "I thank thee that thou has graciously thought me worthy of this day and this hour that I may receive a portion in the number of the martyrs in the cup of thy Christ." Today we still see the evil and persecution of Christians. A news report today tells of a radical group called Isis beheading Christians strictly because of their faith. So we are still living a part of the history of Revelation as it is happening in places around the world in our time.

Jesus said to them, "Fear none of these things which thou shalt suffer; behold, the devil shall cast some of you into prison, that ye may be tried; and you shall have tribulation ten days; be thou faithful unto death, and I will give thee a crown of life."

The tribulation for ten days in Revelation 2:10 given to this church, was probably referring to the ten major persecutions under the future ten emperors. According to history, as many as five million Christians were martyred during the reign of these emperors.

Jesus commanded them by saying in 2:9, "I know thy works, and tribulations, and poverty, and I know the blasphemy of them which say they are Jews, and are not, but are the synagogue of Satan."

The next letter was written to the church at Pergamos. It was the capital of Asia. It was the ancient center of world learning, having the largest library in the world at that time. The library contained 200,000 scrolls-a huge number in an age where every scroll had to be handwritten. It was, however, also the center of worship of Aesculapius, the god of healing. Sufferers were allowed to spend the night in the temple while tame and harmless snakes glided over the floor. It was also a center of many Greek idols.

Jesus first commended them, "I know thy works, and where thou dwellest, even where Satan's seat is: and thou holdest fast my name, and hast not denied my faith, even in those days wherein Antipas was my faithful martyr, who was slain among you, where Satan dwelleth."

He then said to them, "Nevertheless, I have a few things against you: you have people there who hold to the teaching of Balaam, who taught Balak to entice the Israelites to sin. Repent therefore! Otherwise, I will soon come to you and will fight against you with the sword of my mouth." He ends by encouraging those who remained true: "To him who overcomes, I will give hidden manna. I will also give him a white stone with a new name written on it, known only to him who receives it."

The next church is the church of Thyatira. It did not have the political importance of the other cities but was a commercial center during Paul's day. It was not emperor worship that was attacking the church at this time, but conformity to the world for material prosperity. One main reason for its downfall was the worship of other gods. The Christians were eating meat that had been offered to idol gods and drinking wine that had been poured out as a libation to the false gods.

A woman whom Christ calls Jezebel was leading the Christians astray. Jesus addresses them in 2:20, "I have something against you: You tolerate that woman Jezebel, who calls herself a prophetess. By her teaching, she misleads my servants into sexual immorality and the eating of food sacrificed to idols. I have given her time to repent of her immorality, but she is unwilling. So I will cast her on a bed of suffering, and I will make those who have committed adultery with her suffer intensely unless they repent of their ways. I will strike her children dead, and the churches will know that I am he who searches hearts and minds, and I will repay each of you according to your deeds."

The teaching about Jezebel is taken from the Old Testament. You can look it up in 1 Kings, 18:4 and 2 Kings 9:22, if you want to reference it.

He ends with an encouragement to those who do not follow her path, "I will not impose any other burden on you: Only hold on to what you have heard until I return. To him, who overcomes and does my will to the end, I will give authority over the nations."

To the church at Sardis. Sardis was a commercial center but had fallen away from the true faith in the church. Jesus starts out by saying to them, "I know thy works, you have a reputation of being alive, but you are dead." He then commands the few people, "Yet you have a few people in Sardis who have not soiled their clothes. They walk with me, dressed white, for they are worthy. He, like them, who overcomes will be dressed in white. I will never blot out his name from the book of life, but will acknowledge his name before my Father and his angels."

To the Church at Philadelphia: The very name of Philadelphia means brotherly love, and this is a church that remained faithful to Christ and his Word. Jesus praises this church for their faithfulness. He commends them, "I know you have little strength, yet you have kept my Word and have not denied my name. I will make those who are of the synagogue of Satan, who claim to be Jews though they are not, but are liars-I will make them come and fall down at your feet and acknowledge that I have loved you. Since you have kept my command to endure patiently, I will also keep you from the hour of trial that is going to come upon the whole world to test those who live on the earth."

He tells them that he is coming soon and encourages them to hold on to their faith. He also tells them that for those who overcome and stand firm till the end Jesus will make a pillar in the temple of God. He says he will write on them the name of God and the name of the city of God, Jerusalem, which will come down from heaven. This, to me, shows a sign of ownership. Jesus is saying that he is giving a nametag, to those who endure faithfully to the end, and who tells everyone that they belong to him and their address is his address. Much like we do when we send our children to school with a nametag so they are always identifiable. They must have felt very loved and special.

The Church in Laodicea: The name Laodicea means the judgment or rule or will of the people. It is interesting that in each of the letters, our Lord addresses himself to the particular need or spiritual condition of the assembly. To this church, he addresses himself as Amen. This denotes a final, unalterable authority meaning, so be it.

Christ finds nothing to approve of the self-satisfaction and accumulated wealth of this assembly and immediately reveals utter disappointment and nausea at the half-hearted, lukewarm attitude regarding spiritual things. He tells them in 3:15, "I know your deeds, that you are neither cold nor hot. I wish you were either one or the other! So because you are lukewarm-neither hot nor cold-I am about to spit you out of my mouth. You say I am rich; I have acquired wealth and do not need a thing. But you do not realize that you are wretched, pitiful, poor, blind and naked."

Wow! Don't think they can miss the message here. But so many times I fear we are like this church, and we likewise want to straddle the fence to quote an old saying. We say we love the Lord and are committed to him, but we are unwilling to profess him to others. We are embarrassed to pray in public, witness to those around us or to take a stand for what is biblically right when it is not politically correct.

Jesus then gives a beautiful offer for them to repent and turn from their ways. "I counsel you to buy from me gold refined in the fire, so you can become rich, and white clothes to wear, so you can cover your shameful nakedness, and salve to put on your eyes, so you can see." He is trying to show them the way to true wealth, the everlasting kind that does not fade away.

Then he gives them the assurance that he is still standing at the door of their heart and knocking to see who would receive him. "Here I am! I stand at the door and knock. If anyone hears my voice and opens the door, I will come in and eat with him, and he with me. To him who overcomes, I will give the right to sit with me on the throne, just as I overcame and sat down with my Father on his throne."

What a pathetic picture in the life of Christ, standing outside of the door knocking for admittance into his own church. Yet it is a wonderful lesson of Christ's patient love and his respect for the will of man. He will never force an entrance into any heart- he must be invited in. The latch of the door of man's will is on the inside.

One thing to note is the fact that at the end of each letter, he says, "To him, who has an ear let him hear what the Spirit says to the churches." The seven spirits were directing the Words to the churches, just as the Holy Spirit inside us is directing the truths in the Word of God to us.

Discussion Questions:

1. Considering the theme of this book is redemption and regeneration, do you have the assurance in your heart that you and your loved ones have been redeemed?

2. What do you think he meant when he said, to those who have an ear to hear?

3. John starts out this lesson by saying he was in the spirit when he heard this message. What do you think that means, and how can you apply that to your life as you spend time with God?

4. Why do you think John fell down as a dead man when he saw these visions since he had seen so many supernatural things in his ministry before?

5. Has God ever picked you up from a circumstance where you were fearful and given you the assurance that he is the alpha and omega and has everything in control? Explain

6. In each of the churches, he has a message that applies particularly to them. What do you think the message would be if he were to send a letter to you?

7. He talks a lot about the worship of idols being the downfall of so many believers. What idols might be stumbling blocks in our time?

8.. Why do you think the spirit of Jezebel was such an abomination to God and the consequences following her so harsh?

Lesson 70
Revelation: Lesson 3
(Chapters 4-5)

We looked in our last two lessons at the introduction to Revelation. Who wrote it, why and to whom? It is divided into things which were, things to come and things hereafter. In our last lesson, we covered the first stage, which was the things that were; this is laid out in the letters written to the seven churches that described the condition they were in at the time.

Chapter four starts to look at the second stage, which was things to come. In this phase, we are looking from a heavenly perspective. John tells us in 4:1, "After this I looked, and behold a door was opened in heaven: and the first voice which I heard was as it were a trumpet talking to me; which said, 'Come up hither' and I will show thee things which must be hereafter." Everything from chapter 4 to the end of the book is divinely predicted to be fulfilled after the church is taken from the earthly scene. That is good news for those of us who are believers because we will have been raptured up in the air with Jesus before this all takes place.

We hear Paul confirming this when he is talking to those who have turned to God in 1 Thessalonians 1:10, "They tell how you turned to God from idols to serve the living and true God, and to wait for his Son from heaven, whom he raised from the dead-Jesus, who rescues us from the coming wrath."

He talks again about this in 1 Thessalonians 4:16, "For the Lord himself shall descend from heaven with a shout, with the voice of the archangel, and with the trump of God: and the dead in Christ shall rise first."

We see him opening the fourth chapter by saying that at once he was in the spirit and he talks about hearing a trumpet. I find it so interesting that the trumpet was used throughout the Bible. We see it starting in Exodus when Moses was on the mountain with God. Exodus 19:6, "On the morning of the third day, there was thunder and lightning, with a thick cloud over the mountain, and a very loud trumpet blast."

Then in Leviticus, we see there was a feast of trumpets, and the trumpets were used to celebrate the feast and festivals. Numbers 10:10 states, "Also at your times of rejoicing—your appointed festivals and new moon feasts—you are to sound the trumpets over your burnt offerings and fellowship offerings, and they will be a memorial for you before your God. I am the Lord your God."

In Numbers 10, God told Moses to make two trumpets out of silver and to use them to call the community of the tribes together and as a sign when it was time for them to move toward the Promised Land. Moses was also instructed to blow the trumpet to announce the year of Jubilee.

Judges 6:34 states, "Then the Spirit of the Lord came on Gideon, and he blew a trumpet, summoning the Abiezrites to follow him."

Then in Numbers 10:9 we read, "When you go into battle in your own land against an enemy who is oppressing you, sound a blast on the trumpets. Then you will be remembered by the Lord your God and rescued from your enemies."

Joshua 6:4 states, "Have seven priests carry trumpets of rams' horns in front of the ark. On the seventh day, march around the city seven times, with the priests blowing the trumpets."

Then we see it used throughout Revelation as a means of announcing things to come. Revelation 9:1 states, "The fifth angel sounded his trumpet, and I saw a star that had fallen from the sky to the earth."

Paul in the New Testament states in 1 Corinthians 15:51-52, "Behold, I show you a mystery; we shall not all sleep, but we shall all be changed. In the twinkling of an eye, at the last trump, for the trumpet shall sound, and the dead shall be raised incorruptible, and we shall be changed. "

This is just a note of interest. We mentioned earlier that God's favorite number was seven, and I think from these verses, we can safely say that his favorite musical instrument was the trumpet.

Now starting in chapter four, we are getting a view from heaven. As John beheld a door open in heaven, he found himself in the immediate presence of the One upon the Throne. It must have been unimaginable in beauty as he describes the one who sits upon the throne as a dazzling stone of deep red hue, perhaps speaking of the blood of redemption.

A rainbow like unto an emerald enhancing its beauty in an unbroken circle represents the eternal covenant that he has with man and also that his mercy has no end. You can reference back to Genesis 9 when God put a rainbow in the sky and told Noah, "This is the token of the covenant, which I have established between me and all flesh that is upon the earth."

"Surrounding the throne were twenty-four other thrones and upon them sat twenty-four elders. They were dressed in white and had crowns of gold on their heads." There can be little doubt that they represent the church. The white raiment that they wore represented their right to be there. Jesus himself refers to this in the preceding chapter when talking to the church at Sardis and addressing their sins. "You have a few people in Sardis who have not soiled their clothes. They will walk with me dressed in white, for they are worthy."

Then to the church at Laodicea, he states, "I counsel you to buy from me gold refined in the fire, so you can become rich, and white clothes to wear…" White represents purity. We see God's hair was described as white, Jesus will come back riding on a white horse, and his armies clothed in white will ride white horses. Jesus talks about a great multitude of people standing before him from every nation, tribe, and language that were dressed in white. Then we remember when Jesus was transfigured in Mark 9:3, "His clothes became dazzling white, whiter than anyone in the world could bleach them."

The crowns and being seated on thrones denotes their position of leadership. In the Old Testament, twenty-four elders were appointed to represent the entire priesthood. The chief privilege of a priest is access to God. The priest alone was allowed to go into the Holy of Holies and approach the presence of God. But when the veil in the temple was rent, the body of believers became priests and we all now have access to the throne of grace, for as the apostle Peter declared, "Ye are a chosen generation, a royal priesthood, a holy nation, a peculiar people; that ye should show forth the praises of him who hath called you out of darkness into his marvelous light." Then in Revelation 1:5-6, "Unto him that loved us, and washed us from our sins in his own blood, and hath made us kings and priests unto God and his Father."

But as you can see in verse 4:10, "The twenty-four elders fall down before him who sits on the throne, and worship him who lives forever and ever. They lay their crowns before the throne and say: "You are worthy, our Lord and God, to receive glory and honor and power, for you created all things, and by your will, they were created and have their being." This tells us that in heaven, all authority will yield to our Lord and Savior.

Some believe these twenty-four represented the leaders of the 12 tribes of Israel of the Old Testament and the 12 Apostles of the New Testament. The important thing is to know that they represented the authority of leadership given on earth and were now bowing and falling prostrate before the King of Kings. I love that even though they were honored on earth as leaders when they stand in the presence of our Savio,r we are told they fell down before him laid down their crowns. They acknowledged that he was the creator of all things and was Lord over all.

"From the throne came flashes of lightning, rumblings, and peals of thunder." John was now to understand that the beauty of the heavenly scene he was observing was a throne of judgment. Lightning and thundering are the symbols of divine judgment. Such was the case when the Israelites heard the judging voice of God at Mt. Sinai, and we are told they were fear-stricken because of his judgment of them turning to idol worship when Moses was on the mountain. Note Exodus 19:6, "On the morning of the third day, there was thunder and lightning, with a thick cloud over the mountain, and a very loud trumpet blast." I find it interesting that whenever you see a play or go to a movie and the scene needs to be scary or defining fearful drama, they always have sounds of thunder and have lights flashing like lightning to bring emphasis. Perhaps that symbol was taken from this passage.

Before the throne, seven lamps were blazing. These are the seven spirits of God. It is important to remember that seven represents completion and even though it speaks of seven spirits, it is speaking of the completeness or fullness of the person, the works, and attributes of the Holy Spirit. You can read about them in Isaiah 11:2-3, where he is giving a prophecy about Jesus coming. "A shoot will come up from the stump of Jessie, from his root a branch will bear fruit. The spirit of the Lord will rest on him-The spirit of wisdom and understanding, the spirit of counsel and power, the spirit of the knowledge and the spirit of the fear of the Lord." We will see them referred to in chapter five as well, being represented as seven horns and seven eyes.

Then it gets even more confusing because what he sees before the throne was a sea of glass that looks like crystal. This denotes the calmness of God's rule. There is always peace and calm when we come into the presence of God, even when he is judging our deeds. Remember in 23rd Psalm where he says, "The Lord is my Shepherd, I shall not want. He leads me to lie down in green pastures; he leads me beside the still waters, he restores my soul." If you have ever stood beside a still body of water, you know that it looks like a sea of glass that reflects an unspeakable calmness.

Next, we read, "In the midst of the throne and around about the throne were four beasts with eyes in front and behind. The beast had the face of a lion, ox, man and an eagle. This refers back to Ezekiel 1:4-10. We know that Ezekiel was taken up in a vision much the same way John was. In the vision, he says the heavens opened, and he saw a similar vision. He says the hand of the Lord was upon him and, "I looked, and I saw a windstorm coming out of the north-an immense cloud with flashing lightning and surrounded by brilliant light. The center of the fire looked like glowing metal, and in the fire was what looked like four living creatures. In the likeness of their faces, the four had the face of a man, and the face of a lion, on the right side; and the four had the face of an ox on the left side: the four also had the face of an eagle."

Ezekiel goes on in chapter 10 to compare them to cherubim, but the most recognized interpretation is that these are the four major aspects of the person of Christ. He is presented in the gospel of Matthew as a lion.

Mark presents him as the ox (representing the faithful servant). Luke focuses on the humanity of Jesus as a man, and John represents him like an eagle, as the divine Son of God. If these symbols were interpreted as the symbols of Christ, it would imply strength, patience, intelligence, and swiftness in passing judgment.

In thinking of the throne, you can see God the Father on the throne, surrounded by a brilliance of a crystal sea of glass. The Holy Spirit, represented by the seven spirits, and Jesus sitting beside him with eyes looking in every direction as he is interceding for us. "His eyes are going to and fro throughout the earth seeking to whom He might make himself strong." (2 Chronicles 16:9) Another version of the Bible interprets it this way, "The eyes of the Lord range throughout the earth to strengthen those whose hearts are fully committed to him."

I just imagine that he is watching with authority as the king and lion of Judah, and the understanding of a servant's heart as the ox. Remember when he said, "Come unto me all that are burdened and heavy laden, and I will give you rest, take my yoke upon you for my yoke is easy, and my burden is light." That is referring to the yoke that is put on oxen when they are plowing in a field. One ox might be weaker than the other, but when they are yoked together, the stronger one carries the weakness of the other. Then knowing because he was once on this earth as man being tempted in every way we are today he represents our human weaknesses before the Father and at the same time has the keen oversight of the eagle in all the majesty and elegance that great bird displays.

Chapter four has given us an overall picture of the scene John was looking at. In it, we have seen God the creator, but now we are going to look at Christ the Redeemer, as we start chapter five.

Revelation 5:1 states, "Then I saw in the right hand of him who sat on the throne a scroll with writing on both sides and sealed with seven seals." This is not to be confused with the book of life, which is a register of the redeemed. The book, (or scroll) that John saw in God's right hand, I believe was the book that contained the future of human history and the revelation of events that had to take place for the establishing of the coming kingdom of Christ.

The scroll had writing on both sides and was sealed with seven seals. Then John said as he was looking at this scene, he heard the voice of a mighty angel who was saying in a loud voice, "Who is worthy to break the seals and open the scroll?" But no one in heaven or earth or under the earth could open the scroll or even look inside.

Then John said, "I cried and cried because there was no one worthy to open the seals to see what was inside." Then one of the elders said, "Do not weep! See, the Lion of the tribe of Judah, the Root of David, has triumphed. He is able to open the scroll and its seven seals. Then I saw a lamb encircled by the four living creatures and the elders. He had seven horns, and seven eyes, which are the seven spirits of God sent out to all the earth. "

John's sobbing ceased when he was reassured that there was one worthy to open the seals. This was of great importance as the scroll contained the successive judgments of God from the breaking of the first seal to the breaking of the seventh and last seal when the trumpet of God shall proclaim the kingdom reign of Christ.

Then in verse five, we are told that John said he saw a Lamb, standing in the center of the throne, looking as if it had been slain. A slain lamb would bear the wound-prints, and John could not mistake his identity as the Savior of the world, for he was near the cross when the Lamb (Jesus) laid down his life. But John now is seeing him standing alive forevermore in his resurrection and glory-possessing fullness of power. This was displayed by the vision of seven horns and fullness of omniscient wisdom as portrayed by the seven eyes. As the Lamb was slain for our salvation, he alone is worthy to complete the work of redemption by reclaiming the dominion lost by Adam and taken by Satan. Remember, we talked about earlier the central theme of this book is redemption and regeneration. Opening the seals to take a look at the contents is to take a look at the final plan to redeem and restore both man and the earth to the purpose and intent of God. This takes us back to the Old Testament days of sacrifice when they enacted a type of what was to come by taking a lamb without blemish and shedding its blood to cover their sins till the eternal lamb could come and bring eternal redemption.

Then the Lamb (Jesus) comes and takes the scroll from the right hand of God. This is the moment that all creation had been waiting for because it was the preparation for the inauguration of his kingdom. The celebration was enormous. The twenty-four elders fell before him. They played harps, and they had golden bowls of incense, which represented the prayers of the saints. He said they started singing a new song. "You are worthy to take the scroll and to open its seals because you were slain, and with your blood, you purchased men for God from every tribe and language and people and nation. You have made them to be a kingdom and priests to serve our God, and they will reign on the earth."

Then John said he heard thousands of thousands of angels singing as they encircled the throne. They sang, "Worthy is the Lamb, who was slain, to receive power and wealth and wisdom and strength and honor and glory and praise!" This reminds me of what Jesus himself told his disciples when they came to arrest him, and one of them pulled his sword out to defend him. Jesus rebuked him by saying, "Put your sword back in its place for all who draw by the sword will die by the sword. Do you think I cannot call on my Father, and he will at once put at my disposal more than twelve legions of angels? But how then would the scriptures be fulfilled that say it must happen in this way?" Looking back throughout scripture helps put everything in Revelation in context. We are no doubt living in the most interesting of times as we will see as we continue in our next lesson watching the seals being opened.

Discussion Questions:

1. As you think of the tribulations that will come on the earth, do you have assurance that we as believers will already be taken away before they take place?

2. Why do you think God chose the trumpet as his instrument of choice?

3. As you look at the description of the throne of God, which aspect of its beauty most strikes you?

4. We saw that the rainbow circling the throne was a sign of the eternal covenant of God. How does knowing you have an eternal covenant with the God who created the universe affect you?

5. Which of the seven spirits of God that are encompassed in the Holy Spirit are the most meaningful to you?

6. Share what it means to you to understand the four faces of Jesus. Which of these have impacted your life the most and which one do you most identify with?

7. Jesus is described both as a lion and a lamb. Which of these pictures gives you the most comfort?

Lesson 71
Revelation: Lesson 4
(Chapter 6)

In our last lesson, we left John finding that there was one worthy to open the seals, and of course, that was Jesus.

Chapter six begins with the breaking of these seven seals, and the breaking of every seal brings tragedy on the earth. Also, with the breaking of each seal, the redemption of the earth comes one step nearer. The final chapter is being written. The climax was Jesus coming to earth as a man and offering himself as our substitute to allow for our redemption. Now the prophecies are being fulfilled, and John is being shown how the end of the ages will unfold.

He watches the Lamb, (Jesus) open the first of the seven seals. Revelation 6:1-2, "I watched as the Lamb opened the first of the seven seals. Then I heard one of the four living creatures say in a voice like thunder. "Come!" I looked, and there before me was a white horse! Its rider held a bow, and he was given a crown, and he rode out as a conqueror bent on conquest."

The first seal does not reveal the rider of the white horse. I personally believe it was Jesus, the Lion of the tribe of Judah who is now ready to go forth to take over the earth and restore it to its rightful heirs. Remember, the theme of Revelation is redemption and regeneration. Taking back what had been taken from man in the garden, Jesus now stands as the triumphant one who is ready to bring about the final chapter of that redemption.

One reason we can assume the rider is Christ is that white is connected with righteousness. Christ has white hair, the saints have white robes, God's judgment throne is white, and Christ says the overcomers in the church shall walk with him in white clothing as he talks about in Revelation 3:4.

He is coming to take vengeance, and the bow symbolizes conquest. You can reference this in Psalm 7:11-12, "God judgeth the righteous, and God is angry with the wicked every day. If he turn not, he will whet his sword; he hath bent his _bow_ and made it ready."

Next, we are told he was given a crown and was going out to conquer. We know that he was already the king of kings, the overcomer who had come to earth and overcome the enemy on our behalf, that not only would he conquer, but we who accepted him would as well.

Reference some verses that speak of this as I think it is important that we keep in mind this was all done for the benefits of the righteous saints who accepted him as their Lord and king.

Romans 8:37, "Nay, in all these things, we are more than conquerors through him that loved us."

John 16:33, "These things I have spoken unto you, that in me ye might have peace. In the world ye shall have tribulations: but be of good cheer; I have overcome the world."

We know that he had overcome the world and offered Himself as the lamb that was slain for our sins, but now he is coming back as a king with a crown on his head, signifying that he has power and authority to take back ownership of the earth and set up his kingdom; a kingdom that we all will be a part of. He gives us a promise in Revelation 3:21, "To him that overcometh will I grant to sit with me in my throne, even as I also overcame, and am set down with my Father in his throne."

Because we are the ones spoken of that have overcome, I do not think these judgments that are coming on the earth in this time of tribulation applies to the church, and it is nowhere pictured in these earthly scenes. It is not mentioned until chapter 21:9, as Jesus, is portrayed as the bridegroom coming for his bride, (the righteous ones who have accepted his offer of redemption).

Another reference is seen later in Revelation 19:11, "I saw heaven standing open and there before me was a white horse, whose rider is called faithful and true. With justice, he judges and makes war. His eyes are like blazing fire, and on his head are many crowns. He has a name written on him that no one knows but he himself. He is dressed in a robe dipped in blood, and his name is the Word of God." We know that is Jesus. John tells us that himself in John 1:14, "The Word became flesh and made his dwelling among us."

The fact that he comes with his eyes blazing shows that he has come with a fierce determination to now declare war on the evil one who has taken the property that had been created and given to his beloved ones, and he is no longer holding his restraint for vengeance on their behalf. This was spoken by the prophet Isaiah who lived 700 years before Christ was born in Isaiah 34:8, "For the Lord has a day of vengeance, a day of retribution, to uphold Zion's cause." Remember, Zion represented the righteous city of David, representing God's chosen city for his people. The city where his temple was built, where he was crucified, resurrected, and where we are told he will come back. The enemies tried to destroy it many times, but God always restored it. Isn't it interesting that Israel, this small piece of the earth is at the heart of the controversy in the Middle East that we see today? This is part of the prophecies laid out all those years ago.

Some scholars believe the rider of the white horse is the antichrist, pointing out that Christ comes after the tribulation, not before as we read in the verses above.

Then others say the four horses represent the four spirits quoted in Zechariah 6:1-11, "I looked up again and there before me were four chariots coming out from between two mountains. The first chariot had red horses, the second black, the third white, and the fourth dappled-all of them powerful. I asked the angel who was speaking to me, "What are these, my lord?" The angel answered me, "These are the four spirits of heaven, going out from standing in the presence of the lord of the whole world." This would suggest that these horses were representative of the spirits being sent out to complete the work of regeneration. He goes on to say they each go in a different direction, possibly the four-headed representation of Jesus that was seen around the throne. This to me, does not contradict that Jesus was the one who was riding out to begin this time of regeneration. After all, the four winds were a representation of the four natures of Jesus as a Lion, Eagle, Ox, and Man.

So you can draw your own conclusion as to who the rider of the white horse is, but my conclusion is that it is Jesus himself setting the end of ages in motion.

On opening the second seal, "And there went out another horse that was red: and power was given to him that sat thereon to take peace from the earth, and that they should kill one another; and there was given unto him a great sword."

We now see the introduction of a red horse with its rider. The color red denotes war and bloodshed, and this rider was permitted to take peace from the earth. God had warned throughout the Bible that we have a choice, and if we choose not to accept his gift of eternal salvation that we would be making a choice for damnation and all the destruction that comes with it.

It had been prophesied by Isaiah in the Old Testament, Isaiah 19:2, "There is no peace…for the wicked." Then Paul wrote in 1 Thessalonians 5:1-3, "Now brothers, about times and dates we do not need to write to you, for you know very well that the day of the Lord will come like a thief in the night. While people are saying, "Peace and safety," destruction will come to them suddenly, as labor pains on a pregnant woman, and they will not escape." Then the best part for us as believers is in verse 4, "But you brothers are not in darkness so that this day should surprise you like a thief. You are all sons of the light and sons of the day. We do not belong to the night or to the darkness."

The fact that he was given a great sword symbolizes the power to bring about this destruction. Judgment time is here, and by the use of the pronoun "him" we can only assume that the rider was more than a symbol. He was a divinely appointed agent, a man of blood, (I believe Satan himself), who would not only bring destruction but would pit the ones still on the earth against each other. This could include a flood of violence, riots, race wars, nations pitted against nations, genocide, etc. This is all too familiar as we look at the news today although the full wrath has not been declared yet.

As we look at the ambition of conquest of territory set loose by the rider of the white horse, it naturally leads to open warfare and bloodshed incited by the rider of the red horse. We see righteousness coming against the evil one more time for the final conquest. The king of kings must meet face to face with the evil that has ruled over his domain, and once and for all bring restoration.

This just reminds me of the patience Jesus must have had when he was faced with this same evil one on the mountain of temptation. He encountered him as he went up into the mountain after he was baptized where Satan flaunted the fact that he owned the kingdoms of this earth and tried to get Jesus to take him on at that time. Jesus knew the time had not yet come and with more restraint, than I can imagine, looked him in the face and remained steadfast to his plan and purpose. Luke 4:5, "The devil led him up to a high place and showed him in an instant all the kingdoms of the world. And then said to him, "I will give you all their authority and splendor, for it has been given to me, (by Adam), and I can give it to anyone I want. So if you worship me, it will all be yours." Jesus simply said, "It is written: Worship the Lord your God and serve him only."

Then he took him to the highest point of the temple in Jerusalem and said, "If you are the Son of God, throw yourself down from here, and your God will command his angels to guard you and lift you up in their hands so that you will not strike your foot against a stone." Jesus answered, "It is written, do not put your God to the test." Then the devil left him until an opportune time, and I think this is that time. The restraint Jesus had held back was now being released.

This brings us to the opening of the third seal, which sends a black horse and rider to earth. Revelation 6:5, "When the lamb opened the third seal, I heard the third living creature say, "Come!" I looked, and there before me was a black horse! Its rider was holding a pair of scales in his hand. Then I heard what sounded like a voice among four living creatures, saying, "A quart of wheat for a day's wages, and three quarts of barley for a day's wages, and do not damage the oil and wine!"

The average daily pay for a working man was a denarius and would normally buy eight quarts of wheat or twenty-four quarts of barley (which was considered the poor man's grain). The message here is that the famine would be so bad that it would take a man's whole daily wage just to buy his own grain ration, with little left for his family or other needs.

The phrase not to harm the oil and wine, (two other staples of ancient cultures), could mean that God was putting restraints on the horseman not to damage those as he does the grain supply. These were staples that the rich would have in more abundance. It could mean that the rich will still have plenty adding to the frustration of the famine, or it could mean that those were already scarce and therefore care must be taken not to hurt what little remained.

It is interesting that in the Old Testament, black is associated with the effects of famine or starvation. In Lamentations 4:8, we see Jeremiah lamenting about the destruction of Jerusalem remembering the bright and prosperous times, but now he describes it as, "But now they are blacker than soot; they are not recognized in the streets. Their skin has shriveled on their bones; they have become as dry as a stick. Those killed by the sword are better off than those who die of famine; racked with hunger, they waste away for lack of food from the field."

Another reference that had been prophesied to the fact that the rider was holding a pair of scales was proclaimed in Ezekiel 4:16 where God says of Jerusalem's inhabitants, "They shall eat bread by weight and with anxiety, and they shall drink water by measure and in dismay."

The message is clear that the intent and purpose of the black horse is to bring about famine and scarcity, not at all a tactic that is unusual for enemies to cut off the food supply that weakens and brings a new level of frustration and hatred. It is no wonder that this time of judgment is called the great tribulation, for hunger is a living death.

Next, we have the opening of the fourth seal. Revelation 6:8, "Behold a pale horse! Its rider was named, death, and Hades was following close behind him. They were given power over a fourth of the earth to kill by sword, famine, and plague, and by the wild beast of the earth."

Here the pale horse is followed by an assistant called Hades or the grave. It is the place of the dead, and he is there to pick up after death does his work. But notice he is only given authority over a quarter of the earth's population at the time.

The deadly duo is given authority to destroy in four distinct ways, sword (war), famine, plague, and wild beasts. These four forms of death were spoken of by the prophets as found in Ezekiel 14:21, "For this is what the Sovereign Lord says: how much worse will it be when I send against Jerusalem my four judgments-sword and famine and wild beasts and plague-to kill its men and their animals." This, of course, was when God was warning against the continual sinfulness and idolatry of the people at that time.

Something to think about is the spiritual connotation of these passages. Amos 8:11-12 says, "The days are coming, declares the Lord God when I will send a famine on the land-not a famine of bread, nor a thirst for water, but of hearing the words of the Lord. They shall wander from sea to sea, and from north to east; they shall run to and fro, to seek the word of the Lord, but they shall not find it." Spiritual death follows spiritual starvation, so this is a lesson on the importance of not allowing our hearts to suffer from a spiritual famine and not be found ready when our time comes to meet judgment.

The fifth seal takes us from the earthly judgments generated by the horsemen to the heavenly presence of the departed saints. Revelation 6:9, "When he opened the fifth seal, I saw under the altar the souls of those who had been slain because of the word of God and the testimony they had maintained. They called out in a loud voice, "How long, Sovereign Lord, holy and true until you judge the inhabitants of the earth and avenge our blood? Then each of them was given a white robe, and they were told to wait a little longer until the number of their fellow servants and brothers who were to be killed was completed."

Here John identifies those who had been slain for their faith and even as their bodies were placed in a grave, their spirits went to heaven and are sheltered in a sacred and holy place close to God. Paul talks about this in 2 Corinthians 5:1, "Now we know that if the earthly tent we live in is destroyed, we have a building from God, an eternal house in heaven, not built with human hands." Here we see these souls who have poured out their blood as an offering as they held fast to their faith. Their martyrdom as faithful witnesses leads naturally to their plea, "How long, O God?"

It is interesting to note that these departed souls are conscious in heaven, able to address God directly, and able to remember fully their experiences on earth. They are asking God to avenge them and the price they paid, God in all his loving and patient way, gives them white robes to wear and tells them to wait just a little longer than the time will come soon.

So often, we like the saints in heaven, want to take revenge as life seems to be unfair, but as Paul tells the church at Rome, "Do not take revenge, my friends, but leave room for God's wrath, for it is written: "It is mine to avenge; I will repay, says the Lord." This is a lesson we can take from this passage as we sometimes get overly anxious to see justice done in our lives. God is telling us as he did to these saints, be patient and know that I will always be true to my Word.

Then he tells them in Romans 12:21, "Do not be overcome by evil, but overcome evil with good." God has a plan and place for all those who are faithful, and we are told these saints were under the altar. Not going to the altar or standing beside the altar, but had been put in a place under the altar signifying they were sheltered around the throne of God in a place of honor prepared for those who stand steadfast, and true to God and his Word.

Then the opening of the sixth seal abruptly returns us to events on earth with enormous disturbances occurring during the tribulation period. Revelation 6:12, "I watched as he opened the sixth seal. There was a great earthquake. The sun turned black like sackcloth made of goat hair, the whole moon turned blood red, and the stars in the sky fell to earth, as late figs drop from a fig tree when shaken by a strong wind. The sky receded like a scroll, rolling up, and every mountain and island was removed from its place."

I find an interesting comparison to the beginning in Genesis when God first formed the earth, Genesis 1:2, "Now the earth was formless and empty, darkness was over the surface of the deep, and the Spirit of the Lord was hovering over the deep." In the next few verses, we see him forming a perfect structure for the inhabitants he is going to create in His image to live here. Genesis 1: 9, "And God said, "Let the water under the sky be gathered to one place, and let dry ground appear.
God called the ground land, and the gathered waters he called seas. And God saw that it was good." We know he goes on in this chapter to describe the skies and the perfect environment he has created from this deep pit of darkness.

Interesting how, now that we are at the end of times, the breaking of this seal brings indescribable fear upon the people left. They run and hide, begging the rocks and mountains to fall on them and hide them from the wrath of the one who has been teaching and begging them to repent and avoid this terrible day. I also find it interesting that verse 15 states that at this time, "Then the kings of the earth, the princes, the generals, the rich, the mighty, and every slave and every free man ran for cover in caves." There suddenly did not seem to be any amount of status, or wealth, or position that mattered on that day.

Jesus warns of this time in Luke 25:26 when he is teaching of what to expect in the end times. "There will be signs in the sun, moon, and stars. On the earth, nations will be in anguish and perplexity at the roaring and tossing of the sea. Men will faint from terror, apprehensive of what is coming on the world, for the heavenly bodies will be shaken. At that time, they will see the Son of Man coming in a cloud with power and great glory. When these things begin to take place, stand up and lift up your heads because your redemption is drawing near."

Again, we hear Jesus talking about this being a time of redemption, and we see the events taking place on the earth much like a contractor coming in and destroying an outdated and dilapidated building so he can build a new and updated structure. We read more about this in Revelation 21:1 "Then I saw a new heaven and a new earth, for the first earth had passed away, and there was no longer any sea. I saw a holy city, the New Jerusalem, coming down out of heaven from God, prepared as a bride beautifully dressed for her husband."

If we have accepted him as our Lord and Savior, we can rejoice at the coming of the Lord and live in a new heaven and a new earth prepared for us by God. But to those who fail to heed the warnings, it will be a time of fear and desolation.

Discussion Questions:

1. As you look at the opening of these seals, which one speaks more truth to challenge you?

2. The seals were opened in a particular order. How can you compare the opening of the seals in the sequence they came to our personal walk with Christ?

3. As you see Christ coming back as a conqueror, what hope does that give you as you go through your daily life?

4. As you looked at the saints being sheltered under the altar of God, did it inspire you to take a more bold stand for the cause of Christ?

5. From what events that are happening today can you see the time is drawing near? If it were to come today, would you be ready to stand before Christ and give account for the way you lived your life?

Lesson 72
Revelation: Lesson 5
(Chapter 7)

We ended chapter six with the seals being opened and bringing judgment on the earth. It was sure devastation with a great earthquake, the sun turning black, the moon turning blood red and the stars falling from the sky. It went on to say the sky receded like a scroll and every mountain and island were removed from their place.

Keep in mind that the purpose of the book of Revelation is to reveal the time of redemption and regeneration. Redemption means to return to the original owner. God is our original owner, and he is releasing the completion of his plan for us to be restored to himself, the one who designed and created us.

Man lost three things in the fall: his soul, his body and the ownership of the earth.

Man's body was intended to live forever, but God gave him perimeters to live by to maintain the eternal state they were created to live in. Genesis 2:17 states, "But of the tree of the knowledge of good and evil, thou shalt not eat of it, for in the day that thou eatest thereof thou shalt surely die." We know that is exactly what happened. Man started a process of deterioration, and his days became numbered. Genesis 2:19 tells us, "In the sweat of thy face shalt thou eat bread, till thou return unto the ground; for out of it was thou taken: for dust thou art, and unto dust shalt thou return. Listen to Jobs take on it Job 14:1-2, "Man who is born of a woman is few of days and full of trouble. He comes out like a flower and withers; he flees like a shadow and continues not."

God promises us that part of his plan is to restore our body and we find that promise in 1 Corinthians 15:51-52, "Listen, I tell you a mystery: We will not all sleep, but we will all be changed—in a flash, in the twinkling of an eye, at the last trumpet. For the trumpet will sound, the dead will be raised imperishable, and we will be changed."

We know that the moment man disobeyed God the fellowship of their soul, the connection of oneness was broken, and their soul was hungry for the connection they had lost. David expresses it in Psalm 6:3, "My soul is in deep anguish. How long, Lord, how long?" There is a deep void in our being that was created for our relationship with our creator, and the book of Revelation is about the amazing plan of restoration to fill that void in all three areas.

"The Lord, your God, will circumcise your hearts and the hearts of your descendants, so that you may love him with all your heart and with all your soul, and live." (Remember, circumcision was the sign of those set apart for God during Abraham's time to set aside a genealogy to bring Jesus into the world). Since Jesus came and set the plan in motion by being our sacrifice, when we accept him as our savior, the circumcision God is concerned with is the circumcision of our hearts. We are no longer separated from God and now have access to him through prayer. The sign of that was when the curtain was torn from top to bottom that housed the presence of God in the Holy of Holies in the temple. No longer did man have to offer a physical sacrifice or go through a priest to be connected to God. The thing that takes the place of the sacrifices in the Old Testament is explained in Psalm 51:17, "My sacrifice, O God, is a broken spirit; a broken and contrite heart. You, God, will not despise. Psalm 35:9 says, "Then my soul will rejoice in the Lord and delight in his salvation. Then my favorite is found in Psalm 23, "The Lord is my shepherd, I shall not want, He maketh me to lie down in green pastures, He leads me beside still waters, He restoreth my soul."

Now we see the order of restoration. The soul is restored at the time of conversion or salvation, the body at the rapture and the earth at second coming when the earth will be cleansed and restored. We will see that in Revelation 21, "Then I saw a new heaven and a new earth, for the first heaven and the first earth had passed away...."

Regeneration means to restore to the original state. We, as God's children, are the original owners of the earth. It was created for us, and now God is about to restore it back to us. The earth has been in a state of turmoil since Adam gave over his title deed to a fallen angel. God put a curse on the earth at that time which you can read about in Genesis 3:17-18. Now in the book of Revelation, the time has come to reclaim the earth and restore it back to the state it was in when it was God's masterpiece for the children he created in his image. To do that God has to judge those who contributed to the corruption and to cleanse it. Now God is bringing judgments to the earth and all those who do not receive the gift of salvation and eternal life.

Needless to say, this brings panic and fear on all mankind as the last passage in chapter 6 reads, "The kings of the earth, the princes, the generals, the rich, the mighty, and every slaved and every free man hid in caves among the rocks of the mountains."

I believe that before this happens, we believers who are still alive will be taken up from the earth (called the rapture) along with those who have fallen asleep (died). Paul tells us, in 1Thessalonians 4:13-17, "Brothers and sisters, we do not want you to be uninformed about those who sleep in death so that you do not grieve like the rest of mankind who have no hope. For we believe that Jesus died and rose again, and so we believe that God will bring with Jesus those who have fallen asleep in him. According to the Lord's Word, we tell you that we who are still alive, who are left until the coming of the Lord, will certainly not precede those who have fallen asleep. For the Lord, himself will come down from heaven, with a loud command, with the voice of the archangel and with the trumpet call of God, and the dead in Christ will rise first. After that, we who are still alive and are left will be caught up together with them in the clouds to meet the Lord in the air. And so we will be with the Lord forever. Therefore, encourage one another with these words."

I think this is what will happen at the time we see the first seal opened, and the white horse with Jesus comes with a bow and crown riding out to conquest and conquer. He is coming to claim his children, both those who have already died and those who are still alive. After that, the judgments come, and Satan is raging havoc on the earth, as he knows his time is coming to an end. Remember the purpose of the seals (or judgments) is to kick Satan out of the earth and give it back to its original owner. He has established a stronghold and is not going to willingly leave, so God has set the battle plan in motion, and it was written and sealed until the time for implementation was here. Now he is giving John a peek at the battle strategy. John is told to record it for us so we can be prepared and know a time of total redemption is coming.

Keep in mind that in chapter five, we saw God sitting on the throne and in his right hand was a book. Revelation 5:1 tells us, "And I saw in the right hand of him who sat on the throne a book written within and on the backside, sealed with seven seals." I find it interesting that when Jesus ascended into heaven that he sat down at the right hand of God. Now we see God holding the title deed to the earth in his right hand, which would be where Jesus was seated. Jesus is the only one who was worthy to open the seals to reveal the things that must take place for the final redemption and regeneration. Within these seals are the seven judgments that must take place to evacuate Satan.

While we see the sixth seal bringing incredible judgment on fallen mankind, we see in chapter seven God showing mercy upon his people. Chapter seven, starts with a halt of the four angels who had been sent to bring these judgments. We read in Revelation 7:1-3, "I saw four angels standing at the four corners of the earth, holding back the four winds of the earth to prevent any wind from blowing on the land or on the sea or on any tree. Then I saw another angel coming up from the east, having the seal of the living God. He called out in a loud voice to the four angels who had been given the power to harm the land and the sea: "Do not harm the land or the sea or the trees until we put a seal on the foreheads of the servants of our God."

Keep in mind that the purpose of the plagues was to strike hard at Satan and his kingdom-both spiritual and material. They also were intended to hurt the earth because there had to be a cleansing as we have talked about earlier because this is a time of redemption and regeneration, both of mankind and of the earth that had been taken over by an evil influence.

It is interesting to read in Genesis God's account of creating the heaven and earth, hanging the sun to give light by day and the moon by night, etc. Then to see how during this time we see the sun that was intended to give light turning black, the moon turning blood red, the stars falling from the skies, and the skies receding like a scroll. It is truly as if God is bringing about a re-do. It has taken thousands of years to bring this about legally and justly and has cost him the greatest suffering possible of sending his own son to earth and having him humiliated, beaten and crucified to pay the price of redemption for mankind.

Now once again, we see him watching out for his children as the time of redemption is drawing near and the great battle is about to begin. Now we see the four angels standing on four corners of the earth with the power to start the process of regeneration. (Four corners, is a figure of speech viewing earth as a room). In the first century and today, it signifies the sum total or entirety, of the earth and its spaces, or the four major points of the compass.)

Then we see coming out of the east another angel carrying the seal of God in his hand. He tells the angels to restrain themselves until God has provided protection for his servants during this time of judgment, just as Lot was protected from the destruction of Sodom and Gomorrah. Luke 17:28-29 states, "Likewise also as it was in the days of Lot; they did eat, they drank, they bought, they sold, they planted, they built but the same day Lot went out of Sodom it rained fire and brimstone from heaven, and destroyed them all."

We see also this protection in the time of the prophet Ezekiel before the destruction of Jerusalem. You may recall that God caught him up in a vision and showed him the worshiping of idols in the temple, even by the elders. Here God is bringing judgment to the city but tells him in Ezekiel 9:4, "Go throughout the city of Jerusalem and put a mark on the foreheads of those who grieve and lament over all the detestable things that are done in it." Then in verse 6, God gives instructions on releasing his wrath, "Slaughter old men, young men, and maidens, women, and children, but do not touch anyone who has the mark."

This reminds me also of the time when God sent the plagues on Egypt but had the Israelites put a seal of blood on their doorpost so the angel of death would pass over them.

Then when he set aside the lineage of Abraham to be the family or genealogy to bring the plan of redemption to the world by the birth of Jesus, they too were given a mark of circumcision.

One thing is clear. God's plan has not changed since he gave instructions to Adam and Eve in the garden. "Obey and enjoy peace and all the wonders I have created for you, or disobey and you will eat of the tree of destruction." Although they screwed up, he so loved us that he gave us another chance to make a right choice. He even calls that choice being made righteous. That means that we are once again in right standing with God and put back in the place Adam and Eve were before the fall.

We are told in Ephesians 1:13, "And you also were included in Christ when you heard the word of truth, the gospel of your salvation. Having believed, you were marked with a seal, the promised Holy Spirit, who is a deposit guaranteeing our inheritance until the redemption of those who are God's possession." When we accept Christ as our savior, his spirit resides within us as our seal and guarantee of eternal life.

Then we hear Jesus himself in John 6:27, "Labour not for the meat which perisheth, but for that meat which endureth unto everlasting life, which the Son of man shall give unto you: for him hath God the Father sealed."

God is now about to bring closure to Satan's lease on the earth, and it will only come through destruction and a great battle. However, in his great love, once again, we see him setting apart the lineage of Israelites.

The angels are at their stations and have the winds of war ready to go when God suddenly sends another angel to tell them to halt until He once again protects his chosen people. He wants to be sure there are witnesses left to speak the truth of salvation and gives instructions for the angel to place the Lord's seal on 12,000 from each of the tribes of Israel. That totals 144,000. Then he lists the tribes so there can be no question as to who they were. He is setting aside 144,000 Jews to be witnesses to Christ as the true Messiah during this terrible time to come. We don't know what that seal is exactly, but it could be the same as it is for those of us who are believers, which is the Holy Spirit. Perhaps the Holy Spirit descends on them much like the event in the upper room when the Holy Spirit came upon those waiting there.

The 144,000 of verse four and the great multitude spoken of in verse 9 are different, "After this I looked and there before me was a great multitude that no one could count, from every nation, tribe, people, and language, standing before the throne and in front of the Lamb." One is the elect of Israel, and the other is from all nations. With one group, the scene was on earth. With the other, the scene is in heaven.

Then the Bible says that after the tribulation had begun, a great revival had taken place as the witnesses had proclaimed Jesus was indeed the Messiah they had been waiting for. Now we see that they were raptured and taken before the throne and given white robes. They were worshiping God, and one of the elders inquired as to who this new group of people was. "Then one of the elders asked me, 'These in white robes who are they, and where did they come from? I answered, Sir, you know. And he said, these are they who have come out of the great tribulation; they have washed their robes and made them white in the blood of the Lamb." "For the Lamb at the center of the throne will be their shepherd; he will lead them to springs of living water. And God will wipe away every tear from their eyes." These verses are more meaningful now that you see the ones who it was spoken of. These saints were the ones who would have been through the tribulation, and no doubt had shed many tears for what they had to witness.

Reference Jesus' own words about this time in Matthew 24:29-31, "Immediately after the tribulation of those days, shall the sun be darkened, and the moon shall not give her light, and the stars shall fall from heaven, and the powers of the heavens shall be shaken: And then shall appear the sign of the son of man in heaven: and then shall all the tribes of the earth mourn, and they shall see the Son of Man coming in the clouds of heaven with power and great glory. And he shall send his angels with a great sound of a trumpet, and they will gather his elect from the four winds, from one end of the heavens to the other."

As we get a peek into heaven, it is interesting to note that those who come in the first rapture of saints, (some call them the church saints), are seen having harps and holding bowls of incense. "Each one had a harp, and they were holding golden bowls of incense, which are the prayers of God's people." It would indicate that possibly these saints will be in service to God in some form.

Then in the description of the raptured saints from the time of tribulation we are told in 7:9, "After this I looked, and there before me was a great multitude that no one could count, from every nation, tribe, people, and language, standing before the throne and before the lamb wearing white robes and holding palm branches in their hands." Palm branches were a symbol of victory and praise. You may remember when Jesus was riding a donkey into Jerusalem before his crucifixion that people lined up and waved palm branches giving honor and praise to the one who had come to redeem and restore them to God. Possibly they will make up the choir in heaven and lead worship.

Back on earth, those who have believed in Jesus as the Messiah will have his name on their foreheads, and it will be visible at the time of judgment for all to see.

It will be visible to the demons as we see in 9:4, "And it was commanded them that they should not hurt the grass of the earth, neither any green thing, neither any tree; but only those men who have not the seal of God in their foreheads." We will see later that the antichrist will try to emulate God's mark with a mark of his own which will bring anything but safety. The strategy of Satan has not changed since the beginning. He is called the father of lies. Just as he deceived Eve by telling her a lie, he will be doing the same thing when we see him later in chapter 13. Here he is telling people that if they do not take his mark, they will not be able to buy or sell goods, but by taking his mark, they will be protected.

We see the truth of this in chapter 14 when it is revealed in verses 9 and 10, "And the third angel followed them, saying with a loud voice, if any man worships the beast and his image, and receive his mark in his forehead, or in his hand the same shall drink of the wine of the wrath of God which is poured out without mixture into the cup of his indignation; and he shall be tormented with fire and brimstone in the presence of the holy angels, and in the presence of the Lamb."

So now we have been a witness along with John into the throne of God and what is going on in heaven, as well as the future events that will come on earth when the seal is broken on the book that contains the future events that must take place.

We see also God's unbelievable love and protection for those who trust him. He has been warning those through generations, and his Word has not changed. Obey and reap the blessings of his presence and heaven, or rebel, and you will be out from under his protection. We are told over and over in the Old and New Testament that all will come before the judgment seat of God.

As you think back over our past lessons, you'll recall the numerous times God has given instructions and how the rebellious nature of mankind tested his patience. In his great love for us, he made provisions for escape and redemption. We especially see his love and protection for the Jews, who were his chosen people before the Gentiles were given the gospel.

Discussion Questions:

1. As you reflect back on this lesson, what can we learn about what heaven is going to be like?

2. As you read about the rapture of the dead (those asleep) being raptured first, does that give you comfort for those who have gone on before you? Also the fact that if we are still alive, we will be caught up in the sky with them?

3. Which of the horses impacted your thinking about end times and why?

4. As you envision Jesus riding on the white horse with a bow in his hand to conquer the enemy on our behalf, how does that influence your view of him as your savior?

5. God sealed those who received him. How does it make you feel to know that you are sealed in God?

6. Why do you think God paused in the middle of the seals to protect His chosen people?

7. As we reflect on the theme of Revelation being redemption and regeneration, does that give you a clearer understanding of the purpose of the destruction that will take place?

Lesson 73
Revelation: Lesson 6
(Chapter 8-9)

We saw in our last lesson a suspension in the opening of the seals of judgments for God to show his mercy on 144,000 Israelites before the continuation of the judgments to come. This has ended the first three and one-half years of the seven years of tribulation.

Now we see Christ, the Lamb, is to resume the opening of the seals. After opening the seventh seal, there was silence in heaven for about half an hour. The purpose of this pause we do not know, but some think it was for the reading of the now completely unrolled scroll and the preparations that are to be made for their fulfillment. Remember, the scroll is the title deed to the earth with the strategy that is about to be released to win it back for mankind.

It was almost as if at this time, all creation was holding its breath in anticipation of what was to come. During this silence, John beheld seven angels, and to them were given seven trumpets. The seven angels were to sound seven successive trumpet blasts to announce the final judgments that were to come on the wicked of the earth.

Remember we discussed in an earlier lesson how trumpets have always been used to announce special occasions. We see them playing an even greater role as we study the fulfillment of the prophecies.

One of particular interest to our previous lesson comes with the rider of the white horse who had a bow in his hand and is coming for us as a warrior for redemption. Zechariah 9:14, "After the Lord shall be seen over them, and his _arrow_ shall go forth as the lightning: and the Lord God shall blow the trumpet and shall go with whirlwinds of the south."

Again in the prophet Joel, "Blow ye the trumpet in Zion and sound an alarm in my holy mountain: let all the inhabitants of the land tremble: for the day of the Lord cometh, for it is nigh at hand."

After John saw the seven angels with trumpets, he saw a single angel appear. "Then appeared another angel who had a golden censer, who came and stood at the altar. He was given much incense to offer, with the prayers of all God's people, on the golden altar in front of the throne. The smoke of the incense, together with the prayers of God's people went up before God from the angel's hand."

Interesting that there was a pause in heaven, and then there was a prayer meeting in heaven before these judgments were released. That could have been the purpose of the half-hour pause: To allow the saints to offer prayers for what was to come.

We can look back at the worship in the temple and see a censor filled with live coals was used in worship. Incense was poured on the coals, and the incense of sweet-smelling smoke drifted upwards-symbolizing believers' prayers ascending to God.

Then we see in the next verse the angel taking the censer, filling it with fire from the altar, and hurling it on the earth. The result is lightning, thunder, and an earthquake.

We see earthquakes happening at different times in the Bible, always announcing a major event. We see this at the announcing of the law when Moses went up on Mt. Sinai. Exodus 19:18 states, "And Mount Sinai was altogether in a smoke, because the Lord descended upon it in fire: and the smoke thereof ascended as the smoke of a furnace, and the whole mount quaked greatly."

Then there was an earthquake at Christ death. We find in Matthew 27:50-51, "Jesus, when he had cried again with a loud voice, yielded up his spirit. And behold, the veil of the temple was rent in twain from the top to the bottom: and the earth did quake, and the rocks rent."

Then it is always good to hear Jesus' own words of warning on the events to come. Matthew 24:29 says, "Immediately after the tribulation of those days shall the sun be darkened, and the moon shall not give her light, and the stars shall fall from heaven, and the powers of the heavens shall be shaken."

Now we see as the first angel sounds the trumpet that this is announcing the first judgment. "The first angel sounded his trumpet, and there came hail and fire mixed with blood, and it was hurled down on the earth. A third of the earth was burned up, a third of the trees were burned up, and all the green grass was burned up."

Peter talked about this in 2 Peter 3:5-11, "For this they willingly are ignorant of, that by the Word of God the heavens were of old, and the earth standing out of the water and in the water: Whereby the world that then was being overflowed with water, perished: But the heavens and the earth, which are now, by the same word are kept in store, reserved unto fire against the day of judgment and perdition of ungodly men. But, beloved, be not ignorant of this one thing, that one day is with the Lord as a thousand years and a thousand years as one day. The lord is not slack concerning his promise, as some men count slackness; but is longsuffering to us-ward, not willing that any should perish but that all should come to repentance. But the day of the Lord will come as a thief in the night; in which time the heavens shall pass away with a great noise, and the elements shall melt with fervent heat, the earth also and the works that are therein shall be burned up. Seeing then that all these things shall be dissolved, what manner of persons ought ye to be in all holy conversation and godliness?"

Peter wrote that the earth "perished," but he didn't mean that it had totally vanished. The earth was purged by water (flood during Noah's day), and now it will be purged again by fire. People are purged by blood, the blood of Jesus for our redemption, but the physical earth will be purged by fire. All of the last seven plagues have fire.

Interesting to note that five of the plagues of Egypt occur again in Revelation. You can reference them in Exodus 9:22-24.

We also see God raining fire and brimstone on Sodom and Gomorrah. Genesis 19:24, "Then the Lord rained upon Sodom and Gomorrah brimstone and fire from the Lord of heaven."

We are told in this judgment that the hail/fire burns a third of the earth. It mentions the earth's trees, which would include the fruit and timber producing trees, which would impair the lifestyle of those dependent on them. Also, we are told it burned the grass, which would include the crops and man's food supply. All this would make life more miserable for those who remained.

The second angel blows his trumpet, and it affects the oceans and seas of the earth. John sees something like a flaming meteorite striking the earth. It causes a third part of the sea, a third of the animals, and a third of the ships to be destroyed. We also see it turns a third of the waters to blood, again reminding us of the foreshadow found in Exodus 7:20, "And Moses and Aaron did so, as the Lord commanded; and he lifted up the rod, and smote the waters that were in the river in the sight of Pharaoh, and in the sight of his servants; and all the waters were turned into blood."

The third angel blew his trumpet and is similar to the second trumpet, except it affects the land rather than the sea. It causes a third part of the rivers and fresh waters upon the land to be made bitter or poisonous. The meteorite evidently strikes into the ground where there are headwaters for three great rivers. The meteorite and its vapor impart something poisonous to the water of one of the rivers. This was even prophesied by Jeremiah 9:15, "Therefore thus saith the Lord of hosts, the God of Israel; Behold, I will feed them, with wormwood, and give them water of gall to drink." Wormwood represents God's judgment on disobedient people. Wormwood represents a class of bitter plants, which were poisonous.

The fourth angel blew his trumpet and struck the celestial bodies that affect life on earth. A third each of the sun, moon, and stars are darkened, leaving earth's day and night with less light. Interesting that it was on the fourth day of creation God made the light and on the fourth trumpet judgment, he will diminish the lights by one third. Darkness has always been a sign of judgment, and we can again refer back to Egypt being judged by darkness as in, Exodus 10:21-23. The prophets also associated darkness with God's judgments. We find that in Joel 2:2 and Amos 5:18. Then we know that when they crucified Jesus one-quarter of the day was darkened, Matthew 27:45 states, "Now from the sixth hour there was darkness over all the land unto the ninth hour."

When we consider humanity's dependence on light for food, energy, guidance, and daily living, we can appreciate the impact darkness might have on daily living, as well as the psychological depression, as it is a symbol of impending doom.

The first four trumpets are directed toward the earth, the sea, the rivers, and the sun. These judgments are caused by inanimate forces: heat, blood, fire, wormwood, and darkness. The last three will be directed toward people. They are judgments brought by living beings: one comes from the bottomless pit: one from the river Euphrates, and one from heaven.

Now still under the sound of the reverberating trumpet blast, John beheld an eagle. Some say it was an angel flying in the midst of the darkened mid heaven crying, "Woe, woe, woe, to the inhibitors of the earth," because of the previous judgments, as well as the three to come, which will be the most terrifying than any of the judgments. They will cause men to seek death when exposed to these final and full judgments of end times. Some call these the woe judgments, as they are definitely warning of a new level of punishment.

In the blowing of the fifth trumpet, we see a star falling from the sky to the earth. The star was given the key to the Abyss. Revelation 9:2-3 tells us, "When he opened the Abyss, smoke rose from it like the smoke from a gigantic furnace. The sun and sky were darkened by the smoke from the abyss. And out of smoke, locusts came down upon the earth and were given power like that of scorpions of the earth. "

The star represented here was Satan. Looking back at Luke 10:18, we see Jesus describing Satan's fall: "And he said unto them, I beheld Satan as lightning fall from heaven."

Stars were used throughout the Bible for many references. Jesus even called himself a star. "Revelation 22:16, "I Jesus have sent mine angel to testify unto you these things in the churches. I am the root and the offspring of David, and the bright and morning star."

Peter referred to him as well as being the day-star, 2 Peter 1:19, "We also have a more sure word of prophecy; whereunto ye do well that ye take heed, as unto a light that shineth in a dark place, until the day dawn, and the day star arise in your hearts."

We often see angels symbolized as stars. We saw earlier that the angels of the seven churches were referred to as seven stars. Then in Judges 5:20, we see them fighting a battle but referred to as stars. "They fought from heaven; the stars in their courses fought against Sisera."

Also, we see the star being Satan as he is given the key to the bottomless pit and allowed to unleash his wrath on the earth. The locusts released were undoubtedly not common locusts, but a visual for John to see how the destruction of these demons would strike. These would be demons embodying creatures and endowing them with the power to strike painful torment so bad that men will seek death to flee from them. "They were not given power to kill them, but only to torture them for five months. And the agony they suffered was like that of a scorpion when it strikes a man. During those days, men will seek death, but will not find it: they will long to die, but death will elude them."

The description John gave of these swarming demon creatures is almost beyond the power of imagination. He describes them in 9:7-10, "They looked like horses prepared for battle. On their heads, they wore something like crowns of gold, and their faces resembled human faces. Their hair was like woman's hair, and their teeth were like lions' teeth. They had breastplates like breastplates of iron, and the sound of their wings was like the thundering of many horses and chariots rushing into battle. They had tails and stings like scorpions, and in their tails, they had power to torment people five months."

Then we are told that they had a king over them named Abaddon in Hebrew, or Apollyon in Greek, which means destroyer. This, of course, is Satan ,and he has many ranks of angels under him. He seems to have authority over the bottomless pit at this time to let these demons out. Eventually, we know that the key will be taken from him, and he will be thrown into the bottomless pit for a thousand years.

Now we see him being released as the destroyer that his name implies. However, the scope of the demonic activity is limited. Not to attack the vegetation and only to hurt those who have not the seal of God on their foreheads. This also would exclude the 144,000 sealed ones we saw in chapter seven. Also, their activity is limited to five months.

A painful time for those on earth at this time when Satan uses his key to unlock the forces of hell or the abyss, but we know as believers that Jesus tells us ultimately he has the keys. Revelation 1:18 states, "I am the living one; I was dead, and now look, I am alive forever and ever, and I hold the keys to death and Hades." So Satan has the key to cause havoc for a short season, but Jesus has defeated him for us and actually given us the keys. We see him explaining this to Peter when he is telling him that he is going to use him to establish the church. "And I tell you that you are Peter, and on this rock, I will build my church, and the gates of Hades will not overcome it. I will give you the keys of the kingdom of heaven; whatever you bind on earth will be bound in heaven and whatever you loose on earth will be loosed in heaven."

To summarize the judgment under the sound of the fifth trumpet blast, John writes, "One woe is past; and behold, there will come two woes more hereafter."

Next, John sees in his vision the sixth angel sounding his trumpet, and he says he heard a voice from the four horns of the golden altar, which is before God saying, "Loose the four angels who are bound in the great river Euphrates. And the four angels who had been kept ready for this very hour and day and month and year were released to kill a third of mankind. The number of mounted troops was two hundred million."

As we look back at the Euphrates, it is interesting to note that the Euphrates flowed through the garden of Eden and the fact that these angels had been held back in the very place where sin came into the world is of particular interest. Genesis 2:10, "A river flowing from the garden flowed from Eden; from there it was separated into four headwaters." Then it goes on to name the rivers as Pishon, Gihon, Tigris, and Euphrates. So we see the demonic angels that are waiting to release the wrath on the earth actually being held back in the very place where sin originated.

Another interesting fact about the angel holding back the Euphrates is that the Euphrates traditionally divides the East from the West and marks the line between Israel and its pagan enemies, Assyria and Babylon. As we stated earlier, somewhere in the region, Adam and Eve sinned; Cain committed the first murder; and the tower of Babel was built in arrogant rebellion against God. So it is not surprising that Satan's four powerful warriors would be bound there waiting to devastate unrepentant people of the world.

John describes them in 9:17, "Their breastplates were fiery red, dark blue, and yellow as sulfur. The heads of the horses resembled the heads of lions, and out of their mouths came fire, smoke, and sulfur. A third of mankind was killed by the three plagues of fire, smoke, and sulfur that came out of their mouths. The power of the horses was in their mouths and in their tails; for their tails were like snakes, having heads with which they inflict injury. "Wow, I don't think any writer of a horror show could create such a creature.

You would think that after all this the remaining mankind would repent, but they continued to worship demons and idols of gold, silver, bronze, stone, and wood-idols that could not see, hear or walk. We are also told in verse 21 that they also did not repent of their murders, their magic arts, sexual immorality, or their thefts.

Between the sounding of the sixth trumpet and the blast of the seventh, there was a suspension of time, the same as there was between the opening of the sixth and seventh seal while a group of witnesses was sealed from coming punishment. This pause will be the longest one, and we will resume with the events that brought the need for this pause in our next lesson.

Discussion Questions:

1. As you think over the pause between the opening of the seals, what do you think the purpose was? What role do you think the prayers of those believers who are already around the altar played?

2. Read 2 Corinthians 2:14-15. What does the phrase that we are to be an aroma of Christ mean to you?

3. Choose one of the six trumpets and give a life lesson we can learn from.

4. What do you think it means that we have been given the keys, and what is bound on earth is bound in heaven?

5. What do you think was the reason men continued to sin even after such devastation?

6. What lesson can we learn as we think of coming judgment?

Lesson 74
Revelation: Lesson 7
(Chapter 10)

At the end of chapter 9, we saw the first half of the tribulation coming to an end, and half the earth's population is dead. Now we are beginning the final phase of the time of tribulation. We are about to see things go from bad to worse.

We have seen two of what was called the woe judgments, and now we are tracking along with John in his vision and seeing time suspended, as there was a lapse in time between the sixth and seventh seal. Now we are about to experience the third and final woe judgment.

The first two saw the unleashing of fallen angels upon mankind. Demons that had been locked up in the pit of hell and were under the rule of Abaddon, (Satan), came out with vicious plagues of creatures that were like locust to torment those rebellious people who continued to reject God's teaching. There also were released beings of almost indescribable horror to kill a third of mankind.

Although these seem almost too evil to conceive, they were used as instruments of God's judgment upon unrepentant man. Keep in mind that they, as do we all, have a choice to make. It is important to remember that God is a just God and has always stayed true to his Word. Beginning with Adam and Eve in the garden, he provided a way of right and wrong and told them the consequences of a wrong choice.

Let's pause a minute and look back through time when God made this clear in all his dealings with mankind.

Proverbs 10:16: "The wages of the righteous is life, but the earnings of the wicked are sin and death."

Jeremiah 21:8: "Furthermore, tell the people, 'This is what the Lord says: See, I am setting before you the way of life and the way of death.

Deuteronomy 30:15-20: "See, I set before you today life and prosperity, death and destruction. For I command you today to love the Lord your God, to walk in obedience to him, and to keep his commands, decrees, and laws; then you will live and increase, and the Lord your God will bless you in the land you are entering to possess. But if your heart turns away and you are not obedient, and if you are drawn away to bow down to other gods and worship them, I declare to you this day that you will certainly be destroyed. You will not live long in the land you are crossing the Jordan to enter and possess. This day I call the heavens and the earth as witnesses against you that I have set before you life and death, blessings and curses. Now choose life, so that you and your children may live and that you may love the Lord your God, listen to his voice, and hold fast to him. For the Lord is your life, and he will give you many years in the land he swore to give to your fathers, Abraham, Isaac, and Jacob."

I want us to keep a focus on the eternal picture of what is going on during this time. The time of judgment is coming after years of pleading and begging his children to come to him and enjoy the life he intended when he created them. Because of his great love, he gave us a choice so that we would be more than robots and could choose to love and obey him just as any father wants for his children. He went to the greatest degree of sacrifice to give his only son to come and redeem us when we made a wrong choice, but just like Adam and Eve, we have to obey and walk in the path he has laid out for us. Now we are seeing the remnant of mankind having to make that same choice, and even after seeing the destruction being brought on the earth; the people are still worshiping idols and living in a disobedient lifestyle.

Now we are ready for the third and final woe, but before it happens, John sees another angel come who had a little book open. We pick up in chapter 10, "And I saw another mighty angel come down from heaven clothed with a cloud: and a rainbow was upon his head, and his face was as it were the sun, and his feet as pillars of fire: And he had in his hand a little book open: and he set his right foot upon the sea, and his left foot on the earth, and cried with a loud voice, as when a lion roareth: and when he had cried, seven thunders uttered their voices."

There are two trains of thought as to who this angel is but the one that most speaks to me is that he is the Lord Jesus Christ who has come to stake his claim on the earth again.

I will lay out both trains of thought so you can come to your own conclusion. First, let's look at the thought that it was Jesus. The angel is called a mighty angel, and we know he is called the Almighty. Next, he is clothed with a cloud, which refers to deity. Let's look back in both the Old and the New Testaments that clarifies that.

Exodus 19:16 states, this is when Moses went up on the mountain to meet with God. "And it came to pass on the third day in the morning, that there was thunder and lightning, and a thick cloud upon the mount…." We know that God was in that cloud, and that is the way he expressed himself to Moses at that time.

Matthew 24:30 states, "And then shall appear the sign of the Son of man in heaven: and then shall all the tribes of the earth mourn, and they shall see the Son of man coming in the clouds of heaven with power and great glory."

Revelation 1:7, states "Behold, he cometh with clouds; and every eye shall see him, and they also which pierced him: and all kindreds of the earth shall wail because of him."

Next, it says he has a rainbow around his head. We know that at the beginning of John's vision when he saw the throne where the Godhead was seated, he saw a rainbow about the throne. Rainbows always show God's relationship with the earth as in the covenant shown to Noah that the earth would never be destroyed by a flood again. (Genesis 1:26-28.)

Now we see the time has come for Jesus to come and redeem and restore the earth to its rightful owner, and he is the only one who can take that stand. It says he puts his right foot on the earth and his left on the sea as if to say; I am here reclaiming all that has been stolen from mankind. He is repossessing the earth, and he is the only one who has earned the right to do that.

The mighty angel's face is described as the sun. Christ's countenance was described in a similar manner earlier in Revelation 1:16, "And he had in his right hand seven stars: and out of his mouth went a sharp two-edged sword: and his countenance was as the sun shineth in his strength." Also, in Malachi 4:2 in the Old Testament, he is described as the sun of righteousness. "But unto you, that fear my name shall the Sun of righteousness arise with healing in his wings…"

The angel's feet are described as pillars of fire, similar to the description of Jesus' feet in 1:15, "And his feet like unto fine brass, as if they burned in a furnace; and his voice as the sound of many waters."

He is, of course, called the Lion of Judah as we see many times in the Bible. Revelation 5:5, records, "And one of the elders saith unto me, weep not: behold, the Lion of the tribe of Judah, the Root of David, hath prevailed to open the book, and to loose the seven seals thereof."

Other scholars think it could have been Michael since he is referred to in the book of Daniel when the events of end-time prophecy were given to Daniel.

We read about it in Daniel chapter 12. "At that time, Michael, the great prince who protects your people, will arise. There will be a time of distress, such as has not happened from the beginning of nations until then. But at that time your people—everyone whose name is found written in the book—will be delivered. Multitudes who sleep in the dust of the earth will awake: some to everlasting life, others to shame and everlasting contempt. Those who are wise will shine like the brightness of the heavens, and those who lead many to righteousness, like the stars forever and ever. But you, Daniel, roll up and seal the words of the scroll until the time of the end. Many will go here and there to increase knowledge.

Then I, Daniel, looked, and there before me stood two others, one on this bank of the river and one on the opposite bank. One of them said to the man clothed in linen, who was above the waters of the river, 'How long will it be before these astonishing things are fulfilled?' The man clothed in linen, who was above the waters of the river, lifted his right hand and his left hand toward heaven, and I heard him swear by him who lives forever, saying, 'It will be for a time, times and half a time. When the power of the holy people has been finally broken, all these things will be completed.'

I heard, but I did not understand. So I asked, 'My lord, what will the outcome of all this be?' He replied, 'Go your way, Daniel, because the words are rolled up and sealed until the time of the end. Many will be purified, made spotless and refined, but the wicked will continue to be wicked. None of the wicked will understand, but those who are wise will understand. From the time that the daily sacrifice is abolished, and the abomination that causes desolation is set up, there will be 1,290 days, (3 ½ years). Blessed is the one who waits for and reaches the end of the 1,335 days. As for you, go your way till the end. You will rest, and then at the end of the days you will rise to receive your allotted inheritance.'"

Also, we see in Revelation 7:2 that Michael leads the charge against Satan. "Then war broke out in heaven. Michael and his angels fought against the dragon, and the dragon and his angels fought back."

I will leave it up to you to decide what your conclusion is, but it was ordained by God whatever the case and whoever the angel is.

Next, we see the mighty angel standing on the sea and land raising his right hand to heaven. He swears before him who lives forever and ever, who created heaven and everything in it and the earth and all it contains, and the sea and its inhabitants that there should be no more delay but that when the seventh angel blew his trumpet, God's veiled plan would be fulfilled.

Then the voice from heaven spoke to John again and told him, "Go and get the unrolled scroll from the mighty angel standing upon the sea and land." John says he approached him and asked him for the book (scroll). The angel told him he could have it but gave an unusual instruction. "Take it and eat it. At first, it will taste like honey, but when you swallow it, it will make your stomach sour!"

Sure enough, John said he did as he was told and it was as the angel had said, sweet in his mouth but gave him a stomachache when he swallowed it. The little book is the title deed to the earth, and although this means that the time all had been waiting for is drawing near, it also means that the fulfillment of the final judgments are coming and they will be more painful than what has already been done.

We can reference the prophecy of Ezekiel. Ezekiel 3:1-2 states, and he said to me, "Son of man, eat what is before you, eat this scroll; then go and speak to the people of Israel.' So I opened my mouth, and he gave me the scroll to eat. Then he said to me, 'Son of man, eat this scroll I am giving you and fill your stomach with it.' So I ate it, and it tasted as sweet as honey in my mouth." Just like John, Ezekiel was being sent to Israel, and God wanted him to consume the revelation of his Word so he would be prepared to deliver the message he was about to be sent. The Word was like honey, but the aftermath was going to be painful. I compare it to a mother about to give birth. The joy of what is about to happen brings sweet happiness, but the process of pain that must be endured brings anxiety.

Then we remember Jesus himself telling his disciples to eat his flesh as being symbolic of being consumed with the revelation he was giving. John 6:51-54 states, "I am the living bread that came down from heaven. Whoever eats this bread will live forever. This bread is my flesh, which I will give for the life of the world." It goes on to read, "Then the Jews began to argue sharply among themselves, 'How can this man give us his flesh to eat?' Jesus said to them, 'Very truly I tell you, unless you eat the flesh of the Son of Man and drink his blood, you have no life in you. Whoever eats my flesh and drinks my blood has eternal life, and I will raise them up at the last day. Whoever eats my flesh and drinks my blood remains in me, and I in them.'"

So we can see that even though it seems strange to have John eat the scroll, it was a term that was used to be consumed with a truth. Psalm 119:103 states, "How sweet are your Words to my taste, sweeter than honey to my mouth!"

After assimilating the revelation of the little book, John is told he must prophesy again among many peoples, nations, tongues, and kings. He has more prophetic work to do. No doubt this includes the judgments that are soon to come that are in the little book. The fact that he was told to prophesy to many people, nations, tongues, and kings mean he is speaking to all mankind. The seventh trumpet is about to blow, and all mankind is about to be thrown into chaos.

Discussion Questions:

1. As you read about the horrible judgments that are to come in Revelation, does it incite fear in you or present more of a challenge to live a life of righteousness?

2. As you look at the evidence of who the mighty angel who is giving John the book, what are your thoughts as to who he might be?

3. Are the words in the Bible like honey in your mouth or do you sometimes feel like they are more sour and create fear and anxiety?

4. We see that after John consumed the words of the book he was told to go and prophesy. Now that you are getting a fuller grasp of the truth of the Bible, do you feel compelled to share it with more people?

Lesson 75
Revelation: Lesson 8
(Chapter 11)

We left John in our last lesson being told by an angel to go and prophesy to many nations.

The next instruction seemed as strange as the one telling him to eat the little book that was the title deed to the earth. Now the angel gave him a measuring stick and told him to go and measure the Temple of God, including the inner court where the altar stands, and to count the worshipers. Also, he was told not to bother to measure the outer court because it had been turned over to nations and they would trample it for 3 ½ years. The stick was a measuring instrument, but also an instrument of judgment. Judgment was to begin at God's house. We see that mentioned in 1 Peter 4:17, "For the time is come that judgment must begin at the house of God: and if it first begins at us, what shall the end be of them that obey not the gospel of God?"

Some interpreters say this is symbolic of Israel and some say it is the church. There are some facts that suggest, however, that it was the literal temple of tribulation. The fact that he wants the worshipers counted may mean those who were being true to God and who would be protected. The outer court indicates those who will plunder and are disobedient.

The temple at that time was called the tribulation temple, and that was where the final tribulation would start. The temple was the place of worship and a symbol of God's place in the hearts of man.

The history of the temple began with David. He desired to build it, but God only let him prepare for it. His son, Solomon, built the first temple, and the Shekinah glory of God appeared in it. When the Jews would not repent of their idolatry, however, Nebuchadnezzar raided their temple. Seventy years later they returned and built another temple, but it was far inferior to Solomon's temple.

About 40 years before Jesus was born, Herod renovated the temple and added to it. It was then called Herod's temple. You might remember that Jesus prophesied that Herod's temple would be destroyed. That was when he went to the temple where they were buying and selling in the house of God. He was angry and turned over the tables. The Jews then responded to him, "What sign can you show us to prove your authority to do all this?" Jesus answered them, "Destroy this temple, and I will raise it again in three days." They replied, "It has taken forty-six years to build this temple, and you are going to raise it in three days?" But the temple he had spoken of was his body. After he was raised from the dead, his disciples recalled what he had said. Then they believed the scripture and the words that Jesus had spoken. Titus, a Roman general, destroyed Herod's temple in 70 A.D.

God's temple in this dispensation is the church, which is you and me. 1 Corinthians 6: 19-20 states, "Know ye not that your body is the temple of the Holy Ghost which is in you, which ye have of God, and ye are not your own? For ye are bought with a price: therefore glorify God in your body, and in your spirit which are God's."

Jesus prophesied of an end-time temple as well, which we will see fulfilled at the sounding of the seventh trumpet. Revelation 11:15 tells us, "And the seventh angel sounded his trumpet; and there were great voices in heaven, saying, the kingdoms of this world are become the kingdoms of our Lord, and of his Christ, and he shall reign for ever and ever."

We saw this also prophesied by the prophet Daniel, "And the kingdom and dominion, and the greatness of the kingdom under the whole heaven, shall be given to the people of the saints of the most high, whose kingdom is an everlasting kingdom, and all dominions shall serve and obey him." The bottom line is that in the end, God will give his kingdom to the saints as it is their inheritance.

We also know that the Jews, under the antichrist, will rebuild the temple and offer sacrifices again. This will be in the midst of the tribulation period. We also know that in the midst of the tribulation the antichrist will break his agreement with the Jews and set up his idol in the temple. We hear the word abomination used in reference to the temple, and it should be noted that abomination always refers to idolatry.

We read about the antichrist in 2 Thessalonians 2:3-4, "Let no man deceive you by any means: for that any shall not come, except there come a falling away first, and that man of sin be revealed, (antichrist), the son of perdition; who opposeth and exalteth himself above all that is called God, or that is worshipped; so that he as God sitteth in the temple of God, shewing himself that he is God."

Here we see in Revelation 13: 14-15 that the antichrist has the ability to fool people with miracles. "And deceiveth them that dwell on the earth by means of those miracles which he had power to do in the sight of the beast; saying to them that dwell on the earth, that they should make an image to the beast, which had the wound by a word, and did live. And he had power to give life unto the image of the beast, that the image of the beast should both speak, and cause that as many as would not worship the image of the beast should be killed." The beast was the idol set up in the temple to be worshiped.

We are told, that during the time of the antichrist, that the godly will flee to the wilderness. We know the rest of the story is that at the second coming of Christ there will be a great earthquake just as there was at his crucifixion. Zechariah 14:4 tells us that the Mount of Olives will be split in half and the Tribulation Temple, which the Jews will be returning to build, as well as, the Mosque of Omar that stands on the site where Solomon's Temple was built, will be destroyed as part of that territory. Then we know the Millennial Temple will be built.

An interesting point to make is how sacred this temple mound is. We see Jews, Muslims, and Christians all considering it holy territory. We know that some Jews consider it sacred because it is where Abraham went up to sacrifice Isaac, and where the temple stood where they could go and offer a sacrifice and appease God for another year. It was where the holiest of holies was where God met the priest of old to accept the sacrifice. You would think that at the time of Jesus' crucifixion when the curtain was torn from top to bottom and God was no longer veiled from mankind, the Jews would receive him as the Messiah. It was also accompanied by earthquakes and other signs to demonstrate the authenticity of God's son.

It is so sad to go to the Wailing Wall in Jerusalem, which is part of the remaining foundation that the original temple was built on, and see the Jews rocking back and forth waiting for the coming of the Messiah. They even put prayers through the cracks of the wall to be offered up through Old Testament protocol. It is there that the Jews are planning to rebuild the temple and a Jewish research group has already created many of the vessels to be used in temple worship. Also, there is a generation of animals that are being bred to be worthy to be sacrificed at that time. So while they are waiting for the Messiah to come, we believers are waiting for his second and final return.

That was just a little of the history of the temple. Now let's go back to the sounding of the seventh trumpet. Before the seventh trumpet is sounded, two unique witnesses begin their testimony in Jerusalem. We read about this in Revelation 11:3-12, "I will give power unto my two witnesses, and they shall prophesy a thousand two hundred and threescore days, (3 1/2 years)." There is much debate as to who these two witnesses will be. Some think Elijah and Enoch, having as evidence the passage that says it is appointed man once to die, and they both were translated and did not see death. Others say it will be Elijah and Moses, but they are divinely designated as "these two prophets."

Interesting that Elijah is always mentioned. His influence has spanned time and is still being celebrated today during the Easter season. As part of the Jewish families' celebration of the Passover feast, a dinner is served called the Seder dinner where they set an empty place setting and leave an empty seat for Elijah to come and join them. At some point in the meal, a child is sent to open the door to see if Elijah has come to announce that the Messiah has come. This stems from the prophecy in Malachi 4:5, "Behold, I will send you Elijah the prophet before the great and awesome day of the Lord comes."

We also see in Luke 1:17-21 that John the Baptist came, "in the spirit and power of Elijah," to prepare the way for Jesus' first coming. We read his own words in Luke 3:16, "I indeed baptize you with water, but one mightier than I cometh, the laces of whose shoes I am not worthy to unloose: he shall baptize you with the Holy Spirit and with fire." We also see him answering the Jews and Levites who had been sent from Jerusalem to quiz him as to who he was. "And they asked him, who then are you? Art thou Elijah? And he saith, I am not. Art thou that prophet? And he answered, no. Then said they unto him, who art thou so that we can give an answer to the ones who sent us? What sayeth you of thyself?" John answered by saying, "I am the one crying in the wilderness, make straight the way of the Lord, as said the prophet, Elijah." So we can see that Elijah's identity was never questioned as it had been prophesied that he would make an appearance as one of the two witnesses. The important thing is that if God wanted us to know their identity, he would have stated it but the important thing is what God's purpose will be fulfilled through them.

These two witnesses are described as two olive trees and as two candlesticks. This indicates that they are anointed ones and light bearers testifying of God's truth in the darkest days of human history. They are given judgment powers, and no one or scheme can harm them until their testimony is finished. We read in Revelation 11:6, "These have power to shut heaven, that it rain not in the days of their prophecy: and have powers over waters to turn them to blood and to smite the earth with plagues, as they will."

We then see that when they have finished their testimony that Satan will come out of the bottomless pit of hell and make war against them and they will be killed. It is only with God's permission that this happens to fulfill his plan and prophecy. Their death causes great celebration, and their bodies are publicly displayed for three and a half days. However, the party quickly came to an end when the Spirit of life from God enters them, and they stand upon their feet. You can imagine the fear that entered all those who watched and even more when they heard a loud voice from heaven say, "Come up hither." At that, they actually saw the two prophets, whom they had slain, alive and ascending up to heaven in a cloud. This is the third and final rapture in Revelation. The first was the overcoming church we read about in chapter 4. Then the martyred saints in chapter 7 and last the two witnesses in chapter 11.

When the witnesses are raptured, that same hour there will be a great earthquake that levels a tenth of the city. Then everyone that is left will give glory to God. Loud voices from heaven said, "The kingdoms of this world now belong to our Lord and to his Christ, and he shall reign forever and ever." At this the twenty-four elders around the throne threw themselves down in worship, saying, "We give thanks, Lord

God Almighty, who is and was, for now, you have assumed your great power and have begun to reign. The nations were angry with you, but now it is your turn to be angry with them. It is time to judge the dead, and fear your name, both great and small-and to destroy those who have caused destruction upon the earth." We likewise will be part of that judgment, as we all will be judged for our time on earth.

Then in heaven, the temple of God was opened, and the Ark of his Covenant could be seen inside. Remember the ark was a sacred rectangular box, or chest, constructed at God's direction for the Old Testament tabernacle. It was carried by the Levites on poles because it was too holy for human hands to touch. Within it was Israel's most cherished relics: Aaron's rod that budded, the stone tablets of the law given to Moses, and a pot of manna. The Ark of the Covenant was God's most sacred symbol of the Mt. Sinai covenant he had made with the sons of Abraham, and it was placed in the holy of holies where a symbolic sacrificial offering could be made each year until the time Jesus could come as the eternal sacrifice for our sins. By opening up heaven and allowing it to be seen was an announcement that God had not forgotten his promise to the Jewish nation.

Even though a lot of emphases is being put on the Jews at this time, Gentiles are an equal part as they have been grafted into the family of the sons of Abraham by their belief in Jesus Christ as Savior. You can reference this in Romans 11:11-32. When by faith we are grafted into the family of God, we are equal in every way to the chosen people God set apart to bring about his plan of redemption. Galatians 3:29 states, "After faith has come, we are no longer under a schoolmaster. For ye are all the children of God by faith in Christ Jesus. For as many of you as have been baptized into Christ have put on Christ. There is neither Jew nor Greek; there is neither bond nor free, there is neither male nor female: for ye are all one in Christ Jesus." How wonderful to see that we are all branches drawing from the same resources of the root of Jesus when we receive him as our Messiah.

When the ark was seen, lightning flashed, and thunder crashed, and there was a great hailstorm, and the world was shaken by a mighty earthquake. Seven thousand people were killed, and this was a wake-up call to many survivors because we are told in 11:13, that in their terror they "gave glory to the God of heaven."

The effective witness by the two faithful saints, supported by dramatic divine confirmation caused many to begin to be obedient and worship the true Messiah.

We are about to look at the third of the woe judgments. The first you may remember was the demonic locust plague from the pit of hell. This came at the sound of the fifth trumpet.

The second was the demonic army of four unbound Euphrates angels. This came at the sounding of the sixth trumpet. Then we have a lengthy interlude.

Now we see the focus on three events that happen in heaven. First, we hear the loud voices in heaven declaring that the "kingdom of the world has become the kingdom of our Lord and of his Christ." With the sounding of this final trumpet, the declaration of transfer of the title deed to the earth has been delivered back to its rightful owner, and it will so be forever and ever.

After the twenty-four elders fall and worship him, they declare that the dead be judged, which refers to all who have lived and died on earth, whether just or unjust. It is a time for review, "rewarding your servants, the prophets and saints, and those who fear your name, both small and great."

That God will reward his people, in varying degrees, for their faithful service, is a familiar theme in the Bible. In Matthew 16:27, Jesus speaks of varying degrees of rewards. "For the Son of Man is going to come in his Father's glory with his angels, and then he will reward each person according to what he has done." Paul also mentions this in detail in 1 Corinthians 3:10-15 and other parts of his teachings. Far too often we focused so much of our time on getting salvation, and our ticket punched to get into heaven. That is a free gift through grace, but the rewards we will receive are earned through faithful service.

One thing to remember as we go through Revelation is the fact that although it seems like a book of doom and judgment, there is always a worship service in heaven before each judgment. God always honors our worship. We should not overlook the role of the prayers we saw earlier going up as incense from the saints, as well as, the times we see the elders fall prostrate to worship. God always involves his children in the plan as we are called to be co-laborers with Christ.

Discussion Questions:

1. God gave instruction to measure the temple, not the outer courts but the inner holy areas. As you consider yourself the temple of God and are being measured internally, what might you want to hide from the measuring stick?

2. As we compare the instruction not to bother with the outer court, can you see how God is more concerned about the holy of holies that resides in our hearts? How much focus do you spend on physical appearance, as compared to the inner part of your heart?

3. I have heard it said that the price of anything is the price someone is willing to pay for it. The passage in 2 Corinthians we read earlier in the lesson says we were bought by God at a price. How does this affect your view of your worth?

4. The two witnesses are sent as anointed light bearers to the world at the appointed light bearers to the world at that appointed time. We likewise are to be the same today. Does your life reflect this?

5. What lesson can we learn from the two witnesses as they are true to God's instructions, yet seemingly defeated by the devil in the end? God resurrects them in the fullness of his glory. Does their example encourage you to stay true to the Lord, no matter what?

6. Why do you think God opened up heaven to let the Ark be seen?

Lesson 76
Revelation: Lesson 9
(Chapter 12)

Chapter 11 ended with God opening up the doors of heaven and allowing the Ark of the Covenant to be seen. As we discussed in our last lesson, the ark always represented victory and the final conflict is about to take place. God is showing his people that he will be victorious over the enemy. However, the battle goes on but now it is seen from earth's viewpoint. Before we were looking from heaven as to what was happening on earth, but now we are seeing from earth what will take place in heaven.

We see John not only seeing the Ark of the Covenant, but also two other signs. One is the sign of a woman clothed with the sun and the moon under her feet, and a crown of twelve stars upon her head. This woman symbolizes the church, which is made up of born-again believers.

She is said to be clothed with the sun. As we look back at Malachi 4:2, we see Jesus described as the sun. "But unto you that fear my name shall the Sun of Righteousness arise with healing in his wings; and ye shall go forth, and grow up as calves of the stall." Then we see Jesus calling himself the light of the world. John 8:12 states, "Then spake Jesus again unto them, saying, I am the light of the world: he that followeth me shall not walk in darkness, but shall have the light of life."

We know that Jesus gives us his light as we follow him. He gives us his light by his Word and the power of the Holy Spirit. Psalm 119:105 says, "Thy Word is a lamp unto my feet, and a light unto my path."

Matthew 5:14 says, "Ye are the light of the world. A city that is set on a hill cannot be hid." Then we see Peter confirm that the church is clothed with light. 1 Peter 2:9 tells us, "But ye are a chosen generation, a royal priesthood, a holy nation, a peculiar people; that ye should shew forth the praises of him who hath called you out of darkness into his marvelous light."

Then it says of the woman that she has the moon under her feet. The moon here represents darkness and the evil forces of Satan. Men who had mental illness used to be called lunatics because they had supposedly looked at the moon too long. We see Satan's deeds done in the darkness under the dim light of the moon. We know that Satan has power to deceive but can never stand in the presence of the great and beautiful light of Jesus' presence. We can refer back to the passage in Ephesians 1:22-23, where Paul was talking about the church, "And hath put all things under her feet, and gave her to be the head over all things to the church. Which is his body, the fullness of him that filleth all in all." Jesus also tells us in Luke 10:19, "Behold, I give you power to tread on serpents and scorpions, and over the power of the enemy: and nothing shall by any means hurt you. Notwithstanding in this rejoice not, that the spirits are subject unto you; but rather that your names are written in heaven."

She was also said to have a crown of 12 stars on her head. The 12 stars represent the church's leadership. There were 12 apostles who made up the leadership of the early church. Going further back to the Old Testament, there were leaders from the 12 tribes of Israel, who we saw in the previous chapter, seated around the throne. Also, God sealed 12,000 from each of the twelve tribes as witnesses to the people of the tribulation period.

Jesus speaks of this in Matthew 19:28, "And Jesus said unto them, verily I say unto you, that ye which have followed me, in the regeneration when the Son of man shall sit in the throne of his glory, ye also shall sit upon twelve thrones, judging the twelve tribes of Israel." Note that he referred to the regeneration of the time that he would sit on the throne. Always keep in mind that the theme of the book of Revelation is redemption and regeneration.

Next, we see that the woman is with child and is travailing in birth. Knowing that the woman represents the church, we can see the comparison of pain that takes place for the presentation of a child, with what must happen to bring forth a glorified church to live and reign with Jesus forever in his heavenly kingdom.

A woman in labor is a familiar Old Testament metaphor for the nation of Israel. We see that in Isaiah 26: 17, "Like a woman with child, that draweth near the time of her delivery, is in pain, and crieth out in her pain, so have we been in your sight oh Lord." Then we see Paul also used this symbol in 1 Thessalonians 5:3, "For when they shall say, peace and safety; then sudden destruction cometh upon them, as travail upon a woman with child; and they shall not escape."

There appeared another wonder in heaven and that was that of a red dragon with seven heads, ten horns and seven crowns upon his head. Then we are told that his tail drew the third part of heaven and cast them to earth.

Next, we see the dragon standing before the woman about to give birth, just laying in wait to destroy the child as soon as she delivers. "And she brought forth a man child, who was to rule all nations with a rod of iron: and her child was caught up unto God, and to his throne." We know that this is referring to Jesus and the overcoming church. Let's look back at the very beginning in Genesis where this was referenced. Genesis 3:15 states, "And I will put enmity between thee and the woman, and between thy seed and her seed; it shall bruise thy head, and thou shalt bruise his heel."

We know Satan's goal has always been to destroy the Messianic line so the Messiah could not defeat him at the cross. We can look back at the days of Moses when the Israelite male babies were ordered to be killed in hopes to destroy the line this male child would come through. Then during the days of King Herod we see the children of Bethlehem were ordered slain in hopes to find this male child before he could grow up and fulfill his destiny. Satan's goal was to stop the one thing that could bring to an end his reign on the earth. This child did not have the seed of sin passed down through man, but was conceived in a young virgin by the Holy Spirit to preserve a godly seed to restore our union with God. You can see why Satan was in a panic to find this hidden one who could destroy him. We saw God in his infinite wisdom preserving the genealogy and the promised one, and now John is given a vision to see the final fulfillment be this promise.

There is no doubt that this dragon mentioned here is Satan himself. We will see later in chapter 20 that the dragon is described as "that ancient serpent, which is called the devil and Satan." That John describes him as a great red dragon possibly suggests his great power and bloodthirsty brutality. The description of Satan as the red dragon here is a reflection also of the vision that Daniel had of end time events. You can read the account of his vision in Daniel 7 if you want to reflect further on the comparisons of what was shown to both John and Daniel of what was to come.

The fact that Satan swept down a third of the stars of heaven and cast them to earth represents the angels that followed him in his rebellion against God. We have already seen in chapter 9 that a star can be symbolic of an angel, 9:1, "And the fifth angel sounded, and I saw a star fall from heaven unto the earth: and to him was given the key of the bottomless pit."

We see many references also to these fallen angels in the New Testament. Jesus himself refers to them in Matthew 25:41, "the devil and his angels." Also Jude 1:6 states, "And the angels which kept not their first estate, but left their own habitation, he hath reserved them in everlasting chains under darkness unto the judgment of the great day." Then in 2 Peter 2:4, "For if God spared not the angels that sinned, but cast them down to hell, and delivered them into chains of darkness, to be reserved unto judgments."

In this description, we see the power and authority with which the devil operates in our present world system. Jesus referred to him as "the prince of this world." However, in the description of the child here, he says, "he will rule with a rod of iron. "We can look back in Psalm 2:7-9 where God says to his son, "You are My Son. I will make nations your heritage…you shall break them with a rod of iron."

We are then told that the child was caught up to God and to his throne, speaking of Jesus' ascension. Satan now sees that he has failed to destroy the man-child who is now in heaven interceding for those who believe in Him. Hebrews 7:25 tells us, "Wherefore he (Jesus), is able also to save them to the uttermost that come unto God by him, seeing he ever liveth to make intercession for them. "

We see there must have been a gap between 12:5 and 12:6, which is not unusual in prophecy as we are looking at the big picture. This prophetic gap begins in verse 5 with the Lord's ascension and runs its course until the future days of the great tribulation.

Now that Jesus has been taken out of reach of Satan's grip, he now turns on the woman who is the remnant of Israel. Romans 9:5 describe Israel, "Whose are the fathers, and of whom as concerning the flesh Christ came, which is over all, God blessed forever." God has always had a plan of protection for his chosen people. Here we see her flee from the persecution and wrath of Satan to a place God has prepared for her. She is given two wings of a great eagle that she might fly into the wilderness. This symbolizes her speedy and sure flight to the refuge that had been prepared for her. You might remember that God used the same symbol of eagle's wings when he brought the Israelites out of Egyptian bondage. "…I bare you on eagles' wings, and brought you unto myself."

We see Satan's fury against this remnant in 12:17, "And the dragon was wroth with the woman, and went to make war with the remnant of her seed, which keep the commandments of God, and have the testimony of Jesus."

However, his time of power is quickly coming to an end and literally, all hell is about to break loose.(I wonder if this is where that expression came from.) We see in verse 7, that Michael and his angels fought against the dragon and his angels. The result was that Satan was cast out of heaven. "And the great dragon was cast out, that old serpent, called the devil and Satan, which deceiveth the whole world: he was cast out into the earth, and his angels were cast out with him." Victory has been won. Up until now Satan had access to heaven to accuse the brethren before God but now he is cast out to earth.

Rejoicing is heard in heaven as we read in verse 10, "And I heard a loud voice saying in heaven, now is come salvation, strength and the kingdom of our God, and the power of his Christ: for the accuser of our brethren is cast down, which accused them before our God day and night."

Satan has lost his ability to reside in the stellar heavens. He now seems to be trying to rob us of our inheritance. It is interesting to read the next verse as to how the believers overcame him. "They overcame him by the blood of the lamb, and by the Word of their testimony; and they loved not their lives unto the death." Interesting that we now overcome the devil by the same path. We have to accept the blood that Jesus shed for us and then we are baptized and give our testimony as to having been born again. After that we now bear the family name of our new heavenly family. We are then sealed with the Holy Spirit as the guarantee of our union.

There was great rejoicing in heaven because the way had been cleared for the coming kingdom and the rightful owner to reign on earth again. The transfer of the title deed to the earth was taking place.

Even though there was rejoicing in heaven, there was a warning given to those on earth. "Woe to the inhabitants of the earth and of the sea! The devil has come down to you in great wrath, because he knoweth that he hath but a short time." Jesus himself spoke of this in Matthew 24:21, "For then shall be great tribulation, such as was not since the beginning of the world to this time, nor shall ever be." Although this time is more horrible than we can imagine, God had preserved a remnant of his people as he always has. History is a record of the fact that every power that has attempted to wipe out the Jews has been thwarted to their own destruction, from Haman of old to the Hitlers of our day.

We see this in the symbolic imagery of Satan trying to destroy the woman as she flees into the wilderness by casting out water as a flood to cause her to be carried away, but the earth helped the woman by opening up her mouth and swallowed up the flood. Satan could not destroy those who had kept the testimony of Jesus Christ.

Discussion Questions:

1. We see at the beginning of this lesson the passage in Malachi that Jesus comes with healing in his wings. What does that passage mean to you?

2. Jesus is called the sun, or light, in our lives. We read in Psalms that his Word is a lamp unto our feet and a light unto our pathway. Can you give examples how this has been true in your life?

3. Jesus tells his disciples who are rejoicing that the spirits are subject to them not to rejoice over that, but more at the fact that their names are written in the book of life. Are you as excited to have power in your spiritual life or that you will live eternally with him? Sometimes we get caught up in the miracles and miss the main point of our eternal purpose.

4. The plan put forth in Revelation is compared to a pregnant woman. As you compare your walk with the Lord assuming salvation was conception. What stage of pregnancy would you consider yourself to be in?

5. Considering we are told that Satan has access to the throne of God to be constantly accusing you before God, what good things about you far outweigh any of the devil's accusations?

Lesson 77
Revelation: Lesson 10
(Chapter 13-14)

In our last lesson we ended by talking about the woman who is represented as the church, and the dragon representing Satan. We left them with God providing a place of safety for her to run and Satan declaring war against her offspring. Satan realizes his time is short and he only has three and ne-half years left, so he pulls out all the stops.

As we start this lesson it is important to point out that the central figures in the events of the great tribulation are spoken of as beasts. These are not animal monstrosities. The metaphors are actually a description of world powers, having the characteristics of animals portrayed. We use the same language, in a sense, when we speak of the Russian bear, the Chinese dragon, the American eagle, and so on. An example is also seen in Daniel 7:6 in his visions of the swift conquests of Alexander of Greece that is symbolized by the agile swiftness of a leopard.

Revelation 13:1-2 states, "The dragon stood on the sea and I saw a beast coming out of the sea. He had ten horns and seven heads, with ten crowns on his horns, and on each head a blasphemous name. The beast I saw resembled a leopard, but had feet like that of a bear and a mouth like that of a lion."

We know that Satan is a spirit being and can only operate effectively in the human sphere by embodying himself in an earthly organism--the mind and body of man in our case. Here we see his embodiment symbolized in creatures coming out of the sea. As we look at the description of the beast it has many features that are symbolic. The seven heads denotes completeness or the giving of wisdom to this beast. The ten horns represent political power, and the crowns authority to rule. With all these qualifications he will represent all those who rejected Christ and are the restless masses that are waiting for a super power to come in and save the day. This will be blasphemy against God and ushers in the arising of the anti-christ.

As we look back to the beginning, we know God created the earth as the dwelling place for man whom he had created in his image and likeness. God basically gave him the title deed to the earth and all the authority and power to rule and care for it. Adam and Eve were given all the freedom to enjoy this wonderful new home with one exception. They were not to eat of the tree of good and evil. We know from history that they disobeyed when approached by the evil one (Satan) and seduced to give over the title deed and all authority and power over to him.

Satan was now called the god of this age, with full authority over the earth, which was now his to give away with all its power and property rights. Remember when he tried to get Jesus to bow down and worship him? Luke 4:6-7: "And the devil said unto him all this power will I give thee, and the glory of them: for that is delivered unto me; and to whomever I will I give it. If thou therefore wilt worship me, all shall be yours."

Now we see Satan making the same offer to the antichrist. Now at last he will get the worship he so eagerly desires. Revelation 13:4 tells us, "And they worshipped the dragon (Satan) which gave power unto the beast: and they worshipped the beast saying, who is like unto the beast? Who is able to make war with him?"

It is important to stop and look at some references we have in the New Testament as well to see the warnings concerning the coming of the anti-christ.

1 John 2:18: "Little children, it is the last time: and as ye have heard that antichrist shall come, even now are there many antichrists; whereby we know that it is the last time."

Matthew 24: 21, 24, 25: "For then shall be great tribulation, such as was not since the beginning of the world to this time, or ever shall be. For there shall arise false Christ, and false prophets, and shall show great signs and wonders: insomuch that if it were possible, they shall deceive the very elect. Behold, I have told you before."

2 Thessalonians 2:2, 4, 6: "Let no man deceive you by any means: for that day shall not come, except there come a falling away first, and that man of sin be revealed, the son of perdition; Who opposeth and exalteth himself above all that is called God, or that is worshipped; so that he as God sits in the temple of God, showing himself that he is God. And now ye know what withholdeth that he might be revealed in his time."

We also know that Daniel warned the antichrist would use flattery to receive power. Daniel 11:21: "And in his estate shall stand up a vile person, to whom they shall not give the hour of the kingdom: but he shall come in peaceably, and obtain the kingdom by flatteries."

Now we see Satan being symbolized as the dragon, standing on the shore of the sea, laying out his plan for his embodiment into a man who will be the fulfillment of his plan. He knows his time is short and his plan involves giving over his power and authority to this man who will rise to world power from among restless humanity. He will be the world's last tyrannical ruler who will come to doom in the end.

There is no mistaking the identity of this coming sinister ruler of the world. Revelation 12:1-10 is a description of his political sovereignty over the whole world. You can see his portrait being painted throughout the scriptures in both the Old and New Testaments. He is the beast in Revelation 11:7 and 13:1. He is the horn or world power of Daniel 9:27, the abomination of desolation of Matthew 24:15, and the king of fierce countenance of Daniel 8:23-25. These are among many references given to this man who will be Satan's final incarnation. Satan knows that the keys of the kingdom handed over to him in the garden long ago are about to be snatched away from him, and his hold on mankind is about to come to an end.

Next we see the description of the beast. In 13:3 we see that one of the heads of the beast seems to have had a fatal wound, but the wound had been healed. We are told also that he is given a mouth to utter proud words and blasphemies to exercise his authority for the next three one-half years. He uses that authority to slander the name of God, his dwelling place and those who live in heaven. He even had authority to make war against the saints and to conquer them. In fact, we are told in verse 7 that he has been given authority over every tribe, people, language and nation of the earth and that all would worship him that did not have their names written in the book of life. That for us now is good news because hopefully we do have our name written in the book of life and are followers of Jesus.

Next we see another beast coming out of the earth. He has two horns like a lamb, but it spoke like a dragon. We see once again Satan's imitation of God. As the Holy Trinity is the embodiment of godliness, so the embodiment of evil is manifested in this counterfeit trinity. One is the **Dragon**, that old serpent the Devil found in 12:9.

Two is the **antichrist**, the blasphemous leader who takes on the nature of Satan to deceive the world found in 13:1-10.

Three is the **false prophet**, the third person of the evil trio, who is the one that looks like a lamb but speaks like a dragon. He is given the power to perform great and miraculous signs, even causing fire to come down from heaven to earth for men to see. With all his flamboyance and flair he enables the antichrist to set himself up in the Temple of God and also enable an image of the antichrist to be erected.

This image was given power to actually have breath so as to be able to speak and demand worship. The consequence of not bowing down and worshiping him was to be put to death because of disobedience. He then forced everyone, small and great, rich and poor, free and slave, to receive a mark on his right hand or on his forehead, so that no one could buy or sell unless he had the mark of the beast, which was the number 666. Again, this is an imitation of God's actions. Remember the 144,000 that God put his mark on to preserve for witnesses.

Chapter 14 opens talking about this very same group of witnesses. We remember past references in chapter 7 to these 144,000 being 12,000 from each of the tribes of Israel. They were sealed with the protection of God and left here to witness to the Jews who were worshiping the antichrist. God, once again, preserved a remnant to be witnesses to them. They are here on earth and with the seal that they cannot be touched by the antichrist. God sealed them for this time to witness to the Jewish people and give them yet another chance to accept his son.

As we move into chapter 14 we are assured of the triumph of the Lamb and the judgment of the wicked. Chapter 12 dealt primarily with Israel and chapter 13 with the activity of the satanic trinity. Now we are moving into the more victorious times. In this chapter John sees seven different visions, not chronologically arranged, but each complete in itself, yet all related to the whole picture.

In the first vision John sees a Lamb (Jesus) standing on Mount Zion, and with him the 144,000 who had his name and his Father's name written on their foreheads. He hears the sound of harps and a new song being sung that was only learned by this special group of witnesses. They followed the Lamb wherever he went. Verse 4 tells us, "They were purchased from among men and offered as first fruits to God and the Lamb." You can look back at the Old Testament at the offerings and study the significance of the first fruit offering that the Israelites practiced, and some still do till this day. Jesus then called himself the first fruit from the dead meaning spiritually dead men. Now we see this group being called first fruits being offered to God.

Jesus used the example of fields and crops many times in his teaching. Like the parable of the sower, the command was to go out and bring in the harvest. He chose disciples who were the first fruits of his ministry and commanded them to go out and reach others with the gospel. Now he is sending, or preserving, a first fruit of the nation of Israel, restored, redeemed and protected, and to form the nucleus of the living nation of Israel in its place of prominence in the Millennial Kingdom.

This select group had seven unique qualities:
1. They are virgins, called to keep themselves pure.
2. God's name is written on their foreheads.
3. They sing a special song no one else could learn.
4. They followed the Lamb everywhere he went.
5. They are the first fruits of the Jewish people.
6. No lie is found in their mouths and they are blameless.
7. They are before God's throne.

The second vision is a warning that the final judgment is approaching. John says he saw an angel flying in midair proclaiming the gospel to those who live on the earth; every tribe, nation, language and people. He gives a final warning, "He said in a loud voice, fear God and give him glory, because the hour of his judgment has come. Worship him who made the heavens, the earth, the sea and the springs of water." This is an attempt to remind the people that this God they are rebelling against is the God of all creation.

The third vision is the fall and doom of Babylon. Babylon was a center of idol worship. "As a second angel followed and said, "Fallen! Is Babylon the Great, which made all the nation's drink the maddening wind of her adulteries." Jeremiah 51:7 speaks of it, "Babylon hath been a golden cup in the Lord's hand, that made all the earth drunk; the nations have drunk of her wine; therefore the nations are mad." You may remember that the twelve tribes were all taken captive by Babylon. It stands as a symbol of rebellion against God. We will see more about the significance of Babylon in chapter 19 when we see her judged.

The fourth vision is the doom of the beast (antichrist) worshipers. This is a warning to those who might take the mark of 666 offered by the antichrist. "A third angel followed them and said in a loud voice: If anyone worships the beast and his image and receives his mark on the forehead or on the hand, he too will drink of the wine of God's fury, which has been poured full strength into the cup of his wrath. He will be tormented with burning sulfur in the presence of the holy angels and of the Lamb." Receiving the mark is an open testimony of the total acceptance of Satan's counterfeit christ. The warning could not be more severe. Revelation 14:11 tells us the smoke of their torment will rise forever and ever.

The beast is Satan in a brilliant, perfect body. He will appear to people as a glorious being and he claims to be God. He will have many names, all of which are different names for God. In fact, he will have a total of six hundred and sixty-six (666) names. The mark of the beast is the name of the beast or any of his 666 names. In other words, you receive the mark of the beast by taking any one of the beast's 666 names.

So why does he need so many names? The answer is because he wants to appeal to every person on earth. He carefully selects his blasphemous names so that one of his names will appeal to each person on earth. He will come as Allah or Imam Mahdi to the Muslims, Maitreya Buddha to the Buddhists, Jesus Christ to the Christians, Krishna to the Hindus, Messiah to the Jews, Saoshyant to the Zoroastrians, the "Dark Lord" to Satanists, and so on through the whole list of 666 names. His goal is to win the worship and allegiance of every person on earth.

Here we are seeing holy approval of the everlasting punishment of those who turn their backs upon the Creator-Savior to bow down to the worship of the antichrist. This is hellfire and brimstone that we hear preached, but it is also preaches a mercy judgment that every effort is made to offer a way of redemption to those who will receive it.

The fifth vision is one of blessing those who refuse to bow and worship the Antichrist and stand faithfully keeping the commandments found in Exodus 20:3-5, "Thou shalt not make unto thee any graven image...thou shall not bow down to them, nor serve them..." They are called blessed and their works, standing true to their testimony, shall follow them and be recorded in heaven. That applies to all of us who are found true to the Lord until he calls us home.

The sixth vision is the angel with the sickle. "And I looked, and beheld a white cloud, and upon the cloud one sat like unto the son of man, having on his head a golden crown and in his hand a sharp sickle. Then another angel came out of the temple and called in a loud voice to him who was sitting on the cloud, 'Take your sickle and reap, because the time to reap has come, for the harvest of the earth is ripe.' 'So he who sat on the cloud swung his sickle over the earth and the earth was harvested." This reminds me of Jesus' words to his disciples telling them to go out and spread the gospel saying that the fields are white and ready to harvest.

The time of harvest has come to an end and the end of the world or (age) has come.

The reapers are the angels. Let's look at Jesus' own words in Matthew 13:37-43 when the disciples asked him to explain the parable of the weed in the field. "The one who sowed the good seed is the Son of Man. The field is the world and the good seed stands for the sons of the kingdom. The weeds are the sons of the evil one, and the enemy who sows them is the devil. The harvest is the end of the age, and the harvesters are angels. As the weeds are pulled up and burned in the fire, so it will be at the end of the age. The son of man will send out his angels, and they will weed out sin from his kingdom everything that causes sin and all who do evil. They will throw them into the fiery furnace, where there will be weeping and gnashing of teeth. Then the righteous will shine like the sun in the kingdom of their Father. He who has ears let him hear."

Interesting that Revelation 13:9 says the same thing. "He who has an ear, let him hear." This means our spiritual ears tuned into the things of God. After all, we all have ears. If we are not tuned into the spirit of God we cannot hear because the frequency of God's voice is like none other. 1 Corinthians 2:14 states, "The man without the Spirit does not accept the things that come from the spirit of God, for they are foolishness to him and he cannot understand them, because they are spiritually discerned."

The seventh vision is another angel who comes out of the temple in heaven also having a sharp sickle. "Still another angel, who had charge of the fire, came from the altar and called in a loud voice to him who had the sharp sickle, 'Take your sharp sickle and gather the clusters of grapes from the earth's vine because its grapes are ripe.' The angel swung his sickle on the earth, gathered its grapes and threw them into the great winepress of God's wrath. They were trampled in the winepress outside the city and blood flowed out of the press, rising as high as the horse's bridles for a distance of 1,600 stadia (200 miles)."

So we see the angel having power over fire coming forth from the brazen altar, the altar of judgment, commanding the angel out of the temple to gather the clusters of the vine of the earth, as opposed to the true vine and its branches which is what Christ and his own are called in John 15:5.

The winepress being trodden "without the city," again may be in reference to Armageddon. The battle will be fought in the valley of Megiddo.

Discussion Questions:

1. As you reflect on Satan being the god of this age, in what ways have you been tempted, like Jesus was, to surrender to his false offers of prosperity and power?

2. Daniel says the antichrist will use flattery to gain power. How do you think flattery will gain him power, and has flattery ever worked on you as you watched a powerful leader leading you in a way that may not be God's best?

3. Compare the trinity of God, the trinity Satan set up, and the trinity of man we talked about in an earlier lesson.

4. After reading this lesson on the judgment of those who refused until the end, what is your belief about hell?

5. We are given the instruction "if any have an ear, let him hear." What does that mean to you?

Lesson 78
Revelation: Lesson 11
(Chapter 15-17)

We ended our last lesson with God sending the angels to harvest with a sickle in hand. "Another angel, who had charge of the fire, came from the altar and called in a loud voice to him who had the sharp sickle. Take your sickle and gather the clusters of grapes from the earth's vine, because its grapes are ripe." God is saying the end is here and man's time to receive Jesus as the Messiah has come to an end. God has extended mercy and withheld His wrath with long-suffering patience as Satan has been running rampant on the earth. He has continued to send prophets, witnesses, and disciples in a continuous line throughout the ages to announce the redemption for all those who will believe and receive the salvation he has provided. But now we see beginning in chapter 15, that time has run out, and the last seven plagues and judgments are here.

Revelation 15:1 says, "I saw in heaven another great and marvelous sign: seven angels with the seven last plagues-last because with them God's wrath is completed. "These are the last of the tribulation judgments: seals, trumpets, and bowls."

In the vision, John sees what looks like a sea of glass mixed with fire, and standing there are those who had been victorious over Satan and had not taken the number of 666 to appease him. It is important to stop a minute and see how they withstood the attacks and temptations to take the easy way out and just take the mark for comfort's sake. They overcame him not by their own will and might, but by the power of claiming the blood of Christ and their testimony signifying they would face death if necessary rather than deny Jesus as the Messiah.

Chapter 12:11 states, "They overcame him by the blood of the Lamb and the Word of their testimony; they did not love their lives so much as to shrink from death." This is important because we are constantly being put in a compromising position, having to decide as to whether we are going to stand strong and firm in our faith or give in to the way the world lives. The term overcoming by the blood of the lamb just means that we have accepted the fact that Jesus came as the sacrificial lamb to redeem us, and now we have his power living in us. The word of our testimony means that we confess what we believe and let it build up our faith. Jesus was in the very same place when the devil took him up in the mountains and tried to get him to turn his back on God. But every time he was given a temptation, he just said, "It is written." He held firm to his testimony as to his purpose and calling and refused to entertain any other thought. If Jesus had ever compromised himself, we would have been doomed.

Now we see those who remained faithful are being rewarded for their faithfulness. They are standing there holding harps that were given them by God himself. They are singing, and rejoicing, "Great and marvelous are your deeds, Lord God Almighty. Just and true are your ways, King of the ages. Who will not fear you, O Lord, and bring glory to your name? For you alone are holy. All nations will come and worship before you, for your righteous acts have been revealed."

We notice they are standing in what looked like to John a sea of glass mixed with fire. We remember that, earlier in chapter, two that John saw around the throne of God a sea of glass. He described it in 4:6 as being like crystal. But now we see those victorious believers standing beside the sea of glass, which represents God's throne, but now it is mixed with fire representing the fact that it is now time for the final judgment represented by fire.

Next, we see John beholding the scene in heaven where he sees the temple of God. You might remember that earlier John was given a glimpse inside the temple where he saw the Ark of the Covenant and a golden altar. This vision was accompanied by thunder, lightning and an earthquake that came from the temple. John sees the curtains of the sanctuary opened and seven angels coming forth clothed in pure white linen and having their breasts girded with golden girdles.

Next, he sees one of the four living creatures that are around the throne of God giving the angels seven golden vials, (bowls) filled with God's wrath. John says he saw the temple filled with smoke from the very presence and glory of God. No one was allowed to enter the temple until the seven plagues that were represented in the seven bowls were completed. No approach to God by man, angel, prayer or supplication could halt the wrath of the Almighty God now that the time of the end has come.

Starting in chapter 16, John hears a voice coming from the temple saying, "Go, pour out the seven bowls of God's wrath on the earth."

We see the first angel pouring out his bowl and from it came ugly and painful sores upon those who had taken the mark of the beast and worshiped his image.

The second angel poured out his bowl upon the sea, and it turned into blood, and every living thing in the sea died.

The third angel poured out his bowl on the rivers and springs of water, and they became blood. This represents the earth's fresh water system that sustains life because thirst is more terrifying than hunger. The angel then spoke and said, "You are just in these judgments, you who are and who were, the Holy One because you have so judged; for they shed blood on your saints and prophets, and you have given them blood to drink as they deserve."

As we look at these judgments, it reminds us of the Egyptian plagues sent on Pharaoh because of the oppression of God's people during that time in history. God always has, and always will, vindicate his people if they remain true to Him.

The fourth angel poured out his bowl on the sun, and the sun was given the power to scorch people with fire. They were seared with the intense heat, and they cursed the name of God who had control over these plagues, but they still refused to repent and glorify him.

The fifth angel poured out his bowl on the throne of the beast, and his kingdom was plunged into darkness. Revelation 16:10, tells us they gnawed their tongues in agony and still cursed the God of heaven because of the pain, but still refused to repent of what they had done.

The sixth angel poured out his bowl on the great river Euphrates, and its water was dried up to prepare the way for the kings of the East. Next, he said he saw three evil spirits that looked like frogs that came out of the mouth of the dragon, the beast, and the false prophet. These spirits are controlled by the satanic trinity and given power to lure the kings for the great battle to come. "They are spirits of demons performing miraculous signs, and they go out to kings of the whole world, to gather them for the battle on the great day of God Almighty." It is important to realize that it is God, in righteous retribution, who gathers them to this place of judicial judgment, employing the satanic trinity to carry out the divine purpose.

Then we get a warning before the last bowl as we hear from our Lord himself who speaks with loving concern to those who have endured the snares of the antichrist and the lures of the devil himself. "Behold, I come as a thief! Blessed is he who stays awake and keeps his clothes with him, so that he may not go naked and be shamefully exposed."

Interesting that Adam and Eve were made aware of their nakedness and were ashamed after they sinned. Genesis 3:7 tells us, "Then the eyes of both of them were opened, and they realized they were naked; so they sewed fig leaves together and made coverings for themselves. Then the man and his wife heard the sound of the Lord God as he was walking in the garden in the cool of the day, and they hid from the Lord God among the trees of the garden. But the Lord God called to the man, 'Where are you?' He answered, 'I heard you in the garden, and I was afraid because I was naked; so I hid.' And God said, 'Who told you that you were naked?' Have you eaten of the tree that I commanded you not to eat from?" So we see the shame of nakedness was represented as a result of sin in the garden.

Now in Revelation, he is telling his people not to be found naked but to keep their clothes with them so they will not be found naked and ashamed. After Jesus came, we are told to be clothed with the righteousness of God, to put on the breastplate of righteousness, and that would mean to have put sin away and be walking in obedience. Once again God is giving his people the same warning he gave to Adam and Eve in the garden. "Don't be caught living in sin when the time comes because I will come as a thief in the night."

You may remember Paul's warns the church in 1 Thessalonians 5:1-11, "But ye, brethren, are not in darkness, that that day should overtake you as a thief for ye are the children of light. We do not belong to the night or darkness. So then, let us not be like others, who are asleep, but let us be alert and self-controlled. For those who sleep, sleep at night, and those who get drunk, get drunk at night. But since we belong to the day, let us be self-controlled, putting on faith and love as a breastplate, and the hope of salvation as a helmet. For God did not appoint us to suffer wrath but to receive salvation through our Lord Jesus Christ. He died for us so that, whether we are awake or asleep, we may live together with him."

The seventh angel poured out his bowl into the air, and out of the temple came a loud voice from the throne, saying, "It is done!" Then there was lightning, thunder and an earthquake that was greater than any before. It was not poured out to a certain location on earth but in the atmosphere surrounding the whole earth, which caused worldwide destruction. It was so great that it tumbled down cities and swallowed up the islands and mountains. This was followed by a hailstorm that had hail as large as 100 pounds each. All that man had built on this earthly realm without God collapsed.

The important thing about this judgment is the fact that it is poured out over all the atmosphere, and the announcement from the temple saying it is done! This says this judgment is the finish of God's wrath. After all the horrible things we have seen happen, there were still those who were blinded, arrogant and rebellious survivors with hardened hearts. They still blasphemed God's name rather than throwing themselves upon his mercy hoping upon hope that the final gate of grace was not closed.

As we move forward into chapter 17, we see one of the seven angels who had the seven bowls come to John and says, "Come, I will show you the punishment of the great prostitute, who sits on many waters. With her, the kings of the earth committed adultery, and the inhabitants of the earth were intoxicated with the wine of her adulteries." The phrase 'sitting on many waters" just means the prostitute has significant influence over many people and nations. Here he is saying that both kings and commoners have been defiled with her. This just means they violated standards of righteousness and had illicit intercourse with the godless of this world system.

We will now take a closer look at the city of Babylon because so much emphasis is put on this city. We see Babylon being the great city that is split into three parts, "…God remembered Babylon the Great and gave her the cup filled with the wine of the fury of his wrath."

The language in chapter 17 is figurative with Babylon being portrayed as a very powerful immoral woman. Babylon has been the city that is at the center of the dragon and antichrists evil world regime. Babylon of old was the center of early civilization, and we can look as far back as the patriarchal forefather, Noah, and remember this was where the Tower of Babel must likely was. This is where a Satan-inspired conspiracy to centralize the power and influence of a one-world system took place. God had instructed Noah's sons and their descendants to go out and fill the earth after they came out of the ark, but they once again were inspired by the evil one to stay in one place united and build a tower to heaven, indicating they did not need God. We know that God had to intervene and confused their language so they could not understand each other and they had to separate and do as he had commanded. The Hebrews claim the city was named for this confusion of languages. The Hebrew word babel means 'confusion.'

Babylon also appears in the books of Daniel, Jeremiah, and Isaiah, among others. It was undoubtedly the seat of immorality and the place where God was constantly being excluded. You might remember back to the study of the children of Israel where all twelve tribes were eventually taken captive by Babylon. This is where Daniel was thrown in the lions' den for refusing to worship God, and where Shadrach, Meshach, and Abednego were thrown in the fiery furnace for refusing to worship the idols they had set up to oppose God.

Its ruins lie in modern-day Iraq 59 miles southwest of Baghdad. As we think back on our recent history, we can see the evil that is still oppressing the people as we have watched an evil radical group called Isis, beheading Christians and terrorizing everyone in their path. Satan's influence on them has the same goal as the disobedient ones who were trying to build a one-world order excluding God as it tells us in the Old Testament. The stated purposes and goals of this group is to eliminate all Christians and establish the idolatry structure of an evil society set up by a manmade god. It is amazing as we look back through history and see that Satan's goal in the garden was the same as it is today; to set up a one-world political system and religion without God.

Next, John says the angel carried him away in the Spirit into a desert. "There I saw a woman sitting on a scarlet beast that was covered with blasphemous names and had seven heads and ten horns. The woman was dressed in purple and scarlet and was glittering with gold, precious stones, and pearls. She held a golden cup in her hand, filled with abominable things and the filth of her adulteries."

The color scarlet represents royalty because we will see that the seven heads and the ten horns represent kings. It is also referred to in Isaiah 1:18, "though your sins be as scarlet, they shall be white as snow," this Solomon says, was spoken by the Lord himself. Scarlet here represents the nature of sin while we see the saints clothed in white around the throne of God.

Next, she was said to have been covered with blasphemous names. I think it is interesting that her name was a mystery. We find in Ephesians 3:3-6, the bride of Christ being referred to as the "mystery hidden from other ages." Here again, we see Satan's counterfeit being called, "Mystery, the Mother of Prostitutes."

John describes her accessories, "adorned with gold and jewels and pearls." No doubt representing all the world has to offer with its allure of all the things the wealth of this world can offer. Interesting that when we see someone who is overdressed and wearing gaudy jewelry, we might even make the statement that she looks like a prostitute. This adornment is part of the way even prostitutes of our day dress to lure the men into their beds of sin. Here we see this representing the city of Babylon because she is loaded down with material opulence and moral decadence.

Next, we see her golden cup, "full of abominations and the impurities of her sexual immorality." As we look back over the history of Babylon, we know that the corruption of evil manifests itself in every imaginable form of human-even subhuman, animalistic evil.

Then we see she is intoxicated. She is drunk with the blood of the saints, the blood of the martyrs of Jesus. More Christians were martyred in the 20th century than in the previous ten combined. This will pale in comparison to what the great city of Babylon will do to the saints during this time.

Then, the angel tells John where this evil comes from, "…shall ascend out of the bottomless pit, the abyss." This leaves no question as to whom this represents, as this is Satan's domain.

The seven heads of the beast are first said to be, "seven mountains, on which the woman sitteth." The seven-hilled city is a common term used in the history of Rome; this means that the term used here is geographical. (Interesting to note that in John's lifetime Rome ruled the then known world.) Some think that these kings mentioned are associated in some form of Rome's political rule. Some speculate that it represents the seven successive forms of government starting with the rise of the Roman Empire with Nebuchadnezzar's vision found in Daniel 2:40-43. Others say they are individual emperors, one of who is said to have existed during John's writing.

We read in 17:10, "They are also seven kings. Five have fallen, one is, (in John's day), the other has not yet come, but when he does come, he will remain only a little while. The beast who once was, and now is not, is an eighth king. He belongs to the seven and is going to his destruction."

We can look back through history and make many speculations, but one thing we know and that is that the antichrist is the last world ruler and his reign will only be a little while. We see his fate in verse eleven is destruction.

Next, we see the ten horns, which represent ten kings, who have no kingdom as yet, but receive power as kings for one hour with the beast. They will operate as one mind and give their strength over to the beast or antichrist. We can assume that these ten kings and the antichrist are contemporaries. They have joined forces to fight against the Lamb, but the Lamb shall overcome them because he is Lord of lords and King of kings, and with him will be the called, the chosen and his beloved followers."

Meantime, the antichrist and the ten kings will make an all-out assault on Babylon (the prostitute). "The beast and the ten horns (kings) you saw will hate the prostitute. They will bring her to ruin and leave her naked; they will eat her flesh and burn her with fire."

They will do this because they realize that she has used her political power and influence to seduce and intoxicate the world and entrench herself as the governing and controlling power. God uses the enemies of his true church to bring to ruin the false religious system of Babylon.

The final fate of the antichrist and ultimate destruction though is reserved for the coming of the Lord which we shall see in 19:15: "shall smite the earth with the rod of his mouth, and with the breath of his lips shall he slay the wicked." God's plan was given all those years ago to the prophet Isaiah as it is recorded in Isaiah 11:4. This just helps me to know that God is a just God and is faithful to his plan and promises. He did not just wake up one morning and decide to execute judgment. It was a plan full of mercy, patience, and fulfillment of his word. We see that in 17:17, "For God has put it into their hearts to accomplish his purpose by agreeing to give the beast their power to rule until God's words are fulfilled."

The last verse validates who the mysterious woman is, "The woman you saw is the great city that rules over the kings of the earth."

Discussion Questions:

1. As you look at the saints who stood strong and overcame the evil, what does that mean to you as you go about your everyday life? "They overcame him with the blood of the lamb and the word of their testimony." Why do you think it was important to have a word of testimony?

2. We see the saints standing around the throne giving praise and having hearts of thankfulness. Do you incorporate these same attributes as you stand in his presence each day?

3. Jesus says he will come as a thief in the night, but also tells us of signs to look for as we approach the end times. What should we as followers of Christ be doing to prepare others and ourselves?

4. There seem to be two cities that are key to the end time, Babylon and Jerusalem. Why do you think they were singled out, and what do each signify?

5. We learned that the antichrist is coming and we have been warned not to take the mark he offers us. What can you do to build up your faith to withstand that temptation?

6. We are instructed to keep our clothes with us in 16:15. What do you think this means?

Lesson 79
Revelation: Lesson 12
(Chapter 18-22)

In our previous lessons, we have seen Babylon playing a significant role in the discussion of end times. It was described as a mystery, and as we have gone through the book we have read about a mystical woman, but the mystery is unveiled in the last verse of chapter 17, "The woman you saw is the great city that rules over the kings of the earth." 18:2-3 states, "Fallen, Fallen is Babylon the Great! She has become a home for demons and a haunt for every evil spirit, a haunt for every unclean and detestable bird. For all the nations have drunk the maddening wine of her adulteries. The kings of the earth committed adultery with her, and the merchants of the earth grew rich from her excessive luxuries."

Here, we see the downfall of Babylon with a description of the evil that has become a part of its culture and the influence it has on other nations and kings. Now the time of judgment on this great city has come, but God once again is making an appeal by sending an angel to tell his people to repent and turn away from the idolatrous and evil ways. "Then I heard another voice from heaven saying, "Come out of her, my people so that you will not share in her sins, so that you will not receive any of her plagues; for her sins are piled up to heaven, and God has remembered her cries." That same appeal is still going out today to those who are ignoring the Word of God and living in the lust of the flesh, which has been characterized here as the adulterous woman, or Babylon. They are going about ignoring prophecies that tell us the time is short, and I am afraid all too often we are living in the same attitude of ignorance.

We see in chapter 18, a detailed account of this destruction. "In one day her plagues will overtake her; death, mourning, and famine. She will be consumed by fire, for mighty is the Lord God who judges her." Next, we see the kings who have been enjoying the luxury of the sinful city looking on and saying "Terrified at her torment, they will stand far off and cry: Woe! Woe, O great city, O Babylon, city of power! In one hour your doom has come." Amazing how those who seem to enjoy the sinful, luxurious lifestyle are nowhere to be seen when the time of desperation and sorrow come. You may have noticed that people today seem to be oblivious to the precepts of God until tragedy strikes. Then they do not seek out those they have been partying with, or those who have the riches of this world, but they start looking inward and seeking those who have the peace and faith in something bigger than this world we live in.

We also see in chapter 18 the weeping of those who had been trafficking in the abundant merchandise of the great city. "The merchants who sold these things and gained their wealth from her will stand far off, terrified at her torment. They will weep and mourn and cry out Woe! O great city, dressed in fine linen, purple and scarlet, and glittering with gold, precious stones, and pearls! In one hour such great wealth has been brought to ruin!"

How fleeting those things are as we see that in verse 18 as sea captains and those who are looking on from the sea also mourning and saying woe as well. "Woe! O great city, where all who had ships on the sea became rich through her wealth."

Then we see a scene in heaven as God is telling those who are looking on to notice that his judgment on those who mistreated them has come. "Rejoice over her, O heaven! Rejoice, saints and apostles and prophets! God has judged her for the way she treated you." God always brings justice to those who trust him and remain steadfast.

This celebration went on in chapter 19 where we are told that a great multitude in heaven was shouting ... "Hallelujah! Salvation and glory and power belong to our God, for true and just are his judgments. He has condemned the great prostitute who corrupted the earth by her adulteries. He has avenged on her the blood of his servants." As they watched the smoke come up from her destruction, we are told that the twenty-four elders and the four living creatures fell down and worshiped God, who was seated on the throne. They cried, "Amen, Hallelujah!"

Now that this judgment has been brought on the evil prostitute, the true bride who is waiting in heaven can now be brought forth in all of her beauty. She is not arrayed in purple and scarlet that are symbolic of earth's lavish adornments, but she appears in fine linen, clean and white: for the fine linen is the righteousness of the saints. Revelation 19:7 tells us that this is the bride that is ready for her ceremony. Amazing how much we pattern our weddings on this model. The bride wears white showing that she has remained pure and is being presented to the bridegroom by her father. We have a reception that is a supper of celebration of the union that has just taken place, and we give toasts and honor to the bride and the groom. The long-awaited day has come, and Jesus as the bridegroom has come to take his bride (the church or overcoming saints) to live in his house forever.

John says then an angel said to him, "Write: Blessed are those who are invited to the wedding supper of the Lamb!" John was so overcome with the joy of this that he fell at his feet to worship him but the angel said, "Do not do it! I am a fellow servant with you and with your brothers who hold to the testimony of Jesus. Worship God! For the testimony of Jesus is the spirit of prophecy."

Next John describes a glorious scene, "I saw heaven open, and behold a white horse; and he that sat upon him was called Faithful and True, and with the righteousness he doth judge and make war. His eyes were as a flame of fire, and on His head were many crowns; and he had a name written, that no one knew, but him himself. He was clothed with a robe dipped in blood: and his name is called the Word of God. The armies of heaven were following him, riding on white horses and dressed in fine linen, white and clean." Interesting that the first-time heaven is opened it is suggested that Jesus was coming for his people, and the second time it is opened he is coming with his people. We read in 1 Thessalonians 4:16-17, "For the Lord himself shall descend from heaven with a shout, with the voice of the archangel, and with the trump of God, the dead in Christ shall rise first, then we which are alive and remain shall be caught up together with them in the clouds, to meet the Lord in the air, and so shall we ever be with the Lord." Now we see him returning with those faithful saints.

(Interesting to note that up to chapter 19 the judgments have been directed from heaven with the angels carrying out their execution. Now, Christ descends to earth in person for the final execution of judgment against the Satan-inspired conspirators and the leaders of the darkness of this world.)

This is a long-awaited scene that we have read about and is what the book of Revelation is really about; the actual appearance, a literal manifestation, the unveiling of our Lord Jesus Christ. Jesus himself actually tells us of this time to look forward to. Matthew 24:30 states, "At that time the sign of the Son of Man will appear in the sky, and all nations of the earth will mourn. They will see the Son of Man coming on the clouds of the sky, with power and great glory."

We are told that out of his mouth comes a sharp sword with which to strike down the nations. He will rule them with an iron scepter. This reminds me of a passage in Hebrews 4:12, "For the Word of God is alive and active. Sharper than any double-edged sword, it penetrates even to dividing soul and spirit, joints and marrow; it judges the thoughts and attitudes of the heart." Jesus now is that Word, and he is now carrying the scepter of the King of kings to rule and reign. We are told next that on his robe and his thigh are those very words written KING OF KINGS AND LORD OF LORDS.

As King of Kings, he defeated the beast, false prophets, and their armies. The two of them were thrown alive in a lake of burning sulfur. The rest of them were killed with the sword that came out of the mouth of the Lamb. It is interesting to hear what he had planned after the battle. John says he saw, "An angel standing in the sun, who cried in a loud voice to all the birds flying in midair, "Come, gather together for the great supper of God, so that you might eat the flesh of kings, generals, and mighty men, of horses and their riders, and the flesh of all people, free and slave, small and great." Later on, after the battle and bodies were strewn everywhere, we are told, "…all the birds gorged themselves on their flesh." Interesting that birds are part of the end time prophesies. Also, I find it interesting that they could hear the instructions of the angel and follow his commands. Never underestimate the purpose or power of any creature God created. He used the snake in Genesis and the birds in Revelation.

In chapter 20 we see another angel coming down from heaven, having a key to the bottomless pit and he is holding a chain in his hand. We are told that he took hold of the devil and bound him in the pit and put a seal on it so that he would remain there for a thousand years. The earth is finally free from Satan's sinister presence and deceptive influence for a period of a thousand years.

John recalls his vision, seeing thrones of glorified saints who had been given the power to judge. He saw those who had been beheaded because of their testimony for Jesus and standing true to the Word of God, as well as those who had not worshiped the beast nor taken his mark. He gives them special notice for the trials and long-suffering they endured. He states that this is the first resurrection and those who have put their faith in Christ will be the ones who will be resurrected at this time as well.

Those who were not believers are those who will be left until the time of the second resurrection when we will all stand before the throne of God to see whose names are written in the book of life. This is alluded to in 20:11, "Then I saw a great white throne and him who was seated on it. Earth and sky fled from his presence, and there was no place for them. And I saw the dead, great and small, standing before the throne, and books were opened. Another book was opened, which is the book of life. The dead were judged according to what they had done as recorded in the books. The sea gave up her dead that were in it, and death and Hades gave up the dead that were in them, and each person was judged according to what he had done. Then death and Hades were thrown into the lake of fire. The lake of fire is the second death. If anyone's name was not written in the book of life, he was thrown into the lake of fire."

Jesus himself talks about this in John 5:28 where it is talking about the fact that he has been given the authority to judge because he is the Son of Man, "Do not be amazed at this, a time is coming when all who are in their graves will hear his voice and come out-those who have done good will rise to live, and those who have done evil will rise to be condemned." Jesus talks about that time of judgment again in Matthew 7:22-23, "Many will say to me on that day, 'Lord, Lord, did we not prophesy in your name, and in your name drive out demons and perform many miracles?' Then I will tell them plainly, 'I never knew you. Away from me, you evildoers!'" What a sad day that will be for those who were Christ followers in words only, as well as those who rejected him altogether.

As we look back at 20:6 where it is talking about the first resurrection, which is the resurrection of the saints, you may remember that it says. "The second death has no power over them."

This comes after Satan is released from his prison and will once again be allowed to deceive and draw armies from the four corners of the earth to battle against the Lamb. He compares the number to be as sands on the seashore. We are told that they marched across the breadth of the earth and surrounded the camp of God's people. God; however, has a plan and sent fire from heaven and devoured them. The devil then joined the beast and the false prophet in the lake of burning sulfur where all three of them will be tormented day and night forever and ever.

We have seen that this earth, as we know it has been destroyed and passed away. Now, starting in chapter 21 John sees a new heaven and a new earth. "Then I saw a new heaven and a new earth, for the first heaven and the first earth had passed away, and there was no longer any sea. I saw the Holy City, the new Jerusalem coming down out of heaven from God, prepared as a bride beautifully dressed for her husband." Although there will be no sea, we do see that a river of life flowing from the throne of God which we will read about in the next chapter.

The idea of the New Jerusalem being prepared as a beautiful bride validates the purity and beauty of our new dwelling place. It lies in direct contrast to the harlot city of Babylon, which was the epitome of evil. The New Jerusalem is the realization of the city Christ said he was going away to prepare for us. The promise of this eternal home has been a foundational truth that Christ followers look forward to. Jesus' words reassure in John 14:1-6, "In my Father's house are many mansions …I go to prepare a place for you." Looking at Hebrews and the hall of faith we see Abraham was looking for a city, which hath foundations, whose builder and maker is God. Hebrews 11:10 talks about the pillars of faith, "that God had prepared for them a city." So the thought of a new city being prepared was noted in both the Old and New Testaments.

The city is called, "the bride, the Lamb's wife." A city is only a city in the sense of those who inhabit it. The heavenly city is called this because of the ransomed, redeemed and glorified ones who dwell within its walls. God himself announces that he will be with them and be their God, wiping away every tear from their eyes. "There will be no more death or mourning or crying or pain, for the old order of things has passed away" He then tells John to write these things down because they are trustworthy and true. He is told, "It is done. I am the Alpha and the Omega, the Beginning and the End. To him who is thirsty, I will give to drink without cost from the spring of the water of life. He who overcomes will inherit all this, and I will be his God, and he will be my son."

Then he gives a warning to those he calls cowardly, the unbelieving, the vile, the murderers, the sexually immoral, those who practice magic arts, the idolaters and all liars-their place will be in the fiery lake of burning sulfur. "This is the second death." Not a pretty picture if you are not a believing follower of Christ. It is hard to believe of such eternal punishment, but this scripture is quoted directly from the word.

God then gives him a special vision of the city in its entire splendor. One of the seven angels who had the seven bowls said to him, "Come, I will show you the bride, the wife of the Lamb." John says he was carried away in the spirit to a mountain and shown the Holy City coming down from heaven. He said it was shining with the glory of God, and its brilliance was like that of a precious jewel that looked like jasper and was clear as crystal. It had a great high wall and twelve gates, and with twelve angels at the gates. On the gates were written the names of the twelve tribes of Israel. The city also had twelve foundations, and on them were the names of the twelve apostles.

The angel was said to have a measuring rod of gold to measure the city, its gates, and its walls. The city was laid out in a square. It is said to be 1,400 miles square. This is about the distance between Dallas and Los Angeles. Everything about the city is perfect as designed by God. We can go back to 1 Corinthians 2:9 and read the description given to the churches, "No eye has seen, nor ear heard, nor the heart of man imagined, what God has prepared for those who love him." John validates this by his description. The wall was made of jasper, the city of pure gold, as pure as glass. The foundation of the city walls was decorated with every kind of precious stone. The twelve gates were twelve pearls, each gate made from a single pearl.

John says he did not see a temple in the city because the Lord God Almighty and the Lamb are its temple. The city does not need the sun or the moon to shine on it, for the glory of God gives it light.

John says that the gates will never be shut because there will be no night there. Nothing impure will ever enter in, nor will anyone who does what is shameful or deceitful, but only those whose names are written in the Lamb's book of life.

The last chapter is describing the river of life we mentioned earlier. It runs down the middle of the street of the city and on each side of the river stands the tree of life, bearing twelve crops of fruit. The leaves of the tree are said to be for the healing of the nations. There will be no more curses. The presence of God will be there, and we will be allowed to see his face, and we are told that his name will be written on our foreheads. He is claiming us for eternity. I love the fact that I will have his name stamped on me.

The angel then said to John, "These words are trustworthy and true. The Lord, the God of the spirits of the prophets, sent his angel to show his servants the things that must soon take place."

We have the recorded words of Jesus saying, "Behold, I am coming soon! Blessed is he who keeps the words of the prophecy in this book." John was so overwhelmed that he fell at the feet of the angel who had shown him these things, but the angel told him to worship God only because he was a fellow servant. Then he told John, "Do not seal up the words of the prophecy of this book because the time is near. He tells him to let those who are doing wrong continue and those who are doing right continue to do so. This again just shows us that we have free will and God will do nothing to force himself on us.

We end with the words of Jesus, "Behold, I am coming soon! My reward is with me, and I will give to everyone according to what he has done. I am the Alpha and the Omega, the first and the last, the beginning and the end. Blessed are those who wash their robes, that they may have the right to the tree of life and may go through the gates into the city." He then tells John, "I, Jesus, have sent my angel to give you this testimony for the churches. I am the root and the offspring of David, and the bright morning star."

He ends with an invitation again, "The Spirit and the bride say, come! …Whoever is thirsty, let him come; and whoever wishes, let him take the free gift of the water of life."

Discussion Questions:

1. He also adds a warning not to let anyone add anything to the words of the prophecy of this book. He says if anyone takes away from this book that he will take away his share in the tree of life. Interesting that Jesus was the tree of life in the Garden of Eden and is the River of Life in Revelation. Have you seen the thread of His influence throughout our study? Share examples.

2. As you think back over this lesson and think of the city of Babylon, can you see a comparison to the times we are living in today?

3. We can see such a comparison to Sodom and Gomorrah where God spared Lot and his family because of the intervention of Abraham. What can we do to warn those who are walking in the same darkness as they are deceived about what is to come, just like those during Abraham's day?

4. As we think of standing before God at the judgment seat when the book of life is opened, what is he going to read about your life? What do you think your responsibility is to those you love and those God has put in your path to help them prepare to stand before God in judgment?

5. Share any thoughts or insights that have helped you in this study. Do you feel better equipped to understand and share God's Word?

LAST REMARKS

This book is the result of 39 years of my research and study of the Bible. I started this journey utilizing resources such as Halley's Bible Handbook that my dad had given me when I accepted Christ at the age of twelve. As I completed these studies in recent years, I referred to Bible Gateway, Cruden's Concordance and gleamed from the teachings and writings of others in my search for truth and understanding of God's Word. With the help of the Holy Spirit I found we each have the ability to study and understand the truths in the Bible for ourselves. It is only when we embrace it personally that we not only realize our history, but the extent of the love our Heavenly Father has for us and how he preserved this written legacy for all generations to come.

Upon the completion of this study we would like to hear from you. We would like to know how this course has helped in your knowledge of the Bible and how it has added to your spiritual well-being.

For additional information and help:

Contact: Biblestudies@globalministries.org